INSTRUCTION

AS A

HUMANIZING SCIENCE

A series of three volumes to be used to increase learning by increasing the effectiveness, efficiency, and productivity in designed instruction.

Volume I — The Changing Role of the Educator: The Instructioneer

Volume II — A Behavioral Learning Systems Approach to Instruction: Analysis and Synthesis

Volume III — Creating an Emphasis on Learning: Quality Control, Productivity, and Accountability

Volume II

BEHAVIORAL LEARNING SYSTEMS

APPROACH TO INSTRUCTION:

ANALYSIS AND SYNTHESIS

by

DON STEWART

SLATE Services, Publishers
Post Office Box 8769
Fountain Valley, California 92708

iii

Library of Congress Card Number 75-13673
Cloth Cover ISBN 0-913448-08-7
Paperback ISBN 0-913448-09-5
Manufactured in the United States of America

First Printing October, 1975

DEDICATION

I want to dedicate this series to the thousands of teachers who during the past decade or more have indirectly helped me to develop the concepts presented in this book by challenging them and making me justify and defend these concepts over and over again.

I also want to dedicate this series to my deceased Aunt and Uncle, Birdie and Frank Christopher of Wichita, Kansas, who indirectly provided the financial resources necessary to take the time to write the series and the funds necessary to publish the series.

I want to dedicate Volume II to the thousands of students who have already benefited from the concepts presented herein and to the hopefully millions of students who will benefit from these concepts in the future.

Don Stewart

Series Philosophy — "The Socratic Oath"

Most educational institutions in their charters or constitutions have stated a philosophy that is probably very much in agreement with the goals of our society. All too often these statements are so general in nature that they cannot be put into practice by the teachers and other educators whose job it is to develop a curriculum in support of the philosophy. Because the teacher's role is so critical in preparing the learner for life and even throughout life, there are many comparisons that can be made between the role of the teacher and the role of a doctor. Consequently the philosophy of the author can be succinctly stated in the following "Socratic Oath" which parallels the "Hippocratic Oath" which is taken by doctors in the performance of their role with their patients.

THE SOCRATIC OATH

You do solemnly swear, each person by whatever he holds most sacred, that you will be loyal to the profession of teaching and just and generous to its members; that you will lead your lives and practice your art in uprightness and honor; that into whatsoever educational institution you shall enter, it shall be for the good of the learner to the utmost of your power, you will set yourself up as an example to your students by constant efforts to keep abreast of the changes in your field of study, adding what is new and dropping what is obsolete; that you will endeavor to determine the knowledge level of new students and adjust the course to their needs and, if appropriate, remedial studies for some and advanced placement for others; that you will exercise your art in such a manner that every student in your classes regardless of race, creed, or economic status will progress positively through the content of your course; that you will exhaust all available methods, media, and instructional materials if necessary in order to help the student learn all of the objectives of your course; that within your power you will not allow any student in your classes to proceed to subsequent courses without achieving all of the prerequisite behaviors available in your course and necessary for a successful progress in the subsequent courses. These things do you swear. And if you will be true to this, your oath, may prosperity and good repute be ever yours; the opposite if you shall prove yourselves forsworn.

Copyright 1966 - Donald K. Stewart - all rights reserved

Parchment copies of "The Socratic Oath" ready for framing are available for purchase from SLATE Services, Publishers, P.O. Box 8796, Fountain Valley, California 92708.

TABLE OF CONTENTS*

Because the three volumes represent a series and are strongly interrelated, the Table of Contents in each volume contains the chapter and unit headings from all three volumes.

---

*It is customary to place the Table of Contents after the front material (Preface, Foreword, etc.) and usually just before the first chapter. However, in this series, the Table of Contents is placed before most of the front material for three reasons: first, it is recognized that most potential readers skim through the Table of Contents as a preliminary appraisal of the contents of the book; second, in this book, the front material is longer than in most other books and if the Table of Contents was placed in the customary location, it could be difficult to locate; and third, the front material is considered to be important enough that it should be placed after the Table of Contents along with the rest of the book and it should be included in the Table of Contents for ease of identification and location.

PREFACE

or

Why Be Concerned About the Role of the Educator?

Almost one out of every three people in the United States is either a full or part-time student, a teacher, or an educational administrator and at some time in every person's life in the United States, they are directly involved and affected by the educational process. Although the 1974-75 enrollment of almost 59 million students gave evidence of a continued slight decline of less than one percent, the total cost of education of almost $108 billion gave evidence of a continued increase of over eleven percent and accounts for eight percent of our gross national product. There is no other facet of our society that involves so many people and has such a critical affect on the future lives of the people (students) who are the consumers of these educational services. Therefore, the purveyors of these services take on a very critical role in our society. Ideally, this role should be performed in such a manner that the consumers are positively affected by these services. In fact, this is not the case. That is why I wrote my first book *Educational Malpractices: The Big Gamble in our Schools* in which I identified forty-one (41) educational malpractices that are commonly found in most educational institutions and being practiced by a majority of the teachers and administrators. This first book was primarily written for students and parents of students to make them aware of the malpractices being perpetrated on them and to give them some practical suggestions (including actual dialogues) which can be used to alleviate or eliminate these malpractices. Secondarily, this book was also written for teachers as a summary of the solutions to the problems as presented in this three volume series. Ironically, the very same educators who are performing the malpractices against students basically want students to have success in learning. The major problem is the strength of the loyalty that most educators hold for the traditions of education which have been handed down through generations of teachers. The strength of these traditions, even though they are malpractices, gathers support from two areas. Since *teachers tend to teach the way they are taught not the way they are taught to teach,* as long as most of the teachers at all levels of education carry on most of the malpractices, their students who become teachers will tend to do the same. However, the major support for the continuation of these malpractices comes from most of the teacher-training institutions which not only practice the malpractices, but they preach them and demand that their students also perform these malpractices in order to graduate.

If education is a critical aspect of our society and the teachers and administrators in education perform a critical role in the educational process, I can't possibly imagine a more critical role in our society than those faculty in higher education who are teachers of students who are planning to be teachers. In any other discipline at a college or university, the faculty members may affect hundreds of students each semester or quarter and over a lifetime they may affect thousands of students, but teachers of students who are planning to be teachers, indirectly affect millions of students. Because of this, it is critical that teacher-training institutions make the necessary changes to eliminate the malpractices in their own teaching and in how they teach others to teach. As a result, the major motivation behind the writing of this book is to prepare a text that could be used by students who are preparing to teach. *Notice though*, at the present time, only teachers who are planning to teach at the elementary or secondary level are required to take any special training in *how to teach*. All that is needed at most institutions of higher education is an advanced degree. The assumption is made that to require graduate students or non-education faculty to take some education courses or training on *how to teach* and/or *how to test* would not be of much value because it can be easily pointed out that teachers who have had these education courses and the faculty who teach the courses typically don't actually behave much differently in the classroom than teachers who have never had any of these courses.*

Consider for a moment the seriousness of the existing problem in which thousands of higher education faculty are involved in the teaching and testing of millions of students and they are not in the least qualified to perform this critical role of *teaching* and *testing*. Yet, their actions and decisions are permanently affecting the future lives of their students. Therefore, a secondary audience for this book are the teachers who have never had any courses or formal training on *how to teach* and/or *how to test*, but would like to help more of their students learn more and would like to be more honest with students in their instructional evaluation situations. A third group for which this book could be of value are the administrators and teachers who have been trained through the traditional education courses to carry on the malpractices

---

* A recent study funded by the U. S. Office of Education as part of its Targeted Research and Development Program found little research evidence to show that teachers having teacher preparation courses have any greater effect on students' performance than teachers who haven't had these courses.

described in my first book.

Although the titles of the series and each volume were selected to communicate to potential readers the emphasis which I have placed in the series and within each volume, it is possible because of differences in the prior experiences of the reader to misinterpret this emphasis. To minimize possible misinterpretation, the primary emphasis throughout the series is on increasing learning — student learning! In changing the emphasis in the instructional setting from *what teachers do* to *increasing student learning*, two traditional concepts become obsolete: the classroom itself and the teacher's role as a presenter of content in that classroom. Almost every educational institution has somewhere in its charter or constitution the statement *to develop each student to the maximum of his or her ability*. Notice, the statement does not say to develop the *average* student or *most* students or a *curve's worth* of students. The statement specifies EACH student. In other words, the majority of educational institutions are legally committed to the concept and practice of individualized instruction. Since it is practically impossible to have a class of students who are all at the same level and who all learn at the same rate, it is also impossible to individualize instruction on a mass or class basis. Hence, the concept of classes of students is obsolete and since under the concept of individualized instruction it would be rare to gather a group of students together for an instructional experience, the concept of the teacher's role as a presenter of course content to a group of students also becomes obsolete.

As pointed out in my first book, the two major problems in traditional education are the evaluation process throughout education (from evaluating students all the way up to the evaluation of the U.S. Office of Education) and the teacher-training institutions. The reasons that the teacher-training institutions have become a major part of the problem in education instead of being a part of the solution are that most of them are practicing the malpractices, are teaching the teachers-to-be to practice the malpractices, and are training the students for an obsolete role as presenters of course content. Although some of the schools of education think they are being very modern by individualizing their instructional program, the content of the individualized program still emphasizes the traditional role of the teacher as a presenter of course content rather than teaching the teachers-to-be on how to individualize instruction for their students. The new role of the teacher as an instructioneer is the one that should be taught by the teacher-training institutions and should be *practiced by teachers at all levels of education*.

Among traditional educators, there has been a belief for decades that elementary school teachers teach differently and should be trained differently than either secondary school teachers or higher education faculty and that secondary school teachers teach differently and should be trained differently than either elementary school teachers or higher education faculty. The new role of the teacher and the process of designing instruction as described in this series is essentially the same role and involves the same basic behaviors for teachers at all levels of education from pre-school to graduate or continuing education.

The National Field Task Force on the Improvement and Reform of American Education has called for a new leadership to bring about increased effectiveness and inefficiency. In their report, the Task Force states that:

The welfare of this nation requires that schools attain new levels of success, and that this attainment be more inclusive of the population. Although a larger proportion of American youth is enrolled in school than at any other time in our national history, many thousands leave school with inadequate sustaining learning skills — and with insufficient preparation for the transition from school to the work force and effective participation in other aspects of the society.

Although their report calls for administrators to take on the leadership role, I believe successful change can best be brought about by cooperative leadership on the part of both teachers and administrators. Teachers should take the lead in accepting and performing their new role and encourage administrators to accept and perform their new role. Administrators should take the lead in accepting and performing their new role and encourage teachers to accept and perform their new role. Because of the transposition of authority as discussed in Chapter IX, Volume No. 3, it is actually more important that teachers be the first to institute changes which increase student learning. Whereas it is possible for teachers to improve student learning without administrative leadership and cooperation, it is almost impossible for administrators to improve student learning without the leadership and cooperation of teachers.

An important point to remember is that regardless of the teacher's feelings towards behavioral objectives, systems approaches, humanism, etc., practically every teacher evaluates their students and assigns some kind of evaluation mark. Realizing that not all desirable objectives lend themselves to measurement, the intent of this series is to maximize the learning of whatever it is that teachers are presently using as a basis to evaluate students and then to improve the quality, quantity and relevance of the learning objectives for each course.

INTRODUCTION

I expect to hear repeatedly three particular comments about this series. First, I expect to hear comments about the reading level of this series or that it is not very *scholarly*. Second, I expect some traditional oriented educators to be upset because I haven't quoted from or referred to the works of the many *big wheels* in education often enough (name-dropping) or at all. Third, in looking at this series in its present form, some readers will charge that I have not practiced what I am preaching.

With reference to the use of *scholarly* language, I would like to describe an experience which I had about five years ago. I had just completed a two-day seminar at a university when one of the faculty participants approached me and said, *I really liked the Seminar, but one thing has bothered me throughout the Seminar. What is that?*, I asked. *Your language,* said the professor. I asked him, *What is wrong with my language?* He replied, *It was not very scholarly.* I asked him, *What do you mean by saying that my language was not very scholarly?* The participant replied, *I understood everything you said!!!* Particularly in higher education, there is a tendency among faculty to select textbooks that will impress members of an accrediting team or most visiting colleagues even though the textbook may be so *scholarly* that even the teacher has trouble understanding what the author is saying (not to mention the fact that many of the students can't read or learn from it).

The name-dropping syndrome which is found in most *acceptable* papers, articles, and books is supposed to indicate that the author is acquainted with the work done by others in the field. By careful selection of references and quotes from the publications of *big wheels* in almost any major field of study, it is possible to support almost any point of view via inference. This is because in the process of developing a particular point-of-view, many of the *big wheels* have changed their ways of looking at certain concepts. As a partial result of the *publish or perish* dictum in higher education, a trend has developed which at best is questionable. This trend is the writing of articles and books which are primarily built on quotations and references from other writers with little, if any, new contributions actually being made by the person writing the article or book except the collecting of the quotations and references. Under certain conditions, this type of article or book could be of value particularly when it is one of the first in its field. After that, most of the articles and books in this category are just a rehash of one another. Since I have been conducting seminars and classes for over a decade on the topic of this series, the vast majority of the material in this series is original. In fact, the beginning of this series goes back to a 74-page paper entitled *A Behavioral Learning Systems Concept as Applied to Courses in Education and Training* which I wrote in 1964. Over 5,000 copies of this paper and revised editions of this paper have been sold. I have also written a number of articles during the past decade on various aspects of the same basic concept and these have been published in a wide variety of journals, magazines, and books.

There have been a number of publications which have been written about various aspects of developing objectives or developing instructional units which have been written in a format which would illustrate that the author was *practicing what he was preaching.* This would be very laudable if all the readers of the publications had the same needs. Rarely is this a realistic assumption. Although it is possible that some publications will only be read by one type of reader, the majority of publications are read by readers with differing needs. Therefore, the design of this series has been based on an analysis of reader needs and hopefully has built in sufficient flexibility that most of the many reader needs can be satisfied.

A majority of the initial users of this series will probably use this book as a reference source and many of the learners who use this series as textbooks for formal courses will probably also want to use this series as reference sources after they have completed the courses. Since most reference books are of the traditional format, I decided to write this series in the traditional format except for the following:

1. The general objectives (GO) and some of the specific objectives (SO) for each chapter will be listed at the beginning of each chapter.

    NOTE: The GO's and SO's at the beginning of each chapter are those which I believe are particularly important. A teacher who may want to use one or more of the volumes as a textbook for a course, may want to add more GO's and SO's and/or may want to delete some of the GO's and SO's which I have listed.

2. Following this Introduction, there is a list of six categories of readers who might read this book with directed guidelines for each type as to how they might locate what is most relevant for them.

3. Following the list of potential readers and their prescriptions is a list of fifty-one critical new concepts which are suggested in this book with the page numbers where these concepts are discussed in more detail.

4. For those learners who have problems in reading this series because of the reading level and for those learners who learn better from an audio-visual source or like an audio-visual reinforcement, films

covering most of the major topics and accompanying Active-Involvement Forms will be available by late 1975 or in 1976.

As mentioned in the Preface, the primary purpose of my first book, *Educational Malpractices: The Big Gamble in Our Schools,* was to point out to students, parents and educators, specific problems in the traditional approach to the instructional process which interfere with learning and to present a summary of the solutions to these problems which is presented in this series in much greater detail and are designed to eliminate the educational malpractices and to maximize student learning. To accomplish this task, I have divided the series into three volumes.

Volume I   Changing Role of the Educator: The Instructioneer
Volume II   A Behavioral Learning Systems Approach to Instruction: Analysis and Synthesis
Volume III   Creating an Emphasis on Learning: Quality Control, Productivity, and Accountability

In order to help most educators to accept the changes suggested in this series, I have found that it is necessary to present the rationale or reasons which support the need for the changes. Chapters I-III, Volume I, have been written with this view in mind. Chapter I, *Education vs. Instruction: Which is the Profession,* points out some of the major problems in education today and how they conflict with the alleged functions of education in our society. Chapter II, *Instruction or Education: Which is Humanizing,* takes a very critical problem which is of concern to educators, students, parents, and almost every citizen in our country and points out how the present instructional approach in most schools is not very humane and how by changing the teacher's role and by instituting a Behavioral Learning Systems Approach in the instructional process not only makes the process more humane, but can contribute significantly towards developing students who are more humane in their relationships with other people. Chapter III, *Why a Behavioral Learning Systems Approach (BLSA) to Instruction?,* describes various definitions of *systems* and how the application of the systems concept can help to eliminate many of the problems found in the present educational process without being as rigid and inhumane. Chapter IV, *Identification and Development of a Philosophy of Instruction and Theories of Instruction,* describes the six steps to be taken in achieving excellence in instruction and then continues on to develop the first step, identification of a philosophy of instruction and the theories of instruction. Chapter V, *The Changing Role of the Teacher from Educator to Instructioneer,* is the major and last chapter of the first volume and describes the second step in the process of designing effective and efficient instruction. A comparison is made of the new role with the traditional role of the teacher with an emphasis on how the new role helps the teacher and the whole instructional process become more humane in dealing with students. Major differences between the traditional philosophy and the philosophy of the Behavioral Learning Systems Approach (BLSA) to instruction are pointed out particularly as these differences affect the role of the teacher, i.e., whereas tradition considers student errors as a normal student or genetic problem which requires little, if any, follow up, the philosophy of the BLSA considers student errors as a learning problem brought about by student learning differences or problems in the learning environment, both of which can be solved. The Chapter ends with a description of a number of supportive roles which can help the teacher be more effective and efficient.

Volume II, *A Behavioral Learning Systems Approach to Instruction: Analysis and Synthesis,* concerns the next two steps in the process of designed instruction: the identification and specification of learning objectives and matching test items and the development of the instructional environment such that it will facilitate the achievement of the desired objectives. Chapter VI, *Determining the Purpose of the Instructional Event: Objectives and Evaluation,* is the first chapter in Volume II and is primarily concerned with the specifying and evaluation of instructional objectives in all three domains of learning: cognitive, sensory, and affective. In addition, reasons for specifying objectives, and guidelines for writing specific objectives, and the questions to be asked to justify the students' need to learn the objectives are discussed in detail. One of the most important concepts covered in this chapter is the need for and how to identify the minimum common core specific objectives in each course. Another important concept presented in this chapter concerns the need for a high correlation between the statements of what should be learned (specific objectives) and the test items or criteria for evaluation used to evaluate whether or not the desired learning has been achieved. As discussed in the chapter, this need for a high correlation between objectives and evaluation makes most traditional evaluation procedures and formats inappropriate and obsolete including standardized and normed tests and the so-called objective type test items (multiple-choice, true-false, and matching).

Chapter VII, *A Behavioral Learning Systems Approach to the Design of the Instructional Environment,* is the other chapter in Volume II of the series. The Chapter starts out with a comparison between the development of learning environments with and without specific objectives. Next, the development and selection of instructional software and hardware is discussed in detail.

Volume III, *Creating an Emphasis on Learning: Quality Control, Productivity, and Accountability,* concerns the necessity for making learning the major emphasis in our schools rather than the traditional emphasis which may have little relationship with learning. Chapter VIII, *Quality Control, Productivity, and Accountability,* starts out by discussing three important concepts: a critical principle of evaluation, the effects of a problem called *entropic drift,* and an evolutionary (some might call it revolutionary) transposition of authority which takes student learning from the bottom of the authority pyramid and puts it at the top of an inverted pyramid of support functions. Then the evaluation of students, teachers, administrators, etc., are discussed from the point of view of their affect on student learning. Of particular importance is the discussion of the evaluation of teachers as professionals rather than as artists or laborers.

Chapter IX, *Instructional Research: A New Role,* describes the last step in the designing of effective and efficient instruction. Traditionally, educational research has had little, if any, affect on what actually happens in the classrooms of our schools. The reasons for this waste of energy, time, and educational dollars are identified and then, the chapter concerns itself with methods by which instructional research can become a critical partner in designed instruction.

Chapter X, *Changing From Traditional (Chance) Education to Designed Instruction,* concerns the various steps that can be taken to bring about the change in the instructional environment. Included are comments on the implications of the Behavioral Learning Systems Approach on a variety of contemporary innovations in education.

By the time many readers reach this point in the last volume of the series, they will have questions which they want answered. For other readers who want to implement some of the suggestions I have made in this book, their colleagues may have challenged them with some questions about various aspects of the systems concept or about the imagined results of implementing some or all of the systems concepts. Therefore, the last part of Chapter X consists of a number of questions (and my answers to these questions) which typically arise at the Seminars which I have conducted with faculty from a variety of schools, colleges, and universities throughout the United States and Canada.

GUIDELINES TO READERS

In order to minimize the learning time involved in going through this book, I will identify six categories of readers. Categories II and III are further divided into sub-categories. After each grouping there are brief guidelines as to how readers in that grouping can get the most out of this series in the shortest time. (Those readers who have already read my book, *Educational Malpractices*, or have attended one of my seminars, see footnote below.)

I. *Description:* Learners who are planning to be teachers in preschool, elementary, secondary, higher education, or continuing adult education (this also includes people who are planning to teach in training programs in business and industry, military programs, and private schools).

    Prescription: In reading through this series, pay particular attention to the general objectives (GO's) and specific objectives (SO's) found at the beginning of each chapter. If one or more of these volumes are being used as a textbook for a course, it would be particularly helpful if the teacher of the course followed some of the guidelines suggested in the series. Although most of the SO's are rote memory, the major process objective is described in Chapter X, Volume III, under pre-service training. It is very important that you get involved in solving a learning problem such that 90 percent or more of the students learn 100 percent of your SO's as the process will convince you of the practicality of the instructional design process. Also, be sure to use a pretest and post-test of your attitudes towards the four basic concepts of the whole series. This attitudinal instrument is described under the affective domain in Chapter VI, Volume II.

II. *Description:* Teachers who are already teaching and would be

---

My book, *Educational Malpractices*, and my seminars have both emphasized the problems to be found in traditional education and have presented a summary in 68 pages of the book or in two days or more of the seminars what is contained in about 1000 pages in this series. Consequently there is an overlap which is spread throughout the series. Therefore, in addition to the guidelines suggested for the reader category that you fit into, try to program yourself through the reading. Every time you come to a familiar concept, section, paragraph, or sentence which you recognize comes from *Educational Malpractices* or from one of my seminars, skip ahead by skim reading until you encounter new material and then slow down your reading speed to your usual level.

interested in trying out some new ideas and/or approaches to the instructional process. This category can be divided into six sub-groups.

A. *Description:* Teachers who are already trying some aspects of the systems concepts and want to either double check their present approach or expand their application of the systems concept to their instructional activities.

   Prescription: Before reading any of this book, readers in this group should read through the list of fifty-one critical new concepts which follows this section. Any concept which is of interest can be pursued by reading the reference pages listed at the end of each concept. In addition to these specific references, here are some general guidelines. For this group, the first three chapters of Volume I can probably be skipped. You should read through Chapter IV and those parts of Chapter V dealing with learning problems and individual differences. In Volume II, depending upon your experience in specifying objectives and developing matching test items, you may find it best to skim read over those parts you already know and practice and read a little more carefully those parts that are new. You may also find that Volume II will be a very good reference source as you develop and/or select instructional materials. In Volume III, that part of Chapter VIII dealing with the evaluation of students should be of interest and you might want your administrators to read that part of Chapter VIII dealing with teacher evaluation. If your use of various systems concepts is being challenged by your colleagues, you may find the last part of Chapter X useful as it concerns questions and answers about various systems concepts.

B. *Description:* New teachers who have not had any formal training on *how to teach* or *how to test* and also haven't been teaching long enough that they are committed to a particular technique or approach to instruction.*

   Prescription: Readers in this group can probably skim over the first three chapters in Volume I. Because teachers in this group

---

* Quite often, teachers in this group feel guilty about not having any special training or courses on *how to teach and test.* Since few education courses are relevant to the needs of teachers-to-be, not having any formal training actually becomes a benefit. In other words, they haven't been tainted yet!

will have a tendency to teach *as they were taught*, Chapter IV and particularly Chapter V will be very important. All of Volume II will also be very important. That part of Chapter VIII in Volume III dealing with student evaluation is of importance, but the rest of Volume III may not be appropriate at the moment.

C. *Description:* New teachers who have had formal training on *how to teach and test*, but haven't been teaching long enough to be considered as being in the traditional teaching rut.

Prescription: The first three chapters in Volume I will probably be very important for these readers as they may have difficulty in accepting the rationale for the need to change the teacher's role and in accepting the new role itself. Chapters IV and V and all of Volume II will also be of importance to this group of readers. Again, only that part of Chapter VIII dealing with student evaluation is of particular importance; however, all of Volume III could be of value in helping the reader to accept and put into action the Behavioral Learing System Approach (BLSA) to instruction.

D. *Description:* Teachers who have been teaching for a long enough period of time to develop a pattern or style of teaching that is fairly consistent, but haven't had any formal training on *how to teach or test.*

Prescription: Teachers in this group will generally take a little longer to make the transition from the traditional approach to the Behavioral Learning Systems Approach. Because of this, readers in this group should pay particular attention to Chapters I—III in Volume I. Depending upon how traditional your pattern of teaching is (if you fit into this group), it may be useful to read Volume III before finishing Volume I or starting Volume II. The more traditional you are, the more important it may be to read Volume III. After Volume III, it may be best to read through Volume II and then come back to read Chapter IV and V in Volume I. After reading Chapter V on the new role of the teacher, it may be useful to review those sections in the rest of the series which you found most difficult to accept. It would also be useful if you could follow up the reading by attending a seminar dealing with these concepts in order to meet and talk with other teachers who are in a similar situation and some person(s) who is well acquainted with the systems concept.

E. *Description:* Teachers who have been teaching for a long enough period of time to develop a pattern or style of teaching that is fairly consistent and have had formal training on *how to teach and test.*

Prescription: The more traditional the teacher's pattern of teaching the more difficult it may be to make the transition from the traditional approach to the Behavioral Learning Systems Approach. However, an ameliorative factor is that many or maybe even most traditional teachers basically want students to have successes in learning and want to be at least partially involved in helping the students achieve their successes. I sincerely believe that once the traditional teacher is convinced that the concepts suggested in this series will actually help more students learn more that the teacher will be motivated to make the change and will try to be as loyal to the systems approach as the teacher was to the traditional approach. Given this situation, readers from this group should read Chapters I—III in Volume I, skip over Chapter IV, read Chapter V and then read Chapters VIII and X in Volume III. If, at this point, the reader is convinced of the need for specific objectives and matching test items in designed instruction, read Chapter IV and then all of Volume II. If the reader still has doubts about the need for specific objectives and matching test items, it may be best to try to attend a seminar on the systems concepts; to try to meet with some fellow teachers who are applying some of the systems concepts in their courses; and/or identify a learning problem in one of the reader's own courses and while trying to develop a solution to the problem read through Chapter IV in Volume I and all of Volume II.

III. *Description:* This category of readers are involved in trying to help teachers to make the changes and/or to implement some of the suggestions made in this book through in-service sessions which probably include large and small group meetings and individual conferences.

A. *Description:* This subgroup of readers are ones whose primary task is the conducting of in-service professional development sessions.

Prescription: For this group, Chapter X of Volume III will probably be the most important preparation and should be read first. In addition, Chapters I—III in Volume I and the malpractice dialogues at the end of my book, *Educational Malpractices,* should be very useful in answering the faculty questions of the type *Why I shouldn't change!* I assume that if the in-service sessions are to be about the systems concepts, that Chapters IV through VIII will be read very thoroughly. It would be very useful for this person if before any in-service sessions he or she worked with an interested teacher and identified a learning problem and solved it in accordance with the systems concepts. This would not only be a good experience for the in-service trainer, but the problem and solution could be used as a model for similar efforts by other teachers attending the in-service session.

B. *Description:* This subgroup are administrators who have responsibilities for the instructional program but have never had any formal training on *how to teach or test.*

Prescription: During the past decade, this group has been trying to think of themselves as *instructional leaders.* At the present time, this particular group of readers may be hesitant to lead in a direction in which they have not had any formal training. Since most formal courses on *How to Teach and Test* are irrelevant, not having them can actually be considered a benefit. For this group it would probably be best to read Chapters I—III in Volume I and all of Volume III. Before trying to encourage teachers to change, it might be very useful to read through the malpractice dialogues at the end of my book, *Educational Malpractices,* and then to read Chapters IV and V of Volume I. Because the administrator will probably not be as involved in the instructional process as the teacher, it isn't as necessary that he or she knows the contents of Volume II as well as the teachers. However, administrators should be acquainted with the concepts if only to be in a better position to understand what the teachers are doing. Those administrators who want to think of themselves as *instructional leaders,* should know Volume II as well or better than the teachers and since these administrators usually don't have classes of students upon which they could practice the application of the systems concepts, they should work frequently with teachers in their efforts to identify and solve learning problems and to develop instructional materials in accordance with the systems concepts (as presented in Volume II).

C. *Description:* This subgroup are administrators who have responsibilities for the instructional program and have had formal training on *How to Teach and Test.*

Prescription: The main difference between the last subgroup and this one is that the administrators who have been trained as traditional teachers will have a greater tendency to evaluate teachers in accordance with traditional criteria which in turn will tend to keep teachers in their traditional role despite efforts by the administrators to get them to change. As a result, readers in this group may have to pay particular attention to Chapter VIII in Volume III. Otherwise, the prescription would be the same as the last group. If you are a reader in this group and you feel that you are quite progressive and that your faculty have been and are involved in many instructional innovations, you may find that the Exhibits (pp. 143—244) in Part II of my book, *Educational Malpractices: The Big Gamble in Our Schools,* and Chapter X in Volume III of this series may be important in evaluating prior and present innovations. In case your time for reading is limited and particularly if you feel your faculty are already using some aspects of the learning systems concept, you may want to look through the following section on the *Summary of New Concepts* (as suggested in this series) and pick out the concepts which you feel most relevant for you and your faculty and read up on those.

IV. *Description:* This category of readers are in many ways the most important because they are the teachers of students who are learning to be teachers and what they do or don't do with these students will indirectly affect millions of other students that these students will be teaching.

Prescription: This category breaks into two subgroups. The largest of the two subgroups concerns those teachers of teachers-to-be that are teaching any of the subjects these students might take *but not* actually courses on *How to Teach and/or Test.* These readers can follow the prescriptions outlined for them under category II with the following added reminder: students will go out as teachers and they will teach the way they were taught not necessarily the way they were taught to teach (particularly when the way they were taught to teach doesn't match the way they were actually taught)!

The other subgroup, although smaller, is the most critical group of all. These readers are the ones who will decide whether or not to use this book as a textbook in their course(s) on *How to Teach and/or Test.* In previewing this book, look through the following section on the *Summary of New Concepts* (as suggested in this series). Then, you should read Chapter X, Chapter V, and Chapter VIII. If you can accept the concepts and particularly the new teacher's role as an instructioneer, then you might read Chapters I—IV, skim read through Chapter V again, and then read Chapters VI and VII. Of critical importance in the design of a successful course involving the concepts presented in this series, would be the practicing of what is preached and the course project in which each student identifies and solves one or more learning problem units.

V. *Description:* This particular group of readers are primarily interested in doing research which might affect what happens in instructional situations.

Prescription: For this group, Chapters IV and IX will be the most important. Then the reader may want to look through the following section on the *Summary of New Concepts* (as suggested in this series) and also Chapter V for some ideas on what research they might want to do. The balance of the book could be read in any sequence desired.

VI. *Description:* This last category of readers consists of parents of students and students themselves who want to find out in more detail how to go about improving the instructional process so as to be more conversant on the topic when talking with professional educators or when trying to evaluate teachers or schools as to their effectiveness and efficiency.

Prescription: The readers in this group should first read my other book, *Educational Malpractices: The Big Gamble in Our Schools.* Having read that book, these readers might want to read Chapters IV, V, VIII, and X in this series and then whatever concepts in the following section, *Summary of New Concepts* (as suggested in this series, which are of interest to them.

SUMMARY OF NEW CONCEPTS

I consider the following 51 concepts to be essentially new and different from instructional concepts found in most other books of a similar nature. Not all of these concepts are new from the point-of-view that no one has ever heard or thought of them before; but they are new in that most educators, particularly traditional educators, have not come in contact with them before. Even though some of the more innovative educators have thought of and maybe even practiced some of these concepts, the major contribution I think I can make in addition to the concepts themselves, which may be new to even these innovative educators, is that all of these 51 concepts fit together in a package and constitute the Behavioral Learning Systems Approach to Instruction.

Volume I. *The Changing Role of the Educator: The Instructioneer.*

1. As a profession, education is the only one that commits malpractices on its clients by design and tradition. (See pages 27-36).

2. Actually education, as traditionally practiced, is not a profession in accordance with the three primary criteria for evaluating a profession: the existence of a specialized knowledge and skills; high standards of achievement and conduct; and a prime purpose of public service. (See pages 7-20).

3. Although the humanization or dehumanization of the instructional process is a critical issue in our society, most of the teachers of the courses which are claimed to be the major vehicles for humanization actually teach and test in a manner which is not very humane! (See pages 26, 29-31).

4. Given that humanism is concerned with positive interrelationships with other people and the respect for the rights of others, to interpret humanism as the freedom to *do your own thing* is to develop selfism, an emphasis on self regardless of effects on others, which is anti-humanism. (See pages 57-60).

5. Regardless of whether or not a teacher likes the concept of a *system's approach to instruction*, each teacher and each student is already an integral part of one or more systems and these systems

will continue to exist and function as systems. Therefore, the question *is not* do we or don't we want to use a systems approach, but given we are already in an instructional system, do we want to maximize the potential positive benefits and minimize any negative aspects. (See pages 69-78).

6. Although many educators, psychologists, and others have written about and tried to develop a theory of instruction, there hasn't been one which has proved itself in application. There is a theory of instruction, in fact, two theories of instruction: one for teaching and learning in the affective domain and one for teaching and learning in the other domains of learning. (See pages 101-120).

7. Once an educator accepts the concept and need for actually individualizing instruction instead of just talking about it, the classroom concept becomes obsolete along with all of the teacher behaviors associated with the classroom concept, i.e., the teacher as a presenter of content, the topic of classroom management, micro-teaching, practice-teaching (as practiced in most teacher-training institutions, etc. (See pages 129-136).

8. The humanistic role is that of an Instructioneer who helps each student achieve success by identifying his or her learning problems and solving them. (See pages 136-144).

9. Most teachers already practice this role but not in the right place. Notice the following conflict in most traditional teachers' behavior. If a student came up to a teacher in the hallway and said, *I don't understand what you were just saying in class*, not a single teacher in the tens of thousands that I have ever talked with would even think of taking out their gradebook and grade the student down for asking that question. Almost all of the teachers I know would try to solve the student's learning problem. However, in the classroom, when most traditional teachers give tests and students make mistakes which indicate that *they don't know or understand*, most teachers will mark the mistake as wrong and record the score in the gradebook without solving the learning problems. The instructional process can be significantly improved, if teachers will only bring their behavior in the hallways of *trying to solve learning problems* into the classroom and solve learners' learning problems instead of recording grades. (See pages 304-306).

10. In almost all areas of our society, it is an accepted common sense practice to diagnose first and design the appropriate treatment

second. Only in the traditional approach to education is this process reversed. The treatment is given to the students first and then the students are given the test. Not only is the common sense sequence reversed, but the data revealed in the diagnosis (test) is usually ignored except for some kind of score which is recorded. I refer to this behavior of the traditional educators as evidence of the *Backwards Ostrich Philosophy*. Tests should be given first and the treatments designed to fit the needs of the learner as evidenced by the results of the tests. At the end of the treatment, a duplicate test should be given and depending upon the results of that test, subsequent treatments should be revised to facilitate the learning of whatever was missed. (See pages 88,187-188).

11. A learning problem is basically any situation in which a student is expected to learn, but for one reason or another the student hasn't achieved the desired learning (student errors on tests, essays, etc.) As a learning problem, it is something to be solved, not just recorded in a gradebook. (See pages 144-196).

12. When a student leaves a unit of a course or a course not knowing some of the objectives of that unit or course which are a prerequisite for success in subsequent units or courses, his or her chances for success are significantly reduced. This condition is referred to as *cumulative ignornace.* It is not the fault of the learner. The teacher and our present system were the ones that allowed the student to leave the unit or course not knowing the critical objectives. *Cumulative ignorance* is a malignant disease associated with the traditional teacher-oriented educational system and it should be eliminated or at least reduced. (See pages 36-39, 42-43, 64,73).

13. A very common and hence popular misconception among educators and psychologists is the use of the words *ability* and *capacity* as synonyms when referring to intelligence. As a result, evidence of differences in ability and particularly evidence of different levels of ability are reported in such a manner as to indicate that these same differences apply to *capacity* (limits) as well. Most research that is used to suggest or prove that one race or culture has more intelligence than another is based on this popular misconception. As far as I have been able to find out, no one has ever identified the 100 percent full capacity (limits) of the human mind. Therefore, at this point in time, it is not valid to even hypothesize, let alone prove, that there are differences in capacity (limits). Probably the most acceptable hypothesis of the capacity (limits) of the human mind is that it has infinite capacity (limits). Can you imagine a situation in

which the healthy mind stops accepting any further input because it is full? On the other hand, I can't imagine anyone not agreeing that there are individual differences in ability of which part of this difference is genetic and part of it is environmental or learned. Just because there are differences in ability does not in any way affect the concept of capacity (limits). Ability may very well affect how the capacity *is filled* given certain situations but not the capacity (limits) itself. Differences in ability are clues which indicate the need for different learning materials, techniques, and pathways in order for the same learning to occur. For example, most IQ tests tend to be based on verbal ability. Therefore, students who score low on IQ tests have low verbal ability at that point in time. In order to bring about learning, a teacher could either teach verbal ability or use learning techniques that are less verbal and more appropriate for the learner's abilities. You do not have to compromise or change what they learn only how they learn. (See pages 31-35, 75, 88, 92-100).

14. Intelligence is frequently equated to *rate of learning* such that the slower learner is considered to be not as *intelligent* as the faster learner. Given that students learn best in different ways, to compare students intelligence (rate of learning) in a situation where these differences are ignored is unfair and the student's *apparent* rate of learning is not equal to the student's *real* rate of learning. (See pages 204-279).

15. Given that a teacher performs the role of the Instructioneer such that students' learning problems are identified and solved, at least 90 percent or more of the students can learn 100 percent of specified learning objectives. (See pages 111-120).

Volume II. *A Behavioral Learning Systems Approach to Instruction: Analysis and Synthesis*

16. An addition to the two domains of learning, cognitive and affective, the third domain is not the psychomotor domain as is popularly believed. The third domain of learning is the *sensory* domain. (See pages 394-412).

17. All cognitive, sensory, and affective domain objectives are nonmeasurable on a direct basis and, as such, they are all general objectives. (See page 104, Volume I, and pages 351-353).

18. When one specifies a specific behavior which is supposed to signify

indirectly the achievement or existence of a cognitive, sensory, or affective domain objective, the achievement is by inference only and, as such, the specific measurable objective is only a part of the more general non-measurable objective. (See pages 343-348).

19. The measurement of the achievement of specific learning objectives in the three domains of learning refers to different student behaviors: cognitive learning is inferred from psychomotor behavior, sensory learning is inferred from sensomotor behavior, and affective learning is inferred from emotive behavior. (See pages 103-104, Volume I and 367-370).

20. Instead of hiding from students what they should be learning which is traditional, students should know at the beginning of a unit or course what cognitive and sensory learning they will be expected to achieve. (See pages 105, 147-151, Volume I, and pages 336-338).

21. Affective domain objectives are not generally given to the learners ahead of time nor should the achievement or non-achievement of affective domain objectives be used to arrive at grades for learners. The achievement or non-achievement of affective domain objectives by learners is primarily a measure of the effectiveness of the teaching design rather than being a measure of learning. (See pages 105-110, Volume I, and pages 413-424).

22. In contrast to the teaching and learning of cognitive and sensory learning which is done directly, the teaching and learning of affective learning has to be done indirectly. You cannot demand the achievement of an affective objective. If you do, you are liable to develop beliefs, attitudes, and values which are opposite from what you want. (See pages 105-110, Volume I, and pages 413-424).

23. In contrast to cognitive and sensory learning which is achieved best when it is done intentionally and is achieved least when ignored, affective learning goes on all the time regardless of whether or not teachers want to do anything about the development of beliefs, attitudes, and values through the use of a designed systematic approach to instruction. At the present time, most beliefs, attitudes, and values are developing by chance and, as such, some of these emotional tendencies are not necessarily in the best interests of the students, the schools, the community, or our country. (See pages 416-417).

24. Despite the fact that some educators are against the concept of

behavioral objectives, almost every teacher depends on *behavioral test items* for evaluation. In other words, almost every teacher evaluates their students and bases their evaluation on something the student is doing (behavior) or has done (the result of a behavior). (See pages 456-57, 644-648).

25. The learner behaviors which are required to indicate achievement of an objective have to match as close as possible the behavior specified in the unit or course objectives, i.e., objective type test items are inappropriate because rarely does an objective specify the exact behaviors which take place in the objective type test situation. (See pages 458-468).

26. The purpose of most tests which are given in traditional educational settings is to obtain a score of some kind which later can be used as a basis for assigning a grade or can be manipulated in a variety of ways using various statistical instruments in order to generate more data. The purpose of tests under the learning systems concept is to identify student learning problems. If any score is given to a student, it would be when the student has achieved 100 percent of the test. (See pages 461, 490, 500-2).

27. The test items, papers, performances or whatever else a teacher uses to evaluate students' achievement are actually the real objectives of a course or instructional unit. If there is any difference between the learner behaviors described in the professed objectives for the course and the learner behaviors necessary to successfully pass the evaluation instrument (test, paper, etc.), students will generally try to learn whatever is on the evaluation instrument and will ignore the stated objectives. As a result, if there are stupid or irrelevant test items and/or criteria in the evaluation instrument, students end up learning stupid and irrelevant things. (See pages 500-502).

28. It is good to *teach to the test*. In fact, that is what teachers should be doing! If a test actually tests for the achievement of something a teacher wants students to learn, then why not teach what you want the students to learn (the test). If a test doesn't test for the achievement of something a teacher wants students to learn then of course a teacher shouldn't teach to *that* test nor should the teacher use *that* test. (See pages 474-480).

29. There is no place in designed instruction for *normal* or standardized tests because they are not based on a standardized list of specific objectives and the distribution of scores is built into the tests, i.e., a

professional test item writer can take any multiple-choice item and by holding the stem and the correct choice constant and by varying the distractors in the wrong choices can get almost any percentage the writer wants of the people who are answering the test item to answer it correctly or incorrectly. In addition, in *normed* tests, test items are selected primarily because they are good discriminators rather than because they measure the achievement of important learning. A good discriminator is a test item that 50 percent of the students will miss whereas a good test item should be one that is first considered important and desirable. (See pages 513-523).

30. When dealing with rote memory objectives and test items, 100 percent achievement of the objectives is equal to 100 percent achievement of the matching test items because they are on a one to one basis. However, when dealing with process objectives and test items where almost every objective is tested by more than one test item, the percentage achievement of the objective is rarely equal to the percentage achievement of process test items. 100 percent achievement of process objective may be equal to 80 percent achievement of process test items. (See pages 360-365, 495-499).

31. Most innovations in education and instruction are concerned with different methods of doing something. As long as teachers don't know specifically what they want their students to learn, any method should be acceptable. However, once a goal is defined, there may be certain methods which will be more successful in facilitating learning in certain students than other methods. (See pages 662-670).

32. Similarly, as long as teachers don't know specifically what their students should be learning, almost any materials can be selected, particularly for a learning resource center and open classrooms. Under these conditions, learning is by chance and is biased in the direction of the person(s) who selects the materials. Once the desired objectives are specified, there will be certain materials which will be more successful in facilitating learning for certain students than other materials. (See pages 672-679).

33. Instead of having every teacher reinvent their course objectives as if no one else had ever taught the course before and given that the vast majority of students are going to live in the same society, there has got to be something in common in every course with the same name that is considered desirable to learn, regardless of where in the country the course is taught. These minimum common core

objectives can be identified. (See pages 527-537, 632-4).

34. Students may know best how they learn and what they are interested in, but they do not know best *what* they should learn. (See pages 635-643).

Volume III. *Creating an Emphasis on Learning: Quality Control, Productivity, and Accountability*

35. In all evaluation of humans, there is a psychological principle in operation. *Human beings tend to do those things that the person whom they allow to evaluate them wants them to do!* What this means is that as long as teachers are evaluated on a variety of things not including learning, then teachers will tend to be concerned about a variety of things not including learning. When teachers are at least partially evaluated on the basis of the student learning they have helped facilitate, then they will tend to be concerned about facilitating learning.

36. Whenever the goals are unknown or fuzzy, there is a tendency to make the means to the goals the objective or goal. This situation can be referred to as *Entropic Drift.* As long as we don't really know what students should be learning, the process or method becomes the most important. When a teacher doesn't know what students should be learning from reading a book, reading the book (the vehicle for learning) becomes the objective, rather than learning.

37. When identified student learning becomes the focus of schools, there can and will be a transposition of control. Whereas at the present time student learning is at the bottom of the authority pyramid and important (often critical) decisions concerning student learning are being made by people who rarely work with or even see the students, under the Behavioral Learning Systems Approach (BLSA), student learning is at the top of an inverted support pyramid, and everyone's role is designed to support the one above and indirectly to help facilitate student learning.

38. Whereas quality control is a familiar concept in many fields, it is long overdue in the instructional process. Whereas the traditional approach is satisfied with a normal curve's worth of achievement wherein the average student learns about "C" worth or about 75 percent which causes designed cumulative ignorance, under the

Behavioral Learning Systems Approach (BLSA), 90 percent or more of the students have to learn 100 percent of the required specific objectives. Whereas in the traditional approach, time, methods, and materials are constant and learning is a variable, under the BLSA, learning is kept as constant as possible and time, methods, and materials are all variables.

39. In talking with thousands of teachers, I find that they want quality control such that all students should be learning 100 percent of the specified objectives and/or test items instead of the 80-90 percent suggested by many *systems* consultants or the 65-75 percent (or less) which has been considered *normal* under the traditional approach to instruction. If you are a teacher or plan to be a teacher, consider the following situation, the question and your answer to the question:

> You have given your class a test in which there were 50 points possible and 40 points (80 percent) was identified as passing. The question is *If 40 points is passing, which 10 points are not important?* If your answer is that you think all 50 points are important, then you actually want the students to achieve 100 percent. If your answer is that there are 10 points that aren't important, then why are you testing for student achievement of unimportant things and why are you grading a student down for not learning something you now admit is not important!

40. Just as teacher organizations and other employee groups demand the right to have a grievance committee to give them recourse as protection against administrative decisions which are unjust and capricious, and with negative effects on the teachers; students need and should have the same right as protection against teacher decisions, grading, and educational procedures which are unjust and capricious and with negative effects on the students.

41. Once teacher training institutions accept the concept of individual differences in bringing about quality control in student learning, and that tests are diagnostic in nature, the present test and measurement course as offered in most teacher training institutions becomes obsolete. Unless a student is going into research, there is no need for the teacher-to-be to learn how to do statistical gymnastics with students' scores. Even if a student may plan to do educational research, there is no need to teach the student how to

use *distractors* in order to trick students into answering tests in such a way that the test maker obtains the curve of results he wants regardless of what students actually know or don't know. The emphasis in test and measurement courses from the systems point-of-view will be how to write objectives and test items that have a 100 percent correlation and on how to solve learning problems. Whereas in the traditional test and measurement course the best test items are ones that 50 percent of the students who are answering them will answer them wrong, under the learning systems concept the best test items are ones that are first considered important and secondly the ideal situation would be where 100 percent of the learners learn 100 percent of these important items.

42. Since the traditional courses in test and measurement are essentially useless, a critical condition exists in that not only are those teachers who have not had any training in testing not qualified to do testing and evaluation (about 50 percent of elementary and secondary teachers and almost 90 percent of higher education faculty), but even those teachers who have had training in tests and measurement are also not qualified to perform such a critical task in education and particularly in designed instruction.

43. Given an educational situation in which the average student only has to learn 75 percent of the course and a normal or *chance* distribution of learning is acceptable, it is not very necessary for the teacher to know much about teaching and/or testing. In addition, given that the teachers role is to present course content rather than to facilitate learning and that tests can be manipulated to give almost any desired results without affecting student learning, there is even less reason to know anything about teaching and testing. In contrast, in a society where learning has become very important, teaching-learning effectiveness also becomes important. As the costs of education increase, efficiency also becomes a critical issue. Under the BLSA where 90 percent or more of the students have to achieve 100 percent of the required SO's, it is necessary for teachers to know what they are doing. It takes specialized knowledge to be an effective and efficient teacher not only at the elementary and secondary levels, but also in higher education.

44. Individual differences as a concept applies to teachers as well as to students. Teacher negotiations and/or contracts which ignore indi-

vidual differences among teachers are unreal, and inappropriate, i.e., all teachers in a given institution should have the same size class, same teaching load, and paid about the same amount of money.

45. Given that the individual differences in teachers can be recognized and the teachers are performing the role of an instructioneer, teachers will be able to teach multiple levels of the same course and/or multiple courses simultaneously. This would be very similar to the old one-room school concept. No one ever heard of a teacher in a one-room school canceling fourth grade because there wasn't enough students enrolled. This concept becomes more important in view of decreasing enrollments.

46. Given that most teachers have not been taught how to teach as defined in terms of facilitating student learning, nor on how to develop and use diagnostic tests and that very few teachers have ever been hired on the basis of their ability to facilitate student learning, then it is not fair to hold a teacher accountable for student learning unless schools and administrative bodies provide appropriate systematic in-service training first.

47. Given a situation where a teacher is having trouble solving student learning problems, the administrative structure should include an *Instructional Crisis Squad* that could work with the teacher and help solve learning problems such that both the students and the teacher have success.

48. Although teacher salaries were in need of improvement and the teacher union movement has done a great deal to increase teacher salaries and to improve other working conditions, continued emphasis of teacher organizations on the teacher as a laborer rather than as a professional will be at the detriment of the teaching-learning situation. Professionalism and unionism are almost antithetical in their goals and concepts and teachers will have to decide which way they want to go.

49. Educational research has also been affected by entropic drift in that since we don't know what students should be learning (the goals of education), the emphasis of educational research has been on the process of education, i.e., methods, materials, techniques, etc. As such, educational research is a non-science because it deals with man-made phenomenon. In contrast, instructional research is primarily concerned with learning and is a science becuase learning

is a natural phenomenon.

50. Given that there is little commonality in what is being learned in courses with the same title, that tests can be manipulated to give any desired results, and that standardized tests don't match any known lists of specific learning objectives, not only is most educational research irrelevent and useless, most of it is invalid because the data is invalid. Regardless of the power of the statistical instruments used and the validity of the methods used, if the data is *garbage* to begin with, the results are still *garbage*. (GIGO — garbage in — garbage out!)

51. There is a method of evaluating the design of an instructional situation on the basis of three factors: potential boredom factor, the instructional effectiveness factor, and the instructional efficiency factor. Using this technique, it can be shown that *Seasame Street*, which has been heralded as the model for future instructional television, although entertaining, has a high potential for boredom and is not very effective nor efficient from the point-of-view of learning.

CHAPTER VI

DETERMINING THE PURPOSE OF THE INSTRUCTIONAL EVENT: OBJECTIVES AND EVALUATION

General and Specific Objectives:

GO — To understand the importance of having both general and specific objectives in designed instruction.

SO — Define *learning* in terms of it being both nonmeasurable and measurable as listed in the text and cite at least two examples from your own experience that demonstrate the existence of learning in accordance with both definitions.

SO — List the nine reasons for specifying objectives and give one or more examples for each that demonstrate the value and importance for specifying objectives.

SO — Describe the interrelationship between a general objective and its specific objectives as stated in this text.

SO — List the five reasons for having general objectives.

SO — Define a *specific objective* as defined in this text.

SO — Given a specific objective, identify the three basic elements.

SO — In specifying the criteria for achievement of process objectives, state why it is important to differentiate between objectives and test items and why it is important to treat all of the test items associated with the same process objective as a single unit.

GO — To understand the differences, similarities, and interrelationships of the three domains of learning.

SO — Given the interaction chart between the three domains of learning and the three types of consciousness, fill in the interactions in the nine squares and describe these interactions.

SO — List and define the three domains of learning as defined in this text.

SO — Describe the utility of a taxonomy as stated in this text and give at least two examples of this utility.

SO — Describe the characteristics of measurement in the three domains as stated in this text.

SO — Given the chart (Fig. 56), describe each of the four parts in the *Perception to Behavior* process in the sensory domain.

SO — State the major difference between the teaching and learning in the affective domain and the teaching and learning in the other two domains and identify how this difference affects the traditional way of teaching affective objectives. Describe two or more personal experiences which support the existence of this difference.

GO — To understand that the evaluation process in the instructional event is diagnostic in nature and as such has to correlate highly with the objectives of the instructional event.

SO — State the necessary relationship between objectives and test items for effective instruction and briefly describe each of the four categories of correlation problems.

SO — State why the so-called *objective type* test items are inappropriate for evaluation of learning.

SO — Describe the process of preparing a standardized examination and point out why these examinations are inappropriate and irrelevant for evaluating learning.

GO — To understand the process of identifying the Minimum Common Core objectives and to appreciate their value in designed instruction.

SO — Describe the steps and procedures used to identify the Minimum Common Core objectives.

GO — To know the guidelines for writing specific objectives and/or test items and to be able to apply the questions of justification.

SO — State the seven questions of justification and illustrate their use on two or more specific objectives and on two or more test items.

SO — Given a new course, describe the suggested procedures for getting general and specific objectives.

A. INTRODUCTION

Given a philosophy of instruction that assumes that every student can learn, two theories of instruction which provide basic strategies of how to make sure that every student can learn, and a role for the teacher as an instructioneer who can identify and solve student learning problems to facilitate learning, what is needed now is the rest of the elements in the instructional event in which these factors can be applied to students. Of the five elements in an instructional event, the instructioneer and the learner were discussed in the last chapter (Volume I). If the teacher's primary role is to identify and solve learning problems, it becomes critical to know what it is a student should be learning in order to identify whether or not a student is having a problem learning. In using a test to identify whether or not learning took place or in order to diagnose a learning problem, it also becomes critical that the tests (evaluation or diagnostic instruments) actual test for the achievement of what is supposed to have been learned. Without the one to one correlation, the diagnostic data is meaningless. Therefore, this chapter will deal with two more of the elements: the unit or course objectives and the evaluation instrument. These two elements answer the two questions which should be asked of anything called instructional: *What is being instructed?* and *How do you know if it was instructed?* In order to answer the first question, teachers at all levels of instruction need specific measurable learning objectives. In order to answer the second question, it is absolutely necessary to utilize testing procedures which actually test the achievement of these specific measurable learning objectives. This does not necessarily mean that everything that occurs in instructional institutions has to be backed up by specific learning objectives, but it does mean that before students can be involved in activities which are not designed for specific learning, these students should have achieved all of the objectives that are measurable in order that the student will not suffer from cumulative ignorance. As long as students are achieving everything they are supposed to learn, then they may be involved in a wide variety of activities in which the teacher, school district, college, or university feels that in some way the activity may be beneficial to the student, but are not specifically sure how to measure this benefit.

As pointed out repeatedly throughout this book, in order to improve the teaching-learning situation and to make the instructional process effective and efficient, it is necessary to know what it is we are trying to teach. As an illustration, I would like to refer to an incident in the story of *Alice in Wonderland.* Alice came to the crossroads and didn't know which way to go. She noticed a Cheshire Cat in a nearby tree and asked:

ALICE: *Which road should I take?*

CHESHIRE CAT: *Where are you going?*

ALICE: *I don't know!*

CHESHIRE CAT: *Well, then, any road will get you there!*

This incident from *Alice in Wonderland* has implications for instruction, in that if we don't know specifically what we want students to learn, or where we're going, then anything we are doing may be fine. Any learning pathway may be sufficient. But once we have specified where we want to go, or what we want the learners to learn, then there may be specific pathways which will take the learner there.

323

Not only have some research projects ended up with the conclusions that schools and teachers really don't seem to make much difference, now the National Association of Elementary School Principles are reporting that after hundreds of approaches (pathways) have been tried at the cost of millions of dollars to solve the problems in ghetto schools, there is little success. Even the Ford Foundation, in looking back at the decade of the sixties, has concluded that the impact of their millions of dollars invested in a wide variety of projects is negligible. It is difficult to identify any differences in student achievement between free schools, informal schools, open schools, or formal schools. Now suggestions are being made to give bachelor's degrees after three years instead of four and high school diplomas after eleven years instead of twelve. Like Alice, as long as we don't know where we are going, it really doesn't matter which pathway you take or where it ends up taking you!

In looking rationally and reasonably at the evidence, it would appear that there could be four places for problems. There could be problems in that the learners are not able to learn or that the teachers are not able to teach. Hopefully in the last chapter (Volume I), these potential problems were given potential solutions. There could also be problems in that the goals, objectives, or aims of the various educational projects were not identified specifically enough or the tests used to evaluate achievement were not appropriate. As will be pointed out by the end of this chapter, the actual problem is compounded by having both problems: a lack of specified goals and a lack of appropriate tests.

If you were going to build a house, a machine, or almost anything, you would want some kind of directions. The more important, costly, and/or complicated the task, the more critical is the need for specific directions. *Is the education of each student an important, costly, and complex task???* Where are our specific plans or educational objectives?? Very few educators teach from lists of specified objectives. Very few public school districts, colleges, or universities have outlined specific and measurable objectives for the courses they are offering to students. Very few state departments of education have outlined even minimum specific and measurable objectives for the various standard courses offered by the elementary and secondary schools in their state. Is it any wonder that having a diploma or a degree does not guarantee that the student has learned anything. High school diplomas and college degrees only guarantee that the student has spent 12 years getting the diploma and about four years getting the bachelor's degree.

A recent publication of the American Association of Colleges for Teacher Education, *Evaluative Criteria for Accrediting Teacher Education,* states that the most important thing that can happen in any educational institution is *LEARNING.* The only way we can tell for sure that learning is taking place in our schools is to test for it. BUT, if we do not know what the students are supposed to have learned, how can we test them to see if they have learned *IT?* Although most educators do give tests, since they do not really know specifically what they want the students to learn, the test results are used mainly to differentiate between students (curve grading) or to punish students. If *LEARNING* is our most important product in schools, then tests should be used to indicate what the students already know (correct answers) and what they have left to learn (wrong answers). What students already know, teachers can not do anything about. What students do not know, teachers can *teach* instead of trying to do *statistical gymnastics* with the test results. Arthur Coombs made a fitting statement in the ASCD 1970 Yearbook, *Commitment for the 70's.*

A man who has not determined what is truly important is like a ship without a rudder, at the mercy of every fad, fancy, or force which may be exerted upon him. When a person does not know what is important, then everything is important. When everything seems important, one must do everything. Other people seeing us do everything then come to expect us to do everything, and this, of course, keeps us so busy, we do not have time to think about what is important.

B. INSTRUCTIONAL SPECIFICATIONS

Instructional specifications have been and are referred to by a variety of names: purposes, outcomes, goals, objectives, aims, intentions, target, etc. Since words don't have meaning and people are the ones that have meanings for words, it really doesn't matter too much which word is used as long as one communicates the meaning as well as just the word. Frequently, when people have two or more meanings for the same word, these meanings become confused and problems develop. Remember the problem with the word *capacity* for which most people have two meanings: ability and limit. In the confusion of these two, tests which supposedly test abilities of the learner are interpreted as also testing limits. To me, the word that most clearly conveys to the majority of readers and listeners what I mean when I'm talking or writing about instructional specifications, is the word *objective.* I also realize that there are people who think of the word *objective* when it is used as an adjective rather than as a noun. As such, their meaning for the use of the word *objective* refers to something that is impersonal, disinterested, dispassionate, unprejudiced, impartial, nonsubjective, etc. People who are probably subjective idealists or subjectivists who believe that supreme importance should be given to the subjective or human

325

elements in experience and knowledge (Kontionism, Protagoreonism, Berkeleianism, Fichteonism, etc.), confuse the two different meanings they have for the word *objective* and conclude that anything related to an instructional unit or course that is called an *objective* has to lack humanness. As pointed out several times, to keep the goals or aims of an instructional unit or course, vague, ambiguous, and dependent on the whims or humanness of the teacher at any particular moment is inhumane for the learners. To evaluate students' achievement of learning using subjective criteria which reflect the moods and fancies of the teacher at any particular moment is also inhumane for the learners. Maximum humanness for the learners in instruction can be achieved by identifying as specifically as possible the objectives (aims, goals, specifications) that students are supposed to learn in an instructional unit or course; by evaluating or diagnosing the achievement of the objectives (aims, goals, etc.) in the most objective (unbiased, open-minded, uncolored, equitable, etc.) manner possible; and in solving the learners' learning problems, recognize the differences in the human elements in learning experiences and knowledge.

NOTE: The important point to remember is that in discussions pro and con *objectives*, the argument should center on the rights of the taxpayers and parents who pay for the schools and the salaries of the teachers and the rights of the students who give up their time to attend classes and study. Do they have the right to expect something in return from the teachers? I think they do have this right and I also think that the something they have a right to expect is that the teachers and the schools will facilitate learning and that the teachers and schools will be able to establish that more learning took place because of the teachers and schools than if there weren't any teachers or schools and the students learned by chance out in the real world. The objective of instruction, of this book, and of this chapter, is not to have specific objectives, but to facilitate learning. If anyone can do it some other way without any specific objectives and yet still prove that more learning took place, then I'm with them!

1. WHAT IS LEARNING?

In answer to the above Note, the most common responses are *What is learning?* and *You can't really measure learning?* There are a wide variety of definitions of learning that one can read or hear about. Some of these definitions are of the global type and some referring only to narrow areas.

      a.   Learning is the process of acquisition, extinction or modification of existing knowledge, skills, habits, or action tendencies in a motivated organism through experience, practice, or exercise.

b. Learning is the activity of achieving and improving contact with the environment.

c. Learning is a matter of differentiating the input.

d. Learning is an organic process of associating to a receptive process which originally lacked meaning.

e. Learning is something that occurs in the mind and for all practical purposes is not directly measurable.

f. Learning can be likened to the invisible particle traveling through a Wilson Cloud Chamber. Although you can't see the particle, you can see its effects and so you know it was there. Learning is a very personal and internal thing. Although you can't see it, you can see evidence that it has occurred. As such, it can be measured indirectly.

Regardless of what definition you have or can accept, close to 70 million students in the United States and Canada (many more millions around the world) are being evaluated on the basis of tests, observations, performances, themes, etc. and when the students don't achieve all of the items or all of the criteria, they are graded down for a condition that most of their teachers would describe as a *lack of learning.* Therefore, for my purposes at the moment and as a humanist, whatever it is that any teacher is presently using as criteria for evaluation and he or she believes these criteria to be important enough to grade or score students down for not *learning* it, then I will call these criteria indirect measurements of learning! Remember, of the 70 million students probably more than 60 million of them are being given grades or scores that are less than "A's" or 100's!!

2. *REASONS FOR SPECIFYING OBJECTIVES*[1]

As long as any kind of evaluation procedures are carried on by teachers, then it is necessary that these evaluation procedures are as fair as possible to all concerned. In order to be fair, it is absolutely necessary that the person doing the evaluating knows exactly what it is he is evaluating, and what the exact criteria are for doing this evaluating. It is also necessary (to be fair) that the student being evaluated knows exactly what it is he is to be evaluated on and that the student has had time to prepare for this evaluation. If the evaluation is based on

[1] In the National Assessment Project which is supposedly designed to assess the regional and national levels of education, the tests were developed and standardized without the lists of instructional objectives being specific and measurable. Therefore, questions can be easily raised as to whether or not the actual test items are in fact testing for the achievement of the ambiguous and vaguely stated objectives, particularly when test items in standardized tests are included primarily because they discriminate between students rather than because they test for the achievement of specified objectives.

specific objectives, it is possible to treat the evaluation as a diagnosis wherein the objectives which were not learned at the time of the evaluation are identified as needing additional instructional effort. From the teacher's point-of-view and also for students and parents, there are at least ten reasons why learning objectives should be specified.

a. IDENTIFIES THE SUBJECT MATTER FOCUS

The noun in the objective brings into focus the subject matter of the instructional event. If the noun is specific and singular the objective is probably a form of rote memory and/or of limited application. However, if the noun is plural and/or represents a category, type, classification, etc. then the objective is probably concerned with the transfer of learning from one or more members of the category to other members of the category. For example, in a literature course, if the noun in the objective refers to a specific piece of literature, chances are that the objective will be a type of rote memory objective. Even if the objective is a thinking type of objective involving analysis, synthesis, critiqueing, etc., since the learning is associated with a specific piece of literature, any learning will have limited value and application. A very common problem with objectives of this type is that the vehicle for learning the objective becomes the objective. In the study of *Hamlet,* not only is the vehicle for learning the objectives *Hamlet,* but the objectives and evaluation are also only concerned with *Hamlet.* If the student was going to be a specialist in *Hamlet,* this would be fine, but few students are planning to be specialists in *Hamlet,* so the learning of the objectives has limited value and application. However, if the noun of the objective referred to a category or type of plays of which *Hamlet* was one, then Hamlet could be used as a vehicle for learning the objectives, but the evaluation would utilize other plays from the same category or type to see if the student can transfer the learned behaviors to the other plays. This increases the value and application of the objective.

A similar problem can be found in almost every course. In many vocational courses, the project which should be the vehicle for learning becomes the objective: the making of a particular dress in sewing; the making of book ends, broom holder, etc. in junior high wood shop; etc. In social studies, the study of our South American neighbors could be the vehicle of how to study any geographical part of our world in which the objectives would be probably process objectives. However, in most schools, South America is both the vehicle for learning and the concern of the objectives and evaluation.

b. THE NATURE OF THE BEHAVIOR IS REVEALED

The verb in the objective describes how the objective should be taught, learned, and evaluated. Notice the verbs in the following: *list the seven rules for . . ., Recite the following 15 quotations from . . ., Solve problems similar to the following 6 problems . . ., Draw a map of Europe, showing the boundary lines of 1967 . . ., Discriminate between the seven categories of . . ., Identify the following chemical reactions . . ., Critique the film . . ., Direct the . . ., Discuss the development of . . .,* etc. About 50 percent of the learning problems which have been identified by teachers at all levels of education and in a wide variety of subject matter areas in my seminars and workshops have been solved when the teacher was able to identify exactly the behavior which he or she wanted in a particular teaching-learning situation.

These first two reasons for specifying objectives also help to increase the correlation between objectives and evaluation. It is of interest to note the incongruity in the majority of our present educational system's teaching and testing situations. We teach students certain facts, how to deal with facts, how to interpolate certain facts, how to diagnose situations based on certain facts, etc. Then we test their knowledge with multiple-choice tests which test the students' ability to discriminate between answers which may or may not be an important behavior and may not test the behaviors of dealing, interpolating, diagnosing, etc.

c. BEHAVIORS TO BE MODIFIED ARE IDENTIFIED

In comparing the desired behavior of the objective with the results of tests which were used to identify where the learner is (with reference to the desired objectives), it is possible to identify not only which existing behaviors may have to be modified in order to achieve the desired behaviors, but how much modification is necessary. (See Figure 45).

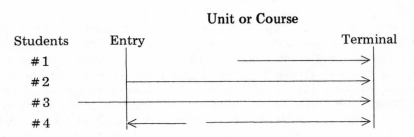

Figure 45 — Modification of Existing Behavior

329

Student #1 already has many of the desired behaviors of the unit or course and usually this student will have the easiest time in learning the rest of the objectives. Student #2 is right at the beginning of the course and probably should not have too many problems in learning the objectives of the course. Student #3 is missing some prerequisite behaviors in order to have success in the course. Although this indicates potential difficulties in learning, if the teacher is willing to solve the student's learning problems, the student should still be able to learn all of the objectives of the course. Student #4 has special problems. Even though the student has already learned some of the desired behaviors in the course, the short arrow pointing to the left indicates that some of what the student has previously learned is in conflict with learning the rest of the course objectives. This student's problems in going through the course will be dependent upon how the teacher handles the *anti-behaviors*. Under our present educational patterns, new behaviors which the students are supposed to learn are imposed on top of existing behaviors, even if the behaviors are opposites and conflicting. The usual result is that the students reject learning the new behaviors and rebel against the whole teaching-learning situation. In order to have success, it is necessary to first either eliminate the anti-behaviors or to circumvent them and then to teach the objectives related to the anti-behavior. Common examples of this problem can be found in many of the vocational courses, i.e., in typing where a student may have picked up some typing habits before starting the course which will interfere with successful learning of the regular typing objectives. If the teacher doesn't eliminate the bad typing habits, the student may never learn to type well. Many other courses are affected by poor study habits or in some cases, problems of discipline interfere with student learning. Since poor study habits and discipline problems are primarily affective domain objectives, the correction of these problems cannot be handled directly. Here are two examples.

A group of about 80 students who were extreme discipline problems in the first and second grades in a large urban school district were brought together during a special summer program. The major purpose of the program was to do something about the discipline problem because it was interfering with learning. The program was designed to apply two concepts: contingency management and Premack's principle. Contingency management is a situation in which learning is dependent upon the reward. Premack's principle is that *a preferred behavior can be used as a reward for the performance of a lesser preferred behavior.* In applying these concepts, the first week or so was spent observing the children at play in a classroom situation and identifying their preferred behaviors. The preferred behaviors for each student were arranged in hierachical order. During the rest of the summer program, as a student was given a learning task or an instructional unit to learn, the student was also told that if he or she completed the task successfully that the student would be allowed to indulge in their most preferred behavior for a certain number of times or minutes, i.e., make lots of noise, tear up drawings, jump up and down on a table, etc. After a negative (preferred) behavior is used as a reward several times, pretty soon the student will say, *I don't want to do that anymore.* Then, the student's second preferred behavior would be used as a reward until it was eliminated as a preferred behavior. This procedure was carried out with each student such that one by one the negative anti-behaviors were eliminated. By the end of the summer program, almost all of these students went back into regular classes as normal children. An additional benefit was that the average I.Q. scores for the students increased 15-20 points during the summer program.

One of my ex-students who had just graduated went into a second grade class as a replacement teacher a month after school started. Within about three weeks she came back to see me because her principal had warned her that she had to do something as her class was too noisy and she appeared not to have any control over the students. She agreed that she didn't have control as she didn't like to yell at the students and she didn't know what else to do. After discussing the problem, she decided to use the same two concepts: contingency management and Premack's principle. She first identified what the problems were in the class in addition to learning problems and then took time to ask each student what they liked to do most of all and what they would see as rewarding. On the basis of these interviews, she ran off on the ditto machine a number of sheets of paper which were ruled off into small squares. She stapled several of these sheets together and made up sort of a trading stamp booklet and then she bought a rubber stamp with an odd design on it. She then posted on one bulletin board the list of student behaviors which would be rewarded with so many stamps in their booklet, i.e., completing the lesson correctly — 10 stamps; cleaning up the play station — 5 stamps; etc. On another bulletin board, she posted the rewards, i.e., to be able to feed the goldfish, to be able to go down the slide out on the playground without standing in line, to take the pet mouse home over the weekend, etc. Within two weeks time she was able to change a difficult chaotic learning situation into a productive learning situation.

An example of circumventing an anti-behavior concerns students in school who speak various forms of pidgin English primarily because that is the way their family, neighbors, and friends speak. These students typically score low on I.Q. tests and have trouble learning in school, particularly in learning via classroom English. The traditional approach is to treat the students as slow learners and possibly as being mentally retarded and to consciously or unconsciously communicate to the students that they are dumb and that anyone who speaks the way they do is also dumb. This attitude is taken as an insult by the students because the students' family, neighbors, and friends speak the same way the students do. Because of the insult, the students refuse to learn which in turn reinforces the teacher's opinion that the students are dumb. In order to circumvent the problem, the teacher essentially says to the students who speak a form of pidgin English, *You speak fine and I'm sure you communicate effectively to your family, neighbors, and friends; but if you leave your group and have to communicate with people who don't speak as you do, you are in trouble. In order to help you communicate effectively in these other groups and also to help you learn in school from regular materials, I'm going to teach you classroom English as a second language!* In this way, nothing negative is implied about the students' families, background, or their intellectual abilities.

NOTE: Some teachers may look on the concept of reinforcement as a problem for psychologists, others may lampoon colleagues who try to apply the principles of reinforcement in their classrooms, others may consider reinforcement as manipulation and as such dangerous in the classroom. The major point to remember is that the concept and principles of reinforcement are operating all the time whether or not it is recognized and controlled. To ignore it, is to hand over reinforcement to chance[2] and in chance there is the possibility that negative attitudes, values, and beliefs will be reinforced and developed. Consider a husband who becomes a little lazy socially and hasn't taken his wife out for a long time. The wife starts nagging the husband and finally when he can't stand it any longer he says. *All right!!, I'll take you out just to shut you up!!* (At that moment, he just reinforced nagging.) Afterwards, if the wife wants to go out on Saturday, she may start nagging on about Wednesday or Thursday depending on how long it takes until the husband gets mad and gives in. Under these conditions, neither one will probably enjoy going out. It is so much easier for the husband and/or wife to control it and reinforce positive situations instead of negative situations and the results will be much more enjoyable for both.

d. FACILITATES INSTRUCTIONAL PLANNING

In order to individualize instruction, it is necessary to know exactly what it is that the students should be learning, how much of it

---

[2] If interested, you may want to view B. F. Skinner's film on conditioning in which he demonstrates the difference between controlled reinforcement and random reinforcement.

each student already knows, and how much of it each student does not know. The more specific and measurable the objectives, the easier it is to plan or design a learning situation that will be successful in taking the student from where they are intellectually through to the goals of the course. Knowing exactly what objectives the students should be learning, makes it relatively easy to identify a learning problem (the student or students are not learning one or more of the objectives). It also is much easier to develop alternate paths to learning when a student runs into trouble in learning a certain objective in the designed sequence.

Traditionally when teachers select textbooks, films, or other instructional materials, the criteria are essentially presenter-oriented, *Does it cover the course content?*, *Does it appear to be interesting?*, *Is it appropriate for the grade level (from a teacher's point-of-view)?*, etc. Under the Behavioral Learning Systems Approach to instruction, the criteria are learner-oriented, *Will this help the student(s) learn the objectives of the course?*, *Will this solve this student's learning problem?* Under the traditional approach, it is very difficult to change the vehicles for learning (usually the textbook) because the way each book presents the content and the sequence in which it is presented is slightly different, so a teacher needs time to go through new materials carefully before using them with students. Under the systems approach, knowing what the students' learning problems are, the instructioneer suggests a particular vehicle for learning, if it doesn't work, the instructioneer tries another vehicle and repeats the process until the desired learning occurs. Changing the vehicle for learning doesn't mean that the objectives are changed. Traditionally, teacher's have a tendency to change objectives to fit the student's capacity (limits). Under a systems approach the instructioneer will change the vehicles to fit the student's capacity (abilities).

NOTE: In changing vehicles for learning, if a teacher can identify alternate vehicles, then let the students pick the vehicle that each one thinks he or she can learn best from. Although students probably can't write the specific objectives that they should learn, they know much more than the teachers about which vehicles they learn best from.

The students' attitudes, values, and beliefs can be affected indirectly by the content of a vehicle, so in changing vehicles, instructioneers should be aware of possible changes which may not be desired.

Not only does having specific objectives facilitate instructional planning in a classroom, but it allows increased freedom in designing the learning environment whether it be in a classroom, a learning resource center, at home, out in the community, in satellite learning

333

centers, or almost any place and at any time.

In the open school concept where the teachers role is to provide a learning environment which will facilitate student learning, many teachers interpret this approach as not needing any specific objectives. Quite the contrary. Because there are so many materials readily available, the teacher has to select some materials and not others. If the selection is based on specific objectives, it is a much simpler task than when it is based on the *gut* feelings of the teacher. In the process of selecting materials, with or without specific objectives, the teacher is indirectly saying that the objectives which can be learned from the selected materials are more important than the objectives which could have been learned from the materials not selected. Why not be honest and spell out the objectives so at least the students can question the learning of an objective and ask the teacher to justify the inclusion of some materials and not others.

When the teachers are directing the students' learning by communicating the specific objectives to the learners, fewer pathways are necessary than when the students are learning by trial and error and learning is initiated only by student interest.

One of the key concepts in the open learning approach is the use of the *teachable moments.* This is a situation in which the student's activity at the moment is ideal for the teaching and learning of a particular concept (or objective). If the teacher doesn't have specific objectives, many ideal *teaching moments* can go by unrecognized because neither the teacher nor the student have identified what they are trying to learn. It is extremely difficult to reinforce a behavior if you don't know what behavior you are looking for.

e. THE OBJECTIVES CAN BE COMMUNICATED

An old story that has been passed around in educational circles for a long time is a good illustration of this reason for specifying objectives.

This teacher was trying to teach a class a certain concept and they didn't learn it. The teacher tried a second time and the students still didn't learn it. The teacher tried it a third time and the teacher learned it. Then on the fourth try, the students learned it!

It is extremely difficult to communicate to someone if you don't know exactly what it is you are trying to communicate. Think of a city that you have never been to, and then consider the difficulty in the task of trying to give directions to someone else as to how to get to a particular place in that city and you don't know exactly where the place is! The greater the degree of specificity of the objectives, the easier it is to communicate the objectives to the learner so that the

334

learner knows what he is supposed to learn. The most common result of courses which are taught in the traditional manner and in which objectives have not been specified is that the learners only learn some kind of a *curve's worth* of what they are supposed to learn. This is because of the guessing game in which the teachers are guessing by their test items as to what it is they are teaching and want to test, and the students are trying to guess in their studying what it is the teachers are going to test. If the students' and the teacher's guesses coincide, the students may answer everything correctly and get "A's". If they do not coincide, the student fails the course and genetics or home environment is blamed. The other grades ("B's," "C's," and "D's") achieved by the other students indicate the degree of overlapping of the student's guess and the teacher's guess, and does not necessarily indicate whether or not the students learned anything by design. The most common result of curriculum projects in which objectives are specified is that the learners learn what they are supposed to learn.

Actually, almost all learning problems can be traced to problems in communication. Sometimes the teacher doesn't really know what he or she wants to communicate. Sometimes the teachers know exactly what they want, but they don't or can't communicate to the students such that the students know what the teachers want. Sometimes the teachers know what they want and are capable of communicating to the students, but the tests they use communicate different objectives than the teachers were teaching. At least with the objectives specified and given to the students at the beginning of the course, it will be possible for the students to discuss them with the teacher. As long as the objectives are vague and ambiguous, the interpretations are left up to the personal biases and selective perception of each individual and in the case of parents or other members of the community this could become a problem. For example, in the sex education debate, the course objectives were so vague and general that the anti-sex education faction had visions of the teachers demonstrating various positions of sexual intercourse on the teachers desk with drafted or volunteer student partners. At the same time and looking at the same objectives, the pro-sex education faction were talking about sane, hygienic, and healthy living. If the pro-sex education group had specified the learning objectives involved, i.e., 230 specific objectives to be learned between kindergarten and twelfth grade, and then sat down and discussed each one with the anti-sex education group, they might have had a hundred or more of the objectives rejected by the anti-sex education group; but that would still leave over a hundred objectives which could be taught and learned instead of keeping out the whole program.

In specifying objectives and making these open and available to students, colleagues, administrators, parents, and other interested people in the community, the sanctity of the classroom can be opened to the daylight of honesty. One of the reasons parents are against some innovations is that they don't really know what's going on in the classroom. Although the parents and community are often given a public relations type description of innovation, they really don't understand how the innovation is affecting learning because the same students are coming home with the same "C's", "D's", and "F's". This is a similar problem to the passing of bonds, tax increase proposals, and increases in teacher salaries. Most of these issues are proposed on the basis of increasing the *quality* of education; but the *quality* is rarely identified and since the same students are coming home with the same low grades, parents and taxpayers doubt any increases in *quality*. The elimination of letter grades is not the solution either, as it makes the whole learning environment even more mysterious and it just covers up the symptoms of learning problems and in no way solves the problems or treats the causes of the problems. By specifying objectives, it is possible to communicate increases in learning and justify innovations.

In recognizing that the instructional process is a system in which each part has some affect on the other parts, it is possible to facilitate the making of this affect a positive one. To ignore this relationship is to facilitate each part having a negative affect on the other parts. Because of the preceding, it is very important that teachers, in recognizing that they are a part of a system, communicate to teachers who have had their students before in prerequisite courses; to other teachers teaching the same courses; and to teachers who will be teaching the students in more advanced courses after they leave their course. Without specific objectives, the value of the communication between teachers is limited, but with specific objectives, this communication can save individual teachers a lot of work and can facilitate effectiveness and efficiency in student learning. At the present time there is very little communication between the various levels of education, i.e., elementary schools and junior high schools, junior high schools and senior high schools, senior high schools and higher education, etc.

Of special concern, as teachers increase their efforts to teach objectives in the affective domain, it is even more critical that communication pathways between teachers and parents are kept open. When teachers start affecting students attitudes, values, beliefs, and opinions by design, they are going to have to be particularly careful that these affective domain objectives are openly a part of the curriculum and are in accord with those desired by the parents, community, and society.

f. HELPS STUDENTS PLAN THEIR LEARNING TIME

(ROLE PLAY) — You are driving on an unknown freeway in the left hand (fast) lane at about 60 miles per hour and looking for a particular exit. The conditions are such that you have to pay attention to the highway, i.e., it is raining or snowing, the traffic is heavy, etc. All of a sudden, in the periphery of your vision, an exit sign flashes by and you have a sinking feeling in the pit of your stomach that you just missed the exit you wanted! So you slow down and move over into the right hand lane. As you pass the next two or three exits, your anxiety builds and finally you pull off on the shoulder of the freeway and stop. When you take out the map to check on where you are and discover that you did miss the exit you wanted, your spouse or whoever is riding with you might make the following comment, *I told you that if you would look at the map we would get there faster and not make mistakes!*

Can you agree with that comment? Doesn't it seem to be a truism, *If you look at a map, you'll get to where you want to go faster and easier than if you don't look at a map?* When students are given the instructional objectives, the objectives become their *instructional map.* Not only does it help students to learn them, it helps them to learn the objectives easier and faster. Obviously, giving the students the specific objectives to be learned in a unit or course solves the students major traditional problem of, *What am I supposed to learn in this unit or course?*

Research has indicated that the student's *knowledge of results* from learning activities helps the student to achieve the objectives which might have been missed in going through the instructional process. When the students know at the beginning of the unit or course what it is that they will have to learn, then the students can almost monitor their own learning and have knowledge of results while in the instructional process. Like a navigator on a ship or plane, knowing where the ship or plane is going the student can plan a course as direct as possible to the destination. Also, like the navigator, if problems arise during the journey, the student can take advantage of knowledge of results and make mid-course corrections in order to still arrive at the destination.

The greatest benefit is that in knowing what it is the student is supposed to learn (required objectives) and what the student wants to learn (voluntary objectives), each student can take advantage of independent study time and direct his or her learning. A common complaint of teachers who teach or have taught in schools using modular scheduling is that the students don't use their independent study time like they are supposed to. A lot of the students tend to waste the time in a variety of activities, i.e., talking to other students, day dreaming, sleeping, etc. When I ask these teachers who are complaining if I can see their course objectives, rarely do they have them. If the teachers don't

337

know what it is they want the students to learn during their independent study modules, how can the students possibly use their independent study time effectively and efficiently. Students that have average to better success in guessing what the teacher wants will use up a lot of time guessing by *shotgunning* the educational materials. By studying a little bit of everything, these students hope to hit on what the teacher wants. Students that haven't had much success in guessing what their teachers want them to learn will tend to give up and not even try to guess. These students would rather spend their learning time in things they can be more successful at, i.e., bullying other students, aggravating the teachers, vandalizing the school, finding ways to violate regulations, etc.

If students are supposed to spend from one to six or more hours a day outside of classes studying on their own, why not give them the instructional map — the specific objectives — and let them all have successes in learning!

g. ACHIEVEMENT CAN BE MEASURED

If we do not know specifically where we are going in education, we will never be able to tell when we are there. The lack of specificity in objectives has led to a very low correlation, if any, between what is taught in the classrooms and what the students are actually tested on. Actually, as indicated previously, once the objectives are specified sufficiently, a slight change of wording can make test items out of the objectives. Another 25 percent of the learning problems identified by teachers can be solved by designing test items that actually test the desired behaviors of the specified course objectives.

In most schools at the present time, achievement of learning is measured in terms of time, i.e., four years of Spanish, two years of math, a semester of logic, etc. A high school diploma means the student spent approximately twelve years in elementary and secondary schools. It is the rare high school principal or superintendent that will be willing to guarantee that every student who graduates from his or her high school with a diploma knows a certain list of things in common with every other student who graduates from that high school with a diploma. The longest list I've been given so far consists of two items; first, all of the students will know the difference between boys and girls and second, they will also know the location of the high school!! A bachelor's degree means that the student has spent approximately 2,000 hours in a classroom in front of a live teacher and in some college or university. A master's degree means approximately 500 hours in a classroom in front of a live teacher and in some college or university. A Ph.D. means another 500 hours plus a dissertation. Since it is very difficult to identify any guaranteed levels of learning achievement for any of the degrees either, it can rather easily be assumed that the diploma and degrees are really awarded for endurance rather than for learning. Notice how we use the phrase *earned doctorate* rather than *achieved doctorate!* After all, credits in higher education are determined by how many times a week a particular class meets and have little, if any, relationship with the actual learning requirements of the course. Under the Behavioral Learning Systems Approach, any measures of performance are based on achievement of specified learning objectives. Hopefully, the time will come when diplomas and academic degrees can represent certain levels of scholarly achievement and the process of awarding the degrees, particularly advanced degrees, will be free from interpersonal conflict and biases and at least simulate the open-minded objectiveness of the true scholarly environment rather than simulating the initiation rites of social fraternities and sororities!

In performing the role of the instructioneer, it is critical to use specific objectives; otherwise, one would never know when a learning problem exists nor when it was solved. It would be extremely difficult to identify the learning value in using various innovations and/or technology.

h. TEACHER ACCOUNTABILITY IS POSSIBLE

As long as teachers (at all levels of education) can avoid specifying what it is that students should be learning, then no one (including the teacher) can really evaluate whether or not the students are learning and consequently no one can evaluate whether or not the teachers can teach. Once objectives for courses are specified, then not only is it possible to evaluate whether or not students are learning, but it also becomes very easy to evaluate whether or not teachers can teach. Obviously, teachers who are not sure that they have the ability to help students learn, are going to have a tendency to resist the whole concept of specifying objectives, teaching with objectives, and evaluating the achievement of objectives. In other words, teachers who are not sure whether or not they can teach (as measured by students' learning) are not going to want to be held *accountable* for the learning that does or does not take place in their courses.

NOTE: Remember, very few teachers in elementary and secondary schools have been taught *how to teach by design* by teachers in the teacher-training institutions who also *taught by design* and used objectives. Also, very few teachers in higher education have been taught *how to teach by design* because all that is necessary to teach in higher education is to have advanced degrees (masters or a doctorate) in the general subject area the teacher is supposed to teach. It is not considered important in higher education that the teachers know anything about how to teach or about how to test for the achievement of what they are trying to teach.

Teachers who are not afraid of being held accountable should welcome the use of specific objectives because it makes the whole concept of teacher evaluation much more objective and open minded. It brings real academic freedom to the classroom. As long as a teacher can prove that learning is taking place, the teacher should have freedom to do what they want and to come and go as they please.

I can partially agree with teachers who resist being held accountable for the learning of objectives that they weren't involved in setting, but then if teachers won't specify the objectives they want students to learn in their courses, then in this decade of accountability, someone else will probably specify the objectives for them. If teachers are getting paid as professionals, then the teachers should accept the professional responsibility and put their reputation on the line and commit themselves as to what is important to learn and what is not so important to learn.

As the concept of accountability based on specified objectives looms ever larger on the horizon of teacher evaluation, many teachers in trying to escape the inevitable try to avoid it by either trying to discredit the whole concept of specifying objectives or to claim that the really important things happening in the teaching-learning situation are the things you can't measure and in particular the things which you can't measure that fall into the affective domain (attitudes, values, and beliefs). Of course the hope for many of these teachers who are trying to avoid accountability is that it will be much harder to specify and measure affective domain objectives. As such, it may become a standard part of teacher evaluation to evaluate key attitudes, values, and beliefs on a pretest and posttest basis, not so much to check on how much the teacher was able to develop desired attitudes, values, and beliefs, but as sort of a fuse or protection against serious subversion of desired attitudes, values, and beliefs. Two important points to remember: first, teachers who are not confident of their ability to teach cognitive and sensory objectives and are probably doing a sloppy job of it, in switching over to the affective domain objectives could very well do as bad or worse in that area; second, in the cognitive and sensory domains, if a teacher is not very affective, the students just won't learn all of the objectives and may develop a negative attitude towards that particular teacher with a slight carryover of a demotivating force towards the school; however, in the affective domain, if a teacher is ineffective,[3] the students

---

[3] Assuming that the teacher wanted to develop attitudes, values, and beliefs which are more or less in agreement with the desires of the students' parents, the community, and our society, to not be successful in developing or increasing these affective objectives or actually develop negative attitudes, values, and beliefs by mistake, would be considered as ineffective. However, if a teacher's personal objective was to develop attitudes, values, and beliefs which are in conflict with those desired by the students' parents, community and our society, then the observed ineffectiveness could actually be a very effective form of subversive teaching.

may not only have problems in achieving the desired affective objectives, but as a result of the teacher's ineffective practices, the students may have some of their positive attitudes become less positive and they may develop negative attitudes, values, and beliefs which will be carried into other courses and out into their homes and social life.

NOTE: With respect to the evaluative terms *positive* and *negative* as used in the affective domain, these are not absolute evaluative terms. The positiveness and negativeness of an attitude, value, or belief is always in reference to those attitudes, values, and beliefs which are considered desirable by the students' parents, the community, and our society. It should be obvious that a certain attitude which might be considered as positive in one society chould be considered negative in another society. In the same way, a value which might be considered positive in one community might be considered a negative value in another community. A belief held by one student's parents and thought of as a positive belief, could very easily be considered a negative belief by another student's parents.

A very common example of this problem can be identified in any elementary school. Whereas almost every teacher and parent would like to have the students like schools and love learning. This attitude is observable among most children in early elementary school. However, by sixth grade there is an obvious change in this attitude and by twelfth grade the change in attitude is even more obvious. Since there are very few people on the outside who tear down the schools to these youngsters, it becomes highly likely that the causes for the change in attitudes occurs in the school itself and principally because of the teachers in the school. Consider one probable cause, in the middle elementary grades, it is very common to punish students with learning activities because of infractions of classroom regulations. In classrooms where the teachers want students to want to write and solve problems, they say things like, *Write 100 times; I won't chew gum*, *Write two punishment essays on citizenship*, *Do twenty extra homework problems*, etc. In the very same physical education class where the teacher wants students to develop positive attitudes towards keeping the body physically fit, students are punished with physical activities, i.e., *Do twenty push-ups*, *Take five laps around the track*, etc. I personally believe that teachers that use learning activities as punishment are having negative affects on the rest of the students' learning activities in other classes and maybe for the rest of the students' learning life. As such, they should be warned of the consequences of their acts and if the teachers persist in punishing students with learning activities, they should be suspended from the classroom until they can develop other methods of punishing (if punishment is needed at all)!

i. FACILITATES THE DEVELOPMENT OF COMMON EXPECTATIONS

Not only is it important for the teacher who is developing the instructional materials to specify the instructional objectives, it is important that the learner be made aware of these objectives, thus establishing common expectations of the learner's performance held by the instructor, the learner, or any other instructor or learner. Consequently, specifying of instructional objectives could reduce learner statements of the type *I didn't know that this is what you wanted, I thought you wanted something else.* Specification of objectives should also reduce the variability from classroom to classroom introduced by having different instructors who may interpret the general objectives differently. One of our biggest problems today in education is that when the same course is taught by two or more teachers, the content of the course varies almost as much as the teachers themselves vary. Yet, as the students go on to subsequent courses which depend on the learning which was supposed to have taken place in prerequisite courses, the students are ultimately punished because of the previous teachers' lack of common expectations with other teachers who are teaching this same prerequisite course with reference to the minimum content of the course which should have been learned by the students.

Back in the day when the average person grew up, lived, worked, and died within about ten miles of where the person was born, common expectations at a state, regional, and national level weren't as important as they are today. Just as we need a common language in order to communicate (which has to be part of the common expectations), there are other things we need as a common base if we are all going to live together in a mobile society such as we have here in the United States. It is very common for families to move one or more times during the formal education of a student. If there are no common expectations in courses with the same name, the lack of continuity develops learning problems which results in punishment of the student in the new community in the form of putting the student back one or more years, or failing the student because of nonlearning of prerequisite objectives.

This in no way suggests that every course in fifth grade social studies or algebra, speech, calculus, Shakespeare, etc., has to be exactly the same throughout the country. But it does suggest that in each of these courses there should be some common core of learning objectives, such that any student completing a course or grade at any school in the country, with any teacher in the country, should have achieved some MINIMAL objectives. Once these minimal learning objectives have been achieved, then the individual school system, school building, department or subject matter teacher can add whatever he or she feels pertinent, necessary, or useful to the student. For a comparison of the two different points of view concerning the concept of a minimum, common core of course content, consider the following:

A certain portion of my course will be useful to my students, no matter where they go in this country.

If any part of my course is useful to a student at any other place in the country, it is because of chance, not by design.

It would be better to have 90 percent or more of the learners who know 100 percent of behaviors which are useful anywhere in the country than to know only 60 to 70 percent ("C" worth) of the behaviors that are useful only in a small, local area.

Obviously, the greatest advantage of having common expectations would be the interchange of instructional materials which are able to present the content for the learning of common objectives. As common learning problems are identified in the learning of the common objectives, these could also be interchanged among teachers. Although the idea of learning packets or modules is widespread, under the traditional approach and in a situation with few, if any, common objectives, not only do teachers feel they have to develop their own learning packets, but each teacher is probably the only one that will use his or her own learning packet. The Ford Foundation, after spending millions of dollars in the packaged curriculum movement, found that the lack of commonality of objectives and the teacher's desire to reinvent curriculum wheels negated the value of having learning packets. Once these common expectations are identified and teachers change their role to that of the instructioneer, the idea of learning packets will become widespread in *use* instead of just widespread in awareness of the idea. Publishers of instructional materials will be able to develop quality materials which will have designed widespread application instead of just hoping someone can use their materials.

Another advantage, if the teachers of courses which are found in both high school and college could get together and identify their common expectations, there is no reason why some of the high school courses couldn't carry college credit, i.e., chemistry, physics, English composition, etc.

j. INCREASING SPECIFICITY, INCREASES CHANCES FOR LEARNING

In writing specific objectives, far to many people look on specific objectives or SO's as something completely different and un-associated with general objectives or GO's. There is not that much difference between them. In fact, all specific objectives or SO's are a part of some general objectives or GO's. However, not every GO has one or more specific objectives or SO's associated with it. The reason for this relationship is that the GO's almost always are identified first and then the SO's are identified later. When SO's are identified first, there is a possibility that the SO's will be predominantly low level, represent simple rote memory, and lack continuity. The most important concept to remember in reference to GO's and SO's is that the degree of specificity and generality of a GO is a continuum with the SO's at one end of the continuum and representing the maximum degree of specificity and zero generality (see Figure 46).

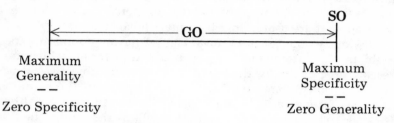

Figure 46 — Specific Objectives as a point on the
generality-specificity continuum.

In classifying objectives with reference to specificity and/or generality, there are just the two categories: either a SO or a GO. It is difficult to break GO's into sub-categories because the degree of generality is undefined. However, it is possible to look at a series of GO's which are related to a single GO and rank them as sub-GO's, sub-sub-GO's, sub-sub-sub GO's, etc. For example in Figure 47, the main objective, to understand —, is three levels away from the measurable SO's. The level of the GO only has relative importance in that as the number of levels of GO's increases, generality decreases and specificity increases. For example, if I were to say to you, *Let's meet for a drink.* What are the chances of the event occurring? Probably very small. If I said, *Let's meet in Kansas City for a drink*, the chances are still small, but slightly better than before. If I said, *Let's meet at the Holiday Inn in Kansas City for a drink*, again the chances are small, but better than before. In continuing the process of adding more and more specificity, the chances of the event occurring continue to increase.

It is very possible that a particular GO cannot be analyzed sufficiently to develop SO's, but even though the results are not measurable, the chances of the desired learning occurring have been increased by analyzing the main GO into sub GO's, sub-sub GO's, etc. In other words, it is necessary in order to have excellence in the teaching-learning situation to identify in all courses specifically and measurably what it is we want students to learn. This does not mean that we would

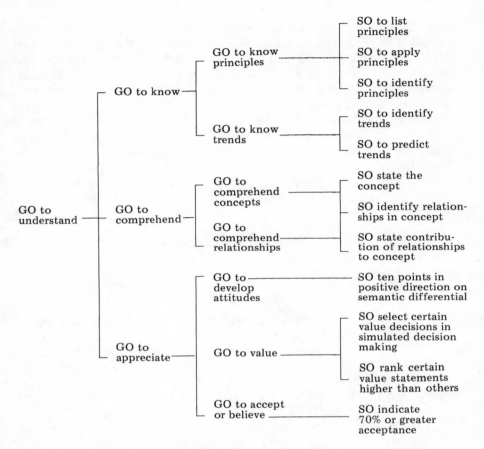

Figure 47 — Analysis of a General Objective into Measurable Elements

eliminate from our courses anything that cannot be measured. But in order for a course to be included in the curriculum and to justify expenditure of funds in order to present the course to the learners and to justify the time and effort of the learner in the course, it should be necessary for all courses to have some kind of measurable, observable SO's.

Another way of looking at GO's and SO's and their interrelationship is from the point-of-view of being operationally defined. SO's are defined and GO's are undefined. Although many course objectives can be indirectly defined in such a way that the objective when stated in behavioral terms and the test item are almost identical, there are also many objectives at the present time which are not directly definable, and as such, usually remain undefined. These objectives are usually the ones that are stated in terms of appreciation, understanding, familiarity,

345

value judgments, etc. These undefined objectives can be indirectly defined if the teacher is capable of identifying how the students behave that seem to have this *appreciation, understanding, familiarity,* etc., and are also able to identify how students behave that do not have the *appreciation, understanding, familiarity,* etc. Whenever the teacher is able to identify as observable and measurable the behavioral differences between the students who have this previously undefinable behavior and other students who do not have it, then it is possible that these behavioral differences constitute an indirect measurement of the undefined objective.

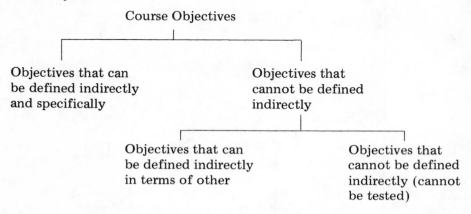

Figure 48 — Classifying Objectives According to Operational Definitions

It should be pointed out, however, that objectives in the teaching-learning situation which are not directly or indirectly definable and still depend on various degrees of chance for learning to take place, should not be included among the objectives for which the student is going to be evaluated on for achievement. The emphasis in this book on measurable SO's should not be misunderstood, misinterpreted, or misquoted as saying that I believe everything that is taught can be measured and/or only those things that can be measured should be taught. Given that almost all teachers are involved with evaluating students and assigning letter grades, I challenge any teacher's right to fail or downgrade a student for not learning *something* when the teacher does not know what that *something* is that the student did not learn (undefined objectives).

(Malpractice Dialogue) A student received a "C" in a course and the parent (or student) went to see the teacher about it.

Parent: *You gave my daughter a "C" in your course. What is "C" worth of your course? Is it 60 percent, 70 percent, 80 percent,*

346

65 percent, 75 percent? What percentage of your course did she learn in order to learn only a "C" worth?

Depending on the teacher's approach to assigning letter grades, most teachers will have trouble answering this question. But if under repeated questioning, the teacher finally says, *About 70 percent*, then the parent (or student) would say,

Parent: *If my daughter only learned 70 percent, could you please give me a list of the other 30 percent that she did not learn in your course?*

Depending on the teacher and the subject, many teachers may be able to come up with most of the 30 percent; but it would be the rare teacher who could identify *all* of the missing 30 percent. In other words, it is common to find teachers who have graded a student down for not learning *something*, when the teacher does not know what that *something* is that the student didn't learn!

I have used this dialogue with thousands of teachers and everyone has agreed that it would be difficult to defend grading a student down for what they didn't learn which in turn indicates that most teachers would have trouble operationally defining what an "A" is in their courses. Let's be honest and humane and spell out what it is that is presently being measured and make sure students learn all of whatever is measurable. After the students learn 100 percent of what is measurable, then teach the unmeasurable or *gut feeling* stuff. Don't be false and inhumane and grade students on their achievement of *something* which even you, the teacher, can't identify! Just because a GO cannot be measured does not mean that it is not important. In trying to compare values of GO's and SO's, it is important to identify the criteria used in making the comparison. From the point-of-view of learning, since SO's are usually a part of a GO and if the SO is considered important, then the GO would have to be as important or probably more important than the SO. This would be particularly true if two or more important SO's are part of a GO. On the other hand, from the point-of-view of designed instruction where measurement is important, the SO is more important than the GO simply because it is measurable. Given both GO's and SO's which are interrelated as in Figure 47, if a teacher accepts that the learning of the GO is more important than the learning of the SO's and as such is sloppy in the instruction of the SO's, the SO's will not be achieved and as a consequence neither will the GO's because the SO's are a part of the GO's. In the example given previously, the idea or concept of meeting as friends over a drink is certainly more important than the specific time, date and location of the meeting, but if 100 percent of the time, date, and location are not achieved, the meeting cannot occur! By designing the instruction such that 100 percent of the measurable objectives are achieved, chances are increased that the GO's will be learned as well. As the achievement level of the SO's decreases, so do the chances for learning the GO's! The more important (for learning) you think the non-measurable GO's are, the more important (for learning) it becomes to analyze the GO into sub-GO's, sub-sub GO's, etc. until you identify some SO's, and the more important (for measurement) it is to have the students learn 100 percent of the SO's. Assuming that the GO's or non-measurable objectives are the most important (learning), then forty million or more students have been inhumanly and unjustifiably punished with letter grades which are less than an "A" for not learning the SO's or measurable objectives which are less important (learning) plus, of course, not learning that *something* which is unknown!

There are some teachers who claim that learning can't be measured and so there is no value in having SO's or tests. Many of these very same teachers still assign letter grades from "A" to "F". If they haven't been measuring anything, then why have they inhumanely treated so many of their students. Why be hypocritical and say there is nothing to measure and then turn around and measure something by giving tests. If it is true that the teacher doesn't have any objectives or only GO's, then the course should be presented in Scholarship sessions, taught on the teachers own time, with no captive audience via registration, and no letter grades given at all.

(1) INTERACTION BETWEEN SO's AND TEACHER'S ROLE IN MAXIMIZING LEARNING

Point "A" in Figure 49, indicates where the highest percentage of the course objectives are defined and measurable. At this point, there is also the possibility for the highest degree of designed instruction and the lowest degree of chance education.

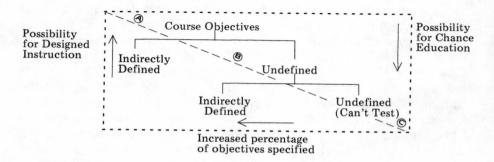

Figure 49 — Relationship of SO's and Designed Instruction

Point "B" in Figure 49 indicates where about half of the course objectives are defined and measurable. At this point, there is just about as much possibility for designed instruction as there is for chance learning.

Point "C" in Figure 49 indicates where there are very few course objectives defined and measurable. As a consequence, at this point, there is very little possibility for designed instruction and maximum opportunity for chance education. (The purpose of Figure 49 is to indicate that the instruction vs. education concept is a continuum rather than dichotomy.)

The role of the teacher should also be thought of as a continuum with the instructioneer's role as a practitioner at one end and the traditional role as a researcher at the other end (see Figure 50).

Practitioner ____Ⓐ_____Ⓑ_____Ⓒ_ Researcher

Figure 50 — Practitioner vs. Researcher as a Continuum

Point "A" indicates the point on the continuum where the instructioneer would be. An operational definition of the role at this point might be suggested by a teacher's comment at the beginning of a course, *How many of you want an "A" in the course?* (all of the students put up their hands) *Okay, you are all going to get an "A". I don't know when it will happen or how you are going to actually achieve it, but my job is to solve your learning problems and get you all there!*

Point "B" indicates the point on the continuum where the teacher has accepted some of the aspects of the instructioneer's role and has retained some of the aspects of the traditional role. An operational definition of the role at this point might be suggested by a teacher's comment at the beginning of a course, *My job is to present the course content to you and whenever I find extra time, I will work with the students who are having serious learning problems. I intend that all of you will get at least a "C" grade or better.*

Point "C" indicates the point on the continuum where the teacher is performing the traditional role of the researcher. An operational definition of the role at this point might be suggested by a teacher's comments at the beginning of a course, *My job is to present the course content and to see to it that all of you have the same opportunity for the necessary experiences during this semester. If you learn, great. If you don't learn, it's your fault. I'll grade on a curve.*

Point "D" in Figure 51 indicates the point at which there are very few SO's and the teacher is performing the traditional researcher role

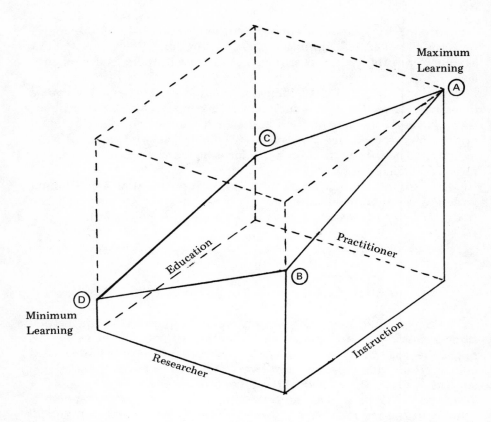

Figure 51 — Interaction between SO's and the Teacher's Role

and only a *curve's* worth of the few available SO's are learned by the students. A position of minimum learning.

Point "C" in Figure 51 indicates the point at which the teacher didn't want to write any more SO's than the few that were available; but the teacher was willing to change his or her role to that of the practitioner such that all of the students learned all of the few SO's that were available.

Point "B" in Figure 51 indicates the point at which the teacher didn't want to change his or her role in the classroom; but the teacher was willing to write more SO's such that even if the students did learn only a *curves* worth of the objectives, the average student at point "B" learned more than the average student at point "D".

Point "A" in Figure 51 indicates the point at which the teacher has written more SO's and is performing the instructioneer's role as a practitioner such that all of the students are learning all of the SO's for maximum learning.

3. REASONS FOR GENERAL OBJECTIVES

There are a number of educators who state their GO's in such superlative terms that one would suspect the consultation of an advertising, public relations, or political platform specialists, i.e.,

— students will be able to listen actively, speak convincingly, and perceive knowledgeably (College Psychology);

— to appreciate the rich heritage of man, his literary and artistic achievements (College English);

— to be able to think critically and reason intelligently (almost all levels of subjects); and

— to be a good citizen and an active contributor to a participatory democracy (almost all levels in the social sciences).

There is really nothing wrong with these GO's, that's why they are used. After all, who could be against them? It would be like being against motherhood, God, country, and apple pie! But, they are so general and represent such a cluster of sub-GO's, it would take a number of levels of sub GO's, sub-sub GO's, sub-sub-sub GO's, etc. before some SO's would appear and in the process the GO's and SO's would cross over many subject matter areas and many more courses. Some people refer to this type of GO as a *global objective* because they attempt to wrap up the whole world in one statement. The major problem with this type of GO is that they are so general that they are useless for practical purposes of the teacher in the classroom.

If a teacher has never been taught how to analyze a GO and break it down, level by level, until some SO's are identified and that GO's and SO's have a direct relationship with tests, then chances are that the teacher looks on lists of GO's as something you write in lesson plans as a practice teacher or as a new teacher to keep supervising teachers and administrators happy. Once a teacher is considered an experienced teacher, the only time the lists of GO's are taken out of their hiding place in a file cabinet or on a shelf somewhere is to make up a catalogue description, to show to accrediting teams or to nosey consultants like myself. Quite typically at the elementary and secondary level the GO's and a few SO's for all grades and courses are put into a book of which most schools will have at least one copy, although in some school districts the copies of the courses' GO's and SO's are kept only at the district offices. Rarely will each teacher have a copy. In other words, these books of GO's and SO's are not actually developed to be used by the teachers in the classrooms. They are primarily developed for show so that the administrators can say, *We have our objectives!* In California and several other states, there is definite pressure on administrators and

351

teachers to spell out their course objectives. To teachers who are accustomed to working without any objectives at all or at best some GO's, to have to write and work with objectives, even if GO's, seems like being confined or being spied on by some mysterious secret agent. This feeling is primarily because the objectives are GO's and being non-measurable, the teachers are unsure as to how they are going to be held accountable for the GO's.

NOTE: Oddly enough, this is just how the students feel in classes where there are no objectives at all or at best some GO's, but tests are going to be given and the students are unsure as to how they are going to be held accountable for guessing what the teacher wants.

At some schools which I have visited, the books of GO's are put away so carefully and referred to so seldom that the administrators can't even find them. In most cases, when I do see a book of GO's, the book is in brand new condition indicating that few teachers, if any, ever look at them.

General objectives are useful and they should be taken out of storage and every teacher should have a copy. There are five reasons for having and using GO's.

    a.   GO's are the best guidelines as to what the SO's and test items should be. By analyzing the GO's and breaking them down, level by level, the SO's can be identified. If the SO's are really specific and measurable, each SO can become a test item by a slight change in wording. The change is essentially from *To be able to do something* to *Do it.*

    b.   The GO's indicate the types of learning desired: cognitive, sensory, or affective. This is particularly important because of the two theories of instruction: one for the cognitive and sensory objectives and the other for the affective objectives.

    c.   A very important point to remember is that once GO's have been identified, they are fairly permanent whereas SO's which are indirectly identified may change when the teacher loses confidence in the SO as measuring what he or she really wants. Quite typically when teachers first start writing SO's, the objectives are usually low level and rote memory. As such, the teachers don't have confidence in them as really measuring very much of what the teachers really want as identified by the GO's. Instead of rejecting the whole concept of SO's, teachers should learn how to write better SO's. The writing of good SO's is not a simple task and cannot be learned by most people just by sitting down for a few hours even with a consultant's help. However, given time and someone who is willing to solve the

352

teacher's learning problems with them (sort of a teachers' instructioneer), every teacher can learn to write SO's. Don't be hesitant to throw away a SO that you feel is inappropriate for the related GO, but try to replace it with a better SO.

d. The use of GO's help to catagorize SO's and to clarify the relationships between other SO's and GO's. If the GO's for a course are on one page and the SO's are on another page, the relationships are not identified. That is why GO's and SO's should be presented together indicating their interrelationships. In this way, if a GO doesn't have any SO's, the teacher knows that they are missing and will try to develop some SO's for the non-measurable GO. Also, sometimes when teachers write SO's without looking at their GO's and then put the GO's and SO's together, they find that some SO's don't relate to any of the available GO's. In that case, either the SO can be dropped or maybe a GO should be developed if it appears that this is a missing area of importance. It is possible to have GO's without any SO's, but it is highly unlikely that a course can have a SO without a related GO.

e. If a teacher hasn't identified any learning or instructional resources, the use of GO's are very helpful in locating and identifying potential instructional materials. Then the SO's can be developed either from the GO's, the instructional materials, or both. Until such time as instructional modules or materials are catalogued by their SO's, lists of SO's only will not be very useful in locating materials. However, lists of SO's can be used to develop sort of *bare bones* instructional modules which will appear fragmented. By developing GO's from the lists of SO's, the GO's will help put some non-measurable *meat* on the SO *bones.*

4. OTHER CATEGORIES OF OBJECTIVES

As pointed out, as far as instruction is concerned there are only two kinds of categories of objectives: specific objectives which are measurable and general objectives which although non-measurable, have varying degrees of generality. Different writers have different names for objectives. Frequently the names are descriptive of their use. For example, *course* objectives can be GO's or SO's, but are usually the main objective of the course. I refer to these objectives as *terminal* objectives. Some writers use the term *enabling* objectives to indicate the objectives which have to be learned in order to culminate in the learning of the *course* or *terminal* objectives. I usually refer to *enabling* objectives as *learning* objectives. A not too common labeling is the use of *open* objectives to refer to general objectives which are almost measurable and *closed* objectives to refer to specific objectives. As long as the objectives are used in the instructional process, the main thing to remember is whether or not the objective can be measured specifically or not.

a. EDUCATIONAL OBJECTIVES

Almost all objectives used under the traditional approach to education are general objectives and in accordance with the traditions of education, most of these general objectives are written in terms of what the teacher should be doing or covering in a course instead of what learners should be doing or learning. Various state departments of public instruction and many large school districts have set up objectives or curriculum guidelines defining the content of each course at each grade level. Because these are so general, the interpretation of any one teacher objective or guideline varies widely from one teacher to another.

Under the traditional approach, about the only objectives that could be interpreted as specific and measurable are *activity* objectives. These are not only specific and measurable, but from a certain point-of-view, they could also be called behavioral objectives because they usually specify the activity in terms of a behavior, i.e., do three projects, hand in four essays after doing the assigned reading, do two book reports, do twenty abstracts of current research, etc. The critical point in differentiating between specific *learning* objectives and specific *activity* objectives is that in learning objectives both the quantity and quality aspects are included in the statement of the objective. For example, take the activity objective: *hand in four essays after doing the assigned reading.* A student could hand in four "A" essays, four "F" essays, four "C" essays, or any other combination of letter grade essays and still achieve the objective. Therefore, in most cases, if part of the statement of the objective does not contain the criteria for evaluation of quality, it should be considered an *activity* objective. The inhumane part of using *activity* objectives is that the teachers who use these objectives actually do evaluate the projects, essays, book reports, etc. on the basis of quality. And as the educational tradition goes, the students are usually not told what the criteria for quality are and in fact, it would be the rare teacher that would take time to even have these criteria written down. After all, if the students don't achieve the hidden criteria, the teachers can always blame it on genetics and/or home environment.

Not only are activity objectives specified for students, they are also frequently specified for teachers. In elementary and secondary schools,

354

the primary emphasis of the teacher is on the completion of an activity. This is regardless of learning mainly because the majority of the activities are not associated with specific measurable learned objectives, so the teacher is not able to determine whether learning took place or not. In case the reader does not quite agree with this statement, then go to almost any elementary or secondary classroom about two weeks before the end of the semester, and if the teacher is behind in the completion of the activities that were supposed to be completed, you will observe teacher efforts directed at completing the activity and catching up, regardless of student learning.

5. WHAT IS A SPECIFIC OBJECTIVE?

Definition: A specific objective is an objective in which *the meaning for that objective is constant* over time from the point-of-view of all students and all teachers using that objective and *the measurment of the achievement of that objective is also constant* over time from the point-of-view of all students and all teachers using that objective.

The reason I define a SO as I have above is that in some of the courses I have consulted on, an objective that looks like a GO to me is looked on by the students and teachers as a SO. The explanation is that I haven't had the prerequisite courses and once the situation was explained, I could see how the students and teachers could see the objective as a SO. In order for instructional objectives to give direction to the learning process and to determine the nature of the evidence to be used in appraising the effects of learning experiences, the terminology must be stated so clearly that the authors of the objectives know exactly what they mean and the readers (students and other teachers) of the objectives have that same meaning.

One of the easiest ways of identifying whether or not an objective is a SO is to imagine how the objective would be tested. If the wording of the objective is such that a test item could be selected which would be more difficult than some other test item and yet both of them fit the wording of the objective, the objective is still a GO. The reason why this situation would not be acceptable is that given an objective which allows for variable difficulty level in the evaluation of the achievement of the objective, it would be possible for a teacher to vary the number of students who achieved the objective without regard to what students have learned. In this way, the results of tests are more affected by what a teacher decides to test (all difficult, all easy, or some curve's worth mixture between the two extremes of difficulty level), than by what the students have learned. This practice introduces dishonesty and inhumanity into the instructional process by telling the students what they should learn, maybe the easy examples derived from the objectives, and then the students are tested with test items of a different difficulty level. A common example of this is the use of a so-called specific objective (SO) worded as follows:

> The student will be able to answer correctly at least 80 percent of the items on a multiple choice test.

As pointed out in detail (in pages 483-495) multiple choice tests can be designed to get any results the author of the tests wants to have, regardless of what students actually know, i.e., a normal curve of results, a positive skewed curve (a majority of the students have success), a negative skewed curve (a majority of the students fail), etc. Therefore, this type of a so-called SO is actually very much a GO. Another very common example is the use of the plural form:

> The student will be able to apply the principles of -------------- in case studies.

There are two problems with the plural form in this example which can be identified in answering these two series of questions:

> How many principles? Two? Four? Six? Are some principles more difficult to apply than others?

> Isn't it possible to select case studies in which the application of the principles would be more difficult than others? If only a few of the principles were selected by the learner to learn, what if the case studies used to measure the achievement of this objective concerned some of the principles the student didn't select to learn?

When the wording of an objective is such that the test items used to measure the achievement of the objective can have varying difficulty level, it is necessary to specify the difficulty level by giving examples illustrating the difficulty level. The following two objectives are typical of objectives thought to be SO's:

> The student should be able to solve *any* quadratic equation. (The word *any* makes this objective a GO.)

> The student should be able to identify the theme of a short story. (The wording of this objective implies the word *any* which makes it a GO.)

The following objectives are in the form that should have been used:

> The student should be able to solve any quadratic equation representative of the following five types of quadratic equations: --------, --------, --------, --------, and --------.

The student should be able to identify the theme in short stories typified by the following examples: --------, --------, --------, (in which the examples illustrate a common difficulty level in identifying a theme of a short story.)

If the objective specifies a performance or a product as the purpose of the objective and it is difficult to find words that will clearly communicate the specifications of that performance or product (particularly in the sensory domain), the use of films, photographs, audio tapes, etc. may be necessary to make the objective a SO.

Two common misunderstandings which are encountered in discussions concerning the specification of objectives are that most SO's are rote memory and that they refer only to products or answers. First thing to remember is that there is nothing wrong with rote memory objectives. Almost every instructional unit and for sure every course has rote memory objectives which are critical for success in the unit or course. Don't make the mistake of equating rote memory learning with *easy* learning. The concept of rote memory is actually a continuum which ranges from very simple rote memory vocabulary objectives to extremely complex rote memory procedural objectives. The negative aspect of a rote memory SO is if it is not followed by an application type SO in which the students apply or utilize what they have rote memorized.

The second common misunderstanding concerns the belief that SO's can only be used to specify end products or answers. At the present time, the production and accumulation of information is increasing faster than anyone can reasonably assimilate it, as such, information or end product SO's have limited utility. What becomes more important and useful are process SO's in which what is considered important is how to process information or the processes used in identifying and obtaining necessary information. Process SO's are ones that readily transfer from the teaching-learning-testing situation to other situations. Whereas an end product So may very well tie the student to a specific vehicle for learning, a process SO usually allows students to learn from a variety of vehicles in which the individual student can select the vehicle he or she wants to learn from. To insure transferability of the process behavior, it is best to test for the achievement of a process SO with a different vehicle than was used in the learning situation.

a. THE ANALYSIS OF A SPECIFIC OBJECTIVE

There are several different ways that a SO can be analyzed. The most common approach is to check the SO for three elements:

- Does the objective specify the behavior that the student who has mastered the SO will be able to do?

- Does it specify under what conditions the SO will be learned and exhibited?

- Does it specify to what extent the behavior will be learned (the criteria for evaluation of achievement)?

If you are interested in learning to evaluate objectives from the point-of-view of these three elements, Robert Mager's programmed booklet, *Preparing Instructional Objectives,* will be very useful. The title is slightly in error however, because it doesn't actually teach the reader how to prepare or write SO's, but it does a very good job in helping learners learn how to evaluate objectives on the basis of whether or not the objectives contain the above three elements.

NOTE: In Mager's booklet and most other books, booklets, pamphlets, and articles dealing with specific objectives, it is considered acceptable to use objective type test items to evaluate SO's. Under the Behavioral Learning System's Approach to Instruction, it is a rare event that a specific objective is worded in such a manner that it can honestly be evaluated with the traditional so-called *objective type* test item (multiple-choice, true-false, and matching). as long as one ignores the parts dealing with evaluation in these sources of information on specifying objectives, the materials are generally useful in learning how to write SO's.

(1) SPECIFYING THE LEARNING ENVIRONMENT

In analyzing an objective, I find that there are usually four steps in SO's and repeated five step patterns in GO's. The first step is optional and if it is physically located at the beginning of the objective, it usually starts out with, *Given* -------- *(a particular learning environment), the learner will be able to* --------. This is the same as the second of the three elements of a SO just described. Examples of this step are:

- Given *the resources of the library, the learner will be able to* —

- Given *nothing but a paper and pencil,* the learner will be able to —

- Given *twenty poems on the following list,* the learner will be able to —

- Given *the following five types of chemical equations,* the learner will be able to —

(2) SPECIFYING THE BEHAVIOR

The second step describes the behavior to be learned in the objective and the behavior which should be evaluated in any testing. This is the verb in the objective. If it is measurable, the objective is a SO and will probably stop at the fourth step. If the verb is non-measurable, the objective is a GO and will have five steps. The following list of verbs indicate an objective which could be a SO depending upon the fourth step:

predict	repeat	compare	dramatize
compose	record	identify	illustrate
design	list	locate	operate
assemble	name	tell	sketch
organize	relate	translate	volunteer
prepare	restate	interpret	choose
solve	discuss	use	select, etc.
question	describe	demonstrate	

The following list of verbs indicate an objective which is a GO, but which can be analyzed into sub and sub-sub objectives and eventually made into SO's:

learn	grasp the essence of	be knowledgeable
understand	be familiar with	deal with
appreciate	possess	comprehend
become aware of	be conscious	propose
formulate	discover	plan
attend carefully	listen	have an acquaintance with
participate	examine	weigh

(3) SPECIFYING THE OBJECT OF THE BEHAVIOR

The third step is the identification of the object of the verb which is usually the noun in the objective. Most of these nouns concern one or more of the following three areas: singly or in various combinations.

objects	actions with the objects	actions with information
actions	information about the objects	information about actions with objects
information	information about the actions	actions with information about objects

In recaping the first three steps, they would be:

(1) (optional) Given a specific learning environment the learner will be able to

(2) do something (a verb denoting action)

(3) with objects, actions, information, etc.

(4) SPECIFYING THE CRITERIA FOR EVALUATION: 100% OF THE OBJECTIVES vs. 100% OF THE TEST ITEMS

There have been many heated discussions over the quality level of learning experiences. Under the traditional approach where there are few, if any, specific objectives and no one worried about the correlations between objectives and test items, if a student achieved 50, 60 or maybe 70 percent of the test items right, it was considered passing. In many of the so-called *tough* courses, students achieving even 30-40 percent of the test items on a test could get a passing grade. Mager in his now almost classic *Preparing Instructional Objectives*, which was written in 1962, used the figure of 80 percent correct as being the passing mark. During the mid-1960's, as the concept of mastery became more and more important (particularly in business and industry), the common theme seemed to be *90-90* which meant that 90 percent or more of the students would achieve 90 percent or more of the objectives. About that same time, I started asking myself and thousands of teachers (with reference to the 80 percent criterion), *which 20 percent aren't important?* or (with reference to the 90 percent criterion), *which 10 percent are not important?* The answer I kept getting from the teachers was that all of the objectives and test items were important. As a result I started using the 100 percent level for a passing grade as far as course objectives are concerned. That is also when I found it necessary to differentiate between course objectives and the test items used to test for the achievement of the course objectives. As long as there is only one test item for each SO as with rote memory SO's, the criteria for evaluation can apply to test items and objectives simultaneously. Most teachers in testing for the achievement of a process objective will use two or more similar items testing the same process behavior. As a result, although there should always be at least one or more test items for each specific objective, there will not be more than one different objective for each test item. In recognizing the differences between the function of the objectives and that of the test items, it is also important to note that the quality control level for objectives and test items can be different but that it is critical to keep the relationship between test items and related objectives identified.

In Figure 52, the criteria for evaluation is 80 percent of the test items. Where this criteria is applied to a test which is testing for the achievement of multiple objectives (five in this case), it is possible to have a wide variation in the achievement of the objectives. To be sure that the students were not just lucky in answering one test item for each SO, the teacher in this example made up 25 test items to test the first SO, 20 test items to test the second SO, 15 test items to test the third SO, 10 test items to test the fourth SO, and five test items to test the fifth SO (see Figure 52). If there are 75 test items in a test which is being used to test for the achievement of five SO's and the criteria for successful achievement is 80 percent, this would allow a student to miss any 15 items. Depending on which 15 test items are missed, it would be possible to have 20 percent, 40 percent, 60 percent, 80 percent, or 100 percent achievement of the SO's and still stay within the specified criteria for evaluation of the *test items.*

SO's	Total No. of Test Items	80% of Test Items	A 20% of SO's	B 40% of SO's	C 60% of SO's	D 80% of SO's	E 100% of SO's
I	25	20	25	19	17	10	20
II	20	16	15	15	13	20	16
III	15	12	10	11	15	15	12
IV	10	8	7	10	10	10	8
V	5	4	3	5	5	5	4
	75	60	60	60	60	60	60

Figure 52 — 80 Percent of Test Items Does Not Necessarily
Mean 80 Percent of SO's

In applying the 80 percent criteria to each of the five SO's, the student would have to achieve at least 20 out of the 25 test items for SO I, at least 16 out of the 20 test items for SO II, at least 12 out of the 15 test items for SO III, at least eight out of the 10 test items for SO IV, and at least four out of the five test items for SO V. In column "A", the 15 test items that were missed were spread through SO's II, III, IV, and V such that that student was able to achieve the 80 percent criteria in only one SO or 20 percent of the SO's.

In column "B", the 15 test items that were missed were spread through SO's I, II, and III such that the student was able to achieve the 80 percent criteria in only two SO's or 40 percent of the SO's.

In column "C", the 15 test items that were missed were spread through SO's I and II such that the student was able to achieve the 80 percent criteria in only three SO's or 60 percent of the SO's.

In column "D", the 15 test items that were missed were only in SO I such that the student was able to achieve the 80 percent criteria in only four SO's or 80 percent of the SO's.

In column "E", the 15 test items that were missed were spread through all five SO's much that the student was able to achieve the 80 percent criteria in all five SO's or 100 percent of the SO's.

In Figure 53 the criteria for evaluation is 80 percent of the SO's. Where this criteria is applied to multiple SO's being tested simultaneously, it is possible to have a wide variation in the number of test items correct. In the example used in Figure 53, 80 percent achievement of the five SO's means that one of the SO's can be missed. Depending upon which SO is missed, 80 percent achievement of the SO's could be met while at the same time achieving from 53-92 percent of the test items if SO-I is missed, from 59-93 percent of the test items if SO-II is missed, from 64-95 percent of the test items if SO-III is missed, from 69-96 percent of the test items if SO-IV is missed, and from 75-97 percent of the test items if SO-V is missed.

			80 Percent of SO's Achieved				
SO's	Total No. of Items	80% of Test Items	SO — I Missed	SO — II Missed	SO — III Missed	SO — IV Missed	SO — V Missed
I	25	20	0-19	20-25	20-25	20-25	20-25
II	20	16	16-20	0-15	16-20	16-20	
II	20	16	16-20	0-15	16-20	16-20	16-20
III	15	12	12-15	12-15	0-11	12-15	12-15
IV	10	8	8-10	8-10	8-10	0-7	8-10
V	5	4	4-5	4-5	4-5	4-5	0-3
	75	60	40-69 53%-92%	44-70 59%-93%	48-71 64%-95%	52-72 69%-96%	56-73 75%-97%

Figure 53 — 80 Percent of SO's Does Not Necessarily Mean 80 Percent of Test Items

Although it is understandable that a teacher may be willing to let a student pass a unit or course without achieving 100 percent of the test items, I can not imagine a teacher allowing a student to pass a unit or course without achieving 100 percent of the required SO's (those that the teacher has already indicated are the important SO's of the unit or course). Therefore, in specifying the criteria for evaluation of a single SO, it is alright to have less than 100 percent achievement of the test items which are testing that SO. Where two or more SO's are being tested in the same test, the test items associated with each SO have to be identified and the criteria for achievement should be applied to the test items of each SO. If no criterion for achievement is specified in the SO, it should be assumed to be 100 percent. In some courses, particularly in the allied health fields, flight training, and others, not only will it be necessary to achieve 100 percent of the objectives, but it will also be necessary to achieve 100 percent of the test items. The 100 percent quality control achievement of the course objectives and test items can be easily defended. For example, I do not think a pilot or the passengers of an airplane would be happy knowing that the navigator was only able to navigate successfully 80 percent of the time. However, to be practical, even the 100 percent achievement should be defined, i.e., by being able to do 10 out of 10 correctly, by being able to do 15 out of 15 correctly, etc. In this way if a student makes a mistake and 100 percent has been defined as 12 out of 12 items correct, the student and the teacher knows how much extra drill and testing is involved before the student achieves the SO. In this example, the student would have to do 12 items correctly or in the case of the compound units, the student would have to repeat the unit (using different vehicles for learning) 12 times with all SO's achieved correctly.

In the traditional educational setting where specific objectives are not usually identified, test items testing the same behavior are not grouped or identified as being essentially the same, and scores on the tests are usually cumulative scores covering the whole test, the problems indicated in Figures 52 and 53 still exist but are usually hidden and any negative effects are ultimately blamed on genetics, home environment, etc., rather than on a lack of the teacher's knowledge about the relationship between objectives and test items. For example, in a class of 30 students being taught in a traditional manner, there will be about 20 students who will get "C" grades. If the "C" grade represents a score of about 70 percent of the tests, the 30 percent that each of the 20 students missed is assumed to be the same. It would be a rare event if all 20 students missed exactly the same test items. A more likely result would be that all of the items that were missed by the 20 students collectively would be the total test. In other words, each test item would probably be missed by one or more students. (Remember, under the traditional approach, a test item that most or all of the students know is considered a bad item because it doesn't discriminate and is usually dropped — even if it is important!) In actuality, the 30 percent that each of the 20 students missed is different from the 30 percent that any one of the others missed. Among the 20 students, there are probably one or more students whose 30 percent missed is like column "E" in Figure 52 in which there is little, if any, cumulative ignorance developed. Among the same 20 students, there are probably one or more students whose 30 percent missed is similar to columns "A", "B", "C", and "D" in Figure 52. Consequently, in not recognizing the relationship between objectives and test items, even though their scores might be the same, the amount of cumulative ignorance that each student takes with him or her could vary from practically nothing to involving the non-learning of over a majority of the course objectives. This particular point challenges the validity of almost every letter grade given in the traditional educational setting. Although the letter grades may show a student's standing relative to his or her classmates in achieving the test items given in a course, the letter grades may have little correlation to the relative standing in regard to the achievement of the stated or unstated course objectives!

It is very important to identify which test items are related to which objective, particularly if the testing procedure is looked on as a diagnostic procedure rather than just a procedure to obtain a score or grade. When using a test as part of a diagnostic procedure and by identifying which items are associated with which SO, the instruction-eer knows which SO's are causing learning problems and can select or design alternate learning pathways. Also, subsequent tests only have to include the SO's which were missed. Even if a teacher only wants to use a test as a means to arrive at a grade rather than as a diagnostic instrument, it is still important to identify which test items are duplicates and are essentially testing the same behavior and which test items are testing different SO's on a one-to-one basis. As can be seen in Figure 52, the same total scores can represent a wide variation in achievement. As such, identifying a score as the number of test items correct in a test covering multiple SO's is meaningless!

An easy way to keep track of the relationship between test items and SO's is to number your test items as follows:

I — 1	I — 6	I — 11	III — 16
I — 2	I — 7	II — 12	III — 17
I — 3	I — 8	II — 13	III — 18
I — 4	II — 9	II — 14	III — 19
I — 5	II — 10	II — 15	Etc.

The first number refers to the SO and the second number to the test item. If desired, Arabic numerals can be used instead of the Roman numerals to indicate the SO. Also, if desired, the numbering of the test items does not have to be continuous. The numbering of the test items could start over with each SO as follows:

1 — 1	1 — 6	2 — 3	3 — 1
1 — 2	1 — 7	2 — 4	3 — 2
1 — 3	1 — 8	2 — 5	3 — 3
1 — 4	2 — 1	2 — 6	3 — 4
1 — 5	2 — 2	2 — 7	Etc.

NOTE: When using the criteria for achievement of 80 percent or higher for each SO, remember that the student that gets 80 percent of the test items correct gets the same grade, score, or credit as the one that got 90 percent or 100 percent of the items correct. If you feel that you want to give extra credit for getting a higher percentage correct, then maybe you should require 100 percent achievement. The guideline is as usual, *Anything important enough to score a student up for learning or down for not learning must be important enough to teach. If it is not important enough to teach then it is not important enough to score a student up for learning it or down for not learning it.* For example, in column E of Figure 52, students achieving scores between 60-75 will all receive the same grade (if any grades are given at all) as long as a student doesn't miss more than the permissible limit for any one SO.

In deciding the criteria for evaluation, the preceeding was concerned primarily with the achievement of problem solving behaviors in which the solving of the problems was of relatively short time duration and each SO could be tested by itself. A similar approach can be used in testing for the achievement of more complex SO's which may or may not be interdependent, but are usually tested simultaneously for achievement. Examples of this category are the complex problem solving of relatively long term duration resulting in reports (essays, case studies, etc.), complex production skills which result in various products (vocational-technical courses, art courses, etc.), and complex projects of the type frequently found in science courses which may result in reports, products, etc. Because of the interdependence of some or all of the SO's in any one of these compound instructional units, it may be difficult to retest only a few of the SO's by themselves. In this type of situation, if at all possible, the student should be able to correct any errors identified in the first evaluation (essay, report, experiment, product, project, etc.). In doing the instructional unit over again, although the objective should be the same, a different vehicle should be used to demonstrate the achievement of the SO's and emphasis should be on the evaluation of the SO's which were incorrectly demonstrated the first time through the instructional unit. This process should be repeated until all of the SO's have been achieved. If in doing the compound instructional units five or more times a student makes a mistake in demonstrating the achievement of a SO during one of those times, the teacher may want to assume the student has learned the SO because it was demonstrated correctly at least four out of five times (or 80 percent).

NOTE: If you are a teacher already, you may find it to be a very useful exercise to go over your tests and identify those items that are duplicates of the same behavior and start grading and diagnosing the results of tests on the basis of objectives achieved rather than on the basis of test items achieved. This change in evaluation usually makes big differences in the scores for some students.

(5) INCREASING THE SPECIFICATION OF THE OBJECTIVE

In case the behavior in the second step of the analysis is non-measurable and at the same time the criteria for evaluation is missing, then the objective is a GO and the next step would be to say *as measured by* and repeat the process, but try to identify a behavior in the second step that is measurable and include criteria for evaluation. At least try to reduce the degree of generality such that after breaking the GO down into sub-GO's, sub-sub GO's, etc. some SO's are identified which have all four steps in each of them (see Figure 54).

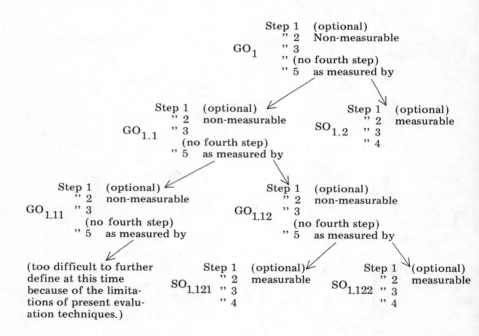

Figure 54 — Increasing the Specification by Analyzing the Objective[4]

---

[4] The numbered subscripts of the GO's and SO's indicate the relationships between the objectives. The number of digits indicate the level or generation of the objectives, i.e., $SO_{1.121}$ indicates that this specific objective is a fourth generation objective (four digits) and is related to the GO, at the first level, to $GO_{1.1}$ at the second level, and to $GO_{1.12}$ at the third level.

6. THE THREE TYPES OF LEARNING: COGNITIVE, SENSORY, AND AFFECTIVE

OPTIONAL: (For those readers who have access to Volume I). For a better understanding of this unit and for a better background for most of the subsequent units in this chapter, you should reread or review pages 101-120 in Volume I concerning the three domains of learning. Although certain critical concepts will be repeated in this unit in order to emphasize their importance and to maintain continuity, not enough of the previous material will be repeated to eliminate the need for review. If you don't review the previous material and you run into a problem comprehending some of the following material in this unit, at that point, branch yourself back and review the previous material.

One of the most important concepts to be remembered in thinking of the three domains of learning is that although learning objectives can be specified in each of the domains a great deal of learning (maybe even most) involves all three types of learning. This means that in designing instruction to help students learn SO's in any one of the domains, chances are pretty good that indirectly learning in one or both of the other two domains may also be occurring plus fringe learning in the domain of the SO's. Because the evaluation instrument in the designed learning situation has been designed to measure the achievement of the desired SO's in the instructional unit, the associated learning in either or both of the other domains will probably not be identified, even if measurable and neither will the fringe learning in the domain of the SO's. The associated learning and the fringe learning may not become noticeable until much later at which time the learning environment which facilitated the development of the associated and fringe learning can no longer be identified even by the learner. As long as the associated and fringe learning is positive and will benefit the learner and society, the problem of associated and fringe learning is not of great concern. However, because the possibility of associated and fringe learning has not been considered in the traditional approach to education, some of the associated and/or fringe learning is negative and becomes a liability to both the student and society. Consider the following examples:

— In the punishing of students in early elementary grades with learning activities (write sentences, paragraphs, or essays, do extra problems, etc.), the purpose of the punishment falls in the affective domain, the vehicle for the punishment is in the cognitive domain, and the fringe learning of the view that learning is punishment is in the affective domain;

- In the teaching of the writing of essays in courses which the emphasis is on the activity of writing a certain number of essays rather than on learning how to write well, the purpose of writing is in the cognitive domain but because quantity is more important than quality,[5] students have to repeat essentially the same course or that part of a course concerning essay writing each year from about fourth grade up to freshman composition at the college level which develops negative attitudes towards English and writing and these attitudes are in the affective domain.

- In art, music, and literature appreciation courses, *appreciation* is too often defined in terms of liking what the teacher *appreciates* which indirectly results in many students claiming externally that they like and appreciate whatever the teacher wants in order to get through the course. Internally, however, the students develop negative attitudes towards what they felt forced to like. The purpose and the results are both in the affective domain but in opposite directions.

- In using the curve grading concept to assign grades on the results of a test which tests for cognitive learning, the students at the lower end of the curve not only don't achieve the cognitive SO's, but many of them develop negative attitudes towards themselves, the teacher, the subject, school, community, society, and maybe even parents because of their lack of success.

The following is an example of positive associated learning:

- In using the Behavioral Learning Systems Approach in which 90 percent or more of the students would be able to learn 100 percent of all of the cognitive SO's, the students develop positive attitudes towards themselves, the subject, the teacher, school, community, and maybe even parents because of their success.

Under the traditional approach to education, the emphasis has been on cognitive domain objectives and in certain courses on sensory domain objectives. Affective learning was ignored or was assumed to be occurring in the appropriate directions. As pointed out in the above examples, this approach may actually develop undesirable affective learning. A current so-called *modern* or revolutionary approach empha-

---

[5] In many schools and particularly in college level composition courses, students can fail the course faster by not turning in one of the assigned essays then by turning in all the essays and they are all of "F" quality.

sizes the teaching of affective learning and ignoring the cognitive domain objectives. Typically in this approach, formal testing of either affective or cognitive learning is dropped. Because cognitive learning is not emphasized, even fewer students than before learn the necessary intellectual and sensory skills necessary to not only survive in our society but to achieve success. As a result, although some of the students may have good attitudes during class because it seems easier and the atmosphere is pleasant, when they discover that they can't read or communicate or obtain work, their attitudes will reverse direction.

In recognizing the overlapping of the three domains of learning, the instructioneer can design instruction to accomplsih SO's in two or more domains simultaneously and can also design instructional units in which the achievement or recognition of SO's in one domain can be used as a means of achieving SO's in another domain. For example:

— In developing appreciation for the skills of specialists in art, music, literature, craft, etc., it is necessary to teach the cognitive and sensory domain objectives associated with the production process and the evaluative process before the students can develop appreciation.

— In trying to solve student's learning problems in the cognitive and sensory domains, it is very useful to vary the vehicles for learning such that the student is motivated to *want to learn.*

— In a situation in which the instructioneer shows concern for the individual by solving each student's learning problems such that almost all students have success, not only does a student learn the desired SO's of the instructional unit and develop positive attitudes, but the student has also learned by example to care about other individuals.

In recognizing that one or more of the three domains of learning can occur simultaneously, it becomes even more important to recognize and take into consideration in the instructional event that each of the domains represent distinct types of learning with characteristics which may be common to two or all three domains and also characteristics which are unique to a specific domain. When two or more types of learning are supposed to occur simultaneously in an instructional event, there is a natural tendency to assume that they can be treated as having the same characteristics. For this reason it is critical to identify and remember those characteristics which are unique to a specific domain. Table V which was presented in Chapter 4 is repeated here to facilitate the awareness of the differences between the three domains.

In addition to the differences noted in Table IX and discussed in pages 000-000, Volume I, there are several other differences which can be pointed out. Although it should be obvious, it may be important to identify the object of the instructional efforts. In the cognitive domain,

TABLE IX (Table VIII, Volume I)

	A Behavioral Theory of Instruction: Cognitive and Sensory Domains		A Behavioral Theory of Instruction: Affective Domain
	Cognitive	Sensory	Affective
Types of Learning	Intellectual Skills	Sensoria Skills	Emotional Tendencies
Types of Objectives	General Only	General and Specific	General Only
How Measured	Indirect	Direct and Indirect	Indirect
What Behaviors Measured	Psychomotor Behaviors	Sensomotor Behaviors	Emotive Behaviors
Purpose of Behaviors	To Communicate Mental Thought	To Communicate the Degree of Sensoria Skills	To Communicate the Intensity and Direction of an Emotion
Objectives Given to Learners at the Beginning of Instruction	Yes	Yes	No
Learners Identified in Evaluation	Yes	Yes	No
Quality Control	100% Achievement	100% Achievement	Best Possible Achievement
How Taught and Learned	Directly	Directly	Indirectly
Instructional Emphasis	Individual	Individual	Group
Primary Purpose of Evaluation	Identify Student's Learning Problems	Identify Student's Learning Problems	Identify Instructor's Design Problems
Secondary Purpose of Evaluation	Identify Instructor's Design Problems	Identify Instructor's Design Problems	Identify Student's Learning Problems
The Effect of an Instructor's Conflicting Attitudes & Values	Minor Effect	Minor Effect	Possible Major Effect
Student's Control over Learning	High	High	Low

the efforts are directed towards affecting the mental senses (common sense, wisdom, judgement, intuition, etc.). In the affective domain, the efforts are directed towards affecting the emotional senses (feelings, attitudes, beliefs, values, etc.) In the sensory domain, the efforts are directed towards affecting the bodily senses (visual, auditory, skin, taste, smell, kinesthetic, and organic).

a. MENTAL, EMOTIONAL, AND BODILY CONSCIOUSNESSES

Bloom and others in their *Taxonomy of Educational Objectives, Handbook I: Cognitive Domain* suggested differences between the domains with reference to the levels of consciousness involved. Whereas they discussed levels of mental consciousness, they did not mention differences in levels of emotional consciousness or differences in levels of bodily consciousness or suggest that these other categories of consciousness existed. Consider the following hypotheses:

Levels of Mental consciousness refers to the varying degrees of internal awareness of mental activity.

— Learning in the cognitive domain is usually associated with a high level of mental consciousness (a high degree of internal awareness of mental activity).

— Learning in the affective domain is usually associated with a low level of mental consciousness (a low degree of internal awareness of mental activity).

— Learning in the sensory domain is usually associated with little, if any, mental consciousness (little, if any, internal awareness of mental activity).

Levels of emotional consciousness refers to the varying degrees of internal awareness of emotional activity.

— Learning in the cognitive domain is usually associated with variable levels of emotional consciousness (varying degrees of internal awareness of emotional activity). The more positive the attitudes, the easier it is for the learning to take place. The more negative the attitudes, the more difficult it is for the learning to take place.

— Learning in the affective domain is usually associated with a proprotionate level of emotional consciousness (proportionate degree of internal awareness of emotional activity). In the development of a *new* attitude, value, or belief,[6] the higher the

---

[6] A *new* attitude, value, or belief is one in which the carrier (topic, concept, idea, thing, etc.) is also new and there has never been a prior attitude, value, or belief associated with the carrier.

levels of emotional consciousness and/or the more frequent the emotional consciousness is aroused or stimulated, the stronger the development of the new attitude, value, or belief. In increasing the intensity of an existing attitude, value, or belief, the higher the levels of emotional consciousness in the same direction and/or the more frequent the emotional consciousness is aroused or stimulated in the same direction, the greater the tendency to strengthen the existing attitude, value, or belief.[7] In increasing the intensity of an existing attitude, value, or belief, the higher the levels of emotional consciousness in the opposite direction and/or the more frequent the emotional consciousness is around or stimulated in the opposite direction, the greater the tendency to weaken the existing attitude, value, or belief.[8]

— Learning in the sensory domain is usually associated with variable levels of emotional consciousness (varying degrees of internal awareness of emotional activity.) The more positive the attitudes, the easier it is for the learning to take place. The more negative the attitudes, the more difficult it is for the learning to take place.

Levels of bodily consciousness refers to the varying degrees of internal awareness of sensory activity.

— Learning in the cognitive domain is usually associated with low levels of bodily consciousness (low degrees of internal awareness of sensory activity).

— Learning in the affective domain is usually associated with variable levels of bodily consciousness (varying degrees of internal awareness of sensory activity). The greater *the rate of change* of the attitude, value, or belief, the higher the level of bodily consciousness.

— Learning in the sensory domain is usually associated with high levels of bodily consciousness (high degrees of internal awareness of sensory activity).

---

[7] Given the same level of emotional consciousness and/or the same frequency of arousal or stimulation, an existing weak attitude, value, or belief will *tend to increase in intensity* more than an existing strong attitude, value, or belief (both being in the *same direction* as the emotional consciousness).

[8] Given the same level of emotional consciousness and/or the same frequency of arousal or stimulation, an existing weak attitude, value, or belief will *tend to decrease in intensity* more than an existing strong attitude, value, or belief (both being in the opposite direction as the emotional consciousness).

A summary of the interaction of the three domains of learning with the three types of consciousness are shown in Figure 55.

TYPES OF CONSCIOUSNESS

		Mental	Emotional	Bodily
TYPES OF LEARNING	Cognitive	High	variable (motivation)	Low
	Affective	Low	variable	variable (rate of change)
	Sensory	little, if any	variable (motivation)	High

Figure 55 — Levels of Consciousness as affected by the different types of learning

Since an instructional situation can and usually does involve more than one type of learning by design or as associated or fringe learning, the instructional situation also involves one or more of the types of consciousness. The interactions between types of learning and the types of consciousness indicated in Figure 55 may very well affect the instructional situation. Remember, however, that these interactions are primarily occurring in a *learning* situation. Once the learning situation is over and whatever was learned is practiced, the levels of consciousness will decrease. At the point where the observable behaviors representing the learning is performed with little if any internal awareness of mental, sensory, and/or emotional activity, then whatever was learned has become a habit. In a sense, the individual has become internally programmed. Although the concept of a person being *programmed* carries with it a variety of negative thoughts, everyone is internally programmed to do certain things, i.e., once a person has learned to drive a car, the behaviors necessary to carry out normal driving are internally programmed; once a person has learned to read, the physical behaviors of reading are internally programmed; etc. It is part of human nature to internally program repeated activities which then reduces the *awareness load* in the mental, bodily, and/or emotional consciousnesses such that other things can be attended to. The negative aspects of the concept of being *internally programmed* are concerned with who directs it, how it is done, under what conditions, and whether or not what i

373

being internally programmed is in conflict with accepted so-called *normal* patterns of behavior.

With reference to *how it is done* and *under what conditions*, the techniques can vary from being very open and with high levels of consciousness to being secretive and with none or subliminal levels of consciousness and the conditions can vary from being very positive and rewarding to being very negative and punishing.

With reference to who directs the programming, as long as the individual is highly conscious of the learning activity, then only the individual can direct the programming. If however, the individual is only slightly conscious or is not even conscious of the learning activity, then whoever sets up the learning situation is directing the programming. Because it is very common to have two and sometimes even all three types of learning occurring simultaneously, an individual can be very conscious of one type of learning and control whether or not the learning takes place and whether or not the learning becomes a programmed behavior. At the same time, the individual may not be conscious at all of another type of learning which is essentially *hitchhiking* a ride along with the known learning activity. The individual doing the learning does not have control over this second type of learning and as such the individual may for one reason or another decide not to learn and make a habit of the learning activity for which the individual has a high level of consciousness, but will learn and make a habit of the learning activity for which the individual has a low or zero level of consciousness. Although this process seems very insidious, most of the time the second or unknown learning is there by chance and no one is directing it, particularly in the case where the second learning is in the affective domain. In most other cases, the purpose behind the use of the process is very worthwhile and acceptable. Common examples can be found everywhere. A mother offers a reward of enough money to go to a movie to a daughter or son if they will do the dishes (which the daughter or son doesn't want to do). The hope of the mother is that the child will be so highly conscious of the reward (affective domain) that the child will only be slightly conscious of the task of doing the dishes (cognitive and sensory domains). The concept of motivation (both positive and negative) is very much a part of the process of utilizing dual or triple consciousnesses to achieve a goal. Notice however, that both the motivation and the activity are known. In most Sunday school programs, the primary objective as identified by what happens in the classes is to learn about the Bible (cognitive), but the real purpose is to develop certain sets of attitudes, values, and beliefs (affective). Although both purposes are known, in the actual classroom, the issue with which the children are highly conscious of concerns the Bible. The fact that the childrens' attitudes, values, and

374

beliefs are being programmed by the church is not openly discussed, it is considered acceptable.

Usually, if the person or persons directing the programming are considered acceptable then whatever is being programmed into the individuals is also considered acceptable. Obviously, teachers, education, and the whole concept of schooling is very much involved in this process. The cognitive learning which is the primary purpose of education and instruction is constantly carrying with it affective domain motivators and demotivators. It is assumed that the teachers' role should be to facilitate the cognitive learning by maximizing the motivators and minimizing the demotivators. Outside of certain issues such as sex education and evolution theories, most of what is being programmed in the students is considered acceptable.

NOTE: Since most teachers at the present time have not really specified their specific objectives in the cognitive, sensory, or affective domain, most of what is being programmed into the students occurs almost by chance — including many attitudes, values, and beliefs which may not be what the majority of parents and teachers want, i.e., notice that the increase in the militancy of students followed the increase in the militancy of the teachers.

In only a relatively few cases, hopefully, the teacher who is directing the programming process has ulterior or hidden motives such that the secondary learning associated with a very low level of consciousness on the part of the learner is in conflict with the concepts and patterns of behaviors which the majority of parents and society would consider acceptable. Usually the way this is accomplished is that a teacher selects vehicles for learning which will accomplish the primary purpose of learning but will also facilitate the teacher's secondary purpose. Among the thousands of teachers I have worked with, I have encountered maybe a dozen or so teachers at the secondary level which fall into this category and probably fifty or so in higher education. For example, in several cases where the teachers' stated primary objectives concerned the analysis of various forms of literature, the teachers had selected as vehicles for learning literary analysis a variety of literature which was anti-democracy and anti-establishment. All of the objectives, discussions, and testing concerned the cognitive aspects of literary analysis and as such were at high levels of mental consciousness. On the other hand, the content of the literature had to be read in order to achieve the public emphasis of the course, and since there was very little, if any, discussion of the content of the literature, there was probably a very low level of consciousness of the attitudes and values being presented in the content. As such, the students had control over the learning of the literary analysis techniques, but they didn't have much control over the subliminal learning of the attitudes and values being presented in the content of the literature. This same approach has been used by several teachers in the teaching of history courses, econimics courses, and civics courses at the secondary level.

Although I have run into more teachers in higher education than in secondary schools that use their classroom as a means of developing conflicting attitudes and values in students, at least the efforts in higher education are much more open. The content of the vehicles for learning is of the same type: anti-United States, anti-democracy, anti-establishment, etc. The difference is that the cognitive content of these vehicles for learning openly constitute the objectives for the courses, the topics for discussion, and the sources of the test items and as such is at high levels of consciousness where the learning is controlled by the learner. However, as before, the attitudes, values, and beliefs presented in the content are not as openly handled and as such are at low levels of consciousness and not subject to the control of the learner.[9]

Regardless of what level of consciousness learning takes place initially, as it is practiced over and over again, the level of consciousness decreases until it becomes a habit at which point the level of consciousness is practically non-existent. This becomes very important in trying to change a learned behavior. If the learned behavior has become a habit, it will be very difficult to change because its occurrence is almost beyond the control of the person possessing it. In trying to change a learned behavior which has become a habit, it is probably necessary to re-arouse the level of consciousness to the point where the learner has control again.[10] It is also important to remember that two or all three domains of learning and their associated levels of consciousness can be involved in the performance of a habit. If they are, it may be necessary to raise the level of consciousness in each of the domains involved in order to bring about the desired change. In some habits, the habit or low level of consciousness is only in one of the domains; whereas the levels of consciousness in the other domains are relatively high. In these situations, the change in the habit could be brought about easier by starting from the domain with the higher level of consciousness.

---

[9] I am not against students being exposed to other points-of-view and other attitudes, values, and beliefs, but I am against teachers who take advantage of the classroom and the captive audience to present only one side of conflicting points-of-view and especially when it is done in such a manner that the students, parents, and others are not aware of the learning that is occurring.

[10] Encounter groups and a lot of psychotherapy are efforts to raise a persons' level of consciousness to the point where problem factors can be identified and possibly controlled by the person or by the individual directing the encounter group or psychotherapy.

- changes in the cognitive domain can often be accomplished by showing the learner data or processes which will be in conflict with the learned behavior to be changed.

- changes in the sensory domain can often be accomplished by using one of the other senses to identify sensory input which will be in conflict with the learned behavior to be changed.

- changes in the affective domain can often be accomplished by identifying attutides, values, or beliefs which the learner already has that are in conflict with the attitudes, values, or beliefs which are to be changed. If you can't identify existing attitudes, values, or beliefs which are in conflict with the attitudes, values, or beliefs which are to be changed, it may be possible to develop them by designing an appropriate learning environment.

- Because two or all three domains may be associated with a behavior to be changed, it may be easiest to identify or develop a potential behavior (decision-making) or an actual behavior which is in conflict with the behavior to be changed and in a domain other than the one in which the behavior to be changed is in.

b. COGNITIVE DOMAIN

Cognitive objectives are ones which emphasize remembering or reproducing something which has presumably been learned, as well as objectives which involve the solving of some intellectual task for which the individual has to determine the essential problem and then reorder given material or combine it with ideas, methods or procedures previously learned. Cognitive objectives vary from simple recall of material learned to highly original and creative ways of combining and synthesizing new ideas and materials.

Taxonomy of Educational Objectives, Handbook I: Cognitive Domain

by Bloom and others

In the cognitive domain, the amount a person can learn is infinite and cumulative. There is no such thing as negative knowledge from the point-of-view of measurement. In other words, a person cannot know less than zero knowledge. Being cumulative, once something in the cognitive domain is learned it is relatively static in that it doesn't change after that. As such, most measurement in the cognitive domain is quantitative and is done to identify whether or not the necessary or desired learning took place as a basis for future instructional decision-making.

NOTE: The major difference between the student and the teacher in the cognitive domain is that if the teacher is a subject matter specialist, the teacher knows much more than the student and they will be involved in a transfer of information, skills, etc., either directly from the live teacher or indirectly via some form of technology. If the teacher is a teaching specialist, then the teacher may or may not know more about the subject than the student, but the teacher knows more about locating sources of information, skills, etc.; more about how to set up an instructional unit which will facilitate student learning; and more about how to solve the student's learning problems.

Most of the testing in the cognitive domain (outside of problem solving) has concerned the remembering of information and under the traditional educational approach, traditional testing has developed four serious problems. First of all, the purpose of testing traditionally is to get a grade rather than to identify learning problems and as such, the tests are usually given during the last few days before grades are supposed to be assigned. This in turn creates the second problem which is the need to evaluate the tests in a short period of time. As a result, the use of objective type tests (multiple-choice, true-false, and matching) spread rapidly among traditional teachers because they can be scored by computers or other machines and even scored by hand very quickly. Another traditional major advantage of the objective type tests (a disadvantage from my point-of-view) is that with a minimum of training, teachers can be taught how to adjust the test items in order to get a curve of results regardless of what students actually know.

The third and fourth problems concern what is being tested. In testing for the memorization of information, if the information is useful, then the testing should involve using the information not just the recall of the information. If the information is not useful, then I see no reason to test the students' recall of something they can't use. The emphasis on the testing of information only has led to charges of irrelevancy which may be valid.

Glasser in his *Schools Without Failure* stated that *Memory is not education, answers are not knowledge. Certainty and memory are the enemies of thinking, the destroyers of creativity and originality.* My reaction to his statement is that just because the present testing of memory is bad because it doesn't go on from there to greater things such as creativity is not sufficient reason to not have any memory objectives. It would be rather disastrous if everyone creatively developed their own individual language, number system, rules for driving, etc. Although the foundation and internal structure of a building is not necessarily the beauty of the building and left unfinished, the skeleton

378

of a building might be ugly and uncreative. It would be better to complete the building creatively then to tear it down and try to build a creative, beautiful, building with no foundation or internal structure to support it. The fourth problem is that in a situation such as we have in our society today where the production of information is like an avalanche, there is just no reason and no way to have students try to keep up with the production of information by memorizing it.

Information that is used a lot can be memorized to save time locating it every time the students need it, but to make sure of relevancy, the tests should include the testing of the students' ability to use the information. In the testing of process SO's, it may be useful to have students memorize some information long enough to learn a process. The processes involved are typically how to analyze a problem, how to identify and locate sources of information dealing with certain parts of the problem, how to retrieve the information from the sources, how to handle or process the information, and then how to store the processed information for anyone else who may have the same or similar problem. Once the process has been learned, however, it would be the ability of the students' to use and apply the process that would be tested rather than the ability of the students' to memorize. Therefore, testing in the cognitive domain would primarily consist of open ended test items which could be answered by a word, phrase, sentence, paragraph, essay, etc. The answer would reflect whatever it was that the student was supposed to *do* as identified in the SO (specific objective) that the test item was associated with.

NOTE: Since the cognitive domain concerns the development of intellectual skills and mental processes, essentially what the student should be writing down in most of the test items is a description of the thinking that took place in response to the stimulus of the test item.

A very common question that is asked at my seminars is, *But what if the students don't remember either the information or the processes dealing with the information?* In reference to the problem of forgetting, the first thing to be sure of is whether or not the student had actually learned something in the first place. All too often, if the students were exposed to a concept when a teacher presented it, the assumption is made that all of the students learned the concept. Then, if a student doesn't know the concept when he or she is tested, it is assumed that the student forgot it. Notice in almost all of the descriptions of year-round school programs they talk about all of the forgetting that takes place during the summer. Since it is not a common practice traditionally to give entry tests at the beginning of the school year to identify exactly what students know and don't know about necessary prerequisite knowledge, skills, etc., the way that teachers usually identify that the students must have forgotten some things during the summer is that some of the students aren't able to answer some of the discussion questions during class or some of the test items in the test given at the end of the first unit. Since not all students by June, under the traditional approach to education have learned 100 percent of their course objectives, then it should be expected and normal to have students who don't know everything they are supposed to know. After all, remember that under the traditional approach, the average students learn about "C" worth or about 70 percent of their courses and collectively all of the things each student in a class didn't learn probably equal the total course. In most situations involving forgetting, the problem is not one of the students forgetting, the problem is that all of the necessary objectives were not learned in the first place. You can't forget something you haven't learned.

In the case of forgetting, it doesn't mean that what was once learned has left the mind, it just means that it has not been used enough to keep it at a conscious level.

NOTE: Habit and forgetting are very similar in that both are associated with very low levels of consciousness and as such are at the extreme ends of the frequency of utilization curve (see Figure 55a).

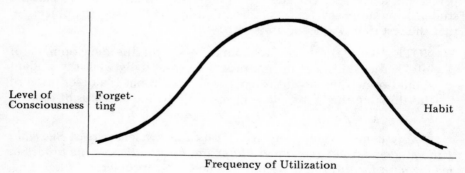

Figure 55a — Frequency of Utilization Curve

In addition to the frequency of utilization affecting the formation of a habit or forgetting, if whatever it is, is associated with positive attitudes, values, and beliefs, forgetting will tend to be delayed and the formation of a habit will be speeded up. If it is associated with negative attitudes, values, and beliefs, forgetting will tend to be speeded up and the formation of a habit will be delayed. Two other factors which affect forgetting and the formation of a habit concern

380

the multiplicity of a stimuli in the consciousness and the relative strengths of the other stimuli. The greater the number of competing[11] stimuli in the consciousness, the longer it will take to develop a habit and the quicker something can be forgotten. The greater the relative strength of a competitive stimulus (higher levels of consciousness), the longer it will take to develop a habit and the quicker something can be forgotten. Forgetting which is caused by either or both of these last two factors is usually momentary or for a relatively short period of time. The length of time being dependent on when the number and/or relative strengths of competing stimuli are reduced.

(1) TAXONOMY OF COGNITIVE OBJECTIVES

A taxonomy refers to a system of classifying things. In any one taxonomy, there are some unifying characteristics which place things into the taxonomy and then other characteristics which are used to separate things within a taxonomy. A taxonomy is not of much value unless you know the guiding principle which was used to separate the things into various categories. The value of a taxonomy is that it facilitates the study of a class of things from a particular point-of-view (the guiding principle). It should be remembered that given a class of things, there are different ways that the things could be classified. For example, given cars as a class of vehicles, they could be classified according to weight, cost, speed, shape, etc. Notice that if given motorized vehicles as a class, cars could be one of the categories.

In reference to a taxonomy of educational objectives, Bloom and others published in 1956 a *Taxonomy of Educational Objectives Handbook I: Cognitive Domain.* Their main purpose was to develop a taxonomy which would facilitate communication between educators and curriculum groups. Since objectives were usually stated in general terms and hence non-measurable, it was very difficult to develop any kind of commonality in what students were learning even if the GO's were the same. The mistake that some curriculum writers and directors of objective writing workshops often make is to look on a taxonomy as having been handed down by some kind of God and as such they feel that every instructional unit must have objectives which reflect each level or category of the taxonomy. From the point-of-view of a teacher who already has objectives, a taxonomy helps the teacher to identify the types of objectives he or she is using. From the point-of-view of a teacher who is writing objectives, a taxonomy facilitates the writing of different types of objectives and helps a teacher avoid writing objectives

---

[11] Competition is in reference to the concept that all of the stimuli in the consciousness are vying for attention and awareness.

which are all of the same type (unless that is what the teacher wants). It is not necessary to have objectives which reflect each category of a taxonomy unless this is what the teacher wants and can justify.

A very common problem was encountered by Bloom and others in the development of their taxonomy and by many others in using the taxonomy. In the very beginning of the book Bloom and others stated:

> For example, some teachers believe their students should *really understand*, others desire their students to *internalize knowledge*, still others want their students to *grasp the core or essence* or *comprehend*. Do they all mean the same thing? Specifically, what does a student do who *really understands* which he does not do when he does not understand?

A little later on Bloom and others also stated:

> It was pointed out that we were attempting to classify phenomena which could not be observed or manipulated in the same concrete form as the phenomena of such field as the physical and biological sciences, where taxonomies of a very high order have already been developed. Nevertheless, it was the view of the group that educational objectives stated in behavioral form have their counterparts in the behavior of individuals. Such behavior can be observed and described, and these descriptive statements can be classified.

Based on the two quotes, it would seem that their efforts would be to make SO's out of GO's, but if you look at most of the examples listed with the taxonomy in the appendix of the book, you will find that their examples are still GO's. For example:

> Familiarity with a large number of words in their common range of meanings.

> Understanding of the continuity and development of American culture as exemplified in American life.

> The ability to understand non-literal statements (metaphor, symbolism, irony, exaggeration).

In addition, many of their examples of acceptable test items are of the objective type test item (multiple-choice, true-false, and matching). The problem is that although the guiding principle of Bloom's taxonomy is the varying difficulty and complexity levels of the learner's behavior in learning educational objectives, the learner's behavior is often confused with the topic of an objective, i.e.,

— Given the following five pieces of literature, --------, --------, --------, --------, --------, the student will be able to perform a literary analysis which will be evaluated on the basis of the following criteria: --------, --------, --------, --------, and --------.

— In literary analysis, the first step according to (some name) is
    a. --------
    b. --------
    c. --------
    d. --------

Although both examples use the term *literary analysis*, they are not the same from the point-of-view of what behavior the learner performs. In the first example, the learner actually performs a literary analysis. In the second example, the learner is being tested on his or her ability to recall the first step of a process given the clues of right or wrong answers. The second example does not test the student's ability to perform a literary analysis and difficulty level of the item is more determined by the distractors put into the right and wrong answers by the writer of the test item than by the performance of the student. It really amazes me when I am asked to preview an instructional unit in which the teacher claims to have included SO's from all of the levels of Bloom's taxonomy yet the test is an objective type multiple-choice test in which all of the items are testing the same behavior.

(a) Bloom's Taxonomy

Despite my negative comments, the taxonomy by Bloom and others is a very useful tool as long as the sample test items of the objective type (multiple-choice, etc.) are skipped over as being in error and you recognize that most of the sample objectives are GO's. The following is the condensed version of the taxonomy of educational objectives in the cognitive domain as presented in the appendix of the book by Bloom and others.

KNOWLEDGE

1.00 KNOWLEDGE

Knowledge, as defined here, involves the recall of specifics and universals, the recall of methods and processes, or the recall of a pattern, structure, or setting. For measurement purposes, the recall situation involves little more than bringing to mind the appropriate material. Although some alteration of the material may be required, this is a relatively minor part of the task. The knowledge objectives emphasize most the psychological processes of remembering. The process of relating is also involved in that a knowledge test situation requires the organization and reorganization of a problem such that it will furnish the appropriate signals and cues for the information and knowledge the individual possesses. To use an analogy, if one thinks of the mind as a file, the problem in a knowledge test situation is that of finding in the problem or task the appropriate signals, cues, and clues which will most effectively bring out whatever knowledge is filed or stored.

1.10 KNOWLEDGE OF SPECIFICS

The recall of specific and isolable bits of information. The emphasis is on symbols with concrete referents. This material, which is at a very low level of abstraction, may be thought of as the elements from which more complex and abstract forms of knowledge are built.

1.11 KNOWLEDGE OF TERMINOLOGY

Knowledge of the referents for specific symbols (verbal and non-verbal). This may include knowledge of the most generally accepted symbol referent, knowledge of the variety of symbols which may be used for a single referent, or knowledge of the referent most appropriate to a given use of a symbol.

> Ex. To define technical terms by giving their attributes, properties, or relations.

> Ex. Familiarity with a large number of words in their common range of meanings.

1.12 KNOWLEDGE OF SPECIFIC FACTS

Knowledge of dates, events, persons, places, etc. This may include very percise and specific information such as the specific date or exact magnitude of a phenomenon. It may also include approximate or relative information such as an approximate time period or the general order of magnitude of a phenomenon.

> Ex. The recall of major facts about particular cultures.

> Ex. The possession of a minimum knowledge about the organisms studied in the laboratory.

1.20 KNOWLEDGE OF WAYS AND MEANS OF DEALING WITH SPECIFICS

Knowledge of the ways of organizing, studying, judging, and criticizing. This includes the methods of inquiry, the chronological sequences, and the standards of judgment within a field as well as the patterns of organization through which the areas of the fields themselves are determined and internally organized. This knowledge is at an intermediate level of abstraction between specific knowledge on the one hand and knowledge of universals on the other. It does not so much demand the activity of the student in using the materials as it does a more passive awareness of their nature.

1.21 KNOWLEDGE OF CONVENTIONS

Knowledge of characteristic ways of treating and presenting ideas and phenomena. For purposes of communication and consistency, workers in a field employ usuages, styles, practices, and forms which best suit their purposes and/or which appear to suit best the phenomena with which they deal. It should be recognized that although these forms and conventions are likely to be set up on arbitrary, accidental, or authoritative bases, they are retained because of the general agreement or concurrence of individuals concerned with the subject, phenomena, or problem.

> Ex. Familiarity with the forms and conventions of the major types of works, e.g., verse, plays, scientific papers, etc.

> Ex. To make pupils conscious of correct form and usage in speech and writing.

1.22 KNOWLEDGE OF TRENDS AND SEQUENCES

Knowledge of the processes, directions and movements of phenomena with respect to time.

> Ex. Understanding of the continuity and development of American culture as exemplified in American life.

> Ex. Knowledge of the basic trends underlying the development of public assistance programs.

385

1.23 KNOWLEDGE OF CLASSIFICATIONS AND CATE-GORIES

Knowledge of the classes, sets, divisions, and arrangements which are regarded as fundamental for a given subject field, purpose, argument, or problem.

> Ex. To recognize the area encompassed by various kinds of problems or materials.

> Ex. Becoming familiar with a range of types of literature.

1.24 KNOWLEDGE OF CRITERIA

Knowledge of the criteria by which facts, principles, opinions, and conduct are tested or judged.

> Ex. Familiarity with criteria for judgment appropriate to the type of work and the purpose for which it is read.

> Ex. Knowledge of criteria for the evaluation of recreational activities.

1.25 KNOWLEDGE OF METHODOLOGY

Knowledge of the methods of inquiry, techniques, and procedures employed in a particular subject field as well as those employed in investigating particular problems and phenomena. The emphasis here is on the individual's knowledge of the method rather than his ability to use the method.

> Ex. Knowledge of scientific methods for evaluating health concepts.

> Ex. The student shall know the methods of attack relevant to the kinds of problems of concern to the social sciences.

1.30 KNOWLEDGE OF THE UNIVERSALS AND ABSTRACTIONS IN A FIELD

Knowledge of the major schemes and patterns by which phenomena and ideas are organized. These are the large structures, theories, and generalizations which dominate a subject field or which are quite generally used in studying phenomena or solving problems. These are at the highest levels of abstraction and complexity.

1.31 KNOWLEDGE OF PRINCIPLES AND GENERALI-ZATIONS

Knowledge of particular abstractions which summarize observations of phenomena. These are the abstractions which are of value in explaining, describing, predicting, or in determining the most appropriate and relevant action or direction to be taken.

> Ex. Knowledge of the important principles by which our experience with biological phenomena is summarized.

> Ex. The recall of major generalizations about particular cultures.

1.32 KNOWLEDGE OF THEORIES AND STRUCTURES

Knowledge of the *body* of principles and generalizations together with their interrelations which present a clear, rounded, and systematic view of a complex phenomenon, problem, or field. These are the most abstract formulations, and they can be used to show the interrelation and organization of a great range of specifics.

> Ex. The recall of major theories about particular cultures.

> Ex. Knowledge of a relatively complete formulation of the theory of evolution.

INTELLECTUAL ABILITIES AND SKILLS

Abilities and skills refer to organized modes of operation and generalized techniques for dealing with materials and problems. The materials and problems may be of such a nature that little or no specialized and technical information is required. Such information as is required can be assumed to be part of the individual's general fund of knowledge. Other problems may require specialized and technical information at a rather high level such that specific knowledge and skill in dealing with the problem and the materials are required. The abilities and skills objectives emphasize the mental processes of organizing and reorganizing material to achieve a particular purpose. The materials may be given or remembered.

2.00 COMPREHENSION

This represents the lowest level of understanding. It refers to a type of understanding or apprehension such that the individual knows what is being communicated and can make use of the material or idea being communicated without necessarily relating it to other material or seeing its fullest implications.

2.10 TRANSLATION

Comprehension as evidenced by the care and accuracy with which the communication is paraphrased or rendered from one language or form of communication to another. Translation is judged on the basis of faithfulness and accuracy, that is, on the extent to which the material in the original communication is preserved although the form of the communication has been altered.

Ex.   The ability to understand non-literal statements (metaphor, symbolism, irony, exaggeration).

Ex.   Skill in translating mathematical verbal material into symbolic statements and vice versa.

2.20 INTERPRETATION

The explanation or summarization of a communication. Whereas translation involves an objective part-for-part rendering of a communication, interpretation involves a reordering, rearrangement, or a new view of the material.

Ex.   The ability to grasp the thought of the work as a whole at any desired level of generality.

Ex.   The ability to interpret various types of social data.

2.30 EXTRAPOLATION

The extension of trends or tendencies beyond the given data to determine implications, consequences, corollaries, effects, etc., which are in accordance with the conditions described in the original communication.

Ex.   The ability to deal with the conclusions of a work in terms of the immediate inference made from the explicit statements.

Ex.   Skill in predicting continuation of trends.

3.00 APPLICATION

The use of abstractions in particular and concrete situations. The abstractions may be in the form of general ideas, rules of procedures, or generalized methods. The abstractions may also be technical principles, ideas, and theories which must be remembered and applied.

> Ex. Application to the phenomena discussed in one paper of the scientific terms or concepts used in other papers.

> Ex. The ability to predict the probable effect of a change in a factor on a biological situation previously at equilibrium.

4.00 ANALYSIS

The breakdown of a communication into its constituent elements or parts such that the relative hierarchy of ideas is made clear and/or the relations between the ideas expressed are made explicit. Such analyses are intended to clarify the communication, to indicate how the communication is organized, and the way in which it manages to convey its effects, as well as its basis and arrangement.

4.10 ANALYSIS OF ELEMENTS

Identification of the elements included in a communication.

> Ex. The ability to recognize unstated assumptions.

> Ex. Skill in distinguishing facts from hypotheses.

4.20 ANALYSES OF RELATIONSHIPS

The connections and interactions between elements and parts of a communication.

> Ex. Ability to check the consistency of hypotheses with given information and assumptions.

> Ex. Skill in comprehending the interrelationships among the ideas in a passage.

4.30 ANALYSIS OF ORGANIZATIONAL PRINCIPLES

The organization, systematic arrangement, and structure which hold the communication together. This includes the *explicit* as well as *implicit* structure. It includes the bases, necessary arrangement, and the mechanics which make the communication a unit.

> Ex. The ability to recognize form and pattern in literary or artistic works as a means of understanding their meaning.

> Ex. Ability to recognize the general techniques used in persuasive materials, such as advertising, propaganda, etc.

5.00 SYNTHESIS

The putting together of elements and parts so as to form a whole. This involves the process of working with pieces, parts, elements, etc., and arranging and combining them in such a way as to constitute a pattern or structure not clearly there before.

5.10 PRODUCTION OF A UNIQUE COMMUNICATION

The development of a communication in which the writer or speaker attempts to convey ideas, feelings, and/or experiences to others.

> Ex. Skill in writing, using an excellent organization of ideas and statements.

> Ex. Ability to tell a personal experience effectively.

5.20 PRODUCTION OF A PLAN, OR PROPOSED SET OF OPERATIONS

The development of a plan of work or the proposal of a plan of operations. The plan should satisfy requirements of the task which may be given to the student or which he may develop for himself.

> Ex. Ability to propose ways of testing hypotheses.

> Ex. Ability to plan a unit of instruction for a particular teaching situation.

5.30 DERIVATION OF A SET OF ABSTRACT RELATIONS

The development of a set of abstract relations either to classify or explain particular data or phenomena, or the deduction of propositions and relations from a set of basic propositions or symbolic representations.

> Ex. Ability to formulate appropriate hypotheses based upon an analysis of factors involved, and to modify such hypotheses in the light of new factors and considerations.

> Ex. Ability to make mathematical discoveries and generalizations.

6.00 EVALUATION

Judgments about the value of material and methods for given purposes. Quantitative and qualitative judgments about the extent to which material and methods satisfy criteria. Use of a standard of appraisal. The criteria may be those determined by the student or those which are given to him.

6.10 JUDGMENTS IN TERMS OF INTERNAL EVIDENCE

Evaluation of the accuracy of a communication from such evidence as logical accuracy, consistency, and other internal criteria.

> Ex. Judging by internal standards, the ability to assess general probability of accuracy in reporting facts from the care given to exactness of statement, documentation, proof, etc.

> Ex. The ability to indicate logical fallacies in arguments.

6.20 JUDGMENTS IN TERMS OF EXTERNAL CRITERIA

Evaluation of material with reference to selected or remembered criteria.

> Ex. The comparison of major theories, generalizations, and facts about particular cultures.

> Ex. Judging by external standards, the ability to compare a work with the highest known standards in its field — especially with other works of recognized excellence.

(b) Gagné's Taxonomy

In presenting another taxonomy in the cognitive domain, my main purpose is to point out that there are other ways of looking at objectives in the cognitive domain. Gagné first came out with seven categories of objectives and later increased the number of categories to eight and changed the hierarchical sequence of the categories. The guiding principle in Gagné's taxonomy is that each category is a building block for the next category in that achievement of the objectives in the first category are necessary in order to achieve the objective in the second category. The achievement of the objectives in the second category are necessary in order to achieve the objectives in the third category and so on. Although I can accept his eight categories, I personally prefer his original sequence. In discussing each category, the

391

concept of the category is Gagné's, but the words are expressing my opinions. As such, any disagreement with a category is probably more a conflict with me than with Gagné.

1.0 Response Learning

This refers to the more or less traditional stimulus-response type of learning. Given a particular kind of stimulus, the student should come up with a specific response. Although this is rote memory, remember that rote memory represents a continuum of difficulty; from simple recall to complex recall.

2.0 Association

This category refers to a stimulus-response type of learning except that when given a particular kind of stimulus, the student should come up with a number of responses which are all associated with that stimulus.

3.0 Multiple Discrimination

Given that a student is able to give a number of responses to a particular stimulus, this category concerns the student now being able to discriminate between the different responses. In other words, although a number of responses are triggered by the same stimulus, the student is able to differentiate between the responses.

4.0 Behavior Chains

Given that the student is able to discriminate between a number of responses, this category of objectives would be concerned with having the student arrange the responses in various hierarchical sequences or procedures. This category of objectives is not just concerned with the student learning the sequence of six steps in order to do something or the ranking of a series of responses according to certain criteria because that could just be a form of response learning or rote memory particularly if the sequence is given to the student. In this category, the student has to be able to identify the criteria for ranking or the reasons for a particular sequence.

5.0 Class Concepts

Once the student has been able to learn a variety of behavior chains (procedures, sequences, ranking, etc.), the student should be able to identify that these behavior chains tend to fall into certain groups or classes. The identified similarities within a group or class essentially describe the class concept.

6.0 Principles

Based on the similarities within groups or classes and the differences between the groups or classes, the student should be able to develop principles which relate to or are based on multiple discrimination, behavior chains, class concepts, and/or previously developed principles.

7.0 Problem Solving

Given a number of principles and a problem, the student should be able to identify the appropriate principles for the problem and carry through to a solution the processes described by the principles.

8.0 Strategies and Theories

Given a number of principles and prior experiences in problem solving, the student when faced with a new situation should be able to come up with a strategy or theory for handling the new situation even though the student may not have the skills at the moment to carry out the strategy or to apply the theory.

(2) THE COGNITIVE GENIUS

In my seminars when I present the concept that 90 percent or more of the student can achieve 100 percent of the objectives, I usually have one or more teachers in each group that will make the following comment, *Do you mean to say that everyone can be a genius?*

First of all, it is necessary to recognize that the development of an ability is in part a result of nature and in part a result of nurture. Given a high level of natural talent, the development of an ability can be achieved with a minimum of nurture and maybe even in spite of any efforts by teachers. Given a low level of natural talent, the development of an ability can only be achieved with a maximum of nurture and only if teachers are willing to design the instructional environment such that it facilitates the development of the ability.

Second, since my statement is that 90 percent or more of the students can achieve 100 percent of the SO's, this assumes that the teacher will perform the role of the instructioneer and will solve the students' learning problems and put forth the effort necessary to help those students who need lots of nurture because they lack the natural ability.

Third, in order to achieve genius level, it would be necessary to have genius oriented SO's that the students could achieve 100 percent of! So far, of the thousands and thousands of SO's I have looked at, I have yet to see a SO at the genius level. Given some of the extremely vague GO's

I have seen, it might take a genius to break them down into all of the important component SO's, but that still doesn't mean that the SO's are at the genius level.

Therefore, what I am really saying is given the SO's and test items which I have seen at all levels of education that fall in the cognitive domain, I have no doubt that 90 percent or more of the students can learn 100 percent of the SO's and test items — provided that the teacher is willing to be an instructioneer and provided that the students want to achieve the SO's and test items. Remember, this last condition is in reference to the problem of motivation which may be solved. It is not in reference to some imaginary capacity (limit). Maybe as time goes on and teachers get better and better at specifying the desired SO's which are continually representing higher and higher levels of ability, I may have to retrench a little on my statement.

A person who might be considered a genius in the cognitive domain would have to have been endowed with or had developed transcendent mental abilities plus the necessary ability to communicate to others such that his or her abilities are recognized. A genius who is unable to communicate evidence to anyone that he or she has transcendent abilities is like the proverbial giant tree in the forest that fell down but there weren't any ears close enough to identify whether or not it made a crashing sound when it fell. In order to really be considered a genius, it is not enough just to communicate to anyone, because the term genius is often used in a relative sense, i.e., among a group of people who have trouble solving simple arithmetic problems, a person who can do calculus problems is considered a genius, yet among mathematicians the same person could be considered almost a beginner. Therefore, to be considered a genius, a group of specialists in the same field would have to be the ones to recognize that the person has transcendent abilities. To be considered a genius, it is not necessary to have all of the cognitive abilities developed to transcendent levels because there are many different types of abilities and many different subject matter areas. As a general rule, the fewer the number of abilities a person has at the transcendent level, the higher the transcendent level has to be above the abilities of other specialists in the same area.

Geniuses in the cognitive domain would include areas such as literature, mathematics, philosophy, etc., which primarily depend on mental abilities.

c. SENSORY DOMAIN

Sensory objectives are ones which emphasize the development of the bodily senses in their ability to perceive stimuli; the development of the sensoria in its ability to identify the stimuli and to select or discriminate between the stimuli; and to increase the effectiveness and efficiency of the sensoria feedback cycle in maximizing the proficiency of the individual in performing sensomotor activities.

(1) INTRODUCTION

For a long time, the third domain was thought to be the psychomotor domain. As I pointed out earlier, psychomotor behaviors refer to the observable behaviors of an individual which are inferred to have been a result of or caused by prior cognitive activity. As such, the term is inappropriate for describing the third domain. Although, there is a substantial overlap between the cognitive domain, the affective domain, and the third domain with reference to observable behaviors, those observable behaviors which are primarily originated by cognitive activity are behaviors in which the primary emphasis is on communicating a variety of cognitive activity. There are also observable behaviors which are primarily originated by emotional tendencies in which the primary emphasis is on communicating a variety of attitudes, values, and beliefs. In examining those observable behaviors in which the primary emphasis is on the behavior itself, the tendency has been to look only at the behaviors without examining the process which involves the behaviors or from which the behaviors evolve.

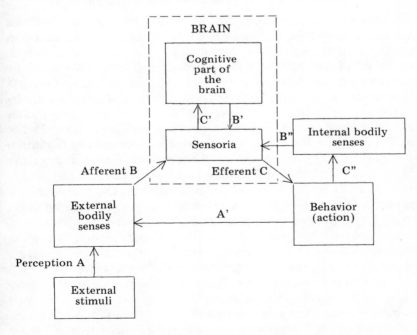

Figure 56 — Perception ⟶ Behavior Process

395

The first part of the process is the perception-afferent stage which involves one or more of the bodily senses perceiving some external stimuli and then the transmitting of associated nervous impulses from the senses to the sensoria. The bodily senses involved could be auditory (hearing), gustatory (taste), olfactory (smell), tactual (skin), and/or visual. In Figure 56, the first part of the process concerns perception at "A" and the afferent sequence at "B".

The second part of the process takes place in the sensoria which is that part of the brain that is concerned with the reception and interpretation of sensory stimuli. The interpretation involves identification, selection and/or discrimination between the various stimuli which are perceived. In addition to the interpretation of sensory stimuli, there may also be a decision for action. This decision may or may not involve the cognitive part of the brain. If it does, the information is sent to the brain (C') and the decision for action may come back to the sensoria (B'). At the same time a decision for action is made, depending on prior experiences and/or the design of the instructional system, a model for the action may or may not be also identified in the sensoria.

The third part of the process is the efferent-action stage in which nervous impulses are transmitted from the sensoria to the effectors in the muscle sense of whatever muscles are involved in the intended action.

The fourth part of the process is the sensory feedback cycle which takes place if a model for the intended action has been established in the sensoria. If no model for the intended action has been established, then this stage of the process probably does not take place and the process stops with the third part. However, most of the time a model is established and the sensory feedback cycle occurs. In this step, the senses perceive the action and the perception-afferent sequence carries the nervous impulse image of the action back to the sensoria. In the sensoria, the image of the action or behavior is compared to the image of the action already established in the sensoria. Depending on the range of acceptability, the process may or may not stop. If the action was perceived to be within the range of acceptability, the process stops. If the action was perceived to be outside of the range of acceptability, then the sensoria (and possibly the cognitive part of the brain) will send out adjusted nervous impulses for a slightly different action. This cycle of perception-afferent to the sensoria and then efferent-action will be repeated until the action is within the range of acceptability.

Notice in this feedback cycle (Figure 56) that it is possible to have part of the feedback come to the sensoria via the internal senses which include organic sense, the labyrinthine sense (balance), and the kinesthesic which are the affectors in the muscle sense. These internal senses report to the sensoria about changes in the conditions of the body.

There are two other possible changes in the model of the process (Figure 56). Because some actions may be difficult to observe for effective feedback, some type of recording device may be used to record audio action and/or visual action. In this case, the feedback cycle would involve the external senses perceiving the action via the media (recording device) rather than the actual action. In many of the behaviors where the emphasis is on the action, the action may be to transport something somewhere (the something could be the individual) and/or to bring about changes in some object. In these cases, the feedback cycle would involve the external senses perceiving the action and the object of the action.

In examining this process, it should be obvious why it is natural to refer to the third domain as the sensory domain.

(2) MEASUREMENT IN THE SENSORY DOMAIN

In looking at the model (Figure 56), there are actually three types of measurements that can be made. Since the process is dependent on the ability of the senses to perceive the stimuli in the first place and then to perceive the action in the feedback cycle, the first concern whould be to find out whether or not the senses are sensitive enough to perceive what should be perceived. Therefore, dependent upon what is to be perceived, tests to test the sensitivity of the appropriate abilities of the senses can be developed. Care should be taken that if some type of standardized test is used, that the test actually tests for the sensitivity level of the right abilities needed to perceive the stimuli and the associated action in any instructional unit. These tests should go from having the senses sense gross stimuli up to having the senses make very fine identifications and discriminations in each of the abilities of each of the senses.

The second area of measurement concerns the sensitivity of the muscle sense to perform the necessary movements of the action. For example, if an individual's level of agility and dexterity is below that needed for the achievement of some action, continuous drill of the action may not solve the problem. It may be easier to train the muscle for the necessary levels of agility and dexterity and then learn the desired action. Therefore, tests could be set up to measure various levels of agility, dexterity, and coordination of the muscles.

The third area of measurement concerns the action itself. Given that there is a specific desired action in a specific instructional situation, then it is necessary to identify the range of acceptability of the action (see Figure 57). There is a tendency among teachers to use words to describe and evaluate action behaviors. As long as both student and teacher can agree on what the action or behavior is supposed to be, words may be acceptable. The best approach would be to use audio

397

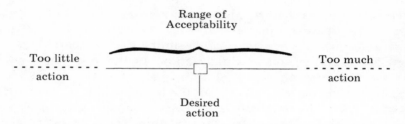

Figure 57 — Range of Acceptability

and/or visual recording media to identify to the students the range of acceptability, i.e., the following three brief films identify the behavior desired, the maximum action acceptable, and the minimum action acceptable. The evaluation instrument should include the same criteria which were set up when describing the desired action.

NOTE: The teachers' contribution to the instructional situation in the sensory domain would be one or both of two situations. First, the teachers' senses are developed to a higher level than that necessary in the instructional unit and the teachers are able to perform any of the actions required in the instructional unit and within a smaller range of acceptability than that allowed in the instructional unit. Second, the teachers' senses would still have to be developed to a higher level than that necessary in the instructional unit, but rather than the teacher having to be able to perform all of the required motions, a series of recorded media could be used as a standard for performance and also to indicate the range of acceptability.

(3) TAXONOMIES OF SENSORY OBJECTIVES

In setting up a taxonomy for learning in the sensory domain, it seems necessary to divide the taxonomy into three parts to coincide with a sensory event: the first part concerns the abilities of the senses to perceive in the stimulus-afferent sequence; the second part concerns the ability of the muscle sense to respond in the efferent-action sequence; and the third part concerns the action itself. The first part of the taxonomy will be quoted in large part from Elizabeth Simpson's *The Classification of Educational Objectives, Psychomotor Domain* which was published in the *Illinois Teacher* in 1965. (The examples of objectives and item 1.3 are mine.)

(a) Classification of Instructional Objectives

Sensory Domain Part I: The Senses in the Stimulus — Afferent Sequence

398

The major organizational principle here is just a listing of the various abilities of each of the senses, but implied in the listing are three different dimensions from the simple or gross perception to high levels of discrimination.

— In each of the senses as the student is able to identify additional abilities, there is increasing difficulty in identifying and discriminating between the various abilities of a sense.

— In each of the abilities of each sense, there is increasing difficulty as the student goes from gross identification and discriminations to higher levels of discrimination.

— As each additional sense is added to the perceptual task, it becomes increasingly difficult to make identifications and discriminations.

1.0 Perception

This is an essential first step in performing a motor act. It is the process of becoming aware of objects, qualities, or relationships by way of the sense organs. It is the first part of the perception — interpretation — action sequence leading to purposeful motor activity.

1.1 Sensory Stimulation

Impingement of a stimulus upon one or more of the sense organs.

1.11 Auditory

Hearing or the sense or organs of hearing.

1.111 Volume
1.112 Pitch
1.113 Timbre
1.114 Patterns of sounds
1.115 Spatial Relations

Examples of objectives:

— Given a language master card with a five note musical sequence recorded on the master track, the student will be able to reproduce the sequence using the same pitch and pattern of the sound.

— Given a tape of twenty paired sounds which are unique to the Spanish language, the student will be able to identify which pairs are identical and which sounds are different.

1.12 Visual

Concerned with the mental pictures or images obtained through the eyes.

1.121 Color
1.122 Spatial Relations
1.123 Shape (line, form, size)
1.124 Motion
1.125 Light
1.126 Shade

Examples of objectives:

— Given twelve color cards, the student will be able to arrange them in the sequence found in the normal solar spectrum.

— Given a microscope and a glass slide with a sample of fluid containing numerous living cells of three types, the student will be able to discriminate between the three types of cells by listing two or more visual characteristics of each type of cell.

1.13 Tactual

Pertaining to the sense of touch.

1.131 Texture
1.132 Temperature
1.133 Shape
1.134 Size
1.135 Pressure
1.136 Position
1.137 State of motion
1.138 Weight

Examples of objectives:

— Given samples of ten grades of sandpaper ranging from extra coarse to extra fine in random order, the student while wearing a blindfold will be able to arrange the samples of sandpaper in the correct graduated sequence.

— Given ten cubes of the same size but of different weights, ranging from 6 ounces to 24 ounces in random order, the student will be able to arrange the cubes in the correct sequence of increasing weight.

400

1.14 Gustatory
Ascertain the taste or flavor of something by taking a portion into the mouth.
1.141 Saltiness
1.142 Sourness
1.143 Bitterness
1.144 Sweetness

Examples of objectives:

— Given the following four samples of treated water, the student will be able to identify by tasting which of the samples is primarily salty, sour, bitter, and sweet.

1.15 Olfactory
To perceive by sniffing a sample of something.
1.151 Ethereal (fruity, lemon)
1.152 Fragrant (violet)
1.153 Burned (tar)
1.154 Putrid (bad fish)
1.155 Resinous (pine)
1.156 Spicy (cloves)

Examples of objectives:

— Given the following ten samples of substances, the student will be able to identify which samples have the same odor and which ones are different.

1.2 Cue Selection
Deciding to what cues one must respond to in order to satisfy the particular requirements of the performance of a task. This involves identification of the cue or cues and associating them with the task to be performed. It may involve grouping of cues in terms of past experience and knowledge. Cues relevant to the situation are selected as a guide to action; irrelevant cues are ignored or discarded.

Examples of objectives:

— Given a ten minute film of a simulated surgical operation, the student will identify all ten instances of contamination.

— Given five samples of mixed odors, the student will be able to identify which ones contain the odor of smoke from burning marijuana.

401

1.3   *Sensoria Decision-making*

This concerns the translation from the perception of stimuli and the selection of cues to the decision as to which motor activity (action, behavior, etc.) would be appropriate. This could be a single decision or a series of decisions in the feedback cycle.

Examples of objectives:

— While taking a practice drive and encountering at least three or more traffic signals in each of the following conditions: green, yellow, and red, the student driver will perform the correct action response to the color of the traffic signal.

— Given a circle on a piece of paper, a pencil, and tracing paper, the student will be able to trace the circle without going off the circle being traced by more than a sixteenth of an inch (the number of trial attempts in achieving this objective is not important).

In the development of the second and third parts of the taxonomy of objectives in the sensory domain, I found it useful to examine the sequence in the development of an action or actions in a situation without systems designed instruction, but possibly under a traditional approach to education. At one time, I even considered these six steps as possibly a taxonomy of the sensory domain objectives:

First step — Given a new stimulus which appears to necessitate a response, the action or actions may be random unless similar stimuli had been encountered before. If this is the case, then the action or actions made in response will also tend to be similar to the responses given to the similar stimuli.

Second step — Depending on the situation, this step or the third step may take place next. Based on an evaluation of what occurred when the random response was made to the new stimulus, an individual may go through a period of trial and error without knowing exactly what is the best response and yet trying to find the best response to the stimulus.

Third step — This step assumes someone wants to help the individual make the right response. This other person could be a teacher, a parent, an employer, a friend, etc. In this step, an external model for the correct response is provided by the other person. During the feedback cycle, the individual now has at

402

least an external model to compare his or her response to. Although, this could still involve several trials, having an external model available reduces the errors and the number of trials.

Fourth step — As the individual learns the response associated with the stimulus, the model in the feedback cycle is internalized such that an external model is no longer necessary.

Fifth step — This step and the sixth step fall into an area which could be referred to as creative responses. Once an individual has developed a repertory of actions and associated results of these actions, the individual may combine two or more of these actions in new ways to achieve a purpose, result, or reaction to a stimulus.

Sixth step — This step involves the invention of new actions in order to obtain the same purpose, results or reaction to a stimulus which previously was achieved by some actions or series of actions available in the individual's repertory of actions and associated results of these actions.

In looking at these six steps, the area best suited to designed instruction would be the third step through to the sixth step. This would indicate that the initial emphasis in designed instruction would be to provide an external model of action to aid the student in learning the desired action. However, the emphasis would be on the weaning of the students from the need for an external model and the development of internal models which are within the range of acceptability. This emphasis is important as long as our instructional goals are ultimately to develop students who are independent learners (independent of external models). This is essentially the same concept as discussed on page 299, Volume I, concerning the development of the independent learner. The fifth and sixth steps in the development of actions are concerned with the same area of creativity as the fourth through the ninth steps in the development of the independent learner. However, in the development of the independent learner, most of the student's responses and actions as an independent learner are the same ones the student made when under the direction of the instructor. In the last two steps in the development of actions, the emphasis is not only on the individual being able to set his or her own goals and being able to identify the means necessary to get there, but on being able to use means that in themselves are creative.

Although from a certain point of view trial and error learning can be considered creative, creativity can be facilitated more effectively and efficiently if the student has already learned the necessary tools and skills as a foundation upon which the creative process can be based.

This puts the major effort of designed instruction in the sensory domain on the third and fourth steps: the development of the action from an external model and then the weaning of the learner from the external model and the development of an internal model.

(b) Classification of Instructional Objectives

Sensory Domain Part II — The Sense in the Efferent — Action Sequence

The major organizational principle here is the listing of the various muscle groups which might be involved in an action and their various abilities which might affect the action. With particular reference to the voice, the production of sound involves the lungs, larynx, mouth and associated muscles in the head and trunk of the body. Since the production of sound is a coordinated activity and an internal process, the measurement of the ability of various elements to produce sound may best be handled by measuring the product (the sound and its various qualities or characteristics). However, it is possible to develop some of the elements of sound production, i.e., breath control.

2.0   Muscle Sense[12]

The various abilities of the muscles to produce an action.

2.1   Head
    2.11 Facial muscles — flexibility, expressiveness
    2.12 Mouth muscles — flexibility, strength, and endurance
    2.13 Neck muscles — suppleness, strength and endurance.

2.2   Sound production muscles — control, strength, and endurance.
    2.21 Direct production muscles (speech and singing).
    2.22 Indirect production muscles (wind instruments).

2.3   Trunk muscles — suppleness, strength, and endurance.

2.4   Limb muscles — agility, strength, and endurance.

---

[12] To clear up a possible misunderstanding, there are three aspects of the muscle sense. One concerns the efferent stage, or the cause of the action, the second aspect concerns the action itself, and the third aspect concerns the internal results of the action. The kinesthetic sense, the organic senses, and the labyrinthine sense essentially report the conditions of the body to the sensoria. Feelings sensed by these senses are a result of some changing condition of the body and as such cannot be trained directly. Like feelings in the affective domain, any changes in these senses have to be handled indirectly. For example, if a person wants to have that good kinesthetic feeling of being in good physical condition during some physical exercise, it wouldn't do any good to try to train the kinesthetic sense directly. A person would have to develop and work with the muscles in the body until the desired kinesthetic feeling was developed indirectly.

404

2.5 Hands and feet suppleness, strength, and endurance.

2.6 Fingers and toes — dexterity, strength, and endurance.

(c) Classification of Instructional Objectives
Sensory Domain — Part III — The Action

Part I and Part II of a taxonomy of instructional objectives in the sensory domain as presented here probably represent about the only way or one of the few ways in which the instructional objectives in the stages of the perception-interpretation-action cycle can be viewed. However, in Part III, the action itself, there are probably many ways that the instructional objectives in this last stage of the process can be viewed and categorized. As indicated in Simpson's review of the literature in developing her taxonomy of educational objectives in the psychomotor domain, a number of people have attempted to categorize action-oriented objectives in some sort of taxonomy. The major problem is in identifying a guiding principle. Simpson's guiding principle was one of increasing complexity with attention given to the sequence involved in the performance of a motor act. Her first category concerned *perception* and has already been quoted as Part I. Her second category is *set* and is divided into three parts: mental set, physical set, and emotional set. Since any taxonomy in the sensory domain should emphasize *action* above any other aspect, the categories of mental and emotional set don't belong in the taxonomy. The third part of *set* concerns physical set which is a part of the action process and as such can be a way of looking at the educational objectives dealing with the action process. However, I feel that Part II concerning the abilities of the muscles to perform the desired actions as being a necessary second step before considering the action process itself. Also, I see the physical set as an integral part of the action process rather than as a separate step.

The third, fourth, and fifth categories of Simpson's taxonomy concern the steps in *learning an action* not necessarily the steps in *performing an action* and as such are not in accord with the guiding principle Simpson set forth. These three categories are similar to the six steps I listed as describing the learning or development of an action.

In developing a taxonomy of instructional objectives for Part III, The Action, the easiest guiding principle to use concerns the function of the action. The sequence of the functions is arbitrary and is not meant to indicate any sort of hierarchy. Within each function, the four subcategories indicate increasing potential for complexity in the learning of instructional objectives. The first subcategory, the individual, involves instructional objectives which deal only with the actions of the individual. The second subcategory, the individual and an object, in-

405

volves instructional objectives which deal with the action of the individual with the object. The third subcategory, an object as an extension of the body, involves instructional objectives which deal with the actions of the individual and the actions of an object acting as an extension of the body. The fourth subcategory, a group action, involves instructional objectives which deal with the actions of the individual in consort with one or more other people. Obviously, within each subcategory there is also the possibility of increasing complexity.

3.0 *Action for the sake of sound production.*
Whereas 2.2 concerned the abilities of the various muscles to produce sound, this category is concerned with evaluating the quality of the sound produced. Since the sound produced is the result of the actions and they both occur simultaneously, the evaluation is also continuous.

3.1 Individual (speaking, singing, etc.)

3.2 Individual and an object (where the sound is controlled directly by the muscle senses of the individual).
3.21 Voice via a microphone
3.22 Wind (bugle, harmonica, etc.)
3.23 Percussion (direct, hand contact)
3.24 String (direct finger contact)

3.3 As an extension of the body (where the sound is controlled indirectly by the muscle senses of the individual).
3.31 Wind via electronics for echo effect, vibrato, etc.
3.32 Wind (indirect control via keys, buttons, stops, etc.)
3.33 Percussion (indirect control via sticks)
3.34 String

3.4 Group action where the individual has to work with one or more other people to produce a coordinated sound.
3.41 Voice with voices
3.42 instrument with instruments
3.43 voice with instruments
3.44 instrument with voices

4.0 *Action for the sake of an art form.*
In subcategories 4.1 and 4.4, the art form is the action itself and as such should be continuously evaluated. In the other subcategories, the art form is generally the product of the action. In this whole category and particularly in subcategories 4.2 and 4.3, the development of the skills involved rely very much on the development of the input senses and the feedback cycle. The major emphasis in evaluation is on the quality of the action or result of the actions.

4.1 Individual (dancing, ballet, pantomine, etc.)

4.2 Individual and objects
    4.21 placement of objects (interior decorating, landscaping, etc.)
    4.22 changing or creating an object with hands (pottery, clay sculpture, finger painting, etc.)

4.3 Using extensions of the body
    4.31 composition of objects (photographs, film making, etc.)
    4.32 changing or creating an object with tools (painting, sculpture, dress design, drawing, etc.)

4.4 Group action where the individual has to work with one or more other people to produce a coordinated action (dancing, ballet, theater, etc.)

5.0 *Action for the sake of a sport or recreation.*
Underlying most sports and even a lot of recreational activities is the concept of a game or competition, even if the competition is with one's self. As such, the primary emphasis is on physical fitness. Whereas successful achievement of objectives in category 4.0 is rather dependent on the successful achievement of objectives in the first category 1.0 (perception), the successful achievement of objectives in this category are dependent on the successful achievement of objectives in the second category 2.0 (muscle sense). The evaluation in this category can be continuous with regard to the form of the action, but the ultimate evaluation tends to be in terms of quantity, i.e., the fastest, the strongest, the winner, etc.

5.1 Individual (gymnastics without equipment, hiking, track, swimming, wrestling, etc.)

5.2 Individual and objects (pole vault, archery, weight lifting, mountain climbing, roller and ice skating, gymnastics with equipment, etc.)

5.3 Using extensions of the body (golf, bowling, fishing, etc.)

5.4 Group action where the individual has to work with one or more other people in a coordinated activity or game.
    5.41 Individuals (swimming teams, track teams, etc.)
    5.42 Individuals and objects (baseball, football, volleyball, etc.)
    5.43 Using extensions of the body (hockey, polo, etc.)

6.0 *Action for the sake of transportation.*

In a manner similar to the previous category, evaluation and objectives in this category can concern the form of the action, but the ultimate evaluation is on whether or not whatever was to be transported arrived at the predetermined destination.

6.1 Individual (walking, running, etc.)

6.2 Individual and object
6.21 Sedentary — object moves (using the arms and hands for transporting the object)
6.22 Locomotion (carrying, pushing, pulling, etc.)

6.3 Using extensions of the body (car, truck, motorcycle, tractor, etc.)

6.4 Group action where the individual has to work with one or more other people in transporting something.

7.0 *Action for the sake of changing something*

7.1 Individual (reducing or building up the individual)

7.2 Individual and object

7.21 Transporting an object to be changed by something else (drill press, hand saw, etc.)
7.22 Changing the object directly without tools

7.3 Using extensions of the body — changing the object by use of tools (grading road, surgery, dentistry, construction, etc.)

7.4 Group action where the individual has to work with one or more other people in a coordinated effort to change or build something.

(4) SOLVING LEARNING PROBLEMS IN THE SENSORY DOMAIN

Although the concept of solving learning problems has already been discussed in Chapter V, Volume I, most of the discussion was directed towards solving learning problems in the cognitive domain. Therefore, in presenting a new domain (at least in name), it is appropriate to point out special learning problems which may occur in the sensory domain.

In any objective which depends on a certain level of sensitivity of the senses, a common problem will be one in which the senses have not been trained or developed to the necessary level to enable the students to achieve the sensory objectives. Under-trained and/or under-developed senses will not only affect the original perception of the stimulus, but they will decrease the effectiveness and efficiency of the feedback cycle. In case the problem is one of physical limitations of the senses, it might be appropriate to correct the problem with glasses, hearing aids, electronic sensing devices, etc. In some cases, the other senses can be trained to aid a sense that is underdeveloped.

Another common problem will be that the model for action which the student is supposed to learn from is not clearly defined in the teacher's mind. If the action is difficult to observe, then it may be appropriate to record the action for study and imitation. In reference to transporting, the *how* of the action may be important but not clearly defined. The result or the *where* something is being transported to may also not be clearly defined and the connection between the *how* of the action and the *where* something is being transported to may not have been clearly established.

Another problem dealing with the external model for action is that although the teacher has a clear picture of the mode for action in his or her mind, he or she is unable to communicate it to the student. As a result, the student's mental image of the external model for action is in conflict with the teacher's model for action.

Even if the external model for action is clearly communicated and particularly when it isn't, a very common problem is the overlooking of the need to communicate to the learners what the range of acceptability is. In other words, given that the model for action is called *good*, how far can the student's imitated action be from what is called *good* without being called *bad*.

Whenever students have trouble identifying the external model for action and the range of acceptability for that desired action, the value of drill becomes questionable and the motivation on the part of the student decreases. A symptom for this problem is when the student's action is outside of the range of acceptability and repeated imitations of the desired action don't seem to improve the action and in fact the action may even get further away from the desired action.

Contributing factors to these problems are when there is lack of agreement among teachers as to the correct model for action and/or the action becomes the objective when it should be a vehicle for learning a concept which is the true objective. For example, in the teaching and learning of a foreign language, if you could visit almost any ten teachers who are teaching Spanish, you may very easily identify ten different accents and ten different pronunciations of Spanish. One may speak Castilian Spanish, another one Mexican Spanish, another one speaks Spanish with a Booklyn accent, yet still another teacher speaks Spanish with a southern accent, and so on. But in the classroom of any one of these teachers, students are drilled and drilled and many graded down because they didn't imitate the teacher's pronounciation of Spanish.

The real objective may very well be to be able to communicate successfully rather than to imitate the teacher's pronounciation. In nursing, an objective in the medical-surgical nursing unit concerns the learning and performance of the scrubbing technique in cleansing the hands. There are a number of different ways the hands can be scrubbed as long as the way or method fits within the principle of the scrub technique. I know of a case in which a nursing student almost didn't become a nurse because she had so much trouble imitating exactly the teacher's method of scrubbing. After graduation, in the very first hospital she went to, the nursing supervisor in surgery became very upset with the ex-student because she didn't use or know the scrub technique desired by the supervisor. As indicated, a particular method of scrubbing which should have been a vehicle for learning the concept, instead became the objective. As a result, the most important aspect was not learned, the concept of maintaining asepsis during scrubbing.

One of the many values in specifying objectives is that the important objectives are identified and they can't get lost among the vehicles for learning. Also, the specification of objectives in the sensory domain will quite frequently (or at least should) include audio and/or visual recordings which help minimize the negative effects of teacher variability in the setting up of a model for learning a desired action.

(5) THE SENSORY GENIUS

A person who might be considered a genius in the sensory domain would have to have been endowed with or had developed transcendent sensory abilities plus the necessary ability to communicate to others such that his or her abilities are recognized. As with the cognitive genius, it is not enough that just anyone considers the person to be a sensory genius. In order to be considered a sensory genius, a group of specialists in the same field of abilities would have to be the ones to recognize that the person has transcendent abilities. Again, as in the cognitive domain, it is not necessary to have all of the sensory abilities developed to transcendent levels in order to be considered a genius. There are too many different sensory abilities and even a greater number of various combinations of these abilities for any one person to have transcendent levels in very many of these abilities. As a general rule, the fewer the number of abilities a person has at the transcendent level, the higher the level has to be above the abilities of other specialists in the same area.

In the sensory domain, however, there is a unique problem. Of the many different abilities represented in this domain, transcendent levels of achievement are not recognized in all areas. It would not be unusual to recognize great painters, sculpturers, singers, speakers, athletes, and other artists, but it would be unusual for someone to be recognized as a

410

genius in the grading of hillsides, in welding, in working on a wood or metal lathe, in landscaping, in construction work, etc. There are two main reasons for this of which one far outshadows the other. The main one is that physical work is looked down on as something less than other occupations. The other is that most of the worker type abilities involve a fair amount of cognitive ability too. From that point of view, the abilities necessary to be a genius in the physical work-oriented occupations is not quite as *pure* as the artists in music, art, and athletics.

Inherited from past generations when only the elite went to school, physical workers had little if any education, and intelligence was measured in terms of verbal ability, our present traditional educational system continues on with this calamitous, nonsensical, pageantry of looking down on physical labor. Although physical workers are now achieving higher levels of education, they are selected by an educational system which uses curve grading, ignores individual differences, utilizes the wrong teacher's role, doesn't solve students' learning problems, and allows and even encourages the development and growth of cumulative ignorance. It is assumed by the present system that when students are at the bottom of the curve, they are obviously dumb and as such in junior and senior high schools and in many community colleges are channeled into vocational-technical courses. As a consequence, most of the students in these courses are convinced they are not very smart. Oddly enough, when the very same literature, math, or *humanities* teacher that failed these students out of the academic curriculum has trouble with his or her car or television set, the car or television set is taken to the *pushed-out* student with supposedly lower intelligence in order to get it repaired because as the teacher looks under the car hood or into the back of the television set, *it looks too complicated for the teacher to understand it!!*

In academia and particularly in higher education, faculty have gone overboard in their attitudes towards the vocational-technical occupations and even against the teachers who teach these courses. For example, in one community college, the so-called academic faculty became so upset about eating in the same faculty lounge with the vocational-technical faculty that they protested and demanded that the vocational-technical faculty be given a *separate but equal* facility away from their lounge. An even more ridiculous example with potentially tragic results concerns medical schools. Before medical schools joined the universities, professors of surgery actually taught the manual and sensory skill of cutting (operating). When the medical schools joined the university communities, their academic colleagues told them that they couldn't do that anymore because that was manual training. As a consequence, few medical schools actually teach the skill of cutting anymore. In the medical schools I have consulted with, invariably when I make the last statement, one or more professors of surgery will object and say, *I know that with the modern audio-visual aids and step-by-step programming, I could probably take almost any students on the campus and train them to be the best cutters in the hospital; but they wouldn't know why they are cutting or how to make the critical decisions necessary during the processing cutting. That is what we teach in the department of surgery, the why of surgery and how to make decisions about surgery.* My answer has always been, *that is great, but after your medical students know all the whys and have all of the decision-making skills, wouldn't it be useful if they knew HOW to cut??* To check on this statement, ask any nurse who has worked in surgery, *Have you ever come away from an operation saying to yourself or to other nurses that the operation just completed was a good one?* Every nurse I have talked to tells me *Yes.* This proves that there are other operations that aren't so good and this is because the actual learning of the cutting is left up to chance because it is beneath the academic environment to teach a manual skill.

As educators and instructioneers, if we really want to be humanists, then we have to get off the *high horse* of academia and look on all learners and learning as respectable. By solving students' learning problems and recognizing individual differences in learning to the degree that almost every student will complete high school with 100 percent achievement of all required objectives in whatever courses they take, students who elect to go into vocational-technical courses will do so because they want to and not because all other pathways to success have been closed off by teachers with phony standards of quality. As the negative image of working with one's hands is slowly sloughed off and more students elect to take vocational-technical courses because that's what they really want to do, it would not be surprising to find people in the vocational-technical areas who are referred to as geniuses by their colleagues because they have developed or were endowed with transcendental abilities in their particular fields of work.

d. THE AFFECTIVE DOMAIN

Affective domain objectives are ones which emphasize emotional feelings, attitudes, values, and beliefs. They are usually stated in terms of how a person will or should act in certain situations and are usually based on observations of the behaviors of people who are supposed to have those emotional feelings, attitudes, values, and beliefs. Affective objectives can vary from simple changes in a single attitude to highly complex changes in a cluster of attitudes, values and beliefs.

412

(1) INTRODUCTION

The most important thing to remember about the affective domain is that learning the objectives in this domain is very different than learning the objectives in the cognitive and sensory domains. Whereas in the cognitive and sensory domain, it is possible to start and stop learning at almost any time; in the affective domain, development and changes in attitudes and values goes on constantly. Whereas in the cognitive and sensory domains, a teacher can say *I'm going to teach these objectives directly to the students;* in the affective domain, a teacher can only say, *I'm going to teach these objectives indirectly.*

During a child's preschool years and in elementary school, it is possible and highly likely that teachers will be developing new attitudes, values, and beliefs towards concepts where there weren't any attitudes, values, or beliefs before. As students progress through junior and senior high school, the number of new attitudes, values, and beliefs that are developed decrease. By the time students are in post secondary education, there are relatively few new attitudes and values to be developed. In contrast to the decreasing number of new attitudes, values and beliefs which are developed as a student progresses through school, there are an increasing number of attitudes, values, and beliefs which can only be changed rather than developed anew. Changing the direction of an existing attitude, value, or belief is much more difficult than to develop new attitudes, values, or beliefs. With reference to affective domain objectives, elementary teachers and particularly pre-school teachers should have the easiest time in teaching these objectives, but because once these attitudes, values and beliefs are developed, they are very difficult to change, it becomes even more critical that these teachers understand the differences between the theory of instruction in the affective domain and the theory of instruction in the cognitive and sensory domain.

NOTE: The teacher's contribution to the teaching-learning situation in the affective domain could consist of one or more of the following four concepts: first, a teacher could ignore the whole problem of teaching and learning of affective domain objectives and let it continue on by chance; second, a teacher could learn the variety of techniques which are successful and apply these to the teaching and learning of affective domain objectives; third, a teacher could use the successful techniques to develop or change the attitudes, values, and beliefs of the students such that they are more in line with the teacher's own attitudes, values, and beliefs; fourth, a teacher could use the successful techniques to develop or change the attitudes, values and beliefs of the students such that they are more in line with those attitudes, values, and beliefs which are

413

desired by the majority of taxpayers, parents, and students regardless of whether or not their own attitudes, values, and beliefs are in conflict or in accord with the desired objectives. A possible compromise, would involve the identification and teaching of the minimum common core of affective domain objectives which could be agreed upon by teachers, administrators, taxpayers, parents and students.

In the cognitive and sensory domains, there are many objectives within which the concept of right or wrong (as it is normally viewed) can be applied. However, in the affective domain, the concept of rightness or wrongness of a particular attitude, value, or belief is a very relative concept. Given that a certain intensity of a particular attitude, value, or belief is considered to be the desired objective, any attitude, value, or belief that is in conflict with the desired objective is viewed as wrong and even a lower level of intensity of the desired attitude, value, or belief can be considered not quite *right.* The rightness or wrongness of objectives in the affective domain are so dependent upon what is desired by the people involved, that there is probably a group of people in some place somewhere in our world that would view almost any attitude, value, or belief as the right or wrong objective.

Although it is possible to isolate a particular attitude, value, or belief, from the point-of-view of predicting how a person would act or behave in certain situations, it is more realistic to think of attitudes, values, and beliefs as being in clusters. It is the resultant effect of a cluster of attitudes, values, and/or beliefs which are behind the decisions for certain actions or behaviors. Given a certain behavior or emotional tendency which is considered desirable by someone or some group, there are some attitudes, values, and/or beliefs which are acting negatively against the performance of the behavior and there are also some attitudes, values, and/or beliefs which are acting positively for the performance of the behavior. If the positive and negative forces are almost equal, it would be very difficult to predict whether or not an individual would behave in a certain way. If the positive forces are much greater than the negative forces, then the confidence in predicting that a person will act or behave in a certain manner is high. If the negative forces are much greater than the positive forces, then the confidence in predicting that a person will NOT act or behave in a certain manner is also high (see Figure 58). It is important to remember that the cluster of attitudes, values, and/or beliefs which affect one action or non-action can only be thought of as a cluster from the point-of-view of one particular action or non-action. Given a slightly different situation, the composition of the cluster of attitudes, values, and/or beliefs affecting the resultant action or non-action will also be slightly different. In the teaching-learning situation in the affective

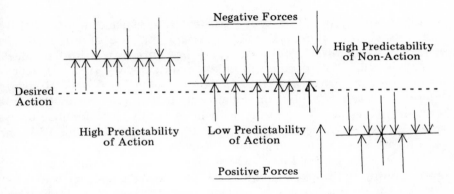

Figure 58 — Predictability of an Action

domain, the goal is to develop or change the forces in such a manner so as to increase the predictability of action or non-action in certain situations.

In putting together all of the highly predictable actions and non-actions of a particular person, you are actually describing a person's character and personality. The common threads found among the highly predictable actions and non-actions form a person's philosophy and can be used to predict a person's actions or non-actions in completely new situations in which there may be no attitudes, values, or beliefs at the moment the person encounters the new situation. When there are groups of people which have similar highly predictable actions and non-actions, then the people in these groups are said to have a common culture, religion, political idealogy, etc.

For anyone to say that the objectives in the affective domain are not important would be almost as preposterous as trying to say that food or air is not important. Over the centuries, millions of people have been killed because of differences in attitudes, values, and/or beliefs. From a certain point-of-view, however, those attitudes, values, and beliefs which destroy a person's or people's self-image and cripple their potential for happiness may be even more important.

The total environment affects the development and/or changing of affective domain objectives. Although the home or external (from school) environment may not have much direct affect on the learning of cognitive and sensory objectives, the external environment can very much affect affective domain objectives and then indirectly affect the learning of cognitive and sensory objectives. Negative attitudes towards aspects or parts of cognitive and/or sensory learning will tend to delay the learning of cognitive and sensory objectives and will tend to increase the rate of forgetting of what has been learned. On the other hand, positive attitudes towards aspects or parts of cognitive and/or

415

sensory learning will tend to increase the rate of learning of cognitive and sensory objectives and tend to delay the rate of forgetting. In reference to the affective domain itself, high intensity attitudes, values, or beliefs will tend to diminish unless maintained by frequent experiences which reinforce the existing attitudes, values, or beliefs. Moderate intensity attitudes, values, or beliefs will tend to remain at the same level over long periods of time with little, if any, maintenance unless acted up by experiences which intensify or are in conflict with the existing attitudes, values, or beliefs.

The environmental forces which give support and maintenance or are in conflict with existing emotional tendencies could occur in other parts of the school besides your classroom and they could be external to the school, i.e., home, street, social groups, etc. If a desired emotional tendency can be practiced sufficiently such that it becomes habitual, this would very strongly affect retention of an affective objective.

(2) INSTRUCTION, INDOCTRINATION, OR BRAINWASHING

There are four characteristics of the teaching of affective domain objectives which make teaching in the affective domain a very sensitive area. Then there are two factors which determine whether or not the teaching is mainly instruction or mainly brainwashing. The four characteristics are:

— The development or changing of attitudes, values, and beliefs goes on continuously, regardless of whether or not anyone is trying to influence, guide, or control the development or change;

— The development or changing of attitudes, values, and beliefs can be taught most effectively when it is done indirectly rather than directly;

— The development or changing of attitudes, values, and beliefs occurs under conditions of low mental consciousness or awareness of what is happening; and

— The development or changing of attitudes, values, and beliefs can be taught simultaneously with cognitive and/or sensory objectives.

What these four characteristics of the teaching of affective domain objectives emphasize is that if anyone wanted to influence, guide, or control the development or change of someone else's attitudes, values, or beliefs, it would have to be done indirectly, i.e., you can't demand of someone, *love me.* One can only create situations which develop the

416

appropriate attitude, value, or belief. Because the development or change is brought about indirectly as a result of other events, there is a low level of mental awareness that the development or change is taking place. Also, because the development or change in the affective domain can hitch-hike on the learning of cognitive or sensory objectives, it is possible in overly emphasizing the learning of the cognitive and/or sensory objectives to even further reduce the mental awareness of any development or change in the affective domain. In very simple works, the development or change of a person's attitudes, values, or beliefs can be accomplished without the person realizing that it is occurring and in the teaching-learning situation, the development or changes can be accomplsihed without anyone knowing about it.

The two factors which determine whether or not the teaching is mainly instruction or mainly brainwashing or somewhere in between are:

— the degree of congruence or conflict of the intended affective objective with which what might be considered desirable by the school administrators, taxpayers, parents, and students.

— and the degree to which the intended affective objective is known to be the emphasis of the teaching-learning event by the school administrators, taxpayers, parents, and students.

The first factor actually determines the importance of the second factor. The smaller the degree of congruence or the greater the degree of conflict of an intended affective objective when compared to what might be considered desirable, the more critical the second factor is in determining whether or not the teaching-learning situation is primarily instruction or primarily brainwashing and the greater the chances are that it might be the latter. As the desirability of an intended affective objective decreases or as the undesirability of an intended affective objective increases (in the opinion of the school administrators, taxpayers, parents, and students) and as the degree to which the intended affective objective is known decreases (to the school administration, taxpayers, parents, and students), the more the teaching of the intended affective objective could be termed brainwashing rather than instruction. This is why it is even more critical in the affective domain to specify the objectives than it is in the other domains.

(3) MEASUREMENT IN THE AFFECTIVE DOMAIN

Since the teaching and learning of affective objectives is a very sensitive area because of the potential of being accused of brainwashing, not only is it important to specify the objectives in terms of emotional tendencies, but it is important to identify the effect of the

417

teachers and the school in developing or changing the emotional tendencies. In order to do this, it becomes very important to measure the direction and intensity of an emotional tendency at the beginning of a course (pretest) and again at the end of the course (posttest). In that way, the development or change in the intended emotional tendencies due to the teachers and school can be more easily identified. Therefore, measurement in the affective domain is concerned with identifying the direction and degree of intensity of an emotional tendency at the beginning and end of a course or unit in order to identify the primary function of teaching affective domain objectives, that of developing or bringing about a change in an emotional tendency.

NOTE: Relying on posttest scores only can be misleading. For example, if a person has a positive score of 10 on a given affective objective at the end of an instructional unit, one could think it was a successful unit. What if the person's pretest score was a positive 30? In other words, the desired emotional tendency actually decreased in intensity during the instructional unit. In another example, a person might have a negative score of 10 on a given affective objective at the end of an instructional unit and one could think that the instructional unit was not very effective. What if the person's pretest score was a negative 30? In other words, the person's negative reaction to the desired emotional tendency was less negative at the end of the instructional unit and as such the unit could be considered successful. Given pretest and posttest data, it is possible to measure the direction of the change and also the change in intensity.

In teaching cognitive and sensory objectives, the teacher should strive to get at least 90 percent or more of the students to achieve 100 percent of the SO's, however, where you can demand achievement in these domains, a teacher cannot demand the achievement of an affective objective. Even the learner can't force himself or herself to achieve an affective objective. For example, there are some white people who can understand and accept the concept of integration and can even actively work for it, but still can't erase some of their emotional tendencies which indicate prejudice. Therefore, if the percentage of students who develop the desired emotional tendency is not what the teacher would like, then the teacher changes the design of the instructional unit by solving the design problems (remember affective objectives are taught indirectly).

The descriptions of desired attitudes, values, and beliefs usually sound like statements about mother, God, country, and apple pie, i.e., to be a good citizen, have respect for the law, to appreciate our rich heritage, etc. Although these types of statements are frequently ridiculed in objective writing seminars and workshops, they are actually good general objectives in the affective domain. The problem is that they are non-measurable. In making specific objectives out of these GO's, it is necessary to set up real or fictitious events in which the student is asked to make a decision which would have to be based on emotional tendencies. These items would usually be in the form of short answer essays which could be used to indicate the direction of emotional tendencies and they might even suggest the intensity of the emotional tendencies. This type of evaluation might be useful in scholarship sessions, but they are actually too imprecise to measure slight changes in an attitude, value, or belief. A much more useful type of test item is one in which the students are reacting to statements with varying degrees of agreement-disagreement, positive-negative, etc. This can be accomplsihed by using Osgood's Semantic Differential.[13] The semantic differential has two parts to it. The first part is usually a brief statement describing a concept or an event and in the second part the student is presented with a series of objectival pairs with three, five, or seven spaces between the words, i.e.,

good _____ _____ _____ bad

inferior _____ _____ _____ _____ _____ superior

positive _____ _____ _____ _____ _____ _____ _____ negative

The center blank is considered neutral in all three of these examples. The other blanks stand for:

good __(good__ __(neutral)__ __(bad)__ bad

inferior __(inferior)__ __(slightly inferior)__ __(neutral)__ __(slightly superior)__ __(superior)__ superior

positive __(very positive)__ __(positive)__ __(slightly positive)__ __(neutral)__ __(slightly negative)__ __(nega- tive)__ __(very negative)__ negative

The more blanks between the two words, the smaller the change in attitude, value, or belief that can be measured. The person taking the test makes a check on one of the blanks between the two words to indicate how he or she feels about the concept or statement. Personally, I have found that the three blank format doesn't allow for identification of small changes in emotional tendencies and the seven blank

---

[13] For further information on the Semantic Differential, read *The Measurement of Meaning* by Osgood, Suci, and Tannenbaum, University of Illinois Press, 1957, and/or *The Semantic Differential: A Sourcebook* by Snider and Osgood, Aldine Press, 1968.

format has too many choices for some people and it takes them too long to decide what their opinion is. Therefore, I usually use the five blank format and ten adjectival pairs. This results in a maximum positive score of 50, a minimum negative score of 10, and a neutral score of 30. For example, the following semantic differentials are the ones I use in my seminars on a pretest and posttest basis.

Concept No. 1 — Role of the Professional Educator

The most important role of the professional educator is to facilitate learning for individual students by diagnosing their learning problems, solving these learning problems, and prescribing appropriate learning experiences, so that students learn. The least important role of the professional educator in designed instruction is to lecture to groups of students.

	Very	Slightly	Neutral	Slightly	Very	
Useless						Useful
Right						Wrong
Skeptical						Believing
Fair						Unfair
Bad						Good
Meaning-ful						Meaning-less
Harmful						Beneficial
Positive						Negative
Reject						Accept
Exciting						Discour-aging
	Very	Slightly	Neutral	Slightly	Very	

Concept No. 2 — Learning Ability of Students

It is possible for 90 percent or more of your students to learn 90 percent or more of whatever you think is important in your courses ("A" and/or "B" worth of your course).

	Very	Slightly	Neutral	Slightly	Very	
Useless						Useful
Right						Wrong
Skeptical						Believing
Fair						Unfair
Bad						Good
Meaning-ful						Meaning-less
Harmful						Beneficial
Positive						Negative
Reject						Accept
Exciting						Discour-aging
	Very	Slightly	Neutral	Slightly	Very	

Concept No. 3 — Learning Objectives

In order to maximize learning and the effectiveness and efficiency of the teaching-learning situation, the learning objectives of your courses have to be specific and stated in terms of observable and measurable behaviors exhibited by the learner.

	Very	Slightly	Neutral	Slightly	Very	
Useless						Useful
Right						Wrong
Skeptical						Believing
Fair						Unfair
Bad						Good
Meaning-ful						Meaning-less
Harmful						Beneficial
Positive						Negative
Reject						Accept
Exciting						Discour-aging
	Very	Slightly	Neutral	Slightly	Very	

Concept No. 4 — Testing

The results of the tests which you give to your students should determine what is to be taught in the teaching-learning situation. Therefore, testing should be a very critical and integral part of the teaching-learning process, instead of being used primarily as an aid in determining students' grades.

	Very	Slightly	Neutral	Slightly	Very	
Useless						Useful
Right						Wrong
Skeptical						Believing
Fair						Unfair
Bad						Good
Meaning-ful						Meaning-less
Harmful						Beneficial
Positive						Negative
Reject						Accept
Exciting						Discour-aging
	Very	Slightly	Neutral	Slightly	Very	

When I first started conducting faculty seminars on the improvement of instruction, I tried the typical evaluation form used in adult or continuing education classes which evaluates the teacher more than it does the course being taught or the students taking the course. These forms usually have questions like, *Did you like the course?*, *Would you recommend it to others?*, *What didn't you like?*, etc. By using good jokes and concentrating on being a good entertainer, I was able to get a high percentage of participants to say that they liked the seminar. But then, not very many of the participants made subsequent changes in their classrooms. I then tried the cognitive approach in which I specified the SO's and designed the seminar such that by the end of the seminar I was able to get 90 percent or more of the participants to achieve 100 percent of the SO's. Although I had more participants that made subsequent changes in their classrooms to facilitate increased learning, I still didn't think that enough of the participants were making changes. I finally realized that the main reason that most of the participants didn't make subsequent changes in their classrooms to facilitate increased learning was that I hadn't significantly changed their attitudes towards the four concepts which are basic to the whole approach described in my seminars (and also in this three volume series). As a result, I started using the semantic differential to identify changes in attitudes and changed the design of the seminars to maximize the changes in attitudes in the desired direction. Although the range of pretest scores from hundreds of seminars has not changed much during the past ten years, I have been able to slowly but continuously increase the posttest scores in the desired direction. Pretests over the years indicated that from 55 percent to 80 percent of the participants in any one group had scores of less than 30 on one or more of the four semantic differentials and as such would be considered negative towards the total concept even though they might be positive towards one, two, or three of the basic concepts. The more traditional the faculty group, the higher the percentage of participants whose scores would indicate negative attitudes towards one or more of the four basic concepts of the total approach. Also, the pretest scores would indicate that only about 10 percent or less of the participants in any one group would be highly positive (scores from 45-50) towards all four of the basic concepts. Although when I first started being concerned with attitude change I was only able to reduce the percentage of participants with negative attitudes to somewhere between 30 percent and 50 percent as indicated by posttest scores and to increase the number of highly positive posttest scores to about 30 percent. During the last year or so, I have been able to reduce the negative posttest scores to between 10 percent and 30 percent. At the same time, the percentage of participants with high positive attitudes as indicated by posttest scores has increased from 30 percent to over 50 percent. As a result of concentrating on attitude change while at the same time maintaining high levels of cognitive achievement, I have had an ever increasing percentage of participants who subsequently make changes in their classroom teaching behavior which increases student learning.

NOTE: Often it is possible to change attitudes, but the prevailing conditions are not conducive to overt changes in behavior to match the changes in attitudes. For example, many people believed for decades in abortion and equal rights for women, but the climate for overt changes in the law and public behavior didn't occur until the early 1970's. In civil rights for minority groups, the same situation occurred. Although many people have believed for a long time in equality of civil rights for everyone regardless of race, the climate for changes in overt behavior didn't occur until the sixties and after many peaceful and militant demonstrations. Habitual behaviors which are not in keeping with a person's attitudes, values, and beliefs may continue to be performed unless,

423

1) the intensities of the person's attitudes, values, and beliefs which are in conflict with the behavior is raised sufficiently high to interfere with the performance of the behavior;
2) the intellectual evidence against the performance of the behavior is too strong to be rationalized away;
3) peer group pressure against the performance of the behavior is too strong; and/or,
4) the performance of the behavior becomes unlawful.

The most critical thing to remember in measuring objectives in the affective domain is that what is being measured is a person's opinion. As such, there is no such thing as absolute rightness or wrongness of an opinion. Any evaluation is in terms of a comparison between the desired attitudes, values, and beliefs and the students' opinions which indirectly indicate the students' existing attitudes, values, and beliefs or emotional tendencies. Because of the possibility of conflict between expressed emotional tendencies and actual actions which may be used to infer emotional tendencies, it may also be desirable to have the students identify situations which they have been in that are similar to the hypothetical situations set up to identify their emotional tendencies. Then the students should be asked to describe their actions in the situations. The evaluation would be concerned with identifying consistency or conflict between expressed emotional tendencies and the students' actions.

Because of the problem of selective perception, under which people see what they want to see and hear what they want to hear, evaluation of attitudes, values, and beliefs can not be based on observations of one person only unless that person has been trained with films or videotapes to recognize certain behaviors which may be associated with certain attitudes, values, or beliefs. For further information on measurement of specific types of attitudes, see:

Measures of Occupational Attitudes and Occupational Characteristics, by Robinson, Athanasiou, and Head, Survey Research Center, Institute for Social Research, The University of Michigan, Ann Arbor, Michigan. February 1969.

Measures of Political Attitudes, by Robinson, Rusk, and Head. Center for Political Studies, Institute for Social Research, The University of Michigan, Ann Arbor, Michigan, May, 1972.

Measures of Social Psychological Attitudes, by Robinson and Shauer. Survey Research Center, Institute for Social Research, The University of Michigan, Ann Arbor, Michigan. August, 1969.

NOTE: Although multiple choice type test items are inappropriate and an educational malpractice when used to measure achievement in the cognitive domain, they can be used in the affective domain as long as it is remembered that distractors should not be built into any of the choices, the choices represent all real possible opinions and as such there are no right or wrong choices, and the results are indicative of factors in the learning and living environment not something good or bad concerning the individual.

(4) TAXONOMY OF AFFECTIVE OBJECTIVES

In identifying a taxonomy of objectives in the affective domain, it is important to keep in mind seven aspects of any affective objective which is meant to be measurable.

— Affective domain objectives are concerned with emotional tendencies and as such are non-measurable by any direct means.

— Emotional tendencies vary in strength and direction (normally thought of as positive and negative in a relative sense) and can be indirectly measured by a variety of paper and pencil tests.

— Measurements of the strength and direction of emotional tendencies as revealed by questionnaires and other paper and pencil tests do not necessarily enable accurate prediction of a person's actions or behaviors which are emotion related (emotive behaviors).

— A person's philosophy and character is made up of two major categories: those things a person will feel (both positively and negatively) and do consistently and those things a person won't feel and won't do consistently.

— Things that a person feels and will do and things that a person won't feel and won't do are usually a resultant of a cluster of attitudes, values, and beliefs rather than the resultant of just one attitude.

— Observations of actual emotive behaviors can be used to infer the existence of emotional tendencies.

— Because of other contributing factors, the observations of a *lack* of emotive behaviors cannot be used to infer the non-existence of an emotional tendency towards action nor the existence of an emotional tendency towards non-action.

The first taxonomy of educational objectives in the affective domain was developed by Krathwohl, Bloom, Masia, and others in a project which was a continuation of the same project which developed

425

the taxonomy of educational objectives in the cognitive domain. Where as the latter was quoted in its entirety of the condensed version (pp 000-000), I will only list the titles of the categories and sub-categories[1] of the former.

The Classification of Educational Goals
Handbook II: Affective Domain

1.0 Receiving (Attending)
   1.1 Awareness
   1.2 Willingness to Receive
   1.3 Controlled or selected attention

2.0 Responding
   2.1 Acquiescence in responding
   2.2 Willingness to respond
   2.3 Satisfaction in response

3.0 Valuing
   3.1 Acceptance of a value
   3.2 Preference for a value
   3.3 Commitment

4.0 Organization
   4.1 Conceptualization of a value
   4.2 Organization of a value system

5.0 Characterization by a value or value complex
   5.1 Generalized set
   5.2 Characterization

Although Krathwohl and others in setting up the above classifica tion suggested that there are negative categories probably dealing with rejection, they didn't identify them. The problem is in confusing the concept of *rejection* with the concept of *negativeness.* I would like to suggest that there are at least two separate dimensions in the affective domain which should be of concern in working with designed instruc tion in the affective domain.

I. Acceptance and Rejection of attitudes, values, and beliefs.

II. Intensity and direction of attitudes, values, and beliefs.

Whereas in the sensory domain, the three taxonomies were concern ed about three different parts of the sensory domain; these two dimen sions exist simultaneously and can each affect an objective in the affective domain.

---

[14] Printed with permission granted by David McKay Company, Inc., publishers o Taxonomy of Educational Objectives, Handbook II: Affective Domain by Davi R. Krathwohl, Benjamin S. Bloom and Bertram B. Masia, copyright © 1964.

(a) Acceptance and Rejection of Attitudes, Values, and Beliefs (Action—Non Action Continuum)

The guiding principle in setting up a taxonomy of instructional objectives in the affective domain is the degree of consistency in the correlation between a given attitude, value, or belief and the corresponding action if accepted and non-action if rejected.

Using the taxonomy as developed by Krathwohl and others as a base, I would like to extend the taxonomy to include the rejection of attitudes, values, and beliefs as well as their acceptance.

The other half of this taxonomy is important because as our personal philosophy develops, it not only consists of feelings we consistently have and of emotive behaviors we consistently perform, but it also consists of feelings we consistently don't have and of emotive behaviors we don't perform. I am also making some other changes in their classification system to maintain consistency and to hopefully clarify relationships between categories and the other dimension. Before an attitude, value, or belief can be accepted or rejected, it has to be noticed. Therefore, the neutral or middle point in the acceptance-rejection continuum has to be awareness. On either side of the center point up to and including 2.3 is the area in which attitudes are accepted or rejected. On either side from 2.2 to 4.2 is the area in which values are accepted or rejected. On either side from 3.2 to 5.2 is the area in which beliefs are accepted or rejected. The overlapping of the three areas is because a complex or cluster of attitudes make up a value and a complex or cluster of attitudes and values make up a belief. Also, starting from the center point and going out to the action end, there is an increasing correlation between a person's attitudes, values, and beliefs and his or her corresponding emotive behaviors. From the center point and going out to the non-action end, there is an increasing correlation between the attitudes, values and beliefs that a person has rejected and the lack of the corresponding emotive behavior.

In writing or identifying objectives in the affective domain, it is important to remember that when most GO's in the affective domain are broken down into sub GO's and SO's that one or more of the SO's will be cognitive and/or sensory domain objectives. For example, a very common GO in the affective domain is *the student will appreciate art (music, literabure, democracy, outdoor life, football, etc.).* In order to develop appreciation, one of the first things to do is to develop the related intellectual and/or sensory skills which are necessary in order to appreciate. Without these prerequisite skills, it will be very difficult if not impossible to develop appreciation.

In writing sample SO's for the taxonomy, you should notice that the same objective topic can be used for all levels of the taxonomy. The differences depend on whether or not the intention is to develop only

427

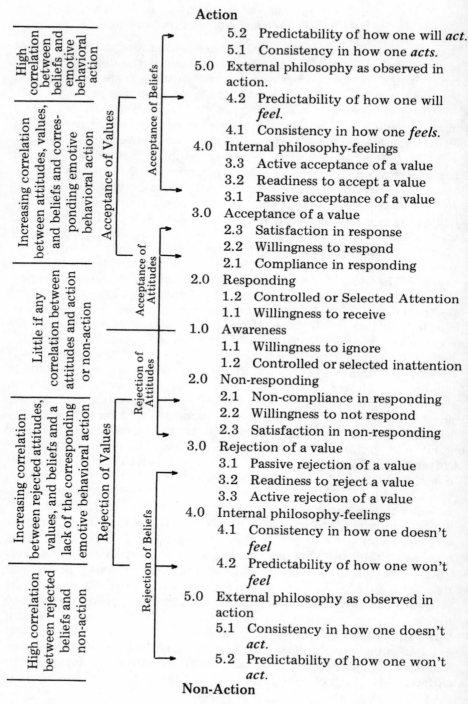

Action

High correlation between beliefs and emotive behavioral action

Increasing correlation between attitudes, values, and beliefs and corresponding emotive behavioral action

Little if any correlation between attitudes and action or non-action

Increasing correlation between rejected attitudes, values, and beliefs and a lack of the corresponding emotive behavioral action

High correlation between rejected beliefs and non-action

Acceptance of Values

Acceptance of Attitudes

Rejection of Attitudes

Rejection of Values

Acceptance of Beliefs

Rejection of Beliefs

5.2 Predictability of how one will *act*.
5.1 Consistency in how one *acts*.
5.0 External philosophy as observed in action.
4.2 Predictability of how one will *feel*.
4.1 Consistency in how one *feels*.
4.0 Internal philosophy-feelings
3.3 Active acceptance of a value
3.2 Readiness to accept a value
3.1 Passive acceptance of a value
3.0 Acceptance of a value
2.3 Satisfaction in response
2.2 Willingness to respond
2.1 Compliance in responding
2.0 Responding
1.2 Controlled or Selected Attention
1.1 Willingness to receive
1.0 Awareness
1.1 Willingness to ignore
1.2 Controlled or selected inattention
2.0 Non-responding
2.1 Non-compliance in responding
2.2 Willingness to not respond
2.3 Satisfaction in non-responding
3.0 Rejection of a value
3.1 Passive rejection of a value
3.2 Readiness to reject a value
3.3 Active rejection of a value
4.0 Internal philosophy-feelings
4.1 Consistency in how one doesn't *feel*
4.2 Predictability of how one won't *feel*
5.0 External philosophy as observed in action
5.1 Consistency in how one doesn't *act*.
5.2 Predictability of how one won't *act*.

Non-Action

428

an attitude, a value, or a belief. The similarities in the wording of the three series of sample objectives indicate that the same similarity will be found in almost all SO's in the affective domain concerned with actions or non-actions related to attitudes, values, or beliefs. The numbers to the left of each objective refer to the taxonomy level.

Sample Objectives

Topic I — To appreciate art (music, literature, etc.)

5.2 Given that the student has appreciated art by doing the following list of things for so long, it can be predicted that the student will continue to appreciate art and do these things.

(This objective is still a GO until accompanied by a list of specific things that a person who appreciates art would do and a length of time substituted for the term *so long.* Both of these unknowns would have to be filled in by the teacher using the objective.)

5.1 The student will consistently appreciate art for a set period of time by doing the following list of things.

4.2 Given that the student has felt for so long that appreciating art is important by doing the following list of things, it can be predicted that the student will continue to feel this way.

4.1 The student will consistently feel for a set period of time that appreciating art is important by doing the following list of things.

3.3 The student will attempt to prove to others that appreciating art is important by doing the following list of things.

(This objective is still a GO until the teacher defines specifically what constitutes *attempts.*)

3.2 The student will accept that appreciating art is important by doing the following list of things before doing these other things when asked by the teacher.

(This has to be achieved under conditions where there are no external pressures such as grades, points, etc.)

3.1 The student will accept that appreciating art is important by indicating his or her preference in doing the following list of things before doing these other things.

(This objective is still a GO until the teacher defines specifically the second list of things which should be less preferred by the student.)

429

2.3 The student will indicate a feeling of satisfaction in doing the following list of things which show an appreciation for art.

(This objective is still a GO until the teacher defines specifically how the student should indicate the feeling of satisfaction.)

2.2 The student will appreciate art by doing the following list of things.

2.1 The student will appreciate art by doing the following list of things when asked by the teacher.

1.2 The student will identify the following aspects of art which are worth appreciating.

(This objective is still a GO until the teacher defines specifically the aspects of art the student should appreciate.)

1.1 The student will indicate that he or she feels there might be something in art that could be appreciated.

(This objective is still a GO until the teacher defines specifically how the student should indicate his or her feelings.)

1.1 The student will indicate that he or she feels there probably isn't anything in art that could be apreciated.

1.2 The student will identify the following aspects of art which are not worth appreciating.

2.1 The student will not appreciate art by not doing the following list of things when asked not be do them by the teacher.

2.2 The student will not appreciate art by not doing the following list of things.

2.3 The student will indicate a feeling of satisfaction in not doing the following list of things which show an appreciation for art.

3.1 The student will reject that appreciating art is important by indicating his or her preference in not doing the following things (first list) before doing the other things (second list).

3.2 The student will reject that appreciating art is important by not doing the following list of things (art-oriented) before doing these other things (non-art oriented) when asked to do them (first-list) by the teacher.

(The first list or the *following list* refers to those things a person who appreciates art would do. The second list or the *other things* refers to things a person who doesn't appreciate art might do.)

430

3.3 The student will attempt to prove to others that appreciating art is not important by not doing the following list of things.

4.1 The student will consistently feel for a set period of time that by not doing the following list of things that appreciating art is not important.

4.2 Given that the student has felt for so long that by not doing the following list of things it indicates that appreciating art is not important, it can be predicted that the student will continue to feel this way.

5.1 The student will consistently not appreciate art for a set period of time by not doing the following list of things.

5.2 Given that the student has not appreciated art by not doing the following list of things for so long, it can be predicted that the student will continue to not appreciate art and not do those things.

In this first example, the desired result would be for students to appreciate art throughout their lives (objective level-action 5.2). In actuality, very few teachers of art appreciation have identified those things that people who appreciate art would do, and consequently they couldn't design their courses in such a manner so as to create an environment in which the students would do those things. As a result, since the students have not learned to do the things that indicate that they appreciate art, most of them don't do them and consequently don't appreciate art (objective level-non-action 5.2). The same problem occurs in music appreciation, appreciation of literature, etc. In literature, the achievement of the lowest objective level, non-action 5.2, is so widespread that a survey taken by the American Library Association indicated that the average non-student American reads only one book per year.

Topic II — Maturity

Whereas art appreciation is a concept which most people would like to have students achieve the objective level of action 5.2, maturity is a concept in which there are some actions which are preferred, but also some non-actions which are desired, i.e., *a mature person wouldn't act that way.*

5.2 Given that the student has reached a level of maturity as indicated by his or her doing the following list of things for so long, it can be predicted that the student will continue to act at this level of maturity.

431

(This objective is still a GO until the level of maturity is specified in terms of the list of things a student would do to indicate maturity. A specific length of time would have to be substituted for the term *so long.*)

5.1 The student will consistently act at this level of maturity for a set period of time by doing the following list of things.

4.2 Given that the student has felt for so long that acting at this level of maturity is important by doing the following list of things it can be predicted that the student will continue to feel this way.

4.1 The student will consistently feel for a set period of time that acting at this level of maturity is important by doing the following list of things.

3.3 The student will attempt to prove to others that acting at this level of maturity is important by doing the following list of things.

(This objective is still a GO until the teacher specifies what constitutes *attempts.*)

3.2 The student will accept that acting at this level of maturity is important by indicating his or her preference in doing the following list of things before doing these other things.

(This objective is still a GO until the teacher specifies the second list of things which should be less preferred by the student.)

3.1 The student will accept that acting at this level of maturity is important by doing the following list of things (first list) before doing these other things (second list) when asked by the teacher.

(This has to be achieved under conditions where there are no external pressures such as grades, points, etc.)

2.3 The student will indicate a feeling of satisfaction in doing the following list of things which show a level of maturity.

(This objective is still a GO until the teacher specifies how the student should indicate the feeling of satisfaction.)

2.2 The student will act at a level of maturity by doing the following list of things.

2.1 The student will act at a level of maturity by doing the following list of things when asked by the teacher.

1.2 The student will identify those things which a person should do to indicate a level of maturity.

1.1 The student will indicate that he or she feels that there are some things a person should do at certain levels of maturity.

(This objective is still a GO until the teacher specifies how the student should indicate his or her feelings.)

At this point, if I continued through the rejection of the actions which indicate a level of maturity, the last level would be:

(non-action)

5.2 Given that the student has not reached a level of maturity as indicated by his or her not doing the following list of things for so long, it can be predicted that the student will continue to not act at this level of maturity.

Again as with art appreciation, since the list of things a person should do to indicate various levels of maturity has not been specifically identified, the students may learn them only by chance rather than by design and many students may not achieve them at all and instead of achieving the objective level of action 5.2, they achieve the objective level of non-action 5.2. As suggested before, the concept of maturity includes desired actions and desired non-actions. The series of objectives concerning the desired non-actions would start with:

(action)

5.2 Given that the student has not reached a level of maturity as indicated by his or her doing those things (which the student shouldn't do) for so long, it can be predicted that the student will continue to act immature by doing those things.

As before, since the list of things a person shouldn't do to indicate various levels of maturity has not been specifically identified, the students may only learn not to do them by chance rather than by design and many students may not learn to do them and instead of achieving the objective level of non-action 5.2, they will achieve the objective level of action 5.2.

Assuming that those things a person should do and shouldn't do at various levels of maturity will be identified and the instructional environment will be designed to bring about an achievement of the actions and non-actions, it is not necessary to list the rejection-non-action half of the series of objectives dealing with desired actions. In a similar manner, it is not necessary to list the acceptance-action half of the series of objectives dealing with desired non-actions. The following

433

series would be the rejection-non-action half of the objective dealing with desired non-actions.

1.1 The student will indicate that he or she feels that there are some things a person shouldn't do at certain levels of maturity.

1.2 The student will identify those things which a person should not do to indicate a certain level of maturity.

2.1 The student will act at a level of maturity by not doing the following list of things when asked not to do them by the teacher.

2.2 The student will act at a level of maturity by not doing the following list of things.

2.3 The student will indicate a feeling of satisfaction in not doing the things which when not done show a level of maturity.

3.1 The student will reject that not acting is not important in showing a certain level of maturity by not doing the following list of things (first list) before doing these other things (second list) when asked not to do them (the first list) by the teacher.

(The first list or the *following list* refers to those things a person at a certain maturity level would not do. The second list or the *other things* refers to those things a person would do who thinks that non-action is not important in determining maturity level.)

3.2 The student will reject that not acting is not important in showing a certain level of maturity by indicating his or her preference by not doing the following things (first list) before doing these other things (second list).

3.3 The student will attempt to prove to others by not doing the following things (first list) that not acting is important in showing a certain level of maturity.

(This objective is still a GO until a teacher specifies what constitutes *attempts.*)

4.1 The student will consistently feel for a set period of time that by not doing the following things that not acting is important in showing a certain level of maturity.

(This objective is still a GO until a teacher specifies the set period of time and how the student will indicate his or her feeling.)

434

4.2 Given that the student has felt for so long that by not doing the following things that not acting is important in showing a certain level of maturity, it can be predicted that the student will continue to feel this way.

5.1 The student will consistently show a certain level of maturity for a set period of time by not doing the following list of things.

5.2 Given that the student has shown a certain level of maturity for so long by not doing the following list of things, it can be predicted that the student will continue to show the level of maturity by not doing those things.

Inconsistency in action or non-action may be because the strength of the attitude, value, or belief is not sufficient to maintain consistency, or it could be caused by other factors which promote or inhibit consistency. Another very important point to remember is that what may appear as inconsistent action or non-action in two similar situations may very well be actually consistent. Because action or non-action is based on the resultant of clusters of attitudes, values, and beliefs which have been accepted or rejected, the slightest change in a situation probably also changes one or more of the attitudes, values, and beliefs in a cluster and may change the action into a different action or into a non-action and change a non-action into an action. Examples of this apparent inconsistency would be where a person believes strongly in non-violence, but in certain situations approves of violence; a person who believes strongly in complete freedom for all, but accepts restrictions for certain groups whose exercise of freedom interefers with the freedom of others; and a teacher who believes in individual differences among the students, but then ignores individual differences in the classroom.

(b) Intensity and Direction of Attitudes, Values, and Beliefs

Given that an attitude, value, or belief has been accepted does not automatically mean that it is also thought of as positive and is of maximum strength. In the same way, given that an attitude, value, or belief has been rejected does not automatically mean that it is also thought of as negative and is of maximum strength. The strength of a person's attitudes, values, and beliefs vary considerably and are in various stages of change. Some emotional tendencies change very slowly and may take almost a lifetime to indicate evidence of change. Other emotional tendencies change very quickly in a matter of seconds or minutes. Because emotional tendencies are almost in a constant state of change, the direction of change is important and can only be determined with pretests and posttests. This makes the direction of an emotional tendency at any point in time dependent upon its strength at a previous point in time.

In addition to the two characteristics, intensity and direction of change, a third characteristic of an emotional tendency should be considered and that is whether or not it is positive or negative. As mentioned earlier, this aspect of an emotional tendency is very relative and depends on the wording or juxtaposition of the concept or stimulus the person is reacting to which in turn is controlled by the person or person's making up or selecting the test items. For example, if I felt that the study of literature was a critical part in a students' education, I could ask the students to react to the following statement:

The study of literature is a critical part in the development of the *whole* person in our society.

If I felt that the study of literature was not a critical part in a student's education, I could ask the students to react to the following statement:

The study of literature is not a critical part in the development of the *whole* person in our society.

A student who reacted very positively to the first statement would probably react very negatively to the second statement.

This second dimension of objectives in the affective domain does not quite fit the usual concept of a taxonomy. However, a guiding principle could be considered as the degree of difficulty in bringing about or aiding the change in strength and direction of an emotional tendency or tendencies.

1.0 Starting a new positive emotional tendency.

2.0 Maintaining change in a positive direction of an emotional tendency.

    2.1 Continued decreasing (positive direction) of an existing negative emotional tendency.

    2.2 Continued increasing of an existing positive emotional tendency.

3.0 Maintaining change in a negative direction of an emotional tendency.

    3.1 Continued increasing of an existing negative emotional tendency.

    3.2 Continued decreasing (negative direction) of an existing positive emotional tendency.

4.0 Starting a new negative emotional tendency.

5.0 Reversing the direction from negative to positive of an emotional tendency.

    5.1 Reversing the direction of an existing decreasing positive (negative direction) emotional tendency.

    5.2 Reversing the direction of an existing increasing negative emotional tendency.

6.0 Reversing the direction from positive to negative of an emotional tendency.

    6.1 Reversing the direction of an existing decreasing negative (positive direction) emotional tendency.

    6.2 Reversing the direction of an existing increasing positive emotional tendency.

The concept of positiveness or negativeness as used in the above statements is dependent upon what is considered positive and negative by the majority of the people in the social environment (in and out of school) within which the new emotional tendencies are to be started and within which the changes in emotional tendencies are supposed to take place. (To help clarify the directions used in the listing of the second dimension, see Figure 59).

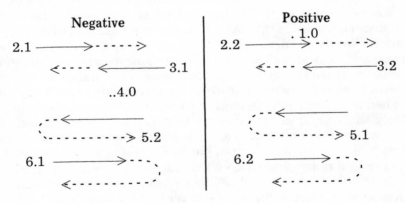

Figure 59 — Starting, Maintaining, and Changing Emotional Tendencies

(c) Other Factors Affecting Emotive Behaviors

    The expression and measurement of attitudes, values, and beliefs is a very sensitive area, particularly if one's emotional tendencies are in conflict with other people in the surrounding social environment. If certain actions are normally associated with an emotional tendency, but the social or cultural environment views these actions as negative, chances are that people who have that emotional tendency may not act out their feelings. The chances of a person acting out his or her feelings in this situation regardless of the social environment are increased as the intensity of the tendency increases and decreased as the intensity of the tendency decreases. The chances are also increased if the emotional tendency is more than just a single attitude, i.e., part of a cluster of attitudes making up a value or part of a cluster of attitudes and values making up a belief.

An opposite situation is when a person is in a social or cultural environment where a particular emotional tendency is considered very positive and important. Even if the person doesn't actually have the emotional tendency or he or she has it, but it is negative, he or she may perform the appropriate emotive behavior associated with the positive tendency in order to be one of the group. In this case, the more neutral a person's tendency, the more apt the person is to perform emotive behaviors which are not consistent with the person's real feelings.

In order to impress certain people favorably or unfavorably, a person may perform certain emotive behaviors which are normally associated with certain attitudes, values, or beliefs even if the actual emotional tendency is non-existent or existent in a direction and/or intensity different from that indicated by the emotive behaviors.

An obvious, but rarely considered factor affecting the performance and non-performance of emotive behaviors associated with various emotional tendencies, is the cognitive and sensory learning of the emotive behaviors. Words of course are used to communicate feelings, but body language and the way we speak or write probably communicates more of our emotional tendencies than words themselves. Children go to school and learn to read and write, but where do we actually teach children how and when to express their feelings and when not to express their feelings via body language, speaking manner, etc. It is not normally considered a part of a formal course. Some art courses are used to allow students to express themselves in an art form, but this is more a means or outlet for self-expression rather than designed instruction on how to communicate feelings to others. Since most of the emotive behaviors are learned by chance, some of these behaviors are never learned, some may be learned partially, and some may actually be learned in such a way as to cause misunderstandings. A parallel sensory and cognitive behavior concerns the learning of the identification and interpretation of the emotive behaviors of others. Although many emotive behaviors are almost universal because as human beings, we all have at least the capacity for similar feelings, various social and cultural traditions may affect the performance or non-performance of these emotive behaviors.

NOTE: As the world's people get closer and closer via electronic communication and transportation, it becomes more and more important in furthering human understanding to teach the performance and interpretation of emotive behavior and the associated emotional tendencies found in our society and culture and found in other societies and cultures.

As pointed out earlier, the teaching of new attitudes, values, or beliefs are relatively easy and particularly with young children and even the maintenance of attitudes, values, or beliefs isn't too difficult, but the changing of existing attitudes, values, or beliefs is a much more difficult instructional task. Of the many factors involved, there are five that are rather important: the credibility and honesty of the teacher involved; the degree of emotional consciousness; the degree of open or closed mindedness; the quantity and intensity of conflicting or complementary emotional tendencies; and the relationship between the desired changes and the social environment.

The more credible and honest the teacher is the easier it will be for the students to accept the teacher's teaching of affective domain objectives. This means the teacher would have to eliminate all or most of the traditional educational malpractices. It also means that the teacher will practice the emotional tendencies he or she is trying to teach.

In keeping with the concept that affective domain objectives have to be taught indirectly, the level of emotional consciousness (with reference to the tendency to be changed) has to be kept low. In maintaining an existing attitude, value, or belief, it is acceptable to have medium to high levels of emotional consciousness; but in changing emotional tendencies, medium to high levels of emotional consciousness just get in the way. The use of the direct approach in teaching and learning in the affective domain usually results in raising the levels of emotional consciousness.

The terms *open* and *closed* when used in reference to a personality or philosophic characteristic of the mind is pretty descriptive of how these characteristics affect the changing of someone's emotional tendencies. The concept was developed by Rokeach. The two extremes of the same continuum can be differiented with these statements:

— the more that a person can make decisions using both internal and external sources, the more open-minded a person is;

— the more objective and rational a person can be in arriving at a decision, the more open-minded a person is;

— the less a person's decisions are controlled by external pressures, the more open-minded the person is; and

439

— the less traditional a person is, the more open-minded a person is.

The reverse of the above statements would be descriptive of the closed-mind. With reference to changing emotional tendencies, the more the change is based on reasoning, facts, logic, and relevant information, the easier the change can be brought about with open-minded people. The more the change is based on authority figures, the easier the change can be brought about with closed-minded people. The degree to which a person is open or closed minded is determined in great part by the environment within which the person grew up (school, home, etc.). Authoritarian environments tend to produce closed-minded people. A very common mistake of the uninformed humanist is to think of a permissive environment as being the opposite of an authoritarian environment and as such should develop more students who are open-minded. A permissive environment may develop some self-directed people, but the self-direction may be towards a *do nothing* or a *do the minimum to get by* philosophy. In order to develop students who are more open-minded, the students have to be involved in an environment where decisions are based on reasoning, facts, logic, and relevant information. For example, very few of the rules in school dress codes are based on reasoning, facts, logic, and relevant information. Most of the rules of dress codes and conduct are set by authorities based on their personal feelings. In the use of objective type tests where the guideline is usually *Select the best answer (according to the teacher or author of the text)*, the student is taught to match the answers of the authority. In most of these tests, the student is never told why the other choices are wrong. Consequently, the use of objective type tests tend to develop closed-mindedness among the students. By having the student go through the complete decision-making process instead of just guessing, it is possible to develop open-mindedness.

In changing a person's emotional tendency, it can be accomplished easier if the teacher can identify other existing attitudes, values, and/or beliefs which are in conflict with the emotional tendency to be changed and complementary to the change to be made. The more existing emotional tendencies which can be identified as being in conflict with the tendency to be changed and/or complementary with the intended change, the easier it will be to make the change. The more existing emotional tendencies which are identified as being complementary with the tendency to be changed and/or in conflict with the intended change, the more difficult it will be to make the change.

A conflict between existing emotional tendencies can be revealed by making the person conscious of both tendencies and then either teach or review any cognitive or sensory skills which are related to the

440

tendencies and which may aid in bringing about a change in one of the two conflicting tendencies.

Changes in existing emotional tendencies are most apt to occur in a social and/or school environment which is highly organized in cooperative efforts to bring about the desired changes. The greater the percentage of people who are in contact with the students that are cooperating in developing the change, the greater the probability the change will occur. Also, the more that the student can be separated from influences which would tend to maintain existing attitudes, values, or beliefs, the greater the chances for the desired changes to occur.

(5) TEACHING AND LEARNING IN THE AFFECTIVE DOMAIN

As our society and the world get more and more involved in confrontations, discussions, and conflicts, the teaching and learning in the affective domain becomes more and more important. The day may not be to far away when more time, money, and energy will be spent by both teachers and students in learning affective domain objectives than in learning cognitive and sensory domain objectives put together. Just because the teaching and learning of affective domain objectives is so critical is also why any proposed solutions to the problem cannot be treated lightly. Just as our society has now become concerned about the ecological effects of many aspects of our society on the present and future quality of our environment, we have to be concerned about the emotional effects of many aspects of our schools in society on the present and future quality of our personal and social lives not only for local and national reasons, but also for international reasons.

(a) The Present Teaching and Learning of Affective Domain Objectives

If there are not very many teachers who have specified cognitive and sensory objectives for their students, there are even fewer teachers who have specified objectives in the affective domain. Although most teachers at least attempt to measure cognitive learning and in some courses the teachers may even measure sensory learning, but it is the rare course that measures affective learning. Where affective domain learning is measured, the results of the tests or observations are generally used to grade the student as if it was the student's fault that he or she has certain attitudes, values, and beliefs. Typical of the affective domain objectives which are presently evaluated are things like paying attention in class, citizenship, class participation, etc. Because these affective objectives are stated in general non-measurable terms, the grading is highly correlated with the teacher's preconceived notions about the student (the self-fulfilling prophecy) and the interpersonal

441

relationship between the teacher and the student. That 20 percent or more of the student's grade which depends on *class participation* is used by many teachers as a buffer such that if the students they like don't quite achieve in cognitive and sensory learning, they can add the 20 percent and pass the students. If the students they don't like happen to achieve passing levels in their cognitive and sensory learning, the 20 percent can be taken off the students grade and they can be failed or at least punished for being insolent (having different opinions).

As a result of not having specific affective domain objectives which are measurable and of not trying to identify the existence or the achievement or non-achievement of emotional tendencies, the learning of any desirable affective domain objectives occurs primarily by chance. However, the achievement of undesirable emotional tendencies occur primarily because of the design unconsciously built into many of our traditions.

In learning affective domain objectives, it is even more critical than in the learning of cognitive and sensory objectives that what the teachers and students do is what the students are supposed to learn. Practicing what is preached is a must. Sad to say, however, this guideline is not the guideline used in schools, homes, churches, and most other aspects of our social life. All too often there is a conflict between what we say and what we do. As a result, there is also a conflict between what we want and what we get.

- A common occurrence in almost every home is where parents want their children to be honest and punish them when they tell lies; but when the telephone rings a parent may say, *If that's Alice, tell her I'm not home!* By their actions, parents are saying that telling lies is okay.

- Students are taught in school that in our system of justice a person is innocent until proved guilty, but the actions by our police, courts, and society is that once accused, a person is guilty until he or she can prove his or her innocence.

- Our prisons are supposedly set up to rehabilitate the prisoners and change their attitudes, values, and beliefs and yet most prison programs violate almost every rule in the changing of emotional tendencies. An obvious result is that most ex-convicts end up back in prison.

- In schools, teachers openly talk about individual differences among students as to their rate of learning, mode of learning, motivation to learn, etc. Yet, in most classes, the students are all treated the same. Individual differences are recognized by accepting different levels of achievement, rather than change

442

how the students are taught. Even the learning unit on individual differences taught in psychology courses is usually taught in such a manner as to ignore individual differences in the students studying the unit.

— In early elementary school classes, a common affective objective is that students will learn to play well together (measured by observing the students sharing with one another) and yet most of the games played in and out of the classroom are designed to have winners.

— Teachers at all levels and particularly in higher education keep demanding academic freedom which they define vocally as, *The freedom to teach and to learn.* Yet in perpetrating the educational malpractices against the students, their actions restrict the freedom of students to learn.

— Teachers voice the goodness of honesty, respect for others, integrity, etc.; but then the militant teachers while on strike say and even do negative things against their non-striking colleagues. Whereas the function of many of the teacher strikes is to improve *quality of education*, when the strikes are over, the students observe business as usual with no change in *quality* except their teachers are working less and getting paid more. Is it any wonder why militant student action followed closely on the heels of militant teacher action!

An increasing request in teacher negotiations is the elimination of the students who are discipline problems and an increasing amount of teachers' and administrators' time is spent in discipline and security activities. Several studies including the report of the President's Task Force on Juvenile Delinquency and Youth Crime (1967) have identified an inverse relationship between levels of achievement and levels of discipline problems, delinquency, and crime. Many educators have observed and known about this relationship for years. In schools where the achievement levels are low, the discipline problems are high. In schools where the achievement levels are high, the discipline problems are low. Principals of schools which were low in achievement and high in discipline problems that decided to have a *real* continuous progress school in which all students had success, noticed that discipline problems were reduced and tend to be eliminated. Our educational traditions have created these problem students for us. The solution is not to eliminate these students physically from the classrooms as that doesn't solve the problem. The solution is to eliminate these students by not creating in them the negative attitudes, values, and beliefs which cause the problems and those who have already been created can be eliminat-

443

ed by teaching them what they need to know to have success in learning instead of having to seek success in anti-social activities. In ignoring the students' learning problems which should be a teacher's primary concern, the students learn by example to ignore some of their more important responsibilities. In New York City unitl recently, it was not unusual for a school to withhold diplomas from students who were disciplinary problems. Whereas in the affective domain, it is the teacher's design of the course that gets the grade not the student, then it should have been the schools and the teachers who had their certificates and accreditation withheld rather than withholding the diplomas of the problem students.

In the now familiar statements by Dorothy Law Nolte in her *Children Learn What They Live*

> If a child lives with criticism,
>   he learns to condemn.
> If a child lives with hostility,
>   he learns to fight.
> If a child lives with ridicule,
>   he learns to be shy.
> If a child lives with shame,
>   he learns to feel guilty.

(b) TWO ILLUSTRATIVE CASES: BOOK BANNING AND RELIGION

According to the American Library Association, the number of attacks on books is increasing at the rate of 150-200 percent per year. The most common problem in book banning relates to sex. The next most common problem is politics and the third highest is religion. Parents and taxpayers are afraid that the attitudes, values, and beliefs that are depicted in the books will be picked up by the students. Even more common are books in which the attitudes, values, and beliefs are so vague and so subtle that anyone can read into the material any emotional tendency they want. Like in most sex education debates, the anti-sex education groups visualize teachers and students demonstrating various positions of sexual intercourse and the pro-sex education groups foresee sane healthful living. The problem is obviously one of a communication breakdown. The same problem exists in book banning. Since teachers of most literature courses have not specified their course objectives, they tend to pick popular books, books with potential high interest, or books which will shock students. The only objective is to read something. When the defenders of public morality hear about the use of certain books, they ask why. The answers are so vague that they can freely imagine almost anything. As a result, most of the demands

444

for book removal succeed. If the teachers had identified their specific objectives and they were able to prove that a particular book was the best vehicle for learning the objectives, I'm sure the chances for keeping the book would be much better. However, any literary objective that can only be learned from one specific book will probably have limited utility. Most objectives of any literature course should be capable of being learned from a number of different vehicles. In other words, the behavior to be learned is transferable to many other books. If this is the case, the book banning issue wouldn't even have to come up. All too often, in picking books for shock value to the students, the teacher also shocks some parents. The more that any teacher or librarian insists on keeping any one book on the basis of freedom, the more that the defenders of public morality suspect the existence of hidden subversive messages in the book.

For example, J. D. Salinger's *Catcher In the Rye* has been attacked for years because of the use of four letter words considered to be obscene and the situations containing disrespect for parental authority. If a teacher wants to have the students read this book because it is the only book that illustrates a particular type of literary technique, then the use of the book might be defended. But once the students have learned to recognize the technique, they'll only rarely, if ever, run into it again; so the value of using the book becomes doubtful. If there are a number of books that illustrate a particular literary technique of which *Catcher In the Rye* is one, then if parents object, select one of the other examples and get down to the business of teaching and learning the important objective rather than arguing over a particular example. If on the other hand, the purpose is to try to find something that will attract students to English courses or to improve the negative reputation of English courses, I can understand this, but it won't solve the problem. The real problem is that students need to learn how to read and to write and it isn't happening for far too many students. Making the literature aspect of the English course exciting because it matches the mood or desires of the students doesn't help students in learning to write. Admittedly, many students may enjoy reading literature that shocks their parents, but if there is no way that this enjoyment can be transferred to subsequent reading, the enjoyment and benefit is short-lived.

As some of the morality defenders may suspect, there are some teachers who use the challenge of parental authority as a model of challenge of any authority, i.e., teachers challenging the authority of administrators or the public. In this case, the book banners are playing directly into the game set up by the teachers. Whereas the book banners should be challenging the books as to their possible contribution to learning, they end up in an issue over authority which indirectly

445

supports the need for some of the attitudes and values supposedly suggested in *Catcher In the Rye.* There is a need to use reason rather than emotion, to be open-minded (not necessarily permissive) rather than closed-minded.

Probably the best example of the wrong ways to achieve affective domain objectives occurs in religion and particularly in the various so-called christian religions. I could be wrong, but in all of my experience in Sunday schools, churches, religious discussion groups, and in reading the Bible, it seems to me that Christ's greatest emphasis and most important message concerned the achievement of a more humane society in which people loved one another and were concerned about the welfare of one another. Yet, in the efforts to carry this message to the people of the world, millions have been killed and injured, families and homes destroyed. We verbalize on how we should *Do unto others as you would have them do unto you*, but our actions too often demonstrate that we should *Do unto others before they do it to you.* Until the civil rights movement, more racial, social and religious prejudice was taught and learned in the churches than in almost any other aspect of our society. Religious movements suffer from many of the same problems which I identified in *Educational Malpractices.*

Whereas the majority of the objectives in instruction concern the cognitive and sensory domains and the first theory of instruction, the majority of objectives in religion concern the affective domain and the second theory of instruction. As such, the design should emphasize indirect teaching and learning and the participants should be involved in the behaviors that they are supposed to learn. In order to maximize the chances for success, the affective objectives should be clearly specified and instruments or techniques for measuring achievement of these objectives should be available and used to identify design problems.

⁻ First problem, there are few, if any, specific affective objectives identified, and consequently no measuring instruments developed. As a result, few, if any, church participants ever learn and achieve the desired affective objectives except by chance.

Second problem, it is the rare priest, preacher, or rabbi that is evaluated on the basis of how much brotherly love he or she has personally given or how much brotherly love have the church or temple members given. Just as some teachers try to claim that you can't measure learning, many church people claim that you can't measure brotherly love. In education, in lieu of measuring learning, teachers measured such things as attendance, tardiness, handing in assignments, sitting quietly when the teacher talks, participating in class discussions, helping to clean the room, length of hair, manner of dress, types of shoes, smoking and drinking, etc. Almost everything but learning. In religion, in lieu of measuring brotherly love, church leaders measure such things as attendance, financial contributions, church size, marriages, baptisms, ritual of worship, use of makeup, manner of dress, smoking and drinking, going to races, etc. Almost everything but brotherly love. The sad part is that people tend to do those things that people whom they allow evaluate them, want them to do. As long as the churches and temples are not concerned with measuring whether or not brotherly love has been given to others, then the members of the congregations are not going to be overly concerned with whether or not they offer brotherly love to their fellow men and women. Given the present emphasis in measurement, it is easy to observe in almost any religious group that if you attend the meetings and contribute financially to the movement, you are considered a good member of the congregation regardless of how you act towards your fellow men and women away from the church or temple.

Third problem, efforts to indoctrinate potential and existing members emphasize the passive mode (sitting and listening), the importance of the particular congregations unique method and ritual of worship, attendance, and financial support. Conflicting examples are frequently observed in which the actions of the church and temple leaders contradict what they say. Love one another, but not necessarily those of a different color, race, or religion (these people aren't allowed in the church or temple or are discouraged from attending). As told to the members: *Don't build up treasures on earth.* As done by the leaders: *Build up bigger and better churches and temples on earth.* In the typical religious service, there are periods of group singing and group prayers which are probably useful in the development of fellowship. However, another common element of the typical religious service is the sermon. In seminars which I have conducted for various religious groups, most pastors, priests, and rabbis have admitted that they know many of the people attending their services are not listening to the sermons. The fact that sermons have developed a negative reputation can be identified by the expressions often used when someone has done something wrong and they expect to be given a lecture or have been given a lecture by a parent, spouse, or boss, *Don't give me a sermon.* or *He gave me a sermon.* Over time, the concept of a sermon has become synonymous with being scolded. Is it any wonder why some people prefer not to listen to the sermons or prefer going on a picnic, playing golf, watching television, going to visit friends, or just having a late family breakfast rather than going to a religious service to be scolded. A person who looks forward to being scolded probably has masochistic tendencies. On one hand, the pastor, priest, or rabbi wants to increase the size of their congregation and yet, in the average sermon, the congregation is verbally punished for coming to the service. Another typical conflict found in the sermon concerns the avowed emphasis of spreading brotherly love

447

and the actual content of the sermons. It is the rare sermon that discusses the advantages and techniques of reducing hate and ill feelings and of increasing love and kind feelings for one's relatives, neighbors, and fellow human beings particularly through actively helping someone. All too often, the typical sermon castigates the congregation for not improving their relationship with God or Christ (rather than with their neighbor). Luckily for most churches and temples, there are sufficient positive rewards in attending to overcome the negative experiences or they would lose their congregations.

Fourth problem, formal religions in general have not succeeded in teaching their congregations to practice brotherly love. In almost any church or temple you want to go to, you'll find people who sit next to one another in prayer and then don't speak to one another the rest of the week. Very religious husbands and wives fight each other and either get divorced or live in misery hating each other. As a nation, we have argued, debated, and become divided and violent over the Vietnam war issue. Yet the Vietnam war is not the real problem. It is just one of many symptoms of a sick society and treating the symptom will not cure the cause. The problem is that as the population increases, as faster modes of travel shortens distances between people, and as various modes of communication decrease our privacy, it is becoming extremely critical to know how to get along with and understand our fellow men and women.

In religion, the techniques for humanization have been known for a long time. The people who are looked up to as real examples of humanitarians are the priests, rabbis, monks, nuns, missionaries, and others who actually work at helping others. Those who are so busy managing the business of the churches or temples and are not actually involved in helping others may talk about the ideal of humanism, but their actions probably conflict with their words. For many rural people, their most *christian* experiences (defined as helping their fellow men and women) occur out of church and in situations where the only reference to Christ may be in some profane statement. These experiences occur when groups of neighbors get together to help harvest someone's crops because the person is ill or to rebuild a house or barn that has been burned down. I have participated in these experiences where Methodists, Catholics, Baptists, Atheists, and others will work side by side and enjoy working up a sweat for their neighbor. It is so pleasurable that *thank you's* are almost embarrassing. In the Mormon faith where the young people give two years of their lives in missionary work, those who actually spend the time helping others in schools, hospitals, etc. very obviously benefit from the experience. Those who spend much of their two years trying to sell their faith by talking from door to door run into so many negative experiences, they also are

448

affected, but not necessarily in a beneficial way.

The same positive results can be observed among many Peace Corps and Vista Corps members who may join the Corps as self-centered individuals wanting to get away from life and end up as humanists wanting to help others get involved with life. It is very difficult not to like your fellow men and women when you have to work at helping them day after day. If we really want to have a humanist society, just think what it might be like if every youngster in our society regardless of race, creed, or sex were to spend at least one summer helping our society — particularly other people! After all, haven't most of our young people been saying that they want to be involved!

If as educators, parents, and citizens, we do not want to put forth the extra effort to teach humanism by design, at least we can decrease our conscious and subconscious efforts at teaching inhumaneness. Children do not pick up negative attitudes, values, and beliefs all by themselves. They are helped. As was so clearly expressed by Oscar Hammerstein II in the lyrics for *Carefully Taught* from *South Pacific*:

> You've got to be taught to hate and fear.
> You've got to be taught from year to year.
> It's got to be drummed in your dear little ear.
> You've got to be carefully taught.

> You've got to be taught to be afraid
> of people whose eyes are ugly made
> and people whose skin is a different shade.
> You've got to be carefully taught.

> You've got to be carefully taught before it's too late
> before you are six or seven or eight
> to hate all the people your relatives hate.
> You've got to be carefully taught.
> You've got to be carefully taught.

(c) Possible Directions for Successful Teaching of Affective Domain Objectives

The best way to start this section is to list the positive statements from Dorothy Law Nolte's *Children Learn What They Live*.

> If a child lives with tolerance,
> he learn to be patient.
> If a child lives with encouragement,
> he learns confidence.
> If a child lives with praise,
> he learns to appreciate.
> If a child lives with fairness,

449

he learns justice.
If a child lives with security,
he learns to have faith.
If a child lives with approval,
He learns to like himself.
If a child lives with acceptance and friendship,
he learns to find love in the world.

Even though repetitious, it is very important to remember that attitudes, values, or beliefs are not static, they are dynamic and subject to change on a second's notice. Like the waves of an ocean, there are times when the beginning, the changing, and ending of emotional tendencies if charted would resemble a storm at sea. At other times, the beginning, changing, and ending of emotional tendencies might resemble the slight swells of a calm sea. When the decision is made to teach affective domain objectives, what is really meant is that someone is going to attempt to *control* the beginning, changing, and ending of one or more emotional tendencies.

A second characteristic concerns the differences in measuring achievement in the three domains. In measuring achievement in the cognitive and sensory domains, you are measuring what a person CAN DO (intellectual and sensory skills). In measuring achievement in the affective domain, you are measuring what a person WILL DO (emotional tendencies). Achievement in the cognitive and sensory domains is generally cumulative, although skills can become rusty from lack of use. Achievement in the affective domain generally fluctuates in both positive and negative directions, although a feeling may stay relatively stable on the positive or negative side. In measuring achievement, there is no known limit of how much a person can learn in the cognitive domain. Achievement in the sensory domain approaches physical limits of the senses and the muscles. In the affective domain, the measurement of emotional tendencies approach a positive or negative limit in intensity caused by the limitation of our measuring instruments rather than a limitation of emotional intensity. In considering the concept of a cluster of attitudes, values, and beliefs, there is probably no limit to the number of emotional tendencies that can be associated in a cluster.

A third characteristic and most critical is that whereas cognitive and sensory objectives can be taught directly, affective objectives can only be taught indirectly. As such, designed development (achievement) of emotional tendencies that is successful means plaudits for the design and the designer (not the learner). This assumes that the emotional tendencies developed were ones desired by the parents, community, teachers, and hopefully the learners. In contrast, the teacher who is successful in designed development (achievement) of undesirable emotional tendencies (according to the parents, community, and other

450

teachers) may be condemned, fired, and possibly even expelled from the teaching profession.

In developing positive emotional tendencies, I would like to suggest a few guidelines. Since most emotional tendencies have been created by chance, the first step should be to eliminate or at least try to minimize the development of negative tendencies and if at all possible try to decrease the intensity of those negative tendencies which have already been developed. In accomplishing this goal consider the following:

— Identify and eliminate all educational malpractices which are constantly developing negative emotional tendencies.

— Like ecological problems, be careful that in making changes, even in eliminating a malpractice, that the changes don't directly develop other negative tendencies.

— In identifying the negative tendencies which were being developed by the malpractices, try to identify how the tendencies were developed and consider the reverse as possible directions for developing positive tendencies.

The second step would be to specify the affective objectives which would be considered desirable. Remember, because of the potential charge of *brainwashing*, it is even more critical to specify teaching objectives in the affective domain than it is in the other domains. It is also more critical to identify those affective objectives that everyone or most will agree as being desirable than in the other domains. In identifying the desirable emotional tendencies, be sure to include other teachers, administrators, parents, other community members, and the students. Although the students who are in an affective instructional unit may not be aware of the actual affective SO's involved in the unit, the pretest should indicate to the students at least the affective GO's from which the SO's were developed.

To give added support to my suggestions for active involvement, consider the following quotes. Herbert Thelen in *Comments on What it Means to Become Humane* (ASCD 1970 Yearbook, *To Nurture Humaneness*) states that:

Humaneness is transmitted through its exercise, and in no other way.

In the same book, Levone Hanna in *An Educational Imperative: Commitment to a Humane and Open Society* states that:

Schools fail to educate students for humane participation in a free and open society when they function as authoritarian bureaucracies. Young people must be surrounded by persons

451

who demonstrate in their actions that they are worthy representatives of a free society, for children assume the dominant habits, language, tools, beliefs, morals, values, aspirations, fears, superstitions, and hates of the people with whom they associate. It is how children are treated in their formative years that determines whether or not they will grow to be free, responsible men and women. *Attitudes are learned by doing:* (my emphasis) by working and playing with others, by sharing, by cooperating in group activities, by solving interpersonal conflicts without resorting to violence, by listening to each other, by learning to accept criticism and failure as well as praise and success. Because skills and attitudes are learned primarily through practice, the young need many opportunities to practice them in new situations and different contexts.

Charles Hoban in *Communication in Education in a Revolutionary Age* (Winter 1970 issue of *A V Communication Review*) states that:

Values are internalized not so much on the basis of what people say but what they do, i.e., the operational norms of behavior of reference groups or models. As the front-line agents of the school, teachers have as their first order of business the serious, searching examination and necessary reordering of the values they act out in their roles as teachers.

Although the best way to teach affective objectives is to involve other emotional tendencies, in efforts to try to have 100 percent of the students learn 100 percent of the objectives, students are also learning indirectly

— that the teacher cares about each individual student,

— that the teacher recognizes the individual differences in each student as to *how* the student learns,

— that every student has the potential for success, and

— that the students needing the most help can get it.

In designing instructional units concerning affective objectives, we should take lessons from others who are so successful. For example, consider the commercial companies that are developing products and advertising for the youth market. Tens of thousands of dollars are spent in motivational research to find out how to change or develop certain attitudes, values, and beliefs of our young people. The results of this research is used to create a demand for a product or to sell an existing product. Consider also the Chinese, we may not like the attitudes, values, and beliefs they are so successfully teaching, but that doesn't mean that we can't copy some of their techniques to teach the desirable attitudes, values, or beliefs. Even closer to home, theater, films, radio, and television have developed techniques to involve the observers and help them empathize with the characters in the stories, i.e., to cry, to laugh, etc.

Simulation games and other simulated events show some evidence of being able to change emotional tendencies by design and to develop at least temporary emotional tendencies as a learning experience. For example, in order to help students have a feeling for *freedom*, Carl De Young, the principal of North Ogden Jr. High School (Utah) simulated a totalitarian society in the school for two and a half days during which a number of the students' freedoms were taken away. As a result, De Young claims that many of the students have a different feeling and a greater value for *freedom.* Other schools have experienced simulated prejudice against all blue eyed people, experimented with not eating in order to know how starving people feel, simulated students with drug problems, etc. In addition, there are a wide variety of simulated games which not only can teach many cognitive objectives, but can also develop an awareness of the feelings involved in the real situations the game is simulating. There has been some evidence to indicate that when the emotional tendencies aroused in the simulated game are incompatible with the students' existing emotional tendencies, change occurs in the direction of the simulated emotional tendencies.

If the results in the evaluation of achievement of affective objectives are not what was expected or desired, then in addition to checking the design of the instructional unit, there are two other possible directions. First, it may be useful to check on the out-of-school environment for conflict and to enlist the aid of parents in the development and maintenance of the desired emotional tendencies. If the problem is that not only are the desired objectives not being achieved, but undesirable tendencies are being developed, it may be of value to check on the vehicles for learning. It is possible that a teacher in trying to select learning vehicles that are contemporary has selected one that not only teaches the desired cognitive and/or sensory objectives, but is also developing undesirable emotional tendencies.

Because the achievement or non-achievement of desirable and undesirable emotional tendencies is so important, it is well worth while to identify those teachers who are consistently successful in developing the desirable tendencies and keeping the undesirable tendencies in check. They should be able to help other teachers improve their techniques and may also be given more responsibility in the teaching of affective objectives to more students. At the same time, it will also be useful to identify those teachers who are not very good at teaching affective objectives and reduce their responsibility in the teaching of affective objectives.

As a closing cautionary note, be very careful in using obvious rewards or punishment in the development of affective objectives. It is too easy to indicate apparent achievement of the objective just to get the reward or to avoid the punishment.

(6) THE AFFECTIVE GENIUS

At first, it may seem difficult to think of anyone being a genius in the affective domain because emotional tendencies are not usually thought of as abilities. A person who might be considered a genius in the affective domain would have to have been endowed with or had developed transcendent affective abilities in communicating feelings to others and in instilling feelings in others. People who might fit into this category could be great actors and actresses, great leaders in politics and religion, anyone with transcendent charisma. Whereas in evaluating geniuses in the cognitive and sensory domains, it was necessary that the evaluation be made by other people who themselves have exceptional abilities in the cognitive and sensory domains; the evaluation of the genius in the affective domain can be equated to the number of people who consider the person to have exceptional charisma. The person who can get the most people to like him or her and do things which are suggested by the person is the greater affective genius.

e. INTEGRATED DOMAINS: THE REALITY OF INSTRUCTION

Learning which concerns only one domain and is affected by only one domain is in all probability a theoretical concept. It probably does not exist in the reality of day-to-day instructional activities.

— Almost all learning has in some part the use of a person's cognitive processes.

— Almost all learning involves the senses in receiving input and/or in producing some form of output.

— Almost all learning is potentially affected by a persons emotional tendencies.

— All SO's have to involve some form of action (behavior) in order to be specific and measurable.

In other words, almost every objective has actually three components to it: the cognitive component, the sensory component, and the affective component. When an objective is labeled as a cognitive, sensory, or affective objective, this really means that the label is referring to the primary or largest component. (See Figure 60). In solving learning problems, it becomes very important to recognize that there are three components to almost every objective. For example, in the learning of a cognitive objective concerning identification and classification of certain items, non-achievement could be caused by lack of cognitive data necessary to make the identifications and classification, non-achievement could also be caused by a lack of visual training necessary to make the identification, or non-achievement could be caused by a lack of motivation or a personal distaste towards the items to be identified. If a teacher was not aware of the potential influence of all three domains on the learning event, it would be easy to try solutions in the primary domain only and if learning didn't occur blame non-achievement on mental capacity (limits).

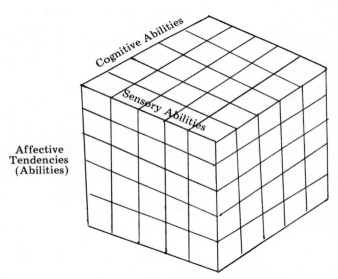

Figure 60 — The Learning Cube

In the specification of the objectives, it may not be necessary to identify all three components unless experience has indicated the need for the additional specific objectives (in the other two non-primary domains) in order to bring about the desired achievement.

(1) THE INTEGRATED GENIUS: JACK-OF-ALL-TRADES

Given that a genius can be identified in each of the three domains and each one is identified by his or her having trancendent abilities in any one domain, it might be reasonable to think of the existence of a genius in the reality of the integrated domains.

455

Consider for a moment the possibility of a theoretical unit of ability called an *abilitun* (ability unit). Also, assume for a moment that there are a finite number of cognitive, sensory, and affective abilities and for the sake of the concept let me say there are 100 abilities in each domain.

An average person might be endowed and/or might develop an average of 20 abilities in each domain to the strength of 10 *abilituns* for a total of 600 abilituns.

A superior person in any one of the domains may have been endowed and/or developed the 20 abilities in one of the domains to a strength of 25 *abilituns* and the 20 abilities in the other two domains to an average strength of 10 *abilituns* for a total of 900 *abilituns* for all three domains.

A genius in any one of the domains may have been endowed and/or developed 10 abilities in one of the domains to a strength of 100 *abilituns* and the 20 abilities in the other two domains to an average strength of 10 *abilituns* for a total of 1400 *abilituns* for all three domains.

A genius in any two of the domains may have been endowed and/or developed 15 abilities in each of two domains to a strength of 40 *abilituns* and the 20 abilities in the other domain to an average strength of 10 *abilituns* for a total of 1400 *abilituns*. This person would collectively have as many *abilituns* as the single domain genius, but because the trancendent abilities are in two domains, the strength of a single ability in one of the two major domains would not be as high as the genius in a single domain.

A Jack-of-all-trades may have been endowed and/or developed 30 abilities in each of the three domains to a strength of 20 *abilituns* for a total of 1800 *abilituns* for all three domains. This person does not have transcendent abilities in any one domain, but the collective ability strengths are greater than the genius in any one domain. Although a genius is and should be considered as an exceptional person, maybe the Jack-of-all-trades is also an exceptional person even though he or she may not be as easily identified. In fact, many more people than we usually think of could actually be exceptional in view of the many abilities which can be developed in one or more of the three domains.

C. EVALUATION OF THE INSTRUCTIONAL EVENT

If the primary purpose of educational institutions is to facilitate student learning, then the efforts of all of the people involved in the institution should be directly or indirectly involved with helping students learn and any evaluation carried out in the institution should also be directly or indirectly involved with identifying whether or not the desired learning took place in the students. Given that there is *something* that should be learned by the students, evaluation of the achievement of that *something* should provide two important facts: how much of that *something* has been learned and how much of it hasn't been learned. The *something* may be called a variety of names, i.e., goals, aims, outcomes, objectives, etc. As indicated earlier, I will call that part of the *something* which is measurable as specific behavioral learning objectives. If the word *behavioral* goes against your grain, use any word you feel good about or even make up your own word as long as the meaning you have for it refers to *something* that students DO and is measurable.

In supporting the existence of the two facts revealed in evaluation, I have asked the following question of almost every teacher I have worked with in reference to the test items in their tests.

— As the teacher of this course, do you want all of your students ideally to be able to answer all of these test items?

As could be expected, every teacher has said in answer to the question, *Yes, I want all of the students to be able to answer all of the test items.* For some teachers, I'm sure they gave me this answer because the other answers don't sound very professional and would be very difficult to defend:

— No, there are certain students that I don't want to be able to answer all of these test items!

— No, there are certain test items that I don't want any of the students to be able to answer!

— No, there are certain students that I don't want to be able to answer certain test items!

Obviously, any one of the above answers would indicate a design for non-learning which would be an inappropriate behavior for a teacher who as a professional is supposedly concerned with helping students learn.

Assuming then that teachers want their students to learn 100 percent of the test items, then any student who achieves anything less than 100 percent still has *something* left to learn. As such, teachers who are concerned about helping students learn will look on their tests as diagnostic in nature and will follow up any evaluation with instructional events designed to help the students learn whatever the *something* was that the students missed on the test. In other words diagnosis is followed by some treatment.

457

1. CORRELATION BETWEEN OBJECTIVES AND TESTS

Since most teachers say that they want their students to be able to achieve whatever they have on their tests, then the test items in reality are objectives. Therefore, any teacher who evaluates learning does have specific objectives which are measurable. Oddly enough, although probably less than 10 percent of teachers at all levels have actually listed the specific objectives for each of their courses, probably 90 percent or more give tests or in one or another evaluate the achievement of their students. This means that 90 percent or more of teachers at all levels of education actually do have specific, measurable, behavioral objectives — their test items. This does not mean that the objectives are good objectives or that the test items are good test items, but there is a direct relationship between test items and objectives. If you have one, you must have the other, and vice versa. Consider for a moment the students in the 80 percent or more of the classes in which the only statements labeled objectives are ambiguous and vague. What do you think students study for and learn in these courses? They try to find out what is on the tests and what is being evaluated and study that. In other words, students study what they think will be on tests and to satisfy other criteria for evaluation (when specified) as *their* course objectives. If what is on the tests happens to match the stated course objectives, then it could be said that the students study and learn the stated course objectives. If what is on the tests doesn't happen to match the stated course objectives, then students don't study the stated course objectives. An increasingly common situation that is also sad, is when school districts, colleges, or universities have inservice sessions, workshops, or courses on the writing of specific objectives and after putting in many hours of work in writing objectives the teachers go back into their classrooms and use the same old tests. Since students learn what is on the tests, very little change in learning will occur in the classrooms. As a consequence, the teachers usually blame the concept of specifying objectives as a useless task rather than recognizing that in specifying objectives they should have also changed their tests to fit the objectives. Since students learn what is on tests, it would have been smarter to have the teacher's write better test items from the point-of-view of the test items as being course objectives rather than spend time writing course objectives and not change the test items. Although most teachers have not had much practice in writing specific objectives, most teachers have had experience in writing test items which would have made the whole task of specifying course objectives (test items) much easier. The major problem is that just as *teachers teach the way they were taught not the way they were taught to teach,* teachers also *test the way they were tested not the way they were taught to test (if they were taught at all)*. So if testing has been a problem, the problem is being handed down through generations of teachers.

a. THE TRADITIONAL VIEW OF EVALUATION

There are three steps in the traditional pattern for unit course or curriculum development. The first step is a listing of objectives, which doesn't seem too much different from the learning systems approach. But there are two major differences. The first is the fact that the typical objectives that are stated in the traditional approach are nonmeasurable, nonobservable kinds of objectives that can be made and nobody will challenge whether they were achieved or not, and generally they are objectives of the type *to make a better citizen of the learner, to have a better understanding of literature, to have a real understanding of the theoretical basis of the problem,* etc. The second major difference is in what happens to these lists of objectives once they are completed. In the learning systems concept, lists of objectives are used and referred to continually throughout the development of the materials. In the traditional approach, once the list of objectives has been written they are filed away and then the curriculum group says, *Now that we've finished the objectives, what should we do in the classroom?*

The second step in the traditional pattern is in answer to the question just stated and takes on the form of prescribing activities to be carried out in the instructional situation. The problem with prescribing these activities is that if we don't know specifically the kinds of learning behaviors that are desired or necessary on the part of the learner, it is difficult if not almost impossible to tell whether the prescribed activities are facilitating the learning of these undefined behaviors. As a consequence, in our guidelines for elementary and secondary education and also in some of the standards set up for accreditation the basis for measurement is *Did you perform the activity?* not *What did the student learn as a result of the activity?* For example, in almost every kindergarten and first grade class, there are two activities that are carried out: (1) fingerpainting, and (2) storytelling. When teachers are asked why they do these things in the classroom, the reply from the teacher who is carrying on the activity of fingerpainting has been *It develops the child's dexterity in his fingers.* My question is *How dextrous do you want the student to be? Maybe the student already has the required amount of dexterity.* The teacher's comment at this point is, *Well, the guidelines say I am supposed to have fingerpainting for 15 minutes a day.* Sometimes a teacher will respond to the question of why fingerpainting with the statement *The learner is learning to express himself in color.* My questions here are, *Expressing himself in how many colors — five, six, ten?, Are you concerned with chroma, hue, intensity?, How do you, the teacher, know that one student is expressing himself and another student is not able to express himself?* Here again, in answer to my question the teachers generally say, *We're supposed to fingerpaint for 15 minutes.* I am not trying to imply that all of our activities that we are carrying on are wrong. What I am saying is that if we don't know what we are trying to achieve by carrying on the activity, we may be wasting the student's time and our time.

The third step in the traditional approach concerns *evaluation.* In most curriculum committees that are developing instructional materials, the evaluation during the development stage never goes much beyond just talking about doing some evaluation. Sometimes the group will actually write some statements about what they think the learner's competencies should be as a result of going through the materials, but these competencies are generally written in vague terms and are non-measurable. Rarely, the curriculum committee will write up a test to go along with the instructional materials and in general when these tests are made up, they suffer from the same problems as most tests which are generally used in education today.

If teachers do not know specifically what they are teaching or what the specific terminal objectives of their courses are, then how can we justify testing students for their achievement of something we have not defined? It is a sad comment on our present educational system that there is little, if any, correlation between what is taught in the classroom and the tests that are given to the students which form the very basis for progress through our schools. Just as sad, is the fact that the activities carried on in the classroom have a low correlation with the vague, ambiguous objectives of the course and also a low correlation with the evaluation of the course.

NOTE: Admittedly, the evaluation may have a high correlation with certain parts of the course, but since these parts are not identified to the student ahead of time and in many cases where teachers make up their tests after the treatment even they don't know ahead of time those parts of the course that may eventually have a high correlation with the evaluation, the correlation has to be considered in terms of two factors: first, the degree to which what is being evaluated was even in the course, and second, the degree to which what is being evaluated and is also in the course is diluted with a lot of things in the course which are not being evaluated and a lot of things in the evaluation which were not in the course.

I suppose a scant justification can be made for most teachers because after all, no one ever told them that there should be a high correlation between what is being taught and what is being tested. Of course the advantage (from the traditional point-of-view) of having a low correlation between objectives and tests is that tests can be designed to give any results a teacher wants — REGARDLESS OF WHAT STUDENTS KNOW!!

As long as the correlation between course objectives and the course evaluation has not been a consideration, whole courses have been developed in departments of education, educational psychology, and psychology on how to manipulate test items, tests, and the results of tests. Since the correlation between course objectives and the course evaluation (and particularly any standardized tests) is low, the test results are primarily meaningful with reference to the test itself and are limited in meaningfulness with reference to the course. As a consequence, traditional tests have very limited use as a diagnostic instrument. Of course, the higher the correlation between course objectives and the course evaluation, the greater the usefulness of the test results as a diagnostic tool and in helping to design subsequent instructional materials.

b. CORRELATION PROBLEMS

Given that a high or perfect correlation between course objectives and the course evaluation would be desirable, anything less than that constitutes a correlation problem. In other words, if the course evaluation does not match the course objectives, the situation represents a problem which besides being an educational malpractice, it affects the integrity of the evaluation of teachers and the learning environment. These correlation problems fall into four categories:

— Problems with *general objectives and subjective* test items;

— Problems with *general objectives* and *specific* test items;

— Problems with *specific objectives* and *subjective* test items; and

— Problems with *specific objectives* and *specific* test items.

(1) PROBLEMS WITH GENERAL OBJECTIVES AND SUBJECTIVE TEST ITEMS

This situation represents primarily the traditional evaluation situation just discussed in which the course objectives are so vague and ambiguous almost anything can be tested. The subjective test items would include essay type items, observation of students' performance or products, and the so-called objective type test items which are objective from the point-of-view of scoring but very subjective from the point-of-view of preparing or writing them. Because of the subjectiveness in the evaluation, this situation is the easiest to manipulate in order to get any results that may be desired.

461

(2) PROBLEMS WITH GENERAL OBJECTIVES AND SPECIFIC TEST ITEMS

In this situation, although the objectives are very vague and ambiguous, the test items ask for specifics. This could include essay type tests and observations *if* the criteria for evaluation were specifically spelled out such that subjectivity in the evaluation process is minimized if not eliminated. The problem in this situation is that because the course objectives are general, almost any specific test item could be used as long as it relates to the same content area as the course objectives. Then, although the items themselves are specific, the actual selection of these items is up to the person or persons making up the test and hence, the selection is subjective, which still allows the manipulation of the selection process in order to obtain almost any desired results.

Whereas in the first situation the subjectivity in both the course objectives and the course evaluation severely limits the usefulness of the results as far as improving learning is concerned, the *specific* test items can be viewed as equivalent to *specific* objectives and subsequent instruction can be designed around the specific test items that were missed. However, if the items were selected to give certain results, it cannot be assumed that the items are also important enough to learn. Selecting test items that will give certain results and selecting test items that will measure the achievement of important concepts and objectives are two very different processes each using different criteria for selection.

Whereas most traditional standardized tests are made without any objectives in mind (one of the many reasons why they are useless), at least the National Assessment of Educational Progress (NAEP) started out with some objectives which is a step in the right direction. The problem with NAEP is that the objectives are general objectives and as such allows freedom to pick the test items that will give the results desired by NAEP (a three-hump curve instead of the traditional *bell* curve) which in turn makes the efforts of NAEP fradulent because the results are predetermined by the design of the test items.[15] Since the results of NAEP's project is supposed to influence the spending of educational dollars, it would have been more honest to drop the masquerade, and expense of all the testing and just have the test item writers tell educators what the results of the tests are designed to be and go on from there. Admittedly, without all the window dressing, educational decision makers probably wouldn't accept the predetermin-

---

[15] See pp. 145-64, *Educational Malpractices: The Big Gamble in Our Schools* by Don Stewart; or *DAIRS and Systems for Instruction Newsletter*, Issue 23-24, October 1970. Published by SLATE Services.

ed results as being valid. Hopefully the day will come when educational decision makers will see through the fallacies of traditional test making.

(3) PROBLEMS WITH SPECIFIC OBJECTIVES AND SUBJECTIVE TEST ITEMS

This has only become a problem during the past decade or so; but it is becoming a more common problem than it should be. This situation is a typical result of traditional educators who voluntarily or by administrative order have specified their course objectives but have not changed the way they test for achievement in their courses. Although there are a few teachers in this category that will specify their course objectives and then use essay tests or observations without specific criteria to evaluate student achievement, the major problem in this category are the teachers who spend a lot of time specifying their course objectives and then use the subjectively written *objective* type test items to measure student achievement. The sad part of this problem is that the teachers worked so hard on specifying their course objectives and because they used the same old so-called *objective* type tests, there probably wasn't any increase in student learning. In fact, under these conditions, there could actually be a decrease in learning. Given that students aren't usually given specific objectives but they know they are going to have an *objective* type test, most students know that the best way to study for this kind of test is to not study very hard as they might fall into the trap of the distractors. By cram studying at the last minute and paying attention to names, dates, definitions and other rote memory items (without rote memorizing), students have a good chance in getting a passing grade and particularly if they also use the technique of eliminating the obvious wrong choices. When students are given a list of specific course objectives and at the same time know that the test will be of the so-called *objective* type, most of the students will study as they would in any course using this type of test. However, a few students (maybe quite a few until they discover the deception) will believe the teacher and will study the specific course objectives. Since the specific course objectives do not match the subjectively written *objective* type test items (except in very rare cases), students who spent time learning what the teacher specified they were to learn, end up with lower scores than the other students on the *objective* type test. In the process, these students *do learn* not to trust teachers.

There are many specialists in teaching and learning whose instructional activities fall into this category including most of the educators who have written books, workbooks, and pamphlets on *How to Write Specific Objectives.* Even Robert Mager uses *objective* type test items and obviously believes they are alright. Imagine for a moment that you are a teacher who doesn't have any specific course objectives and you

463

normally test for achievement in your course with the so-called *objective* type test items. You attend an objective writing workshop and after working for days to get some specific objectives listed, you find out that you can still use the same old test items. At that point, you will probably suspect that all that work writing specific objectives was wasted and when the results of using the specific objectives in your classes indicate not much change in achievement or in fact less achievement than before, you will probably be convinced that the efforts at writing specific objectives is a waste of time and just *busy work*.

To help prove that the so-called *objective* type test items rarely match specified course objectives, the following are examples of matching course objectives and course evaluation.

| SO | Test Items |

(True-False)

| The learner will be able to identify whether or not the following statement is true or false —*The server in volleyball may stand anyplace behind the back line while serving.* | The server in volleyball may stand anyplace behind the back line while serving. |

In order for a specific objective to be measured by a True-False test item, the objective would have to be worded in the following manner. *The learner will be able to identify whether or not the following statement is true or false, "--------".* The actual true-false test item would have to be in the statement of the objective.

| SO | Test Items |

(Multiple-Choice)

| Given the following stem of a statement, *A major uprising of slaves in 1831 was led by*, the learner will be able to identify the correct completion of that statement from among the following four choices: (1) Uncle Tom, (2) Abraham Lincoln, (3) Nat Turner, (4) Booker T. Washington. | A major uprising of slaves in 1831 was led by (1) Uncle Tom, (2) Abraham Lincoln, (3) Nat Turner, (4) Booker T. Washington. |

In order for a specific objective to be measured by a multiple-choice test item, the objective would have to be worded in the following manner, *Given the following stem of a statement, "--------", the learner will be able to identify the correct completion of that statement from among the following four (five, six, etc.) choices: (1) --------, (2) --------, (3) --------, and (4) --------.* Of the tens of thousands of specific objectives I have looked at, I have never seen objectives written in either of these formats. Yet, the achievement of many of the specific objectives I have seen is measured by the so-called *objective* type true-false, multiple-choice, and matching test items.

This type of problem is commonly found in the courses which should be humanizing but because of this problem, these courses are more likely to be taught and tested in inhumane ways (using distractors): history, sociology, psychology, and other social science including professional education courses. Probably the subject area most deeply involved in this problem category is the allied health field: medicine, nursing, denistry, medical technician, etc. The main reason for the allied health fields having this problem is that the external evaluation and certification agencies use *objective* type tests, i.e., American Medical Examinations, state and national nursing examinations, etc. In a situation where there is an external evaluation agency and the evaluation used is the subjectively written *objective* type test which rarely, if ever, matches the course objectives, there are four alternative courses of action:

— The teacher or teachers could decide to concentrate on teaching and testing what the students need to know to be successful in their particular field, but then, although the students would know enough to be successful in their field, they would in all probability never pass the external examinations and be certified to work in their field.

— The teacher or teachers could decide to concentrate on teaching and testing what the students need to know to be successful in passing the external examination; but then, although the students in all probability would become certified to work in their chosen field, they wouldn't know the things that they need to know to be successful in their chosen field.

— The teacher or teachers could decide to concentrate on teaching what the students need to know to be successful in their field and testing in a form that tests what the students need to know to pass the external tests and get certified. This is the procedure that is followed in most of the allied health schools and other schools that have an external examination which doesn't match their course objectives. The problems with this approach is that first, the students are never tested on whether or not they have achieved what was taught; second, they are tested on their

465

achievement of something that hasn't been taught (that the wrong choices are wrong); and third, because of the mismatch between the test items and the course objectives, it is extremely difficult to use the tests in a diagnostic manner and achieve quality control (90 percent or more of the students learn 100 percent of the course objectives).

— The teacher or teachers could recognize that they have two separate responsibilities: a long term responsibility to the students and any eventual patients or clients they may work with to be sure that the students know what they need to know to be successful in their field and a short term responsibility to the students to get them through the external examinations such that the students can get certified. In recognizing that these are two separate activities, the teacher or teachers would teach and test what the students need to know to be successful in their field and then also teach and test what the students need to know to pass the external examination and get certified. This procedure is more expensive and time consuming, but it is also the only honest way to go until such time as the external certifying examinations match the desired course objectives.

Examples of the mismatch

The desired course objective (Literature)

Given any one of the following short stories, the student will be able to identify the theme of the story and prove the identification by quoting two or more excerpts from the story that support the identified theme as being the theme of the story.

The typical test item

(The student has supposedly read the short story)
The theme of the short story, "--------", is
   (a) --------
   (b) --------
   (c) --------
   (d) --------

The objective that fits the test item

Given the following stem of statement, *The theme of the short story*, '--------', *is*, the student will be able to complete the statement correctly (according to the author of the test) by selecting one of the following four (a) --------, (b) --------, (c) --------, and (d) --------.

The test item as it should be

The student picks any one of the short stories to read and is then asked make or write a statement identifying the theme of the story. The student will then be asked to quote two or more excerpts from the short story which support the student's statement as being the theme of the story.

The desired course objective (reading-word clues)

Given an unknown word in a sentence or paragraph, the student will be able to identify the word clues and then using the word clues write or state a synonym or definition for the unknown word.

The typical test item taken from commercial reading materials

Circle the letter of the best meaning for *exclusive*
- (a) open to the public
- (b) shutting out all others
- (c) high in cost
- (d) forbidden

(The words used in the tests are generally the same words used in the reading program materials so they are no longer unknown and the concept of word clues isn't even a part of the test)

The objective that fits the test item

Given the following stem of a statement, *Circle the letter of the best meaning for "exclusive"*, the student will be able to complete the statement correctly by circling the letter of one of the following four choices: (a) open to the public, (b) shutting out all others, (c) high in cost, and (d) forbidden.

The test item as it should be

First, it would have to be identified that the word *exclusive* is unknown to the student. Second (like the desired objective states), the student would be given the following statement (or one similar to it containing word clues) and asked to underline the word clues

One will find no Western goods on the floor devoted to the *exclusive* sale of Japanese goods . . . Only such things as beautiful kimonos, sukiyaki tables, and lovely wall hangings are found there.

Third, the student would be asked to state a synonym or definition based on the underlined word clues.

The desired course objective (Anatomy course)

The student will be able to define the term *Kinesiology*.

The typical test item

Kinesiology is the study of

    (a) bones and their movement
    (b) muscles and their relation to skeletal movement
    (c) structure of the body using X-ray techniques
    (d) cell structure and function

The objective that fits the test item

Given the following stem of a statement, *Kinesiology is the study of*, the student will be able to complete the statement correctly by circling the letter of one of the following four choices, (a) bones and their movement, (b) muscles and their relation to skeletal movement, (c) structure of the body using X-ray techniques, and (d) cell structure and function.

The test item as it should be

Define the term Kinesiology.

The desired course objective (Sociology)

The student will be able to describe two or more non-verbal symbols which both animals and mankind use to communicate and state what the symbolic actions are supposed to communicate.

The typical test item

Communication among men is different from that among animals, because men have no non-verbal symbols. (True-False)

The objective that fits the test item

The student will be able to identify whether or not the following statement is true or false, *Communication among men is different than that among animals, because men have no non-verbal symbols.*

The test item as it should be

Describe two or more non-verbal symbols which both animals and mankind use to communicate and state what the symbolic actions are supposed to communicate.

(4) PROBLEMS WITH SPECIFIC OBJECTIVES AND SPECIFIC TEST ITEMS

A *specific* test item is when the test item asks for specific things. Normally, this would be the appropriate type of test item to have for a specific objective. But under certain conditions it is still a problem. For example, it is fairly common where the specific objective asks for the student to define a number of words to find test items in which a list of definitions is given and the student is to supply the term that fits the definition which is just the reverse of the behavior asked for by the objective.

Another common problem in this category is where the *specific objective* refers to a set performance of some kind, but rather than watch what the student is supposed to do or possibly because the teacher thinks he or she has to have a paper and pencil test, the test is a paper and pencil test in which the student describes the *specific* behavior or some aspect of the behavior the student is supposed to be able to do. There is quite a difference between being able to do something and just describing the action. Frequently, the student has already been evaluated on his or her physical performance, but the teacher feels pressure to have paper and pencil evidence of achievement and gives an inappropriate test and duplicates the evaluation process.

A similar mismatch situation is where the course objectives involve identification, discrimination, decision-making, etc. based on audio and/or visual stimuli but the test depends only on printed verbal stimuli. Of the thousands of educators who have participated in my seminars and workshops, about 75 percent have indicated that they utilize some form of audio-visual media in their instructional activities, but only about 20 percent indicated that they used audio-visual media in their testing. This would indicate that we are teaching one type of behavior but not testing this type of behavior. If you use a film, or slides, or a demonstration to teach, why not use parts of the film or a slide or a portion of the demonstration to test? Verbal tests of behaviors which were learned in response to more concrete forms of simulation may not only be testing the learned behaviors of the learner, but may also be testing the learner's ability to interpret correctly the instructor's verbalization of the desired behaviors. The same general considerations which go into the decisions of what to include in a course should also go into the decisions of what to include in a evaluation of the course.

c. BEHAVIOR CORRELATION vs. CONTENT CORRELATION

In giving reasons for specifying objectives, the first reason concerned the noun in the objective which identifies the topic or subject of the learning event. The second reason concerned the verb in the objective which identifies the learner's action in the learning event. The desired objective and consequently the desired evaluation should involve the same nouns and verbs. A common traditional error is to assume that as long as the topic or content of the test item is the same as the topic or content of the objective, it should be acceptable to change the verb not only between the course objective and the course evaluation, but also among the various test items which might be used to test for the achievement of the course objective. This assumption is built into many standardized tests. Since the verb in the traditional course objective is usually non-measurable, it is necessary to change the verb such that it is measurable in order to make up a test. The problem arises when the teacher teaches the topic using one behavior and then tests the topic using a different behavior. Since what students DO with a topic is what students LEARN about a topic, if the noun or topic is the same in the objective and in the test items, but the verb or behavior is different, then the results of the achievement of the test items could be a result of chance learning because the behavior tested was not taught. If a particular curve of results was desired, it would be easy to change the verb or behavior in the test items sufficiently different from that of the objective or from other test items used to test the same topic to get almost any result desired. The manipulation of results is not as easy in this type of a situation as it is when the so-called *objective* type test items are used wherein the professional test item writer can utilize distractors. In the multiple-choice test item, it is possible to put in wrong choices that are so obviously wrong that even if the student doesn't know the right answer, by eliminating the wrong answers, the student can get the right answer (the only choice left). In changing the behavior of a test item, if a student doesn't know the behavior and it is not an *objective* type test item, the student will probably miss the item.

Examples of objectives and test items where the topic is kept the same, but the behavior is changed:

GO — The student will be able to solve linear equations. (This is a general objective because the difficulty level of the linear equations to be solved is not specified.)

$$\begin{aligned} \text{Test items} \qquad & X + 5 = 0 \\ & 2X + 4 = 0 \\ & 3X + 5 = 0 \\ \sqrt{13}X + 7 = {}& \sqrt{31} - 6X \end{aligned}$$

If a student can subtract, he or she can solve the first equation. A student would have to also know how to divide to solve the second equation. A knowledge of fractions would be needed to solve the third equation. The last equation would require that the student can solve square root problems or would know how to use a square root table.

GO — The student will understand the short story

Test items —

— What is the theme of the story?

— List the critical events (caused a change in one or more of the characters) and describe the changes that took place in the characters because of the critical events?

— Is the theme of the story relevant to our society today? If yes, prove it by citing two or more contemporary events in which the theme can be identified of applied. If no, state two or more reasons why the theme is irrelevant in our contemporary society?

The behaviors necessary to achieve each of these test items are different and if they weren't specifically taught, the students probably couldn't answer them correctly unless by chance a student happened to learn it on his or her own time.

In my seminars, I often refer to this type of problem as one of *hidden objectives*. In addition to the multiple-behavior testing of a topic of a general course objective, there are some test items that aren't even related to a course objective. For example, students are often asked to perform the taking of tests within a given time limit, when in fact the learning took place without time limitation. For example, a teacher may give a homework assignment of ten problems, and one student may be able to complete these ten problems in ten minutes, a second student may be able to complete these ten problems in twenty minutes, and a third student may complete these problems in thirty minutes. The students were all able to complete the homework problems when they were able to do it without time limitation. In a subsequent timed test, the students were given ten problems and asked to do them in ten minutes. In this type of situation the students' chances for achievement are not *equal*, because the teacher is really testing the student's *rate of performance*, and is expecting the students to perform at the rate of solving one test item per minute. In this example, before the test is given you can expect one student to complete all ten, the second student to maybe only complete five, and the third student to maybe only complete three or four of them. If this rate of answering test items is really that important, then the students should have been taught that way in the learning situation. For

471

example, the teacher could have given the students fifty homework problems and told them to keep solving the problems until they could solve any ten of these problems in ten minutes. In this instance, the first student who solves ten problems in ten minutes would stop after ten problems. The second student may have to do thirty problems before he can do ten of them in ten minutes. The third student may have to do all fifty problems and go through them a second time before he can solve ten problems in ten minutes. In this way, when the teacher gives a timed test of ten problems in ten minutes, the students have *equal opportunity for achievement.* In most subject matter areas, the time or rate of answering questions is not that important and is not usually one of the specified objectives of the course. Consequently, the hidden objective of *rate of performance* should be left out of the testing situation. Where *rate of performance* is an important objective, it should be taught by design, i.e., automotive repair, typing, preparing income tax returns, etc.

Another very common example of hidden objectives is found in tests which are given in science, mathematics and literature courses. In going through these courses, the students are taught a number of discrete learning objectives. On the final exam, the students are asked to combine everything they have learned during the semester or quarter or year, and solve or answer the problem. The learning objective is obviously to combine all of the individual concepts that were presented throughout the course and this objective is most likely one of the most important behaviors to be learned in the course. The reason that it is considered a hidden objective is that at no time during the course were the students asked to combine all of these individual concepts together, until they arrived in the final testing situation. This combining behavior should have been taught in a designed teaching-learning situation, in which the students learned this behavior on purpose, rather than by chance in the testing situation. Tests for grading purposes should only test those behaviors which have been presented previously to the learners in a teaching-learning situation.

Although the changing of the behavior is acceptable and frequently done under the traditional approach as long as the topic is kept constant, the reverse is generally not quite as acceptable and is not done as often under the traditional approach. This is where the topic is changed and the behavior is kept the same in going from the course objective to the course evaluation. This type of change is usually done when a teacher wants the student to transfer a learned behavior to other topics which is a very good objective, but the course objective is not often worded that way.

Examples of objectives and test items where the topic is changed but the behavior is the same:

Traditional GO — To have a better understanding of our Latin American neighbors.

Test items during the course are all on various aspects of Latin America.

Test item(s) on the final examination: apply one or more of the techniques used to analyze and study Latin America to a country not in Latin America and not previously analyzed or studied.

Revised SO (process objective) — Given a country or a specific area of a country or of the world, the student will be able to apply the following techniques of analysis which will result in the following data: (this should be followed by lists of techniques and resultant data which in a way are actually lists of sub-SO's).

> In achieving the above SO, the teacher could use one or more of the Latin American countries as a vehicle for the students in the learning of the process objective. For the purposes of motivation, the teacher could allow each student to pick two or more countries he or she is interested in and save one for the final mastery examination and use the other one or more as vehicles for learning the process of geographical and/or cultural analysis and study.

Traditional GO — To become familiar with the great philosophers

Test items during the course are all on various aspects and quotations of the great philosophers.

Test item(s) on the final examination: (Given the writing of some person). Identify this person's philosophy from his writing and compare and contrast it to the philosophies of the following four philosophers: --------, --------, --------, and --------.

Revised SO (process objective) — Given any one of the following essays, the students will be able to identify the writer's philosophy (as evidenced by statements in the essay) and then compare and contrast the writer's philosophy to the philosophies of the following four philosophers: --------, --------, --------, and --------, according to the following criteria: (this should be accompanied by a number of essays or a list of titles of writings or publications by various writers with about the same degree of difficulty level in the identification of the writer's philosophy and also a list of criteria for comparing and contrasting.)

> In achieving the above objective, one or more of the writings could be used as vehicles for learning the process of identifica-

tion of a person's philosophy and then any one of the remaining essays could be used to test for mastery of the objective. Notice in the above objective, not only was the topic changed, but the behavior was also changed in going from the traditional objective to the final examination item.

Traditional GO — The student should have a good understanding of the RCA television receivers and be able to repair them.

Test items and trouble shooting during the course are all on RCA television receivers.

Test items and trouble shooting on the final examination are on television receivers made by companies other than RCA.

Revised SO (process objective) — Given any television receiver which operates on the basis of the following principles, the manufacturer's handbook, and schematic drawings, the student will be able to answer the following questions and to locate and repair the following problems: (This objective would be accompanied by three lists: the principles, questions, and the repair problems.)

In achieving the above objective, RCA television receivers could be used as a vehicle for learning as long as the learning included the using of the manufacturer's handbook and schematic drawings. To memorize procedures on any one company's product without reference to handbooks or schematics is to limit the application of the process to similar products. This is a common problem in many vocational technical courses.

d. "DON'T TEACH STUDENTS WHAT YOU WANT THEM TO LEARN" OR "DON'T TEACH TO THE TEST"

Consider very seriously the following statement: *Don't teach students whatever it is you want them to learn.* Does it sound contradictory and absurd to you? It certainly does to me. If a teacher wants his or her students to learn certain facts, concepts, relationships, etc., then it seems most reasonable and logical that the teacher should teach the students whatever it is he or she wants the students to learn.

The converse of the title seems even more ridiculous: *Teachers should teach students whatever it is you don't want them to learn!!!* Yes, I know that both of these statements seem out-of-place in such an important part of our society as the education of our young people, but both of these statements are implied by certain situations commonly found in traditional educational practices. I have pointed out that in order for any materials or situations to be called *instructional* there are two questions that should be asked:

474

What is being instructed? (Is there a list of objectives available?)

How do you know whether or not the instructional experience was successful? (Is there a test available that tests for the achievement of the objectives?)

In an instructional situation where the objectives are vague, ambiguous, and nonmeasurable, the problem of the correlation between objectives and tests is critical, but it is very difficult to identify (the test items are measurable but the objectives are not measurable). However, it should be the goal of an HONEST educator to try to have the correlation between objectives and test items as high as possible in order to measure as accurately as possible the actual achievement of the students in the instructional situation.

In an instructional situation where the objectives are specific and measurable, it is very easy to have a 100 percent correlation between test items and stated objectives. In this case, the usual correlation problem does not exist unless the educators who are evaluating the instructional situation purposely want to ignore the fact that specific objectives are measurable and they decide to test the students with test items which have a correlation with the stated objectives of something less than 100 percent (the more negative the educators who are evaluating the instructional situation want the situation to appear, the lower the correlation between the test items and the objectives).

Among traditional educators where the *normal curve* of achievement is looked on as *GOOD*, it would be undesirable to test students on exactly what the students were supposed to learn especially if the students had been told or had a list of the instructional objectives because most of the students might learn most or all of the objectives (90 percent or more of the students might learn 100 percent of the objectives). By adjusting the correlation between the objectives and the test items (inserting *detractors*), it is possible to have the results of the tests approximate a *normal curve* in spite of the objectives and the fact that the results do not necessarily indicate achievement of those objectives.

Assuming that most educators are more concerned with ALL students learning what they are supposed to learn (objectives) than with trying to obtain a *normal curve* of achievement scores (which means the teacher will have to design the test items such that some students will miss them — designed failure), then the following statement should be acceptable:

Teachers should teach students what they want the students to learn (objectives) and should test students for the achievement of those objectives by using test items that have a high, if not 100 percent, correlation with the stated objectives.

475

In view of the above statement, consider the following situations which exemplify the traditional educators attitude found throughout our country and which also imply the statement used as a title for this section.

Situation No. 1

Dorsett Educational Systems had a performance contract to operate the *remedial*[16] center for the Texarkana School District on a basis of guaranteed learning for selected students in the subjects of math and reading or the company would not receive any money. The project had been operating for one year when Dean C. Andrew, Associate Director of the Arkansas Regional Education Center (the agency responsible for evaluating the Dorsett-Texarkana Project), said, *There's enough evidence to indicate that Dorsett was TEACHING TO THE TEST.* This statement is a very common statement in traditional education and is looked on as referring to a situation that is tantamount to a criminal act and very unethical. In reference to the previous paragraphs in this section, we should be able to make the following premises:

1. Learning objectives are statements concerning what students should learn and what teachers should help students learn through teaching.

2. Test items on tests used to evaluate student achievement in an instructional situation should test for the achievement of the specified objectives in that instructional situation.

Conclusion: Test items on tests should test what students should learn and what teachers should help students learn through teaching.

The only conditions under which this conclusion would not be a true statement is when one or both of the two premises are false. Therefore, in order for the Arkansas Regional Education Center to believe that Dorsett was in the wrong, they would have to believe in one or both of the following negative statements of the above premises:

---

[16] It is common to refer to students who are going back over material which was presented to them in previous years as being *remedial students*. Since the vast majority of these students did not learn what they were supposed to learn when it was first presented ("D" and "F" students), it should be obvious that it is not the students who are being remedied, it is the ineffective and inefficient teaching-learning situation that the students are in. Notice how the students are given the negative label while the teachers and schools are considered blameless. This error in labeling is based on an unstated belief that if the teacher has presented the course content then the students should have learned it. In conflict with this assumption is a common statement found in training centers of business, industry, and the military, *if the student hasn't learned, the teacher hasn't taught!!!*

1N. Learning objectives are statements concerning what students should NOT learn and what teachers should NOT help students learn through teaching.

2N. Test items on tests used to evaluate students achievement in an instructional situation should NOT test for the achievement of the specified learning objectives to be learned in that instructional situation.

If the Arkansas Regional Education Center believes that the first premise is negative and the second premise is positive, then the conclusion is *that test items on tests should NOT test what students should learn and what teachers should help students learn through teaching.* As ridiculous as this last conclusion sounds, consider the following statement made by John O. Wilson, OEO's Assistant Director for Planning, Research, and Evaluation: *in order to prevent a repetition of the Texarkana experience (Dorsett's teaching to the test), safeguards will be built into the system and a large enough variety of tests will be used to make it all but IMPOSSIBLE for a company (or a teacher) TO TEACH TO THE TEST* (or to teach whatever it is we want students to learn — assuming the test is testing what we want students to learn). If the tests are not testing for the achievement of what we want students to learn, then why use the tests at all??? Educators have known for decades that the easiest way to fail students (discredit a teacher — or a company in this case) is to test the students for achievement of something you know they don't know.

This, of course, is why the concept of performance contracting has had difficulty in showing that it can *make a difference.* As long as it is considered unethical and wrong to teach what it is the students are going to be tested on, teachers, schools, performance contracting, etc., will continue to indicate that they don't *make a difference.*

Situation No. 2

A very similar situation exists around the country in school district where they have critical reading problems with their students as identified by standardized tests. Teachers and school districts who subsequently show increases in reading achievement beyond the average increases of the other teachers and school districts are suspected of *teaching to the test.* If the reading tests really test *reading achievement*, then why not teach the students what is on the tests (reading). On the other hand, if the tests don't really test *reading achievement*, it would be wrong to teach what is on the test, but it would also be wrong to use the tests if the tests are testing for the achievement of something you don't necessarily want the students to learn. Sad as it may be, the latter statement represents the real world. Very few reading tests actually test

477

for reading achievement as it is actually practiced in the real world. Consider the following: how many times in your reading of the newspapers, novels, etc. have you found multiple-choice or true-false items on the margin of the page or in a footnote to help you identify or clarify what was important on that page???

Situation No. 3

Any reader who is living or has lived in the state of New York should be familiar with the Regents' Examinations. For about six weeks prior to the exams, there is probably more directed learning going on in New York than at any other time of the year put together. The teachers know what it is that they have to teach and the students know what it is they have to learn (the tests). Assuming that the tests are really testing for the achievement of important objectives, then it should be great that the teachers are teaching the right things and students are learning the right things. Again, as before, school districts and teachers who teach their students what is on the tests are considered to be unethical (could it be that what is on the tests is so unimportant that it shouldn't be taught — or tested???).

Situation No. 4

Ex-students, students, and teachers in the professional and occupational fields where there are state and/or national examinations (nursing, medical, dental, teaching, cosmetology, real estate, etc.) should also be very familiar with this attitude. These state or national examinations are kept very secret and changed frequently enough so that it would be difficult for teachers to *teach to the test.* In fact, in most of our schools it is considered bad if students find out what is on tests early enough in the instructional situation such that they might have a chance to learn what is on the tests (after all, most of the students might learn enough to get "A's" and "B's" and then the teacher wouldn't have a *normal curve" of grades.)* In many schools, students can be suspended from school if they are caught with a copy of an exam before it is given and teachers can be fired if too many students learn (high percentage of "A's" and "B's") because that means that the teacher *taught the test!!!*

NOTE: The traditional belief that it is wrong *to teach to the test* was started by psychologists and standardized test makers. Since the validity of a test is based on whether or not the results fit a predetermined curve, if some teachers taught what was on the test, the results would no longer fit the curve which would then make the test invalid. In order to re-validate the test, the test makers would have to go to a lot of work finding new test items that discriminate (not necessarily important) and to build in more distractors in the old items to trick the students such that the results of the test would again fit the predetermined curve. Rather than do all that work, it was a lot easier to convince teachers that they shouldn't teach what is on the test. Over the decades, no one questioned the validity of using these standardized tests to measure the achievement of something the teachers weren't supposed to teach!

With reference to the previous section where I pointed out the differences between achieving course objectives and achieving test items, the critical concept to remember in this section is that a teacher should teach to the course objectives (process objectives) which indirectly is the same as teaching to the test (of those objectives), but not necessarily to teach to specific test items. For example, if an item in an algebra test asks the student to solve the linear equation $2 X + 4 = 0$, it would be a disservice to the student to teach the student to answer only that test item. On the other hand, the behavioral objective that fits that equation is:

> SO — the student should be able to solve a linear equation in which the coefficient of "X" can be evenly divided into the constant term.

and the teacher should teach to this objective by having the student practice solving equations which fit the SO. Since this is a process objective, it is the process of solving the equations that the students are to learn not just a specific item. In measuring for the achievement of this objective, the mastery test items should be different than the practice items and there should be a sufficient number of items that the teacher is confident that the student has learned the process. Other items which fit the SO are: $3X + 6 = 0$, $6X + 12 = 0$, $5X + 20 = 0$, $8X + 64 = 0$, etc.

The same situation can be found in almost every course or subject in which the desired objective is a process objective. In literature courses, a common process objective is to perform a literary analysis or critique. All too often under the traditional approach, the literary vehicle used to teach the process of literary analysis becomes the objective and the literature used in the teaching situation is also used in the testing situation. What keeps these teachers from being accused of *teaching to the test* is that they generally don't have any SO's and rarely do they know what it is they are going to test until almost the end of the course. As a result, few students really learn the process of performing a literary analysis. To really teach and test for the achievement of the process, the SO's would have to be identified and because there are different levels of difficulty in performing a literary analysis,

479

lists of literary works representing the various levels would have to be prepared. Then, starting at the lowest level (or wherever the students' achievement level is), the teacher could select one or more of the literary works at that level to use as vehicles for teaching the process. The mastery tests should utilize literary works from the same level but they should be ones that the student hasn't been exposed to before. Not only does this test for the achievement of the process, but also if the students can transfer the process to vehicles which are not the same ones used in the teaching of the process.

EXCEPTION: When the SO's or the test items are only concerned with rote memory, then the teaching, practice, and mastery vehicles are all the same. For example, if the SO concerns remembering a certain person's name and possibly what the person did, this is a rote memory item and it would be taught, practiced, and tested just as it is. *The teacher should teach to the specific test item.*

2. TYPES OF TEST ITEMS AND TESTS

Ideally, in setting up an instructional situation, the objectives are identified and made specific in order to know what should be taught and learned during the instructional event. these objectives are the instructional specifications which the instructioneer uses to design the instructional environment so as to facilitate their achievement. The evaluation process should relate to whether or not the instructional specifications or objectives were achieved. However, under the traditional approach to education, relatively few teachers have specified their course objectives and even among those who have, fewer still have tried to maintain a high correlation between course objectives and tests. As a result, the purpose of the evaluation process traditionally is to arrive at some sort of a grade. Since the available objectives are usually nonmeasurable, the grades can't actually represent a measure of achievement with reference to the content of the course. Therefore, the grades generally represent a measure of achievement with reference to a student's classmates wherein the best students of the group get the top grades, the poorest students get the lowest grades, and most of the students get grades in between the two extremes. This traditional approach to grading is based on the assumption that intelligence (I.Q.) is mostly genetic and that in any given group of students there will be close to a normal distribution of intelligence levels (the familiar *bell* curve). In addition to evaluating students in order to get grades, some teachers give tests to find out whether or not students have studied (the *pop* quiz), some teachers use tests to punish students, some teachers use tests to sift out either certain students or to sift out a certain percentage of students, and some other teachers use the tests as an ego trip to prove how smart they are and how ignorant the students are. Without the instructional specifications upon which the tests should be based, the making, giving, and scoring of tests can be based on almost any criteria and can be done for almost any reason.

The evaluation process in arriving at a traditional grade can be divided into two parts: the major part of this evaluation consists of students' scores on formal tests, essays, projects, term papers, laboratory performance, etc.; the second and generally minor part of the evaluation is a subjective evaluation of the student by the teacher, which is very often affected by the personality interrelationships between the student and teacher. In some courses where there are minimum, if any, formal tests, papers, or projects to evaluate, the teacher's evaluation of the student may be primarily based on a subjective basis, rather than on an objective basis.[17] Although in certain instances there may be a definite value for having a teacher's subjective evaluation of a student's performance in reference to the student's enthusiasm, study habits, social and mental maturity, etc., these subjective evaluations should be limited and should not be used as controlling factors to stop a student's academic progress through his courses. The major problem is that the subjective and objective evaluations are combined into a single letter grade and no one besides the teacher knows how much of each is represented in the grade. Ten percent could be a result of subjective evaluation and 90 percent a result of objective evaluation or it could be reversed and only ten percent is objective and 90 percent subjective.

From my point-of-view, I think that every teacher has the right to make subjective comments about a student and have these recorded in the students record; *but,* these comments should be labeled personal comments and not be confused with the objective part of the evaluation process.

a. ESSAY ITEMS AND TERM PAPERS

At first glance, it would seem that most essays, test, projects, etc., which are evaluated by the teacher are evaluated on a fair basis, such that if the grading is low, it is really the student's fault that it is low. But actually, even in the grading of tests, essays, term projects, laborabory performance, etc., there is a great deal of subjectiveness involved in the evaluation. Most teachers, students, and parents realize that the evaluation of essays, term papers, and projects are very subjec-

---

[17] The use of the word *subjective* is in reference to vague measurement of students' performance based on feelings, attitudes, opinions, etc. which generally results in wide variations in grading by different teachers for the same performance. The use of the word *objective* in this instance is in reference to a more specific measurement of students' performance based on achievement of specific measurable objectives (skills, goals, etc.) which results in uniformity in grading by different teachers for the same performance.

tive. In fact, in in-service seminars, thousands of teachers at all levels of education were given the following multiple-choice question:

If each teacher in a group of teachers graded the same essay, the grades would:

1. All be the same
2. Be almost the same
3. Be mostly different
4. All be different

In response to this question, 99 to 100 percent of the teachers have indicated choices 3 and 4, which not only indicates that teachers are very much aware of not only the fact that grading essays is subjective, but also that there is a great variation in the way that teachers grade essays. The major problem that exists is that teachers, knowing that they grade differently from their fellow teachers, will go into the classroom and grade essays and term projects and assign these grades as if they were arrived at objectively. These grades very often affect the students' academic progress through the schools. The results of such a subjective grading situation indicate that a student who would receive "D" or "F" grades with one teacher may receive "A" or "B" grades from another teacher, using the exact same essays or projects. This situation is particularly critical when two or more teachers are teaching the same course, so that a student's grade depends more on which teacher the student is assigned to than on what the student is able to learn. It is very possible to make subjective tests more objective. This can be done if teachers will establish the exact criteria which will be used for grading the essay. When teachers agree on the criteria for evaluation of essays, papers, projects, etc., the grades can be almost unanimous, and with at least a minimum of variation between teachers in the subjective grading process. (For more detailed information see pp. 182-194, Volume I).

In addition to the variability among teachers on the criteria used for grading essays, students are not informed as to what these criteria are. As a result, students use the *shotgun* approach to writing an essay, hoping that they will hit the right criteria. Ask any student who is about ready to start writing an essay or term paper (if you are a student — ask yourself), *What are the exact criteria which the teacher will use to evaluate this essay or paper?* Very few students can answer this question. On the other hand, if students are told what the criteria are, then most students will achieve what they are supposed to ("A's" and "B's") and teachers can't end up with a *satisfactory* grading curve (which would include "C's", "D's" and "F's"). *According to the traditional educational philosophy, it is better not to let the students know what they are supposed to learn because they are liable to learn it.* It is this very same philosophy that indirectly promotes the sale of commercially prepared term papers. Since the students don't usually know the criteria for evaluation (which too often is whether or not it was handed in, how big is it, how long is the bibliography, etc.) and there won't be a chance to rewrite and improve the paper after grading, why not play an unfair game with matching unfair practices. If the development or writing of this term paper is that important in achieving the major objectives of the course, then teachers who allow students to turn in papers that are less than "A" or "B" quality are fostering mediocre quality, and conditioning the student to "C" achievement. Using the learning systems approach, once you have identified what the student did not do in the paper in order to have a "C", "D" or "F" quality (assuming that the teacher knows specifically the behaviors the student should exhibit in the preparation and writing of the paper), then the paper should be turned back to the student, and the student should complete the paper correctly even if he has to go over the paper two, three, four, or more times. The teacher should not accept the paper until it represents "A" or "B" quality. In this way, the preparation and writing of the paper can be considered a successful learning experience.

NOTE: If for any reason, a teacher suspects that a student hasn't done his own writing in a term paper, I believe it is acceptable to ask the student to prepare a brief essay in class to check on whether or not the student can produce the same quality. If the student can't, rather than suspend or fail the student, the teacher should just ask the student to do the term paper over again and then rewrite it as many times as necessary in order to achieve the "A" or "B" quality.

As soon as teachers start treating the writing of essays and especially term papers as a learning experience (every student is helped to achieve the desired quality) and are honest in their dealings with students (the students are told the exact criteria that will be used to evaluate the essay or term paper), the commerical sale of term papers will fade away because the need for them will be eliminated.

b. *OBJECTIVE* TYPE TEST ITEMS AND EXAMINATIONS: AN EXAMPLE OF INSIDIOUS SUBJECTIVITY

There will be several different points of view held by readers concerning the topic of this section. During the first four or five years after publication, I expect that the majority of the readers of this book will be teachers who are already teaching and have probably developed certain attitudes, values, and beliefs about *objective* type test items and examinations (multiple choice, true-false, and matching). These teachers will fall into four groups.

483

(1) There will be those readers who already look on objective type test items and examinations as faulty and avoid using them. They will agree with most of what I will say, so I am not too concerned with their reactions.

(2) There will be those readers who look on objective type test items and examinations as faulty, but use them anyway because it's an *easy way out* of their obligation to evaluate and assign scores or grades. Although they will agree with most of what I will say, they may not want to read it as it will increase their feelings of guilt and their own guilt might force them to stop using the *easy way out* and become honest in their evaluation procedures. I am concerned about this group and DARE them to read this section and then try to defend to themselves their continued use of objective type test items and examinations.

(3) There will be those readers who use objective type examinations because it's traditional and many or most of their colleagues in similar positions use them and they haven't actually considered the thought that something could be wrong with them. I am also concerned with this group as I think they will read this issue with an open mind and accept that evidence that makes sense to them and as a result many or most readers in this group will either stop using the objective type test items and examinations or will shift from this group of readers into group (2) with the accompanying guilty conscience which hopefully will be great enough or will continue to build up within them until even these readers cease using objective type examinations.

(4) There will also be those readers who have accepted the concept of the objective type examinations with such blind faith that they will refuse to read or listen to any arguments against their continued use. Many of these readers will not read past the first page if they even read that far. At this point in time, I realize that it is probably almost futile to try to change their minds with just written words. These readers may have to be sued for malpractice before they will change and even then it may be done begrudgingly. Yet, within this group, there are some readers who are very dedicated people who believe themselves to be very honest and humane in their dealings with other people. This particular group may refuse to read this section because if I succeed in creating a doubt in their minds as to the value of using objective type test items and examinations, then the resultant guilt of remembering the hundreds and perhaps thousands or people whose futures they have directly or indir-

ectly affected by their decisions which were based on faulty and fraudulent objective type examinations, may be too much guilt for the humanitarian mind to cope with and continue teaching. I am very concerned about this group of readers and I hope they will read this section and keep in mind the following concept. Before reading this section, they were doing the best job they knew how to do and any problems resulting from their decisions based on data from objective type examinations were not with malice aforethought. Hence, any guilt feelings can be faced with the realization that they didn't know better at the time. However, once this particular group has read this section, then if they continue to make decisions regarding people's future lives based on data from objective type examinations, I hope their guilt conscience consumes them until they either stop using objective type examinations or they resign their positions.

Although a minority of the readers of this book during the first few years will be students who are training to be teachers, I expect that in five or more years, the majority of the readers will be students training to be teachers. The student readers will probably fall into at least four groups.

(5) There are many students who dislike *objective* type test items and examinations because of the trickery and guessing involved and will be glad to find evidence against their continued use, so I am not too concerned about this group.

(6) There will be a certain group of graduate students who may dislike *objective* type test items, but because the faculty members on their graduate committees like this type of test items, the students will have to use them in their research work. In using this type of test items in research, the students are liable to find them *convenient* because they can be manipulated (reworded) to bring about almost any kind of results a researcher desires regardless of the actual learning levels of the sample used in the research. I worry about this group of students because they may, like many educational researchers before them, start to favor the use of the *objective* type test items as they facilitate the proving or disproving of almost any theory or hypothesis (regardless of actual conditions).

(7) A potentially large group of students could be those who have learned how to take *objective* type examinations and like them because studying for them is much easier than having to really know something as would be the case in tests using open ended

short answer essay items. I worry about this group because they have favorable opinions towards *objective* type test items and as such, may tend to use them regardless of the inappropriateness of the items. My hope is that their enthusiasm to be a teacher will help them read this section with an open mind.

(8) The fourth group of students represents hopefully only a small group. These students will tend to be closed minded and authoritarian. As such, they will tend to want to test their students as they were tested by their teachers and will also want to stick to the traditional ways of testing. I particularly worry about this group because as teachers and authority figures they will continue to impress other students in a cycle of *the blind leading the blind.*

Of the many negative aspects of objective type test items that make them unsuitable for use in an honest instructional system, the most critical is the concept of *detractors.* This concept concerns the use of words, phrases, and/or choices (in multiple choice items) which are put into the test item to either detract the student from getting the right answer or to detract the student from selecting any of the wrong answers. The use of *detractors* is partially based on the concept of selective perception in which a person sees what he or she wants to see and hears what he or she wants to hear. We do not always see and hear what is actually there.

NOTE: If you did not read pages 000-000, Volume I concerning the concept of selective perception, please skip back to it now if you have it.

This is why students don't study very much for objective type examinations. If a student knows the content too well, he or she will fall for the detractors and make mistakes. The best way to study for an objective type examination is to not study throughout the course, but cram just before the test and pay attention to names, dates, and other trivia. As examples of the two types of detractors, consider the following:

Given a test item is to find out if the student know the normal temperature of the human being and you want the students to miss the item, then you select wrong alternate choices that are very similar to the correct choice.

Item — The normal temperature of the human being is
   a.   96.8 degrees Fahrenheit
   b.   96.8 degrees Centigrade
   c.   98.6 degrees Fahrenheit
   d.   98.6 degrees Fahrenheit

If you wanted to make sure the students would get the right answer, then you would select alternate wrong choices that are so obviously wrong that the student could select the right answer even if the student didn't actually know it.

Item — The normal temperature of the human being is
a. 20 degrees below zero
b. 1500 degrees above zero
c. 98.6 degrees
d. zero degrees

Of course, these two examples are extreme examples and wouldn't be considered good test items because too many students might miss the first item and too many students would get the second one right. In professional testing circles, test items that approximately 65% or more of the population taking the test answer correctly are considered not very good items because they don't *discriminate*. At the other extreme, test items that approximately 35% or less of the population taking the test answer correctly are also considered to be not very good items because they don't *discriminate*. The best test items in professional testing circles are ones in which from 35% to 65% of the population taking the test answer them correctly. These test items are considered good *discriminators*, and when used with a normally distributed group (according to ability) then the results of the test should approximate a normal probability curve (bell curve). As a result, complete courses have been built up in which the emphasis is on how to develop, identify, and modify objective type test items which will result in the correct distribution of scores.

Although these test items are referred to as objective type test items, they are only objective from the point-of-view of scoring or grading. A professional test item writer can take almost any multiple choice item and by keeping the stem and the correct choice constant can vary the detractors and wrong choices in such ways as to get almost any percentage of students to answer the item correctly from almost zero to almost 100%. This fact reveals that the writing of the so-called objective type test item is very subjective. And what makes it worse is that the subjectivity is hidden and in most cases the degree of subjectivity is unknown. In looking at the distribution of scores resulting from a so-called objective type test, the actual distribution of scores is more affected by the person or persons who made up the test than by what the population taking the test knows about what is supposedly being tested by the test. In other words, the author or authors of objective type tests knowingly or unknowingly have already built into the test the distribution of scores before the students even take the examination.

In using *objective* examinations where the emphasis is on the distribution of scores, validity and reliability are determined with reference to the distribution. If the distribution of the results of an *objective* test fit a predetermined curve, the test is considered to be valid and if it repeatedly gives these results, it is also considered reliable. This, of course, is why great care is taken in the selection of test items and why it is necessary to know all about *distractors* and how to use them to increase or decrease the scores on certain test items.

In order to arrive at a curve based on the students' performance, the traditional teacher designs evaluation instruments on the basis of the following three types of test items: a small number of test items or criteria which all or most students can answer correctly (this is to encourage students); a small number of test items or criteria which very few, if any, students can answer correctly (this is supposed to separate the *men* from the *boys*); and a majority of test items or criteria which have varying degrees of difficulty (this gives the curve). By varying combinations of these three types of test items or criteria and by varying the number of items of different difficulty level, teachers are able to establish any standards they wish, regardless of what students have learned, and yet be able to defend the results on the performance of the students on the test.

Based on this approach, if teachers feel that they should increase the percentage of "D" and "F" students, they include more test items that are difficult or impossible for the students to answer. If the teachers want to have more "A" or "B" students, then they include test items or use criteria which more students are able to get correct or achieve. As proof of this concept, ask any teacher at any level of education the following two questions:

1. In your course, if you wanted to, could you design a test in which you could fail or almost fail every student in your class?

2. In your course, if you wanted to, could you design a test that would pass or almost pass every student in your class?

I have asked these questions of tens of thousands of teachers and the answers to these two questions have been unanimously *yes.* Teachers can make tests that will either pass or almost pass all of their students or fail or almost fail all of their students (regardless of what the students actually know). Because of this arbitrary variation, the question that should be considered next is:

If a teacher can make a test that would pass or almost pass all of the students, or if the teacher could make a test that would fail or almost fail all of the students, then where does the teacher get the magic which helps him or her to select test items that will pass the students that should pass and fail the students who should fail (if students should fail at all)?

This magic ability does not exist. No teacher has it, at any level of education. In a teaching-learning situation in which the major goal of the teacher or institution is to sift out or eliminate students, then it is very necessary to have an evaluation system in which the teacher can fail as many students as they want or to pass as many students as they want (regardless of student learning). An evaluation system that can be manipulated is also useful in a school where the teachers are expected to have a particular distribution of letter grades and too many high grades or too many low grades is considered bad. Under this approach, it should be rather obvious that the quality of teaching and student learning could be excellent, average, or very poor. It doesn't really make much difference, because it is the evaluation system that ultimately affects who gets through the program and what their grades are!

When the emphasis in a teaching-learning situation is on learning and the purpose of evaluation is to find out which objectives the students haven't learned in order to solve their learning problems such that 90 percent or more of the students will learn 100 percent of the objectives, the evaluation system can not be manipulated unless there is a low correlation between the course objectives and the test items. Under this approach, validity and reliability refer to the correlation between objectives and test items. If a teacher is teaching from specific measurable learning objectives *and* is using test items which specifically measure those objectives, then the teacher cannot make the test items any harder or any easier without changing the instructional objectives. In other words, the results of the tests have a direct behavioral relationship to the achievement of course objectives or learning rather than the results having only a chance relationship with the behaviors taught in a course.

Under the traditional approach where there are few if any specific objectives, both the teachers and the students have similar problems in now knowing exactly what should be taught and learned. But since the evaluation system (using *objective* type test items) is what determines the grades almost regardless of what is taught or learned, having objectives is really not that necessary. In fact, teachers who try to combine the two methods by having specific objectives and also *objective* tests that can be manipulated, may have problems with their students. With general objectives or no objectives, it is relatively easy to claim that the *objective* type test items are testing what you want because the correlation between course objectives and the test items is based on similarity of content. Once the objectives are specified as far as the desired behavior is concerned (what the learner is supposed to be able to do), then the dissimilarity between the desired behavior and the behavior being tested becomes readily apparent, i.e., an objective which specified that the student should be able to list, define, analyze, or perform is tested by a multiple choice or true-false test item which is testing discrimination. Within my experience of critiqueing tens of thousands of objectives, I have yet to see an objective that matches the format necessary to be tested by multiple choice or true-false test items and maintain a high or perfect correlation between the objectives and test items. If a teacher is concerned about testing for the achievement of what he or she is teaching, there is no place for the *objective* type test item.

In questioning thousands of teachers, one of the questions I ask is, *Do you think it is fair and honest to test students for the achievement of something you haven't taught and that they have had no chance to learn before taking the test?* Every teacher has answered, *No.* What do you think? If you agree that it wouldn't be fair, consider the fact that in giving students multiple-choice test items, the students are not only being tested on their ability to identify the correct answer which hopefully has been taught and learned; but the students are also being tested on their ability to identify that the wrong choices are wrong! Where have any students had the opportunity to learn that the wrong choices are wrong? As evidenced by the results in most classrooms, teachers have enough trouble trying to teach the correct answers, let alone trying to teach that the wrong choices are wrong. In other words, the students are being tested on something that they haven't had a chance to learn!

Given that under the traditional approach the primary purpose of testing is to get a score or grade, than the use of *objective* type test items is very advantageous because they can be scored by machines and computers. Even without the hardware, a teacher using a key (showing the correct answers) can grade *objective* type tests much faster than a teacher grading other types of test items. However, if the purpose of testing is to find out what the students don't know in order to teach it, than it is critical that the test items have a high correlation with the subsequent teaching materials so the teacher know what to teach. If there is only a small correlation between the test items and subsequent learning objectives, the results of the tests offer very little help or guidelines as to what should be learned. If *objective* type test items are used and the students are to be taught whatever they missed, then the honest teacher would have to teach one or more of the following:

— how to identify the distractors used in the test that tricked the student into making mistakes and if a so-called equivalent form will be used in a second test, teach the students how to identify the distractors used in the new form;

490

— teach students which choices were wrong choices in the test and if a so-called equivalent form will be used in a second test, teach them which choices are wrong in the new form; and/or

— teach the content of the concept which the missed test items were concerned with but be careful not to teach a behavior other than identification and discrimination and don't teach identification too well because the student may become a victim of *selective perception* and fall into the trap of the distractors.

Obviously, if a teacher were actually to teach one or more of the above, the students would score too high on a subsequent test which would make the test invalid because the results would no longer fit the curve and would also make the individual test items invalid because they no longer discriminate. In addition, since the *objective* type test items rarely have a high behavioral correlation with course objectives (either GO's and/or SO's — listed or implied by the course description), the teaching of the behaviors necessary to have high achievement in the tests becomes wasted effort on the part of both teacher and learner. The time and effort would have been much better spent teaching, learning, and testing for the achievement of the real objectives of the course.

Some teachers claim that they want to use the multiple-choice test item because it teaches the student how to make decisions (discussed in more detail on pages 151-154, Volume I). As pointed out earlier, the multiple-choice test item only tests for one step in the decision-making process, that of making a choice. The problem is that the choice the students pick is not really their choice, because at the beginning of almost every multiple-choice test is the statement, *pick the best answer.* According to who? According to the teacher or whoever made up the test. Certainly it is not the best answer according to each student. Consequently, students who consistently do well on multiple-choice tests may not be the ones who have studied the subject matter content the most, they are probably the ones who have learned to *out psych* the teacher or the author of the tests. Everyone who has ever been a student has answered multiple-choice test items in which, depending on the student's point-of-view, two or more of the answers could be right. But according to the teacher's grading key or the grading machine, there is only one right answer. If a teacher is trying to teach decision-making, at least the students should have the opportunity to select a choice they think is right and then to defend it.

The most amazing thing about many teachers who want to use *objective* type tests because they can be graded or scored in minutes is that they will spend hours and perhaps days preparing the multiple-

491

choice test items according to the criteria taught in most test and measurement courses which in turn make the items inappropriate to test for the achievement of any general, specified, and/or implied course objectives. It would be so much easier, if once a teacher has specific objectives, to make up the matching test items by just a slight change of words and then the hours or days can be spent diagnosing the students learning problems rather than making up trick test items that are irrelevant.

There are two primary reasons why most teachers want to grade or score tests in a hurry. First, because of the number of students taking a test, if a teacher really tested the students the way they should be tested, the teacher would probably be swamped with work. This problem is caused by the lock-stepping of learning in which all students start and stop learning at the same times. Under the approach described in this series where individual differences in *rate of learning* are recognized, it would be a rare event to have all students ready for the same test at the same time. When students are allowed to progress at their own pace, only a few students at any one time are ready for a test. Under these conditions a teacher can use test items whose format really test for the achievement of the desired objectives of the course and can take the time to diagnose the results and prescribe appropriate subsequent learning activities for the test items which were missed. A second reason why most teachers may want to be able to score tests in a hurry is that many schools, colleges, and universities require final examinations and then also require that the grades be turned in within 24-48 hours after the tests are given. Again, when students are progressing at their own pace, there won't be that many students ready for a final examination during that last week. Many students will have already completed the course and taken the final examination before the last week. If a teacher is a little worried about *bucking* the system, remember that although a final examination is required, nothing is usually specified as to what has to be tested during that time. If a teacher is allowing the students to progress at their own pace, the time set aside for a final examination could very well be used to give the affective domain tests concerning attitudes, values, and beliefs which may have been changed one way or another during the course.

NOTE: Remember that tests concerning affective objectives have to be given on a pretest and posttest basis, anonymously, and whatever the scores are, they cannot be used to grade the students.

There are several different versions of this multiple-choice format; one teacher may be interested in which one of four or five choices does not complete the statement acceptably. Another teacher may wish to know which one or more statements will complete the statement correctly, or another teacher may wish the student to identify none of the given statements as correct, or that all of them could be correct. The choice of which multiple-choice format to use is not the problem. The problem is, should I even be using a multiple-choice format? Is the learner behavior of *discrimination* the behavior which I am really concerned about? In many of the sciences where the discrimination behavior may be important, it is not important with reference to the verbal discrimination, but it is very important in reference to visual discrimination, in which the learner is exposed to multiple-choice photographs or diagrams in which he chooses the correct response from a visual mode, rather than a verbal mode, which is more in keeping with the desired learning objectives of the course.

It is also important to remember that the answering of objective type test items involves the element of chance. In multiple-choice items, the percentage chance of guessing the right answer is dependent upon the number of choices available. For example when there are four choices and one is correct, the student has a 25 percent chance of guessing the right answer. When there are five choices, the student has a 20 percent chance of guessing the right answer. Since in most traditional testing the major purpose is to get a grade or a score rather than teaching, elaborate proposals for scoring have been designed to minimize the chance factor. The extra effort would have been better spent in teaching.

True-false test items are really just two choice multiple choice test items and all of the problems with multiple choice test items apply to true-false test items. In addition, in true-false items, there is a fifty percent chance of guessing the right answer and by following a few simple rules, most students can get a passing score and they don't have to study at all.

1) If the true-false item is an absolute — all of, none of, etc. — chances are good that the item is false.

2) If the true-false item includes words like — few of, several of, etc. — chances are good that the item is true.

3) If the student flips a coin on the rest, chance will probably give him or her a passing score.

Matching test items, although still a multiple choice item (with many choices) do fit some specific objectives as long as the desired behavior is a *matching* behavior. The problem is that rarely do teachers include the words and/or phrases that are to be matched in the specification of the objective. The matching behavior in matching test items, if really desired, is nothing but rote memory. By not letting the students see the words and/or phrases to be matched until the time to take the test, it is possible to trick students into missing some of the items. Particularly if the teacher picks words or phrases which are very similar. As with regular multiple-choice, the use of *distractors* in matching test items can raise or lower the scores regardless of what students actually know.

Under certain circumstances, there are three forms of the multiple choice question which would be acceptable.

(1) As a in-between step in developing the decision-making behavior, it could be reasonable to provide the learner with the realistic alternate choices. If this is the case, then the following conditions should be met:

   (a) detractors are not mixed into the choices to affect the students choice one way or the other;

   (b) the number of choices depend on the conditions in the real world, it could be any number but it would be rare that all of most of these multiple-choice items would have the same number of choices;

   (c) after the student has selected a choice, the student should be asked to defend his choice according to the logic and principles of the subject matter being tested;

   (d) in the grading or scoring of the item, more emphasis is placed on the evaluation of the defense of the choice rather than on the choice itself; and

   (e) before the course is over, the student is weaned from this crutch in decision-making and is asked to carry out each of the six steps in the decision-making process as described earlier on pages 151-154, Volume I.

(2) The second form is when the objective concerns the student learning approximations rather than exact facts. This form is only acceptable under the following conditions:

   (a) the choices collectively include the total population of choices;

   (b) detractors are not mixed into the choices to affect the students choice one way or the other; and

   (c) each choice is equal to each of the other choices. An example of this type of item:

   > The percentage of space taken up by advertising in the average issue of Newsweek is
   >
   > a—0-25%   b—26-50%   c—51-75%   d—76-100%

(3) The third form is when the item is asking for an opinion (affective domain) and is acceptable under the following conditions:

(a) any choice could be the right answer;

(b) the correctness of an answer is determined by whichever choice the student picks;

(c) the item is clearly labeled as an opinion item;

(d) detractors are not mixed into the choices to affect the students choice one way or the other; and

(e) as an affective domain test item, any scoring or grading is used primarily to evaluate the design of the environment affecting or developing the opinion rather than used to evaluate the student.

An example of this type of item:

If a student's essay was given to a group of teachers and each of them was to grade the essay independently, the grades would be:

a—	all the same	b—	mostly different
b—	mostly the same	d—	all different

c. ROTE MEMORY AND THINKING TEST ITEMS

Rote memory objectives and test items are looked on usually as being relatively easy to learn and once memorized, they are considered to involve a minimum of mental activity in the testing situation. As such, most educators look on rote memory objectives and test items as low level and generally not very desirable.

Every instructional unit I have developed, critiqued, or even looked at involves some rote memory objectives and corresponding rote memory test items. It is a mistake to look on rote memory objectives and test items as a single level concept. There are many very easy rote memory items (facts, names, dates, etc.), there are many very difficult rote memory items (complex processes) and there are rote memory items that represent all levels of difficulty between these two extremes. In addition to there being rote memory items of varying levels of difficulty and complexity, the learners that have to rote memorize these items represent wide variations in their ability to memorize.

NOTE: Remember, the ability to memorize is a learned behavior and as such, it can be taught and it can be learned. Generally, the behavior itself is rarely taught, but it is frequently tested. Rote memory test items are not only testing for the remembering of certain items they are also testing the ability of the student to rote memorize.

The negative aspect of rote memory objectives and corresponding rote memory test items is that if the learner doesn't retrieve what was memorized from his memory often enough, the learner may forget how to retrieve it. The positive aspect of rote memory objectives and corresponding rote memory test items is that for each one there is or should be almost an automatic higher level objective and corresponding test items concerning what the student will do with whatever was memorized (a thinking objective). If it is not possible to think of anything that can be done with the memorized item, maybe it is of such low value that it is not worth memorizing and should be dropped. For example, in many fields the students are asked to memorize certain processes and procedures which are generally rote memorized such as the making of a bed in nursing instruction. The thinking objective in this case would concern the adaptation of the standard procedure to the individual needs of each patient.

First Objective

The student will be able to list the 12 (or more) steps in the making of a bed.

Second Objective

The student will be able to perform the 12 (or more) steps in the making of a bed in a simulated clinical situation (the criteria for evaluating the quality of the performance of each step should also be included).

Third Objective (from the first objective)

Given a list of 20 common patient problems which would affect the bed making procedure, the student will be able to identify which steps in the bed making procedure will have to be changed to accomodate the patient's problem, describe the change to be made, and then defend the change in terms of the patient's problem and one or more principles of nursing practice.

Fourth Objective (from the second objective)

Given the patient records in a certain clinical area, the student will be able to identify which patients have problems which will affect the bed making procedure, will identify which steps have to be changed to accomodate the patient's problem, will defend each change in terms of the patient's problem and one or more principles of nursing practice, and then will perform the bed making procedure in accordance with the identified changes (the criteria for evaluating the quality of the performance of each step should also be included).

Because there is a tendency among some readers to believe that the concept of developing thinking objectives from rote memory objectives is only useful in career or vocational areas (because of the above example), I would like to include another example in the area of literature.

First Objective

The student will be able to list the six (more or less) steps in preparing a literary critique (or analysis).

Second Objective

Given one of the following examples of literature containing all of the literary aspects necessary to prepare a complete literary critique, the student will be able to prepare a literary critique according to the six (or whatever number) of steps. (The criteria for evaluating the quality of each step would have to be included. In addition, a list of literary examples would be provided which are selected because the literary aspects to be critiqued are very obvious.)

The emphasis in this objective is on the learning of the preparation of the literary critique.

Third Objective

Given an example from each of the following forms of literature, the student will identify which of the steps in the preparation of a literary critique will be affected by that particular form of literature (if any) describe the changes to be made, defend the changes in terms of the characteristics of that particular form of literature, and then prepare the literary critique. (The criteria for evaluating the quality of each step would have to be included. In addition, the student should be given a list of literary works representing each of the various forms of literature which are selected because the literary aspects to be critiqued are very obvious.)

The emphasis in this objective is in the learning of the adaptation of the standard literary critique format to different forms of literature.

Fourth Objective

Given an example from each of the levels of increasing difficulty within each of the following forms of literature, the student will

497

prepare a literary critique in accordance with the six steps learned in the second objective and reflect the adaptations learned in the third objective. (Again, the criteria for evaluating the quality of each step would have to be included. In addition, the student should be given lists of literary works which are first, divided into sub-lists representing each of the various forms of literature and second, divided into sub-sub-lists representing a sequence of increasing difficulty in identifying the elements in the literary work necessary to prepare a literary critique.)

The emphasis in this objective is on the learning of how to identify and extract the information necessary to prepare a literary critique from literary works which represent the varied levels of ambiguity and obscurity found in literature.

Problem solving objectives and test items are usually process objectives in which the process is rote memorized and the adaptations to real life situations represent thinking objectives and test items. As with other rote memory objectives and test items, there is great variation in complexity from very simple problems to very complex problems.

In most courses, the majority of test items being used presently are in reality just rote memory items. By not letting the students know exactly what should be rote memorized until the students are in the testing situation, by not allowing the students extra chances to take the tests, and by hiding the rote memory items in various forms of the so-called *objective* type tests with its distractors designed to trick students, it is possible to obtain variations in student achievement in teaching-learning situations in which if handled in an honest and straight forward manner could easily end up with 90 percent or more of the students achieving 100 percent of the objective and test items.

In rote memory tests concerning facts, names, dates, etc., for each objective there will be only one test item and 100 percent achievement of the objectives will also be 100 percent achivement of the test items. In tests concerning processes, it is common to use multiple test items to test the students ability to use the various processes. In testing for the achievement of 100 percent of process objectives, the student may only have to achieve 80-90 percent of the test items (depending upon the quality control demands of the teacher).

Once objectives and test items are identified as rote memory items and differentiated from process of thinking test items, teachers should divide their testing situations into two parts. The first part would be the testing of the rote memory items and the students would have to achieve 100 percent of these objectives and test items before going on to the next part. During the rote memory part of the testing, no notes or references should be allowed. However, once the student has shown that he or she is able to rote memorize whatever the teacher wanted, during the second part of the testing situation, the thinking part, students should be allowed any notes or references they want. Thinking can not be copied from notes or references and after all, in the world, people frequently use references in making decisions and solving problems. Any time a teacher is worried about the students cheating by copying answers from notes or other sources of reference, chances are very good that what the teacher is testing for is the achievement of rote memory objectives rather than the achievement of thinking objectives.

d. THE BEST TYPE OF TEST ITEMS

In almost every Seminar that I have conducted for teachers, the question arises, *What is the best type of test item?* In order to answer that question, I usually ask the question, *What is it you are trying to evaluate?* The best type of test item is that item that is measuring exactly what you want students to learn. This of course assumes that the purpose of instruction is learning. Under the traditional approach to education where the objectives or learning is not specified, than the function of testing can be about anything the evaluator wants. Frequently under the traditional approach the purpose of testing is to spread the students achievement out on some sort of curve. As such, an important criterion for use of a test item is whether or not the item discriminates between the students taking the test. Whether or not an item is important to learn is not even a consideration.

I can readily agree with the criteria of discrimination in terms of measuring attitudes, values, and beliefs in the affective domain because it wouldn't make sense to use test items that were answered in the same manner by those who are for a concept and those who are against the same concept. In identifying which items are good discriminators, attitude measurement items are tried out (or should be) on samples of people who actually have those attitudes and samples of people who don't have those attitudes.

In keeping with the common problem of the traditional educator in treating all three domains of learning the same, criteria useful in selecting test items in the affective domain are assumed to also be useful for selecting test items in the cognitive and sensory domains. If the same procedures were used, it might be true in this case. In other words, if items used in the cognitive and sensory domains were selected on the basis of discriminating between samples of people who had already achieved *what was wanted* and samples of people who hadn't achieved *what was wanted*, then these items would both be important and discriminating. But since few schools have identified *what was wanted*, their selection process is based only on items that discriminate regardless of whether or not the items are important and almost regardless of what the students have learned. The trying out of test items is to see whether or not the results fit the desired curve of results. No attempt is made to identify samples of students who have or haven't learned *what was wanted*.

The traditional emphasis in the cognitive and sensory areas is on the test and the results of the test relative to the group, whereas the system's emphasis is on learning and the achievement of the individual relative to the objectives of the instructional unit.

In developing the best type of test item (one that measures a specific objective), special care should be taken in identifying the real stimulus for the behavioral response asked of the students. It is very common to find courses that are highly visual that write verbal objectives and test items. For example, most science courses are highly visual and one of the major functions of the laboratory sessions, demonstrations, films, etc. is to help the students develop the eyes of the professional, yet, most science objectives and tests are verbal. As a rule, whenever a teacher uses audio-visual experiences in the learning environment because he or she thinks they are important, then it should also be just as important to have objectives and test items involving the audio and/or visual experiences.

In a similar manner, if a teacher believes that group learning experiences are important, then it should be important enough to identify what should be learned in the group experiences and to set up an evaluation situation which will measure whether or not the group learning objectives have been learned.

NOTE: In a situation where there is individual continuous progress, it is still possible to have group learning objectives. Decide where the group learning objective fits in the sequence of learning and then whenever enough students (four to eight) complete the prerequisite objectives they can work on the group objective. If possible, the students in the group who finish the prerequisite objectives early should be allowed to continue on learning the individual objectives until enough other students have achieved the prerequisite objectives in order to have the group learning event.

e. FUNCTIONS (PURPOSES) OF TESTING

Traditionally, the function of formal tests and examinations is to arrive at some score or grade and since the traditional philosophy is that individual student differences are reflected in these scores, the design of the test is to spread students out on a curve which supposedly represents a *normal* distribution of the students abilities (limits). Whole courses are offered and many textbooks have been written on the methods and techniques of manipulating the test items in tests to get predetermined results and then the other half of the courses and textbooks are devoted to statistical gymnastics and interpretations of the predetermined data. The major emphasis in this traditional approach is on the manipulation of the tests and resulting data almost regardless of whether or not the tests are measuring anything important to learn and whether or not the students have really learned what is important. The traditional approach to testing also assumes that the tests are measuring *limits* of learning ability so very little effort, if any, is directed towards helping students learn what they missed on the tests.

NOTE: It is important to point out that under conditions where a *normal curve* of grades is what is expected and considered desirable, teachers will actually avoid being to good at teaching (helping students learn) because if too many of the students had success, the results would not fit a curve and the teacher would be suspected of having an easy course, of falsely reporting the results, or worst of all — of teaching to the test (a disaster under the traditional approach because the students learn and consequently ruin the expected curve of results).

Of interest, in the traditional approach, informal evaluation based on observations of students and conversations with students is not so restricted to a curve of results as is found in the formal testing procedures. Because no records are kept of informal evaluation, there is no pressure on the teacher to adjust the results to fit some predetermined curve. As a result, informal evaluation is frequently accompanied by teaching activities aimed at helping the student learn more of whatever the evaluation indicated the student was missing or had not learned.

From a systems point of view, there are three functions of evaluation: guidelines for teaching and learning; measurement of where the student is relative to what should be learned; and verification of the student's mastery of what should be learned. The same test can be used for all three functions. If there is a very high or complete correlation between the SO's and test items, then in giving the students a list of SO's or a copy of the unit or course tests at the beginning of an instructional unit or course, these serve as guidelines for what the students should be learning and what the teacher should be teaching.

Given that the tests represent what students should be learning, the tests can be taken by the student to find out where the student is intellectually. Under the measurement concept, the emphasis in the scoring of the test is to identify which test items and related objectives the student does not know in order to set up subsequent instructional activities such that the student can learn what was missed.

Under the mastery function, it is assumed that the student has already learned all of the SO's, but in order to avoid problems of cumulative ignorance, the tests are administered to verify that in fact the student has actually learned 100 percent of the SO's. In case the results indicate that the student missed some of the test items and SO's, then the measurement function automatically applies and the student is given the necessary instructional environment to learn what was missed.

In essence, all testing under the systems point of view is diagnostic in nature within which it is assumed that instead of just recording the results of scores of the tests and go on to the next unit as is done traditionally, the teacher is going to do something about helping each student learn 100 percent of whatever it is the students should be learning (whatever is missed in the tests).

f. FORMATIVE VS. SUMMATIVE TESTING

As with many educational innovations where the major differences tend to be in terminology only rather than in action, the use of the terms *formative* and *summative* evaluation have been introduced into education with little effect except to introduce *mod* terminology in reference to traditional concepts.

Formative evaluation is supposed to refer to the developmental phase of the student, of the instructional materials, and/or of the tests to be used in summative evaluation. The use of the results of formative evaluation as feedback or as diagnostic information is in keeping with the systems concept *IF* the teacher actually teaches the students whatever they missed such that the students eventually learn 100 percent of the SO's. However, if the results of formative evaluation are used to adjust test items so they are more or less discriminatory (to spread students' scores over a curve), then this version of formative evaluation is not in keeping with the system's concept.

If the feedback in formative evaluation is used to evaluate instructional materials and to make changes such that more students will learn more from the materials, this version of formative evaluation would be in keeping with the system's concept.

If formative evaluation is primarily diagnostic, then it is critical that the test items have a high correlation with the unit or course SO's. There is absolutely no place for the so-called *objective type* test items (multiple-choice, true-false, and matching) in formative tests because they have low correlation with any SO's and also, the feedback information is practically useless. Given a student missed a particular multiple choice test item, how does that feedback help the teacher? Did the student miss the item because he or she did not know it or because the distractors led the student to select one or more of the wrong choices. In teaching the students what they missed, should the teacher not only teach which choice is the right one and why it is the right choice but also which choices are wrong and why they are wrong? Should the teacher also be honest and point out the distractors that were designed to trick the students? Personally, even if there was a SO that matched a multiple-choice test item, I think it is a waste of time for the students and teacher to spend time to learn about contrived wrong choices when there are so many students that are having trouble learning the right choices. The presence of *objective type* test items (multiple-choice, true-false, and matching) in formative tests is an indication of low correlation between SO's and test items, of a lack of any SO's, of an ineffective and inefficient teaching-learning situation, and/or of the presence of designed trickery and dishonesty.

Summative evaluation is primarily looked on as an *end of course* type evaluation and is generally used to assign grades or to certify acquisition of skills. Standardized tests are considered to be a type of summative evaluation. As with formative evaluation, any summative evaluation that uses the so-called *objective type* test items (multiple choice, true-false, and matching) is actually useless because the scores do not relate to any SO's with a high correlation and as such are meaningless as far as certifying any level of skill achievement. Because summative evaluation supposedly evaluates the achievement of multiple objectives, a single score of anything less than 100 percent is even more meaningless as far as communicating any level of achievement. Identical scores of less than 100 percent achieved by two or more students in summative evaluation can in actuality represent a variety of results. (See pages 360-365 on 100 percent of objectives vs. 100 percent of test items). For example, the standardized national test given to nurses to supposedly certify that they have achieved minimum safety standards for the nurse and patients, has about 900 points and they are practically all multiple-choice. First of all, none of these test items match any specific objective I have ever seen in nursing instruction. Second, since the test supposedly tests for the achievement of multiple skills and knowledge, what does a score of 500 mean? Surely if the nursing student missed 400 points, this indicates that the student must have missed achieving some skills and knowledge. If the items missed represented a duplication of the items the student got correct, then the potential of danger to the nurse and future patients is minimized. However, if the items missed represent a lack of achievement of 44 percent of the skills and knowledge considered to be minimum safety standards for the nurse and patients, then the potential of danger to the nurse and future patients is very high. In recognizing that the standardized national test for nurses is meaningless, one might be tempted to view the meaninglessness as a deliverance from the danger in letting nurses who had scores of less than 100 percent go out and practice nursing. The problem is that since the achievement of the real critical skills and knowledge has not been evaluated, no one really knows how dangerous the situation is.

NOTE: This same problem exists in all professional areas in which the summative evaluation has low correlation with the SO's of the curriculum and is primarily made up of the so-called *objective type* test items.

A second and very serious humanitarian problem with these meaningless summative evaluations is that thousands of students who have spent years studying to be a professional have failed these tests and have not been permitted to practice. The mental and spiritual agony caused by failing to pass these meaningless tests is unmeasurable and also indefensible.

Formative and summative evaluation are generally considered to be related in that formative tests might be thought of as the unit tests in a course and the summative tests might be thought of as the midterm and final examinations of a course. However, the basic philosophy of the two do not match. If formative evaluation is really diagnostic in identifying what students did not learn such that teachers can then teach it, then formative evaluation is essentially mastery oriented. If summative evaluation is really equated to normative testing, then summative evaluation is essentially curve (achievement) oriented. Given this conflict in orientation, if the use of formative evaluation was successful and most or all of the students learned all of the SO's of a course, then the subsequent summative evaluation could not show a curve of results unless the summative evaluation tested for the achievement of hidden or nonexistent SO's and/or utilized the traditional trickery of distractors. If the summative evaluation was honest and represented in reality a curve achievement of the SO's of a course, then this would have indicated an ineffective use of formative evaluation because the students did not achieve mastery of the SO's of the course. In other words, given the basic conflict of orientation or philosophy, it is impossible to have effective formative and summative evaluation simultaneously in the same course.

Summative evaluation that has a high correlation with course SO's and is designed to identify achievement of critical skills and knowledge (mastery oriented) rather than being designed to give a predetermined curve of results could be very useful in instruction and could exist effectively with formative evaluation which is also mastery oriented.

g. CRITERION VS. NORMATIVE TESTING

In many ways, the discussion of the differences between criterion referenced tests (CRT) and norm referenced tests (NRT) is similar to the discussion of the differences between formative tests and summative tests except that the differences are much greater. The ideal formative test should really be the same as the ideal criterion referenced test (CRT) in that both are concerned about mastery and a high correlation between SO's and test items. The ideal summative test which is defined in terms of end-of-course SO's would also be a criterion referenced test (CRT). However, the summative test which is defined in terms of its ability to discriminate between students who have completed a course or its ability to discriminate between groups who used different treatments (pathways, methods, etc.) to complete a course is much more a norm referenced test (NRT) than a criterion referenced test (CRT). In other words, whereas formative tests are almost always criterion referenced tests (CRT), summative tests can be either CRT or NRT depending upon its design.

Basically, criterion referenced tests are tests which are measuring a student's achievement with reference to a standard of learning under conditions where the standard of learning is further defined as a list of one or more SO's concerning intellectual and sensory skills and emotional tendencies.

Basically, normative or norm referenced tests are tests which are measuring a student's achievement with reference to a standard of achievement under conditions where the standard of achievement is further defined in terms of a predetermined curve of achievement scores on that particular test of a representative sample of students at the local, district, state, regional, or national levels.

Probably the best way to differentiate between criterion referenced tests (CRT) and norm referenced tests (NRT) is to list the multitude of applicable factors and then identify the characteristics of CRT and NRT with reference to each factor.

(a)   Basic philosophy of the learning ability of students.

   CRT — all students can achieve the required criterion if the teachers will recognize individual differences and identify and solve the students' learning problems.

   NRT — There is a normal distribution of intelligence and ability (limits of learning) among students and nothing can be done about these differences.

(b)   Basic assumption of the test with reference to unit or course content

   CRT — There are some specific things in every unit and course that every student taking the course must learn in order to have success in the course and not to develop cumulative ignorance for subsequent units or courses.

505

Specific unit or course objectives are a critical prerequisite.

NRT — There is no one thing in any unit or course that should be learned by every student. Random achievement at or above a minimum level is sufficient where the minimum level is defined in terms of the predetermined curve rather than in terms of the course content. General objectives are acceptable, but not necessary.

(c)   Basic purpose of the test.

CRT — To identify or diagnose what a student does not know or has not achieved in order to design subsequent instructional activities.

NRT — To identify how a student compares in achievement on a given test in reference to how his classmates achieved on the same test or on how a group of students compares in achievement on a given test in reference to how other groups achieved on that test.

(d)   Relationship between course objectives and test items.

CRT — High or perfect correlation between SO's and test items with reference to the topics (nouns) and desired behaviors (verbs).

NRT — Since objectives are not even necessary, the correlation between any existing general objectives and the test items is purely chance or less with reference to the *behavior* being tested. There could be a better than chance correlation in reference to the *content or nouns* in any general objectives and in the test items.

(e)   In order to change the results of the tests

CRT — Given the high correlation between SO's and test items, the only way to change the results is to manipulate student learning by solving learning problems of the students.

NRT — By eliminating the low or nondiscriminating test items and by manipulating the distractors in the test items, almost any distribution of scores can be achieved by the test maker almost regardless of what the students taking the test have achieved.

(f)   Possibility of being part of a science.

CRT — Given that a minimum level of achievement is established, the efforts of the instructor are concentrated on
manipulating the environment in order to bring about
the mastery level of learning. Since learning is the
emphasis and is also a natural phenomenon, the use of
CRT can be part of a science of instruction.

NRT — Given that achieving the predetermined curve is the
major emphasis, the efforts of the test maker is to
manipulate the test items until the desired curve of
results is achieved. Since the desired curve is determined by man and as such is not a natural phenomenon,
the use of NRT can not be a part of a science of
instruction.

(g)   Definition of a *good* test item.

CRT — A *good* test item is one that tests for the achievement
of an important objective with a perfect correlation
between the test item and the objective with reference
to the content and behavior specified in each.

NRT — A *good* test item is one that 50 percent of the students
miss which makes it a good discriminator (the correlation between the test item and any objectives is not a
relevant concept.)

(h)   What would be considered *good* results in the testing situation.

CRT — A *good* situation is when all of the students tested have
achieved 100 percent of all the test items and SO's.

NRT — A *good* situation is when the results of the test fit the
predetermined curve of results (usually a normal
curve).

(i)   Value of having SO's

CRT — Without SO's, it would be impossible to make a CRT.

NRT — With SO's, it would be very difficult to make a NRT
because students would know what they are supposed
to learn and enough would learn it so the possibility of
getting a normal curve of results would be minimized.

(j)   Validation of the test.

CRT — Validity is in terms of the correlation between the SO's
and the test items.

507

NRT — Validity is when the results of using the test fits the predtermined curve the test was designed to achieve.

(k)   Honesty between the teacher and students.

CRT — Emphasis is on openness and honesty and both the teacher and the students know what should be learned (the SO's) and what is going to be on the test (the test items). The situation eliminates or at least minimizes the tendency to cheat.

NRT — Emphasis is on deception (distractors) and secretiveness and the student rarely, if ever, knows what is on a test. In district, state, regional, and national tests, even the teacher does not know what is on the tests. The situation develops the tendency to cheat.

(l)   The teacher's role with reference to the test.

CRT — The teacher recognizes individual differences in learning and uses multiple pathways in helping all students learn all of the SO's. The teacher is supposed to teach the SO's and what is in the test. The teacher identifies and solves student learning problems (diagnoses and prescribes).

NRT — The teacher presents course content to the average student (in order to get a normal curve of achievement) and ignores individual differences in learning. It is considered bad if a teacher teaches what is on the test because it would be too easy for the students to learn enough to ruin the validity of the test (would not result in the predetermined curve.) Since the students are already different, the best way to maintain these differences is to avoid teaching (defined as helping students learn).

(m)   The uses of the students' scores on the tests.

CRT — Since the tests are looked on as diagnostic when given during a unit or course, the scores themselves are not relevant or useful. What is important is to identify which SO's the students missed so the teacher knows what to teach or prescribe in subsequent learning activities. When the CRT tests are given at the end of a unit or course, they should be mastery tests in which all test, more distractors are put into the test.

students taking the tests should achieve 100 percent of the SO's and consequently, the scores again are not important because everyone gets the same score.

NRT — Depending upon the purpose of the test, the scores could be used to assign letter grades, to assign *apparent I.Q. scores*, as guidelines for placement into certain courses, for ranking or ordering students, for predicting success in subsequent courses, to indicate achievement levels, to evaluate the performance of teachers, to evaluate curriculum programs, to evaluate educational innovations, etc.

> NOTE: Of interest is that the NRT are used to evaluate curriculum achievement, yet the SO's of the curriculum are not actually a basis for the development of the NRT. This relationship makes about as much sense as using a car's performance on miles per gallon of gas as compared to some curve of performance of a number of cars on this factor (miles per gallon of gas) to predict how fast the car can go, what it costs, how much oil it uses, how much it weighs, etc.

(n) Value of test in a situation where selectivity is the primary purpose.

CRT — In using this type of test in the selection process, it is critical that the test items have a high correlation with the SO's of the task, role, position, etc., to be performed by the one or ones selected. In that way, the top ones on the test will also be the top ones on the job. In order to increase the selectivity of the test, it is necessary to have a more detailed task analysis and to expand the test to cover more of the details. Also, in addition to demanding high achievement of the SO's, the percentage achievement of the test items could be increased.

NRT — These tests are frequently used for selecting purposes. The major problem is that since there is usually very low correlation between the SO's of the job or task analysis and the test items in the test, the top one or ones in the test may or may not be the top one or ones on the job. In order to increase the selectivity of the test, more distractors are put into the test.

(o)   Variability in scores.

CRT — Since the goal is to have all students learn all of the SO's of the unit or course, the less variability in scores at the high end, the more successful the instructional materials are for the most students. This also means that there are fewer individual learning problems to be solved.

NRT — Since the goal is to have a curve or a spread of student scores, test items that do not discriminate or increase variability are dropped from the test. As the variability in scores decreases, the amount of work necessary to increase variability increases.

(p)   Validity and Reliability of tests.

CRT — Since validity of the CRT refers to the behavioral and content correlation between the SO's and the test items, then a valid CRT would have to have high reliability if defined in terms of the same person getting the same scores in different forms of the same test. The SO's would be the same, so the behavior and content measured by the test items in alternate forms of the same CRT would also be the same even though the test items might be different (rote memory items of facts, names, dates, etc. would be exactly the same in alternate forms).

NRT — Validity and realibility are not related. A NRT is considered valid when the actual results of trying out the test on a sample of the intended population gives the results which it was designed to give. A NRT is considered reliable when the same person gets about the same score on different forms of the same test or the same people's scores rank in about the same order in similar tests.

> NOTE: Almost all factors considered important in developing a NRT are intrinsic and are primarily concerned with internal relationships in the test whereas in developing a CRT, the important factors are extrinsic and are primarily concerned with external relationships.

(q)   Importance of what is being tested.

     CRT — Since the SO's are identified and justified on the basis of being important and the test items of the CRT are based on the SO's then it can be assumed that what a CRT is testing for is important.

     NRT — Since the test items are not related to SO's and in most cases even GO's and the most important criteria for selection of an item is its ability to discriminate and its ease of scoring rather than its importance, then it can be assumed that what a NRT is testing for is of doubtful importance.

(r)   The significance of changes in scores over time.

     CRT — When the socres of an individual or the average scores go up or down, the instructor, administrator, students, parents, etc., know that the learning of the SO's is increasing or decreasing in a direct relationship.

     NRT — In using a curve relationship centered around an average student, classroom, school, etc., in order for one to go above average, another one has to become below average regardless of whether or not there was any actual change. Because the NRT scores are always relative, the absolute average learning levels as might be measured on a CRT could be going up or down over a period of years and educators would never know it as long as there weren't changes in the ordering or ranking of the individuals, schools, etc., relative to the average.

(s)   Ability to identify whether or not schools and teachers *make a difference.*

     CRT — Since the CRT are related to what is important and the scores and the tests are absolute with reference to the SO's of units or courses, if the schools and/or teachers are making a difference in helping the students learn the SO's of the units or courses, these tests should be able to identify it.

     NRT — Since the NRT are not necessarily related to any unit or course SO's and since most NRT are referenced to a normal curve of results (normal probability curve) which reflects *chance*, it would be very difficult to identify any difference beyond *chance* or to be able to reject the null hypothesis.

The very existence of the concept of testing or evaluation assumes that whoever is doing the testing wants to know one or both of the following two areas of information:

— that *something* has occurred or is present at that particular point in time, and/or

— that *something* has not occurred or is not present at that particular point in time.

The *something* that has or has not occurred or is or is not present may be called a variety of names by different people, but from my point of view, I prefer to call it *learning*. An instructional unit, course, or program that is designed to bring about *learning* must therefore have *learning objectives*. Any evaluation of the *something* or *learning* that is supposed to occur has got to be related to the *learning objectives*. In other words, in instructional activities, the *only* type of evaluation acceptable are criterian referenced tests (CRT) defined in terms of being highly correlated to the learning objectives. In view of the 18 comparisons just reviewed, *there is no justifiable reason to use the traditional normative referenced tests in instructional activities primarily concerned with cognitive and sensory learning.*

Because of the traditions of decades of testing; because of the investment of time, energy, and dollars in many textbooks and courses devoted to it; because of the investment of time, energy, and dollars in the decades of educational research based on it; and because of the many companies and consultants whose livelihood depends on it; the use of the traditional normative referenced tests will probably drag on even if they are useless, inappropriate, and inhumane. (It is practically impossible to comprehend the totality of the damage that has been done to millions of people on the basis of the results of normative referenced tests.)

There are at least four aberrations of criterion referenced tests which indicate attempts to combine some of the characteristics of the traditional NRT with CRT. The first is a misinterpretation of the definition of CRT. Instead of thinking of the word criterion as referring to SO's, some educators have interpreted criterion as referring to a level of proficiency. For example, any test in which the student has to achieve 80 percent is thought by some to be a CRT regardless of whether or not the test items relate to any SO's. Although these tests may be *tests with a criterion for proficiency*, they are not the same as *criterion (SO's) referenced tests*. Another very common aberration is the use of the so-called *objective type* test items (multiple-choice, true-false, and matching) in a CRT. These test items may be very easy to grade, but since it is rare, if ever, to find a SO that matches one of these test items, any tests containing multiple choice or true-false test items can not be considered as a CRT. A third aberration is the use of a single score in reporting the results of a test which is evaluating the achievement of multiple SO's. A true CRT would have to be scored in such a way as to indicate the achievement of each SO. A recent and more subtle aberration are tests which claim to be developed from objectives (GO's) and are actually designed to have a high correlation in content between the GO's and the test items. The problem is that since the behavior in the GO is not specified, the behaviors asked for in the test items can be manipulated to give almost any results desired.

h. STANDARDIZED TESTS: A DESIGNED MIRAGE

A normative or norm referenced test which is used throughout a state, region, or the nation is frequently and possibly more often referred to as a *standardized* test. In many schools, and in particular in elementary and secondary schools, standardized tests are used in addition to the teacher-made tests, in an effort to evaluate the progress which students have made in particular courses. In some cases, the standardized tests are designed not only to evaluate students and particular courses, but are used to evaluate the total curriculum of a school, school district, or region. Standardized tests came into common usage primarily for the purpose of measuring a student's *intelligence.* For a long time, it was thought that these tests were very useful in indicating a person's ability to learn, and it was thought by most people that the results of these *intelligence* tests were true indicators of a person's ability to learn anything. Confidence in the results of standardized *intelligence* tests was supported by the fact that the scores in the tests remained rather constant over a period of years for the same person. During the past decade there have been a variety of programs which have been designed to help the person who has had trouble in learning. As a result, the individual student's scores on the *intelligence* tests may change over a period of time. In other words, as long as schools did not teach what *intelligence* tests tested, then the scores of individual students remained almost constant over a period of time. But, when schools make efforts to teach the behaviors which are tested in the *intelligence* tests, then the scores for the individual students do not remain constant.

Since standardized tests are normative or norm referenced tests, they both have the same characteristics, i.e., a good test item is usually considered to be one that about 50 percent of the students will not answer correctly (regardless of whether or not the test item is important or critical). Therefore, good tests consist of items which are primarily selected on the basis of their ability to discriminate between students; second, the test items are easy to grade or score; third, the items represent a variety of formats (multiple-choice, true-false, matching, etc.); fourth, the items represent a variety of difficulty (this helps to get results that fit a curve); and fifth, the items represent a *sample* of the total number of test items which could be used.[18]

The ease of grading or scoring is usually in reference to whether or not a test item can be scored by machine. This secondary criterion, ease of grading or scoring, usually limits most standardized tests to multiple-choice, true-false, or matching test items. In working with thousands of teachers concerning their objectives and tests, it is very unusual to find a multiple-choice test item which a teacher believes actually tests the behavior which he wants the student to exhibit.

The actual development of standardized tests generally consists of three steps: the development or collection of potential test items; the elimination of items which do not discriminate very well; and the validation of the remaining test items such that the results of using these items on a random group of students will fit some kind of curve. For example, see Figure 61.

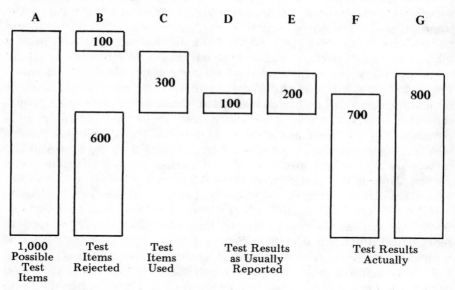

Figure 61 — Development of Standardized Tests and the Interpretation of the Results

[18]Of the thousands of teachers I have talked to, no one has been able to scientifically, rationally, and logically defend his or her *sampling* technique in arriving at the test items for the final examination. This is mainly because it is a guessing game or the *Big Gamble* in which the teacher guesses what he is going to test and the students try to guess what the teacher is going to test. If the guesses match, the students get good grades. If the guesses do not match the students may fail.

Column A in Figure 61 represents the first step of developing or collecting a thousand possible test items. These items could be supposedly testing students' achievement of a specific course or a sequence of courses or over a period of time the students' achievement of a total curriculum. Although the content or nouns in the items may have a high correlation with the content or nouns in the topics covered by the course or courses being evaluated, the most important criteria in the selection of these items are their ability to discriminate between students and are they easy to grade or score.

Column B represents the second step in which the thousand test items are tried out on representative samples of students in order to eliminate two categories of non-discriminating items: those items that 65 percent or more of the students in the sample got correct and those items that 35 percent or less of the students were able to get correct. These percentages are used when the predetermined curve is to be a normal or bell shaped curve. If the predetermined curve was to be skewed in the positive direction in order to show more positive results (a false condition of high achievement), then the upper and lower percentages for acceptability would be increased. If the predetermined curve was to be skewed in the negative direction in order to show negative results, (a false condition of low achievement) then the upper and lower percentages for acceptability would be decreased. In other words, the results of the test are determined ahead of time. In this particular example, I am indicating that 600 of the 1000 items were eliminated because too many students answered them correctly and 100 of the items were eliminated because not enough students were able to answer them. Consequently, these two groups of items were eliminated from the potential standardized test because they did not discriminate between students.

Column C represents the remaining 300 test items which are now refined such that the results of using these items on any sample of students fits the desired curve. This refinement is accomplsihed by changes in the wording in the test items such that a few more students will get it wrong or a few more students will get it correct. The very process of refining the test items in order to get a certain percentage of students who can answer them correctly is proof that the items are very subjective. Remember, in the case of a multiple-choice item, a good test item writer can hold the stem and the correct choice constant and by varying the wording of the wrong choices, the writer can get almost any percentage of students to get the item correct or to miss the item practically regardless of whether or not the students know the correct choice.

Columns D and E in Figure 61 indicate possible test results when this hypothetical standardized test is used with two students, two classes, two schools, two schools from two different school district, etc. In Column D, the student or students who took this test averaged only 100 test items answered correctly. In Column E the student or students who took this test had an average of 200 test items correct. Usually, the results of the use of this standardized test would be reported in such a way that the student or students represented in Column E have learned twice as much as the student or students represented by Column D, which has been the case in many instances in our country. Results of standardized tests have been used as the basis for millions of dollars in changes in curriculum materials and even in some instances the firing of superintendents, principlas, teachers, or even the replacement of some school board members. The results of the comparison of the two students, two schools, etc., as represented by Columns D and E are a mirage. Remember, the test items which are used are those which emaphsize discrimination between students, so the selection of test items exaggerate the differences and consequently the results of the test. The student or school represented by Column E is not twice as good or 100 percent better than the student or school represented by Column D. How about the 600 items in Column B which were eliminated because most or all of the students knew those items? A more realistic comparison of the two students or schools would be Columns F and G, which now only represent a 14 percent difference, rather than a 100 percent difference. In some standardized tests, the original population of test items could consist of thousands of items. As long as the makers of the test can eliminate the non-discriminating test items in order to magnify the differences, it would be possible for an apparent 100 percent difference in test scores to actually be only a few percent difference if the total original population of test items were used.

In reference to Columns A, B, and C, consider the following two questions:

> Column A — Remembering that the primary criterion for selection of items was that they discriminate and a secondary criterion that the test items are easy to grade or score, *what if very few of the test items represent important learning objectives?*

Most testing companies would try to insist that most or all of the original group of 1000 test items are important. Obviously, they would have to say that because if they said some of the items were not important then they could be asked why they are testing students for the achievement of non-important test items.

> Column B — Remembering that the criterion for elimination of the test items is based on the fact that too many students can answer the item, or not very many students can answer the

item, and since all of the test items are supposed to be important (according to the testing companies), *what if those items which were eliminated represent critical learning objectives?*

Surely, if all of the 1000 items are important and 700 of them are eliminated, some of those 700 must have been important. Representatives of test companies that prepare standardized tests insist that not many of the real important items are eliminated. In other words, out of the original 1000 test items, the remaining 300 which are used in the final test are also the most important in addition to being the best discriminators. If this was truly the situation, then the student who only got 100 test items right on the test should be taught the remaining 200 items and the student who got 200 test items right should be taught the remaining 100 items in order that they both can learn all 300 of the professed *important* items. If these tests actually tested for the achievement of identified important learning objectives, then teachers could teach the students what was on the tests and a good result would be when all students achieve 100 percent of what professional educators and test makers believe to be important. In actuality, the students would not be taught the items they missed because that would ruin the curve and invalidate the test. That is why standardized tests are hidden from teachers and students. This is also why testing companies and textbooks and courses on NRT have done such a good job convincing teachers that it is wrong to teach what is on a test. Yet these very tests are used to evaluate the teaching-learning situation. No wonder the research evidence indicates that schools and teachers do not make a difference and the results of *no difference* will continue until it becomes an acceptable teaching practice to teach whatever it is that *makes a difference.*

Robert L. Ebel, Vice President for General Programs, Educational Testing Service, has stated that:

Every important outcome of education can be measured. In order for an outcome of education to be important, it must make a difference. The behavior of a person who has more of a particular outcome must be observably different form that of a person who has less. Perhaps one can imagine some result of education which is so deeply personal that it does not ever affect in any way what he says or does, or how he spends his time. But it is difficult to find any grounds for arguing that such a well concealed achievement is important. To say that any important educational outcome is measurable is not to say that satisfactory methods of measurement now exist.

Ebel's last statement should be taken in the context of the traditional forms of educational measurement used by most commercial

517

testing companies wherein there are few if any SO's and the skills involved are skills in manipulating the test items to get the desired results rather than in the context of a learning system's approach to instruction wherein there are lots of SO's and the skills involved are skills in identifying what is wanted (the SO and test item) and skills in manipulating the learning environment such that the students learn all of the SO's.

(1) EXAMPLES OF HOW STANDARDIZED TESTS ARE FRAUDULENTLY AND/OR MISTAKENLY USED

The primary problem in the use of any form of evaluation is the recognition that there should be some relationship between the evaluation and what is being evaluated. This is the problem which I have referred to and discussed frequently and at length already in this chapter. It is such a critical problem and also such a common problem that I believe the redundancy is necessary. To repeat then, any form of student evaluation carries with it an assumption that the evaluation is testing for the achievement of some objective which may or may not be identified. When the evaluation is used with two or more groups of students (who have different teachers), the evaluation also carries with it an assumption that the teachers have agreed on some common objectives to be evaluated by the common evaluation.

Ideally, teachers should have lists of GO's and SO's to teach to and to use as a reference in making up any form of evaluation such that there is a perfect correlation between the SO's and the test items. Since the majority of teachers do not have lists of SO's to teach to and to make up tests from, the teaching activities, the evaluation activities, and what is *sort of wanted (GO's)* may or may not have any correlation. In the case of a common test used to evaluate the achievement of the teaching and learning in two or more classes with different teachers and where there is no common agreement of what should be evaluated (SO's), the results are really an indication of the correlation between the implied SO's of the common test and the implied SO's of the various teachers' teaching activities. For example, consider the following situation, the common evaluation (standardized test) was based on the achievement of 100 implied SO's (identified by looking at the test items) and two teachers each of whom implied in their teaching activities that they wanted their students to learn 100 SO's (identified by observing the teaching-learning situation) but only 30 of the implied SO's of one teacher matched the implied SO's of the common test and 60 of the implied SO's of the second teacher matched the implied SO's of the common test. The apparent results would tend to indicate that the first teacher's students were pretty low in achievement and most of them would probably fall into the lower tertile (one-third of the distribution of scores) whereas the second teacher's students would most likely fall into the second tertile and be considered much better than the first teacher's students. Depending on the curve built into the common test, the second teacher's students could be average (distributed around the high point of the curve) or they could also be considered below average if the average teacher using the common test had more than 60 of their implied SO's matching the implied SO's of the common test. The only way that the *real* results of the evaluation could be determined would be if the test makers and the teachers identified the implied SO's and compared them. In the absence of any identified commonality, the value of standardized tests is even further negated (in addition to the points brought out previously).

At a conference sponsored by Educational Testing Service in 1972 on testing problems, Henry Dyer, one of the speakers, suggested that the key problem was,

> How does one get the users of tests — especially those who use tests as instruments for determining educational policy — to know enough about the innards of the tests they are using to have some clear ideas of what the test scores are saying about what the children are learning and schools are teaching?

Dyer may or may not have realized it, but the *innards* of the tests are really the implied SO's. Once these SO's are known, then the test users and makers will *have some clear ideas of what the test scores are saying about what the children are learning and schools are teaching.*

Consider the use of proficiency examinations to test out of courses if a student can get a high enough score. The concept is one that I fully agree with IF the tests really test for the achievement of the important SO's of the courses as determined by the teachers of the courses. The CLEP (College Level Examination Program) tests were supposedly designed to do this. First of all, most of the test items were multiple choice test items which automatically reduces any possible correlation with any course SO's. Second, the use of multiple choice items indicates that the results or distribution of scores are already built into the tests such that certain percentages will pass and fail regardless of what the students actually know. Third, the development of the CLEP tests assumes that there is agreement among teachers of the courses as to what the students should be learning in the courses. Few of these teachers at the college level have specified what they want in their courses let alone share these SO's and agree on the importance of a common set of SO's. Of course, another way of looking at it (at least for the students who test out of having to take the courses), as long as the teachers do not really know what it is that students should be learning in their courses, neither the teacher nor the students will know

519

what or if they missed anything. For the unlucky students who failed the CLEP tests, whatever it was they did not know probably will not be taught to them in the course they have to take because of the low correlation between the tests and any desired course objectives (specified or implied by the teachers actions).

The only value of the ACT, SAT, or most other standardized college entrance examinations is that these tests are considered good predictors along with high school grades for success in college. Actually, these predictions are only good as long as the college teaching is carried on in a traditional manner where students have to guess what teachers want them to learn and to guess what they are going to be tested on. Students who have learned to *out-psych* or *out guess* their teachers in high school and to *out guess* the multiple *guess* test items in the college entrance examinations will probably be pretty good at *out guessing* their college teachers. Once teachers become honest and straight forward and cut out the guessing games, high school grades and college entrance examinations scores will no longer be good predictors of success in higher education.

An extremely critical use of *normed* or standardized tests are the so-called IQ tests. Being standardized in the traditional form, most of these tests suffer from the same problems as other standardized tests. In addition, given that there are many (Guilford claims 80) different learning variables, to test only one or even several learning variables and claim they represent a person's intelligence is to ignore individual differences. Even to test all possible learning variables and give some composite single score is not very meaningful because it does not indicate in which variables the person presently has high abilities and in which variables the person presently has low abilities. The biggest mistake of all so-called IQ tests is to assume that the scores of whatever abilities that are being measured represent *limits* of ability. In other words, these tests assume that abilities are static and as such are all or almost all due to genetic influences. What makes these tests so critical, particularly in view of their serious faults, is that the scores are used by teachers as a basis for the *self fulfilling prophecy* and are used by teachers and other educators for tracking purposes (college, vocational, retarded, etc.). The only value that these tests can have is if the scores are interpreted as follows:

Given the following test which is a measure of the following abilities,--------, -------- etc., *(name of student)* was able to achieve on this date _____ the following scores:

Ability No. 1 *(items correct)* out of a possible *(total items)*
Ability No. 2 *(items correct)* out of a possible *(total items)*
ETC.

(The items in the tests would have to be selected because they measure the various dimensions of the ability and represent important aspects of each dimension rather than being selected because they are easy to grade, are good discriminators, and help get predetermined results.)

Another very important use of standardized tests is in educational research. Since a major portion of educational research is based on the results of standardized tests, the problems and faults with the tests reflect on the validity of the research. In addition, since most educational research in the cognitive areas that do not use standardized tests still uses primarily the *objective* type test items (multiple choice, true-false, and matching) which have the faults indicated previously, this makes almost all educational research in the cognitive areas practically useless. Luckily, very few teachers in the classrooms try to apply the results of educational research in their teaching activities. As a result, the fact that educational research is mostly useless is not too critical an issue. Of course, all the educational research that has been done in the cognitive area does represent a lot of wasted time, energy, and dollars. In Chapter IX, I will go into more detail as to the problems of educational research and possible future directions of instructional research.

A special application of research and use of standardized tests is the National Assessment of Educational Progress (NAEP). Although NAEP has made a definite step forward by at least trying to relate the test items in their tests to objectives, the stated objectives are not SO's and so the test items can only be selected because of a content correlation not because of a behavioral correlation. As such, the traditional criteria of a test item's ability to discriminate and ease of grading were second only to content correlation in the selection of test items. Another positive feature of the NAEP tests is the use of a variety of innovative techniques in testing which were not so easy to administer and to grade. However, the tests still include a high percentage of multiple choice items which invalidates the results of the tests.

Since the primary purpose of the NAEP is to give direction and assistance in the spending of future educational funds, the results of these tests may be very critical in terms of funds available for the solving of instructional problems. From that point-of-view, the validity of the NAEP tests also becomes a critical issue and for that same reason, I claim that the NAEP is a fraud on the taxpayers, educators, and students. I have published this charge in detail in my *DAIRS and Systems for Instruction Newsletter* (Issue No. 23-24) and also in my book, *Educational Malpractices,* so I will not go into the details of the points of fraud here. The main issue is that since the test items are selected because they give certain results, the results are predetermined ahead of time (a three hump curve is used for validity instead of the usual normal curve). As such, the test item writers are the ones who are really making the decisions as to the directions of future educational emphasis and funding because they are the ones who are predetermining the results of the tests. For example, according to NAEP's own information, the test items in the tests will fall into three categories: those that only about 10 percent of the students can answer, those that about 50 percent of the students can answer, and those that about 90 percent of the students can answer. Remember, these results are built into the test items. Now, when the tests are taken in a certain area and the results indicate that 54 percent of the students in that area got a particular item right, what do the results mean? If the item was supposed to be a 10 percent item and it turned out to be 54 percent, either the students are a lot better than the test item writers thought or the students in that area could be pretty smart (with reference to that item). If the item was supposed to be a 50 percent item, the test item writers guessed pretty good. If the item was supposed to be a 90 percent item, either the students were a lot worse than the test item writers thought or the students in that area could be pretty bad (with reference to that item). Given that any one of the results could have three different interpretations depending upon its relationship with the intended results, the value of NAEP — if any — becomes even more doubtful when the NAEP refuses to interpret their own findings and also does not tell the people brought in to interpret the results what percentage results were built into the test items.

i. SUGGESTIONS TO IMPROVE THE VALUE OF THE RESULTS OF STANDARDIZED TESTS

In order to increase the value of the results of tests, the test items should be highly correlated with specific learning objectives which have been identified as important and/or critical.[19] In being highly or perfectly correlated, the test items should concern the achievement of the same behavior in the same content area as described in the related SO. Also, the items in the tests should represent minimum acceptable achievement under conditions where the minimum achievement is in reference to national, regional, state, and local standards (see pages 527-542). Under these conditions, the only way the results can be predetermined is by teaching the students to the mastery level of the tests rather than just manipulating test items. As long as the test items represent important SO's, then the results are good indicators

---

[19] A critical objective is one that if the student does not learn it, he or she will have cumulative ignorance which will inhibit necessary subsequent learning.

of what is happening in the schools and classrooms. If almost all of the students are achieving mastery level of the tests (100 percent), then whatever is happening in the classrooms and schools, it must be successful. If there is some kind of curve of achievement occurring, chances are that individual differences are not being taken into consideration. If most students are missing the same test items and related SO's, whatever is happening in the classrooms with reference to the teaching and learning of these SO's, it must be wrong. Do something about it! If almost all of the students are not achieving any of the test items and related SO's, then something is very wrong with the teaching-learning situation and in particular something is wrong with the teaching activities. The teacher needs help!

j. ATTITUDES TOWARDS TESTING

Under the traditional approach to education where the tests are hidden; they may have little, if any, correlation with what is important to learn; are used to evaluate teachers, students, and instructional programs and yet it is considered wrong to teach what the tests test; and the results can critically affect a person's educational progress and may in turn ultimately limit a person's social and financial progress. Over the years, I have encountered hundreds of students who are so afraid of tests that when they take a test, their mind goes blank. For some students the mere mention of a *test* is enough to set off psychosomatic symptoms of physical aches and pains. On top of all the anxiety produced in the educational testing environment, parents frequently load more stress on the student in their desire to have a successful child. It should not really be a surprise to find lots of students cheating and to find that the stress of tests and grades force some students to drop courses, to drop out of school, and some students to commit suicide. Even many teachers feel negative towards tests, some because they do not feel qualified to make up the tests, some because they feel insecure about testing when they realize that the test items may not match what they want students to learn, some because they feel guilty about the tricks involved in traditional testing, and some because as a humanitarian they feel bad about how the results of tests have negative effects on students.

As tests begin to be used as diagnostic tools, both student and teacher attitudes will improve. this will be particularly true under the mastery concept because eventually 90 percent or more of the students will achieve 100 percent of the tests they take. Even when not achieving 100 percent of the SO's in a test, at least something is done about the students' non-achievement and mistakes after taking the test rather than just receiving a score or grade with no further chances to learn what was missed. The stress associated with traditional testing that

523

leads to cheating and attempted suicides, will not be present because the emphasis is an openness and honesty rather than secrecy and deception.

3. TEACHERS' QUALIFICATIONS FOR EVALUATION

Consider for a moment the concept of testing. There are many different areas of our society in which the concept of testing is used. For example, if you were told by your doctor that there was a possibility that you might have heart trouble and he directed you to go to a medical laboratory for an electrocardiogram (EKG) test. When you arrived at the medical laboratory, the medical technician happened to be out to lunch, but the receptionist who had been there for several years volunteered to give you the EKG test on the basis that she had observed the test many times. Would you allow the receptionist to give you the EKG test and interpret the results? So far, every person to whom I have directed this question has answered that they would not allow the receptionist to give them the EKG and interpret the results of the test because the receptionist was not qualified to do this. When you take your car to a garage, are you worried about whether or not the mechanics are qualified to diagnose the problems in your car, or if you take a television set to a repair store, are you concerned whether or not the repairman is qualified to diagnose the problems of your television set? Almost in every area of our society in which people are involved in diagnostic procedures the clients or recipients of these procedures are concerned about the qualifications of the person doing the testing.

In instructional activities, students are being asked to learn a variety of behaviors. Some of these behaviors can be evaluated with paper and pencil tests, some can only be evaluated by observation of the students' performance, some can only be evaluated by inspecting the students' products, and some of these behaviors can only be evaluated by oral evaluations. If all of these different types of learning objectives are important, the question can be raised, *are the teachers qualified to evaluate the achievement of these objectives?*

Under the traditional approach to education, where the typical teacher has few, if any, SO's, the problem is not so much *how to evaluate the non-existent SO's*, but since almost all teachers give tests of some kind, the problem becomes, *what is it that teachers are evaluating when they do test?* In the absence of not knowing specifically what it is students are supposed to learn, then the teachers tend to be evaluated on whether or not they can make up and give tests to their students that will result in an expected or predetermined distribution of scores. The distribution of scores is based on assumptions about: the ability levels of the students, the difficulty of the subject, the level of education, the ability of the teacher to teach (usually concerned with presenting the course content and the ability of the teacher to evaluate learning). It is generally assumed that in elementary, secondary, and undergraduate (higher) education, the students' ability (limits) is normally distributed, therefore, it is *normal* to have a curve of grades. Some teachers, particularly in science courses, believe their subject matter area is more difficult than other subjects, so it is *normal* to have a negatively skewed distribution of scores (more "D's" and "F's"). Because of the *sifting* role in which some teachers believe it is their job to eliminate a certain percentage of students and because many teachers believe the higher the education level the more difficult it should be, there is a tendency to decrease the higher grades ("A's" and "B's") and increase the lower grades "D's" and "F's") as students go higher up the educational ladder. The trend is so evident, that in higher education a large percentage of faculty equate *quality* of a course or school to the *percentage of failures* (particularly in science oriented courses)!! However, during the past few years a countertrend is developing in which some teachers in higher education (particularly in the humanities) are giving higher grades (more "A's" and "B's") without observable increases in learning. This *grade inflation* has become a problem for the traditional educator who believes that the *percentage of failure* is equated to *quality*.

Most teachers consider themselves *good* teachers to the extent that when students do not achieve, it is assumed to be the fault of the learner. Since there is little difference in the observed teaching behaviors of teachers who have had special training in *how to teach* (almost all elementary and secondary teachers) and teachers who have not had any special training in *how to teach* (almost all higher education faculty), it is difficult for a teacher to identify when he or she is not a *good* teacher and also to defend the need for special training. As long as the courses on *how to teach* are primarily concerned with *how to present course content* and *classroom management* rather than on how to help students learn more, it will continue to be difficult to defend the need for courses on *how to teach*. This is particularly true when a curve of student achievement is the expected result. Since students come to a class already different with respect to their ability to learn, the easiest way to end up with a curve of student achievement at the end of a course is to make sure you do not teach (as defined in terms of helping students learn)! If the higher in education the more negatively skewed the results of student achievement should be, then it also follows that the higher in education, the less important it is to know *how to teach!* Because some teachers may accidently be successful in helping too many students learn and upset the expected results in higher education, the emphasis of the teachers' role is placed on *publish or perish* and that part of the teachers' role concerned with teaching students is downgraded. The higher you go in higher education, the less concerned the teacher is supposed to be with the teaching of students (lighter teaching loads and smaller classes) and the more a teacher should be concerned with research and publishing.

Since the expected results of student achievement is a curve and it is so easy to obtain these results, the pressure to be trained in *how to test* is even less than the pressure to be trained in *how to teach.* As a result, not very many teachers have had formal training on how to evaluate student achievement, particularly in reference to the SO's of the courses and to the different forms of evaluation. According to a survey I conducted of over 7,000 elementary and secondary school teachers, 43 percent admitted that they had never had any formal training on how to make tests. A similar survey of faculty in higher education would probably reveal that 90 percent or more of the faculty have never had any formal training in testing. (Remember, in higher education, all a teacher needs is an advanced degree in his or her subject matter area; teachers are not required to know anything about how to teach or how to test for the achievement of whatever they have been teaching.) These results would indicate that a rather large percentage of teachers, who are presently testing students and assigning grades which very drastically affect the future of students' lives, have not had any training and hence, are not qualified to do this kind of testing. This does not mean that all teachers should be required to take courses in testing and measurement as these courses are presently being conducted, or that the teachers who say they have had formal training in testing are necessarily qualified to do testing. In order to learn how to manipulate the tests and raw score results, whole courses and numerous textbooks have been written on *tests and measurements.* As a result of having these courses, teachers may be qualified to give normative tests which have no place in an honest instructional situation; but they are not qualified to give criterion tests or tests which may be used in an honest designed instructional situation. In fact, teachers who have had these courses may be even less qualified to give criterion tests than teachers with no training whatsoever because they have been trained to trick and deceive students and to manipulate tests and test results regardless of actual student achievement.

In talking to teachers around the country, there are few, if any, courses in test and measurement in which the relationship between tests and objectives is emphasized. As a result of this lack of emphasis in most test and measurement courses and textbooks, most teachers try to develop tests that will spread the student scores over some kind of curve, rather than measuring how much of a course or unit the students have actually learned. One of the reasons for this lack of emphasis on the need for test items to be testing the exact behaviors specified by

526

objectives is that the whole concept of *standardizing* tests (design the test items so that the results fit a curve) would be literally destroyed and along with it the value of most of the courses and textbooks on tests and measurement. Once students learn the need for a close relationship or a perfect correlation between SO's and test items, any test item that tests those objectives cannot be changed without changing the original objectives, so if important objectives are specified for a particular course or curriculum, the results of any tests which test those behaviors would just have to represent the actual behaviors which the students have achieved. There is absolutely no place for the manipulation of test items and test results which hide the actual achievement of of the students and consequently, also hid the need for the teaching of any test items and matching SO's which were missed.

There is a very definite need for teachers at all levels to be trained and qualified in *how to teach* (defined in terms of helping students learn) and in *how to evaluate* (defined in terms of diagnosing learning problems). This training should concern the identification and specification of what the students are expected to learn in units, courses, and programs (the GO's and SO's). Since there is a high or perfect correlation between the SO's and the test items, the specification of the learning objectives automatically includes the specification of the test items to be used to evaluate the achievement of the SO's.

Teachers who are involved in research will still have to know how to statistically deal with data, but they will no longer have to know or they should not even know how to manipulate the tests to get the results or data they want. Teachers who are instructional practitioners need to know primarily how to identify and solve learning problems by manipulating the learning environment rather than knowing how to manipulate the test items or the results of tests. Given that the results of a test indicate that certain students did not learn certain SO's, all of the knowledge about stanines, Q-sorts, parametric or non-parametric statistics, medians, modes, etc. will not solve the learners' problems. It is useless information for the practitioner.

NOTE: When educational research changes from being concerned with the study of man-made methods and techniques which makes it a non-science to the study of learning which is a natural phenomenon and as such is a science, then it may be important for the practitioner to learn sufficient statistics to be able to differentiate between relevant and irrelevant research as it is reported in the various instructional research journals.

D. MINIMUM COMMON CORE LEARNING

Although our Country is dedicated to freedom, complete freedom can only be gained in isolation. In a social context, freedom becomes a relative term in which a person's freedom is limited by the freedom of others. This relative freedom is usually expressed in terms of privileges and responsibilities. For example, in driving on a freeway, if one driver took complete freedom to do anything he or she wanted to do, it could very easily endanger the freedom and safety of other drivers and their passengers. In fact, individualism on the highways cause over 50,000 traffic fatalities and over 250,000 permanent disabilities annually. Whenever the freedom of one person carries with it the possibility of interfering with the freedom or safety of others, then the group or society involved has the right and obligation to establish rules and responsibilities for all concerned. As the population grows and as mobility and modes of communication increase, there will be a proportionate increase in conflicts with individualism. Although there may be a few people who want to live in complete isolation for all of their lives, practically everyone will be living in some form of social environment for their entire lives. As such, their freedom is restricted by their responsibilities to others in the social group. If members of the group are willing to communicate to an individual, then the individual has the responsibility to learn to communicate effectively to other members of the group. If members of the group are willing to provide services to the individual when needed (unemployment, welfare, highways, parks, police and fire protection, etc.) Then the individual has the responsibility to contribute to the group so these services will be available to others in the group when they need them. This in effect says that an individual has the responsibility to learn sufficiently in some area to either contribute financially or with services to the group. The group in turn has the responsibility to provide the learning environment whereby the individual acquires the necessary intellectual and sensory skills and emotional tendencies which will minimize the individuals need for the services of the group. By making sure that everyone in the group has the necessary minimum skills, this will minimize the need for the services of the group which in turn minimizes the cost in time, effort, and money to the individual and ultimately results in more time, effort, and money left over for individual freedom.

In addition to minimum commom core learning that is associated with a person's responsibilities to the other members in our society, there is also minimum common core learning associated with the increasing freedom. To some, this last statement might appear to be in conflict with itself because they look on any required learning as an infringement on freedom. Since the time of the ancient Greeks and before, education and learning has been viewed as essential to real freedom. Ignorance is looked on as a barrier to freedom. The minimum common core learning could be considered as the necessary tools in any subject matter area which will allow an individual to study and work

528

independently and creatively. For example, take two people who are interested in art but know nothing about art and have never studied or done any art work. If one is put into an *art environment* and told to do *his own thing* without any help or training and the other person is trained to the 100 percent level of all the measurable SO's in the craft of art and then put into the *art environment*, I claim that the first person's ignornace will limit his or her freedom in art while the second person's minimum common core of learning will allow and facilitate as much freedom as the person wants to use.

In the days when a majority of the population grew up, lived, worked, and died within 25 miles of where they were born, the amount of minimum common core learnings necessary to survive and contribute in that much simpler society was not very much. Most of the survival skills were picked up in the home or outside of school. In this day and age, the situation is reversed. The majority of the population will move several times to different cities and to different states, into different cultural and/or social groups. As a result, the amount of minimum common core learning has increased considerably. In keeping with this change, whereas in decades past the emphasis has been on local autonomy in the control of the curriculum, the minimum common core has to refer to national, regional, and state, and local minimums.

Although there has been and is a lot of discussion about a national curriculum and a national evaluation, most of this discussion is very negative towards these concepts. Oddly enough, educators can accept the concept of a national evaluation easier than they can accept a national curriculum; yet, to have a standardized national evaluation assumes that there is a standardized national curriculum. In a teaching-learning situation where the teacher is primarily concerned with presenting the content of a course, it is understandable that the development of a national curriculum could endanger this role, because it would be relatively easy to develop either textbooks, films, video tapes or audio tapes that could take over the presentation of content. Once a national curriculum is established and a national evaluation is carried out, it will become quite obvious as to who is a good teacher and who is not a good teacher. If the teacher is only performing the role of a presenter of content, then the results of this evaluation would naturally bring only fear, distrust and resentment against people who suggest such things as a national curriculum and a national evaluation. On the other hand, if teachers accept the role of facilitating student learning as their primary function in the teaching-learning situation, then the more materials that are available to present the content of the course, the more release time the teacher has to spend helping more students learn whatever they are supposed to learn. An instructional system in which the teacher has more time to spend with students who need help would benefit not only the slow learners and the gifted students, but it would also benefit the average student. It is extremely important to point out with reference to the local schools and to the individual teacher in a classroom, that the national regional, state, or local objectives are always classified as the minimum learning objectives, never the maximum learning objectives. The maximum objectives should be left up to the individual teacher in the teaching-learning situation and to the student in the teaching-learning situation.

Another way of looking at the minimum common core SO's is that already most of our schools have a common curriculum. Certainly if given a dozen schools located in different parts of the country that offer a course called *Seventh Grade Geography*, there must be more in common than just the title of the course. For the sake of numbers, possibly 10 percent of the course might be the same nationally. In the regional areas, maybe 20 percent of the course might be the same, in the state areas, maybe 30 percent of the course might be in common. In the local areas where there are two or more teachers teaching the same course, there may be 40-50 percent or more in common. As a general rule, the more teachers involved and the larger the areas involved, the fewer SO's there will be in common among the teachers.

If there are minimum common core SO's established at the national, regional, state, and local levels, there would also be matching criterion tests at the national, regional, state, and local levels. In contrast to the traditional standardized tests, the minimum common core criterion tests would contain enough test items to test for all of the SO's instead of just a *guessed* sample of the objectives. Also, when a teacher identifies one or more students that did not get the 100 percent on these tests, the teacher would teach the students what they missed by looking on their roles as facilitators of learning who identify and solve learning problems.

NOTE: A very important point to emphasize is that the minimum common core SO's are identified by the teachers involved in using them in their classrooms. The process of identifying them starts from the classroom in a local area and as more and more teachers get involved in the process, fewer and fewer SO's will be agreed on. The national minimum common core SO's would be the last to be identified except under conditions where a national effort is made to involve thousands of teachers in the identification of these minimum common core SO's.

During most of this century, the percentage of our population with high school diplomas, bachelors degrees, masters degrees, and doctorates has been steadily increasing, but, as of this writing of this book, there are few, if any, diplomas or degrees that are awarded on the basis

530

of the achievement of any particular level of specific knowledge or skills. The primary criterion has been and still is the amount of time spent in classes, i.e., twelve years for a high school diploma, about 2000 classroom hours for a bachelors degree, about 500 classroom hours for a masters degree, and about another 500 classroom hours for a doctorate. It is critical that diplomas and degrees mean something more than just awards for endurance in completing the educational obstacle track. Because of the lack of a relationship between the diploma and learning, it is not uncommon for high schools to graduate functional illiterates. In fact, Pacific Telephone Company states that about 40 percent of the high school graduates that apply for jobs are lacking basic training in reading, writing, and arithmetic. If schools could only guarantee the learning of one SO per year, high school diplomas would stand for the learning of at least twelve things (concepts, processes, facts, etc.) which would be twelve more than can be guaranteed now.

Given that our young people are required to stay in school until a certain age, it should be acceptable that society and professional instructors be required to identify what it is that the young people are supposed to learn during that time. Also, if the concept of individual differences can be acknowledged by our society and professional instructors, then it should be acceptable for students who can demonstrate that they have learned 100 percent of this minimum common core of required learning (which has been identified)that they should be allowed to leave earlier. In other words, instead of using time as a measure of the length of the students' stay in the instructional environment (regardless of the learning that takes place — both positive and negative), why not have learning as the measure (regardless of the time taken or the variety of learning pathways used)!

On a smaller scale, any instructional program (two or more courses) department, or school that requires students to take a particular course or courses should be required in turn to identify specifically what it is in the course or courses that has to be learned. In other words, instead of requiring courses, as professional instructioneers, we should be requiring SO's which may or may not be learned in a particular course. Any course or courses that are required, but the teachers are not able to identify what the required SO's are, should be challenged as to the reasons for the requirement.

In a situation where two or more teachers are teaching the same course (with the same title) in the same school, the teachers should be required to identify the minimum common core learning to be achieved in the course regardless of who teaches the course. This should be a critical requirement of any multi-teacher course which is considered to be a prerequisite for subsequent course or courses. At the present time, the only requirement, if any, is that the teacher present certain content in a course. As a result of the varied achievement and no guaranteed learning of SO's, the conscientious teacher in subsequent courses feels obligated to go back over what the students should have learned in the prerequisite course in order to eliminate cumulative ignorance. Not only is the duplication of presenting inefficient, it can also be boring and ineffective.

1. HOW TO IDENTIFY MINIMUM COMMON CORE LEARNING

In traditional education, attempts to identify commonality or the contents of new courses are usually handled by curriculum committees in a series of group meetings. Because of frequent personality conflicts, these group meetings usually develop much more *heat* than *light*. Consequently, the best guidelines to keep in mind while identifying the minimum common core learning is to minimize or avoid completely any group meetings. However, in going through the four steps in identifying the minimum common core learning, it may be convenient to hold a brief meeting (about 30-45 minutes) of the teachers involved to carry out the first step.

The first step consists of three parts: describing the procedures to be followed in the process; selection of a coordinator;[20] and the identification of the group's *degree of agreement*. The first two parts are self-explanatory. The third part is very important and it is critical that this part be completed before going on to the next three steps. The *degree of agreement* is usually dependent upon the degree of friendship among the members of the group and on how willing they are to trust the judgement of the other members of the group. The *degree of agreement* is defined as that number of members of a group who will say that a particular objective is a required objective and the rest of the group will accept their judgement and require the learning of the objective even if they individually do not believe the objective is that important. It is critical that there is unanimous agreement on the *degree of agreement*. For example, if there are 20 teachers teaching the same course and they get along pretty good except for one teacher, 19 of the teachers may agree that if 12 or more of the group say an objective should be required as a minimum common core objective, the rest will accept their judgement and require all of their students to learn that objective. However, the one teacher may not be so willing to trust the judgement of his or her colleagues. Then the coordinator increases the number to 13, 14, 15, etc. until there is unanimous agreement including the one dissident teacher. Suppose that in this group, the dissident

---

[20] The larger the group involved in this process, the more work it is for the coordinator to put the lists together. Therefore, it may be appropriate to give the teacher-coordinator some release time from his or her regular duties for the duration of the process.

teacher finally agreed to 18 as being the *degree of agreement*. This would mean that any objective which 18 or more of the 20 teachers indicated that it should be a required or minimum common core objective, all 20 teachers would agree to require the learning of that objective. The *degree of agreement* will vary from group to group. In some groups that have a lot of trust in one another, the *degree of agreement* could be as low as 50 percent of the group and in other groups where there is not very much trust in one another, the *degree of agreement* might have to be 100 percent of the group.

At any time that the process of identifying the minimum common core learning is to be repeated, the *degree of agreement* should be re-established. The reasons for repeating the process might be to update the required learning on an annual basis, to include new teachers, or to include a larger group (another school, another district, statewide, or national).

The second step also consists of three parts: the collection of objectives, test items, and criteria for evaluation (these are the same as test items — just a different form); making up the first list; and brainstorming. In the first part of this step, all of the teachers in the group send to the coordinator their GO's, SO's, test items, and criteria for evaluation that are related to the course. In the second part, the coordinator makes up a composite list of all the GO's, SO's, test items and criteria for evaluation (including his or her own GO's, SO's, test items and criteria for evaluation) that are different as far as the implied or described behavior is concerned. Duplicate GO's, SO's, test items, and criteria should be left out. If the coordinator is in doubt as to whether or not a GO, SO, test item, or criterion is a duplicate of another one, then leave it on the composite list. In this process, it is better to err in the direction of duplication than to err in the direction of exclusion. This composite list is then duplicated such that a copy can be sent to each teacher of the group (including the coordinator).

NOTE: It is very important that no notation of any kind identifies the teacher or school that submitted a particular GO, SO, test item, or criterion. Only the coordinator will have this information and it should be treated as confidential. In that way, the GO's, SO's, test items and criteria for evaluation will be evaluated on their own merits rather than on the merits or demerits of the originator of the GO's, SO's, test items, or criteria for evaluation.

In the third part of the second step, each teacher on his or her own, without collaborating with any other teacher in the group, evaluates the lists of the GO's, SO's, test items, and criteria for evaluation from the point of view of what is missing or what else should be learned. This is brainstorming on an individual basis and it is important during this part not to spend time evaluating the worth of each GO, SO, test item, and criterion. Evaluation will come in the next step. Upon the completion of this part of step two the lists plus any GO's, SO's, test items and criteria which have been added by the teacher should be sent back to the coordinator.

The third step consists of two parts: the first part is the preparation of a second composite list which includes the original GO's, SO's, test items, and criteria for evaluation plus any additional GO's, SO's, test items, and criteria added by the teachers in the group and the second part is the evaluation of the GO's, SO's, test items, and criteria by putting each one into one of four categories. The second composite list is duplicated and a copy is sent to each teacher (including the coordinator). Again it is important that the GO's, SO's, test items, and criteria that have been added to the original list are not identified as to which teacher or school contributed it. In the evaluation phase, each teacher, in privacy and without the collaboration of other teachers, places each GO, SO, test item and criterion into one of four categories. This is usually done by placing the number (or other symbol) of the category beside each GO, SO, test item, and criterion on the list. The categories are:

1. *Must know or minimum common core learning.* No student should be allowed out of the course without achieving this objective, test item, or criterion.

2. *Nice to know.* This objective, test item, or criterion is important but not critical for achievement in the course. The student will not develop cumulative ignorance which will inhibit the subsequent learning of *must know* objectives, test items, or criteria.

3. *Frill or enrichment.* The learning of this objective, test item, or criterion is neither important nor out of place. It may be of interest to some students.

4. *Rejected.* These objectives, test items, and criteria should not be included in the course because they are obsolete, inappropriate, belong in another course, etc.

After categorizing each of the GO's, SO's, test items, and criteria for evaluation into one of the four categories, each teacher should send the lists back to the coordinator.

The fourth step consists of four parts; identification of the minimum common core learning; identification of the rejects; the adjustment or structuring of the relationship between the GO's, SO's, test items and criteria; and the identification and filling of any gaps in the structure of the minimum common core learning. When all of the second composite lists have been returned from the teachers, the coordinator matches them up and identifies the minimum common core learning in accordance with the *degree of agreement.* In the example mentioned earlier where the *degree of agreement* was 18 teachers out of 20 teachers, the coordinator would look across the lists and identify any GO, SO, test item, or criterion in which 18 or more of the 20 teachers indicated that it was in the first category (must know). These GO's, SO's, or test items, and criteria would be put on a separate list and would be the minimum common core learning for the course.

NOTE: Because of the prior committment of the teachers to the *degree of agreement,* the minimum common core learning can be identified with a minimum of disagreements, disputes, and personality conflicts.

The second part of the fourth step is similar to the first part of this step except the emphasis is on identifying those GO's, SO's, test items, and criteria which should be rejected from the course in accordance with the *degree of agreement.* In the example mentioned earlier, the coordinator would look across the lists and any GO, SO, test item, or criterion in which 18 or more of the teachers indicated that the GO, So, or test item was in the fourth category of rejects, then the coordinator would eliminate these GO's, SO's, test items and criteria from the lists.

The third part of the fourth step would be to adjust or structure the relationships between the GO's, SO's, test items, and criteria that are on the minimum common core learning list. GO's that are sub-GO's or sub-sub-GO's are set up accordingly in an outline form which would identify any interrelationships (see Figure 54, page 366).

NOTE: At the present time, because of the inability of many teachers to write SO's that are really specific many of the agreed on SO's will really be GO's although not as general and vague as the objectives labeled as a GO.

The coordinator would then place the SO's (or nearly SO) under the appropriate GO in the structure. The coordinator would then do the same with the test items and criteria for evaluation by placing them under the appropriate SO.

Ideally, the test items and criteria and the SO's on the minimum common core learning list should match up such that there is at least one or more of the required test items and/or criteria for each SO and there should also be one or more SO's for each GO on the list either directly under the GO or indirectly after the sub-GO, the sub-sub-GO, or etc. Actually, the GO's, SO's, test items and criteria may not match up so neatly. Therefore, in the last part of the fourth step, the coordinator will identify gaps in the structure. For each test item and criterion on the minimum common core learning list that does not match a required SO, a SO should be written so as to match the test item or criterion. For every SO on the list that does not have one or more matching test items or criteria, these should be prepared. For every SO that is labeled a SO, but is still not quite specific enough, attempts should be made to specify the objective and then make up matching test items. If there are any required test items, criteria, or SO's that do not fit under any of the required GO's in the structure, then some new GO's should be identified that will include the required test items and SO's. If there are any required GO's that do not have SO's or test items associated with it either directly or indirectly, then, if at all possible, some SO's and test items should be generated. The development of any additional SO's and/or test items should go through the whole process in order to get agreement. In the brainstorming phase, the directions would be, *Given the following GO's which have been identified as required learning, develop SO's and test items that you think describes or measures what it is you think the students should learn in order to achieve the GO's.* Again, the coordinator would put all of these added SO's and test items into a composite list for evaluation according to one of the four categories. As a result of these adjustments, most or all of the gaps in the structure should be filled in such that it will be closer to the ideal situation.

In order to help you understand the process better, let me illustrate an example with some representative numbers. For example, given a mathematics course where there are ten teachers who want to identify the minimum common core learning and where any one of the teachers might have 10 GO's, 50 SO's, and 300 or more test items (many of these would be duplicates because of the process objectives). There probably wouldn't be any criteria for evaluation included in this example unless there were some essay questions to be answered and/or projects to be evaluated. The first composite list representing the present GO's, SO's, and test items of the ten teachers might contain 15 GO's, 80 SO's, and 80 or more test items (no duplicates). The second composite list which includes the additional GO's, SO's, and test items generated during the brainstorming phase might contain 18 GO's, 110 SO's, and 110 or more test items and the coordinator has identified the ones that are required in accordance with the *degree of agreement*, the minimum common core learning may consist of 11 GO's, 55 SO's, and 55 or more test items (no duplicates). The coordinator might have also identified 1 GO, 8 SO's, and 8 or more test items that the ten teachers agreed should be rejected.

Another example might concern an English composition course where any one teacher might have 3 GO's, 15 SO's, and 15 criteria for evaluating a composition (there might not be any test items as the emphasis is on the composition). In the first composite list of ten teachers' GO's, SO's, and criteria for evaluation of a composition there might be 4 GO's, 21 SO's, and 21 criteria for evaluation. The second composite list which includes the results of the individual teachers brainstorming might have 5 GO's, 26 SO's, and 26 criteria for evaluation of a composition. After completing the process, the minimum common core learning might be 3 GO's, 14 SO's, and 14 criteria for evaluating a composition.

As a general rule, the more teachers involved in the process, the greater the number of GO's, SO's, test items, and criteria for evaluation in the first and second composite lists and the fewer the number of GO's, SO's, test items, and criteria that the group will agree belong on the minimum common core learning list.

NOTE: In cases where there are a large number of objectives, test items, and criteria and also a large number of teachers, it may be useful to use a computer or a card sorter to identify the minimum common core learning.

2. FUNCTIONS OF ADVISORY GROUPS

To help make the GO's, SO's, and test items on the minimum common core learning list more relevant, it is useful to involve various advisory groups where appropriate. In occupational or career courses, it would be appropriate to include potential employers, people who have been working in the particular career area for years, and maybe even ex-students who are employed in the career area. In service courses like writing, reading, and mathematics, it may be appropriate to include the teachers of some of the other courses in which the students have to practice their writing, reading, and mathematics skills. In high school courses that have matching college level courses (chemistry, biology, physics, etc.) it may be appropriate to include some of the college faculty. For courses that serve as a prerequisite for subsequent courses, it may be appropriate to include some of the teachers of the subsequent courses even if they are at a different school. Ex-students of the courses could be included in any of these groups.

These advisory groups will not dictate to the teachers what should or should not be taught and learned in their courses, but the results of applying the whole process to the advisory group should be made available to the teachers involved. For example, if an advisory group were in agreement that a particular SO should be a required objecitve and the teachers were in agreement that this same objective was a frill, then at least it might be worth a second look at the SO or it might be worth asking the advisory group to justify the SO. The same would be true if the advisory group were in agreement that a particular SO was obsolete or should not be taught in a particular course and the teachers were in agreement that the same objective should be required learning, in this case, the teachers should check on their justification for thinking that the objective should be required.

In the development of affective domain objectives and evaluation, it would be critical to involve a representative sample of parents, taxpayers (for tax supported schools), and students (where they are old enough to be involved) in the advisory groups. If any teacher or teachers teach openly, covertly, or unconsciously certain attitudes, values, and/or beliefs which an advisory group is in agreement should be rejected (category No. 4), the teacher or teachers and the school will probably be in trouble and accused of brainwashing or subversion of the local attitudes and values if the rejected attitudes, values, and/or beliefs continue to be taught.

NOTE: Remember, in the affective domain, the minimum common core learning can not be required because you can not demand the development of attitudes, values, or beliefs. However, those affective objectives which are considered minimum common core learning should be evaluated on a pretest and posttest basis. Any deviations of the group of students from the desired levels and direction should be identified and subsequent instructional activities should be designed to establish or re-establish the desired levels and direction.

3. THE CAFETERIA OF LEARNING

In several of the innovative approaches to education during the past decade, teachers and schools have used the phrase *cafeteria of learning experiences* from which the student demonstrates freedom by selecting what he or she wants to do. In some of the schools that I have visited, the so-called *cafeteria* exists almost in name only. The student's freedom to choose is pretty limited if there are few, if any, choices from which to pick. In schools where there are a variety of learning experiences from which to choose, the student's freedom to choose is limited by what the teacher or teachers select to put in the cafeteria. Also, few of the teachers or schools where they have a variety of learning experiences have identified what it is that students should be learning and what SO's are available for learning in the *learning experiences*. As a result, any learning that takes place is by chance and is primarily directed by interest instead of need. Consequently, the students ignorance limits his or her selection and also his or her freedom.

One of the important side benefits of identifying the minimum common core learning is that the balance of the GO's, SO's, test items, and criteria which are not required or rejected can be made available to the students as a cafeteria of *learning* not just of learning experiences.

As a general rule, the more teachers involved, the more extra GO's, SO's, test items, and criteria there will be left over to be put in the cafeteria of learning.

4. IDENTIFYING COMMONALITY PROMOTES INDIVIDUALITY

As teachers talk about or actually do identify the minimum common core learning or as some teachers even just talk about this part of this book, there will undoubtedly be some people who will accuse the concept of being mechanistic, production line oriented, etc. In fact, the opposite is the truth. In the process of identifying the minimum common core learning, it is possible to promote individual differences by design.

Under the traditional approach to education, diversity was and is accomplished by ignoring individual differences in learning abilities and allowing varying levels of cumulative ignorance (non-achievement) to develop as a result of an ineffective and inefficient learning environment. Given a common content to be presented in a course by the teachers, the evaluation of learning is designed to force the results into a variation of non-achievement which in turn causes problems in subsequent courses or in real life, then traditional individuality is gained at the sacrifice of humaneness.

With reference to the concept described in this unit, the required minimum common core learning usually includes the prerequisite tools of learning which are necessary to be free to go on learning whatever the student may want to learn. The GO's, SO's, test items, and criteria which are left over in the cafeteria of learning can be used to promote not only individual differences among the students, but also to promote the individual differences among the teachers of multi-teacher courses. In addition to the minimum common core learning agreed upon by the teachers of the same course, there will probably be some additional GO's, SO's, test items, and criteria that each individual teacher still thinks is important and critical for success in the course even if the majority of the other teachers do not agree. There will probably be other GO's, SO's, test items, and criteria in the cafeteria of learning that each teacher will recommend to the students in his or her classes as *nice to know* (not required) which will probably reflect the individual teacher's interests. Depending upon the teacher's persuasiveness and enthusiasm, a number of students may elect to learn some or all of these recommended objectives.

In each course, now that a population of GO's, SO's, test items, and criteria have been identified, in addition to specifying the minimum common core learning for all students who take the course, it will now be possible to add to that minimum additional GO's, SO's, test items, and criteria which should be required of certain students who are taking the course and are going in different directions (or majors) than other students in the course. For example, consider a course in high school chemistry. In addition to the minimum common core learning required of all students taking the course, students who are going on to major in chemistry should learn some more as a minimum, students going on to major in biology should learn more as a minimum (different than the added minimum for the chemistry majors), students going on to major in science but not in chemistry or biology should learn more GO's, SO's, and test items which are different than the extra learning required of the chemistry and biology majors.

Actually, there are seven categories of GO's, SO's, and test items which can be learned in addition to the basic minimum common core learning in each course (to review these categories, see pages 209-212, Volume I). The key point to remember is that under the traditional approach, individuality is gained by variations in *non-achievement* whereas in the learning systems approach, individuality is gained by variations in *achievement!*

In addition to the differences in achievement promoted by these techniques, it should also be noted that under the learning systems approach, individual differences in learning are recognized such that students will use different lengths of time to complete their individually different amounts to be learned; as more methodological pathways for learning are developed, the students can choose how they want to learn; and wherever possible, the students can choose the vehicle for learning that matches their individual interests. If the learning situation involves a variety of reinforcements, the student will also be able to choose his or her own reinforcers.

NOTE: At about this point, those very same faultfinders who were objecting to the concept of a minimum common core of learning in every course and program as not allowing for individual differences, will now probably change their accusation to the fact that there is too much individualism and that the students will miss something by not being in group situations (like classes). Remember, some of the required learning may involve objectives which have to be learned in a group situation. Also, if the teachers are willing to have the *Scholarship* sessions, these provide very good opportunities for group interaction and there are no objectives, tests, or required attendance to worry about by either the teachers or students.

5. CONTEMPORARY EFFORTS TO ESTABLISH MINIMUM COMMON CORE LEARNING

Some educators may want to equate the minimum common core learning concept with what is called *Performance Based Education* or

Competency Based Education. If one can go by the implied meanings of the titles, there could at least be a relationship; but in examining the projects carried out under these titles, they can not be equated. Few, if any, of the projects using either one of these two titles have identified their course or unit objectives along the lines suggested in this section. Also, the performance, competency, or criterion required is not usually 100 percent achievement of the objectives. The achievement is often a *pass* or 80 percent of a multiple-choice and true-false test in which the test items do not match the objectives and the 80 percent refers to a *random* 80 percent achievement.

Some teacher training institutions have set up a performance or competancy based education approach in some of their courses as a result of the requirements contained in Teacher Corps contracts. One of the stipulations in the contracts is that the techniques used in training the Teacher Corps trainees should also be applied to the regular students in the education program. In these schools, individual learning units or modules have been developed to allow the student to go through them at their own pace. It sounds good, until upon further examination, one discovers that the tests are usually the multiple choice — true-false variety and the objectives are not as specific as they could be. Saddest of all the aspects, the students and trainees are learning on an individual basis to be a presenter of course content (which ignores individual differences) and a classroom manager (of discipline not learning) both of which are obsolete roles. What these schools should be doing is having their students learn on an individualized basis *how to individualize instruction.* In that way, the method of teaching and learning supports what is being learned.

Several states and countries have used examinations at the end of certain grades from the point of view that students have to achieve certain scores on these before they are allowed to continue on in their education. The problem is that the examinations are normative oriented and are designed to eliminate students. They are not criterion type tests. California passed a law that no student would be able to get a diploma from high school unless the student could demonstrate eighth grade achievement on a *standardized* (normed) achievement test. In addition to all of the problems of using normative tests which have only a content relationship with the curriculum and the use of standardized achievementment tests in a situation where there are not any standardized lists of objectives in use, the California legislature was embarrassed by the low standards (eighth grade level), so the law was repealed.

Probably the closest contemporary effort to the process of identifying the minimum common core learning as described in this section can be found in California. As a result of another law called the Stull Bill which is concerned with the accountability of teachers and schools, school districts are supposed to involve the community in the identification of educational goals. Again, it sounds good and the right words are used, so it is impressive. The problem is that the legislators understood the concept of accountability but they did not know about or understand the concept of specificity of objectives and their relationship with test items. As a result, a lot of time, effort, and money is being put into the identification of these educational goals by educators, parents, taxpayers, and even students and it will have little if any affect on what happens in the schools or classrooms. Consider the following list of educational goals which were identified in one school district:

— To develop a positive attitude toward learning as a process for systematic problem solving.

— To be a responsible, participating member of society.

— To listen carefully and express oneself effectively through written and oral language.

— To recognize one's self-worth and develop an awareness of his potential contribution to society.

— To respect, conserve, and enjoy nature.

— To build a positive, realistic self-image in order to accept the rewards of success and the consequences of failure.

— To express, develop, and appreciate artistic talent (painting, music, etc.).

— To understand the effect of history on the past and present peoples of the world.

— To develop a sense of honesty and fairness with respect toward other people.

— To develop the skills necessary to enjoy a balance between relaxation and productive leisure time activities.

— To develop competency in math skills to the best of one's ability and apply them to everyday life.

— To develop and maintain a healthy body.

— To develop the skills of reading to the best of one's ability in order to enjoy the benefits of reading.

— To appreciate the value of scientific discoveries and apply scientific skills to everyday life.

— To adjust easily to social relationships and be tolerant of the opinions and actions of others.

— To value the personal and material rewards gained from a well chosen vocation.

All of these objectives are GO's and fall into the category I refer to as *Motherhood, God, Country, and Apple Pie* objectives. Who would ever want to be against them? The fact that makes the whole effort an empty gesture is that the wording of the goals is so general that no one including the teacher is able to prove that any student has achieved any of these goals and also no one including the teacher will be able to prove that any student has not achieved any of these goals. As far as accountability is concerned, goals of this type are useless unless they are further defined into more specific GO's and finally into some measurable SO's. Although the Stull Bill gave some hope to the legislators, taxpayers, and parents and frightened a lot of teachers (who also do not know the difference between a GO and a SO nor the relationship which should exist between SO's and test items), the students in the classrooms will and have observed *business as usual*.

E. JUSTIFICATION OF INSTRUCTIONAL OBJECTIVES AND/OR TEST ITEMS

Professional ethics demands of any professional that he or she be able to justify his or her actions which concern or affect the client or recipient of the professional's services. Because of the possibility of professional negligence, the professional should make it a practice to at least consider how he or she might justify his or her actions. Whereas in law, medicine, theology, psychology, and other professions, it is common to consider how the results of the professional's actions will affect the client; in education, we have not asked ourselves often enough to justify what we do with students. Think of the millions of students who have been failed out of courses and out of school and what that failure has done to their perception of society and of themselves. Is it possible to justify the damage? If the non-achievement of test items or of criteria is important enough that a teacher will grade a student down for it, then the teacher who is attaching that much importance to the test item or criteria should also be ready to justify the importance in terms of benefits to the learner. Under the traditional approach, the students do not know exactly what they should learn until they take the tests. At that time, it is too late to challenge the importance of an item because the instructional time is over (the diagnosis comes after the treatment). Under the learning system's approach, where the students are given the lists of required SO's and test items at the beginning of the courses and/or units, it is possible for the students to challenge the importance of certain SO's and test items. If a teacher is unable to justify the learning of all of the required SO's and test items, then those

543

that are undefensible should be put under voluntary learning instead of required learning.

In a situation where time is held constant rather than learning, there is a tendency to pad courses to make them fit a time slot. It is utterly unreal to accept that all courses in a particular school fit into the semester or quarter time slot. Ask any teacher (if you are already teaching, ask yourself) what problem they worried about most when starting to teach a new course for the first time? Most will say that they were worried about what they would do to fill up all the hours allotted to the course. I was in a high school faculty lunch room one time when one of the English teachers came in raving about a great film on Hamlet he had just shown to his class. A bookkeeping teacher asked if he could borrow the film for his next class because he did not have anything planned for it. During the next several days, that film on Hamlet was shown in at least six classes that I know about including a physical education class. One student told me that he had seen the film three times. Where the emphasis is on filling up the time, teachers learn very quickly how to pad their courses. We become so good at padding, that after several years of teaching a course the problem changes from having too much time to one of not having enough time. As a consequence, many courses have become overloaded with varying degrees of trivia. Under the learning system's approach, a new teacher will start a course with a list of GO's, SO's, and test items which have been developed by other teachers who have taught the course. Instead of worrying about how to fill the time, this new teacher can worry about helping students learn the required SO's and test items which probably have been justified by some other teachers in order for them to be categorized as must-know objectives.

In justifying course or unit objectives and/or test items (remember that SO's and test items should be practically synonymous), not only will it help to eliminate the padding in a course or unit and justify the remainder of the course or unit, but the process of justifying objectives and/or test items will help teachers to clarify what they really want students to learn, it will help communicate to students the relevance of the learning task, and it will also help teachers to design a more effective teaching-learning-evaluation environment. The process of justifying a SO and/or test item involves the asking of seven questions. Not all seven questions will be appropriate for every SO and test item, but they should be asked anyway because the answers will be useful even if the answer is *not appropriate.* However, three or four answers of *not appropirate* may start to indicate that the objective or test item itself may be *not appropriate!* The seven questions are:

1. Why should anyone learn this SO (or test item) or of what value is the learning of this SO (or test item)?

2. Under what conditions or in what type of situation will the learning of this SO (or test item) be useful to the learner?

3. Given the learner is in that type of situation and the certain conditions are in existence, what will the learner be expected to do as a result of learning this SO (or test item)?

4. How long will it be after leaving a course before the learner will apply or use the SO or test item that has been learned in the course?

5. At the time that the learner starts applying or using what was learned in achieving a SO or test item in a course, how frequently will the learner use it?

6. If the learner is not able to achieve this SO (or test item), what will happen to the learner which might not have happened if the learner could have achieved the SO (or test item)?

7. How will the learning of this SO (or test item) contribute to the quality of the learner's life?

In going through the process of justifying learning, it is very useful to ask these questions in reference to the total course and the units of the course. The answers will usually be in terms of general statements or GO's which in turn also act as very good guidelines in evaluating subsequent SO's and test items in the course or unit of the course.

The first question when asked in reference to a SO or test item will usually result in one or more general statements which indicate benefits for the learner. Obviously, if the answer is similar to any one of the following, the value of the SO or test item should be seriously doubted: *It is in the book; I learned it when I was a student; I've been using it for a long time;* or *The student should learn it because I said so!* Another aspect to consider in the asking of the first question is to ask, *Is the SO (or test item) an end's value or a mean's value?* Is the learning of the SO (or test item) valuable for itself, an end or terminal objective, or is its value in that it helps or is a means to the achievement of other objectives?

The answers to the second and third question may overlap and tend to be an answer to a more general question, *Once the student has learned the SO (or to answer the test item correctly), how is he supposed to use this behavior?* In breaking this more general question into two more specific questions, the answer to the second question should refer to the nouns and noun phrases in the SO and/or test item while the answer to the third question should refer to the verb in the SO and/or test item.

The second question should result in a description of a situation which should match the situation described in the SO and/or test item.

545

If the two descriptions do not match, then the SO, test item, or answer should be changed because one or more of the three are wrong. If the SO or test item is a rote memory item, the answer to the second question should indicate in the description of the conditions, what the application or utility of the rote memorized item would be. To further justify the rote memorized item, there should be other SO's and test items dealing with the application or utility of the rote memorized item.

The third question is primarily concerned with the learners behavior as stated in the SO, the test item, and in some future situation. The answer to this question should describe the learners behavior in the future situation and that behavior should match the SO and the test item. If they do not match, one or more of the three are wrong. In the case of a rote memory SO or test item, the answer to the third question should describe how the learner is going to use the rote memorized item. The answer should also reflect the verb used in the SO's and test items which are concerned with the application of the rote memorized item.

Because different groups of students may use or apply the same learning in different ways, the teacher should try to identify what the students goals, related experiences, and interests are as this information could be very useful in solving learning problems for a group or an individual. For example, in a given foreign language class, some students may be taking the foreign language because they are planning to visit a country where the language is spoken. Other students may be taking this foreign language because they want to read literature from the country. Some other students may be atking this language because they want to translate scientific journals written in that particular language. In each instance, what the students are planning to do with the behavior once they have learned it is sufficiently different from the other students' use of the behavior that it should be taught and tested differently for each of the different students, even though all of the students may learn the same basic common objectives. As another example, which might be more realistic in light of today's instructional problems, students are being assigned to special reading programs; yetc, depending on the age of the student, why they are learning to read and how they will use this skill will vary from student to student. Some students may be learning to read in order to read vocational or technical materials. Some adult students may be learning to read just in order to be able to read the newspapers. Other students may be learning to read in order to read college level technical textbooks, and some students may be just learning to read in order to read the material they encounter in their everyday school life at whatever level they are at. As it is presently, the special reading programs are taught and tested (in most cases) as if the students should be learning to read for the sake of reading rather than learning to read in order to have a tool to learn more about some other topic or subject. By asking the second and third questions, the teaching of reading and for sure the testing for achievement in reading should reflect *how the student is going to use a particular reading behavior.*

If the answer to the second and/or third question is similar to any of the following, the value and use of the SO and/or test item should be doubtful: *I can not think of how the student could use what would be learned in this SO or test item; I learned the same thing when I was a student and I've never used it;* or *I can see how this could be used, but these students will probably never be in that situation.*

Similar to the second and third questions, the answer to the fourth and fifth question may overlap and tend to be answers to a more general question, *Once the student has learned it, how long do you want the student to remember it?* The reason for breaking the general question into two parts is that the answers to the two separate questions will be a little more specific and as such, will provide better guidelines for action. Notice, how the answers to the second and third questions affect the answers to the fourth and fifth questions. Obviously, if the learner will not be using what has been learned by achieving the SO or test item, the fourth and fifth questions are useless and do not apply. In answering the fourth question, if the delay before using the learned behavior is very long, there is a good chance that the learner will forget the learned behavior before there is a chance to use it. If this is the case, then it may be more important to teach and have the student learn the following:

— How to know when you need to know the behavior to be learned in the SO or test item?

— Once you know that you need to know the behavior in the SO or test item, how can you relearn it or how can you retrieve it from other sources?

In other words, if the learner is apt to forget a learned behavior before he or she has a chance to use it, it may be better to teach the learner information retrieval and processing skills and also make sure the learner has learned to be an independent learner. These skills will be used more often and will be easier to retain and maintain.

If the answer to the fifth question is that the behavior will not be used very frequently, then the teaching and learning of information retrieval and processing skills would be much more efficient than having the learner relearn the behavior each time it is needed. However, if the answer to the fifth question is that once the learner starts using the behavior, it will be used frequently, then it might be better to teach the learner how to relearn it when needed and the frequent use will maintain the behavior.

NOTE: If whatever is to be relearned was actually learned once before, then the problem is not to learn the same thing all over again, but to learn how to retrieve what was once learned from the memory part of the mind. This can be done usually by a quick review to strengthen the retrieval associations. If whatever is to be relearned was not actually learned before, then it will have to be learned completely instead of relearned. Frequently, teachers assume that if students have had a prerequisite course that the students should know 100 percent of the course and if they do not, the students must have *forgotten* whatever they do not know. The fact that the students received "A's", "B's", "C's", "D's", and maybe even "F's" indicates that the students did not learn parts of the course in the first place. Although the phrase *forgetting something* is commonly interpreted by most people as the *something* has disappeared from the mind, if the *something* was ever actually learned, that *something* is still in the mind and what is actually lost are the retrieval connections that are necessary to locate or recall the *something*.

A secondary importance of the fourth and fifth questions may be in pointing out that these questions of retention raise another question concerning the present traditional practices: Are educators only interested in students learning something long enough to pass tests? The failure that an educator may give a student remains on the student's records for the rest of his life and may seriously affect the student's future. If the failing student's classmates would not be able to answer these same test items three months, six months, a year, or two years later, can educators really justify the potential damage they may do to a student's future by giving "F" grades?

The sixth question has two functions. If the first five questions had satisfactory answers which tended to justify the relevance of the SO or test item, then the answer to the sixth question may just be a reinforcement and will help indicate the importance or priority in the learning of the SO or test item. If the answers to the first five questions were not as helpful as desired, it could be because the item is not very good or not clearly stated. In specifying what a person can not do as a result of not achieving the SO or test item, you should actually be restating the behavior described in the SO or test item. If they are not the same, what was specified that the learner can not do is really what the SO or test item should be if the learner can do it. By changing the SO or test item to match the answer to the sixth question (in a positive sense) and then go back and check out the revised SO or test item with the first ive questions again. The answer should be much more help in justifying he revised SO or test item.

The answer to the seventh question should be primarily concerned with the affective domain. In reference to SO's and test items dealing with career skills, the answer might be that the learning of the SO's and est items will help the student be more proficient in his or her job and consequently will help develop a more positive self-image. In some of the humanizing courses, the achievement of the SO's and test items should be defended in terms of how the learning will help the student get along and interact with his or her fellow human beings. In other courses, the achievement of the SO's and test items might be defended on the basis of improving the students' level of self-satisfaction or on the basis of improving the students' skills at self-expression which in turn may lead to increased freedom in creativity and then greater self-satisfaction. Although certain SO's and test items may not have any importance or utility as far as career goals or daily survival are concerned, the achievement of these SO's and test items may be socially useful in particular social groups, i.e., manners, traditional expressions, conversational topics, etc.

1. APPLYING THE QUESTIONS TO COURSES

One of the first things that became apparent when you start asking these questions of courses is that there are many situations where the utilization of the achievement of certain SO's and test items depend on the achievement of SO's and test items in other courses. In other words, most problems in life do not lend themselves to solutions which are arrived at by thinking English for a period of time, mathematics for a period of time, history for a period of time, chemistry for a period of time, etc. The concept of courses is an artificial way of looking at life and is primarily a convenience for teachers and the traditional form of teaching (presenting course content). Because of the integral relationship among the courses as they affect life, there is an overlap and duplication in courses — particularly in the humanities area. For example, for a good understanding of a certain period in history, it is necessary and useful to study the actual history and politics of the period; the literature, music, and arts of the period; the economics and geography of the period; and the psychology, philosophy, and sociology of the period. Competent and concerned teachers in any one of these subjects who are covering a particular period of history emphasizing their own subject area, will also bring in aspects of other relevant subjects to help the students understand the problems of that period.

As mentioned earlier, in applying the questions of justification to courses, the answers will usually be in the form of GO's which in turn can be very useful guidelines for the evaluation of subsequent SO's and test items.

Literature Courses:

In response to the first question, I usually get the following answers: to have a better understanding of the different types of litera
ture; to be able to identify different literary styles and techniques; tc
appreciate good literature; to have a better understanding of people and
places here and around the world in the past and in our contemporary
society; etc. Of interest, is that very rarely do I ever get an answer that
specifies a particular piece of literature even though the course may be
concerned with only one literary piece. For example, when I ask the
first question of teachers of a course on Hamlet, they usually say, *to
have a good understanding of Shakespeare* or *to appreciate Shakespeare*
in addition to one or more of the other statements. What this points
out, is that the vehicle or vehicles for learning are not that critical in
learning the GO's and SO's of the courses. However, in conflict with
this, is the fact that most examinations in literature courses are primarily concerned with the vehicles for learning rather than with the
learning that the vehicles are supposed to convey to the students.

The first answer, *to have a better understanding of the different
types of literature,* suggests subsequent SO's and test items dealing with
the identification of the different types of literature, the comparing and
contrasting of the characteristics of the different types, the analysis of
examples of literary works to identify the characteristics, etc. The next
answer, *to be able to identify different literary styles and techniques,*
suggests subsequent SO's and test items dealing with the identification
of the different styles (not from memorized selections but based on an
actual analysis of the styles) and techniques, the advantages and disadvantages of each style and technique, the reproduction of the styles
and techniques, etc. The next answer, *to appreciate good literature,*
suggests subsequent SO's and test items dealing with the listing and
identification of characterisitcs of *good literature, the evaluation of
literary works according to a set of criteria, the evaluation of a persons
own literary* tastes (affective domain)[21] etc. The next answer, *to have a*

---

[21] If a teacher is concerned about affecting the students' literary *tastes,* then the
teacher should try to evaluate whether or not he or she is actually having an
affect. This can be done by selecting a set of ten or more literary works
(paperbacks or hardcover) ranging from what the teacher would consider very
bad to very good. The students are asked to rank these literary works (anonymously) from the one they would read first to the one they would read last. Be
sure the literary works are available for the students examination and are
arranged in random order. The lists of the literary works on which the students
indicate their rankings should also be in random order. By adding up the rankings
of all of the students for each of the literary works, the teacher will have a class
ranking of the literary works from the lowest number which is the literary work
the class would tend to read first to the highest number which is the literary

(continued on next page)

better understanding of people and places here and around the world in the past and in our present society, suggests subsequent SO's and test items dealing with the comparison of people and places in the literary work with people and places out in the real world.

The answers to the rest of the questions tend to support the value of the GO's and the divergent application of the learned behavior in the courses. In asking these questions in reference to the typical test items in literature courses which are usually concerned only with the vehicles of the course, the answers tend to indicate the inappropriateness of the test items and the limited or convergent application of the learned behavior. If a course on *Hamlet* only deals with *Hamlet* and the test is only on *Hamlet*, then the application of the learned behavior is very limited and short range and the majority of the test items are probably rote memory. However, if a course on *Hamlet* uses *Hamlet* as a vehicle to teach behaviors which can be transferred to many other literary and real world situations and the examinations test for the transference of these learned behaviors, the application of the learned behaviors is unlimited and long range and the majority of the test items will be thinking items. To do this, the vehicle of the course might be *Hamlet*, but the examinations would use other literary works or real world situations.

History Courses:

In response to the first question, I usually get the following answers: to have a better understanding of today and tomorrow by a study of yesterday, to be able to profit in the future from our mistakes in the past, etc. Almost all of the answers I get indicate about the same thing but may be worded differently. Rarely do history teachers expect students to study history for the sake of history. It is rare for me to find a teacher of history that does not feel that a study of history has contemporary and future utility. This would indicate that the SO's and test items would tend to deal with problems of today and potential problems of tomorrow which are mostly thinking test items. This does

---

work the class would tend to read last. This ranking activity should be done both at the beginning and at the end of the course. By comparing the pretest and posttest class rankings with the teacher's ranking, it is possible to identify whether or not the students as a class are coming closer to the teacher's ranking. If the class ranking on the posttest is getting closer to the teacher's ranking, the the teacher is being successful in transmitting the teacher's *good tastes*. If the class ranking in the posttest is further away from the teacher's ranking of the literary works, then the teacher is doing something wrong in the design of the course. In order to eliminate or minimize the possibility of students trying to *polish the apple* by selecting the teacher's ranking, the literary works used in the evaluation should not be mentioned in the class and the evaluation should be anonymous.

551

not mean that history teachers are going to become *fortune tellers* even though history does have a tendency to repeat itself; but they will be concerned with teaching the process of studying a problem which will have utility at any time. Of interest is that rarely in history tests do I find the word *today* or *tomorrow*. Most of the test items are factual and rote memory and deal with what happened *yesterday*.

As an example, a participant in one of my problem solving seminars was a dean of liberal arts division and a teacher of an ancient history course. I asked him the first question and he gave me the usual answer that the study of ancient history had utility in understanding today. He added that he thought the course was exciting because of this utility. He also complained because students usually failed to make the connection and see the utility of the course since in many aspects, the problems of people in ancient history are not much different than the problems of today. I asked to see one of his tests and the first test question I saw was, *What was the name of the emperor who started a dynasty that lasted 300 years?* When I asked the teacher how knowing that emperor's name would help the student understand the problems of today, it became obvious to the teacher that most of his test items were irrelevant. He claimed that in his classes he talked about the utility of studying ancient history and gave examples to students. The problem, of course, was that students study what is on tests and if the tests are irrelevant, in the students' minds, the course is irrelevant. As a result of the problem solving seminar this teacher identified the various process objectives he was concerned with and then went back to his ancient history class and asked them to list the problems they were concerned with at the local, state, regional, national, and international levels. In looking over these problems, he picked those that had parallels back in ancient history. In the revised course, the students studied the problems they were concerned about from the point of view of how they occurred and were resolved in ancient history. Under this approach, the problems were just vehicles for learning the processes of historical and contemporary problem analysis and synthesis.

A situation which closely parallels the teaching of history is the preaching of the gospel of various religious faiths. In seminars with priests, rabbies, and pastors of different denominations, concerning the improvement of communication, we generally identified three types of priests, rabbies, and pastors: the reporter type, who in the sermon is reporting what happened two thousand or more years ago; the interpreter type, who in the sermon is reporting what happened two thousand or more years ago but tries to find something contemporary to associate with what is being reported; and the communicator type, who after identifying the problems of his congregation, tries to find something that happened two thousand or more years ago that will help solve the problems and then reports this in the sermon. The sermons of the *reporter* and the *interpretor* types are usually determined by the topics selected and distributed from some central office regardless of the problems and needs of the congregations. However, the topics of the sermons of the *communicator* type can never be determined ahead of time because it depends on the problems and needs of the congregations.

Of interest, is the experience of the *communicator* and the history teacher who also starts with the problems of today in that over a period of a year, almost the same historical content is covered that would be traditionally covered. The difference is that the emphasis is on today with reference to yesterday rather than the emphasis on yesterday with reference to today. Of critical importance is that although the content of the classroom discussions and the sermons under this approach is more relevant to the listener, they are just vehicles for learning the process of analyzing today's problems in light of yesterday's experiences. If the teacher (pastor, priest, or rabbi) concentrates on the vehicle rather than the process, the presentations have only contemporary relevance and are not necessarily transferable to new or different problems. In order to develop people who are independent thinkers, it is critical to teach the process.

As in the case of literature, the answers to the other questions of justification tend to support the need for the teaching and testing of the process rather than this historical content of the course. As such, most of the tests would be of the thinking type rather than rote memory (and for sure the tests would not be of the multiple-choice type) and would either be a *take home* type test or one taken in a part of a library where a variety of reference sources are available and which act as an integral part of learning the *process*.

Social Studies (the study of a particular country or region of the world)

This is in reference to the elementary or junior high courses where the students study *Our Latin American Neighbors* or some similar title. In response to the first question, I usually get the following answers: to have a better understanding of that particular country or region of the world; to gain an appreciation for the differences among countries and regions of the world; or to learn the process of stydying a country or region of the world. With reference to the first answer and to the fourth and fifth question of justification (concerning retention), the study of these countries or regions in elementary school for use at a much later time really limits the utility of the courses because by the time the students need the information, they have probably forgotten most of it. The second answer indicates a need for simultaneous study of several different countries or regions. With reference to the second and third questions (conditions for utility), the second answer is extended to include the idea that at sometime in the future the students will want to know more about a particular country or region of the world or even a region of our own country. This results in making the second answer fall into the same problem of retention as the first answer.

The third answer becomes the only acceptable answer because the process of analyzing a problem (a country, region of the world, or many other problems) is something that will be used many times and as such will be retained. This indicates that these courses could use the study *of our Latin American neighbors* (or any other country or region of the world) as a vehicle for learning the process. Under this approach, the SO's and test items would not be concerned with the vehicles as they are in the present approach, they would be concerned with applying the process, i.e., given the following list of countries or regions of the world, select one that you (the student) are interested in and apply the process you learned in the study of Latin America (or some other vehicle used in the course) to the analysis of this country or region of the world according to the following criteria (the SO's of the process): etc.

Psychology (basic course or courses)

In response to the first question, I usually get one or more of the following three answers: to have a better understanding of self; to have a better understanding of others; and/or to improve interpersonal communication. If any one or more of these GO's are really why students should take psychology, then the course (or courses) should be required of everyone who *expects to live!* The use of the SO's would be so immediate and continuous that questions four and five (retention) would not have to be considered and the answers to questions six and seven become obvious.

The answers to questions two and three with reference to all three answers to the first question suggest a need for teaching and testing via a variety of simulated situations. For example, if one of the values of studying psychology is to have a better understanding of self, then the teaching and testing should be concerned with a series of simulated situations in which the student has to identify his or her reactions, feelings, and/or opinions in regard to the situations (which is the self at the present time) and then realizing that almost all of these reactions, feelings, and opinions are learned rather than innate, the student should attempt to identify how this learning took place, i.e., state two or more examples in which your family or social milieu helped you to develop your present reaction, feeling, or opinion, state the psychological principle(s) involved in each example, and prove that the principle(s) was involved by underlining the words, phrases, or sentences in your ex-

mples which illustrate the principle(s). If another one of the values of
tudying psychology is to have a better understanding of others, then
he teaching and testing should be concerned with a series of simulated
ituations (could be the same ones used with understanding self) in
vhich the student is given the reaction, feeling, and/or opinion that
omeone else might have in regard to the situation (both extremes of
eactions, feelings, and opinions should be included) and then the
tudent is asked to hypothesize how the learning of the others' reac-
ion, feeling, or opinion took place, i.e., state two or more examples in
vhich the family or social milieu of the other person helped to develop
hat person's present reaction, feeling, or opinion, state the psychologi-
al principle(s) involved in each example, and prove that the princi-
ple(s) was involved by underlining the words, phrases, or sentences in
he examples which illustrate the principle(s). If the third value of
tudying psychology is to improve interpersonal communication, then
he teaching and testing should be concerned with a series of interper-
onal situations in which there is a potential problem. The student
ould then be asked to role play both sides of the situation by taking
ne at a time and identify the person's communication goal(s), write a
prief dialogue (including the non-verbal communication), defend each
ine of the dialogue (and each non-verbal action) used by the role being
played by citing the psychological principle involved, and describe how
he verbal and non-verbal dialogue will achieve the goal(s) of the
nterpersonal communication.

Oddly enough, most basic psychology courses are tested with mul-
iple-choice test items which are very inappropriate (in addition to all
f the other things mentioned previously wrong with using multiple-
hoice items) because in answering them, the students do not really
tudy their own self, they do not really study others (except to
ut-psych the maker of the test) nor do they learn how to improve
nterpersonal communication. Since students learn what is on tests and
he tests are inappropriate the basic psychology course as it is presently
aught and particularly tested in most schools is not a very useful
ourse and certainly should not be required of all students.

Sociology (basic course)

In response to the first question, I usually get variations of the
ollowing answer, *to learn how to interact with groups*. Technically,
ociology is supposed to be the study of groups; but if it was limited to
his, sociology would have limited utility for the individual. Therefore,
pasic courses in sociology are often combined with social psychology
vhich is concerned with the interactions of the group and the indivi-
luals in the group, i.e., how the group affects the individual and how
he individual can and does affect the group. As with psychology, if

555

learning how to interact with groups is really the value or GO in taking sociology, then this course should be required of every student who expects to live in any social group. Again, the use of the SO's of the course would be so immediate and continuous that questions four through seven would not even have to be asked.

The answers to questions two and three suggest that the teaching and testing of a basic sociology course should utilize a variety of simulated and real social groups within which the students can learn to interact and to apply the principles of sociology. Whereas the basic course in psychology provides an environment within which the student can learn how an individual's attitudes, values, and beliefs are developed, maintained, changed, and extinguished, a basic course in sociology should provide an environment within which the student can learn how group attitudes, values, and beliefs are developed, maintained, changed, and extinguished in addition to the interactions between the individual and the group.

If psychology and sociology are taught and tested along the lines indicated by the GO's given in answer to the first question of justification, these two courses would have a major impact on developing humaness in students. The problem is that the basic course in sociology like the basic courses in psychology are too often tested with multiple-choice test items which are inappropriate in reference to the GO's and SO's of sociology and inhumane with reference to the students.

Philosophy

In response to the first question, the answers I get from teachers of philosophy vary more than the answers I get from teachers of other subject matter areas. The present emphasis in most basic philosophy courses appears to be on the study of the writings of famous philosophers. Although the knowledge gained from studying the words and ideas of great philosophers may be useful as conversational topics, there is not much utility beyond that. As a consequence, some philosophy teachers respond to the first question with answers like *to broaden an individual's understanding of the world* or *to help develop a student's intellectual background*. These answers are so general that they are of little value in trying to determine a more specific direction. However, a few philosophy teachers respond with answers like, *to help students identify their own philosophy* and *to be able to identify the philosophy of others*. In a basic philosophy course where these two answers are the GO's of the course, the course joins psychology and sociology in that it should be required of every student who expects to live in a social context. If a person's philosophy can be defined as the sum of all the persons habitual attitudes, values, and

556

beliefs, it can be readily seen that because of their very close inter-relationships these three courses form a triad. Of special interest about these three courses, almost everyone tries to apply the SO's of the courses regardless of whether or not they have ever had the courses and of whether or not they have learned the SO's suggested by the GO's (responses to the first question). The problem is that too often the applications are faulty as far as principles are concerned, used on an intuitive or almost subconscious basis, and controlled more by emotional tendencies than by reason. For example, everyone operates according to a philosophy (their habitual attitudes, values, and beliefs) even if they don't know what it is. A very important part of understanding one's self is to be able to identify one's own philosophy which then enables you to predict your reactions and emotional tendencies in certain situations. If for some reason you don't want to react in certain ways, by being able to predict your reactions ahead of time, you can control your reactions by reason before emotion takes over. In being able to identify the philosophy of other people by what they do, say, and write, it is possible to predict their reactions and emotional tendencies. This information together with the knowledge of your own philosophy can be used to predict the degree of conflict or accord in interpersonal relationships which in turn can be used to facilitate rational discourse rather than building emotional barriers.

In accordance with the general guidelines of *to help students identify their own philosophy and the philosophy of others*, a course in philosophy could use the study of famous philosophers as vehicles for learning how to identify philosophies and also as sources for labeling certain types of philosophies. However, the testing should include the identification of a person's own philosophy and the identification of other peoples' philosophy based on an analysis of what they do, say, and/or write. For example, given an editorial in a newspaper or a magazine, the student should write down his or her first impression of what the author of the article is trying to day, (conclusions, judgements, verdicts, etc.) then the student should identify and differentiate between the statements of fact and the statements of opinion in the editorial (the statements of opinion are usually indicators of the author's philosophy), and then the student should reevaluate the acceptability of the editorial on the basis of the following criteria: do the statements of fact support the statements of opinion are there sufficient facts to make conclusions, are the stated conclusions valid with reference to the statements of fact, and are the valid conclusions based on the facts equivalent to the stated conclusions. If a student has learned how to identify a person's philosophy based on the person's stated opinions and selection of facts,[22] the student should be able to analyze the person's process of arriving at conclusions and identify whether or not the person is being honest or subversive in his or her discourse. Using this process, the student can avoid being brainwashed and/or manipulated without his or her knowledge of what is happening. This same procedure can be used to evaluate printed promotional brochures and advertisements.

Because of the continuous barrage of audio and/or visual statements aimed at influencing young peoples' minds and subsequent actions by advertisers, peer groups, political groups, etc., a very important survival skill if we want our young people to be independent thinkers is to help them learn to listen and evaluate audio or oral statements *on-the-run*. By using audio tapes and essentially the same procedures as used with printed materials, students can learn to evaluate taped oral statements. Of course, in learning to evaluate on-going presentations, the student will not have time to list all of the statements of fact and the statements of opinions; therefore, since the critical relationships concerns the conclusions and statements of fact, students can be trained to identify audio statements of fact and to evaluate whether or not the conclusions are valid based on the statements of fact.

The other questions of justification when asked in reference to a utilitarian type of a philosophy course tend to support this type of a course. When these questions are asked of the typical philosophy course which emphasizes the writings of the great philosophers only, the answers tend to indicate that there is not much value or utility in the course.

Integrated Courses

Traditionally, most courses not in a sequence of related titles (Basic Accounting, Intermediate Accounting, Advanced Accounting; Spanish I, Spanish II; etc.) are taught as isolated courses or sequences which have little, if any, interrelationships, particularly when tested as most courses are traditionally tested. Some colleges and universities have experimented with integrated courses such that the students study certain topics or periods of history from a variety of viewpoints as to the contributions of the various fields of study to the topics or periods of history. The emphasis is on how the various fields of study complement each other. Another way of looking at certain fields of study is on how they contribute to and/or build on the other areas. For example,

---

[22] Given a population of facts which could be stated, the selection of certain ones to be used (usually ones that will appear to support certain opinions and conclusions) and the exclusion of other facts (usually ones that tend to refute certain opinions and conclusions) are also good indicators of a person's philosophy in addition to the person's stated opinions.

psychology could be the study of a person's (self and others) *individual* attitudes, values, and beliefs from the point of view of how they were developed (past) and how they are demonstrated (present). Philosophy could be the study of a person's (self and others) *collective* attitudes, values, and beliefs which are habitual (low level of consciousness) from the point of view of identification of the philosophy and predictions of future actions and reactions of the individual alone or interacting with other individuals. Sociology could be the study of the interactions of individuals with certain attitudes, values, beliefs, and a philosophy with groups which reflect a consensus of certain attitudes, values, beliefs, and a philosophy. History could be the study of the interactions of individuals and groups with other individuals and groups during the past from the point of view of *present* attitudes, values, beliefs, and philosophies. Literature could be the study of the interactions of individuals and groups with other individuals and groups during various periods of the past, present, or predicted future from the point of view of the prevailing attitudes, values, beliefs, and philosophies *at the time the literature was written.*

Other Courses

The same situations exist for most courses when the questions of justification are asked which also points out that the GO's that are given to substantiate having courses in the curriculum are in conflict or forgotten when the courses are actually taught. *Modern math* is often defended on the basis that it is designed to help the student become a more creative problem solver; yet, few students are evaluated on the basis of their ability to solve problems creatively and many students are failed because they don't solve problems in the manner suggested by the teacher.

Almost every Latin teacher states that a study of Latin will help the student learn English; yet, it is the rare Latin teacher who tests students on their understanding of English via their knowledge of Latin. Most foreign language teachers claim that a study of a foreign language helps the students understand how the person thinks that is raised in the foreign language and culture; yet, it is the rare foreign language teacher that actually teaches and tests his or her students, on what the language and cultural influences are on thinking patterns and on how these influences affect personal and group intercultural relationships. In countries such as Canada where there are two or more major cultural groups, the development of mutual cooperation, understanding, and respect between the cultural groups is critically dependent upon the foreign language teachers within each group who are teaching the language and culture of the other group. If they do not teach and test how the language and culture of the other group affects their thinking patterns, the teachers may succeed in teaching the language but they will fail to develop an understanding of the people who use the language.

Most art teachers will state that everyone has a need to express himself or herself in some artistic manner, i.e., interior decorating, clothes, landscaping, mechanical customizing (cars, motorcycles), etc; yet, all too often the student who doesn't have talent in the traditional arts (painting and sculpture) doesn't stay in art because his or her way of expressing isn't traditional. The method of expressing artistic principles is the vehicle for learning not the SO. Generally speaking, the students who are not in the art classes could probably profit most from being in the art classes (assuming the teachers were willing to nurture the students' artistic abilities). The students who are in the art classes now generally have talent (nature) and will probably learn in spite of the teachers (assuming the teachers won't inhibit the students' natural abilities).

Although most botany and biology teachers admit that unless students are majoring in some area of science, their courses could be rather irrelevant, in asking the questions of justification, there are some areas in both courses which with some changes in emphasis could become very relevant. Almost every person, at some time in their life, will be involved with trying to grow plants, shrubs, and/or trees. Practical courses in botany could be developed which would include soil analysis, plant pathology, landscape design, etc. The same kind of changes could be made in biology courses. Although not many students in high school biology courses will go on to major in one of the biological sciences, all of them have to take care of themselves (physically) and most of them will take care of other people and animals at some point in their lives. As such, there is a need for a practical course on physical health needs, problems, and solutions.

Although speech and drama courses are considered by most of the teachers who teach them as courses in communication, rarely are the students in these courses evaluated on their ability to communicate. Similar to teacher training courses, students in most speech and drama courses are evaluated on the basis of how they presented their message (regardless of whether or not the message was received). For example, when a student gives a typical speech *to inform*, the student is evaluated on his or her stance, eye contact, voice inflection, etc., and rarely are the students who listened to the speech tested to find out whether or not they were actually *informed* by the student giving the speech. According to the answers giving to the questions of justification, the types of speeches given by students in the speech course can be justified, but not the way these speeches are presently evaluated. Just as the student teacher during practice teaching should be evaluated on the results of his or her teaching (did the students being taught learn what they were supposed to) rather than on his or her performance; students giving speeches to *inform* should be evaluated on the results of whether or not they *informed*; students giving speeches to *demonstrate* should be evaluated on the results of whether or not they demonstrated well enough to communicate key points of the demonstration and/or well enough for a random sample of listeners to be able to perform the activity in the demonstration; students giving speeches to *persuade* should be evaluated on the results of how much the average listener was persuaded as measured by the difference between pre and post attitude tests; etc. In a parallel situation, almost all teachers of drama state that drama or theater is a form of communication; yet, it is an extremely rare event to find a teacher who evaluates the student actors and actresses on the basis of whether or not the students communicated to the audience via their acting. Student actors and actresses are usually evaluated on the basis of their acting rather than on the results of their acting.[23] Teachers and particularly students find it exciting to realize that they can actually affect the communication of the author's message by their actions and enunciation and without changing any of the author's words. They also find out that in order to communicate successfully to different audiences it is necessary to change their actions and ennunciation. These discoveries are in line with the answers to the questions of justification regarding the taking of a drama course.

In applying the questions of justification to physical education courses, the use and teaching of team sports becomes almost inappropriate because few people are actually involved in team sports after leaving their formal schooling. Two general objectives which are emphasized by the answers to the questions of justification are *to maintain a healthy body throughout a persons life* and *to enjoy physically active leisure time activities*. The first GO indicates a continuity in physical education courses which is not present in most school programs. In observing most physical education programs in action, it appears as if the SO is to keep the students busy and to help them get rid of *excess* energy. Once the criteria for a *healthy body* are identified, there is no

---

[23] In order to evaluate the results, the students and/or the teacher should determine what the author of the play is trying to communicate or what the director of the play and/or the actors are trying to communicate, then they should make up a series of questions which, if answered correctly, would indicate the person received the correct message. At the end of the play, the audience would be asked to respond to the questions anonymously and in writing. If the vast majority of the audience were successfully communicated to, then whatever the author, director, and actors did, it was good. However, if a number of the members of the audience answered the questions incorrectly, then something is wrong in the communication process. (The greater the percentage of the audience that answers the questions incorrectly, the greater the communication problem.

reason why physical education courses could not be aimed at helping students achieve this level of physical fitness and then to maintain it at that level. For example, a student who is excessively overweight and lacks physical fitness would probably put in more hours per week than other students and the teacher would work with the student's parents and family doctor in a continuous long range (over a number of years, if necessary) program designed to correct the problems. On the other hand, a student that is physically fit would not have to take any physical education courses designed to improve physical fitness as long as the student maintains his or her own physical fitness through his or her own activities outside of school.

With reference to the second GO, there would probably not be any specific leisure time game, sport, or activity which should be required, but students might be required to learn one or more games, sports, or activities within each of several categories. Although many critics of the schools have been against such courses as archery, horseback riding, etc., these courses may well be the ones that would be appropriate for some students if these are the activities that they would like to perform in their leisure time. Courses which may be appropriate because they are popular adult leisure time activities but are only offered in a few schools might be, hiking, camping, boating, motorcycling, skiing, skating, etc.

2. APPLYING THE QUESTIONS TO NON-SPECIFIC TEST ITEMS

The non-specific or general objective (GO) has been defined earlier as being an objective which is not measurable. The non-specific or general test item can be defined in the same manner except that it usually is measured anyway because it is given in a testing situation. Although most test items are specific in that the teacher or whoever is doing the testing knows ahead of time what to look for in evaluating the students' responses to the test items, some teachers ask *general* test items or questions and at the time of the test have not identified what the answer or answers should be. As a result, this type of test item or question is frequently evaluated very subjectively and is very much affected by the interpersonal relationship between the student and the teacher. Because these general test items are most often created during the last few moments before a scheduled test period, there is usually little, if any, relationship between the test items and the course objectives (either GO's or SO's) and they are usually open-ended essay type questions. (Many term papers and essays fit into this category of general test items.) Measurable criteria, if any, which may be used in part to evaluate the students' responses, are generally identified just before the evaluation process or often even during the evaluation process, i.e., *This is a good answer. The other students should have thought of it too.* (Responses which were evaluated *before* the new criteria was discovered are okay; but the responses which are evaluated *after* the new criteria was discovered are evaluated in accordance with the new criteria.) Because of the capriciousness involved in the creation and evaluation of the general test items or questions, there is hardly any foundation from which a person could generate relevant specific objectives and/or specific test items. Therefore, most general test items or questions can be considered irrelevant and of such little value to either the teacher or the students that they should just be discarded.

Some teachers will try to defend the use of the general test items or questions from the point of view that whatever the students' answers are, they should be acceptable and as such, there is no need for measurable criteria. Under these conditions, the situation should not be considered as a test nor should any evaluation or grades be given to the students. In fact, under these conditions, a student should be able to hand in a paper without any responses on it at all. However, chances are that the student would be evaluated negatively for not responding because almost all teachers actually do have criteria for evaluating general test items or questions even though they aren't aware of them. Therefore, the general test items or questions asked by those teachers who claim they are not going to evaluate them should also be discarded as busywork and non- productive.

3. APPLYING THE QUESTIONS TO NON-SPECIFIC OBJECTIVES (GO'S).

Although non-specific or general test items are created capriciously and as such are not worth the energy it takes to question them, there are three good reasons for questioning non-specific or general objectives. First of all, by applying the questions of justification, it is possible to determine if the general objective is what is really wanted by the teachers. Secondly, by questioning the amgibuous terms in the general objective, it is possible to redefine the general objective in more specific terms. Third, the answers to the questions can serve as a defense of why the newly derived SO's should be learned and may also bring out bases for motivating students to want to learn the SO's.

The objectives discussed in this unit have been taken from state guidelines for elementary and secondary instruction and from materials developed by teachers at all levels of instruction (including colleges, universities, and technical post-secondary schools). These objectives are typical of the kinds of objectives used in almost all areas of instruction; although during the past few years, a small but increasing number of educators, individually and in groups, are developing much more specific and measurable learning objectives. The biggest problem with non-specified learning objectives is that teachers do not know what it is they are supposed to do to teach the objectives or how they are supposed to measure the achievement of the objectives. As a result, most educators do not pay much attention to these nonspecified objectives once they have been written. It is also important to point out that quite often, these nonspecified objectives are directed towards what the teacher should be teaching, not what the learner should be learning. Teacher objectives usually contain such words and phrases as: to assist students, to help students, to provide, to present, to cover (certain content), to create (in students) an attitude, etc. Nonspecified learning objectives, as indicated earlier, usually contain such words and phrases as comprehend, understand, to thoroughly understand, appreciation for, an awareness of, an interest in, familiar with, knowledgeable about, to know, etc.

Another common type of objective is one that is specific, but it is specifying an activity rather than learning, i.e., write four essays after completing the assigned reading (H.S. English); participate in class discussions; complete three projects; answer a 20-item multiple-choice test. In order to relate the above objectives to learning, it would be necessary to specify the criteria for evaluation and in the case of the test, the test would have to be included in the objective (the student will be able to answer correctly the following 20-item test).

Because the emphasis of teaching at most levels of education is on the teaching of a particular subject matter rather than on the teaching of students, many teachers do not recognize the commonalities in instructional practices regardless of the subject matter area or the instructional level (from preschool to graduate level). As a result, teachers have a tendency to be defensive about their own particular subject matter area and equate the differences in subject matter to differences in teaching practices. This reaction can be identified in a seminar with teachers when after describing a teaching practice using mathematics as an example, an English teacher will say, *that may be true in mathematics, but it doesn't happen (or it won't work) in English.* In a subsequent seminar with a different group of teachers, if the same teaching practice is described using English as an example, a mathematics teacher will say, *That may be true in English, but it doesn't happen (or it won't work) in mathematics.* The same problem exists in reference to the different levels of instruction. Preschool, elementary, secondary, undergraduate, technical, graduate, and continuing adult education teachers generally equate the differences in educational levels to differences in teaching practices. This reaction can be identified in a seminar with teachers of different levels when after describing a teaching practice using a secondary level subject as an example, teachers at the other levels will say, *That may be true at the secondary level, but it doesn't happen (or won't work) at the elemen-*

tary (undergraduate, graduate, etc.) level. In a subsequent seminar with a different group of teachers, if the same teaching practice is described using an elementary level subject as an example, teachers at the other levels will say, *That may be true at the elementary level, but it doesn't happen (or won't work) at the secondary (undergraduate, graduate, etc.) level.*

In order to overcome these problems, in describing a particular practice to teachers, I have found that it is necessary to cite examples in different subject matter areas and at different instructional levels. Therefore, the following objectives (and test items in subsequent units) have been taken from many different subject matter areas and at different levels of instruction. Since the questions to be asked are the same regardless of the subject matter or the level, it is not necessary for the reader to read all of the examples. Just read those that you feel are relevant to your interests. Actually, the importance in reading the examples is not in the subject matter or instructional level, but in the process of asking the questions. After you have read the answers to the questions of justification for three or four of the objectives, you may want to practice asking the questions of justification of subsequent objectives and see if your answers are similar to the ones I have written. In increasing the specification of objectives, you may want to try the same procedure. After reading the questions which I have asked in order to increase the specificity of three or four objectives, you may want to cover up the questions which I have asked of subsequent objectives and guess what kinds of questions you would ask; then compare your questions with my questions. If you practice these behaviors in going through the objectives listed in this unit, you should be able to look at other nonspecified objectives and even specified objectives and by asking the questions of justification, identify whether or not the objectives are stated are what is really wanted and to increase the specificity of the general objectives by questioning the ambiguous terms and ask the right kinds of questions which will help you as a teacher to be more specific in what you really want your students to learn. (When you have read as much as you want of this unit, skip to page 585).

a.   To understand about the nature of the terrain over which the padres traveled. (California; fourth grade; Social Studies.)

JUSTIFICATION — Of what value to a student would be this understanding? Probably not very much as it is presently worded. Under what conditions would this understanding be useful? Possibly in being concerned about contemporary transportation problems, it could be useful to study the various modes of transportation used over the decades (centuries) and examine the problems encountered and their solutions from the point-of-view of learning the process of solving transportation problems and the effects of solutions on society. If this would be the case, the emphasis would not be on the padres or only that period of time. The other questions of justification tend to support the emptiness of the GO as stated and the need to change the GO to emphasize something different.

INCREASING SPECIFICATIONS — Assuming the GO is what a teacher wants, the answers to the following questions will help to derive SO's from the GO. How many padres are you concerned with? During what period of their lives or what particular trips that they took are you concerned with? In reference to the nature of the terrain, which facets of the nature of the terrain are important? What is meant by *understand?* How does a teacher know when one student *understands* and another student *doesn't understand?*

b. *To list some reasons for, and formulate some rules to protect wildlife. (Alaska; seventh grade; Science.)*

JUSTIFICATION — Of what value to a student would it be to be able to achieve this GO? By involving the student in this GO, the student would most likely develop positive attitudes towards the conservation of wildlife. Under what conditions would the learning be useful? If the emphasis was only on Alaska, the learning would have limited application. However, if the GO was changed to include the protection of wildlife anyplace where they are in danger of being annihilated, the learning would be more useful. What is the person supposed to do under the conditions where the learning of the GO is useful? Answers to this question might tend to indicate that what is important for the student to learn is the process of identifying a species of wildlife in need of help, identifying the causes of extinction, and the identification of courses of action to slow, stop, or reverse the trend towards extention (which changes the GO). Answers to the other questions tend to support the change in the objective and the importance of the GO.

INCREASING SPECIFICATION—Which wildlife are you specifically concerned about? Why do you want to protect them? What are the criteria for evaluating a rule? How many rules are *some rules?* How many reasons are the students supposed to list — five, ten, twenty?

c. *To have an acquaintance with vocabulary items that bring content into structure of sound, form, order, etc. (Alabama; Foreign Languages.)*

JUSTIFICATION — This GO is so general, it will have to be broken down into more specific GO's before the questions of justification can be applied advantageously.

INCREASING SPECIFICATION — What is meant by *acquaintance* with vocabulary items? How does the teacher know when one student has this *acquaintance* and another student doesn't have this *acquaintance?* How many vocabulary items are involved — 100, 200, 1,000? Are all the vocabulary items concerned with sound, form and order, or are just some items concerned with sound and some with form and some with order, or some with all three? What is meant by bring *content* into the structure of sound, of form, and of order? What else is included in *etc.?*

d. *To understand that when the Mexicans became independent in 1821, the frontier conditions were neglected in favor of problems nearer Mexico City. (Arizona; History and Government.)*

JUSTIFICATION — Of what value is it for the students in Arizona to understand this? As the objective is presently stated, there is probably little value in learning this objective. Under what conditions will be learning of this objective be useful? Again, as the objective is presently stated, the learning would probably not be useful. However, the objective tends to indicate that as a result of the frontier conditions that were neglected something happened in the Arizona territory. Are there some specific conditions in Arizona today that are a result of the situation described in the objective? If yes, the more appropriate objective would deal with the conditions existing today which affect the students (how did the conditions develop, what are they today, how do they affect the people today, and what should a person do to cope with or minimize these affects). The other questions tend to support that this objective is inappropriate as it is presently stated.

INCREASING SPECIFICATION — What frontier conditions were neglected? In what ways were they neglected? What were the results? What is it that a student should do in order to *understand?*

e. *Students should be able to know the plants and animals which have lived on the earth for a long time. (Georgia; Grade 4; Science.)*

JUSTIFICATION — Of what value is it for students to know these plants and animals? As the objective is presently stated, there is probably not much value. Under what conditions will this knowledge be useful? As presently stated, the knowledge would probably not be very useful under any conditions. Does this refer to plants and animals that have a long life span, or that the species itself has remained unchanged over a number of years, or do we want the students to know the evolution of certain plants and animals with the specific changes in mind? I tend to believe that the objective is aimed at helping the students understand that environment causes changes in most plants and animals over long periods of time. If this is correct, it would be more appropriate to have the students trace the evolution of several plants and animals up to today. The emphasis would be on the process of evolution and adaptation to environment rather than on specific plants or animals. Because of the emphasis and the grade level, it would probably also be appropriate to use locally known plants and animals if possible. The other questions tend to support that the objective as presently stated is inappropriate.

INCREASING SPECIFICATION — How many plants — 10 plants, 100 plants, 200 plants? How many animals — 5, 20, 50? How long is a *long time?* What should the student know about the plants and animals — should they just know their names and list them or recite them orally, should they be able to recognize photographs, should they be able to list identifying characteristics, should they be able to compare and contrast plants and animals: should any relationships be established between the plants and animals and the needs of human beings for clothing and food?

f. *To understand that we are protected, and protect others from coughs and sneezes by staying home when ill. (Idaho; Kindergarten; Health and Safety.)*

JUSTIFICATION — Of what value is this understanding? From the standpoint of individual, family, and community health, this objective would seem to be of value. Under what conditions would this understanding be useful? It is rather obvious that when a student starts coughing and sneezing, it would be useful if the child and his or her parents had this understanding. Notice, that this suggests that the instruction should include parents. Also, because the students probably don't read or write very much at this age, the instructional activities should include visuals (what does a child look like that has a cold) and audio (what does it sound like when a child coughs and sneezes). What is a student (and parents) supposed to do under the conditions of the objective? Not only should the student stay home, but the student and/or parents should initiate a series of steps to protect the child from getting sicker, protect others from getting sick, treat the sickness, watch for symptoms of complications and/or side effects of the treatment, know when to consult outside medical advice and who to consult, etc. Most of these actions involve the parents and could be accomplished in adult education sessions for parents (again using audio and visual aids for audio and visual learning objectives). How long before the learner

568

will apply or use the understanding? This will vary for individuals. For those students who are not sick very often, it may be appropriate to have visual handouts as reference sources for students and parents when the coughing and sneezing occurs. For those students who are sick more frequently, the utilization of the understanding may be frequent enough to not need the additional reinforcement of the handouts. Because of the differences, it would probably be best to make the reinforcement handouts available to all students and parents. What if not learned? The results of the non-learning of this understanding is such that it affects almost every student and should be considered very important for both students and parents to learn. It is also important to point out that this general objective contains both cognitive and affective elements. The symptoms and results of coughing and sneezing and the steps to take in prevention and treatment tend to primarily concern cognitive and sensory learning. However, the motivation to actually react to the symptoms and do these things primarily concerns affective learning. As such, teachers concerned with this objective should remember that it will involve both theories of instruction.

INCREASING SPECIFICATION — In what ways are we protected by staying home when ill? Are all students protected by staying home when ill? What are the criteria for a home that will serve as protection? Why should we be protected from coughs and sneezes? How much of this information should the kindergarten student know? What does a kindergarten student do to indicate that he understands that he should stay home to protect himself and others in contrast to what another student does not do which indicates he does not understand that he is supposed to stay home to protect himself and others? Are there different kinds of coughs and sneezes? Are coughs and sneezes the only symptoms which would cause us to stay home to protect ourselves and others? What are the actions the student should take in a case of coughs and sneezes relevant to a parent or to a teacher or to a school? Should the student know what happens when he is not protected?

g. *To recognize the effects of rhythm, cadence, form and mood in the meanings of oral language. (Maryland; elementary; Language Arts.)*

JUSTIFICATION — This objective is similar to objective No. 3, but is sufficiently more specific that it can be questioned with useful results. Of what value is it to recognize these effects? Almost obviously, if a person doesn't learn to recognize these effects, the person will encounter many communication problems by misinterpreting the meanings of people he or she is talking to. Under what conditions will it be useful to recognize these effects? Practically everytime that the student talks or listens to other people. Given that the objective refers to *oral* language, it should be obvious that the teaching, learning, and evaluation of this objective would involve audio tapes and if the effects are affected by nonverbal body language, then the teaching, learning, and evaluation of this objective should involve visuals also. What is the person supposed to do under the conditions where the effects of rhythm, cadence, form, and mood affect communication? Not only is it important for the student to learn to recognize these effects, but the student should also be able to utilize these effects in his or her own communication to others. This indicates that the objective as stated is insufficient. Answers to the other questions support the immediate importance of this objective. However, because this objective is so basic to successful communication, many students have already achieved the recognition and performance of these effects before starting formal schooling. As a result, there is usually wide spread individual differences among students with reference to the achievement of this objective and it becomes even more critical that these individual differences are recognized through individualized instruction rather than ignored as in the traditional class approach.

INCREASING SPECIFICATION — What meanings of oral language are you going to be concerned about? How many words, phrases or sentences are going to be involved in demonstrating the effects of rhythm, cadence, form and mood? How many effects will rhythm have? How many effects will cadence have? How many effects will form have? How many effects will mood have? What are the criteria for determining an effect? How do you measure the effect? How do you know when one student recognizes these effects, and another student doesn't?

b. *To know what is the work of the many helpers needed to make woolen clothing. (Minnesota; third grade; Social Studies.)*

JUSTIFICATION — This objective is like a number of other objectives which are directed towards an understanding of the work done by many people in our society. This type of objective is similar to the career objectives except the emphasis is different. The old emphasis is on the *knowing about* and *appreciating* the various types of work done by other people in our society and how it takes many different kinds of workers to provide the needs of our society. The career emphasis is more on exploring a variety of potential work areas in an effort to help the student make career decisions later on in life. Of what value is the learning of this objective? As it is presently stated, there probably isn't much value in learning this objective. Under what conditions will knowing this information be useful? Unless a person is going to be working in the wool or clothing industry, it would be difficult to justify the learning of this objective as it is presently stated. What might be more important if the purpose is to appreciate the joint efforts of many people in the production of a product, is to have the students learn the process of identifying all the workers involved with the production of any product. Knowing the process of how to identify the various people involved with the production of any product could be much more relevant than knowing facts about the production of a particular product because with the fast changes being made in almost all industries, the facts may become obsolete and forgotten whereas the process can remain current. If the purpose is to explore career oportunities in production, the learning of the process becomes much more appropriate because the student can apply the process in any field at any time whereas the learning of facts about any one particular field may be inappropriate because jobs change and facts are easily forgotten if not used. Answers to the other questions support the inappropriateness of the objective as presently stated and the appropriateness of the suggested changes in the objective.

INCREASING SPECIFICATION — How many helpers are going to be studied — everyone that is actually involved, or only the major helpers? How much detail in the work of the helpers should be included? What kinds of woolen clothing are involved — 10 types, 15 types, 20 types? Should the student be able to list the helpers and describe their work from memory? Should they be able to make drawings of the work the helpers do, or given a piece of woolen clothing, should they be able to work backwards through the number of steps that were involved to arrive at that particular piece of clothing? Should they know where the workers live, where the wool comes from, what the factories look like? Should they be able to perform some of the tasks of the workers? Should they know the income of the various workers?

i. *To know from where our ancestors came — Spanish settlements and explorers? (Missouri; Grade 4; Social Studies.)*

JUSTIFICATION — Of what value will it be to know this? It would probably not be very valuable to know this information particularly if it was not associated with the present day effects of where our ancestors came from. Under what conditions would this knowledge be useful? Unless the objective was reworded to reflect the present day effects of the culture and origin of our ancestors, it would be difficult to identify conditions under which this knowledge (as presently stated in the objective) would be useful. The answers to

571

the rest of the questions again indicate the irrelevance of the objective as it is presently stated, but support the importance of a restated objective which would concern the learning of the process of recognizing the contributions of one or more cultures in a variety of aspects of our society, i.e., language, food, furniture, mannerisms, etc.

INCREASING SPECIFICATION — How many Spanish settlements — 6, 10, 50? How many explorers — 3, 10? What is the learner supposed to learn about the Spanish settlements? What should the learner learn about the explorers? What is the observable and measurable difference between a student who knows where his ancestors came from in reference to Spanish settlements and explorers, and another student who does not know where his ancestors came from in reference to the Spanish Settlements and explorers?

j. *To have an understanding of the variety of ways both two and three-dimensional media and tools can be explored and controlled to obtain special visual qualities and effects. (Ohio; high school; Art.)*

JUSTIFICATION — What value is in the achievement of this understanding? This could be very valuable in our society where visual communication is everywhere. Under what conditions will this understanding be useful? The principles, media, and tools involved in this understanding would be useful to anyone that wants to express themselves artistically, (painting, sculpture, interior decorating, etc.) to create a visual mood, to recognize and understand better the artistic works of others, etc. The answers to the other questions support the importance of this objective.

INCREASING SPECIFICATION — How many ways are *a variety of ways?* How many two-dimensional media are involved — 2, 6, 10? How many two-dimensional tools or three-dimensional tools are involved? What is meant by exploring and controlling a two or three-dimensional medium or tool? What are the special visual qualities and effects that should be studied? If there are an infinite variety, are there certain ones that the student should be held responsible for? What is the difference between a student who understands the variety of ways and another student who doesn't understand the variety of ways?

k. *To develop a thorough understanding of the principles of modern automobile engines. (Post high school; Automobile Technology.)*

JUSTIFICATION — Of what value is this understanding? For those students who are majoring in automobile technology, the import-

572

ance of understanding the principle is obvious. Under what conditions will this understanding be useful? Since the majority of these students will be primarily involved in repair rather than design, the understanding of the principles of automobile engines should emphasize diagnosis or trouble shooting, i.e., given a defective engine, why isn't the engine operating according to the appropriate principle. In some cases, the mechanic will be involved with design problems, i.e., given a defective engine and lacking the appropriate parts (tools, etc.), what other ways can the engine be repaired keeping in mind the principle involved or given an operating engine, what can be done to increase the effectiveness and/or efficiency of the engine in keeping with the principles of its operation. What is the person supposed to do under these conditions? The answer to this question concerns the whole program of automotive technology. The relationship between the conditions and what a person does is very important in any diagnostic role, i.e., an instructioneer, doctor, dentist, etc. All too often, the instructional program stresses *what the person does* and overlooks the *conditions (or symptoms)* that cause a person to do something. For example, a mechanic could be a fantastic overhauler of carburetors but if he or she doesn't recognize the symptoms in the performance or non-performance of the engine, the mechanic may not have an opportunity to demonstrate this competence. The answers to the other questions support the importance of this general objective.

INCREASING SPECIFICATION — How many principles are involved — 5, 10, 15? What is the difference between an understanding and a thorough understanding? What are *modern* automobile engines? How many different types of engines are going to be involved? What is the difference between a student who has already developed a thorough understanding of the principles and another student who hasn't developed a thorough understanding of the principles. Would it only be necessary to list these principles, or should they be demonstrated by repairing and/or designing an automobile engine?

l.   *To appreciate the rich heritage of man, his literary and artistic achievements. (Freshman College English.)*

JUSTIFICATION — Of what value is it for a student to develop this appreciation? The answer to this question could vary considerably depending upon the answers to the other questions. If appreciation is defined as students being awestruck by the deification of man's literary and artistic achievements, I can see little value in this objective. If appreciation is defined as teaching the student whatever is necessary in order for the student to be able to look at man's literary and artistic achievements and evaluate them according to accepted professional aesthetic criteria plus his or her own aesthetic criteria, then I can see value in this objective. Under what conditions will the learning of this objective be useful? As mentioned previously, if the sub-objective of this objective relate to learning criteria for evaluation of literary and artistic works, then these same criteria should be useful not only to evaluate the achievements of the masters, but to evaluate the person's own literary and artistic efforts. These criteria should not only indicate what is good, but also what is not so good such that the individual can improve his or her own efforts. A very common problem in composition and art courses is that the criteria for evaluation are so vague that the teacher has trouble communicating these criteria to students. Since the students don't really know exactly what is wanted, they find it difficult to achieve the ambiguous criteria. As a result, achievement is all too often by chance and is interpreted as indications of talent. What is a person supposed to do under these conditions? The learner should be able to evaluate literary and artistic works, to be able to communicate the evaluation so that others who also have learned the criteria can understand the evaluation, and possibly to make changes in his or her own literary and artistic efforts. The answers to the other questions support the practical application of this objective as being important while the unsupported emotional (gut feeling) application of this objective has little importance.

INCREASING SPECIFICATION — What is meant to appreciate? What are the literary and artistic achievements that consitute the *rich heritage of man?* What are the criteria used to identify these literary and artistic achievements? What is the student supposed to know about the literary and artistic achievements? What does a student do who appreciates this rich heritage that another student who doesn't appreciate the rich heritage doesn't do?

m. *Students should be able to recognize and understand the limits of tools and equipment. (College Physics.)*

JUSTIFICATION — This objective is typical of ones that I frequently find in technical and vocational courses. In trying to justify the objective, it will be noted that the objective is written with the wrong emphasis. Of what value is the achievement of this objective? By itself, the knowledge of the limits of tools and equipment is of little value. However, if given certain tasks to accomplish, the knowledge of the limits of available tools and equipment help the individual to select appropriate tools and equipment for specific tasks. Therefore, the important objective is to learn how to match the right tools and equipment to the task and to the quality control specifications of the task, i.e., you wouldn't want a student to measure the size of a room with a micrometer or the diameter of a hair with a yardstick. Under what conditions would this knowledge be useful? For almost any task a student might perform, this knowledge would be helpful. What is the student supposed to do under these conditions? The student should be able to examine the task or problem and select the most appropriate tools and equipment from among those available.

> NOTE: In any one occupation involving the use of tools and equipment, it would be very unusual if all of the places of employment were equally equipped. Consequently, a very important category of decisions to be learned in these occupations (doctor, dentist, mechanic, etc.) concerns the selection of appropriate tools and equipment from among those *available*. My suggestion to schools has been to set up three hypothetical working places: the ideal place with all the tools and equipment which might be found in an exceptionally well equipped place, an average *real-world* place with the tools and equipment which might be available in an average place, and a *bare bones* place with the tools and equipment which might be found in a place that is minimally equipped. Students are then asked to perform a series of tasks (they have previously learned to do correctly) in each of the three hypothetical places and listing the tools and equipment they would use to achieve each task. Any compromise using different tools and/or equipment other than the ideal ones found in the best equipped place should be defended by the student as to how the quality of the task has not been compromised also. An important part of this experience is for the student to recognize that for certain tasks the compromises made in tools and equipment affects the quality of the performance of the task to such an extent that the student should refuse to do the task or at least communicate the problem to his or her superiors or clients.

The answers to the other questions support the unimportance of the objective as presently stated and the importance of the revised objectives as suggested by the answers to the questions.

INCREASING SPECIFICATION — How many tools are involved — 10, 15, 25? Is this in reference to the equipment of a college physics laboratory or the equipment found in a research scientist's laboratory? All the equipment or just some of the equipment? What kinds of limits are being considered? What is meant by *to recognize and understand* these limits? What does a student do that understands and recognizes the limits that another student who doesn't understand and recognize the limits doesn't do?

n. *You will provide for patient hygiene, either doing for or assisting*
the individual to do for himself, including the following: bathing,
hair grooming, mouth and denture care, normal care of eyes, ears
and nose. (College Nursing.)

JUSTIFICATION — The answers to the questions of justification
support the importance of this general objective. Therefore, it
would appear that all that is necessary is to specify the behaviors of
the student nurse in carrying out the tasks described in the objective. However, because this objective was probably written as a
separate GO rather than connected (as in a flow diagram p. 345) to
broader GO's which include this objective, the critical thinking
objective has been overlooked. In a way, the answers to *Under what*
conditions will these behaviors be useful? and *What is the student*
nurse supposed to do under these conditions? indicate the missing
objective. A very important guideline in nursing education is *to help*
the patient become self-sufficient. This guideline suggests that a
nurse should do less and less for a patient depending upon what is
wrong with the patient and how fast the patient is recovering. In
combining this guideline with the objective, the students would
have to learn the steps in each of the areas included in patient
hygiene. Then, the students would have to learn to prepare a
patient's hygiene plan with increasing responsibility. To do this, the
following objectives would have to be achieved:

— Given a patient's record (real or simulated), the student will be
able to identify which steps of the patient's hygiene the patient
will be able to do and which steps the nurse will have to do.

— Given a patient's record (real or simulated) and the data from
the last objective, the student will be able to make up a
patient's hygiene plan which would indicate the proposed hygiene steps which would be added to patient's tasks each day.
Each step added to the patient's daily task should be defended
on the basis of the patient's projected recovery.

— Given a patient's hygiene plan which includes a schedule for
increasing responsibility based on the patient's projected recovery and actual or simulated patient conditions which are different than the projected recovery schedule, the student will adjust
the patient's hygiene plan to reflect the patient's actual conditions and defend each change based on the changes in the
patient's condition.

INCREASING SPECIFICATIONS — In many nursing programs,
this objective would be considered specific by the nursing instructors because any nurse that is qualified to be a nursing instructor

should know exactly what is meant by this objective. If the objective was meant to be a *teaching objective* for teachers, it would be acceptable; but as a *learning objective* for students, it is still a general objective. As indicated earlier, the steps for each of the hygiene areas would have to be specified and the criteria for evaluating the quality of each step would also have to be identified. In addition, there are three different sets of behaviors implied by the objective: the behaviors necessary if the nurse has to do the steps (one or more); the behaviors necessary if the nurse is assisting the patient to do the steps (one or more); and the behaviors necessary if the nurse is supervising and/or checking to see if the patient was able to perform the steps on his or her own.

o. *Objectives of the course are firstly, to develop the students' knowledge of business organization, production management and internal economics, secondly; to be able to make application of the knowledge in case analysis and to be able to reserach information relative to the subject. (College; Business.)*

JUSTIFICATION — This objective is very typical of course objectives which are listed in school catalogues. The first part of the objective is really a teaching objective *to develop the student's knowledge*, whereas the second part is closer to a learning objective *to be able to make application* and *to be able to research*. Of what value is this knowledge (as indicated in the first part of the objective)? As indicated, the value should be to be able to spply the knowledge to case analyses and to research information relative to the subject. Although the process of researching for information relative to problems is a very useful behavior, being able to apply knowledge to case studies is probably only useful to the student and not of much value to a person out in the business world. Under what conditions will this knowledge (application and/or researching) be useful? Given that the course is supposed to result in some practical skills to be used in the business world, then the knowledge (application and/or researching) will be useful if it is related to realistic business problems. This indicates that the course objective could have been stated as follows: *As a result of taking the course, the student should have enough knowledge of business organization, production management, and internal economics to be able to identify problems in these three areas and to suggest one or more potential solutions to the problems through the use of case studies and research.* The answers to the other questions support the need to reword the objective.

INCREASING SPECIFICATION — As the objective is presently stated, it is very general and has to be subdivided a number of times before identifying specific objectives. For example, take the first topic *business organizations.* Should the student be able to identify different types of business organizations? Should the student be able to describe the structure of these different types? Should the student be able to identify the affects on a business of different organization structures? Should the student be able to identify divisions of responsibility in the different organizational structures? Should the student be able to identify relationships between the various units in each of the organization structures? Similar questioning could subdivide the other topics. The following questions could be asked to increase the specification of objectives and in the same topic area. What organizational problems should the student be able to identify? What knowledge, techniques, and research is necessary for the student to learn in order for the student to suggest one or more solutions to these organizational problems? Given related case studies, how should the student analyze these in order to identify the organizational problems and to maximize transfer of this identification to real world problems? What are the criteria for evaluating good solutions to organizational problems? Given related case studies, how should the student analyze these in order to identify whether or not the solutions used were the best ones, whether or not other solutions would have been better, and how to maximize transfer of this analysis to selecting solutions to real world problems.

p. *To develop a clear understanding of some of the basic terminology used in accounting. (College; Accounting.)*

JUSTIFICATION — Of what value is this clear understanding? In order to take the course and/or to be associated with the field of accounting, the student will need an understanding of accounting terminology. Under what conditions will this understanding be useful? In answering this question, it is important to recognize that in all objectives relating to learning vocabulary, there are three implied sub-objectives: Given the words, the student should be able to define them (spelled correctly); given the definitions, the student should be able to state the word which is being defined; and given an example of what the word and its definition refer to, the student can identify the word associated with the example and also give the definition of the word. These three sub-objectives are necessary because sometimes the same *understanding* will be triggered by a word, the definition of the word, and/or an example of what the word refers to. Learning just one of these three sub-objectives does not mean that the other two have also been learned.[24] An understanding of accounting terminology will be useful if the student has to read or write verbal materials containing these terms. It will also be useful in talking or listening to other people when the topic is accounting. This would indicate that the teaching and testing of the students' understanding of the terminology should be in the context of a statement or paragraph rather than as an isolated word. What is the person supposed to do under these conditions? This would depend on the context within which the terminology was used. The context may or may not call for an action. If the student was asked to prepare a financial statement from a variety of given data, the student would actually prepare a financial statement. If the student didn't have an understanding of the terminology, the student wouldn't know what was being asked for and would probably have trouble sorting out and reporting the given data in categories which would be meaningful to someone else in accounting. The answers to the next two questions of justification concerning when and how often the terminology will be used indicates that only those items which are used frequently should be memorized. The learning and testing for achievement of terms which are seldom used should concern the students' ability to look up this information in appropriate sources rather than a rote memorized understanding of the terms.

INCREASING SPECIFICATION — What are the basic terms used in accounting? Which *some* of this basic terminology should the student learn? What is the difference between the *some* that should be learned and the other terms that aren't that important? What is meant by a *clear understanding* of *some* of the basic terminology. What will a student that has this clear understanding be able to do that a student that hasn't this clear understanding not be able to do?

q. *To develop a greater understanding and appreciation for the five forms of literature: the essay, the short story, the novel, drama, and poetry. (all levels; English.)*

JUSTIFICATION — I have found this objective or slightly different versions of this same objective in English courses in elementary schools, junior and senior high schools, and in colleges and universities. The way this objective is usually taught and tested in most

---

[24] Sometimes in order to prove that students are dumb or to lower the curve of grades, traditional teachers will tell their students that they want only one of these objectives, but then they will test the students' learning of one of the other objectives. For example, the students will be told to learn the definitions of a list of words, but then the students will be tested by giving them a list of definitions and they are to state the words being defined which is a reverse behavior of what the students were told to learn.

schools is that the teacher picks his or her favorite literary works in each of the five forms of literature and the students are supposed to read them and they are usually discussed by the teacher during one or more class sessions. The tests are usually designed to test whether or not the student read the assigned literary works. As such, the questions or test items are all about the specific literary works. As a result, the objective in practice is changed such that the students are to develop a greater understanding and appreciation for a specific list of literary works (selected by the teacher). The common problem is that the vehicle for learning the objectives of the course have become the objectives. Another very important point to emphasize is that whereas *understanding* is primarily in the cognitive domain, *appreication* is primarily in the affective domain. In accord with earlier statements, it is possible to teach the desired understanding directly, but appreciation can only be developed indirectly and usually by successfully helping the students gain understanding. Rarely will the students develop appreciation on a base of failure or ineffective understanding.

Of what value is this understanding and appreciation (of specific literary works)? About as useful as learning facts and information in a history course. Depending upon the literary works picked, the student may remember and *understand* whenever the works are mentioned in conversation in the years that follow. However, if the objective remained in a generic sense rather than concerned only with specific literary works and the students' understanding and appreciation concerned the unique characteristics of the five forms of literature as vehicles of communication and how different authors used these forms in unique ways, then the appreciation and understanding might transfer to other literary works. Under what conditions will this understanding and appreciation be useful? For the specific literary works, the use would be very limited and the understanding would become difficult to mentally retrieve because of a lack of use. For literary works in the generic sense, the understanding and appreciation could be useful whenever the person did any reading throughout the rest of his or her life.

The answers to the other questions support the short term relevance and use of the objective when it refers to specific literary works. However, the answers in reference to the objective when it refers to the generic sense supports its importance and usefulness. For example, *What is the person supposed to do under these conditions?* Since the person will rarely run into or reread the specific literary works, whatever, he or she might have done under these conditions are forgotten behaviors. In the generic sense, if the student has actually learned to identify various literary styles and techniques, has learned to recognize the meanings and messages that the authors were trying to convey, is able to incorporate, where appropriate, meaningful ideas into his or her own lifestyle, and/or is able to vicariously enjoy other lifestyles and places, then the student will increase his or her understanding and especially his or her appreciation for literary works.

INCREASING SPECIFICATION — In order to increase the specificity of this objective, the five forms of literature are going to have to be defined in much more detail, i.e., What are their unique differences?, When would one form be used over the other form?, What are the characteristics of each form?, What commonalities exist among the forms?, etc. In the development of *greater understanding and appreciation for the five forms of literature*, does this also include understanding and appreciation of different styles of writing in each of these forms? If yes, then these styles will have to be identified as to their characteristics and uniqueness. It will probably also be appropriate to identify one or more authors who use these styles. It might also be appropriate to identify how the styles and norms affect communication. Finally, it is necessary in reference to the answers to these questions to identify what is meant by *greater understanding and appreication* or put in another way, what does someone do who has this *greater understanding and appreciation* that someone who doesn't have it, doesn't do?

r. *To be able to describe methods of analyzing an audience to determine choice of topic and method of presentation with which to communicate with that audience. (College; Speech.)*

JUSTIFICATION — Of what value is this? Since almost everyone will at sometime in his life be asked to speak in front of a group of people, being able to describe the methods of audience analysis should be useful. However, being able to describe the different methods may not be as important as being able to apply these methods. It might also be important to identify the advantages and disadvantages of each method and possible to know when to use one method and not another or when to use more than one method.

Under what conditions will it be useful to be able to describe the methods of audience analysis? Unless the students plan to teach speech courses or to be in a position where they would be helping others do audience analyses, the conditions where it would be useful to know how to describe methods of audience analysis may never occur for most students. In other words, the objective as it is

581

written is irrelevant. As suggested above, being able to *apply* one or more of these methods could be very useful because almost all students will be involved in making presentations to groups. What is a person supposed to do under these conditions? As before, being able to describe the methods does not insure that the student is able to apply the methods of audience analysis. In changing the objective to indicate that the student should be able to apply the methods of audience analysis, there are at least two other variables to be considered: the objectives for giving a speech and the different groups to which the same speech is to be given. In reference to the first variable, it is a continuum with a situation at one end where the objective is to please the audience and say what they want to hear. At the other end of the continuum, the objective is to get the audience to do something that they may not want to do or to tell them things that they may not want to hear. The variable of the continuum is the degree to which the objective or objectives of the presentation are in conflict with the attitudes, values, and/or beliefs of the audience. The second variable concerns the degree of differences on the continuum between the various groups that the same speech is to be given to. Generally, when students are asked to apply methods of audience analysis, they are asked to prepare a speech for each of three or more groups (each speech is different and reflects the interests of the group being presented to). A more difficult and maybe a more appropriate task or objective would be to take a specific speech and prepare it for presentation to three or more different groups. (The speech is pre-designed to contain material which may be in conflict with the attitudes, values, and/or beliefs of many different groups.) Every change in the speech has to be defended by the student on the basis of an audience analysis and the student also has to prove that the objective(s) of the speech have not been changed. By the time students prepare and can then compare three or more versions of the same speech, you will find that students become very aware of the need to do an audience analysis.

The answers to the next two questions concerning *How long before the student will apply the learned behavior?*, support the irrelevancy of the objective as presently stated. However, given the revised objective dealing with application rather than just describing, the answers to the questions support the relevancy depending upon the student. Some students may only be involved in presenting to groups infrequently, whereas other students may be involved in presenting to groups frequently. For students who will only be presenting to groups infrequently, it may only be necessary for them to apply one of the methods and know where to locate descriptions of the other methods. For these students it may be more important that they can recognize situations in which a speaker has or hasn't made an audience analysis because they will hear other speakers frequently. Being able to recognize the advantages of having done an audience analysis and the disadvantages to the speaker when it is not done, will help these students develop positive attitudes and a high value for audience analysis. For the students who will be presenting to groups frequently, they should probably apply more than one method of audience analysis in addition to learning to recognize when other speakers have or haven't done an audience analysis.

NOTE: Given that the function of audience analysis is to facilitate communication, why not think of the groups being spoken to as consisting of one or more persons. From this point of view, everyone needs to know how to do audience analysis because we are always trying to communicate to others. The techniques of audience analysis are very useful in interpersonal communication and knowing them will increase the chances of a person becoming a well liked conversationalist and listener. Being able to apply these techniques on an interpersonal level is a very critical behavior for professional people, sales people, politicians, or anyone dealing with the public.

INCREASING SPECIFICATION — If the objective is going to be used as it is presently stated, then to increase the specification, the different methods of doing an audience analysis would have to be identified first. Secondly, the relationship between audience analysis and selection of topics and methods of presentation would have to be identified. It may also be appropriate even before the second question to identify the different methods of presentation. It will probably also be necessary to identify the criteria or characteristics to be used in analyzing audiences.

s. *The student should be able to name and define the five elements of music: melody, rhythm, mood, harmony, and form. (College Appreciation)*

JUSTIFICATION — Of what value is this? Given that the course is primarily concerned with music appreciation as listening rather than talking about music or performing in music, then being able to rote memorize the definitions of these words may not be very useful.

Under what conditions will it be useful? As presently stated, it would be a rare situation where the student would be expected to be able to name and define the five elements of music. What is probably wanted is that the student, in listening to a variety of musical selections, can identify the five elements and changes in these elements. The student may also be expected to evaluate varying quality in these five elements while listening to various selections. This objective is quite typical of teachers in music, art, and physical performances (dance, physical education, gynmastics, etc.) who believe that they have to give paper and pencil tests even though most of their objectives are non-paper and pencil oriented. Most objectives in a music course should include or refer to records, audio-tapes, audio-visual media, or any other audio media. Consequently, any evaluation of student achievement should include the same audio-media. In the same way, most of the objectives and evaluation in an art course should include or refer to visuals and visual media.

Answers to the other questions support the irrelevance of this objective as presently stated unless it is accompanied by other related objectives which concern the recognition of these elements in a listening situation.

INCREASING SPECIFICATION — This objective as it is presently stated is specific and measurable as long as verbal dictionary definitions are acceptable.

t. *Activity objectives — the student should do at least two projects, the student should give an oral report on any topic of his or her choice, the student should turn in a research paper of about 17 typewritten pages, the student will write five essays after the assigned reading, etc.*

JUSTIFICATION — Of what value are these activities? It is very difficult to answer this question, because the quality of the activities has not been specified. As presently stated (with reference to the oral report) one student could tell a 30 second joke without any prior preparation while another student could give a 30 minute presentation representing months of preparation and they should both achieve the same credit. The value of performing activity objectives varies considerably and occurs almost by chance rather than by any design of the teacher. These objectives which can be questioned with useful results if the criteria for evaluating the activity are identified. The listing of the criteria to be used to evaluate the quality of the students' performance of the activity also makes the objective a specific *learning* objective. As pointed out previously, activity objectives are frequently considered as *specific objectives* or as *behavioral objectives* because the activity is measurable. For example, to turn in a 17 page typewritten research paper is specific and measurable, i.e., it was or was not turned in and it did or didn't have 17 typewritten pages. The problem is that almost every teacher who uses activity objectives also has quality objectives in mind, but they are not specified and available to the student.

4. APPLYING THE QUESTIONS TO SPECIFIC TEST ITEMS WHICH LACK KNOWN SPECIFIC OBJECTIVES

Specific test items are often created for a variety of reasons besides trying to find out whether or not a student has learned something important, i.e., in order to get a score for grading purposes, in order to fill a time slot scheduled for testing, in order to punish students, in order to prove how ignorant the students are, etc. Many of these items can be quickly rejected by applying the questions of justification. Of interest however, is the fact that buried in many of these irrelevant test items are useful objectives and matching test items. In my working with teachers, I have found that I can usually derive higher quality objectives and matching test items from a teacher's existing test items (even though they appear irrelevant as they are presently stated) then from a teacher's list of general or specific test items.

At the present time, most test items consist of true-false, multiple choice, matching, fill-in-the-blank, problem solving, physical performance and short and long essays. The long essays as test items are usually referred to as term papers and as such are frequently the general non-specific test items which I discussed earlier in which neither the teacher nor the student knew the criteria that would be used for evaluation of the essay at the time the essay was written. The criteria are developed as needed during the correcting of the essays. As a result, most students use the *shotgun* approach in writing these essays which is based on the belief that if you write about enough things, hopefully, some of it will coincide with what the teacher was looking for in the evaluation. Short essays and performance type test items can rather easily be associated with matching specific objectives which are known to the teachers, but all too often are not known to the students. Problem solving and fill-in-the-blank type test items can be easily equated to matching specific objectives because the format of the test item and the objective is practically the same.

The use of standard true-false, multiple-choice test items are not as easily associated with objectives, and teachers utilizing these kinds of test items have not usually thought of a test item as testing a specific objective. Yet, when teachers are asked if they give their students any test items which they don't want the students to answer, almost every

585

teacher says that they want all of their students to answer all of the test items correctly.[25]

In other words, if the teachers want the students to answer all of the test items correctly, then the test items must represent specific objectives (SO's) of the course. When the specific objectives for true-false or multiple-choice test items are identified, it is very unusual for teachers to agree that the resulting specific objectives are what they want their students to learn. If the objective associated with multiple-choice, true-false, or matching test items does represent what the teacher wants, it is usually considered by the teacher as a very low level objective. It is bad enough that teachers have not specified what they want their students to learn in their courses, but it is worse when the test items they are using to evaluate student achievement are actually testing for the achievement of objectives which are not relevant or important. Remember, the results of such tests are used to determine grades, which in turn control a student's progress through our present educational system. Therefore, the emphasis in this section will be on true-false and multiple-choice test items, although other test items will be included. The procedure in analyzing each of these test items will be to state the test item as it has been used with students, and then to re-state the test item in terms of its matching specific, measurable learning objective (SO), and then to question the test item, the objective, or both as to the justification of its inclusion in a test. As before, in answering the questions of justification, I will suggest some test items and/or objectives which may be more appropriate in representing what the teachers really wanted their students to learn. In reading my comments on some of the test items, it should become almost obvious how irrelevant and unimportant some test tiems are which in turn may make you wonder about the qualifications of the teachers who make up such bad test items. Remember, relatively few teachers at any level of education have been taught the critical skill of specifying objectives and developing matching test items. Under traditional education, it is not important that a teacher tests for the achievement of what has been taught. In fact, the easiest way to get a curve of grades is to teach one thing and test for the achievement of something else. Teachers who test for the achievement of what they have taught have difficulty in getting low scores as most students learn in an honest teaching-learning situation. This, of course, is why in traditional test and measurement courses students are taught that a good test item is one that fifty percent of the

---

[25] If any teacher said that he or she gave students test items which the teacher didn't want the students to answer correctly, then the teacher would be against students learning which would be considered a malpractice. Actually, in order to achieve a grading curve of some kind, a teacher has to include items in a test that they don't think students can answer correctly, but this is not something that most teachers will admit publicly.

students can't answer. Testing for the achievement of something a teacher hasn't taught and that half of the students don't know may not be an honest teaching-learning situation, but it sure helps get a curve of grades!

Under the behavioral learning systems approach, it is important to remember that test items are given to evaluate the achievement of stated important objectives and is diagnostic in nature. The function of the test is not to obtain a score for grading purposes. Test items which are answered correctly indicate the students' achievement of the matching objectives. Test items which are answered incorrectly indicate a diagnosis of a learning problem which has to be solved. (When you have read as much as you want of this unit, skip to page 608).

a. *(True-False) The Forehand Grip on the racket in badminton forms a "V" by the thumb and the forefinger on the top plate of the handle. (High School; Physical Education.)*

MATCHING SO — Given the following statement, *The 'Forehand Grip'on the racket in badminton forms a"V" by the thumb and the forefinger on the top plate of the handle*, the student will be able to identify whether this statement is true or false.

JUSTIFICATION — Of what value is the ability to answer this item correctly? In an honest testing situation where the students have seen the objective ahead of time, many students might be tempted to associate *true* with the above statement without internalizing the statement. In the traditional testing situation where the students don't know what they are supposed to learn, the value of the item could be whether or not the students are able to recognize the correct definition of a *forehand grip*.

Under what conditions will it be useful to be able to identify whether the statement is true or false? Since the students will probably never come across the statement again, the value of the test item is negligible and it should be considered an irrelevant item.

In talking with instructors in physical education concerning this particular test item and the concept involved, what seems to be important is not necessarily that the student knows a verbal definition of the *forehand grip*, but that the student is able to recognize when someone is holding a racket with a *forehand grip*, is able to hold the racket using a *forehand grip*, is able to state why a *forehand grip* is used, and in what ways it is a better grip for certain situations than other ways of holding the racket. Therefore, the student's ability to indicate true or false doesn't really begin to approach what may be important in this particular test item.

587

More relevant objectives (and implied test items) might be:

SO_1 — Given the following photographs of people holding badminton rackets, the student should be able to identify the grip being used and state why the person might be using that particular grip. (Useful for predicting an opponents actions.)

SO_2 — Given a badminton racket, the student should be able to demonstrate each of the following grips and state the advantages and disadvantages of each: (list of the grips the student should learn).

SO_3 — Given a short film showing the shuttlecock being hit back and forth over the net several times, and the film stops just as the shuttlecock is coming over the net towards the viewer, the student should be able to state what grip should be used and why — including a description of the student's strategy for the subsequent plays in order to win the point. (This objective gets into the intellectual depth of physical instruction which is too often left out in favor of the more standard rote memory type items.)

b. *A major uprising of slaves in 1831 was led by (a) Uncle Tom, (b) Abraham Lincoln, (c) Nat Turner, (d) Booker T. Washington. (High School; History)*

MATCHING SO — Given the following stem of the statement, *A major uprising of slaves in 1831 was led by*, the student will be able to identify (recognize, discriminate, etc.) the correct completion of that stem from among the following four statements: (a) Uncle Tom, (b) Abraham Lincoln, (c) Nat Turner, (d) Booker T. Washington.

JUSTIFICATION — Of what value is it to be able to complete the statement correctly? Learning this historical fact by itself has little if any value. Under what conditions will it be useful to be able to complete this statement correctly from among these specific four choices? Since the students will most likely never run into this same situation (statement and choices) again, the relevance of the test item and matching SO is about as low as it is possible to be which provides another reason why the multiple-choice format is unacceptable in an honest and relevant teaching-learning situation. Although it may be important to know that Nat Turner was the one who led the major uprising of the slaves in 1831, it would be very possible for a student to eliminate the other three choices by the usual process of elimination and end up with the right answer and not even know who Nat Turner is. In talking with teachers who are concerned with black history, there are several other areas that are

588

much more important than remembering that it was Nat Turner who led that particular uprising. It may be more important for the student to know what the causes were which led to the uprising, and what happened after the uprising was over, and possibly, what the conditions are today that are similar to the causes of the uprising in 1831.

More relevant objectives (and implied test items might be):

SO$_1$ — The student will be able to list the (number) causes for the major uprising of slaves in 1831, and will then identify which of these causes are still present today. In addition to listing the causes, the student will cite for each cause two or more events described in any book concerning that period of our history (citing book and page) which demonstrate that the cause actually existed in or prior to 1831 and two or more contemporary events for each cause which demonstrates that one or more of the causes are still present today.

SO$_2$ — Given the list of causes for the major uprising of slaves in 1831, the student will identify which of these causes are not present today and make one or more statements concerning how the causes were eliminated (citing sources of information).

Notice, in both of these suggested objectives, the student would take the test for achievement of these objectives in a library or at least in a place where reference sources are available. This is in accord with one of the major general objectives of history courses which concerns the process of researching the literature for information. As such, the achievement of these objectives has value and is important not only for the content but for the achievement of the process of being able to dig out the necessary information. In other words, these objectives are really vehicles for learning the primary process objective.

c. *The Mexican War, the Fugitive Slave Law, the Kansas Controversy, and the Dred Scott decision all helped to speed the interest in (a) abolitionism, (b) Manifest Destiny, (c) a re-chartering of the Bank of the United States, (d) Temperance reform. (College; History)*

MATCHING SO — Given the stem of a statement, *The Mexican War, the Fugitive Slave Law, the Kansas Controversy, and the Dred Scott decision, all helped to speed the interest in*, the student will be able to identify (recognize, discriminate, etc.) the correct completion of this statement from among the following four choices: (a) abolitionism, (b) Manifest Destiny, (c) a re-chartering of the Bank of the United States, and (d) temperance reform.

JUSTIFICATION — As with the last test item — objective, the multiple-choice format can not be justified and the basic objective really concerns the students' ability to research historical material to find information. In addition to the primary process objective, buried in this objective is another basic history objective. The question concerns how a series of events contribute to the development of a movement.

More relevant objectives (and implied test items) might be:

SO_1 — The student will be able to state how the Mexican War, the Fugitive Slave Law, the Kansas Controversy and the Dred Scott decision helped to speed interest in abolitionism. (The criteria for evaluation of the statements should be included in the objective)

SO_2 — Given the following list of movements, the student will select three or more of these and identify three or more events which contributed to the formation of each movement including citations of the sources of information and descriptions of how the events contributed to the formation of the movement: (a list of movements).

Since most of the leaders of our country have told militant groups that they should bring about change within the system rather than by destroying the system, then a general objective of the school system should be to actually teach the processes which can be used to bring about change. In accord with this concept and the implied content of the revised objectives, an individual or even small group learning objectives could be:

SO_3 — Given a contemporary movement, which is essentially static, suggest three or more events which might contribute to the activation of the movement. Defend the contribution of the suggested events by citing parallels of similar events which helped activate some other movement in history.

d. *(True-False) Feelings of nausea caused by certain sights, smells, and tastes are responses which are culturally determined. (College; Sociology)*

MATCHING SO — Given the following statement, *Feeling of nausea caused by certain sights, smells, and tastes are responses which are culturally determined*, the student will be able to identify whether this statement is true or false.

JUSTIFICATION — Of what value is the learning of whether this statement is true or false? As before, since this statement will probably never be encountered again by the students, the test item

590

and matching objective are irrelevant and of little value. In addition, if a student was testwise, and used logic, it is possible to get the right answer and not know anything about the content of the test item. The correct answer for this true-false test item is *true* because the word *certain*, means *some* sights, smells, and tastes, and whenever the word *some* or another similar word is involved in a true-false test item, the test item is generally a true statement. Whenever a true-false test item involves the words *all* or *none*, the true-false test item is usually false, because there are very few absolutes in our world.

What a teacher in sociology might be more interested in the students learning is that certain sights, smells, and tastes which may cause one or more social groups to have feelings of nausea may be considered as favorable sights, smells, and tastes for one or more other groups.

More relevant objective (and implied test item) might be:

SO$_1$ — Given the following sights, smells, and/or tastes (this could be verbal descriptions, or it could be actual photographs, actual smells or tastes), the student will be able to identify which social or cultural groups would look upon these sights, smells, and tastes as favorable, and what other social or cultural groups would experience feelings of nausea and to explain why these differences occur.

e. *If the inventory at the end of the current year is overstated and the error is not caught during the following year, the effect is:*

a. *To understate income this year and overstate income next year*

b. *To overstate income this year and understate income next year*

c. *To overstate the income for the two-year period*

d. *To understate income this year, with no effect on the income of the next year. (College-Accounting)*

MATCHING SO — Given the stem of a statement, *If the inventory at the end of the current year is overstated and the error is not caught during the following year, the effect is:*, the student will be able to identify the correct completion of this statement from among the following four choices: (a) To understate income this year and overstate income next year, (b) To overstate income this year and understate income next year, (c) To overstate the income for the two year period, (d) To understate income this year, with no effect on the income of the next year.

JUSTIFICATION — Again, the multiple-choice format is not defensible in terms of the questions of justification. The concept of the test item concerns the relationship between inventory and income and the resultant affect on taxes. Of interest, in the classroom the teacher probably wanted the students to realize that if a company's inventory is overstated one year resulting in an understatement of income for that year that the following year or whenever the error was corrected the income would be overstated which could put the company in a higher tax bracket.

However, in the test item, probably because too many students might have learned what the teacher wanted (choice a), the teacher put in a distractor *the error was not caught during the following year* which now makes choice (d) the correct answer. Although the test item will probably be a better discriminating item (more students will miss it), what the students that got the item right will remember is that *If the inventory is overstated, the effect is (choice d) to understate income this year, with no effect on the income of the next year* which is not what the students were supposed to learn.

More relevant objectives (and implied test items) might be:

SO_1 — The student will be able to state the effects on a company's income of understating or overstating the inventory. The statement should include the effects on income for the current year involving the inventory errors and for the subsequent year in which the errors were corrected.

SO_2 — Given the income tax returns (real or simulated) of a company covering a two year period, the student will overstate and then understate the inventory of the first year by at least 20 percent, refigure the taxes due in each situation, make appropriate corrections in the second year return to correct the inventory errors for both situations, refigure the taxes due in each of the two situations and then compare the following results: the sum of the taxes paid for the two years on the original returns, the sum of the taxes paid for the two years when the inventory was overstated the first year and corrected the second year, the sum of the taxes paid for the two years when the inventory was understated the first year and corrected the second year.

f. *Internal hemorrhage in the patient can be identified by the following symptoms:*

   (a) decreasing body temperature, restlessness, decreased pulse, paleness;

   (b) decreasing body temperature, flushed, increased pulse, decreasing respirations

(c) decreasing body temperature, paleness, increasing pulse, thirst

(d) increasing body temperature, paleness, apprehension
(College; Nursing)

MATCHING SO — Given the stem of a statement *Internal hemorrhage in the patient can be identified by the following symptoms*, the student will be able to identify the correct completion of this statement from among the following four choices: (a) decreasing body temperature, restlessness, decreased pulse, paleness; (b) decreasing body temperature, flushed, increased pulse, decreasing respirations, (c) decreasing body temperature, paleness, increasing pulse, thirst, (d) increasing body temperature, paleness, apprehension.

JUSTIFICATION — As before, the multiple-choice format is not defensible in terms of the questions of justification, i.e., if a nurse suspects a patient is hemorrhaging, they will never find these same four choices written on the patient's face or body or anywhere in the patient's room or even in the hospital. In addition, the stimulus — response sequence is in reverse. In the majority of situations, the nurse or doctor identifies the symptoms first and then comes up with a diagnosis based on the symptoms. This process is really a decision-making process in which the more relevant objectives would involve the learner in each step of the decision-making process (see page 000, Volume I).

g. *What saw cuts like small chisels?*

a.	*Crosscut saw*	c.	*Rip saw*
b.	*Backsaw*	d.	*Coping saw*

(High School; Wood Shop)

MATCHING SO — Given the question, *What saw cuts like small chisels?*, the student will be able to identify the correct answer from among the following choices: (a) crosscut saw, (b) backsaw, (c) rip saw, (d) coping saw.

JUSTIFICATION — Again, the answers to the questions of justification reveal this test item to be irrelevant as it is presently stated. The concept involved in this test item concerns the characteristics of the saws while cutting. This information only becomes relevant in reference to the characteristics of the material being sawed.

More relevant objective (and implied test item) might be:

SO_1 — Given the following saws which might be found in an average woodshop: (a) crosscut saw, (b) backsaw, (c) rip saw, (d) coping saw, the student will name each one and list its primary characteristics and functions.

SO_2 — Given the following saws which might be found in an average woodshop: (a) crosscut saw, (b) backsaw, (c) rip saw, (d) coping saw, and a list of sawing tasks, the student will be able to select the correct or most appropriate saw to be used for each task and defend the selection by citing the characteristics of the material being sawed, how these characteristics affect the task to be performed, the characteristics of the saw to be used, and how these characteristics make the saw more appropriate for the task than other available saws. (A more detailed SO might require the student to defend why the other saws are not appropriate in terms of their characteristics as they relate to the characteristics of the material to be sawed and the task to be performed).

b. *You should normally begin and finish a right turn in:*

    (a) The lane nearest the road center
    (b) The lane nearest the right curb
    (c) The same lane as for a left turn
(Driver's test; California)

MATCHING SO — Given the stem of a statement, *You should normally begin and finish a right turn in*, the student will complete the statement correctly by identifying the correct ending from among the following three choices: (a) The lane nearest the road center, (b) The lane nearest the right curb, (c) The same lane as for a left turn.

JUSTIFICATION — This test item is typical of the test items given in drivers tests in almost every state. Of what value is the ability to answer this item correctly? If it can be assumed that there is a high correlation between answering this item correctly and being able to actually begin and finish a right turn, then there is value in learning to answer it correctly. However, the correlation between the two is very low. A person could be able to perform a very good right turn while driving a car (which is the desired behavior) and not be able to answer this test item correctly because he or she can't read the item, misread it because of nervousness, are tricked by the distractors, are visualizing a different situation than the test item writer (turning from a one-lane country road into another one-lane country road), etc.

Under what conditions will the ability to answer this item correctly be useful? Since the person taking this test will probably never run

594

into the same test item again except in taking another driver's test and there are no real driving conditions that result in a verbal multiple choice test item suddenly appearing on the windshield of the car, being able to pass this item and other similar test items is practically useless. What is really desired by state motor vehicle agencies is that if a person is going to make a right turn while driving a car, the person should know how to do it legally and safely.

What is the person supposed to do under the conditions implied by the test item? Not only is the person supposed *to know* how to make a right turn, the person should be able to perform the right turn while driving a car. Ideally, the actual driving test is the only way to ascertain whether or not the person can drive a car. But the typical drivers test is insufficient in at least three critical areas: only a bare minimum of driving situations and laws are involved; the driving skills necessary to pass the test are enough to get the driver out on the streets and highways to learn by *trial and error* how to drive under more realistic conditions; and in many states, a person can fail one or two of the critical skills in the driving test and still get a driver's license even though the lack of that skill potentially could kill the driver and/or other people the next day.

With the availability of sophisticated computer based car simulators, there is no reason why driver's tests could not be given on a simulator which could test a variety of driving situations and at various points in the test, the person taking the test could be required to answer questions concerning points of law which affect driving.

More relevant objectives (and implied test items) might be:

SO$_1$ — Given diagrams depicting the following combinations of one-way and two-way streets intersecting each other, the student will draw lines to indicate the correct procedure in making a right turn (and left turn if desired): (a series of appropriate diagrams).

SO$_2$ — The student will be able to list the (number) steps in making a right turn including the preparation and the execution of the right turn.

SO$_3$ — The student will be able to perform while driving a car each of the (number) steps in making a right turn including the preparation and the execution of the right turn.

i. *Sterilization by intermediate heating is accomplished in the:*

a. *autoclave*

595

b. *incubator*
c. *dry oven*
d. *Arnold sterilizer*
e. *x-ray chamber*
(College; Micro-biology)

MATCHING SO — Given the following stem of a statement, *Sterilization by intermediate heating is accomplished in the*, the student will select the correct device from among the following five choices: (a) autoclave, (b) incubator, (c) dry oven, (d) Arnold sterilizer, (e) x-ray chamber.

JUSTIFICATION — This test item is typical of the ones in which several objectives are supposedly being tested by the one item. Students are supposed to know the sterilization function of each of the devices and the characteristics of the sterilization process associated with each device. What teachers really want the students to know is that each device is best for certain tasks. The important point to remember is that on the job, a person does not start with a sterilization device and then look for tasks to do. A person starts with a task, selects the sterilization device that best fits the task and the item to be sterilized, and then does it. As presently stated, the test item is irrelevant and of little value.

More relevant objectives (and implied test items) might be:

SO_1 — Given the following list of sterilization devices commonly found in a laboratory setting, the student will be able to describe the sterilization function of each, the unique characteristics of the sterilization process used by each device, and describe the operation of the device: (a) autoclave, (b) incubator, (c) dry oven, (d) Arnold sterilizer, (e) x-ray chamber.

SO_2 — Given the following sterilization devices in a laboratory setting, the student will identify the device and operate each one according to specified criteria: (a list of sterilization devices and specific criteria for evaluation of effective and efficient operation of each one).

SO_3 — Given the following list of sterilization tasks and a list of sterilization devices commonly found in a laboratory setting, the student will select the best device for each task and defend the selection based on the characteristics of the device, the characteristics of the item to be sterilized, and the criteria for evaluation of the sterilization task: (a list of sterilization tasks and a list of sterilization devices or possibly a photograph of laboratory setting in which the student has to recognize which devices are available.)

596

j. *(Matching test items) As with the other so-called objective type test items, this format is found in all subjects and at all levels of education and consists of two lists of items in which the items on one list are matched to the items on the other list. As with multiple-choice and true-false items, the percentage of students who match the items correctly can be varied considerably by the person making up the matching test item depending upon the design of the test item and almost regardless of what the students know about the content of the lists to be matched.*

MATCHING SO — Given two lists of items, the student will be able to match the items on the first list with the related items on the second list.

JUSTIFICATION — This type of test item is usually used to test rote memory objectives such as the definitions of words and terms; associating people with certain events; associating characters with certain plays, operas, novels, etc. The actual format of the matching test item is irrelevant because there will rarely, if ever, be similar conditions in the real world of a person being presented with the same identical lists in which the person is to match up the lists. The individual related items may or may not be relevant depending upon whether or not the rote memorized association is used or applied in real life situations.

More relevant objectives (and implied test items) might be:

SO_1 — Given the following list of words the student will be able to define them:
　　(a list of words)

SO_2 — Given the following list of definitions, the student will be able to state the word associated with the definition:
　　(a list of definitions)

k. *(True-False) Botony is the study of animals. (College; Botany)*

MATCHING SO — Given the following statement, *Botany is the study of animals*, the student will be able to state whether the statement is true or false.

JUSTIFICATION — Since the test item is false, it is very irrelevant. Obviously, what a teacher wants is that in a botany class the student is able to define what the study of botany is concerned with. Actually, what most teachers really want is for the student to be able to differentiate the study of botany from the other fields coming under the broad label of biology and yet realize that all these fields are concerned with the study of living organisms.

More relevant objectives (and implied test items) might be:

SO_1 — The student will be able to define botany.

SO_2 — Given the following list of biological fields of study, the student will be able to define each in terms of the content area to be studied: (a list of biological fields of study).

SO_3 — Given the following list of fields of study dealing with living organisms, the student will be able to construct an organizational (or flow) chart which indicates the relationship between these fields of study: (a list of biological fields of study).

l. *(True-False) Gordon Allport defines personality as the dynamic organization within the individual of those psychophysical systems. (College; Psychology)*

MATCHING SO — Given the following statement, *Gordon Allport defines personality as the dynamic organization within the individual of those psychophysical systems*, the student will be able to state whether the statement is true or false.

JUSTIFICATION — As before, the item as presently stated is not very useful. What the teacher probably wants is for the student to be able to state the definitions of personality which are suggested by certain people and/or groups. The teacher may also want a student to differentiate between these definitions. These objectives would be rote memory and as such, their value would be dependent upon whether or not what is memorized is applicable to real situations. If not applicable, possibly what is really important is that the student is able to locate sources in which the student can look up these definitions when wanted rather than committing these definitions to memory and then be unable to retrieve them from the memory when wanted because of the lack of sufficient use of the retrieval mechanism. Ostensibly, knowing these definitions should help a person understand his own personality and the personalities of others. If this is correct, then the application objectives could concern certain actions by a person from which inferences (based on personality definitions) could be made about that person's personality and about subsequent actions by that person which will be consistent with his or her personality.

More relevant objectives (and implied test items) might be:

SO_1 — Given the following list of names of people and groups, the student will be able to state the definition of personality suggested and/or commonly ascribed to these people and groups:

(a list of names)

SO_2 — Given the list of names and associated definitions of personality from the last objective, the student will be able to differentiate the definitions from one another in terms of the emphasis of each definition. Ideally, it would be useful to differentiate between these definitions of personality on the basis of observable behaviors which represent a person's personality, i.e., Given the following behaviors which represent a person's personality, the student will be able to differentiate between the definitions of personality on the basis of how each definition explains the same personality behaviors.

m. *What is cadence? (High School; Music Appreciation)*

MATCHING SO — The student should be able to define the term *cadence.*

JUSTIFICATION — This objective in its present form which asks for a verbal definition is basic, but a much more useful objective in music might be concerned with whether or not a student is able to identify the cadence in various selections of music. The identification could consist of the student naming the cadence and/or to copy (reproduce) the cadence with an instrument, hands, or feet. This ability would not only be useful in listening to music, but it would be useful in playing a musical instrument and in dancing. This test item and matching objective is typical of the traditional verbal testing in courses in which the desired objectives are really concerned primarily with seeing, listening, feeling, and performing. In other words, the test items and objectives are primarily cognitive rather than being primarily sensory. In courses dealing with sensory skills, the test items and objectives should also be concerned with sensory skills.

More relevant objectives (and implied test items) might be:

SO_1 — Given the following musical excerpts, the student will be able to identify the cadence of each, label it, and be able to reproduce it by clapping his or her hands: (accompanied by an audio tape containing the musical excerpts).

n. *In a sentence or less, give me your definition of good nutrition. (High School; Home Economics)*

MATCHING SO — The student will be able to define good nutrition.

JUSTIFICATION — Just being able to define good or poor nutrition verbally is probably not very useful. However, if the student can apply the definition to a given meal or sequence of meals, and

599

identify whether the meal or meals represent good or poor nutrition, this could be useful. The conditions under which this ability might be useful could include looking at verbal menus (as most people eat out in restaurants at varying frequencies), but should emphasize looking at a photograph of a meal or a series of photographs of meals. The application of this ability is not only concerned with identifying the nutrition value of a meal, but ultimately with what changes can be made to improve the nutrition of poor meals and to improve the unappetizing appearance of meals.

More relevant objectives (and implied test items) might be:

SO_1 — Given the following types of meals (or photographs of meals), the student should be able to identify which meals represent good or poor nutrition; to defend the identification based on a definition of good nutrition; in the case of the meals that are poor, to suggest one or more ways to correct the nutrition level and balance; and to defend each change in terms of the definition of good nutrition; (a list of menus and/or a series of photographs).

o. *Write the shorthand for each word in the space provided. Be sure to insert the necessary vowel symbol in all single words because the words are not in context.*

1. *power* _____	5. *correspond* _____
2. *action* _____	6. *spread* _____
3. *doing* _____	7. *slowly* _____
4. *outcome* _____	8. *inspire* _____

MATCHING SO — Given the following list of words and phrases, the student will write the shorthand for each word.

JUSTIFICATION — The chances of a secretary being given a list of single words or phrases and being asked to translate them into shorthand symbols, is very rare. Learning the behavior of translating printed words and phrases into shorthand symbols is not relevant to the actual tasks of most secretaries. Also, although there are times when a single word might be given in dictation such as a title of a paragraph or of a person, but the words in the test item would probably not even be given singly in dictation which makes the item even more irrelevant. The teacher who made up this test item realized part of the problem by stating *Be sure to insert the necessary vowel symbol in all single words because the words are not in context* which means that what the students will be writing down for this test item is not what they would be writing down if the words were in context. This indicates that the students' response is not even what would normally be desired when the words are dictated and in the context of some message. A very important behavior for a secretary to learn is to be able to identify words in context in which the shorthand symbol is incorrectly made. By identifying and remembering the phrase and sentence patterns of the person doing dictation, it will be easier for the secretary to identify any misformed symbols. Misspelled words and incorrectly formed shorthand symbols may be the correct spelling or form for different words. For example, in spelling, if the correct word was *farther* and a student wrote *father*, by itself, the word seems correct; but if given to the student in the context of *The store is father than two miles down the road*, the error in spelling or incorrectly formed shorthand symbol will be easier to identify.

More relevant objectives (and implied test items) might be:

SO_1 — Given the following audio tape (or cassette) of a series of sentences containing the following list of words and phrases, the student will be able to write out the sentences in shorthand notation correctly forming the assigned words and phrases while listening to the audio tape. (Only those words and phrases in this lesson and in previous lessons should be evaluated).

p. *(Spelling lists) A very common test consists of a list of words which are dictated to the students singly or in sentences and the students are supposed to write down the key words from the week's assignment correctly spelled. In addition, correct spelling is one of the criteria used in the evaluation of written assignments in most subjects and at almost all levels of education.*

MATCHING SO — Given the following list of words dictated by the teacher singly or in sentences, the student will be able to write the words down and spell them correctly. (Traditionally, students can pass the weeks spelling list by achieving 50-60 percent of the words correctly spelled.)

JUSTIFICATION — If a person was to live in such a way that reading or writing was not involved, it might not be important to learn to spell correctly. As long as our society utilizes the skills of reading, writing and even speaking and listening as means of communication, it will be important and for many people, it will be critical to be able to spell correctly. Misspelling in writing may cause the following problems in reading: the reader may not understand the message at all; the reader may misinterpret the content as communicating a different message; the reader may feel that the writer is uneducated and/or is not concerned with detail or the communication of his or her message; and depending upon the

601

degree of misspelling and the lack of familiarity of the reader with the content of the message and the words misspelled, it may be difficult or impossible for the reader to look up the misspelled words in a dictionary in order to develop a meaning for the unknown words and possibly even a meaning for the written message itself. Misspelling in writing may also cause similar problems in speaking and listening. If the writer is also the speaker, misspelled words will probably lead to mispronounced words which may cause the listeners to have the same problems as the reader of the written message.

> NOTE: Most teachers in correcting spelling errors cross out the word, circle the word, write *sp* near it, and/or spell the word correctly. Although these actions may correct the error, they do not necessarily help the student learn to spell better. As described under Learning Problems in Volume I (pp. 190-191), the spelling behavior which has to be taught is that a word *doesn't look right* when it is misspelled. The easiest way to teach this is when the misspelled word is in the context of a sentence or paragraph and then indicate the line in which there is a word misspelled and ask the student to locate the misspelled word and then to correct it. No student will look up each word in the line, he or she will study the words in the line and decide which word *doesn't look right* the most and look that one up.

Although not very many students will be secretaries who will have to take down dictation, almost everyone will take notes while listening. Under the traditional approach to education, the behavior of taking notes is very important and in many classes even critical in helping students to remember what was presented in the lectures. Even under the Learning Systems Concept, note taking is important when listening to recorded lectures and to scholarship sessions. Throughout most people's lives, there will be many times in conferences and meetings when it would be useful if a person could take notes. Taking down notes which involve words which the listener is familiar with is not too much of a problem; but taking down notes which include words which the listener is not familiar with and has no meaning for, creates problems in receiving the message. In trying to look up these unknown words in a dictionary it is particularly difficult if the person has not learned to translate audio sounds (words) into written letters (probably phonetically or using the Initial Teaching Alphabet — ITA) and doesn't know the various letters or combinations of letters that give similar sounds. Although students are usually taught the sounds of the letters singly and in combinations, they are not usually taught the reverse, which letters or combinations of letters give what sounds.

NOTE: Some of the so-called *mod, progressive,* or *creative* English teachers claim that they don't care about whether or not students spell correctly as long as they have *fresh* ideas. This philosophy may make these teachers temporarily popular with students who haven't learned how to spell; but when the students find out that they can't communicate their *fresh* ideas to others via written misspelled words, the popularity of these teachers who should have helped them learn to spell may be shortlived. As long as mankind continues to be a social creature, creative ideas will have to be communicated in a conventional language based on habitual or traditional rules of grammar and spelling. Creative spelling, grammar, and language may be fine for self-communication, but it probably won't be very useful in communicating to other people who don't understand the *newly created language!*

More relevant objectives (and implied test items) might be:

SO_1 — Given the following list of words recorded in sentences, the student while listening to the audio tape (cassette) will write out the sentences spelling the assigned words correctly. (The student would have to achieve 100 percent of the words to pass).

SO_2 — Given the following sentences in which there are misspelled words (the students are familiar with the words when spelled correctly) and the words as presently misspelled are still recognizable, the student will be able to locate the misspelled words and correct them using a dictionary when necessary.

SO_3 — Given a student's own sentences (paragraphs, essays, etc.) in which there are misspelled words, the student will be able to locate them and correct them using a dictionary when necessary. (In multi-paragraph essays or papers, the teacher should indicate the line or paragraph in which the misspelled word is located.)

SO_4 — Given a series of recorded sounds, the student will be able to write the letters and/or combinations of letters which match the sound. (This could be done with the regular alphabet, the Initial Teaching Alphabet, or phonetically.)

SO_5 — Listening to recorded message containing unknown words, the student will be able to spell out the unknown words based on the sounds. The student will also be able to spell the unknown words in different ways where different letters or combinations of letters have the same or similar sounds. The student will then locate the unknown word in the dictionary and confirm the correct spelling. (It should be remembered that there are at least three levels of difficulty in this SO; words that are spelled like they sound; exceptions to the rule; and words starting with or containing letters which are silent when the word is pronounced.)

q. *There should be* _____ *clearance between the touch tuning plate universal bar arm and the key lever spring plate. (Vocational; Typewriter Repair)*

MATCHING SO — The student should be able to quote from memory the clearance between the touch tuning plate universal bar arm and the key lever spring plate.

JUSTIFICATION — This is typical of many test items found in vocational-technical courses dealing with maintenance and/or repair of equipment, motors, etc. Because the numbers, the pieces involved, and their location change from one typewriter to another and from one year to another, this type of rote memory objective is representative of a design for obsolescence. If the student had to depend on rote memory for this information, the student would have to go back to school each time a new machine came out. As a result, this test item in its present format is of little value. The much more appropriate behavior to be learned would require the student to consult the manufacturer's handbook whenever this information is necessary.

More relevant objectives (and implied test items) might be:

SO$_1$ — Given a typewriter, the manufacturer's handbook, and a list of points to be checked in servicing the typewriter, the student should be able to locate the specifications for each checkpoint in the handbook, check to see if the typewriter is up to those specifications at each check point, and, if not, to adjust or correct the problem so as to be in accordance with the specifications. (Included with the SO would be a list of check points.)

This objective could be broken down into three separate objectives: one concerning the use of the handbook, a second one concerning the diagnosis of the typewriter, and the third concerning the actual repair or adjustments. Even each of these three objectives could be further sub-divided into smaller objectives — particularly the last one concerning the actual repair and adjustment. Since most typewriters consist of many complex parts and assemblies, it would be easier for student learning if there was a separate SO for each repair and adjustment task.

r. *What are the four fundamental economic questions which every society must attempt to answer? (College; Economics)*

MATCHING SO — The student will be able to state the four fundamental economic questions which every society must attempt to answer.

JUSTIFICATION — It should be obvious that this item is a rote memory item. A student would be able to memorize rather easily the four questions which are probably listed in a textbook. The problem in answering whether or not the test item is useful depends on whether or not the student is asked to do anything with these four questions. If not, the four questions will be memorized in order to pass the test and then forgotten about as fast as they were memorized. The GO that this SO is a part of would probably be stated as follows: *The student should understand why every society must attempt to answer these four questions.* Listing the four questions might be the first SO; but the subsequent SO's should go into more depth in order to substantiate the value of memorizing the four questions.

More relevant objectives (and implied test items) might be:

SO_1 — The student should be able to state briefly why these four fundamental economic questions should be answered by every society. (Included in the statement for each question should be a reference to what might happen if a society doesn't attempt to answer each question in contrast to the situation if the society did attempt to answer each question.

SO_2 — The student will be able to give two more examples of societies which did attempt to answer the four questions and two or more examples of societies which did not attempt to answer the questions and will describe the resultant effects on these societies.

s. *Which of the following is NOT a necessary ingredient for communication? (a) noise (b) encoder (c) channel (d) thought (e) receiver (College; Communication)*

MATCHING SO — Given the following five items: (a) noise (b) encoder (c) channel (d) thought (e) receiver, the student will be able to identify which one is not a necessary ingredient for communication.

JUSTIFICATION — This item is representative of a common form of multiple choice test items in which the teacher would like the student to know two or more things but rather than test for each of the important things, it is easier to test the student, as in set theory,

605

on his or her ability to identify which one of the choices is incompatible with the rest. Notice, the emphasis is on the one choice that doesn't belong in the set not necessarily one of the ones that do belong in the set. Since the emphasis is on what the teacher doesn't want the student to learn and the student will rarely ever run into the same set with the same non-member of the set, the item has to be irrelevant and useless. In most cases, what the teacher really wants is for the student to list the members of the set. In this item, the teacher wanted the students to list the parts in the process of communication. It would have been much more relevant to just ask the student to list them (a rote memory objective). As in many test items of this type, the four choices which are supposed to constitute the set are not complete, so the teacher doesn't really know if the student knows all the members of the set which is the implied objective even though not tested by the item. This type of negative multiple-choice item is also used as a trick item because in the rush of answering a number of multiple-choice questions in a timed test where the emphasis is on finding the one choice that is right (according to the test-maker), it takes a mental shift to look for the one choice that is wrong and as a result, some students will miss the item because they forgot to make the mental shift in emphasis.

More relevant objectives (and implied test items) might be:

SO_1 — The student will be able to list the (number) parts of the communication process and make a brief statement about the function of each part in the process.

SO_2 — The student will be able to identify two or more factors in each part of the communication process and make a brief statement about how each factor affects the effectiveness and efficiency of the communication process.

SO_3 — Given the following list of communication problems, the student will be able to identify the part and factor of the communication process primarily contributing to each problem and will suggest a solution to each problem based on the function performed by the factor and/or part. Since the correct choice that doesn't belong in effective communication is *noise* it could be possible that the teacher wants the student to learn about *noise* and how it has negative effects on communication. In that case, the objectives might be:

SO_4 — The student should be able to define *noise* in communication.

606

SO$_5$ — Given the factors in the communication process, the student will be able to describe the effects of *noise* on each factor, if any, and give one or more examples.

t. *Name seven of the twelve Olympian Gods using their Greek names. Do not use their Roman names.*

MATCHING SO — The student will be able to name seven of the twelve Olympian gods, using their Greek names, not their Roman names.

JUSTIFICATION — The first problem in justifying the test item is to find out which five gods are not important (the test item asked for *any* seven out of the twelve). This is a common type of test item found in many science and humanities courses, i.e., *answer any three out of the following five questions.* If all of the questions are equal in value and testing the same behavior, this type of test item would be acceptable. However, in most of these tests, the test items are not equal and are not testing the same behavior. If all five questions are important, then the students should answer all five questions. In the case of this test item, the students should know all twelve if all twelve are important. Teachers accept less for one of two reasons: first, the teacher may feel that all of the items have limited importance and as such don't feel that it is necessary for students to learn any one of the items (shouldn't be required learning in the first place then); second, the teacher wants to be fair and knows that the students couldn't guess what all of the questions would be on the test and study for them, so the teacher hopes that the students have at least guessed three out of the five items. (In an honest situation where the students are told ahead of time what they are going to be tested on, guessing is not a part of the game and the students can be required to learn all of the important test items.)

If there are certain gods which are more important than the others, then the test should be aimed at these specific gods. As the item is presently stated, it is a rote memory item of very limited value and relevance. I can't quite believe that it is the names of the gods that are important. What the teacher may have really wanted was that the students should know what the gods were the god of. Since some modern advertising makes use of visuals depicting the Greek gods which is supposed to imply that the article being advertised has the properties of the Greek god, i.e., speed, strength, etc., maybe the teacher would like the students to associate the name of the god with a visual of the god and then with the properties associated with the god. As there are still contemporary references to the

607

Greek gods in literature and some festivals which can be traced back to the Greek gods, it may be that these aspects may help to make the content of the item relevant.

More relevant objective (and implied test items) might be:

SO_1 — The student will be able to list the twelve Olympian gods, using their Greek names, and identify what they are the gods of, and will also identify with supporting evidence which of the gods are still represented in contemporary literature, festivals, etc. (it may also be appropriate to have the student identify the gods from pictures).

5. APPLYING THE QUESTIONS TO SPECIFIC TEST ITEMS AND RELATED OBJECTIVES WHICH HAVE LESS THAN 100 PERCENT CORRELATION

Although it should be apparent that the evaluation of an instructional event should reflect what should have or was expected to have occurred during the event, the problem of the correlation between objectives and related test items is very critical in education. Under the traditional approach, where only general objectives were available and almost anything could be tested, tests were designed to give grades and to reflect comparative learning levels regardless of what the content and behavior of the learning level consisted of. The belief in the existence of a *normal* distribution of learning abilities in all classes supported decades of testing in which obtaining a curve of grades or results was much more important than what the tests were testing for. Now, as more and more educators, students, parents, and taxpayers became concerned with the negative effects of the normative testing concept and with the need to become accountable in education such that schools and teachers emphasize designed success rather than designed failure, there are more schools and teachers who are concerned with identifying what it is they are supposed to be teaching and students are supposed to be learning. Many of the teachers who are writing good specific objectives have not identified the need to have their test items match their objectives and as a consequence, many of these teachers are still using their old tests and test item formats even if the test items do not measure the achievement of the new objectives. Since students try to learn whatever it is they are going to be evaluated on and if a teacher's tests don't match the teacher's stated objectives, then the students will ignore the objectives and try to find out or guess what the tests are like. In turn, since the objectives haven't affected what the students are learning, the teacher is discouraged from writing any more objectives and regrets all the energy expended in writing the objectives the teacher has already written. As teachers increase the correlation such that the test items are

608

changed to test for the achievement of the specified objectives or the specified objectives are changed to represent what the test items are testing for the achievement of, teachers will notice increases in learning without really making many other changes in what happens in the classroom. By being consistent, teachers are really just bringing honesty back into the classroom after decades of the designed trickery of normative testing.

The following examples again represent a variety of subjects and levels of education. The emphasis will be on justifying either the change in the test item to match the objective, the change in the objective to match the test item, or changes in both. (Again, when you have read as much of this unit as you want, skip to page 622).

a. *Implied Objective — Value free sociology is a study for truth and results in insights into daily life.*

Test Item — (True-False) Sociology is value free. (College; Sociology)

MATCHING SO — (To the test item) — Given the statement, *Sociology is value free*, the student will be able to identify whether or not the statement is true or false.

JUSTIFICATION — Although the implied objective suggests that the student should understand that *value free* sociology is a study for truth, this doesn't really indicate that this understanding can be tested by a series of true-false statements. The test item is irrelevant and of little value.

More relevant objectives (and implied test items) might be:

SO_1 — The student should be able to define the term *value free sociology* and give two or more examples to illustrate the definition.

SO_2 — Given the following two principles of *value free sociology*, the student will be able to cite one or more events in his or her own life in which each principle could be applied.

b. *GO — The student should be able to show the relevance of literature to life in the school and in the community.*

Test Items — A series of test items requiring rote memorized information from the novel Ice Station Zebra. (Junior High School; English)

MATCHING SO — (To the test items) — Given a series of questions on the content of the novel *Ice Station Zebra*, the student should be able to answer the questions by remembering the correct information.

609

JUSTIFICATION — Unless the student is going to make some kind of an extended study of the novel *Ice Station Zebra,* this test item has limited value. Notice that the GO does not specify the vehicle for learning, yet the test concerns only the vehicle and ignores the GO. This is a very common problem in literature in which the vehicles for learning the course objectives become the objectives. If the GO is what is really wanted, then the teacher should be able to select a list of literature in various forms which meet the criteria of having relevance to life in schools and in the community. Each student should be free to pick which ever book on the list that interests him or her most. The test would primarily be concerned with the student proving that the book actually had relevance to life in the schools and in the community. Learning that literature can be relevant is probably a much more important objective than learning details about the content of any one novel or literary work.

More relevant objectives (and implied test items) might be:

SO$_1$ — Given a list of literary works, the student will be able to show that literature is relevant to life in the schools and in the community by reading one or more of the literary works and by comparing two or more events in the literary work with similar events in schools and/or in the community. (Should be accompanied with a list of literary works representing similar levels of ease of comparison, but varied interest areas and reading levels. In subsequent courses, the difficulty level of identifying comparable events could be increased. The criteria for evaluating the comparison should be included.)

c. *SO — Student should be able to list three Renaissance painters, name one or more of their outstanding works and the characteristics of each painters' work that marks it as Renaissance.*

Test item — Which of the following was not a painter? (a) Cervantes, (b) Rembrandt, (c) Raphael (d) daVinci (High School; History)

MATCHING SO (to the test item) — Given the following question, *Which of the following was not a painter?,* the student will be able to answer the question correctly by choosing one of the following four choices: (a) Cervantes, (b) Rembrandt, (c) Raphael, (d) daVinci.

JUSTIFICATION — This objective and test item were taken from a Learning Activity Packet on the Renaissance. It should be obvious that the test item is not testing the SO which was stated in the program. Being a multiple-choice item, the test item is irrelevant by design and of very little value particularly when the emphasis is on a non-painter rather than on the painters.

Although the SO is specific and measurable, the test item that would match the objective would be asking for rote memory learning which would have limited value because knowledge of the kind asked for in the objective would not be used very frequently and hence, might become difficult to retrieve from the memory. If there are specific characteristics which identify Renaissance painters and their works, it might be much more appropriate to have students learn how to identify these characteristics not only in the paintings of the Renaissance painters, but in the paintings of anyone else since then who utilizes these characteristics. This same approach may be appropriate concerning Renaissance music, literature, furniture, clothing, etc. If the facts of the Renaissance are useful in part, it may be appropriate to have the students learn how to locate sources of information on the Renaissance and then learn how to extract whatever information they want rather than commit to memory a multitude of seldom used data.

More Relevant Objectives (and implied test items) might be:

SO_1 — Student will be able to list the (number) characteristics of Renaissance paintings and will be able to identify these characteristics in the paintings of Renaissance painters.

SO_2 — Given a series of photographs of paintings representing a variety of styles, the student will be able to identify those paintings which have characteristics of the Renaissance paintings and will point out and describe each characteristic which is used in identifying the painting.

d. *GO — Given an unknown word in a sentence or paragraph containing word clues as to the meaning the student should develop for the unknown word, the student will be able to identify the word clues and then using the word clues state a synonym or definition for the unknown word.*

Example: I had expected some <u>vibration</u> during the takeoff. I was pleasantly surporsed to find it as <u>smooth</u> as gliding through water.

Test Items — A series of multiple-choice vocabulary test items completely out of context in which the words to be matched to one of the choices are no longer unknown to the student because the words are the same ones which were used in the programmed unit.

Example: <u>Vibrations</u> means (a) quivering movement, (b) great activity, (c) <u>moving forward</u>, (d) great speed. (Junior High School; Commercial Reading Unit)

611

MATCHING GO (to the test item) — Given a (supposedly known) word, the student will select from among four choices a word or phrase which is the closest to the meaning the student has for the given word.

JUSTIFICATION — The GO and the matching GO are general objectives only in the sense that specific words, sentences, and multiple-choice items are not included. Notice the two major differences between the objective and the test item: first, the objective concerns unknown words while the test item concerns a known word; second, the objective concerns having the student look for word clues in the context of a sentence or paragraph while the test item concerns isolated words out of context without any other words for possible word clues. The concept of learning how to look for word clues in the context of what the student is reading, is a very important behavior for all students and critical for students whose reading abilities (at the moment) are two or more grade levels below the materials they are reading. Therefore, the objective can be easily justified in terms of usefulness to the student and in terms of what the student is supposed to do when encountering unknown words in context. However, the test, as with all multiple-choice test items, can not be justified and is particularly irrelevant and useless with reference to developing meanings for unknown words based on identified word clues.

In order to make the commerical materials even more relevant, the teacher or reading specialist could identify words that students are having trouble with in their daily class work. Then tests could be made up which would include these words in excerpts from their reading assignments. Care should be taken that the excerpts selected actually have word clues which will help the students develop meanings for the unknown words.

More relevant objectives (and implied test items) might be:

SO$_1$ — (Pretest) Given the following list of words, the student will indicate which words are known and which words are unknown by defining those which the student has meaning for and leaving the others blank.

This objective should be followed by a list of words used in the reading program. This procedure is necessary because if the student works with words for which the student already has meanings, the learning of the critical behaviors (identifying word clues and using word clues to develop meaning for an unknown word) would be seriously limited or hampered.

SO_2 — The same objective (GO) which was stated at the beginning of this item except with specifics involving the unknown words identified in the pretest (SO_1).

e. *SO_1 — The student will be able to define the following terms; neuroanatomy, cytology, organology, asteology, and histology.*

Test item — (True-False) Neuroanatomy is the study of the functions of the brain. (College; Medical Technology)

MATCHING SO — for the test item — Given the following statement, *Neuroanatomy is the study of the functions of the brain*, the student will be able to state whether the statement is true or false.

JUSTIFICATION — As should be expected by now, there is no way that the use of the test item can be justified on the basis of being useful and relevant for students. Obviously, students will never again run into this same false statement and be asked to state whether it is true or false. With reference to the desired vocabulary objective, the way it should be tested is to just ask the student to define the words. As with most objectives concerning vocabulary, the objective and revised test items represent rote memory learning. There is nothing wrong with memorizing definitions if the words and/or the definitions are going to be used soon and frequently. If this is not the case, it would be better to do one of two things; first, the students could be taught how to locate sources (dictionaries, etc.) and how to look up needed definitions; and second, since many words in medical and related fields are made up of various combinations of Latin words, prefixes, and suffixes, it might be very useful to have the students memorize certain basic words, prefixes, and suffixes and practice developing meanings for words containing various combinations of these word elements. Both of these learned behaviors will be used frequently in the medical fields.

Revised Test item — Define the following terms: (a list of basic words which are frequently used).

More relevant objectives (and implied test items) might be:

In addition to SO_1 listed at the beginning of this item.

SO_2 — Given the following sources commonly found in a medical laboratory and a list of unknown medical terms, the student will be able to locate the correct source for the definitions, will look them up, and copy them down for each word.

SO_3 — Given the following list of basic Latin words, prefixes, and suffixes, frequently used in medical technology, the student will state or write the English equivalent for the word element.

SO_4 — Given the following list of unknown words which are made up of Latin base words, prefixes, and suffixes (specified in SO_3), the student will state or write out a definition for the unknown words based on a composite meaning of the word elements.

f. *GO — To develop a philosophy in the (dental) students that will enable them to see, appreciate and understand the total concept and value of community health activity; to realize that as practicing dentists, they will have a role to play in the health matters of the community, the state and the nation, and how to relate such matters to their profession and to their practices.*

Test Item — The state level would have primary responsibility for which of the following dental public health activities?

> a. *Determination of the dental needs in an institution for mentally retarded children.*
>
> b. *Periodic examination of children's teeth in a school district.*
> c. *Monitoring of dental x-ray units to limit unnecessary radiation.*
>
> d. *Investigation of methods for the financing of dental care.*
> e. *Two of the above.*

(University; Dental School)

MATCHING TEST ITEM — Given the following question, *The State level would have primary responsibility for which of the following dental public health activities?* the student will be able to answer it correctly by selecting one of the following four choices:

> a. Determination of the dental needs in an institution for mentally retarded children.
> b. Periodic examination of children's teeth in a school district.
> c. Monitoring of dental x-ray units to limit unnecessary radiation.
> d. Investigation of methods for the financing of dental care.
> e. Two of the above.

JUSTIFICATION — As before, since the test item is a multiple-choice item, it is irrelevant and of very little value (although being able to answer this type of test item is the basis for certification of dentists, doctors, nurses, etc.) In addition, note that the objective is primarily concerned with the roles of the dentist while the test item is primarily concerned with the roles of the state dental unit. Actually both of these areas are important, but they should represent separate objectives and test items.

A common problem encountered when writing objectives and test items concerning the role or roles someone or some agency should

614

perform is that the role descriptions are like general objectives in that they are usually statements depicting boundary lines within which certain actions take place. Specific objectives, in reference to roles, are usually spelled out in terms of specific tasks performed by the roles. It is possible to list the various areas of responsibility a particular role might encompass and at one time or another this list should be prepared or at least seen by the person or persons performing the role. However, the conditions under which this knowledge will be useful are when a particular question is raised about a certain task, i.e., who or what agency is responsible for this task.

More relevant objectives (and implied test items) might be:

SO_1 — The student will be able to state his or her role as a dentist in the health matters of the community, of the state, and of the nation. In addition to a description of his or her role in each of the three areas (community, state, and national), the student will be able to specify two or more tasks to be performed by each role.

SO_2 — The student will be able to list the five most important functions of the state dental public health unit and place them in a hierarchical order of importance and state the criteria for evaluating the importance of the functions. The student will also be able to specify two or more typical tasks which would be performed in each of the functions of the state dental public health unit.

SO_3 — Given a list of 20 dental needs and problems stated in the form of questions (simulated inquiries), the student will identify whether the individual dentist or the state dental public health unit should be primarily responsible in taking care of the need or of solving the problem. The identification should be defended in terms of the roles performed by the individual dentist and the state dental public health unit.

g. *GO — To be able to recall the specific names of individuals, places, and events which were instrumental in the political, social, and economic development of Europe during the Age of Absolutism.*

Test Item — What is the name of the dynasty which ruled France from 987 to 1328 expanding the Ile-de-France into a large nation? (High School; History)

MATCHING SO — The student will be able to answer the following question. *What is the name of the dynasty which ruled France from 987 to 1328 expanding the Ile-de-France into a large nation?*

JUSTIFICATION — This is a good example of how a test item can reflect the objective. However, the objective is not specific enough to really let students know what the teacher wants. In order to make it more specific, the teacher should have included a specific list of names, places, and events which should be remembered. This list would then be given to the student at the beginning of the course or unit. A common oversight in the writing of the objective is that whereas the objective states that the student should just remember the names, the test item states by its format that the student has to remember the names in association with what the names represent in reference to political, social, and economic development of Europe during the Age of Absolution. A more appropriate version of the GO would ask the students to recall the names when given the significance of the names or to recall the significance of the names when given the names.

However, even if the relationship between the test item and the GO is fairly good, the questions of justification indicate that unless a student is going to major in history, both the GO and the test item are of little value and irrelevant. For the student majoring in history, it may be necessary to commit to memory a variety of facts, names, and dates in order to carry on conversations with other historians; but, for the non-history majors, they could live out the rest of their lives and rarely, if ever, would they come across the need to recognize the names of the people, places, or events involved with the GO. Admittedly, some historical names of people, places, and events are referred to from time to time in contemporary communication (conversation, lectures, newspapers, magazine articles, books, etc.) because the significance of what is associated with the name helps to communicate an idea, concept, or feeling (if the receiver of the communication is familiar with the significance), i.e., a certain event was like the *Trojan Horse.* If these famous names which have become a part of our language are the names to be remembered, then the objective and the test items should reflect the use of the names. Otherwise, it is probably much more important that the student can locate approproate sources and retrieve any information desired which is a process objective learned through practice rather than an information objective learned by rote memorization.

If a teacher's objective is for the students to be able to apply to contemporary problems some of the techniques or solutions used in history, then the objective and test items should be so stated. Process objectives of this type are the easiest to justify because there are always a multitude of contemporary problems to be solved. Although some contemporary political, social, and economic problems are unique and have no parallel in history, most problems are not that unique because people over the centuries are not that unique and different. It is possible for us to benefit from studying our past mistakes and good fortunes; but only if the emphasis is on the process which led to the mistake and the process which led to the good fortune rather than emphasizing the names of people, places, and events.

More relevant objectives (and implied test items) might be:

SO$_1$ — (For students majoring in history) Given the following list of names of people, places, and events and the accompanying annotations describing the significance of the names in the political, social, and economic development of Europe during the Age of Absolutism, the student will be able to recall the significance of the name when presented with the name and/or will be able to recall the name when presented with the significance of the name.

SO$_2$ — Given the following list of historical names of people, places, and events which are commonly found in contemporary communication, the accompanying descriptions of their significance in history, and paragraphs similar to the following paragraphs taken from newspapers, magazines, books, etc., the student will be able to describe how the significance of the historical name helps to emphasize a concept being communicated in the paragraph. (The test items should utilize different paragraphs then those accompanying the objective so that the student learns the process of applying the significance of the historical names to different situations rather than memorizing the situations in the paragraphs given as examples with the objective. Be sure, however, that the new paragraphs do not introduce historical names which are not on the list given with the objective.)

SO$_3$ — Given the resources of a library and a list of historical names of people, places, and events, the student will be able to locate in the library, sources of information about these names and will be able to retrieve or extract information from these sources regarding the significance of these names, places and events concerning the political, social, and economic development of Europe during the Age of Absolutism (or any other historical period or movement).

SO$_4$ — Given the following list of contemporary problems, the students will select two or more of the contemporary problems, analyze them according to the following list of factors, will identify two or more historical problems which are similar to each of the

selected contemporary problems, will analyze the historical problems according to the same factors as used to analyze the contemporary problems, will prove that the historical and contemporary
problems are similar by comparing the factors of both which were
analyzed, and then will suggest solutions for the contemporary
problems in terms of applying the solutions of the historical problems if the problems were solved satisfactorily and/or in terms of
not applying the solutions of the historical problems if the problems were not solved satisfactorily, i.e., do these things and don't
do these other things. (The student should identify his or her
criteria for satisfactory solutions to both historical and contemporary problems. It is likely that two different students might interpret
the solutions to the same problem differently or they might both
agree that a solution was satisfactory or unsatisfactory but for
different criteria or reasons.)

b. *GO — To develop in students an understanding of themselves in
    relation to their physical needs.*

   *Test Items — The text mentions two objectives of a physical condi-
   tioning program. Which of the following is not an objective of a
   physical conditioning program?*

   *a. General objective   b. to reduce the level of muscle endurance
   b. specific objective   d. none of these*
   (College — Physical Fitness Program)

   MATCHING SO — Given the following statement and question, *The
   text mentions two objectives of a physical conditioning program.
   Which of the following is not an objective of a physical conditioning program?*, the student should be able to answer the question
   correctly by selecting one of the following four choices: (a) general
   objective, (b) specific objective, (c) to reduce the level of muscle
   endurance, (d) none of these.

   JUSTIFICATION — The test item format and the content of the
   item is of little value and irrelevant in terms of the GO. In addition,
   the test item was written by a teacher who has had limited training
   and practice in writing test items, the choices were selected such
   that students would select choice (c) and it would be considered as
   the right answer even if they didn't remember the two objectives in
   the text. In addition, the choices are almost without any relationship to the concept of physical conditioning.

   In many schools at all levels, students in physical education courses
   are given a physical fitness test at the beginning of school in the fall
   and another physical fitness test at the end of the school year in the

spring. Supposedly, the results of the fall test should indicate whether or not the student needs physical conditioning, if not, the student should be exempt from required participation in the program. However, the student could voluntarily participate in the program and/or could be involved in other aspects of a physical education program. If the student needs physical conditioning, the physical fitness test should be considered as a diagnostic tool which indicates the student's physical needs. The subsequent physical conditioning program should be based on each student's individual needs. Because of individual differences among students, it would be highly unlikely that all students would need the same exercise, at the same time, and in the same amount. Therefore, the concept of a class (all students doing the same thing) should not exist in a physical conditioning program. The program should be individualized such that as students achieve the desired physical condition, they can drop out of the required activities and stay out until such time as the student is unable to pass the physical fitness test. The ideal program would start in early elementary levels and be continuous at least through high school in which the objective would be to help a student reach a certain level of physical condition and then to help the student when necessary to maintain this level throughout the student's school years. Under this approach, some students might be able to stay in good physical conditions because of their out-of-school activities and never have to participate in the conditioning program except to take the physical fitness tests to verify their good physical condition. At the other extreme, there would be some students who would probably participate in the program every year from early elementary to their last year in high school and they still might not be in *good* physical condition. However, this latter group of students would be much more physically fit under a program which is trying to deal with their individual needs than under a traditional program where the individual needs are ignored and there is no continuity from year to year. All to often, what happens in the traditional physical conditioning program bears little relationship to the results of the physical fitness tests.

A key point to remember is that almost all objectives and test items in a physical conditioning course would be performance objectives where the students would have to perform physical activities rather than the paper and pencil objectives and tests found in most other courses. This means that the objectives might very well include a series of single concept films which would demonstrate the quality of the exercises. During the last year in school, in order to help students maintain a good physical condition throughout their lives

619

or to continue to improve their physical condition, it might be appropriate in a physical conditioning course to teach the students how to diagnose their own physical fitness needs and to be able to prescribe the right physical conditioning exercises.

More relevant objectives (and implied test items) might be:

SO_1 — Given a physical fitness chart, the student should be able to determine the level of good physical condition for his or her age, height, weight, body build, etc.

SO_2 — Given a physical fitness chart (or test) and accompanying visuals which indicate the quality level of the exercises, the student will perform the indicated exercises at the appropriate level or the best he or she can do.

SO_3 — After taking a physical fitness test, the student should be able to identify areas of need and to identify the exercises that will benefit the body in the areas of need.

SO_4 — The student should be able to reach and maintain a good physical condition or at least be able to make steady progress towards attaining a good physical condition.

i. *GO — To acquaint the student with her duties when the executive travels.*

Test Item — Which kinds of tasks should an executive secretary expect to perform?

_____ *a. Assigned tasks*
_____ *b. Routine, flow-of-work duties*
_____ *c. Original, creative work*
_____ *d. All of these*
(College — Executive Secretary)

MATCHING SO -- Given the following question, *Which kinds of tasks should an executive secretary expect to perform?*, the student will be able to answer the question correctly by selecting one of the following four choices: (a) assigned tasks, (b) routine, flow-of-work duties, (c) original, creative work, (d) all of these.

JUSTIFICATION -- Although the teacher of the executive secretary course at first thought the test item and the GO were correlated, upon closer study, note that the GO is concerned with the additional tasks the executive secretary may have to perform while

620

the executive is traveling whereas the test item is concerned with the different types of tasks which the executive secretary can be expected to perform at any time. With reference to the test item, the format of the multiple-choice makes the item irrelevant and of very little value. In addition, the test item is designed such that almost every student would select choice (d) which is the right choice and yet the student might not be able to list a single specific task the executive secretary should perform.

Although the GO is not specific, the wording of the objective implies that a subsequent SO would consist of the student being able to write out a list of specific tasks which the executive secretary should perform while the executive is traveling. The problem with this type of rote memory objective is that it assumes all executives are alike and will want the same tasks performed by their secretaries while they are traveling. Although it might be important for the students to know the kinds of common tasks which they might be asked to perform, other objectives are also important. In addition to being able to list the common tasks, the student should be able to perform them, the student should be able to identify what tasks an executive wants done while he or she is away traveling, and if any of the desired tasks are not among the list of common tasks, the student should be able to learn the new tasks with maximum speed and minimum interference in the performance of the other tasks. Also, the tasks which may be performed while the executive is traveling may vary depending upon the length of time the executive will be gone and the frequency of contact during the trip between the executive and the secretary.

More relevant objectives (and implied test items) might be:

SO_1 — The student will be able to list and perform the following list of common tasks which an executive secretary may be asked to perform while the executive is away traveling.

SO_2 — On the basis of a simulated interview with an executive, the student will prepare a checklist of tasks which the executive might wish performed while he or she is traveling.

SO_3 — Given the following list of tasks which an executive may wish his or her secretary to perform (none of which are on the list of common tasks), the student will select two or more tasks that have not been previously learned and will prepare a detailed description of how he or she would learn the tasks and then the student will learn to perform the tasks.

621

6. APPLYING THE QUESTION TO SPECIFIC TEST ITEMS WHICH DON'T RELATE TO COURSE OBJECTIVES IMPLIED BY THE TITLE OF THE COURSE

Under the traditional approach to education, a course title is identified; some general objectives are written which may concern what the teacher is to do in the course, what the course is to cover, or more recently what students are supposed to learn in the course; the activities or assignments are identified and programmed to fill the time slot, i.e., 50 minutes per day, five days per week, and for 36 weeks; the classes are held; and usually towards the end of the unit or course, tests are prepared. The important point to remember is that under the traditional approach it has never been a requirement that the course title, course objectives, assigned activities what actually happens in the classroom, and the tests had to have any particular relationship. Each part of the course could be rather independent of the other parts and nothing much would be said to a teacher as long as students appeared interested, not too much noise or confusion occurred in the classroom, and the grades given approximated the normal curve. However, since the course title and general objectives might be observed by department chairmen and other administrators, these two usually related to one another. Since the general objectives were vague and non-measurable, almost anything could be assigned as learning activities without worrying about whether or not they related to the course title and the course general objectives. However, since course syllabi listing the assignments, activities, and grading criteria are usually carried around by students and are in many ways available for observation by parents, colleagues, and administrators, even most course syllabi tend to bear a relationship with the course title and the general objectives of the course.

Just because the syllabus of a course relates to the course objectives, it cannot be assumed that what actually happens in the class has any relationship to the course, or the course syllabus, the general objective of the course, or the course title. What happens in the classroom is *academic freedom* and is considered by some teachers as their private platform to expand on their views to captive audiences about any subject. As long as these teachers keep to the cognitive and/or sensory domain and don't try to force their attitudes, values, and beliefs on the students, the biggest problem is that the students aren't learning what they should be in these classrooms. Given the *mod* concept of letting the students *do their own thing*, some teachers have essentially turned over the classrooms to the students and the students talk about and do whatever appeals to them. Some students prefer this non-directional type class because there are no requirements, but when these students go on to subsequent courses in which successful learning

622

is dependent upon what should have been learned in the course where the students were allowed to *do their own thing,* the students and the teachers of the subsequent courses suffer for the lack of responsibility and professionalism of the *mod* teachers. As more and more teachers claim that they are going to start teaching attitudes, values, and beliefs (affective domain), what happens in the privacy of the classroom begins to take on much more importance. In part, because more teachers will become lax in their teaching of important cognitive and sensory objectives and in part, because few, if any, of these teachers have actually been taught or have learned how to teach in the affective domain. However, the greatest problem will be the actual attitudes, values, and beliefs the students develop in these classes. Since most of these teachers won't have their affective objectives specified, it is possible that in their ignorance, the teachers may very well develop attitudes, values, and beliefs that even they don't want the students to have. In some classes, teachers may very well try to impose their attitudes, values, and beliefs on their students in the full knowledge that these attitudes, values, and beliefs are in conflict with those held by the parents and the majority of the people in the community. I am not necessarily against the teaching of conflicting attitudes, values, and beliefs because some of these may need changing in order to promote humaneness. What I am very much against is the teaching of these conflicting attitudes, values, and beliefs in the secrecy and privacy of the classroom and the avoidance of specifying these affective objectives and making them public. After all, the students are going to be the ones who will be alienated from their parents and the community by these conflicting attitudes, values, and beliefs not the teacher. Remember, students are able to control whether or not they learn cognitive and sensory objectives; but they cannot control the learning or development of affective domain objectives.

The problem with classroom activities are very similar to the problems in testing and evaluations. Tests are usually made up at the last minute and are treated as if they were highly confidential military secrets and nobody but the teacher has the right to see them except at test time when the students typically see the test for the first time. In many classes, students aren't even allowed to keep the tests after they have been graded. Because of all the secrecy associated with tests and testing, there is very little pressure to make sure the test items relate to any other parts of the course. Tests are considered as sort of a private territory in which only the teacher and his or her students are allowed to tread. As a result, it is not uncommon to find test items on tests that have little if any relationship to the course title and the general objectives. Whereas in classroom activities, the students can control whether or not they want to learn what is being presented, if the tests are used to determine the students grades and the tests match what happens in the classroom but not necessarily what is implied by the course title and objectives, students that want to get good grades can be pressured into learning what is being presented even if they don't like the content or agree with it. There are many cases in which teachers of literature have insisted on using controversial books in the name of *academic freedom*, yet the course titles and objectives have little relationship to the controversial content of the books, i.e., *Catcher in the Rye*. As indicated earlier in this book, if the literary techniques of any one of these controversial books are so unique that no other book has the same techniques or style and this reason is used to defend the study of these books, then from the point of view of transfer, the study and learning of the unique literary techniques is a waste of time and irrelevant because there aren't any other books like the ones studied. If a teacher claims that there are other books which contain these techniques, then the use of the specific controversial book is not a must for learning the special literary techniques as any one of the *other* books which may not be so controversial could serve as a vehicle for learning. However, if a teacher claims that it is not that the literary techniques are unique, it is really the content that is important, then the title and objectives of the course should be changed to fit the situation. Instead of a course entitled *Ninth Grade English Literature*, why not tell it like it is and be honest. When the content of *Catcher in the Rye* is the required vehicle and the tests are going to evaluate the students learning of the content, the name of the course should be *Rejecting Parental Authority* or some similar title. In a *few cases*, I have come across English teachers who are supposedly teaching literature, but the essays being studied and tested have titles like *Why Democracy Can't Succeed*, *Police Brutality in Urban America*, etc. Again, I am not necessarily against students studying these essays, provided that relevant learning objectives can be identified, they are learned in an open environment which presents both sides of a problem, the course title fits the content *(Democracy: Pro and Con, Police Brutality: Pro and Con*, etc.), and the test items are not used to coerce the students into learning any one particular point of view.

It is not unusual to find history teachers who in trying to be relevant concentrate on contemporary events with little, if any, reference to history. Frequently, in these classrooms and in the tests, the discussions are biased in the direction of the teacher's opinions, i.e., (test items) *List the four reasons why United States shouldn't be in Vietnam, Discuss the humanitarian philosophy that substantiates evading the draft*, etc. If these biased opinions and information are in accord with the feelings of the students, parents and the community and are listed openly as objectives for the course, I could possibly accept the

624

situation if in addition the course title was changed from *History* to something like *Contemporary Issues.*

As an example, while writing this chapter, I conducted a seminar at a college in which I came across the following test item in a mid-term examination for a business management course: *Identify in a short statement the following people: Herbert Marcuse, Huey Newton, Danny Cohn-Bendit, Abbie Hoffman, William Kunsther, Eldridge Cleaver, Jerry Rubin, and Andy Worhol.* Although the identification of these people may be appropriate in a political science or political action course, I think it would be difficult for a teacher to defend the relevance of discussing these people in a business management course.

Not all of the problems in the *Truth in Packaging* (of courses and tests) concept concerns politics and the affective domain. Because of the secrecy associated with tests, teachers frequently put test items in their tests that they wouldn't if they knew that the tests would be openly available for anyone to see them. For example, I came across the following test item in a test for a Civics course: *What is the last word in the book?* I asked the teacher why he used this test item. He answered, *I had 98 points and I needed two more points to make it an even 100 points.* Among other nonsense test items which have little, if any, relevance to the course the test item was used in, I have found test questions asking about the score of a world series baseball game, the name of a character in a cartoon strip, etc.

As tests and testing become an open and honest concept where the tests are available to students, parents, administrators, and visiting colleagues, I believe that most of the problems described in this unit will be eliminated. As teachers individualize instruction to the extent that students are working independently or at most in groups of two and three, there will be no classes as we know them in the traditional sense and the problem of classroom activities which have little or nothing to do with the course will also be eliminated. This does not mean that teachers cannot talk to and discuss sensitive issues with students. That is the function of the Scholarship sessions in which any topic can be discussed, with any person (student, teacher, parent, etc.) who voluntarily wants to attend (no captive audience), for any length of time, on any day of the year, and there are no objectives or tests involved.

F. GUIDELINES FOR WRITING AND/OR OBTAINING SPECIFIC OBJECTIVES AND/OR TEST ITEMS

In the past decade and particularly during the past few years, a number of writers have published their version of *How to Write Behavioral Objectives.* Although most of these books, handbooks, pamphlets, and articles are useful in learning how to write specific objectives, most of them also have two problems in common: the value of GO's and the evaluation of SO's. The value of GO's as stated in most of these publications is indicated by a statement which is also often repeated at objective writing workshops: *If you can't specify it and measure it, throw the objective out!* As indicated earlier in this Chapter, I reject that point of view. GO's are very important. They usually represent what is actually desired in the three domains of learning and the GO's are usually very stable as far as what is desired. The major problem with GO's is that they can't be measured. That is why teachers need to write SO's and/or test items in order that they can attempt to measure the achievement of the desired GO's. SO's and test items are only useful as long as the teacher accepts and believes the achievement of them is helping the students achieve the GO's. If a teacher loses confidence in the SO's and/or test items as measuring the achievement of what he or she wants the students to learn (the GO's), then the teacher throws out, changes, or adds more SO's and/or test items. The teacher will rarely throw out, change, or add more GO's. If the SO's and/or test items are written without reference to GO's or separate from existing GO's, it will be easy to develop a lack of continuity in the SO's with gaps and overlaps in the curriculum and a series of SO's and test items that are low in quality. Not knowing what is really wanted (the GO's), teachers writing SO's and test items may be satisfied with their first efforts which will probably be low level rote memory factual and information objectives. If not satisfied with their first efforts, the teachers are more apt to reject the whole concept of writing objectives as having little if any, value.

NOTE: Almost all teachers and particularly those that are supposedly against specifying SO's, still evaluate learning via tests, essays, observation, etc. To evaluate a student is to evaluate whether or not a student has achieved something the teacher thinks is important. In other words, almost every teacher has SO's — their test items and criteria for evaluation. Although most traditional teachers don't look on their test items and criteria for evaluation as SO's, as long as grades are dependent on the students' achievement of the test items and criteria for evaluation, test items and criteria for evaluation are the real SO's that students want to learn. Just as low level SO's should be considered for rejection, so should low level test items and low level criteria be considered for rejection.

Because SO's and test items are essentially the same thing with only a slight difference in wording, it doesn't really matter which a teacher does: write SO's or write test items. Although many teachers have difficulty writing SO's because they haven't had much practice at it. Almost every teacher has written or prepared test itemss. So it may be much easier for many teachers to write test items instead of writing SO's. The guideline to remember is one that should also be used with students — *start instruction at a point where the learner is.* Where most teachers are at the present moment is in the process of writing or preparing test items and criteria for evaluation. If given a choice of writing SO's or test items, the writing of test items and criteria for evaluation will affect student learning faster than the writing of SO's.

NOTE: In the writing of learning system test items, remember the object is to develop test items or criteria which evaluate the achievement of something you want students to learn. The object is NOT to have test items that are easy to grade, represent a variety of formats (multiple-choice, true-false, matching, etc.), represent a variety of difficulty levels (to *separate the men from the boys*), are good discriminators (designed deception), and result in a normal curve of scores regardless of whether or not the students learned what they were supposed to (the traditional approach).

The second problem with most of the available publications on writing SO's concerns the relationship between the SO's and the test items. Even though most of the publications are very up-to-date in their arguments for using SO's and can be useful in learning how to write SO's, most of the authors of these publications let their traditional *long underwear* hang out when it comes to evaluating the achievement of the SO's. Most of these authors still approve of *objective type* test items and normative testing. If a teacher is going to use these types of test items, there is very little value in writing SO's because as soon as students identify that the teacher is not testing for the achievement of the SO's, the students will ignore the SO's and study for the non-related or low correlated *objective type* test items. As stated before, it is very rare that a multiple-choice, true-false, or matching test item correlates with a SO and even rarer that the item can be justified in terms of the questions of justification. There is just no place in honest teaching-learning situations for *objective type* test items and normative testing. This does not mean that the publications on *How to write behavioral objectives* are not useful. Use them, but remember to start with your GO's first and then in the process of breaking the GO's down into smaller units is where the skill in writing SO's becomes useful. Also, remember to ignore any suggestions for using *objective type* test items as your test items should match as close as possible the SO's which have been written. If you started with test items first, then your SO's should match the test items you have written. The main difference between the two approaches is that in writing SO's, you ask yourself, *What should the student be able to do as a result of this learning experience?* or *what should the student be able to do in order to perform this role or task?;* whereas in writing test items first you ask yourself, *what questions, test items, or criteria should I use with the students to evaluate whether or not the students have the necessary or desired skills, emotional tendencies, or behaviors?*

A key guideline to remember regardless if you write SO's first and then develop your test items, or if you write test items first and then develop your SO's, is to use the questions of justification in order to verify whether or not the SO and/or test item is really what you want and is worded in the manner that describes best what you want. Most teachers in writing their first SO.s and/or test items, tend to ask for rote memory or information type SO's and test items. There are times that these items and SO's are exactly what is needed and this need will be revealed in the process of justifying the SO's and/or test items. However, in this age of information pollution, most rote memory and information type SO's and test items are not what is needed or useful to the learner. The most useful type test items and SO's tend to be process objectives.

NOTE: From a certain point-of-view, even process objectives and test items can be considered as just rote memory. After all, the same process is applied each time the process is used. The difference is that the problem or vehicle to which the process is applied is different each time.

1. GUIDELINES FOR ON-GOING COURSES

I am defining an *on-going* course as a situation in which the person who is presently teaching the course is the one who is planning to apply one or more of the behavioral learning system concepts to that course in order to improve student learning. I am also assuming that the teacher has previously taught the course one or more times and has copies of tests which have been used in the course (if no paper and pencil tests are given, then I assume the teacher has the criteria for evaluation of the students' essays, performances, or products). It is also possible that a teacher may already have some SO's, but wants to develop better continuity among the objectives or wants to develop better quality SO's. If a teacher is presently teaching a course for the first time and hasn't developed any tests, criteria for evaluation and/or SO's, then I would consider the course as a new course (at least for the teacher teaching the course) and I will suggest the guidelines for new courses in the next unit. If this course concerns the development of specified skills for a specific role, I would consider the course as an on-going course if the course designed to teach the role had been offered previously or is presently being offered and a task analysis of the role had been performed. I would consider the course a *new course,*

628

if the course concerns the teaching of a specific role which may or may not exist at present, no task analysis has been performed, and no course has been offered previously concerning the role.

In order to develop continuity in the objectives and test items, it is critical to have GO's. If you already have the GO's available, then you may not need to write GO's. If not, look through the materials being used in the course (textbooks, films, field trips, syllabus, daily or weekly assignments, etc.) and then write out the general objectives (GO's) or goals of the course. Most courses will have at least three to ten very general objectives. These can then be sub-divided into less general objectives and possibly even some specific objectives. Put each GO on a separate sheet of paper (keeping in mind their interrelationships) then take each existing test item, criterion for evaluation, and each SO and put them with the appropriate GO (use scissors and tape).

During this process, if there is any test item, criterion for evaluation, or SO that doesn't fit any of the GO's, this tends to indicate that the item, criterion, or SO is inappropriate and has a low correlation with the existing GO's. As such, the item, criterion, or SO should probably be rejected. If, however, you can justify the item, criterion, or SO in terms of the questions of justification, you will have to write a GO to fit.

After the process of matching test items, criteria for evaluation, and SO's with the GO's, any GO's that don't have any items, criteria, or SO's associated with it should be considered for rejection. If, however, you can justify the GO as being an important goal of the course, you may want to concentrate on specifying new SO's, test items or criteria for evaluation that will match the GO.

Although all of the GO's in any one course can probably be related directly or indirectly, try to identify the importance of the GO's by ranking them in hierarchical order on a separate sheet of paper. Does the emphasis in the course as indicated by the number of test items, criteria, and SO's associated with each GO match the emphasis as indicated by the ranking of the GO's? If not, then it may be necessary to create the proper or desired emphasis by writing more test items, criteria, and SO's for the important GO's.

As a last step, be sure to qualify test items, criteria, and SO's by asking the questions of justification of each one to be sure they represent in their present form what is really desired. As indicated earlier, this process of justification may also result in higher level objectives, criteria, and/or test items.

2. GUIDELINES FOR NEW COURSES

In defining *new courses*, I am including courses that are *new* to the teacher who is teaching the course along with courses that are new to the curriculum of a school. Under this definition, most of the *new* courses are ones in which it is actually the teacher that is new to the course. There are many *new* courses that are new in a particular school but not new on the instructional scene as they are and have been taught at other schools. There are also courses which are traditionally offered at one level, but are newly being offered at a lower instructional level. There are some *new* courses which are really the same as one or more existing courses; but a new title has been selected to make the course sound different, modern, or more relevant. (If the title is really all that has been changed, then treat the course as an on-going course rather than a new course.) Although there are a few really *new* courses, these will be the exception rather than common occurrences because there isn't that much that is completely new. However, in the efforts to identify the minimum common core SO's that students should learn in order to exist with maximum freedom in our society, some new courses may have to be created; not because the content and SO's would be new, but because the content and SO's have been ignored as being relevant and necessary. Courses of this latter type should include such titles as *How To Be a Compatible Marriage Partner (legal or living together), How To Raise Your Children, How To Live With Internal Organizational Politics, Your Legal Rights and Responsibilities, How To Enjoy Your Leisure Time, How to Make Purchasing Decisions Concerning Common Items (Houses, Cars, Clothes, Gifts, etc.), Maintenance of Personal Possessions (Houses, Cars, Clothes, Lawns, Appliances, etc.),* etc.

If all a teacher has is a title of a course or a concept which the course should be concerned with, then the first step is to generate some *global* GO's. This can be done best by individual brainstorming[26] or better yet, by two or more people who are concerned about the same course or concept getting together and brainstorming as to the needs the course is supposed to satisfy, what the students taking the course *will learn* during the course that will be of value in fulfilling their needs, and what the students will be able *to do* as a result of taking the course that will be of value in fulfilling their needs. At this point, it is not necessary to develop specific test items, criteria for evaluation, and/or SO's. If they come out in the brainstorming and evaluation processes, they will be useful, but the emphasis should be in the development of general statements concerning desired cognitive and sensory skills and emotional tendencies. Using these *global* GO's, the teacher should

---

[26] Brainstorming refers to the process of generating ideas, concepts, problems, etc., without regard to the evaluation of the contributions at the time they are generated. Evaluation of the contribution is a second process which is carried out after all participants in the brainstorming session have exhausted all possible suggestions.

gather together available materials (textbooks, films, etc.) which relate to these GO's. If you already have the materials relating to the new course, then it won't be necessary to get them together, but it is still necessary to state some *global* GO's and then go back through the materials in more detail.

As a result of studying these available materials, the teacher should now start to break the *global* GO's down into smaller GO's and ultimately into test items, criteria for evaluation, and SO's. In the case of a course which is concerned with the teaching of a specific role, the teacher should locate people who are already performing the desired role and do a task analysis of the role. Since task analyses usually result in descriptions of specific observable behaviors (SO's), it is necessary to work backwards to obtain the necessary GO's. By looking at specific behaviors in the task analysis, an instructor or instructors can brainstorm about the necessary cognitive and sensory skills and emotional tendencies which would enable a person to perform the SO's efficiently and effectively. Then from these GO's, it is possible to identify related skills which may be associated with the observed behaviors but not necessarily observed at the time of the task analysis.

The next step would be to ask the questions of justification to qualify the specified test items, criteria, SO's and even GO's as to whether or not they are stated in the desired format and are at the desired quality level. Be sure to check whether or not the desired emphasis in learning is represented by the test items, criteria, and SO's. It is not unusual for certain aspects of a course that are easier to specify and measure to not be the most important aspects of a course. If the emphasis is misdirected, it will be necessary to concentrate efforts to make the desired measurable results of the course (test items, criteria, and SO's) be more in line with the desired non-measurable results of the course (GO's).

3. UTILIZING TAXONOMIES OF OBJECTIVES

In some objective writing workshops and courses, the participants or students are told that they have to have objectives in every instructional unit that represent each and every level in a particular taxonomy. This point-of-view is based on the concept that the taxonomy is absolute and almost God-like in character. Taxonomies are just one person's or a group's way of looking at certain phenomena, objects, plants, animals, etc. Taxonomies are useful in that they give interested people a way of organizing and discussing things. They are usually developed on the basis of already existing entities and can be used to organize and study the existing entities or to predict the existence of other entities which fit into the organizing principles of the taxonomy. This latter function is the most useful function of the taxonomies of

631

educational and instructional objectives. The different levels in any one taxonomy are useful during brainstorming sessions to expand the mind as to the kinds of GO's and SO's that might be desired in achieving the *global* GO's of a particular course or role. Taxonomies are also useful in trying to realign the emphasis of a course in order to match what is measured to what is desired.

Once the test items, criteria, and SO's have been identified and justified, it is useful to take a particular taxonomy and evaluate the levels of the items, criteria, and SO's from the point-of-view of the organizing principle of the taxonomy. If most or all of the items, criteria, and SO's are at what is considered to be low levels or basic levels of the taxonomy, you may want to generate items, criteria, SO's and GO's which are at the higher levels of the taxonomy IF still appropriate in terms of the desired *global* GO's of the course or role.

4. DON'T REINVENT CURRICULUM WHEELS

The vast majority of courses have been taught and/or are being taught by one or more teachers in some school or in some instructional situation. For most of the standard courses offered in elementary schools, there are over 100,000 teachers who are presently teaching them and over a million teachers that have taught these courses over the past several decades. For most of the standard courses offered in secondary schools, there are probably 50,000 or more teachers who are presently teaching them. For most of the standard courses offered in higher education, there are probably as high as 10,000 teachers who are presently teaching them. In elementary and secondary schools, there are probably over 100 curriculum committees meeting at any one time in different parts of the country trying to develop the same curriculum.

An utterly fantastic situation is that in most schools, at all levels, a new teacher or an experienced teacher teaching a standard course for the first time are expected to reinvent the curriculum for the course as if no one had ever taught the course before. The duplication of effort on a national scale and even in large school districts, colleges, or universities is a terrible waste of time, energy, and money which should have been spent solving student learning problems rather than reinventing *curriculum wheels.* Of course, the basic reason for this situation is that teacher education courses and the evaluation of teachers emphasizes the teacher as a presenter of course content. As such, no one wants to cooperate with any other teacher because the other teacher may learn to present as good as the first teacher and who knows, they might videotape or film the second teacher and then one or both of them might be replaced. When the emphasis is on the teacher's role as a presenter of content, each teacher's goal is to be a little different from the other teachers in order to be needed and to keep the teacher from being bored from doing the same thing over and over again. On the other hand, if the teacher's role is to identify and solve learning problems, every teacher could teach essentially the same basic course. The emphasis in teacher education courses and in the evaluation of teacher education courses and in the evaluation of teachers would be on whether or not students were learning and learning problems were being identified and solved. A medical specialist might work with only four or five health problems throughout his or her career. If the emphasis was on the problems, the specialist would get bored very quickly and would probably not be very effective. However, the emphasis is on the patient who has the problem and since people are all individually different, the specialist could work with a thousand patients who all have the same problem, but the specialist is trained to look on the situation as a thousand different versions of the same problem. When teachers are teaching students rather than teaching a subject, they will not get bored and there will be no need to reinvent the *curriculum wheel* in order to be different.

There is nothing wrong with cooperation in the development of course objectives, test items, and criteria for evaluation. An old cliche is very true and appropriate in this context: *Many hands make for light work!* Ideally, it would be a tremendous step forward if the minimum common core objectives for the standard courses at all levels of instruction could be developed at a national level. Then all the local teachers would be concerned with is the identification and specification of the extra SO's to reflect the state and local needs (required SO's) and the majority of the teachers time could be spent identifying and solving student learning problems and helping students identify what they personally would like to learn (volunatry SO's). Since it will be some years before the state and national education units make this kind of effort, the potential cooperation will be at the local levels. Even if only one other teacher is willing to cooperate, that cuts in half the amount of work involved. Making the transition from the traditional approach to the Behavioral Learning System's Approach requires a lot of energy and time particularly during the first year. After that, since reinventing the curriculum is not the goal, the time and effort necessary will decrease while the effectiveness and efficiency of the approach will increase.

Given that two or more teachers have decided to cooperate in the development of course objectives, criteria for evaluation, and test items, it would be useful to refer to the unit on the development of minimum common core objectives (pp 527-542).

As aids in avoiding the need to start from scratch in the development of course objectives, there are sources of objectives which can be contacted. The objectives for a number of college courses is avilable on microfiche from the Educational Resources Information Center

(ERIC), Ann Arbor, Michigan. Elementary and secondary objectives for most standard courses are available from the Instructional Objectives Exchange, Center for the Study of Evaluation, UCLA Graduate School of Education, Los Angeles, Calif. 90024.

Several of these sources of objectives also provide sample test items. Many of the test items are of the so-called *objective* type (multiple-choice, true-false, and matching) and as such are irrelevant in their present form. By applying the questions of justification to both the objectives and the test items, you will be able to reject the ones that are inappropriate and to develop a good base from those that are acceptable.

Another source for objectives are the teachers' edition of some textbooks. During recent years, more and more publishers of textbooks have asked their authors to list objectives. These are frequently listed in the teacher edition of the textbook. In fact, to save duplicating the objectives on separate sheets of paper, order copies of the teacher edition of the textbooks for the students. Most of the extra information included in the teacher edition is designed to help the teacher teach the course and as such, will probably also help students learn the objectives of the course.

5. PRIORITIES IN WRITING OBJECTIVES

Given that an individual teacher or even a group of teachers have limited amounts of time to develop these course objectives, criteria for evaluation, and test items, it is useful to develop a list of priorities. The most important SO's and related criteria and/or test items to develop are ones that I classify as being critical for learning. These are the ones that if a student doesn't learn and achieve them, the student will have difficulty in having successful learning experiences in subsequent courses (cumulative ignorance). Although many teachers will be able to identify which SO's, criteria, and test items fit into this category, one of the best sources for this information are the teachers of subsequent courses. In other words, if you are a third grade teacher, check with several fourth grade teachers. If you are a first year algebra teacher, check with several second year algebra teachers. If you are a ninth grade English teacher, check with several tenth grade English teachers. In checking with the teachers of subsequent courses, ask them to help you list the skills, knowledge, etc., that students should have when they start their course and are so important that if they don't have these skills, knowledge, etc., the students will have trouble learning the important concepts (SO's and GO's) of these subsequent courses.

A second category which is really only secondary in importance in the lower grades and as students approach the termination of their formal education this category should take precedence over the first

634

category. These objectives, criteria, and test items are ones that I classify as critical for survival out in the real world. Hopefully, most teachers will be able to identify these SO's, GO's, criteria, and test items; but it might be useful to meet with a group of adults in the community and enlist their help in identifying those skills, knowledge, etc. which are necessary in order to live as independently as possible in our society and which might be available in your course.

The third category in priority concerns the balance of the required SO's, criteria for evaluation, and test items. After this comes the measurable SO's, criteria, and test items associated with voluntary learning and finally the nonmeasurable GO's and activities. Putting the nonmeasurable GO's at the bottom of the list does not mean that all of the GO's are in this category. Remember that most of the GO's are indirectly being measured by SO's, criteria for evaluation, and test items which are in the higher levels. I know that some critics of specifying objectives claim that many of the nonmeasurable GO's are more important than the measurable SO's. Actually, they are right because all SO's are sub-divisions of the nonmeasurable GO's and if the SO's are important then the GO's they are a part of must be as important or more important than the SO's. However, GO's which are not measurable and also don't have any SO's associated with them can only be subjectively important in that it is not possible to identify the importance of the GO's from the point-of-view of what advantages the person has who has achieved the GO's or the disadvantages a person has who hasn't achieved the GO's. If the achievement of the GO's doesn't make any differences in what people can or can't do, it is very difficult to defend the imagined importance of the GO's. In other words, the importance of the non-measurable GO's is dependent upon the existence and importance of the measurable SO's associated with the GO's.

G. FREEDOM AND WHO SHOULD WRITE OBJECTIVES: STATE, DISTRICT, TEACHERS OR STUDENTS?

Freedom: The quality or state of not being coerced or constrained by fate, necessity, or circumstances in one's choices or actions. (Webster's Third New International Dictionary).

There is no place that a person could go and have complete freedom. In outer space, your freedom is restricted by life support equipment. On earth, you are limited by gravity, your own physical characteristics, and even in isolation, your freedom is restricted by the non-living environment. If there are living plants and/or animals in the vicinity of the person, these things start to influence and restrict your freedom. As a person lives in the vicinity of one or more other people, his or her freedom is influenced and/or restricted by the desires for freedom by the other people. As the living space around a person

635

decreases, the influence and restrictions on a person's freedom increases. This is true even if only the physical presence of the other people is considered. As more and more mental and emotional relationships develop between the person and other people, the more and more a person's freedom is restricted by the desires of other people for freedom of their mental and emotional expressions. There are two types of freedom to be considered: internal freedom which is affected by the psychological state of mind and external freedom which is affected by the environment within which one lives. Actually these two freedoms affect each other. The knowledge and frustrations of the limits of a person's external freedom affect a person's ability to think of other things and as such affect the person's internal freedom. The attitudes, values, and beliefs that a person has in connection with the external environment affect a person's actions in the external environment and as such affect the person's external freedom. Given that complete freedom is impossible to achieve, the more that a person can learn how to accept those external restrictions which cannot be changed without affecting someone else's freedom, the freer the person's internal and external state will be in order to concentrate on exploring the freedom that is left. Freedom is like sex in that when everything is going good it may only occupy 5-10 percent of our conscious mind. On the other hand, when things are going wrong, freedom like sex may affect 80 percent or more of our conscious mind. When one concentrates on the things you can't do, can't do anything about, or the aspects of freedom one doesn't have, life becomes static and filled with negative decisions (the better of two or more negative choices). When one concentrates on the things you can do or the aspects of freedom one has, life becomes dynamic and is filled with positive decisions (the better of two or more positive choices). Increasing cognitive and sensory skills by design increases the things a person can do. Continued ineffectiveness and chance learning of cognitive and sensory skills increases the student's awareness of what he or she can't do. Increasing the understanding of self and others in the affective domain by design increases the interpersonal relationships that bring joy, comfort, and the extending of one's self, and more freedom. Continued ineffectiveness and chance learning about self and others in the affective domain increases the interpersonal relationships that bring sadness, discomfort, a withdrawing of one's self, and less freedom. Freedom is the ability to decide one's own life in terms of the consequences to self (both positive and negative). The more a person has to relie on others in order to make a decision, the less freedom the person has. The less a person knows about available alternatives, the less freedom a person has. The less a person knows about realistic consequences, the less freedom a person has.

Skinner has claimed that almost all of our actions are predetermined and conditioned which limits our freedom of choice or *will.* The important point to remember is that most of our actions that are predetermined and conditioned have arrived at that status almost by chance. By increasing a person's understanding of how society and others have consciously and unconsciously programmed those around them, it is possible to help the person have more self-control and change the program. Actions which are willed because of an outside force are not free actions. Actions which are willed by emotions or impulse are not free actions because a person can not control the development or change in his or her attitudes, values, or beliefs. Only those actions which are controlled by cognitive and sensory decisions can be free. Therefore, if, in fact, most of our actions are already programmed by the influences in our environment, then it is necessary to help students learn how to make rational internal positive decisions based on knowledge, skills, etc., if our goal is to give them more freedom. Conversely, if teachers delay or avoid teaching students what they need to know to make rational decisions, their ignorance limits their freedom. Accepting authority and conforming to the norms of a community is not a loss of freedom if the acceptance and conformance is based on rational decisions of the individual. To accept or reject authority based on non-rational or emotional decisions is to lose a person's freedom to society. Behavioral objectives which have to be learned but can not be adequately justified and do not contribute to rational decision-making detracts from a person's freedom. Behavioral objectives which have to be learned and can be justified and do contribute to an individuals rational decision-making enhances a person's freedom.

Under the traditional approach to education, it is *normal* for teachers not to have specific learning objectives for students to learn. Since state and/or district education agencies are responsible for educational programs, they usually set up certain requirements concerning the learning environment in the hope that these requirements will facilitate student learning. These requirements, among other things, specify (in public schools) the certification of the teachers; the minimum number of hours per day; the number of days per year; basic course offerings; and for many schools even the textbooks and what content the teachers should *cover in their presentations.* In addition, most teacher training institutions train teachers-to-be to be *presenters of course content* and most administrators evaluate teachers on the basis of *how good a presenter they are.* The emphasis on *presenting course content* as being equivalent to *teaching* has led to the development of several models of the ideal teacher which usually consist of a checklist or an analysis of the teacher's *teaching (presenting)* behavior in the classroom. These models ignore the fact that each and every teacher is different and a technique that works for one teacher may not work for another. From the point-of-view of teachers, the specification by external authorities of the courses to be offered, the content to be covered, the textbooks to be used, and the teacher's behavior in the classroom, restricts the freedom of the teacher in the classroom. From the point-of-view of the state and district education agencies, to relax the requirements for the educational environment and teaching would be to abdicate their responsibilities for educating the students as there would be no way of knowing what was happening in the classrooms. Although student learning is used as a justification for the restrictions placed on schools and teachers, the emphasis throughout the traditional approach is on teachers and teaching (defined as presenting course content).

It is and will continue to be a very difficult problem to change the situation such that the teachers will have more freedom until the teachers identify the GO's and SO's of their courses which in turn will identify what students are supposed to learn as a result of being associated with the teachers. Once the teachers have identified the GO's and SO's of their courses, the state and district education agencies will be able to become instruction agencies. The same justification of indirect responsibility for educating students that is used to restrict the freedom of teachers can now be used to free teachers from the traditional restrictions. Remember, the traditional approach ignores the individual differences in teachers and the individual differences in students, and emphasizes the teacher as a presenter of course content almost regardless of whether or not learning is taking place. Under a system where individual differences of teachers and students are recognized and the emphasis is on the teacher as one that can guarantee student learning levels which are higher than those achieved under the traditional approach, the whole line of authority is inverted (see Figure 62) and changes from one of authoritarian rule and restrictions to one of supportive cooperation and freedom; from one in which each level resists the authority of the level above them to one in which each level supports the level above them; from one in which the goals and evaluation of each level demonstrate conflict and a lack of continuity to one in which the goals and evaluation demonstrate cooperation and continuity. In the traditional approach where the purpose, student learning, is not specified, each level sets its own goals. In the Behavioral Learning Systems Approach where the purpose, student learning, is specified, each level's goals can directly or indirectly support student learning. In other words, under the Behavioral Learning Systems Approach, each level is essentially free to do whatever it wants as long as it facilitates student learning directly or indirectly.

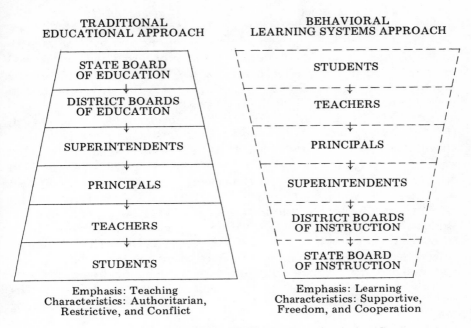

TRADITIONAL EDUCATIONAL APPROACH	BEHAVIORAL LEARNING SYSTEMS APPROACH
STATE BOARD OF EDUCATION	STUDENTS
DISTRICT BOARDS OF EDUCATION	TEACHERS
SUPERINTENDENTS	PRINCIPALS
PRINCIPALS	SUPERINTENDENTS
TEACHERS	DISTRICT BOARDS OF INSTRUCTION
STUDENTS	STATE BOARD OF INSTRUCTION
Emphasis: Teaching Characteristics: Authoritarian, Restrictive, and Conflict	Emphasis: Learning Characteristics: Supportive, Freedom, and Cooperation

Figure 62 — Line of Authority: Traditional vs. Learning Systems

In line with the teacher's resistance to the authoritarian rule above them, some teachers suggest that they shouldn't extend this authoritarian rule to the students. These teachers see the specification of student learning objectives as an example of authoritarianism and in the name of freedom for the student, reject the concept of specifying student learning objectives. However, these very same teachers evaluate and grade the students in their classes. Since test items and criteria for evaluation are actually specific objectives, these teachers are rejecting the concept vocally while at the same time accepting the concept by their actions. There is quite a difference between authoritarianism and acting as an authority. An authoritarian wants to command and control action in a situation where there is little recourse and with the goal of increasing power and dependence and diminishing conflict by repression and decreased freedom (the traditional classroom). An authority wants to command learning in a situation where there is increasing student knowledge and with the goal of decreasing power and increasing student independence and freedom. In the Behaviorial Learning Systems Approach, the teacher specifies student learning objectives so that students can have maximum freedom in learning and eventually can become the authority and be independent learners.

639

There is another group of teachers who reject the concept of specifying learning objectives in the name of *academic freedom.* Their main problem is the growing demand for accountability. As long as no one knows what learning should take place, no one will be able to evaluate whether or not the desired learning occurred and no one will know whether or not the teacher can teach. In their anxiety to escape accountability, some of these teachers may join the anti-authoritarian group while others may join the third group which I will describe next. The sad part is that as the accountability movement gains momentum, the fear and anxiety of these teachers detracts much more from their freedom than would be the case if they were being held accountable for student learning. As pointed out before, by being willing to be held accountable for learning rather than being evaluated in the traditional sense, teachers will have more freedom than ever before. Teachers who refuse to specify student learning objectives and to do any evaluation of student learning and achievement probably have nothing to contribute to the students anyway and as such, these teachers should quit or should be removed in order to give freedom to the taxpayers, parents, and students from having to support these educational parasites. Frequently, teachers in this group claim that attitudes, values, and beliefs are much more important than the cognitive and sensory learning objectives in the cognitive and sensory domains. If affective domain objectives are so much more important, then at least these objectives should be specified. To ignore that affective domain SO's and GO's can be taught in a scientific manner with reason and rationality is:

a) to bury your head in the shifting sands of subjectivity and to let those in the know control by design the attitudes, values, and beliefs of our youth;

b) to want a life controlled primarily by emotions and capriciousness rather than a life controlled primarily by reason and rationality; or

c) to be one of those who wants to control by design the development and change of attitudes, values, and beliefs, of our youth but doesn't want other adults in or out of schools to discover what they are doing. Just like a professional test item writer can make up multiple choice tests that will yield any results desired, there are those who give oral multiple choices concerning attitudes, values, and beliefs and they want to control the results.

Because students (or anyone else) are not able to control the development or change in their attitudes, values, or beliefs, their only defense in order to remain free is to maximize the learning of the intellectual and sensory abilities needed to make reasoned and rational decisions. In this way, it will be possible to minimize the decisions made on an emotional basis and particularly those emotional decisions that others may want to control. In the name of freedom, some teachers may alienate students from their parents or from their community, the results of such actions actually reduces the students' freedom by restricting the students' interrelationships with their parents and their community.

The third group of teachers who tend to reject the specification of objectives are not so much against the teacher specifying learning objectives as they are for letting and encouraging the students to spell out their own objectives. The characteristic slogan associated with this group is that students should be free to *do their own thing*. Ideally, one of the major goals of our educational system is to develop the independent learner who can set his or her own goals and can also achieve them. However, if teachers have as much trouble writing SO's as they say, how is it possible that students are able to write their own SO's without any training? If students have had trouble in achieving the teacher-set objectives, how can it be assumed that the students won't have trouble in learning their own SO's (if they could write them)? I refuse to accept the concept that children are born all-intelligent and then slowly regress until they die ignorant. I believe that teachers should know more about what ever it is they are teaching than the students. I can agree and support the thesis that students know better than the teachers as far as what they are interested in; but this only affects the vehicle for learning, it does not necessarily affect what students learn. I can also agree and support the thesis that students know better than the teachers as far as how they learn best; but this only affects how students learn, it does not necessarily affect what students learn. Just as it is a waste of time and energy for each teacher to reinvent the *curriculum wheel*, it is even a worse waste of time and energy to have every student reinvent basic skills and knowledge necessary to live in our society. As Kenneth Boulding commented in his *The Knowledge Explosion,*

> *We may be pushing forward into a great continent of knowledge, but if every generation has to start from the coast and if the frontier is so far off that a man dies before he gets there, there will be nobody left to push the frontier forward.*

Given that the teacher has justified the SO's that the students are required to learn, these SO's can act as tools for subsequent learning and open up new areas for potential learning. For centuries, learning has been looked on as the keys to unlock the gates to freedom and ignorance has been looked on as the bars of mental incarceration. To allow students to leave courses not learning what they need to know to be successful in subsequent courses or to survive and flourish in life is to restrict their freedom. To let students learn primarily by chance and by trial and error instead of design, is not only to restrict and delay the achievement of their freedom, it is also professional negligence of the role teachers are expected to perform.

Supporters of the *open school* movement look on their approach as having a lot of freedom. However, as teachers select materials to be placed in the *free* environment, their biases are reflected in the selection of materials. If these teachers have not listed any student learning objectives, their selection of materials carries with it hidden restrictions of the students' freedom. At least by having lists of objectives which can be learned from the materials, if the student doesn't want to learn any of them, the teacher and student know the available materials are inadequate and can then seek out more appropriate objectives and materials. A concept which has been associated with the *open schools*, elementary schools and other innovative programs is the use of the *teachable moment*. The idea being that when the student asks the right questions, the teacher should be ready to jump at the situation and take advantage of the student's interest. This is a great idea, but if the teachers have not specified the course objectives, they will not recognize the *right* question when it comes along. For example, if I am in a city with a variety of mass transportation and I don't really know where I want to go, hundreds of buses, trains, subways, etc., could go by and I would never know which one or ones are the *right* ones because I don't know where I'm going anyway. To continue the analogy, if the teacher feels their job is to provide lots of materials without any identification of the objectives that could be learned from the various materials, it would be like being in the large city where none of the mass transportation vehicles had any signs on them to indicate where the bus, train, subway, etc., is going. The selection of a vehicle would be determined by its appearance rather than by where it is going which is contrary to the function of the vehicle. In other words, if instructional and educational resources which are really just communication media are selected by their appearance rather than by what is being communicated (learned), then the students' freedom is restricted by the correlation between external aesthetic appearances and internal quality, i.e., television programs that may be very entertaining and help to pass time pleasantly are not necessarily good learning experiences. In constantly selecting *means* regardless of *goals*, students will find it difficult to become independent learners who are able to select their own goals and are able to select the most approrpiate means of arriving at their goals. They will also have difficulty accepting responsibility because of the emphasis placed on present actions (selection of materials) rather than on the consequences (goals of the actions).

In contrast, in specifying the objective to be learned, teachers can select materials which will offer multiple pathways for learning the objective. The students will be free in the selection of a method and a vehicle for learning. The more success the student has in learning the teacher-set objectives, the more time and the sooner the student will be freely setting and learning his or her own objectives. Given that there are basically two factors involved: the environment and the learning which is supposed to occur as a result of the students being in the environment, there are four possible combinations which could be set up: a structured environment and structured learning (which would not work because of individual differences among students); a structured environment and an open learning system (this is the traditional approach in which differences in achievement are blamed on genetics); an open environment and an open learning system (no need for teachers or schools as there are no goals): and an open environment and a structured learning situation (which recognizes different students need different environments in order to learn the same things — the required objectives).

The pseudo-humanists who think that students should be free to *do their own thing* and enjoy the beauty of the world, are restricting the students freedom of enjoyment of his or her leisure time when they don't teach the students the necessary skills needed to appreciate beauty. Remember, appreciation of beauty is a learned behavior. Given more leisure or *free* time to do whatever a person wants to do, a person whose self image is low and who has been made aware of his or her inadequacies and failures and whose ignorance limits the free use of his or her free time, this person in his or her frustrations will seek a time filler in order to minimize the amount of free time which may necessitate decisions, i.e., television, alcohol, drugs, etc. A person whose self image is high, who has a history of successes in learning and who has learned and developed many skills and interests, will seek out ways to increase the free use of free time.

From time to time, statements and articles appear which suggest our society is over-educated. For example, *a certain percentage (usually high) of people holding a particular non-skilled job have a high school diploma whereas all they needed was an eighth grade education* or *our society does not offer enough jobs that require a college education for all those who are now graduating.* These statements are based on the assumption that the people who are over-educated for their present jobs will never be promoted into a job where they will need their education. To reduce or limit a person's education to the level of available jobs is to place severe restrictions on a person's future vertical freedom.

In reference to teachers who are against or reject the specifying of objectives as imposing on the students' freedom,

643

— any teacher who gives a student a grade or score of less than "A" or 100 percent and is not able to identify specifically what it was the student didn't learn or achieve is restricting the students freedom to improve himself or herself;

— if a teacher can accept that the learning of more cognitive and sensory skills enables students to have greater freedom in their choice of subsequent learning and activities, then for this teacher to not specify objectives to aid the students in learning cognitive and sensory skills is the same as being against the student gaining greater freedom;

— if a teacher can accept the fact that students can't control the development or change in their attitudes, values, and beliefs and this teacher wants to teach in the affective domain without specifying the affective objectives to be created or changed, then this teacher not only wants to restrict the freedom of the students, but wants to have hidden control over the students' minds.

H. THE DEBATE: TO USE OR NOT TO USE SPECIFIC BEHAVIORAL OBJECTIVES

Arguing that planning imposes values on the future, the anti-planners overlook the fact that non-planning does so, too-often with far worse consequence. Angered by the narrow, econocentric character of technocratic planning, they condemn systems analysis, cost benefit accounting, and similar methods, ignoring the fact that, used differently, these very tools might be converted into powerful techniques for humanizing the future.

(Future Shock by Alvin Toffler)[27]

The debate should not be to *use or not use specific behavioral objectives.* Given that taxpayers and parents set up schools, and send students there, implies that they expect something to occur in the schools and when they hire teachers and devote a vast majority of the annual school budget to teachers' salaries, implies that they expect teachers to facilitate the occurring of the something (learning). The real debate should center around whether or not learning should be *increased.* The objective is not to have specific behavioral objectives, the objective is to facilitate learning. The Behavioral Learning Systems Concept is just a way of facilitating learning. If some teacher is able to

---

[27] Permission for quotation given by Random House, Inc. Publishers of *Future Shock* by Alvin Toffler, copyright 1970.

prove that he or she is able to facilitate more learning by more students of those things that students should learn and the teacher never used any part of the systems concept or behavioral objectives, this would be great. The problem is that in order to compare two or more methods in facilitating the same learning, the learning would have to be specified in order to be measured and what would be measured would be students' behaviors.

Many of the traditional oriented educators and also many of the new pseudo student-oriented educators who try to appear as if they are on the side of the students, challenge the need for objectives and claim that the specifying of objectives limits the creativity and *humaness* of education. These very same teachers will then turn around and give examinations, assign papers, evaluate students' products and performances in which the students are expected to achieve a certain level of proficiency, or they are graded down accordingly. If the teachers want a certain level of performance (objectives) at the end of their courses, then why not be honest and tell the students at the beginning of the courses by specifying these objectives (the behaviors tested by the test items or described by the criteria used to evaluate any papers, products, or student performances). To claim there are no objectives in a course and then turn around and evaluate students is to be dishonest, deceitful, duplicitous, and against facilitating learning. To give tests in which the teacher doesn't know the objectives that are related to the test items (particularly those that are missed) is to impede learning (of the items missed). Objectives are not only necessary to facilitate learning, they are also necessary to identify and solve learning problems. It is very difficult to identify and solve a learning problem if neither the teacher nor the student knows a problem exists.

NOTE: Anything important enough to grade a student down for not achieving should be important enough to specify and to help the student learn it. If it is not important enough to specify and to help the student learn it, then whatever it is, it is not important enough to grade the student down for not achieving it. Remember, the vast majority of students are presently being given grades of less than "A", 100 percent, or any other symbol that indicates complete learning. To assume that students enjoy being graded down is to assume that students are masochists. For a teacher to enjoy grading students down is sadistic. Either one or both of these assumptions is inhumane.

Lee Cronback of Stanford states, *The person who wants to specify the acts the learner is to perform as a result of instructions is deluding himself when he talks of history, science, or other non-skill subjects.* Yet, almost every history and science teacher I have worked with talks of developing intellectual *skills* and gives tests in which the students should be able to achieve high scores if they have learned the intellectual *skills* which were supposedly instructed during the course. To claim that there are no intellectual skills to be learned in history courses or intellectual and sensory skills in science courses is to be at odds with a majority of teachers who teach these courses.

In writing specific objectives, far too many people look on specific objectives or SO's as something completely different and unassociated with general objectives or GO's. There is not that much difference. In fact, all specific objectives or SO's are a part of some general objectives or GO's. However, not every GO has one or more specific objectives or SO's associated with it. The reason for this relationship is that the GO's are almost always identified first and then the SO's are identified. When SO's are identified first, there is a possibility that the SO's will be predominantly low level, represent simple rote memory and lack continuity.

It is very possible that a particular GO cannot be analyzed sufficiently to develop SO's, but even though the results are not measurable, the chances of the desired learning occurring have been increased by analyzing the main GO into sub-GO's, sub-sub GO's, etc. In other words, it is necessary in order to have excellence in the teaching-learning situation to identify in all courses, specifically and measurably what it is we want students to learn. This does not mean that we would eliminate from our courses anything that cannot be measured. But in order to be included in the curriculum and to justify expenditure of funds in order to present the course to the learners and to justify the time and effort of the learner in the course, it should be necessary for all courses to have some kind of measurable, observable SO's.

By designing the instruction such that 100 percent of the measurable objectives are achieved, chances are increased that the GO's will be learned as well. As the achievement level of the SO's decreases, so do the chances for learning the GO's! The more important (for learning) you think the non-measurable GO's are, the more important (for learning) it becomes to analyze the GO into sub-GO's, sub-sub-GO's, etc. until you identify some SO's and the more important (for measurement) it is to have the students learn 100 percent of the SO's. Assuming that the GO's or non-measurable objectives are the most important (learning), then forty million or more students have been inhumanly and unjustifiably punished with letter grades which are less than an "A" for not learning the SO's or measurable objectives which are less important (learning), plus, of course, not learning that *something* which is unknown (the GO)!

NOTE: Behaviorism is a field of psychology and as such, the use of *behavioral* objectives in the *Behavioral Learning System's concept causes people who can't accept behaviorism to also reject anything else associated with the concept of behavior.* Behaviorism as a psychological theory is essentially claiming that only what is observable is important and what is happening inside a person isn't important. As such, the pure behaviorist would only want specific measurable objectives and would have no place for general objectives. In opposition, most other psychological theories are essentially claiming that what happens internally in a person and what causes the person's behavior is what is really important and the actual behaviors are not as important. As such, the pure internalist would only want general objectives and would reject specific observable objectives as unimportant and representing concessions to the behaviorists. The Behavioral Learning Systems's concept is based on the belief that, yes, what is happening internally is most important, but you don't know when anything has happened internally unless a person does something externally. Therefore, the external behavior is important because it is the only way one can infer that something is occurring internally. This is why both general and specific objectives and their interrelationships are important in the Behavioral Learning System's concept. Specific objectives are a part of general objectives and if either one is important, the the other has to be important — possibly more or less important, but still important.

NOTE: Many educators become agitated about the use of the word *behavior.* However, almost every teacher who evaluates students is evaluating something that the students are doing or observable evidence of something that the students have done. The very same teacher that condemns the term *behavior* or *behavioral* as in *behavioral objectives* turns around and evaluates their students on some of their behaviors, i.e., answering an objective type test by *circling* letters or numbers, *by writing* an essay or report, by *performing* in someway, by *making* a product, etc. By slightly altering Dewey's comment *students learn what they do,* it could be stated, *students should do what they are supposed to learn.* In order to find out what students should do, one would, have to first identify the observable and measurable behaviors related to that desired learning.

A slight variation of the arguments over GO's and SO's concerns the time of achievement because the GO's and SO's of many courses deal with delayed achievement, i.e., the student will be a good citizen. Although, I can agree that there are long range objectives which may only be evaluated at a much later time, there are still an awful lot of test items and criteria that students are not achieving which are related to present needs. When almost all teachers are achieving 90 percent or more of their students learning 100 percent of the immediate learning needs, there will be time enough to worry about the long range objectives. A significant aspect of this problem is that most of the long range objectives are in the affective domain and represent a whole group of related affective objectives which are developed over a period of time and being in the affective domain, these objectives can not be taught direcly.

A parallel relationship exists between the teaching and learning of GO's and SO's and the teaching and learning of affective objectives and cognitive and sensory objectives. Just as GO's are taught and learned indirectly by teaching and learning SO's, affective objectives are also taught and learned indirectly and frequently in association with the teaching and learning of cognitive and sensory objectives. Also, just as it might be assumed that a teacher who has trouble helping students learn SO's will tend to be ineffective in teaching GO's, it may also be assumed that a teacher that has trouble helping students learn cognitive and sensory objectives will tend to be ineffective in teaching affective objectives. The very fact that affective objectives are so important makes the recent trends of teachers *talking* and *writing* about teaching affective objectives disconcerting. Ineffectiveness, inefficiency, irrelevance, and just plain mistakes in the teaching and learning of cognitive and sensory objectives are and have been serious problems, but students can learn in spite of schools and teachers and often have multiple opportunities to learn. These same problems in the affective domain where student's can't control the learning event could be disastrous to the students and our society. If the affective objectives are taught directly rather than indirectly, it is likely that emotional tendencies will be developed which are opposite to the ones which were desired by the teacher. In addition, if the change in emphasis from cognitive and sensory objectives to affective domain objectives includes a de-emphasis of the already badly taught cognitive and sensory objectives, the effects on our society may be incalcuable. We already have enough students who have trouble reading, writing, and doing simple arithmetic tasks.

1. REASONS WHY SOME EDUCATORS ARE AGAINST SPECIFYING OBJECTIVES

During fifteen years of working with teachers in seminars, institutes, workshops, and individually, I have encountered a variety of reasons why some educators resist specifying objectives.

a. Many consultants and leaders of objective writing workshops and teachers of courses concerning the writing of specific objectives tell teachers or students in these workshops and courses that if an objective is non-measurable it is unacceptable and should be discarded. Because they can't have what they really want, the GO's, some teachers will reject the SO's. As mentioned before, there is nothing wrong with GO's except they can't be measured. The GO's perform very useful functions as guidelines for specification and evaluation and should be retained. They also provide a structure upon which the SO's can be organized.

b.   Many teachers dislike SO's because their first efforts at writing specific objectives result in low level rote memory objectives and the teachers are convinced that their courses have much more quality than is represented by the specific objectives they have written. As a consequence, some of these teachers reject the whole concept of SO's without really learning how to write good SO's. It is the rare teacher that in his or her first attempts is able to write high quality thinking type objectives. It takes time to learn how to write good objectives.

c.   As long as the teachers' role was to present enough content to fill up the time given to the course, almost any course could be padded or trimmed to fit a quarter, semester, or year schedule. However, as teachers started specifying their course objectives, some teachers realized that they didn't really have very much in the course and others realized that they had far too much in a course and shouldn't have expected the students to learn all of it. In either case, when faced with the realities of the course content as identified by the SO's they have identified, some teachers reject the concept of using SO's rather than adjust the learning time for the course.

d.   As mentioned before, one of the most common reasons for not specifying objectives is to avoid accountability. It is not actually accountability that is being avoided. Teachers who are confident that they can teach and help students learn successfully don't worry about accountability because they know they are going to be evaluated positively. Teachers who are afraid that accountability measures will show them up as incompetent teachers are afraid of specifying objectives. As long as no one knows what the students are supposed to be learning, no one will know whether or not the teacher can teach. In a traditional situation where there are GO's and very few SO's if any at all, accountability can be a fearful concept because what the teacher is going to be held accountable for is unknown. By specifying what should be learned, the teacher can bring measurable *light* into the unknown and reduce or eliminate their fear of accountability.

e. There is no doubt about it, the writing of SO's is time consuming and a lot of work and some teachers just don't want to put in that much effort. That is why I strongly suggest that teachers cooperate. Reinventing the curriculum wheel of SO's on an individual basis is a waste of time, energy, and money.

f. Many teachers worry that if students know the SO's they are supposed to learn, they are liable to learn all of the SO's and consequently the teacher will be unable to grade on a curve and will be evaluated as an easy teacher (no "C's", "D's", or "F's") because many administrators also tend to be traditional in their evaluations of teachers. If enough teachers in any one school do the same thing, the school could be in trouble with accrediting committees as being a diploma or degree mill (easy school) because national, regional, and state accrediting associations tend to be traditional in their accrediting criteria.

g. As long as students don't know what the SO's are for the course, a teacher can use any test items he or she wants and can also design tests to produce any results (curve) regardless of what students really know. When students see the SO's for a course, inappropriate test items become fairly obvious and the test results can not be manipulated to give desired results.

h. Once students are told the SO's of a course, teachers have to stick fairly close to what should be taught and learned in a course and they may also have to justify the teaching and learning of the SO's.

i. At the present time, a teacher's colleagues informally evaluate his or her scholarship level by the title of a course, the textbook (the more difficult the textbook, the higher the assumed scholarship), and what the teacher says is presented or covered in the classroom. (Levels of student achievement are usually not a factor in the traditional educational scene unless they are too high or too low in which case either condition is considered as a slightly negative factor.) If a teacher starts using SO's, the SO's and the level of student achievement of the SO's can easily be used as an indicator of scholarship particularly if the SO's are not very impressive and look too easy.

j. Many teachers are afraid that if they have SO's they will not be able to take advantage of the spontaneous *teacheable moments*.

Actually, without SO's, neither the teacher nor the student will recognize that ideal moment when it occurs. If a prospector is out looking for something valuable but doesn't actually know what he should be looking for, he could trip over gold nuggets and sleep among diamonds and he would never know it.

k. Some teachers are worried that the use of SO's will make the instructional process like a factory. Remember, in a factory, the same units get the same treatments in order to end up with identical products. At the present time under the traditional approach, different teachers are expected to give the same treatments in the same way regardless of the fact that students are all different which is more like a factory than what I am suggesting. Individual differences in the traditional setting are identified on the basis of *varying degrees of non-achievement* (less than "A's" or 100 percent). Under the systems concept, different teachers will teach the same minimum common core SO's in different ways to suit their own personalities and different students will successfully learn all of the SO's in a variety of different instructional patterns. Individual differences are identified on the basis of *varying degrees of achievement* (less than "A's" or 100 percent).

I. *DO YOUR OWN THING:* TRAGEDY OR A MODE FOR MAXIMIZING MOTIVATION AND SERENDIPITY

If you can agree that as long as a child is going to grow up and live in a social environment that there is some common core knowledge that must be learned as survival skills (reading, writing, speaking, and listening in a common language; understanding one's self and others; humanism; etc.), then the primary responsibility of a school environment is to make sure that the necessary learning takes place. If the concept of *do your own thing* is defined as being an independent learner who learns the necessary skills at his or her own pace, at a place selected by the learner, and using whatever methods and materials the learner wants, then the concept definitely has a place in schools and designed instruction. However, if the concept of *do your own thing* is defined as allowing students to have complete freedom to learn what they want, when they want, where they want, and even if they want to learn at all, with no guidelines given at all by the teachers or the school, then the concept represents a tragedy in schools for all concerned students, teachers, parents, taxpayers, and the rest of our society.

The most serious problem is that the students won't learn what they need to know to stand a chance for finding happiness in a social environment. In addition, the students are being allowed to develop to live in a world that doesn't exist. As a very young child, it is expected that the student will be self-oriented and selfish. Growing up in a social environment supposedly helps the young child make the transition from being self-centered to being other-oriented. Up to the present time, humanism has been primarily learned by chance and hopefully or luckily there has been enough other-oriented people to take care of and worry about the comfort of the self-oriented people. However, if the predominant philosophy in our schools becomes one of letting students and teachers *do their own thing* regardless of the effects on others, our society may become very maladjusted because there won't be enough *other-oriented* people to take care of the self-oriented people who are being produced by a designed lack of direction. For example, notice the increasing number of people with *do your own thing* orientation that believe that their parents and society owe them a living, i.e., food stamps, medical care, welfare, unemployment, etc. At the same time many of these same people refuse to accept any responsibility towards their parents or society. Some of the *do your own thing* oriented people are supposedly searching for a fuller and more rewarding life in serving society and their fellow man, but as long as their emphasis is on satisfying themselves, they will be unhappy serving others and will continue searching for an idealistic goal that they couldn't be happy in anyway.

NOTE: There are some people who have been in the *do your own thing* environment who have interpreted the emphasis as helping others and society in any way they can, i.e., Peace Corps and Vista Corps volunteers. These people are other-oriented and want to be self-sufficient and performing a service to society rather than being *free-loaders.*

Humanism should not be confused with selfism. To claim that students should do what they want regardless of any family and social responsibilities and regardless of how their exercise of freedom affects the freedom of others is to promote selfism not humanism.

Selfish — concerned excessively or exclusively with oneself, seeking or concentrating on one's own advantage, pleasure, or well-being without regard for others.

(Webster's Third New International Dictionary)

Selfism — concentration on self-interest, a system of selfish ethics.

(Webster's Third New International Dictionary)

Humane — marked by compassion, sympathy, or consideration for other human beings or animals.

(Webster's Third New International Dictionary)

Humanism — devotion to human welfare, interest or concern for man (others). A philosophy that regards man as a natural object and asserts the essential dignity and worth of man and his capacity to achieve self-realization through the use of reason and scientific method.

(Webster's Third New International Dictionary)

A continued emphasis on *do your own thing* or *self* as being the most important entity not only promotes selfism, but it provides a fertile ground for the development of other emotional tendencies which are negative for both the individual and society:

— a person who puts self first will find it difficult to believe in God and may be open for atheism (decreasing church and temple attendance);

— a person who puts self first will find it difficult to love someone else because in a time of conflict with the other person, self will win at the expense of the relationship; if married, a self-oriented person would see a divorce as desirable (increasing divorce rate and decreasing marriage rate);

— a person who puts self first will find it easy to commit a crime against others as long as it benefits self (increasing crime rate and particularly juvenile crime);

— a person who puts self first will find it easy to be passive and apathetic about issues where it concerns others;

— a person who puts self first will find it easy to try to manipulate others at their expense (increasing dissatisfaction in interpersonal relationships);

— when a group in which the majority are self-oriented sits down at the bargaining table to negotiate, they behave much differently than a group in which a majority at least show a concern for the effects of their demands on others (increasing number of strikes in which the demands cause hardships on others); and

— given a nation in which a majority of the people are self-oriented, spiraling inflation, increasing demands for benefits, decreasing acceptance of responsibility, and decreasing patriotism could very easily weaken a country to a point beyond repair making it vulnerable to both an internal and/or an external take over.

In reference to the teachers who promote the *do your own thing* concept in their classrooms, most of those that I have met don't really

653

mean what they say as they really do have things that they want the students to learn. They still give assignments, tests, and grades so their acceptance of the *do your own thing* philosophy is just vocal and is voiced in order to be *mod*. There are some teachers who really claim to believe in the *do your own thing* philosophy and show it by not giving any directions or guidelines to the students for learning, by not giving any tests or doing any evaluation, and by giving all the students the same grade (usually "A's" where possible). If a teacher really embraces the *do your own thing* philosophy and refuses to impose his or her objectives, opinions, etc., on the students because of this concept, I can accept it and respect his or her freedom to believe what they want *provided* the teacher is honest and admits to the school that he or she has nothing to contribute to the students and resigns. For a teacher to accept employment and money under conditions where the employer and people financing the school expect the teacher to contribute to the education of the students and *make a difference* in their learning while at the same time the teacher believes that he or she has nothing to contribute and actually plans *not to make a difference* in the students learning, is to be deceitful and fraudulent. Of interest, the educators who write articles and books espousing the *do your own thing* philosophy are still holding jobs as *educators* despite their contention that they shouldn't make a difference in the learning of their students! I have come to the conclusion that most teachers who claim to believe in the *do your own thing* philosophy are really trying to escape the increasing push for accountability.

Actually, once a student has achieved what he or she is supposed to learn or is progressing successfully towards the SO's of a course, the student has a variety of options for alternate activities. The student could continue on vertically and learn the next unit or course. The student could go back to any SO that was particularly interesting and expand horizontally to any depth desired. The student could also decide to study other subjects or courses and take a learning vacation from the course in which achievement has already occurred. The student could also study or enjoy any other activity of his or her choice. The student would even be free to temporarily stop learning if so desired and just do nothing.

1. SCHOLARSHIP SESSIONS

The scholarship sessions are really the place for the *do your own thing* philosophy. Their function is to facilitate as complete a freedom as possible of topic and presentation with a minimum of restraints. Teachers, students, and even people in the community should be able to conduct these sessions. Because of the lack of restraints and the variety of topics and people presenting them, the opportunity for serendipitous learning, group interaction, and motivation is maximized. The important things to remember about these sessions is that there are no SO's, no tests or evaluation, no grades, no requirements for attending, no registration (no captive audience), no assigned homework, no time limits, and *no one is paid.* Teachers and students who present or attend these scholarship sessions, do it on their own time and at little or no cost to those who financially support the school. These supplemental scholarship sessions should be made an integral, yet informal part of any school's instructional program. Remember, if students are really learning at their own pace, there would not be any classes held at specific times. Therefore, the scholarship sessions could be held at any time and there wouldn't be any problem of bells ringing and stopping a highly dynamic serendipitous learning situation. Students and teachers could really get into *doing their own thing!*

CHAPTER VII

A BEHAVIORAL LEARNING SYSTEMS APPROACH
TO THE DESIGN OF THE
INSTRUCTIONAL ENVIRONMENT

General and Specific Objectives:

GO — To understand the interrelationships between the *Instructional Environment* and the other elements in the instructional event.

    SO — Describe the interrelationships between the elements in an instructional event when there are specific objectives and when there aren't any specific objectives.

    SO — List the four reasons for using technology.

    SO — List any four of the six reasons why technology hasn't made an impact on the educational event.

    SO — Given a particular form of technology, describe how one teacher could use it and in the process dehumanizing the event where another teacher using the same technology, can humanize the instructional event (use a form of technology other than the one used in this Chapter).

GO — To understand the relationship between the *software* and the *hardware* in an instructional event.

    SO — Describe the relationship between the *software* and *hardware* in the traditional educational event and in a systems designed instructional event.

GO — To know how to design software for an instructional event that is effective and efficient.

    SO — List the ten guidelines for designing the instructional environment on page 696 and describe each of these concepts as they are found in traditional education.

    SO — List and describe each of the seven steps in the behavioral analysis and defend the value of doing the seventh step before selecting or developing materials.

    SO — Describe an instructional event as if it was a communication event (use the six steps in Figure 64).

    SO — In using the *medical* model, describe how in a systems designed instructional event, the student is tested like a patient in at least four ways. Also, describe the parallel in strategy used by the doctor and the instructioneer.

SO — Given the 28 guidelines on p. 735, give practical examples from your own experience which supports ten or more of these guidelines from the point-of-view of facilitating learning.

SO — Given a matrix similar to Figure 70, resequence the objectives so as to maximize the number of relationships along the diagonal.

SO — Describe the two major benefits in using an Active Involvement Form. Give two or more examples from your own experience in which these two benefits would have facilitated your learning if your teacher had used an Active Involvement Form.

SO — Describe the validation step in the design of the instructional environment from the point-of-view of achieving mastery learning for 90 percent or more of the students.

SO — Given at least two commercially prepared instructional units, evaluate them according to the ten questions, criteria, and guidelines on pp. 787-791.

SO — Given at least two traditional educational research reports, evaluate the design in accordance with the three factors on pp. 791-796

GO — To know how to select appropriate hardware to maximize the designed effectiveness of the software.

SO — State the five interdependent relationships between hardware and software and give an example of each.

Because of the length of this chapter and as an aid to the reader, I am including that part of the Table of Contents that covers this chapter.

SUBTABLE OF CONTENTS

658

A. INTRODUCTION

In the Behavioral Learning Systems approach to instruction, there are the five basic elements that have to be taken into consideration: the learner, the instructor, the purpose of the instructional event, the evaluation of the event, and the instructional environment within which the instructional event occurs. Chapter V emphasized the first two elements; the changing role of the instructor, the individual differences in learners, and their interrelationships. Chapter VI emphasized the second two elements; the objectives of the instructional event, the evaluation of the event, and their matching interrelationship. In this Chapter, I would like to discuss the last element, the instructional environment, and its relationship with the other elements.

The instructional environment consists of three sub-elements: the software which the student uses to learn the objectives of the instructional event, the hardware which contains and/or transmits the software, and the physical facilities which contain the instructional event.

Software refers to the film that goes through a motion picture projector or the transparency that is placed in an overhead projector, or the slides that are placed in slide projectors, or the computer program and information that are put into the computer. It is also the print on the pages of a book. *Hardware* refers to the projectors themselves, or to the computer machinery, to the tape recorder itself, and in the case of a book, it refers to the book covers and the paper that when bound together help to identify what we call a book. Although many people may wish to separate books from technology, books are a form of instructional technology, and consequently need to be included.

There is a very important interrelationship that exists between the *software* and *hardware.* If the *software* has been developed following the Behavioral Learning Systems Approach, i.e., is based on specific measurable objectives, is associated with test items that really test the desired behaviors, and has been revised to the point where 90 percent or more of the learners will learn 100 percent of the objectives, but the *software* depends on a form of *hardware* which does not function properly and is broken down and being repaired so often that it is almost incapable of being used, then the effectiveness of the software is almost irrelevant and the instructional event will be essentially ineffective. No matter how good the *software* is, if it needs *hardware* and the *hardware* doesn't work, the *software* cannot be effective. On the other hand, if the best engineers and technicians have developed a beautiful conglomeration of *hardware* that works very efficiently, but the *software* utilized with it has not been designed to facilitate learning, then the high quality and effectiveness of the *hardware* is rendered ineffective in the instructional event and the students won't learn. Because of this very close interrelationship between *hardware* and *software*, it is very difficult to talk about one without talking about the other.

The first two sub-elements, software and hardware, are frequently lumped together under the terms *technology, educational technology* or *instructional technology.* Among audio-visual specialists and learning systems promoters, the phrases *instructional technology* or *educational technology* usually refer to the instructional hardware used to store, transmit, and present the instructional software and also to the design process (analysis and synthesis) in the development of an instructional environment which is directed towards the achievement of certain end goals or objectives in as efficient and effective manner as possible, taking into consideration the economics of the situation. However, the majority of classroom teachers at all levels of instruction tend to associate the word *technology* with only the instructional hardware.

The problem is that many educators believe technology is capable of some degree of teaching by itself. The behavior of a teacher who believes that technology can or can't teach by itself is evidenced by statements which evaluate the teaching capability of an entire category of technology, such as *I have used overhead projectors and they don't work, I have used single-concept films and they're great, I tried programmed instruction and it's terrible, I have used dial-access systems and they're not effective, I use computer-assisted instruction and it's tremendous,* etc. In effect, the teachers are attributing the capability or lack of capability of the software to teach as also reflecting the ability or lack of ability of the hardware to teach. The *hardware* in the instructional event, as long as it is operational, occupies a neutral position because by itself it can neither facilitate learning nor inhibit learning. Its physical presence could, of course, develop curiosity or be physically in the way, but it does not directly contribute or detract from the achievement of learning objectives. It is only the *software* which is used in conjunction with the *hardware* that does or does not directly affect learning. Hardware such as the overhead projector, the single-concept film projector, the programmed instructional machine or dial-access hardware or the computer, does not have any capability to teach by itself. Someone has to perform the role of teacher and develop the *software* to be used with the *hardware.* What the educators are really saying is that *I have used the overhead projector and the transparencies I used didn't work, I used single-concept films, and the films I selected were great, I used programmed instructional materials and the programs I selected were terrible, I used the dial-access system and the tapes that I used were not effective, I used computer-assisted instruction and the computer program that I used was tremendous.* It is the software that is good or bad or has the capability of teaching, *not the hardware.*

661

Another problem with the traditional use of technology in the teaching-learning situation is the misuse of technology. The misuses of technology generally occurs when teachers want students to learn one type of learning behavior but in the use of technology are unknowingly really teaching the students a different type of learning behavior. To further complicate the matter, the teachers may end up testing the students for a third type of learning behavior. To illustrate the point, look back over the courses in which you have been a student and in which the teachers used an assortment of films, slides, filmstrips, demonstrations, etc. How many of these same media were used in the testing situation? In working with educators, it is quite common to find a rather high percentage of educators who use some form of media in the presentation of their course content. But when asked how many use these same media in their testing, only a small percentage of the educators indicate that they use the same media in their testing. In more direct references to the misuse of the technology, it is not uncommon to find educators who are presenting course content of highly visualized subject matter areas, such as botany, biology, chemistry, nursing, art, etc. through the use of verbal oriented media, such as lectures, audio tape recorders, or books that are almost devoid of realistic photographs. It is not uncommon to visit a dial-access installation in which a teacher will make a comment that the audio dial-access system is not very effective in the teaching of botany. When asked, *Why don't you think this is effective?* the teacher may say, *Well, the student isn't able to identify any of the plants in the greenhouse or from drawings in the book.* It should be obvious that here is a situation where someone is trying to teach a visual behavior with audio-only materials. It is also possible in some areas that the learning behavior required of the learner is only a verbal behavior but the presentation involves both visual cues and verbal cues. Depending on the student and the visual materials, it is possible for the visual materials to get in the way of learning the verbal behaviors that are required. If you are using transparencies or slides or films to teach, then you should be using the same audio and/or visual forms in your testing. Of course, in the testing, only selected segments of a film would be used, or selected slides, or parts of the transparencies.

As pointed out repeatedly in the last chapter, the main reason for having SO's and matching tests is that without them, the instructional event becomes directionless and as in *Alice in Wonderland,* any (educational) road will work as long as neither the teacher nor the student knows where they are going. To point up the need for SO's as their presence or absence affects the instructional environment, I will present some of the traditional problems encountered in educational situations where there are few, if any, SO's and matching tests. Although educational technology (particularly the hardware) and the physical facilities of educational institutions should be an integral part in the design of the instructional environment, they have not contributed significantly to the learning situation because of some traditional assumptions, points-of-view, and the traditional role of the teacher in education. These traditional barriers to progress can be changed or eliminated such that the instructional hardware and physical facilities can facilitate student learning by also taking advantage of the differences in how, when, and where students learn best.

I will then review a situation in which all five elements of the instructional event are present and acting in consort for a more effective and efficient instructional event. If all students learned the same way, the development of the instructional unit might be rather simple. However, because every student should be considered a unique individual who could possibly learn slightly different than anyone else, it is necessary to have an instructional environment which will facilitate maximum learning for each and every student. Therefore, although the analysis or preconstruction stage of the instructional event indicates that all the students in a given course should learn the same minimum SO's, the function of the construction stage in the development of the instructional environment is to synthesize the instructional materials (software) such that they facilitate learning by taking advantage of the differences in how and why students learn. The third stage concerns the development of the carriers (hardware) for the instructional materials and the development of the locations where and within which the learning takes place.

B. INTERRELATIONSHIPS BETWEEN THE ELEMENTS OF AN EDUCATIONAL EVENT WHEN THERE ARE NO SPECIFIC LEARNING OBJECTIVES

The major problem in an educational event when there are no SO's is that the purpose of the event is subrogated. Although the original purpose of the educational event is to facilitate learning, the learning that is supposed to be facilitated has not been specified and hence whether or not it occurs is unknown. This condition tends to develop entropy (uncertainty) which is in conflict with one of the basic needs of man which is to reduce entropy by making order and structure out of uncertainty. Ordinarily, it would be expected that the easiest way to reduce entropy would be to increase the specification of the learning objectives. However, this involves effort and could possibly interfere with the autonomy of the role of the educator (accountability) and the role of evaluation (force evaluation to relate to the purposes of the educational event rather than to the statistical whims of the evaluator). As a result, there is what Robert Hawley in his *Human Values in the*

Classroom calls *entropic drift* which is the shifting from an ends value to a means value such that the means value becomes a false ends value. Whereas what should be learned, the SO's, would be the desired ends value of an instructional event and the teacher combined with the learning environment would be the means value, in an educational event without any SO's, the ends value becomes so vague and non-achievable that the means for achieving the unknown ends becomes the false end values. In other words, the objective of the educational event becomes the use of the teacher and in some situations the use of technology (the hardware) or some particular method (usually some new innovation). However, since the educational event is supposedly to facilitate learning, it is still considered necessary to evaluate the educational environment. Not knowing what should be learned by the students, test makers (teachers and standardized test makers) made up tests based on certain implied assumptions.

— Intelligence is entirely a result of nature (genetics) and can't be changed by nurture or environment.

— Intelligence is randomly distributed in any class, school, district, etc., and is represented by a distribution approximating the normal probability curve (bell curve).

— The role of the teacher and any technology is to present course content to the students and let learning occur when, where, and to whom it may (by chance).

— No matter what happens in the classroom and because of the *normal* distribution of intelligence, the results of any testing should approximate the normal curve. Therefore, tests were considered valid when the distribution of test results matched the distribution of intelligence that was assumed to be in the educational event (regardless of whether or not the test was related to what was being taught in the class, school, district, etc.)

— Test items used in the tests should primarily be of the type that can be manipulated such that almost any percentage of results can be obtained regardless of what students know (multiple-choice, true-false, and matching).

— Objectives, if any, are GO's and primarily concerned with what teachers are supposed to do rather than what students are supposed to learn and in either case, being nonmeasurable, no one can determine whether or not the objectives are being achieved.

— In order to make it easier to obtain a normal curve distribution of results, it is best not to test what is being taught to the students (the students might learn and get too many right), to keep the tests hidden so no one will know what is being tested, and make it an educational crime of misconduct for a teacher to teach the students what is on the tests (designed so teachers can't make a difference).

As a result of these implied assumptions, evaluation in an educational event is not very much affected by the other elements and in turn does not affect the other elements very much. As such, evaluation as an element of an educational event is practically autonomous.

In an educational event where there are no SO's and the evaluation is autonomous, the only elements left are the learner, the teacher, and the learning environment. As a result of *entropic drift*, the means for learning has become the false end goal of the educational event. In other words the *presenting of course content* has become the emphasis in the educational event. In order to maximize the achievement of this fake end goal, teacher training institutions have emphasized the role of the teacher as a presenter of course content and the educational environment has been designed to aid the teacher in the presenting of course content. For example, classrooms are teaching spaces rather than learning spaces and the classrooms and lecture halls are designed to facilitate the teachers' presentations.

1. THE TEACHER AS THE EMPHASIS IN THE EDUCATIONAL EVENT

There are two situations which emphasize the teacher and can occur in the educational event. The first is where the teacher presents the total course content directly to the students and the second is where the teacher presents some of the course content via teacher oriented hardware and software. Although there are not many teachers in the United States and Canada who present the total course content, this situation is very common in many other countries where the educational event is even more traditional than it is here. Most of the teachers that I have encountered who insist on presenting the total course content are in higher education and only a few in secondary education. The teacher comments which indicate this type of situation are usually along the line of *There just aren't any books or materials that present the course content in the way I think it should be done!* or *There aren't any books or materials that cover the content that I present in my course!* What with all the books being published at this time, it is practically impossible to find a course or topic that hasn't been covered in one or more books or at least in magazines, journals, monographs, etc. It is rather obvious that teachers who are in this type of educational event are very protective of their role in the classroom. They believe that their major contribution to the educational event is their ability to present course content.

In the second situation, although the teacher shares some of the presenting with Technology, the hardware and software is selected and used because they aid and maintain the emphasis on the teacher. If there are objectives, they are usually descriptive of what the teacher will or is supposed to do, i.e., to provide to the students --------, to help the students --------, to present to the students --------, to cover --------, etc. Examples of teacher-oriented hardware and software include the blackboard and chalk, overhead projectors and transparencies, opaque projectors and the materials used with them, 16mm motion picture projectors, film strip and slide projectors when used for classes of students, textbooks when selected because the teacher likes them and particularly if selected to impress a teacher's colleagues and visiting teachers as to the high *quality* of a course (usually means hardly anyone can understand it!), etc. Generally, the software is selected or developed to supplement or amplify parts of the teachers' presentations and the selection of the software determines the hardware to be used. Sometimes in schools where there is a hardware system already available, teachers will try to find a place in their presentations where they can use the hardware system. In these instances, the hardware available determines the software to be used.

In both of these situations where the emphasis is on the teacher as a presenter of course content, teachers are typically evaluated on the basis of their ability to present the course content and the evaluation is generally interpreted by the principal, department head, or whoever evaluates the teacher in terms of *does the teacher present the course like I would if I were teaching the course.* The major problem of the presenting role is that it forces the teacher to ignore individual differences among students and lock-steps the learning experiences of the students to the presenting style of the teacher and at the rate the teacher presents.

The role of the teacher as a presenter of course content also predestines that the teacher will resist anything else that might endanger the performance of that role. During the past several decades, innovations in education concerning the utilization of some form of *hardware* usually has been met with very little success when sold on the basis of *replacing* the teacher, because too often, the word *replace* carries with it connotations of being fired. As a consequence, most *hardware* innovations, including programmed instruction, have been introduced as *aids* to the teacher in the performance of the presenting function. As a result, the hardware innovations have had limited acceptance but have not made much impact on the educational event. Until such time that the teachers start accepting their new and much more important role as an instructioneer, the use of technology in the classroom will remain rather limited and with minimal affect on learning.

Just as there may be thousands and perhaps even hundreds of thousands of teachers who have expressed a resistance to technology, there are hundreds of thousands, and perhaps millions of teachers at all levels of education, from kindergarten through graduate school, who are resisting *books*. Teachers are not actually resisting the USE of books, but they are resisting the possibility that learners can LEARN from books. Teachers do not resist the USE of the books because in cases where a teacher has never actually defined what it is students are supposed to learn in a course, the easiest approach to teaching the course is to follow essentially what is presented in one or more books, which may be used in the *presentation* of the content of the course. The resistance to the fact that students may LEARN from the books comes from the point-of-view of the role of the teacher in the teaching-learning situation.

The behavior of a teacher who resists technology is rather easy to identify, because this teacher will not use very much, if any, of the available instructional technology in his courses, and second, will probably make statements which include negative comments towards technology and its use in the teaching-learning situation. The behavior of a teacher which would indicate that the teacher is resisting the possibility that the book could teach by itself is evidenced by the teacher who reads directly from the book to the students, or lectures to the students on essentially the same material covered in the book. If the material is already available in the book, the students should have a chance to learn from the book, and then, if they can't learn from the book, the teacher should teach them what the book can't. In a recent monograph published by the Association for Supervision and Curriculum Development, the results of a survey indicated that 85 percent of teachers teach from textbooks.

Of course, role competition is not the only reason why many teachers resist technology. There are many teachers who resist technology because they are not really convinced that technology will help them in the teaching-learning situation, which is a very justifiable reason for not using technology. However, if the teacher resists technology because he doesn't know how it will help him teach better and continues to teach courses in which student learning follows the *normal* patterns in which the majority of the students are getting "C", "D", and "F", then this teacher not only doesn't know the possible contribution of technology to his teaching-learning situation, but probably is not too much aware of the contribution of his own efforts to the teaching-learning situation.

2. TECHNOLOGY AS THE EMPHASIS IN THE EDUCATIONAL EVENT

Since the approval of the National Defense Educational Act and the Educational Facilities Act, the input of educational technology into the schools has increased significantly. With the advent of the Elementary and Secondary Education Act of 1965, this rate of acquisition of technology has increased even faster. The budget for the United States Office of Education is approaching ten billion dollars of which a very significant portion of these funds will be concerned in some way with the use of technology in our schools. Why is it that educators are turning to technology? With all of the money, time, and effort being put into the integration of technology into the teaching-learning situation, there must be some reasons why educators want to use this technology. I have identified five reasons why most educators use technology.

The first reason for using technology in the teaching-learning situation was particularly popular during the late 1940's, the 1950's, and throughout the 1960's. This reason is best illustrated by the educator who is conscious of the problems in the teaching-learning situation. When this type of educator observes at an exhibit some technological idea or concept that can be utilized or reads about this technological concept in a professional journal or other magazine, he is motivated to try out these technological concepts from the point-of-view of wanting to be innovative or for the novelty effect. This is particularly true in higher education, where there is a push for publishing and every new technological concept presents one or more potential articles, even if only to say that the technological concept is not useful in the teaching-learning situation.

The second reason why educators use technology in the teaching-learning situation is very similar to the reason that many people have color television in their houses, a second car, or a second house; because everyone else is doing it. In other words, many educators in school districts, colleges, and universities are concerned with keeping up with the *educational Joneses.* For example, a very high percentage of proposals in recent years and probably during the rest of this decade will contain references to computer assisted instruction, because it is the latest *educational fad* to be integrated into the teaching-learning situation.

A third reason and one at the present time which prompts more use of educational technology than probably any other reason, is that educators are involved in a pedagogical conflict between what they

668

believe and how they act in the classroom. For example, every teacher at all levels of education believes that there are individual differences among students and subscribes to the belief that each student should be developed to the maximum of his or her capability in our schools. But, if you examine their behavior in the classroom, they are assuming by their actions that everyone is the same by giving them the same materials, the same learning experiences, and the same length of time in which to learn, and the resultant differences in achievement are attributed to the maximum capability (genetic limits) of the student. In reality, the resultant differences in achievement may be the maximum capability of the instructional materials or the teaching-learning situation for those students during that specified period of time. This doesn't mean that if the students were exposed to something different or for a longer period of time that they are not able to do much better. As a consequence of the pedagogical conflict between what they believe and how they act in the classroom, some educators turn to various forms of technology, hoping that it will somehow magically correct the situation.

A fourth reason for educators using technology in the teaching-learning situation is based on the results of educational research. Of interest, the results of educational research are cited as reasons why educators want to use technology, and educational research has also been cited as reasons why some other educators do not wish to use technology. For example, Wilbur Schram of Stanford University, in a review of 393 research studies comparing televised instruction with regular face-to-face classroom instruction found that 65 percent of the studies showed no significant differences, and 21 percent of the studies showed that televised instruction was superior. Therefore, 86 percent of the studies resulted in conclusions that the televised instruction is as good as or better than regular classroom instruction, which would indicate that there can be no doubt that students can learn effectively via television. Educators who want to use television will cite the fact that 86 percent of the studies resulted in conclusions that television was as good as or better than regular classroom instruction. Educators who do not want to use television can site the fact that 65 percent of the studies showed no significant difference, 14 percent of the studies showed that face-to-face instruction was superior. Therefore 79 percent of the studies resulted in conclusions that face-to-face instruction is as good as or better than televised instruction, so why waste the money on television (this would be particularly true when the educator looks on his role as a presenter of content and television as competition for this role).

In these four reasons, it should be noted that technology is being used for the sake of technology and that the software is primarily determined by the hardware which has been selected for the presenting role. Similar to when the teacher is the major emphasis, the evaluation of the use of technology in the educational event is based on the presentations made by the hardware. The technical excellence and full utilization of the medium are the important criteria rather than learning. As a result, the development of the software is generally controlled by technical experts in the medium of the presenting hardware rather than by experts in solving learning problems. The increased costs of the technical excellence may or may not be necessary for learning, but the increased costs certainly retard the utilization of technology. In spite of the research showing no significant differences in learning, there are significant differences in the time, effort, and costs to develop the software. For example, compare the preparation time of an hour or so for a live one hour lecture versus about 15 hours needed to develop one hour of audio tape, 40-45 hours needed to produce one hour of video tape, 100-150 hours needed to develop one hour of programmed instruction, and 100-300 hours needed to develop one hour of computer assisted instruction. If in an educational event utilizing hardware there still are no SO's and matching test items, then all the extra costs, time, and energy may very well be wasted.

3. WHY TECHNOLOGY HASN'T MADE AN IMPACT ON THE EDUCATIONAL EVENT

In reference to research, the United States Office of Education survey report, *Equality of Educational Opportunity,* which was released during the summer of 1966, stated the conclusion that equipment and technology in schools accounted for very little difference in student achievement. The important point to remember is that technology *as it is presently being used* contributed only slightly to student achievement. The following six statements are suggestions why according to research, educational technology has not been as successful as the advocates of technology have believed it would be:

a. In almost every situation involving technology in schools, the technology was identified first and the educators' and/or students' needs second. This problem of identifying the technology first and the needs second is in part caused by the procedures involved in getting grants from the USOE, or any other funding agency that sponsors educational research. All too often, schools that are successful in getting grants do not start out by identifying a need and then trying to write a proposal to obtain funds to study the need and to find solutions to the need. Professional educators who are successful in getting grants for their schools start out by surveying the funding agencies that they are going to submit the proposal to. They find out what is the current area of interest of the funding agency and then they submit proposals in that area which they think will be funded, remembering that the major objective is to get money, not necessarily to solve problems.

b. In projects where the needs were identified after the technology had been specified, the project objectives were heavily influenced by the technology available and the results may not contribute much to academic achievement. For example, if the technology identified is television or computers, then the project objectives are written around the USE of television and computers, and these projects are generally evaluated on how much USE was made of the technology which was identified as the central theme of the project.

c. The evaluation of the contribution of audio and visual technology to student achievement generally does not include audio and visual testing of the students' learned perceptual behaviors. Of the hundreds of research projects involving technology which have been reviewed by the author, only a few of the projects included in their testing for achievement the testing of the audio or visual learned behaviors which were presented by the technology. The usual pattern is to use paper and pencil, multiple-choice tests which suffer from all of the problems pointed out earlier concerning the so-called (very subjective) *objective* tests used in education.

d. Very often, technology is used in schools, classes, and in subject areas where the student achievement is already average or better than average, so increases in achievement are small. This is covered by the fact that when teachers or even educational researchers have to prepare a unit to demonstrate or utilize some form of technology, they tend to pick a unit they already know quite well, then even without the technology, the students probably are already learning most of what they were supposed to learn. Therefore, the addition of the technology would not necessarily result in students learning significantly more. If teachers and researchers identified a learning problem (students not achieving) and solved the problem in the process of developing a unit to utilize some form of technology, it would be very easy to find significant increases because of the technology (actually the increase is because the learning problem was solved).

671

e. The teachers may or may not have even been shown how to use the technology and even if shown how to use it, they are not usually shown *when* to use it (decision-making). When you use it, is generally when whatever a student or students are using to learn from isn't effective (a learning problem). If the objective of a research project is to use the technology, then it is not necessary to worry whether or not any learning problems exist. On the other hand, if we are concerned about learning, then it is necessary to be aware of learning problems and in order to be aware of learning problems, it will be necessary for the teachers to specify learning objectives to the degree that they will be able to tell whether or not students are learning. Obviously, it is much easier to only worry about whether or not the technology was used, regardless of learning.

f. The generalized statements by technologists regarding the use of technology for large groups, small groups and individuals leave the teacher's role in relation to students' academic achievement vague and often creates negative attitudes within the teachers toward technology. Notice how in most of the research concerning face-to-face teaching versus some other form (usually technology), the other form doesn't have any role for the teacher. To my knowledge, there has only been a few research projects in which the design compared face-to-face teaching versus some form of technology doing the presenting of the unit content and the teacher working with those students who couldn't learn from the technology. This research design could not help but prove that technology plus the teacher is superior to the teacher alone or the technology alone. Promoters of technology would be much more successful if their emphasis and priority was first, on student learning; second, the more important role of the teacher as an instructioneer; and third, the technology which will facilitate the achievement of the first two.

4. TECHNOLOGY AND ACCOUNTABILITY

When most educators and non-educators think of accountability, they most often think of students, teachers, administrators, and school board members being held accountable. Yet, in the educational event, almost all teachers use materials and almost all students learn from materials (both software and hardware). In making the materials accountable for learning, the educators and students can also be accountable. Kenneth Komaski, the Director of the Educational Products Information Exchange (EPIE), testified before the United States House of Representatives Subcommittee on Education:

672

At this time of national concern over consumer protection, the largest single group of unprotected consumers is made up of the 50 million school children who are being required to learn from educational materials almost all of which have been inadequately developed and evaluated.

... EPIE estimates that there are nearly 250,000 textbooks, workbooks, films, filmstrips, transparencies, audio tapes, video tapes, programmed instruction materials, simulation games, paperbacks, and multi-media instructional *systems*. ... We estimate that 99% of the materials school children are now required to use have not been field tested and put through even the initial phases of the learner-verification and revision cycle.

Surveys consistently point out that most teachers feel their biggest problems in the classroom are irrelevant materials and inadequate resources. Militant teachers throughout the country are asking for a bigger say in the selection of materials and resources. The unspoken question that should be asked is *To do what?* Without any SO's, it is difficult for any materials or resources to be relevant while at the same time, any one material is about as good as the next one because the teachers aren't sure what should be learned anyway. At least when state and/or district administrators specify certain materials, there is some commonality in the presenting even if not in the learning. If teachers were completely free to select anything they wanted in a situation where there are no SO's, there would really be chaos in the classrooms and in the schools. In order to have greater freedom in the selection of materials and resources, the teachers are going to have to specify what the students are supposed to learn. Then in the process of solving student learning problems, the teachers should be free to select different materials and resources as long as it can be shown that the new materials and resources contributed to the solution of the learning problems. Also, as soon as the learning objectives are specified and the minimum common core content of similar courses identified, the producers of materials and resources will know what is needed and can develop relevant materials.

Without an identified minimum common core of learning objectives in even one course over any part of the country, the techniques, materials, and technology used to solve the learning problems which students might encounter in learning the minimum common core SO's can't be shared or transferred to other classes or schools. This points up the big difference between education as an art or non-science and instruction as a science. The study of a technique or technology concerns man-made phenomenon which is a non-science. The study of how to solve the problems such that a given group of students can learn

673

a set of SO's concerns natural phenomenon (learning) and as such is a science.

The same problem of accountability of materials and resources affects all areas of hardware and software and in particular the more sophisticated technology like television, computers, and dial-access systems. William Harley, President of the National Association of Educational Broadcasters (NAEB), stated at the 1970 NAEB Convention:

Educational broadcasting must be evaluated not only by what is broadcast but by what happens in the lives of people as a result of broadcasting. It must make a difference.

However, at the 1973 NAEB Convention, Rex Lee who is the Commissioner of the Federal Communications Commission stated:

Never have so many well-intentioned, dedicated and experienced people been given so great an opportunity to use these modern means of communications and yet had so little effect on education. He said, *Never have so many public entities and organizations cajoled, argued and maneuvered for their own points of view with so little impact on their audiences. Never have so many people spent so much time talking about what public broadcasting might become — and had so much trouble translating their words into action.*

At the same Convention, Roger Heyns, President of the American Council on Education said:

Anyone who has studied the relative failure of faculty and administration to seize firmly and make elaborate use in their instructional programs of such promising devices as radio, television, cassettes and computers is forced to conclude that the basic problem has been and remains content — or, as some prefer, software. One must, of course, pay tribute to culprits such as fearful teachers, mechanical primitives in the teaching profession, defective equipment and devices that were oversold to potential users with resulting disappointment, to the discovery that supposedly cost-saving devices turned out to be enormously expensive, still, one is obliged to conclude, however, after giving proper weight to all of these villians, that the primary problem in educational technology is the same as in other technologies whether educational or entertainment namely, the message.

Frederick Breitenfeld, Jr., Executive Director of the Maryland Center for Public Broadcasting and a member of the NAEB Executive Board, wrote in the October-November issue of *ITV Field Report* (a publication of the Great Plains National Instructional Television Library):

Widespread use of classroom television remains a dream. ITV is a mess. We're disorganized — with dozens of national efforts, hundreds of local projects, and let's face it, no great commitment on the part of the big decision makers in education. It's a mess because we are still squabbling about content people versus media people, and it's a mess because we continue to define it as supplementary in too many instances. Most tragically, it's a mess because we haven't been able, universally, to win the backing of teachers, specialists, administrators, and policy makers. What do we have to show for the first 20 years of ITV? The inescapable fact is that television has made very little impact on classroom instruction nationally and locally.

Breitenfeld suggested that there was a need for new administrative patterns which would facilitate the integration of ITV into total learning systems, rather than merely superimposing ITV into traditional classroom procedures and that educational materials have to be more precisely designed so that their results are measurable. A similar statement was made by Representative Orval Hansen from Idaho at another convention when he identified two major problems which he felt were holding technology from making an impact on the educational event:

a. Educators must learn to describe their needs with greater precision, and

b. Educators face a serious *information gap* when making purchases because of inadequate product assessment and consumer information.

In a seminar in Washington, D.C., *Standards and the Educational Consumer*, sponsored by the United States Office of Education and the Educational Media Council (EMC), the participants outlined three types of standards necessary to make technology more effective:

a. Instructional quality standards which would require that books, films, tapes, and kits be proved to help students learn what they purport to teach.

b. Performance standards which would cover the specifications for equipment and their efficiency.

c. Compatibility standards which would allow materials produced for one brand of equipment to be used with other models or makes.

These standards sound great, but one very critical standard that is missing and is the key to the whole problem:

675

d. Learning standards which would specify the minimum common
core SO's of similar courses which would then allow materials
produced for one class of students to be used with other classes
of students in other schools, districts, states, and even countries.
Without this last standard, progress in achieving the other three standards will be slow and probably technology oriented rather than learner-
oriented. In order to make a hardware system *accountable* in terms of
learning, it is necessary to emphasize learning and the instructional
process and to de-emphasize the hardware. If this would have been the
approach used by technologists in the past, the growth and acceptance
of technology (both hardware and software) would have been phenom-
enal compared to what it has been and hundreds of directors of
hardware systems would not have had to *beat the bushes* in order to
find some teachers who will use their systems. Of course, it is not only
the technologists that are going to have to emphasize learning, all
educators are going to have to emphasize learning effectiveness and
efficiency in the instructional process for each and every student during
this decade of instructional accountability. With the increasing demand
for accountability and the advent of performance contracts which are
written in terms of *guaranteed learning or no money*, it is becoming
very important, if not critical, that the decision to install a hardware
system be based on identified specific learning needs. The system
should be designed to solve these specific learning needs and the system
should be capable of being evaluated on the basis of whether or not the
expected learning took place after the system was installed.

On pages 668-669, I listed four reasons why educators use technology. There is a fifth reason for using technology and it represents a
small but growing group of educators who have identified learning
problems in their courses and in the solution of these learning problems
have had to use some form of technology. In this way, the need is
identified first, and the technology is identified to satisfy a need. This
last reason for using technology can be classified as educators using
technology for the sake of learning. An important point to remember
though, is that if the technology is being used at least most of the time
to achieve specific learning objectives, and the students have learned all
of these objectives, then it seems reasonable to utilize the technology
for an *educational experience* which is not based on specific learning
objectives. The utilization of technology in learning activities without
objectives should not form the major basis for purchasing new technology or to justify the maintenance of existing technology in instructional systems. In using computers for instructional purposes, this is even
more important, because the purchase of computers or computer time
and the development of instructional programs to be stored in the
computer, is a very expensive instructional situation. If, in fact, the

676

students are not able to learn any other way, then it is entirely justifiable; but if these other ways have not been tried, then the expenditure for the computers and computer programs may be and should be questioned.

There are two questions which should be asked in reference to the effective utilization of technology. The first one concerns the continued expenditure of funds to maintain existing technology already purchased. The question is, *What is it that students are learning now that they won't be learning if the technology is not maintained and utilized?* The answer should then be related to the maintenance costs to determine whether or not the technology should be maintained. Serious reservations should be made if the answer is something like, *No one knows exactly what the students are learning now, so obviously there is no way to tell what learning will be lost if the existing technology is not maintained!*

The second question concerns the purchase and installation of new technology. The question is, *What is it that the students are not learning now that after the purchase, installation, and operation of the new technology, the students will be learning (as a direct result of the new technology)?* Again, the answer should be related to the costs of purchasing, installing, and operating the new technology. As in the other question, serious reservations should be made if the answer is something like, *No one knows exactly what the students are learning or aren't learning now, so obviously, there is no way to tell whether or not the students will actually learn more after the technology is purchased, installed, and operated!*

The more costly the technology, the more imperative it is to ask one of these questions. In a recent survey of high schools conducted by the American Institutes for Research, 13 percent indicated that they were using computers for instructional purposes. According to the National Association of Educational Broadcasting, in excess of 80 percent of our country's school children have educational television available. Too often, as with other technology, the motivation for using instructional computers and television, is to enable the school district to be modern for public relations rather than to solve some learning problem which can't be solved some other way.

It is true that the use of computers in instruction will motivate some students to learn who might not have wanted to learn in the more traditional setting, but to have all of the students in a class use the computer when a majority might have learned on their own from a book and an audio tape, increases the cost of using a computer to a prohibitive level. One of the major problems in the evaluation of learning resulting from the use of computers in instruction is the use of multiple choice questions because they readily fit into the standard format of computer programs.

Television has a great potential for instruction, but as long as instructional television programs are developed without objectives, this potential might just as well be forgotten. As of 1974, the number of instructional television programs that have been developed according to a systems concept with objectives, testing, etc., could almost be counted on two hands. One such program, *Sesame Street*, has been acclaimed as fantastic, the greatest thing in television, and a model for all instructional television! If other television programs use *Sesame Street* as a model, then instructional television will continue to move into the 20th century in a horse and buggy with both the driver and the horse wearing blinders to keep from seeing what is happening around them. Yes, in comparison with other instructional television, *Sesame Street* is great; but so is the horse and buggy great in comparison to walking! To back up these statements, consider the evidence as presented in the evaluation report of *Sesame Street* prepared by the Educational Testing Service. The conclusions of the report from the point of view of traditional education were that the series was a success. By looking at the same data from the point of view of a systems approach, the success is pretty empty. According to their own data, the average pretest score of all children in their study was 42 percent which means that the children already knew almost half of what *Sesame Street* was supposed to teach which would obviously result in a high level of intellectual boredom for most children. This does not mean that the students would stop watching it, it just means that the students would be passively involved intellectually even though highly entertained. If the series was designed so that the children could start from wherever they were intellectually, then the pretest score for each child should be somewhere between zero and 10 percent (because of individual differences in what they know, some children would have to see more of the programs than others). The boredom factor should be 1.0 for an ideal instructional situation. With an average pretest score of 42 percent, the boredom factor for *Sesame Street* is 8.4 or about eight times higher than it should be.

Under the current concept of designed instruction, the learners should have learned between 90 percent and 100 percent of the objectives of the series in order to be considered effective. The average posttest score of all the children was 59 percent which means that the series was only successful in teaching 59 percent of what the series should have been able to reach. In most classrooms, a student achieving 59 percent would receive an "F" or at best a "D". Therefore, with a desired effectiveness of 95 percent and an actual effectiveness of 59 percent, the effectiveness factor for *Sesame Street* is 59/95 or about .62 which is not very *fantastic*.

In looking at the efficiency of the series, an ideal program which minimizes the boredom and starts each learner with a pretest score of from zero to 10 percent and maximizes learning by having the learners learning 90-100 percent of the objectives would result in the average learner gaining 90 percent. The average child in the *Sesame Street* study gained 17 percent. Therefore, the instructional efficiency factor (17/90) is only .19, which is pretty bad. The publicity for the program claimed that students viewing the programs gained two and a half times as much as the students who didn't view the programs. Sounds good, doesn't it? However, the actual data indicated that the average non-viewer gained about seven percent while the viewing students gained 17 percent and 17 is two and a half times seven. A good example of manipulation of statistical data to obtain desired results.

With a little more analysis of the data it is rather easy to uncover that it took the average child five hours of viewing *Sesame Street* to gain the answer to one test item. As if that isn't bad enough, in isolating the data for the advantaged children in the study, it turns out that they were so bored (passively involved) that it took them an average of seven hours of viewing *Sesame Street* in order to gain enough knowledge to answer one additional test item correctly. Now that is fantastic.

C. INTERRELATIONSHIPS BETWEEN THE ELEMENTS OF AN INSTRUCTIONAL EVENT WHEN THERE ARE SPECIFIC OBJECTIVES

As pointed out in the last section, in an educational event where there aren't any SO's, the elements of the event have minimum relationships and the teacher evaluation, and learning environment as elements of the event can actually be almost autonomous. The results of such a chaotic situation has had negative effects on almost every student going through it and has caused problems for almost everyone connected with the educational event including the teachers, the parents of the students, and the taxpayers.

In an instructional event where there are SO's, the interrelationships between the elements become very important and the functions of each element can be identified and evaluated in terms of its contribution to improving the student learning of the SO's.

1. TECHNOLOGY: HUMANIZING OR DEHUMANIZING?

During the past several decades, the increasing numbers of learners, increasing needs of these learners in order to participate fully in our society and in life, and society's demands that the professional educators become more effective and more efficient in the instructional process, have established a place in our educational institutions and in the instructional process at all levels of education for technology.

However, a reference to *technology* in the course of a discussion about instruction in almost any group of educators brings varied impressions to the minds of the participants ranging from a utopian vision to a catastrophic vision. Under the condition where there are no SO's, the extreme impressions generally break the group down into the technologists versus the humanists. Under the condition where there are SO's, maximizing learning for the students becomes the emphasis and a unifying force because to be against *learning* would not be an acceptable situation for either the technologist nor the humanist. Where the learning environment can be varied to maximize learning, it is possible under the Behavioral Learning Systems Approach to instruction to have the most effective and efficient *system* be composed of all live people interacting with the learner and it would also be possible for the most effective and efficient *system* to be all technology. In contrast to what the traditional-oriented humanist may say and believe, there are students who actually prefer learning from technology because their prior educational experiences have been negative and associated with non-achievement and a variety of the traditional educational malpractices.

Nevertheless, some educators and non-educators have made the charge that using technology in the instructional event and particularly to do the presenting of the course content tends to dehumanize the event. The addition of technology neither dehumanizes or humanizes the instructional event because technology is essentially neutral. Only the teacher can humanize or dehumanize the instructional event by *their use* of technology.

During the past decade, the acceptance of the presence of technology in the teaching-learning situation has changed some teachers into coordinators or supervisors of the technology. When this occurs in a situation where learning objectives have not been specified and the emphasis of the administrators is on the use of the technology rather than an increasing learning, it is possible to come to the conclusion that the use of technology could dehumanize the teaching learning situation. For example, in Figure 63, the center of the two cubes represents whatever amount of technology that is presently being used in a particular classroom situation. In cube "A", the teacher wants to perform the instructioneer role and uses some form of technology (a textbook, audio or video tape, etc.) to take over the presenting role in the class such that the teacher is free to work with the students who have trouble learning all of the SO's of the unit being presented (learner-oriented).

NOTE: Think of the typical traditional classroom and the teacher has given a test on Friday covering the past weeks work. It would be a rare event if all the students achieved 100 percent on the test.

680

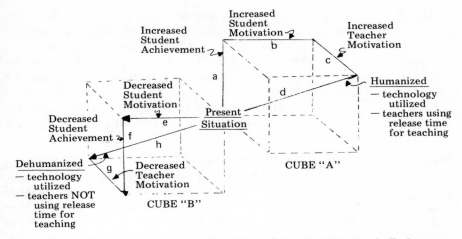

Figure 63 — Humanization as Affected by the Teacher's Role

A more likely result would be some sort of curve of achievement. The following week. those students who had achieved all of the previous week's SO's would continue on and receive the course content by reading a textbook, listening to an audio tape, viewing a film or video tape, etc. The teacher, who is now released from the presenting role, uses the release time to work with those students who didn't achieve all of the previous week's SO's and by solving their learning problems, helps them achieve the SO's and consequently makes a difference in student learning by the design of the learning environment.

Because the teacher is working with individual students, there would have to be an increase in student achievement (see "a" in Figure 63). As a result of the increased achievement and the observation by the students that this new approach is helping the teacher to have time to work with those students who need help at the time when they need help, the students develop more positive attitudes and motivation to learn (see "b" in Figure 63). As a result of the increased student achievement and the increased positive attitudes and motivation of the students, the teacher develops positive attitudes and motivation about the whole learning event. Basically every teacher wants his or her students to learn and be positively motivated, so when it happens, the teacher can't help but be motivated (see "c" in Figure 63). As a result of students achieving, students being positively motivated, and teachers being positively motivated, the instructional event is classified as a humanized teaching-learning process (see "d" in Figure 63).

681

NOTE: This is based on a definition of *humanization* in the teaching-learning process that is concerned with individualization and the degree to which students who need a teacher have access to a teacher for help (learner-oriented). The popular concept of *humanization* held by educators who are resisting technology is based on a definition that is concerned with the degree to which students are *exposed* to the live teacher, regardless of resultant learning, inappropriateness of content for student needs, and whether or not the students need the teacher (teacher-oriented).

Starting again at the center of Figure 63, look at cube "B". The teacher in this situation is a traditional teacher who has decided to use some form of technology to present the course content. Since the teacher believes that his or her role is to present the course content, when that function is taken over by the technology, the teacher looks on the release time as *free time* to do what the teacher wants (teacher-oriented). Very quickly, the students identify that in this situation the technology is substituting for the teacher and removing the teacher even further away from the students and the teacher is not visibly earning his or her salary which the students, their parents, and other taxpayers or financial contributers have paid for. As a result, the students develop negative attitudes and demotivators (see "e" in Figure 63). As a result of the students' negative attitudes and demotivation, the students achievement is negatively affected (see "f" in Figure 63). As a result of the students' negative attitudes, demotivation, and decreased achievement, the teacher develops negative attitudes and demotivation about the whole learning event. Also, because the teacher is not performing the role the teacher believes he or she should be performing (presenting the course content), the teacher feels guilty about letting the situation continue (see "g" in Figure 63). As a result of the students' negative attitudes, demotivation, and decreased achievement and the teacher's negative attitudes, demotivation, and guilty conscience, the instructional event is classified as a dehumanized teaching-learning process (see "h" in Figure 63).

NOTE: During the teacher's *free time* in this last situation, the teacher could be reading or correcting papers, attending a meeting, having a coffee break, or in higher education, the teacher might use this free time to write an article for some journal about how-using technology to replace the teacher in the classroom dehumanizes the teaching-learning process!

In comparing the two situations, the role of technology is exactly the same in both cases. The only difference is what the teacher does with the release time. When the teacher uses the release time to help individual students by solving their learning problems, the instructional event is a humanized teaching-learning process. When the teacher uses the release time to be further away from students and their learning problems, the instructional event is a dehumanized teaching-learning process.

NOTE: Only the live teacher can humanize or dehumanize the teaching-learning process. If the teacher uses technology to give him or her release time to work with individual students and help more students learn more, it is the teacher who is humanizing the teaching-learning process. If the teacher uses technology to give him or her release time to get away from students, it is the teacher who is dehumanizing the teaching-learning process it is NOT the technology.

As an illustration, I have published a Newsletter about Dial-Access Information Retrieval Systems (DAIRS) for Instruction since 1965 and language laboratories fit into the DAIRS concept. From time to time, I have received letters from school districts, colleges, and universities describing their successful language laboratories in which students are achieving and both students and teachers are positive about the teaching-learning experience. When I go to visit these schools, without exception, I find the teacher in the language laboratory working with individual students who are having learning problems. I also receive letters from school districts, colleges, and universities describing their unsuccessful language laboratories in which students aren't achieving, they are committing acts of vandalism, and both students and teachers are negative about the teaching-learning experience. When I go to visit these schools, without exception, I find either some technician in charge of the language laboratory or if the teacher is there, the teacher is reading, grading papers, or doing some other activity and ignoring individual student learning problems. Frequently, I find exactly the same equipment in both the positive and the negative situations. It is only the teacher's role that is different.

If technology is added to the teaching-learning situation without changing the teacher's role, a competitive situation is created between the teacher and the technology in which both are trying to present the content of the course. The result of this competition is usually that the teacher wins by a small margin or there are no significant differences, the teacher's attitudes towards technology are decreased, student learning may or may not increase, and depending upon the quality and utilization of the software, the whole arrangement may become relatively expensive.

2. GUIDELINES FOR THE UTILIZATION OF TECHNOLOGY

Traditionally in education, educators have acted as if the degree of student achievement was a function of individual differences inherent within the student. This teaching-learning belief will continue to exist as long as we teach with traditional methods where-in the *time* for learning is held as a constant and the amount of student *learning* is treated as a variable, and individual differences are something to talk about rather than something that affect the teaching-learning situation.

With available technology and methodology, educators can achieve almost any desired level of student learning. It is entirely possible to have 90 percent or more of the students learning 100 percent of the specified course objectives. The era of equating high percentage of student failures with high quality of teaching efforts is obsolete. It is a case of *malpractice* of the art and science of teaching that results in failure rates over four or five percent. The greatest barrier to more effective and efficient teaching-learning situations is our loyalty to the tradition of *presenting content* rather than manipulating the environment to facilitate learning. A recent publication of the American Association of Colleges for Teacher Education, *Evaluative Criteria for Accrediting Teacher Education,* states that the most important thing that can happen in any educational institution is LEARNING. Therefore, as educators, we should be willing to do everything within our power to raise the levels of student LEARNING.

The results of the traditional teaching methods can be evaluated by the facts that:

— 29 percent of our students who start first grade are unable to complete a high school education (almost a million dropouts annually at a loss of about nine billion dollars of society's investment in education);

— 25 percent of our college freshmen become dropouts or push-outs on or before the end of their first year (over 500,000 freshmen dropouts annually at a loss of 600 million dollars of society's investment in higher education); and

— only 18 percent of our young people are able to obtain a college degree.

A cursory examination of the *Help Wanted* ads in any metropolitan newspaper should convince us that almost 100 percent of our young people should have a high school education and probably close to 50 percent or more should be able to complete some type of post high school education or training.

It would be elysium or paradise if it were possible to have an alive, loving, patient and understanding teacher for each and every student in a face-to-face situation, but this condition is not possible and yet teachers and schools are committed to *develop each student to the maximum of his or her ability (both innate and learned).* Given that the teacher has accepted the committment to maximizing learning for each student, there are three factors which become important: first, the identification of SO's and matching tests (discussed in the last chapter); second, the identification of the functions of technology which will directly facilitate the learners in the performance of their role in learning; and third, the identification of the functions of technology which will directly facilitate the teacher in the performance of his or her role as an instructioneer.

NOTE: In contrast to teacher-oriented technology which is used to help the teacher in the presenting of the course content, learner-oriented technology is used to help the learner learn on an individual basis when and where the learner wants to learn, i.e., individual audio and/or video playback devices, textbooks written for learners, individual kits of learning materials, etc. When teacher-oriented technology is used by learners at their discretion, it becomes learner-oriented by function and purpose.

In a continuous progress learning environment where students are actually learning at their own rate, using vehicles which are the most appropriate for each student, and at a place and time convenient to the student, it is the individualized technology which allows this to occur. To do this, the technology has to be flexible enough to provide three functions: first, the pacing of the presentation of the course content has to be available in various levels of simulation (verbal, visual, etc.), utilizing a variety of methods (inquiry, discovery, convergent, divergent, etc.) and in languages appropriate for the learner (reading level, dialect,etc.); and third, the technology has to be portable and available at all times.

In a more traditional setting, the technology can be used for one or more of three areas. For those students who are learning slower than average, instead of being lost and left behind as is the case in most traditional educational situations, the technology could be used to present the regular course content when the student is ready for it, to present the course content using alternate vehicles for learning which are more appropriate to the learner's learning characteristics, and/or to present the content of units of prerequisite courses which are needed to eliminate the student's cumulative ignorance which is interfering with the students' successful learning of the regular course content. A teacher could decide to use technology for the majority of students who might be able to learn at an average pace with average materials and with minimum learning problems in order to be free to personally work with the students who are having critical learning problems. In this situation, if the differences are not too great, the technology would be group paced and aimed at the average student. Technology could also be used with students who are faster learners or with students who just want to learn more.

With reference to the teacher's role in the almost traditional instructional event, the guideline to remember is that the effectiveness and efficiency of the instructional event is almost proportionate to the degree to which technology is utilized to free the teacher from the traditional role as a presenter of course content in order to help individual students learn. At the lowest level, technology could be used only as a supplementary presenter of prerequisite or enrichment material. The next higher level would concern the use of technology to learn whatever SO's that are expected to be learned in the process of doing homework or studying out of the classroom. The highest level of potential individualization occurs when technology is used to release the teacher from presenting course content in the classroom. Not only does this free the teacher to work with individual students who are having learning problems that need solving, but the use of technology to present the course content also frees the student from the lock-step of the teacher paced presentations.

The guidelines to follow in utilizing technology in the instructional event are as follows:

— try to maximize individual student freedom in learning, but build in necessary group experiences where and when appropriate to achieve all of the course SO's;

— try to minimize the teacher's live involvement in presenting the course content in order to minimize the lock-step of teacher paced group learning and to maximize the availability of the teacher to work with individual students;

— as learning problems are identified and solved, try to set up procedures such that students can be involved in self directed diagnostic testing and prescriptions which will give the teacher more time to identify and solve new learning problems.

3. ULTIMATE GOAL OF DESIGNED INSTRUCTION

Almost every list of goals for education contains one or more statements concerned with the development of the learner for life or the development of the learner into an independent learner. Since contemporary life is everchanging and modern man expects to change occupations at least two or three times during his or her life, then the preparation of the learner for *life* has to include the development of the learner into an independent learner. In other words, the ultimate goal of designed instruction is to free the student from dependence on formal learning experiences.

Before going into more detail, let me state my meanings for three terms which are frequently confused and used interchangeably.

An *independent learner* is a person who can make his or her own decisions, can set his or her own goals, can identify and utilize the means which are appropriate in order to achieve the goals, and is able to achieve success in this process as an independent person.

Learning independently technically refers to all learning because all learning is done on an independent basis. No one can learn for someone else. However, learning independently usually is used to refer to students learning by themselves and is in contrast to *group or class* learning. The emphasis is on the number of people involved in the learning experience and does not necessarily refer to the actual learning that is taking place.

Individualized Learning refers to a situation in which the emphasis is on the learning of the individual regardless of whether or not the learner is learning alone or in a group. In order to individualize a learning experience, it would be necessary to find out a lot about the student so that the learning could start where the learner is (intellectual, sensorily, and/or emotionally) and the learning environment (materials, technology, and facilities) would reflect the individual's characteristics, interests, and abilities.

Given that the professional teacher's task is to develop each student into an independent learner and because of individual differences among students, this developmental process has to be done on an individual basis, then it is going to be necessary to recognize and eliminate four traditional FALSE assumptions upon which most of our present education is founded. First, most educational situations are based on the assumption that learning can only happen in a school building; second, that the learning can only happen in front of a live teacher; third, that students should be able to learn from the same materials (if not, it is a genetic or non-school problem which can't be solved); and fourth, that students should be able to learn at the same time and place (if not, it is a genetic or non-school problem which can't be solved). Once these four assumptions and the related rules and actions resulting from these assumptions are eliminated, it will be much easier to achieve the task of developing the independent learner. The critical concept to accept as a guideline is that being an independent learner is a learned behavior which can be taught. It is not successfully taught in a situation where the student does not have an opportunity to experiment and practice with independent learning. It should also be remembered that in the typical, teaching-learning situation, the student learns in a school, in front of a teacher, and from prescribed materials. In developing the independent learner it is necessary to wean the student from each of these three factors. Because of individual differences among students, some students might be weaned easier from one factor than the other two, in one subject easier than other subjects, and at one grade level easier than other grade levels. There should be a constant effort to encourage students to learn independently (on an individualized basis.) There are some students even at the kindergarten level who can learn on their own if given the SO's. At the very latest, students in their last year of secondary education should be learning one or more of their courses on an independent basis. It is a sad commentary on higher education that almost all undergraduate and even graduate courses are conducted just like elementary and secondary courses. However, there is a small but growing trend towards letting students take proficiency examinations and get credit for courses regardless of how they learned the content.

> NOTE: This idea is exactly what I am suggesting except that few of the courses that students can test out of have SO's and as a result, the proficiency tests are more often designed to give a certain distribution of scores (by using multiple-choice and true-false test items) rather than testing for the achievement of important SO's of the courses. As a result, students who pass the tests may not actually learn what they need to know to be able to apply any implied objectives which could have been learned in the course, which ultimately may make the student have negative feelings about learning independently. Teachers who subsequently have students who have passed these proficiency tests may also develop negative attitudes towards the concept because the students haven't really learned what the teacher expected (implied objectives) them to learn.

As more and more schools experiment with off-campus and out-of-school learning and as more and more teachers experiment with writing GO's and related SO's (particularly the minimum common core objectives), the probability of these two trends coinciding increases. When that happens, the quality, effectiveness, and efficiency of out-of-school learning will also increase and more students will be prepared to become independent learners. As a result of these consequences, the teachers in the schools will be able to work more effectively with the students who still have to learn in a school and in front of or with live teachers because as an increasing number of their students are able to learn without their help, the number of students needing their help decreases which allows the teachers to concentrate their efforts where they are most needed and will do the most good. In other words, instead of decreasing the class size or number of students assigned to the teacher which reduces the teacher's productivity and increases the costs of education (and under the traditional approach there is little or no change in the quality of *education*), it might even be possible to increase the number of students assigned to a teacher which would increase the teachers productivity and decrease the costs of education. The points to remember is that because many of the students would be learning on their own, the number of students the teacher actually has to work with could easily be less than in the traditional classroom and because of the behavioral learning systems approach to instruction, the effectiveness and efficiency of learning is increased!

Another critical concept which can act as a guideline is that the more a student believes he or she can learn successfully on his or her own, the more the student will be able to learn as an independent learner. The reverse is also true. The more a student believes he or she can't be successful learning on his or her own, the more dependent the student will be on schools, teachers, and prescribed materials. Because most students have encountered negative experiences under the traditional approach to education, most students tend to like the step-by-step learning of programmed instruction and computer assisted instruction. However, as their confidence builds up, the students tend to find the step-by-step learning too slow. Advocates of these forms of learning frequently make the mistake of thinking *all* students should learn this way *all* the time. These forms are very useful for students who have trouble learning other ways; but again, as soon as possible, the students should be weaned from any dependence on this or any other particular style of learning.

Therefore, if formal instruction is to prepare the student for success in later life and that success is dependent upon being able to be an independent learner, than the ultimate goal of schools should be the development of the independent learner by design in action and experiences not by choice or in words only and certainly not by a design that is based on the assumptions that learning can only occur in a school, in front of a live teacher and with a particular vehicle for learning.[28]

NOTE: To avoid a potential misunderstanding, although I am completely in favor of developing the independent learner who can set his or her own goals, identify the best means to achieve the goals, and can successfully do it, I am not contradicting myself by suggesting such complete freedom of learning. The goal of developing the independent learner is a designed learning process and the

---

[28] During the changeover from the traditional approach to the Behavioral Learning Systems Approach to instruction, it may be necessary to simulate a traditional classroom environment for those students who have difficulty learning in a freer environment. But the simulation should be limited to the physical environment and only those aspects of the traditional approach which enhance learning for this type of student, i.e., required attendance, scheduled study times, deadlines, etc. Special care should be taken not to include in the simulation any of the traditional malpractices and to constantly attempt to wean the student from his or her dependence on the traditional environment.

freedom of learning comes after the learning of the minimum common core objectives in whatever courses the students take and after the learning of the minimum common core objectives in the minimum common core of courses which are necessary to not only survive in our society, but to find personal success and happiness, to minimize interference in other peoples' achievement of success and happiness, and hopefully to maximize facilitating other people's achievement of success and happiness.

Remember, even in the learning of required SO's, students have or should have freedom in selecting the method of learning, the vehicle for learning, the time and place for learning.

4. THE PHYSICAL FACILITIES OF THE INSTRUCTIONAL ENVIRONMENT

Once we start emphasizing learning in such a way that learning is maximized for each individual student, teachers are being paid on the basis of learning and on how many students they are able to help learn, and technology is being utilized to help the teachers perform their task and to help learners learn, then some interesting concepts come to light in reference to educational facilities which are to be designed for learning.

One of the first things that will develop when we start individualizing instruction is that we will discover that very few students have exactly the same degree of each of the various learning variables and that students should be able to start school or a course at any time and complete the course or school at any time. Not only should students have *open entry* and *open exit* to and from courses, they should also be free in the time for learning. At the present time, classes are scheduled for the convenience of schools and some teachers. There are students and teachers who would prefer to study, teach and learn at times other than those traditionally offered. For example, a college in the midwest installed a dial-access system such that students could call in to the system from their own telephones in the dormitories or at home for recorded class lectures at anytime — 24 hours a day and seven days a week. The director of the system found that the greatest use of the system was from midnight until about 3:00 a.m. when there was no television available and not many other students available for socializing! Some students may learn best in quiet places, some like noise. Some students may like to eat and drink while learning, others may not. As a result, the concept of classrooms becomes almost obsolete, except for the needs of small groups to get together for certain learning activities or scholarship sessions. Second, as we start recognizing the individual differences among teachers we will find that some teachers

690

are able to manage the instruction of hundreds of students at the same time; however, they will not necessarily be in the same classroom at the same time. We will have to recognize that learners can learn independently, not only in schools, *but out of school.* When certain forms of technology are used for the sake of learning, one of the ways in which this technology may very well be used is to take informational materials and learning experiences to the learner, wherever the learner is, *in school or out of schools.* If learning can take place on an independent basis, in school or out of school, then this starts to affect what the instructional facilities would look like. For example, if most students are learning on an independent basis, then libraries, learning resource centers, study halls, will probably take up most of the space in the new buildings, minimizing the number of classrooms. Also, if students can learn *out of schools* it is very possible that school buildings which are designed for 1,000 students today may actually have 2,000 or 3,000 students using the building, but maybe only 500, 600, or 700 students will be in the building at any one time. The need for building school buildings so that each student has a chair in some classroom is not really necessary under an instructional system that maximizes individual instruction. The concept of learning *out of school* may very well become an increasing part of the home activity. What with parents who may be involved in continuing their education for a major part of their lives either for degrees or for personal interest, the home learning concept, which has been talked about during the past several years, may very well become a reality. In addition to allowing students to learn independently, the home learning center may also encourage students and their parents to learn together, which may ultimately contribute to an elimination of the generation gap. Since not every student is going to have a home environment conducive to learning, it may be a function of the school to provide these students with a suitable learning place in the school, where the student can carry on independent learning activities. In certain situations, it may very well be that instructional institutions will set up learning centers in large apartment or housing complexes, in which students who cannot study in their homes will have a place near to them where they can study. Here again, these expenditures will be based on identifiable learning needs of the students, and the justification of these learning centers in the apartment or housing complexes could be verified on the basis of measurable increases in student learning. In the case of young children, who are too young to be left in their homes because both parents are working, then the instructional institutions may just as well admit the fact that part of their role in society is to perform a public babysitting service. If this is the case, then facilities should be designed for babysitting, or keeping the children out of mischief. Obviously, this approach to the teaching-learning situation *decreases the need for more and more school buildings,* particularly when these buildings are designed to fit into a system of individualized instruction.

The decision to use certain methodological or technological concepts in a new school building can cause major changes to be made in the design of that school building. For example, a new community college is planning to emphasize independent study and continuous progress for their students; consequently, there is little, if any, need for the traditional classrooms. Since a lot of the independent learning will be done off campus, the amount of space needed in the buildings will be substantially less than in the traditional campus where the design of the buildings is based on the assumptions that students have to be on campus, in front of a live teacher, and in a classroom in order to learn. On the other hand, once a building is designed and built, the design may affect whether or not certain technological concepts can be used effectively and efficiently. For example, lots of window space in the classrooms tends to make it difficult for the teacher to use films, slides, etc. because it is difficult to black out enough of the natural light coming in through the windows to enable the students to view the projected visuals clearly. Because these two concepts are so closely related, the most important guideline in designing school buildings is to build in flexibility such that the design has a minimum effect on the utilization of any present or future instructional technology or methodology and if possible the design should enhance and facilitate the utilization of technology which in turn may facilitate the utilization of certain methodologies which in turn should facilitate student learning.

During recent years, a very extensive survey (the Coleman Report) indicated that differences in school facilities (including technology) had very little effect on the achievement level of the students. But remember, this is in reference to the present instructional situation in which few teachers have specified what students should be learning, the majority of teachers are presenters of information, and the tests used to measure the achievement level of students are standardized normed tests which are useless and have all the drawbacks pointed out in the last chapter. Changes in the use of technology and in school building design should be initiated because the students are not learning something that they should be learning. The value of the change should be supported by the fact that after the change, the students did learn what they weren't learning before.

If any one travels around the country visiting all levels of schools, he will find a wide variation in the design of the newer school buildings, while most of the older school buildings are quite similar in design. Administrators of many school districts, colleges, or universities will claim that the teaching-learning situation cannot be improved because they have to operate from the old buildings. If teachers have not specified what students are supposed to learn in the old buildings, just transferring the teaching-learning situation to a new *modern* building will not necessarily help improve the teaching-learning situation because what the student is supposed to learn has still not been specified. As a result, most of the changes in the use of technology or in school building design are changes in order to be *modern, futuristic,* or just plainly to develop a good public image.

In order for a school to be up to date according to some of the latest criteria, the school should have a *Learning Resource Center* or an *Instructional Materials Center.* These centers are supposed to be filled with a variety of alternate instructional resources. The first question that should be asked is *alternate instructional resources for the teaching of WHAT?* If teachers haven't specified what it is students should be learning, then how does anyone know that an alternate resource is needed? In truth, the alternate resources are available for teachers to change their ways of presenting the course content. Where there are a variety of student-oriented materials in these centers, it is a situation in which the centers are filled with thousands of solutions to problems that nobody has identified and then when a teacher identifies a learning problem and wants to produce the solution for students to use, there is no money available to produce and duplicate the solution to identified learning problems because all the money was spent on buying solutions to unidentified learning problems. My suggestion to schools wanting to put in a Learning Resource Center is to open up the Center with empty shelves and bank the money which was to be used to purchase materials, Then, as teachers identify and solve real learning problems, there will be money available to purchase, develop, and duplicate the solution. In that way, the shelves of the Learning Resource Center fill up with real solutions to real problems for real students.

The utilization of technology follows the same pattern. Probably as high as 90 percent or more of the technology being used in our schools at the present time is being used primarily as a new or different way of presenting the same thing. In working with hundreds of school districts, colleges, and universities, it is the rare occasion in which technology is utilized to specifically increase learning. In fact, if the purchase of technology was based on whether or not it would measurably improve the learning situation, then very little technology would be in use. This does not mean that technology cannot help the learning situation, because in most instances it could very definitely be of help to the learner if the instructional programs were designed to be effective and efficient. Although various forms of audio-visual equipment have been in our schools for almost half a century, it has only been since the late 1950's that technology in education has enjoyed such a positive reaction from teachers, students, and parents. This does not mean that everyone likes technology, but at least the majority look on technology as *good*.

According to the report, *To Improve Learning*, which was the result of a federal study on the impact of instructional technology on education they found that technology has not contributed very much to learning. The conclusions of the report were that educators are failing to capitalize on the great potential of instructional technology and that there needs to be a far greater investment in instructional technology. As expected, the traditional educators associated with the study have failed to see that the real problems with the utilization of technology are the same problems as can be found throughout education: lack of specified instructional objectives, lack of training of the teachers regarding their role in instruction when using technology, lack of appropriate testing, and the lack of a systematic approach towards the selection of the most effective, efficient, and economical way to achieve maximum learning for each and every student.

NOTE: Although many colleges and universities are beginning to allow and even to encourage off-campus learning, this does not mean that these efforts are also associated with a systems approach to instruction which involves SO's, matching tests and *individualized learning*. Most of these efforts and most correspondence instruction suffers from many of the problems of traditional education.

D. DESIGNING THE SOFTWARE FOR THE INSTRUCTIONAL EVENT

NOTE: Since I started conducting courses, seminars and workshops on the systems concept in 1961 and especially during the past decade, I have encountered a variety of descriptions of a *systems approach* ranging from a simplified version consisting of just specifying objectives to very complex versions consisting of twenty or more steps arranged in complicated flow charts. Some of these versions are so complicated that they are not practical and are only of theoretical value and some are so simple that they don't recognize the complications of individual differences among students and teachers. Those that are useful have in common three basic characteristics: the purpose of the instructional unit is defined in terms of specific measurable objectives; the evaluation instrument has a high correlation with the objectives; and the designed learning environment and strategies are successful in getting a high percentage of students to achieve the objectives. My version of the *systems approach* as described in this chapter is a result of preparing and conducting many workshops, seminars, courses and the writing of a number of papers and articles over the past 13 years.

The actual design and development of the instructional environment utilizing the Behavioral Learning Systems Concept includes most of the steps which are usually followed when preparing a *programmed instructional unit.* Programmed instruction, referred to also as programmed learning, auto-instruction, teaching machines, etc., refers to the utilization of programmed materials (a program) to achieve educational objectives. A program consists of a sequence of carefully constructed items leading the student to mastery of a subject through self-study.

The change from programmed instruction to the *Behavioral Learning Systems Concept* is a matter of greater degree of sophistication. The name change is necessary because *Behavioral Learning Systems* is more descriptive of the process involved and because the stereotype already established by those familiar with the term *programmed instruction* limits the mode of presentation to some kind of verbal format presented in a textbook form or by a teaching machine. *Programmed instruction* does not evoke the same meaning to those unfamiliar with the term as to those who are familiar with it. In fact, people who are unfamiliar with the term, upon hearing or seeing it, often confuse it with computer technology. For those who are uninformed about the progress of programmed instruction, there are over 5,000 programs available today as compared with about 100 programs that were available in 1961. Recent surveys indicate over 16 percent of educators at all levels are using programmed instructional materials for remedial, regular, and enrichment purposes. Almost every major publisher is involved in publishing programmed instructional materials. (This fact in itself may contribute to the stereotype of a verbal format when most people think of *programmed instruction.*)

The major differences between the Behavioral Learning Systems Approach to Instruction and most *programmed instruction* is that the emphasis is placed on student learning rather than on the characteristics of programmed instruction, i.e., frames, fading, reinforcement, cues, blanks to be filled in, multiple choice to select, etc.; secondly, whereas the systems concept can accommodate and utilize any media and even a live teacher for presenting course content, most programmed instruction tends to utilize a single mode of instruction; third, whereas the systems concept makes use of readily available materials as long as they result in the desired learning (existing textbooks, films, slides, audio and videotapes, correspondence instruction and even programmed instruction), most programmed instruction has to be created from scratch which includes a lot of effort to re-invent content wheels; and fourth, whereas in the systems concept the use of GO's is desirable and necessary, in most programmed instruction, GO's are not acceptable because they are not measurable.

In order to maximize the positive effects of the instructional environment on student learning, the following guidelines should be used irrespective of the subject matter content and/or the instructional level (pre-school to graduate school and adult instruction).

— The requirements or objectives of the system will control the design of the system.

— The system will maximize learning efficiency by adapting the system to the learner rather than making the learner fit the system.

— The design and procedures of the system will reflect the instructional philosophy consistent with the requirements of the system and society.

— The design will utilize more fully our instructional resources and the teaching learning environment.

— The system will develop course patterns so that students can pursue their instruction or training as much as possible at their own pace, on their own schedule, and at a convenient site.

— The system will maximize learning effectiveness through quality control procedures such that 100 percent of the stated learning objectives of the system are achieved by 90 percent or more of the learners.

— The system will place the responsibility for learning on the student and will be directed towards the ultimate development of the independent learner.

— The system will utilize practical principles of learning that actually increase learning.

— The system will emphasize the achievement of the needs and desires of each individual student (even if only one student wants one course).

— The system should reflect the importance of student learning by making everything else subordinate to it, the teachers, the materials, administrators, school boards, regents, buildings, state and federal offices of education.

1. BEHAVIORAL ANALYSIS: THE IDENTIFICATION OF THE BOUNDARIES OF THE INSTRUCTIONAL EVENT

Frequently, as teachers identify the GO's and specify the SO's of a particular course or unit of a course, the SO's represent what the teacher wants the students to have achieved by the end of the course or unit of a course. In order to develop an instructional unit that will be successful for different students, just knowing the end achievement objectives or *terminal behaviors* and having matching test items is not enough. All students are not at the same place with respect to the desired terminal behaviors. In doing a behavioral analysis of an instructional event, it is possible to identify the beginning, ending, and content of the event in terms of the students who might be involved in learning the instructional unit or course.

The behavioral analysis of an instructional unit consists primarily of seven steps which are designed to analyze and delimit the course or unit content from the point-of-view of what is expected of the students at the end of the course or unit (terminal behaviors) and where the students are at the beginning of the course or unit (entry behaviors).

1) Specify the terminal behaviors (GO's and related SO's) that the students should be able to exhibit upon completion of the course or unit and as a consequence of the content of the course or unit (See Figure 64).

The reasons for this first step have been discussed in detail in the last chapter and it should be sufficient to say that in an instructional unit, if the teacher doesn't specifically know where it is the students are going (terminal behaviors), then there is no reason for instruction or for the presence of the teacher because anything that is learned is as good as anything else if no one knows where they are going anyway.

2) Prepare a posttest that will evaluate the achievement of the terminal behaviors. (See Figure 64).

For most readers, the term *posttest* refers to any test given at the end of something. Under the Behavioral Learning Systems Concept, the meaning you may have for *posttest* is slightly changed. Throughout this chapter, a posttest refers to a test that tests for the achievement of the terminal behaviors of an instructional course or unit regardless of when it is given.

Now that you have decided where you want the learner to go, or what you want the learner to learn, and you have a test to test whether or not they have arrived there, what would be the next most appropriate step? If someone came to visit you from out of town and called you to ask directions as to how to get to where you are, what is the first question you would ask your visitor? Most likely you would ask the visitor, *Where are you now?* Although it may be obvious to many people that before we can take anyone any place, we have to know where they are, in classes throughout the country and at all levels of education, teachers begin on page 1 of the textbook without ever finding out *where the students are* before they start the course.

3) Specify the entry behaviors (GO's and related SO's) that the students who are going to take the course or unit are assumed to have as they begin the course or unit. (See Figure 64).

4) Prepare a preentry test that will enable the observer to determine whether or not the assumed entry behaviors can actually be exhibited by representative learners who would most likely take the course or unit. (See Figure 64).

5) Specify the enabling objectives[29] necessary to take the students from where they are when they start the course or unit (entry behaviors) to the completion of the course or unit (terminal behaviors). (See Figure 64).

NOTE: Sometimes in the process of specifying the enabling objectives, the instructional analysts go to far and identify more enabling objectives than are actually necessary to achieve the desired terminal behaviors. This results in learning steps that may be to small for the learners. A practice that is used in developing good programmed instruction is to purposely leave out some of the enabling objectives to see if the learners can learn the terminal behaviors without them. If they can, leave them out. If the students can't achieve the terminal behaviors, put back in the design those enabling objectives that are necessary to bring about the desired achievement. If some students can achieve the terminal behaviors without some of the enabling objectives and others need the objectives to achieve the terminal behavior, then a form of branching has to be designed into the instructional event to accomodate these differences.

6) Prepare a pretest that will enable the observer to determine whether or not the enabling objectives and the terminal objectives which constitute the content of the course or unit have been achieved. (See Figure 64).

---

[29] I refer to these objectives as *enabling* objectives because their function is to enable the learners to achieve the terminal behaviors. I may also refer to some of these objectives as *scaffold* objectives in that not only are they used to learn the desired terminal behaviors, but once the terminal behaviors are achieved, the *scaffold* objectives can be forgotten. An example of *scaffold* objectives are the various grammar rules students have to learn to write correctly. Once a student learns to write correctly and it becomes a habit, it is no longer necessary to remember all the grammar rules.

For most readers, the term *pretest* refers to any test given at the beginning of something. Under the Behavioral Learning Systems Concept, the meaning you may have for *pretest* is slightly changed. Throughout this Chapter, a pretest refers to a test that tests for the achievement of all of the learning objectives (enabling and terminal) of an instructional course or unit regardless of when it is given.

NOTE: Practical examples of these tests as they relate to course objectives which are implied by the use of test items and criteria for evaluation in ongoing courses would equate posttests to final examinations, pretests to all of the unit tests put together, and preentry tests to items and criteria for evaluation selected from the final examinations of prerequisite courses. Before use however, the test items and criteria for evaluation in these tests should be justified in terms of the questions on pages (544-549).

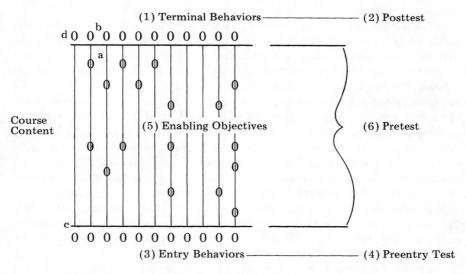

Figure 64 — Steps in the Behavioral Analysis

In reference to the relationships between the steps, two points should be made. First, if a student has already achieved enabling objective "a" (See Figure 64) and is now in the process of learning the last step of the sequence, terminal behavior "b", the learning and achievement of "b" is a part of the course and as such would be tested by the pretest. In addition, "b" is a terminal behavior and as such would be tested by the posttest also. In other words, the posttest is actually a particular part of the pretest. All of the test items in the posttest would be included in the pretest. Remember, however, that the

699

posttest items are unique in that they represent the last steps in a series of learning sequences. For example, if there were 150 enabling objectives in a course, there might only be 15 or 20 terminal behaviors and the pretest would have at least 150 test items whereas the posttest would have at least 15 or 20 test items.

NOTE: For every rote memory objective, there would be only one test item. For every process objective, there would most likely be multiple (not multiple choice) test items in order to find out if the student can apply the process to different situations.

Identifying the relationship between terminal behaviors and the enabling objectives necessary to achieve the terminal behaviors is very useful. Not only will the achievement of the enabling objectives facilitate student learning of the terminal behaviors, but in testing, once the students have achieved the terminal behaviors (posttest), it is not necessary to give the whole pretest because the students would have to have achieved all of the enabling objectives in order to achieve the terminal behaviors. In the example just stated, once it is proved that the instructional unit is effective with most students, instead of using the 150 + item pretest, a teacher could use just the 15-20 + item posttest. If a student missed one or more of the posttest items which indicates the student didn't achieve the terminal behaviors represented by the items, then the teacher would have to selectively test all of the enabling objectives associated with those terminal behaviors that were missed in order to find out where the student needed help. This would still represent a considerable saving in testing time and effort for both teacher and students. Second, if there was only one step from an entry behavior (see "c" in Figure 64) to the terminal behavior (see "d" in Figure 64) for all of the entry behaviors (no enabling objectives between the entry behaviors and the terminal behaviors) the achievement of the terminal behaviors would constitute the content of the course and the pretest and posttest would be identical from the point of view of the objectives being tested. If all the terminal behaviors were rote memory, then the pretest and posttest would be identical. If one or more of the terminal behaviors were process objectives, the testing of the objectives in the posttest and pretest could use different vehicles for testing the achievement of the same process objectives. For most terminal behaviors that are process objectives, the enabling objectives leading to the terminal behaviors represent the various steps in the process.

Not all relationships between enabling objectives and terminal behaviors are linear as in Figure 64. The interrelationships between terminal behaviors can be very complex. The key point to remember is to know which enabling objectives are directly or indirectly associated with a particular terminal behavior (see Figure 65). The easiest way to keep track of the interrelationships between terminal behaviors and the enabling objectives of an instructional course or unit is to identify these relationships with a flow chart or diagram at the time when the enabling objectives are being identified, similar to Figures 64 and 65. Once the desired terminal behaviors and existing entry behaviors are specified, the enabling objectives can be identified by breaking the terminal behaviors down into component parts until you connect with the entry behaviors, by building on the entry behaviors until you connect with the terminal behaviors, and/or by working down from the terminal behaviors and up from the entry behaviors until you connect somewhere in between the two course or unit boundaries.

If you have difficulty in identifying the enabling objectives of the course or unit even if you already have the terminal and entry behaviors specified, then look at available course or unit materials for hints or cues as to the necessary enabling objectives keeping in mind that they must lead towards the achievement of the terminal behaviors. In going through the course or unit materials, it is possible that you may want to add one or more terminal behaviors and if needed, additional required entry behaviors.

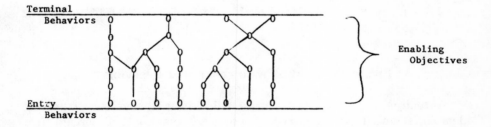

Figure 65 — Interrelationships Between Terminal Behaviors and Learning Objectives

7) A tryout of the three tests (the preentry test, the pretest, and the posttest)[30] on a sample of students that are representative of the students who might actually take the instructional course or unit.

It is important to remember that in this seventh step, only the tests are being tried out. The actual instructional materials have not been

---

[30] It should be pointed out that these tests are not necessarily just verbal tests. They could be visual tests involving static or motion visuals, they could be performance tests, they could be observation tests, etc.

701

developed or selected yet and they will be tried out later on. The primary purpose of this step is to identify the actual boundary lines of the instructional unit from the point-of-view of where the students are in relation to the course or unit, the lack of or existence of the assumed entry behaviors, the lack of or existence of terminal behaviors, and the lack of or existence of knowledge concerning the enabling objectives which constitute the course content.

Ideally, the learners would score 100 percent on the pre-entry test and zero on the pretest and posttest (See Figure 66). This would indicate that the entry assumptions made by the course instructor were correct.

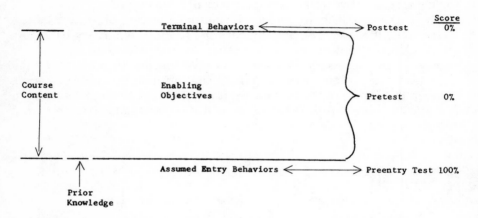

Figure 66 — Ideal Assumed Entry Behaviors

Actually, the tryout test scores will almost always vary from the ideal situation. If the preentry test scores are less than 100 percent, it is an indication that the course instructor's assumptions regarding student entry behaviors were overstated and the students weren't where it was assumed they were. (See Figure 67).

In order to lower the assumed entry level of the instructional unit to match the actual entry levels of the intended audience, the entry behaviors which have been tested by pre-entry tests items which *none of the learners were able to answer* should be deleted from the entry behaviors and added to the course content as enabling objectives. The teacher who believes his or her role is to teach a particular course may be upset when the adjusted course entry level includes some basic concepts that should have been learned in prerequisite courses. However, the teacher who has accepted the role as an instructioneer and is concerned about teaching *students* rather than *courses* will include whatever is necessary to help the students be successful learners. In

702

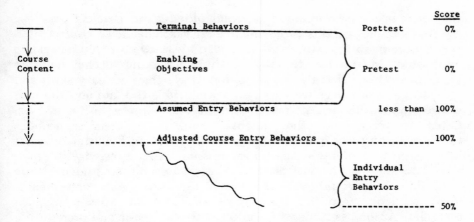

Figure 67 — Results of Trying Out Tests With Assumed
Entry Behaviors Too High

order to take care of individual differences between students, those
entry behavior test items which some students answered and others
weren't able to answer indicate the need for some type of branching[31]
to allow for individual differences in entry behaviors. A teacher could
have each student start where they are as indicated by the preentry test
which would mean that in a class situation, few, if any, students would
be working on the same enabling objectives. A teacher could also start
the class at the adjusted entry level (see Figure 67) and then as a
student reached a point in the course where the missing entry behavior
was needed, the student could be branched back to pick up the missing
objectives (See Figure 68). For some students it would be more meaningful and motivating to learn the missing entry behaviors at the time

Course Enabling Objectives

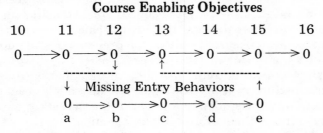

Figure 68 — Branched Sequence for Missing Entry Levels

[31] *Branching* refers to a technique of designing self-paced instructional materials
with alternate learning pathways so that the students' time is spent most
efficiently and effectively, allowing the student to enter a course when appropriate to the learner, skip over portions of the course the student already know,
sent to a developmental path for missing entry behaviors, or sent to an enrichment path for individual choices.

they were necessary and used in learning other enabling objectives.

As examples of this problem, in first year chemistry courses, it is very common to find students who haven't learned how to use negative exponents. In the traditionally taught course, the teacher and the students find out that the students don't have the necessary skills and knowledge about negative exponents when it is too late and the unit where these skills and knowledge are necessary prerequisites is over. Often the teacher and the students blame the problem on genetics rather than on prior instructional ineffectiveness. In English courses, it is common to find students who are missing basic knowledge in grammar. Too many traditional teachers refuse to teach their students these basic skills as it would lower the level of the course. As a consequence, many students never do learn some of the basic rules of English grammar. As long as students are allowed to learn basic and prerequisite courses with less than 100 percent of the implied objectives (missed test items and criteria for evaluation), there will be students whose cumulative ignorance (lack of entry behaviors) necessitates the need for the branching concept.

If you were to write programmed instructional materials without testing for the existing entry behaviors of your intended audience, chances are that in the tryout of the completed program many students would make mistakes because of their lack of necessary entry behaviors. Most program developers would then tend to expand the program by making the steps smaller and by overcueing the required responses to make up for the missing entry behaviors. Very seldom will a program developed under these circumstances be successful. In addition, there will probably be a high percentage of dropouts. If the authors of a program keep breaking the frames down into smaller and smaller units in order to bring about the desired learning, students who go through the program will make comments about how dull the program was and how it was an insult to their intelligence, etc. Actually, under these circumstances, the students may not really achieve the desired behaviors as their responses occurred only in the presence of overcueing.

A second situation could also occur as a result of trying out the tests. This situation would most likely be more common than the last situation (assumed entry levels too high) because many teachers recognize that some of their students don't have the necessary entry behaviors so they extend their course by re-teaching (to the whole calss whether they all need it or not) the most common missing entry behaviors. In trying out the tests (preentry test, pretest, and posttest) in this situation, the students might score 100 percent on the preentry test which indicates they have all of the necessary or expected entry behaviors and scores of greater than zero on the pretest and posttest which indicates that the students already know parts of the course and have already achieved one or more of the terminal behaviors of the course (see Figure 69). These results indicate that the teacher under-estimated the students entry behaviors.

In order to raise the assumed entry level of the instructional unit to match the actual entry levels of the intended audience, the enabling

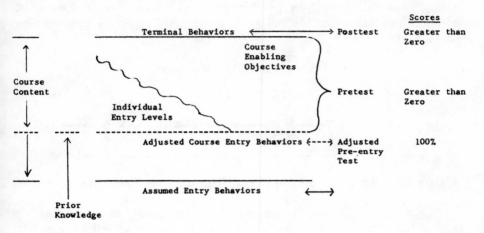

Figure 69 — Results of Trying Out Tests With Assumed
Entry Behaviors Too Low

objectives in the course content represented by test items in the pretest which *all of the learners knew* should be eliminated from the course and added to the pre-entry behaviors. As in the first situation, the teacher who believes his or her role is to teach a particular course may be upset when the adjusted course entry level eliminates parts of the course, particularly if any of the parts eliminated contained some of the teacher's favorite topics, jokes, etc. However, the teacher who has accepted the role as an instructioneer and is concerned about teaching *students* rather than *courses* will be glad to eliminate the course SO's which have already been learned as the teacher will have more time to solve the learning problems of the students and more time to help students learn more of what they individually want to learn above and beyond the course SO's. In order to take care of individual differences between students, the pretest items that some students were able to answer and other students were not able to answer indicate the need for branching within the course content such that the student could skip over the enabling objectives which had already been achieved (see Figure 70).

705

Examples of this problem are common in courses which overlap with other courses. English composition is essentially the same course from about fith or sixth grade up to and including freshman college composition courses (the literature covered in these courses change, but not necessarily the literary objectives to be learned). High school and college level chemistry, physics, biology, and botany courses have a lot in common. Some high school and college level technical courses also have a lot in common.

Course Enabling Objectives

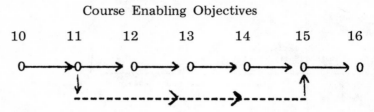

Figure 70 — Branched Sequence for Skipping Over Learned Objectives

If you were to write programmed instructional materials without testing for the existing entry behaviors of your intended audience in this situation, although the learners might reach the terminal behaviors, you have a built-in boredom factor because of over-learning which will inhibit the positive growth of motivation as learning takes place during the program.

Programs of this type are exemplified by situations where learners are able to score high on the posttest without going through the program. A review of the literature on research concerning programmed instruction (or almost all educational research) will reveal that most programs fall into this category. Almost every research article where the pretest data is given indicates that students knew from 30 percent to 75 percent of the content of the program before even going through the program. Generally, if the program is written before the students are tested, the excess frames stay in the program regardless. It is not surprising that many students make the statement about programmed instruction being boring and repetitious to them.

NOTE: It is possible to use available programmed materials where students already know some of the objectives of the program without the boredom problem. By giving the student a pretest of the program (or the posttest as a pretest), the student can program himself or herself through the programmed materials. By letting the student keep the test while the student is going through the program, as soon as the student encounters part of the program that he or she already knows, the student can then scan read ahead until he

706

or she encounters unknown materials. Then the student can back up a few frames and then proceed normally through the program until he or she encounters material dealing with known objectives which can be skipped over using the type of branching indicated by Figure 70.

NOTE: Conceptually, the branching indicated in Figures 68 and 70 are actually the same. The major difference is in the learning pathway taken by the majority of the students. In Figure 68, it is expected that the majority of the students will take the short path and a minority will have to take the extra learning steps. In Figure 70, it is expected that the majority of the students will take the longer path and only a minority will be able to skip over some of the learning steps.

A third situation is actually the most common situation of all and is a combination of the two situations just discussed. Given the typical heterogeneous group or class of students, there will be students who are at varying levels below (lacking) the assumed entry behaviors, some students who are close to having the assumed entry behaviors, and some students who not only have the assumed entry behaviors, but already know parts of the course or unit. The more heterogeneous the students are, the greater the need for some branching in order to avoid losing students who don't have the expected entry behaviors and boring the students who already know parts of the course or unit. Given the traditional approach to education where time in class is a constant and learning is the variable, the higher the grade level, the greater the heterogeneity among students and the greater the problems created when the teacher ignores these individual differences and teachs (presents course content) to the mythical *average* student who may or may not even exist in the classroom.[32] If there are *average* students in the classroom, the number could vary from only one or two students to almost all of the class. The only way to find out where the students are with reference to what is to be learned in any course or unit is to start out the course or unit with diagnostic tests consisting of the pre-entry test and/or the pretest. In ongoing courses, if a teacher is convinced by past experiences that the students have the necessary entry behaviors, it

---

[32] Cutts and Maseley in *Providing for Individual Differences In The Elementary School* (Prentice-Hall, 1960) described a sixth grade class that they said was similar to hundreds of other sixth grade classes they had visited in all parts of the country.

"The twenty-nine pupils showed a range of more than 3½ years in chronological age, 104 pounds in weight, 14 inches in height, 62 points in I.Q., and 8 years 4 months in mental age. Their achievements, as measured by the Iowa Every-Pupil Tests of Basic Skills, ranged from 4.3 to 9.9 in grade average, from 4.4 to 9.5 in reading, and from 3.5 to 11.4 in spelling."

may only be necessary to give the pretest covering the content of the course or unit. If a teacher is convinced by past experiences that none of the students know anything about the course or unit, it may only be necessary to give the pre-entry test to check on the variability in entry behaviors.

NOTE: It should be obvious that the diagnostic testing at the *beginning* of a course or unit is very critical in helping students be successful and motivated in learning the desired SO's of a course or unit. The reason why most teachers do not use diagnostic tests (besides the fact that few teachers were ever taught to use them) is the conflict that is raised between their philosophy in teaching and their role in teaching. The use of diagnostic tests is in keeping with the philosophy of individual differences and concern about students; but if the teacher actually knows that the students are all different, the teacher would ethically not be able to teach them as a class using the traditional role as a presenter of course content because it would ignore these differences and indicate indifference about what happens to the students. Since the traditional role as a presenter of course content is much more ingrained in the teacher's internalized programmed behaviors than the behavior of using diagnostic tests, most teachers don't or won't use diagnostic tests. After all, of one doesn't know for sure that the students are different, it is okay to assume they are the same, present the course content, and then blame the different levels of achievement and motivation on the students (genetics, home environment, etc.)! Because I believe that most teachers are humane individuals and are concerned about their students, if I can get teachers to give diagnostic tests, they will let their philosophy win the conflict and will accept the much more appropriate role as an instructioneer who individualizes instruction and rejects the traditional role as a presenter of course content who ignores individual differences.

In addition to trying the tests out on students who represent a sample of the students who might actually take the course or unit, it is also very useful if these same tests can be given to some students who supposedly already have learned the terminal behaviors of the course or unit. Even better, if the course or unit is designed to teach behaviors which will be used out in the *real world* of work and/or social living, then try the tests out on some people who are out in the *real world* and supposedly already have and use the terminal behaviors of the course or unit. This procedure will verify whether or not these students and non-students actually have the terminal behaviors. If they actually have the terminal behaviors, but they don't have some of the entry behaviors or they can't indicate achievement of some of the enabling objectives of the course or unit, maybe this means that those entry behaviors and enabling objectives are not really necessary to achieve the desired terminal behaviors (unless the missing entry behaviors and enabling objectives are scaffolding objectives which can be forgotten after achieving the desired terminal behaviors).

Among most of the systems approaches suggested by other writers, this step of trying out the tests is overlooked. The trying out stage is after the materials have been developed. The problem with this is that once the materials are developed, it becomes harder to make changes which are based on the results of the try out of the tests. As an extreme example, back in the early 1960's, an aircraft company was in the process of changing from aircraft to missiles and the training staff developed programmed instructional units for the engineers to help them learn the necessary skills to make the transition. Although they gave a pretest before the engineers started on the programmed materials, the training staff was primarily concerned with the effectiveness of the materials they had developed rather than with where the trainees were at the beginning of the training. After the trainees finished the programmed materials, the training staff gave and scored the posttest and found that almost every trainee scored over 90 percent. Elated, the training staff ordered the printing and production of the programmed materials. Several months later, one of the staff took the time to score the pretests and found that most scores were over 80 percent. In other words, almost all of the work in the development of the programmed materials was actually not necessary. By trying out the pre-entry test, pretest, and posttest first before any materials are developed, a lot of time, effort and money can be saved in addition to developing more effective and efficient materials.

Whatever the results of trying out the tests happens to be, it will probably necessitate some changes in the objectives and tests developed during the first six steps of the behavioral analysis. These changes should be made before going on into the second stage in the development of the learning environment: the synthesis of the instructional event. All of this testing, juggling of objectives, and need for branching appears to be (and is) a lot of work. But it is very critical for successful instruction on an individual basis. Of some consolation, it should be remembered that much of the work is necessary because of the traditional approach to education in which time is the measurement of learning and is kept constant almost regardless of the actual intent to be learned, i.e., two years of English, three years of science, elementary school is six years, etc. Once learning becomes the emphasis regardless of time, the terminal behaviors of one course will become the entry behaviors of the next course and no student will finish one course until he or she is ready to start the next course. Instead of students having a homogeneous time to start a course regardless of the heterogeneous differences in their learning levels, the students will be starting courses and units at different times but at homogeneous levels with reference to the course or unit content. In other words, at the present time teachers know when their students will start and stop their courses, but they don't know what the learning levels of the students are when they start or stop the courses. Under the Behavioral Learning Systems Concept, the teachers won't know when the students will be starting or stopping their courses, but they will know as *a minimum* the learning levels of the students when they start a course and when they finish a course. (See Figure 71).

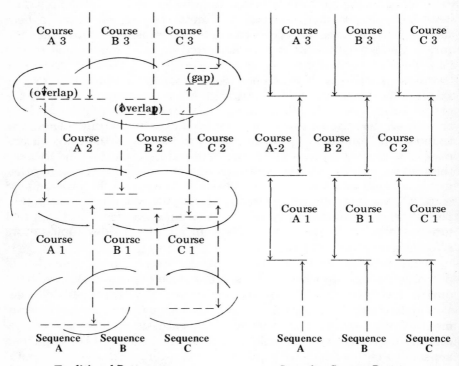

Traditional Patterns

Typified by obscure entry and terminal course behaviors permitting gaps and overlaps in the sequence of courses, but the entering and learning time is the same for all students in each course.

Learning System Patterns

Typified by defined entry and terminal course behaviors such that the terminal behaviors of one course are the same as the entry behaviors of the next course, but the entering and learning time for each course is different for each student.

Figure 71 — Patterns of Course Sequences

710

Under the present traditional approach where the emphasis is on presenting course content for a specified period of time (a quarter, semester, etc.), teachers have had to make their presentations and coverage of the course content fit the time slot. In some cases, the teachers had to trim important content in order to fit the time slot which is a detriment to the course. In other cases, the teachers had to pad a course in order to fill up the time slot which generally also became a detriment to the course. It is virutally impossible that all courses can be covered in the same amount of time. In changing over to the Behavioral Learning Systems Approach, it should not be surprising to find the average time taken by students to achieve the terminal behaviors of their courses to be very different from the traditional time slots. Some courses may be learned in an average of 8 weeks and some may be learned in an average of 47 weeks and be better courses because important objectives were not trimmed off to fit a time slot or useless make-work objectives added to fit a time slot.

Most remedial and compensatory courses are supposedly designed to bring students who are really lacking critical entry behaviors for certain courses up to levels such that they are more homogeneous with other students starting these certain courses. The problems are that the entry behaviors for the certain courses have not been specifically identified so the teachers of the remedial and compensatory courses are not able to specify the terminal behaviors of their courses. In addition, most remedial and compensatory courses are taught in a traditional manner, keeping time and course content constant regardless of individual differences and needs. Because the word *remedial* tends to elicit a meaning in most people that it is the students who need to be remedied instead of the ineffective instructional environment the students were in, many students lose their motivation to learn as soon as they find themselves assigned to a remedial class. By placing the blame where it belongs, by calling these classes *developmental* (developing the student from where ever he or she is), and by truly individualizing these classes, it would be possible for these classes to be very effecitve. However, in order to individualize the courses, it would be necessary to identify the necessary entry behaviors for the regular courses and then do extensive diagnostic testing with the students to identify all of the cumulative ignorance that might cause the students trouble in the regular courses. It is critical that the teachers of these *developmental* courses be instructioneers rather than presenters of course content. Under the Learning Systems Approach, students in these *developmental* courses would do a lot of branching, would use a variety of materials, and would complete their need for the *developmental* course at different times.

Another area where there is a critical need for the use of diagnostic pre-entry pretests, and posttests is in adult or continuing education because of the extreme heterogeneity of the students in what they bring to a course in terms of their entry behavior, what they already know about the course, and what they may actually want to take as terminal behaviors from the course. At the present time, most adult education programs avoid giving any tests because the use of tests creates psychological problems for the adult students and they drop out of the courses even faster than usual. As it is, adult education courses already have a reputation of having a high drop out rate. The ironic aspect of the problem is that the reasons for the high drop out rate could be positively affected by the use of diagnostic tests. The major problem is that most adult education courses are taught in the traditional manner (without tests and homework which are thought to be negative) which ignores the extreme individual differences and adult students are not as willing as younger students to be bored by the gaps and overlaps in the learning process. Their time and energy is too valuable. The problem with tests is that traditionally tests are used to punish and to let a student know what he or she doesn't know and to give the teacher evidence to grade the student down or to fail the student regardless of actual student learning. (Remember, traditional tests are usually designed to give certain results and because of the lack of SO's, they may or may not have any relationship with the implied objectives of the course.)

If tests were used in a diagnostic sense to help identify student learning problems which would be solved such that the students would have successes in learning, the adult student would not be afraid of taking tests. By using lists of terminal behaviors which could be learned in a course, the adult student could pick those he or she wanted to learn and not have to learn all the rest of the SO's unless the adult student wanted to take the course for credit or as a prerequisite for another course in which case, the minimum common core of SO's would have to be learned plus whatever else the student wanted. If adult education courses were taught in an individualized manner which recognized the extreme heterogeneity of adult students, the high drop out rate would be eliminated.

Some adult students sign up for courses in order to meet other people and to get out of their environment for a few hours and they really don't want to learn anything specific. Since courses which are taught in an individualized manner minimize or eliminate group learning, a critical part of adult education efforts should include the Scholarship Sessions in which there are no tests, no objectives, no grades, and no registration or required attendance. These Scholarship Sessions could be used as a motivational take off point or base for a series of designed instructional units. Those adults who only wanted the group meetings would just not sign up for the instructional units.

712

2. THE INSTRUCTIONAL PROCESS: A FORM OF COMMUNICATION

If as a teacher, you are concerned with either chance education or designed instruction, you have to be concerned with the concept of communication. Depending upon your purpose, you may be concerned with any one of the four basic levels of communication. The most basic level of communication is the independent level in which a person is concerned with communicating to himself or herself and is not concerned about anyone else. Everyone uses this level when they talk to themselves. This level of communication can be completely internalized such that no one can observe the evidence of its occurrence; it could be partially external (non-verbal) in that others could observe external evidence of internal communication, i.e., body movement, lip movement, etc.; or it could be partially external (verbal) in that others could hear actual words being spoken. Most of us have had the experience of talking out loud to ourselves.

A second level of communication is essentially the same level of self communication except at this level there is a need for the physical presence of one or more other people. There is no purpose in the communication as far as the other person or persons are concerned. The emphasis is still on the person doing the communicating. Typical of this level of communication is when two or more people are talking simultaneously without either one being aware that the others are talking. During extremes in weather, it is common for someone to come into a building and if anyone is there, the person will comment on the weather. It isn't necessary that the other person answers the comment or even acknowledges that the comment was heard. The person making the comment just had to relieve his or her feelings about the extreme weather, but in the presence of other living human beings. This level of communication is also represented by situations in which the people observing the person doing the communicating say, *He just likes to hear himself talk.* Sad to say, in some traditional educational situations, teachers who are lecturing fall into this level of communication in which they wouldn't give their lecture to an empty classroom or lecture hall, but as long as some students are there, the lecture is given regardless of any effect on the students. The same problem is found in some religious meetings in which the speaker is more concerned about how he or she looks and sounds to himself or herself than how he or she looks and sounds to the people listening or what effects he or she is having on the audience.

A third level of communication involves not only the need for one or more other people, but a purpose for the communication in which the person communicating is trying to have some affect on the people

713

receiving the communication. The distinguishing feature of this level of communication is that the affects the communicator wants to have on the receivers have not been specified to the point where the communicator can tell whether or not the affects actually occurred. Because the affects are not identifiable, the emphasis and efforts in trying to improve the communication event at this level are concerned with the communicator and what the communicator does. If there is some form of technology utilized in the communication, then the emphasis and efforts in trying to improve the communication event at this level could be concerned with the technology and how it is used. In other words, at this level of communication, the content, method, or vehicle for the communication becomes the objective of the communication rather than the non-specified affects of the communication event. In educational situations where the communicator is convinced that the ability to learn is all genetic and there is nothing that the communicator can do to affect the students achievement, the emphasis and efforts to improve the communication event are again concentrated on the communicator or the content, method, or vehicle for the communication without regard to the affects on the learners.

In a situation where there is a purpose in the communication event, but the purpose is not specific enough to be observable and measurable and the communicator and/or the content, method, or vehicle for the communication becomes the purpose, it is very possible for the *medium to become the message* as McLuhan has suggested. In these situations, the real message affecting the receivers is generally a hidden message being communicated by the educational environment. For example, it is common in educational situations to communicate that learning is not as important as other things. After all, the learning hasn't been specified but the other things have, i.e., attending classes regardless of whether or not learning occurred; sit quietly regardless of whether or not learning occurred; ask the questions the teacher wants (so the teacher appears smart) regardless of whether or not learning occurred; give the teacher the answers the teacher wants (agree with the teacher's opinions) regardless of whether or not learning occurred; dress and act correctly according to teacher and administrators regardless of whether or not learning occurred; etc.

These three levels of communication are actually taught in courses which are considered to be concerned with communication. For example, in many art, drama, and some *mod* English composition courses, the emphasis is on the medium and/or the one doing the communicating rather than on the receivers of the communication. Although the students may be aware of what they are communicating to themselves or possibly to their teachers, rarely are they taught to be aware of what they are communicating to potential receivers of their communications.

714

The fourth level of communication is where the purpose of the communication event has been specified in terms of the affects on the receivers of the communication and the objective is to bring about the desired affects in all of the receivers or at least as many as possible (90 percent or more). If one doesn't really care whether or not the receivers achieve the desired affects of the communications, then almost anything goes in a communication event. However, the more concerned a person is that the receivers of a communication are affected in certain ways, the more concerned the person should be about that level of communication which is evaluated on the basis of whether or not the receivers were affected. When the emphasis changes from the medium, content, or vehicle for communication to the results of the communication as they affect the behavior of the receivers or learners, then the whole analysis or study of the communication process has to be viewed from the point-of-view of the affects on the receivers or learners.

Because the purpose of the fourth level of communication is to have an observable affect on the receivers of the communication, it becomes necessary to evaluate whether or not the observable affects occurred. Whereas the emphasis in any evaluation in the third level of communication is on arriving at some resultant score and recording it as the end of the process, evaluation in the fourth level is used as diagnostic information or feedback which in turn is used to make whatever changes in the process that will help more learners learn more. This same contrast between the third and fourth levels of communication is the same as the contrast between education and designed instruction and the contrast between the study of the content, method, or vehicle of education (a non-science study of man-made phenomenon) and the study of learning of SO's (a scientific study of a natural phenomenon). The process of trying to improve the communication event at the fourth level can be thought of as a continum of fidelity. At one end of the continum, the communication event is so well designed that the meanings for the communication event held by the communicator exactly match those held by the receivers of the communication and all of the affects on the receivers which were desired by the communicator actually occurred. At the other end of the continum, the communication event is so badly designed that the meanings for the communication event held by the communicator have little, if any, coincidence with the meanings held by the receivers of the communication and none of the affects on the receivers which were desired by the communicator actually occurred. In between these two extremes are a wide variety of levels of fidelity of meaning in the communication event.

In reference to *meanings*, it is critical to realize that *meanings* are in people. Words, visuals, sounds, tastes, texture, etc., do not have or carry meanings except as the person perceiving them may have *meanings!* Teachers who believe that everyone has the same *meanings* for the same perceptions are involved in what is called *syntactic communication.* These teachers usually utilize the third level of communication in which they assume by their actions that all students learn the same way and any differences in achievement are genetic or external to the teaching-learning situation. Teachers who believe that different people may have different meanings for the same perceptions are involved in what is called *semantic communication.* These teachers realize that there are two types of meanings which contribute to the differences in meanings held by different people for the same perceptions. The first type of meaning is *denotative* meaning which refers to a meaning held in common by most of the people in a given vocational, social, or cultural group for a particular perception. The second type of meaning is *connotative meaning* which refers to the personal meaning an individual may have for a particular perception and is based on personal experiences of the individual. For example, most people who speak English will have a denotative meaning for the word *ball* as being something spherical. However, because of personal interests and experiences, some people may add different connotative meanings to this meaning for the word *ball.* Some may be thinking of football, baseball, a ball (dancing), or *having a ball* etc.

Because *meanings* are in people, in order to try to improve the fidelity of a communication event, a teacher has to be concerned with the observable affects of the communication and infer from these affects as to the fidelity of the meanings held by the communicator and the receivers of the communication. Teachers who believe that different people may have different meanings for the same perceptions and believe that these meanings can only be identified practically by observing the affects of the communication in terms of the behaviors of the receivers are involved in what I shall call *pragmatic communication.* Although in both semantic and pragmatic communication the teachers are aware of differences in meanings held by different students, in semantic communication, the observable behavioral differences have not been specified and hence cannot be identified. As a result, in semantic communication, any evaluation of student achievement is based on subjective criteria which is more strongly affected by interpersonal conflict or congruence between the teacher and students than by the actual fidelity of the communication event.

In contrast, in pragmatic communication, the desired observable behavioral differences have been identified and specified and evaluation of student achievement is based on objective criteria (not the so-called objective type tests which are really very subjectively written) which minimizes and hopefully eliminates the affects on learning of interpersonal conflict between teacher and student and represents more accurately the fidelity of the communication (instructional) event.

In developing instructional materials or the instructional environment at the fourth level of communication in a pragmatic sense, the instructioneer will evaluate the results of students using the materials or being in the environment. Non-achievement of the desired results is looked on as a learning problem which can be solved by a re-analysis of the learner and the learning environment and then a re-design of the learning environment. This action philosophy is in contrast to the traditional approach which blames non-achievement (non-communication) on genetics and outside factors which cannot be affected by the teacher which is a *do-nothing* philosophy.

In viewing the instructional event as a communication event, the interrelationships among the five elements (the learner, the instructioneer, the objectives, the evaluation, and the learning environment) critically affect the efficiency and effectiveness of the event. In looking at these relationships and how they affect the elements, it is convenient to think of the communications event as consisting of only four elements (see Figure 72).

Instructioneer — Instructional — Instructional
  Teacher   Intent   Environment —   Learner
              (Objectives and
               evaluation)

Figure 72 — The Instructional Event as a Communication Event

Since meanings are in people and are developed by their experiences and since no two people have had the same experiences, it follows that no two people have exactly the same meanings. As a result, if the Instructional Environment was designed from the point-of-view of the teacher, the fidelity of the communication event will be less than if the instructional environment was designed from the point-of-view of the learner. In order to maximize the fidelity of the event, it is necessary to design the instructional event from the point-of-view of meanings held by the learner. What this means is that the instructional environment should reflect the communication skills, the intellectual skills, the sensory skills, and the attitudes and values of the learner. A common misunderstanding is that a learner-oriented environment is frequently defined as a situation where the learner controls everything including the setting of objectives. Obviously, in a situation like this, there would be no need for a teacher, no need for schools, and no need for design except as the learner may design his or her own learning. However, in a learner-oriented (designed) instructional environment, the teacher sets up the objectives and matching evaluation and then designs the environment to maximize the fidelity of the communication and to maximize the achievement of the objectives by each learner. However, in viewing the instructional event as a communication process governed by the instructional philosophy (pp. 91-101, Volume I) and guided by the theories of instruction (pp. 101-120, Volume I) there are at least six elements and in case of non-achievement, cyclic repetition of five of the elements until the intent of the instructional event is achieved (see Figure 73).

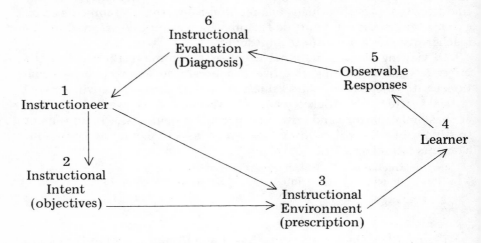

Figure 73 — The Instructional Event as a Communication Process

In the traditional teaching event, the objectives are aimed at what the teacher should do, the environment is designed for the teacher, and any diagnosis of the event concerns what the teacher did or didn't do. The learner and learning is there, but is considered to be more affected by outside factors than by anything the teacher can do. As such, the traditional event is at the third level of communication and is linear (no repetition). Teachers use communication skills they are familiar with and assume their meanings are what is important. They also use intellectual and sensory skills and attitudes and values which reflect the teacher's influence more than the learners influence. As should be expected, the fidelity is low and consequently achievement is varied and proportionate to the level of fidelity. For example, in a traditional teaching event, it is acceptable for the teacher to use a language which is completely foreign to the students. Whereas in a communication event, in order to maximize fidelity, the instructional environment has to utilize a language the learner understands which in turn increases achievement.

NOTE: As this book went to press, the Supreme Court finally ruled that students who speak a language different from classroom English have a right to learn in a bi-lingual environment. During past decades, millions of students who spoke a language or dialect other than classroom English were considered to be genetically incapable of learning — after all, they scored low in all of the English IQ tests! It is utterly fantastic that after all these years of teaching and research in teaching carried on by millions of intelligent teachers and educational psychologists that it took the Supreme Court to tell us that if a teacher teaches a student in a language the student understands that the student might learn better than when a teacher teaches a student in a language the student doesn't understand. [33] Many traditional schools are now interpreting the ruling as being limited by whether or not they have bi-lingual teachers and by whether or not there are enough students with the same language problems to make up a class. This interpretation is based on the assumption that learning has to take place in classes and only from live bi-lingual teachers. There is no reason why the instructional environment can not be designed to reflect the individuals language whatever it is. A teacher as an instructioneer could handle a number of students who each speak a different language as long as the instructional environment is individualized and reflects each student's language needs. The teacher doesn't need to be proficient in all languages, he or she only needs to know enough of each language to diagnose and prescribe. However, in cases of learning problems where there are no solutions available, it would be difficult to solve a problem and to develop a prescription if the teacher was not proficient in the language of the student (or didn't have an interpreter available).

a. THE LEARNER'S ENVIRONMENT AS A FACTOR IN COMMUNICATION

It should be very obvious that the communication skills necessary to learn from the designed instructional environment should reflect those of the learner. It may not be so obvious that other factors which reflect the learner's personal environment may also affect learning. One of the most critical of these factors is whether or not the student will even pay attention to the instructional event. If the student doesn't

---

[33] Just a year before the Supreme Court action, the legislative body in Massachusetts ruled essentially the same concept which affected about 40,000 students in Boston schools alone. In other states where the bilingual problem was even more severe than in Massachussetts, educators were still experimenting with the concept and not quite accepting the fact that non-English speaking students can learn as well as anyone else if the instructional environment reflects their language rather than the teachers' language.

perceive the message of the instructional event, the student won't receive the message and consequently won't achieve the objectives of the instructional event. A student's attention is closely associated with a filtering mechanism which controls which messages get through. In *Future Shock,* Toffler reported that the average adult is assulted by a minimum of 560 advertising messages everyday. Of these 560 messages, the adult only pays attention to 76. A person's filtering mechanism uses a variety of criteria for filtering. The most common filtering criteria concerns whether or not the person is personally interested in the content of the message. This is why some teachers try to get students' attention by letting them do *their own thing* regardless of learning. For most SO's, it is possible to vary the vehicle for learning in order to get attention without changing the SO's. For example, in learning to identify a particular literary technique, there are a variety of authors who write on different topics who may use the technique (if not, then the technique is not significant enough to be singled out to be identified). By matching up the student's high interest with an appropriate author and topic, it would be much easier to gain the student's attention without changing the SO. Theoretically, it should be possible to have 30 different students learning the same SO from 30 different vehicles. It is important to remember that although the teacher knows best which SO's should be learned in a particular course, the student knows best what he or she is interested in and how he or she learns best. Students can and should be involved in deciding the vehicles for learning the teacher-set SO's.

NOTE: Because most students watch a lot of television, some English teachers have found that the scripts of television shows have a high interest value and can be used to teach a variety of literary concepts to students who normally *tune-out* from the learning messages in the traditional classroom using classic literary works.

All too often in the traditional classroom, the vehicle for learning becomes the objective and as such the vehicle can't be varied without changing the objectives. In addition to interest as a factor in attracting attention, many people, particularly the so-called disadvantaged, include in their filtering criteria the probability of whether or not the content of the message is *obtainable* or *achievable*. The lower the probability of obtaining or achieving the content of the message, the greater the probability that the message will be filtered out. Students who have had a series of negative experiences in learning begin to filter out messages concerning learning because they don't believe they could learn it anyway so why pay attention. This is why it is necessary to utilize the mastery concept wherein the student learns 100 percent of all objectives in a unit before going on to the next unit. As cumulative ignorance increases, the probability for achievement of subsequent SO's is decreased and the probability of the learning message being filtered out is increased. Students who are consistently "D" and "F" students finally *tune out* all learning messages and leave school. In order to rebuild a students self confidence which has been destroyed by non-achievement, it may be necessary to utilize very short instructional units with only one or two SO's. As a student's perceived probability of achievement increases, the probability of learning messages being filtered out is decreased.

As self confidence increases, *adaptive perception* occurs in which a persistent abnormal condition becomes the normal condition:[34] the easy to learn becomes obvious; the difficult to learn becomes normal; and the impossible to learn becomes only difficult. In reverse, as self-confidence is destroyed and the probability for achievement decreases: the obvious or assumed learning may still be easy to learn; the normal learning becomes difficult to learn; and the difficult learning becomes impossible.

Even after a student has decided to pay attention, there are social and cultural factors which may affect learning. If the instructional environment contains social and/or cultural factors that are in conflict with the student's personal environment, the learning message may be filtered out. For example, a student who is accustomed to passive learning in front of a live teacher in a formal environment may find it difficult to learn independently and actively in an informal environment. As such the student may have to be weaned from dependence on the teacher and from the formal environment before the student will be able to learn successfully on an independent basis in an informal environment. In some cultural groups, a younger person never questions an older person and particularly a teacher. Yet, in some of our traditional classrooms, students are evaluated negatively if they don't participate in discussions by asking questions.

After a student has decided to pay attention and has followed through the instructional environment, the student is expected to respond in certain ways which in turn is used to evaluate whether or not the student achieved the desired objectives of the instructional event. Although the communication in the SO's and in the instructional environment may indicate specific responses, the student's reactions to the instructional environment are also affected by three factors from the students past personal environment; prior experiences with other similar situations, personal psychic needs of the student, and the social

---

[34] In the fall, when the temperature drops to just above freezing it is subjectively interpreted as being very cold. By spring, when the temperature raises up to just above freezing, it is subjectively interpreted as being almost warm — shirt sleeve weather.

and cultural modes of response considered acceptable, allowable, and not acceptable. For example, if successful achievement of a unit before the majority of a class has achieved that unit results in the teacher giving the student busy work to fill in the spare time, some students may learn not to learn to fast. In another situation, a student may not indicate achievement because non-achievement results in personal attention and the student's psyche needs the personal attention of the teacher. The third factor is exemplified by peer group situations in which it is the *in thing* not to learn and a student may make a wrong response to maintain an image in his or her peer group even though the student may have actually achieved the desired objectives.

As indicated by the theories of instruction, unless the learner has unique characterisitcs which point to specific instructional environments for successful learning, the instructioneer starts out with that instructional environment that seems to be the most successful with the most students. After the evaluation or diagnosis, the students who didn't achieve are cycled to the next best instructional environment. This process is repeated until either the desired learning occurs or the instructioneer runs out of prepared materials or alternate instructional environments. Then the instructioneer may have to solve the learning problem by developing new learning pathways.

In solving most learning problems in the instructional environment, there are five options an instructioneer can use; try different available pathways (same SO's); change or improve existing materials to fit the learner (same SO's); develop a new instructional environment which will be more appropriate for the learner having the problem (without changing the SO's); develop alternate instructional environments which are designed to teach the learner the abilities necessary to learn from the existing instructional environments in which the learner encountered the original problem; or a combination of a little of each of these approaches.

Until instructional research has been done to identify the best instructional environment for the most students for any given course, it will be most practical to use whatever materials are easily available. These tend to be verbal materials in the form of textbooks or instructional pamphlets or booklets. The next most available form of instructional materials consist of audio or video tape recordings of on-going teacher presentations. Most AV or TV technical specialists don't like to use tapes that are not technically correct and that don't utilize the fullest capability of the medium. However if students can learn from the teachers live on-going presentations, they can also learn from the recorded on-going presentations. As learning problems are identified, the tapes can be edited and changed to solve learning problems rather than being changed to be technically perfect. The time deemed necessary by the technical specialists to develop *good* (technical) audio and video tapes may discourage teachers from utilizing the medium and may also increase the costs to prohibitive levels.

As a general guideline for solving learning problems, the pyramid in Figure 73a can be used. It is based on the concept that the more concrete the learning experience, the more likely the student will learn the SO's associated with the experience and also, the more input senses that can be involved in the learning experience, the more concrete the learning experience. The top two levels are what might be

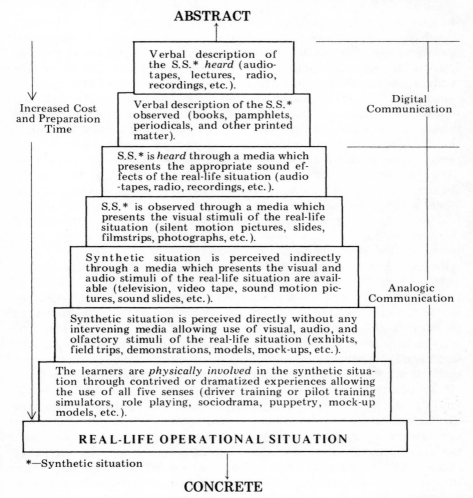

ABSTRACT

Verbal description of the S.S.* *heard* (audio-tapes, lectures, radio, recordings, etc.).

Verbal description of the S.S.* observed (books, pamphlets, periodicals, and other printed matter).

S.S.* is *heard* through a media which presents the appropriate sound effects of the real-life situation (audio-tapes, radio, recordings, etc.).

S.S.* is observed through a media which presents the visual stimuli of the real-life situation (silent motion pictures, slides, filmstrips, photographs, etc.).

Synthetic situation is perceived indirectly through a media which presents the visual and audio stimuli of the real-life situation are available (television, video tape, sound motion pictures, sound slides, etc.).

Synthetic situation is perceived directly without any intervening media allowing use of visual, audio, and olfactory stimuli of the real-life situation (exhibits, field trips, demonstrations, models, mock-ups, etc.).

The learners are *physically involved* in the synthetic situation through contrived or dramatized experiences allowing the use of all five senses (driver training or pilot training simulators, role playing, sociodrama, puppetry, mock-up models, etc.).

REAL-LIFE OPERATIONAL SITUATION

Increased Cost and Preparation Time

Digital Communication

Analogic Communication

*—Synthetic situation

CONCRETE

Figure 73a — Abstract-Concrete Continuum as a Guide in Solving Learning Problems

723

called *digital communication* because they utilize primarily verbal communication. The other levels utilize a variety of modes of communication and might be referred to as *analogic communication*. Although it may be easier for learning to occur as one utilizes learning materials from the more concrete levels, the more concrete the learning experiences, the more costly and time consuming it is to develop the materials.

3. BEHAVIORAL SYNTHESIS: CONSTRUCTION OF THE INSTRUCTIONAL EVENT

The development of the traditional educational event is primarily based on what the teacher is supposed to *cover* during a course and centers around the teacher's presentations of whatever is to be *covered*. If there are any statements associated with the event which concern student learning or *outcomes*, these statements are GO's and as such are non-measurable. If the traditional educational event is evaluated, the evaluation primarily concerns the teacher and what the teacher does during the event. Because student learning in the traditional educational event is considered to be primarily affected by genetics and the students' external (from the school) environment, such that there is very little teachers and school environment can do to change the results, evaluation of student learning usually occurs at the end of the educational event and is designed to produce the results the teachers expect, i.e., a curve of grades. During the process, all of the educational malpractices described in my book *Educational Malpractices* are perpetrated on the students to the detriment of their learning and to their self-image and ultimately negatively affecting their entire lives. The students who did make it through the educational system and went on to greatness were and are a monument to the persistance and ingenuity of the students to learn in spite of the traditional educational event and to a few of their teachers who were able to inspire and help them and who in turn were also able to learn *teaching as an art* in spite of the traditional teacher training programs (elementary and secondary levels) or the lack of any teacher training programs at all (higher education).

The current trends in the development of the educational event tend to be divergent in their approach, but unified in their emphasis on the learner rather than on the teacher. Although there are numerous innovations to be found in the current educational scene, they tend to fall into two groups which are in conflict with one another such that excesses in one group are matched by excesses in the other group. With the advent of programmed instruction, industrial systems analysis and accountability, a growing group of pseudo-behaviorist educators got on the bandwagon of having SO's. In this movement, there is no room for GO's because they are nonmeasurable. As a result, the SO's had to stand or fall by themselves. Frequently, because the interrelationships between the SO's were missing (which would have been represented by the GO's), many SO's were trivial, represented rote memory, and didn't lead anywhere. The justification or evaluation of the SO's was and is concerned with the degree of measurability and whether or not the SO's contained the three critical parts: a statement of the conditions of the learning event, a verb denoting the behavior to be demonstrated, and the criteria for evaluating the performance of the behavior. As such, the concern was more for quantity than for quality.

As this last group started making an impact on the educational scene, a counter group of pseudo-humanist educators started developing and got on the bandwagon of *do your own thing* with no GO's or SO's for student learning. Although most of the more vocal defenders of this approach concentrated their defensive statements on the narrowness and triviality of the SO approach and the openness and humaneness of the *do your own thing* approach, the basic issue concerned the quality of learning in the educational event (which they wanted) and being held accountable for the quantity of learning in the educational event (which they didn't want). However, in avoiding any measurement, not only do the educators in this group avoid being held accountable for the quantity of student learning, they also leave the quality of student learning up to chance and as such *don't make a difference* in student learning which in turn makes the taxpayers reluctant to permit increased spending of educational dollars for higher teacher salaries, and supposedly *improved* learning environments where the *improvement* is based on subjective opinions rather than on objective evidence of results.

As these two groups argue over their differences, they and others overlook their similarities. Both groups are concerned with the learner which is a good change from the emphasis on the teacher and both groups have allowed the means for achieving their objectives or goals to become their objectives. In other words, the first group is more concerned with the importance of having measurable quantity (the SO's) than they are with what the SO's help the students achieve (the GO's) and the second group is more concerned with avoiding measurement and the importance of non-measurable quality (do your own thing) than they are with what the non-directed environment helps students to achieve (by chance). For example, in curriculum projects using SO's and programmed instruction or SO's and almost any other individualized sets of materials, the emphasis is on the use of the program or the set of materials rather than on what the students are learning as a result of using the program or the set of materials. As such, the vehicles for quantifiable learning have become the objective of the learning environment. In classrooms and schools where the emphasis is on the students' *doing your own thing*, the emphasis is on the openness and non-direct-edness of the environment rather than on what the students are learning as a result of being in the open and non-directed environment. Again, the vehicles for qualitative learning have become the objectives of the learning environment. Therefore, both groups fall back into one of the traditional pedogogical conflicts in which they are both saying that students are individually different but by their actions, they are saying that all students learn best the same way.

In the development of the instructional environment under the behavioral learning systems approach as described in this book, the two most important rules to remember are:

— No one method or vehicle for learning will be appropriate and best for all students.

— Don't let any one method or vehicle become the objective of the instructional environment.

Given that there are at least 80 different learning variables which can affect an individual student's learning, the chances of anyone develop-ing a particular vehicle for learning that will be perfect even for one individual student, let alone, for a mixed group of students, are so miniscule as to be practically impossible. Therefore, every learning pathway is in effect a compromise and less effective and efficient than the ideal pathway for any one student or group of students. As such, no one learning pathway should be considered as ideal, perfect, or as the objective of an instructional event. The best learning pathway or combination of pathways for any student is the one or ones (among those available) that works more effectively and more efficiently for that student than other available pathways or combinations of path-ways. For example, if a particular student learns more of whatever he or she is supposed to learn in a closed environment in which a single pathway or combination of pathways are used, than the student should be able to learn that way. If yet another student learns more of whatever he or she is supposed to learn in an environment which is developed in conflict with most or all of the guidelines set forth in this chapter, then the student should be able to learn that way. As should be obvious, learning is the emphasis and not the vehicle for learning. However, in order for learning to become the emphasis, the desired learning has to be identified in terms of objectives. As pointed out in the last chapter, the GO's represent what is really wanted in each of the three domains of learning and the SO's just happen to be the only way one can infer that the GO's are being achieved. In this way, the SO's promote the measurement and accountability for learning and the associated GO's and the process of justifying the inclusion of the SO's promote the quality of learning.

Efforts in this direction can be seen by the growing trend of allowing students to test out of courses on the basis of demonstrated proficiency rather than demanding the completion of a specific amount of time and the use of a particular method (usually sitting in a classroom in fornt of a live teacher). The major drawback to these efforts is that the proficiency tests are not developed from any agreed upon list of GO's and SO's and so the achievement or passing of the proficiency tests is not definable in terms of identified learning. In fact, most of the proficiency tests being used are primarily made up of the so-called objective type test items (multiple choice, true-false, and matching) which are easy to score or grade, but are not matched to any known SO's and are subject to all of the insidious practices found in standardized testing as described in the last chapter. Also, passing of these proficiency tests is not at the 100 percent or mastery level. Therefore, students taking these tests are allowed to miss a random percentage of items, i.e., if 70 percent is passing, the students can miss any 30 percent. If the concept of proficiency tests was tied to an identified and agreed upon minimum common core list of GO's and SO's, the test items were matched to the SO's, and in order to pass the test, the student had to achieve 100 percent of all the SO's or test items, then the concept would be in agreement with the concepts put forth in this book and would be a giant step forward for designed humanized instruction.

Another effort in the direction suggested in this book are the attempts to identify a student's *cognitive style* of learning and then matching the student with certain learning pathways which utilize that particular *cognitive style*. Externally, the idea sounds great. However, in those schools that are experimenting with the concept, most of them keep time as a constant; allow less than the mastery level of learning; are not based on GO's, SO's, and matching tests; and the method tends to become the objective of the program rather than learning.

As the present time, because students learn *how to learn* in a random fashion and generally they learn *how to learn* before they ever start school, there are too many variables to take into consideration to suggest any one pathway or method as being the preferred or best way. The only possible solution to the problem is the use of a process that has built into it maximum flexibility such that almost any pathway ,or method can be used and justified as long as it actually helps a student learn more of whatever he or she is supposed to learn. Under this approach, non-achievement is looked on as a learning environment problem which we may or may not be able to solve due to the primitive state of the science of designed instruction. Non-achievement is not looked on as a genetic student problem which can't be solved.

a. INSTRUCTIONAL MODELS: THEORIES OF LEARNING vs. THEORIES OF TEACHING vs. THEORIES OF INSTRUCTION

In a learning event, there are at least three parts which can be studied: the environment which involves and precedes the learning event; the learning event; and the consequences of the learning event. Theories of learning concern one or more of these parts and tend to be based on non-observable occurrences within the learner. As such, most learning theorists could be observing the same identical learning event and would claim that what they were observing supported their particular theory. Since the emphasis in most of these theories is on *learning* and not on learning *something*, the utility of most learning theories in helping teachers help students learn *something* is very minimal. However, assuming that all theories of learning must be based on some elements of truth and observation, then actually all of them must be useful in some instructional situation. Rather than getting involved in long discussions over non-measurable differences among the various learning theories, any theory which can be applied such that the results indicate that the student or students are learning more of what they are supposed to learn should be considered a good theory for those students in learning those particular SO's (which does not mean that it might be a good theory of learning for other students and/or in the learning of other SO's). Conversely, any theory of learning which cannot be applied to an instructional event or when applied does not result in as many students learning as much of what they should be learning as some other theory of learning should be considered as not a very good theory for those students in learning those particular SO's (which does not mean that it might not be a good theory of learning for other students and/or in the learning of other SO's.)

Theories of teaching which are primarily concerned with what teachers do in presenting course content or in managing the classroom and are not directly related to improving the measurable learning of students are *useless* for designed instruction. Theories of teaching which are directly related to improving the measurable learning of students are in reality theories of instruction. Conversely, theories of instruction which are primarily concerned with what teachers do and are not directly related to improving the measurable learning of students are in reality theories of teaching and, as such, are useless for designed instruction.

Because most theories are stated in rather abstract terms and consequently tend to be difficult to define or describe specifically and even more difficult to apply in practical situations, theorists frequently utilize mathematical formulas, flow-charts, and/or models to communicate the theoretical concept more clearly. Because the theories are just theories, it is important to remember that the formulas, flow-charts, and models are just a way of looking at a particular process. There may be many different ways of looking at any one process. The value in using the formulas, flow-charts, and models is to improve and clarify the communication of the theory. If a particular formula, flow-chart, or model doesn't improve and/or clarify the communication of the theory, this doesn't mean that the theory is bad, it means that the selection of the particular formula, flow-chart, or model was not very appropriate to use in communicating the theory. Frequently, people will identify negative aspects of a formula, flow-chart, or model and apply these to the theory to *prove* that the theory is wrong. Others may select a particular model which has positive or negative aspects and use it to *prove* a particular theory is right or wrong. The rightness or wrongness of a model should relate to the ability of the model to affect communication of the theory rather than to the subjective rightness or wrongness of certain aspects of the model itself.

Many people have looked at the traditional education process and likened it to what happens in some industrial factory. These people view the process from the point-of-view of inputs and outputs wherein children start school at a certain age and most of them finish school at about the same age. In between the starting and finishing of school, about the same things happen to all students (as if it were a factory). The mistake in applying the industrial model to education is that it fits what teachers do and the parallel can be drawn between the teachers doing the same things to all students and factory workers doing the same things to the products in the factory, but the model is inappropriate in reference to the product. In the factory, the products come out the same. In a school, if learning is our product, no two students (let alone a whole class of students) come out with the same learning. Intellectually, emotionally, and sensorably the students are never the same at the beginning of school, at the end of schooling, nor at any point inbetween. From the point-of-view of the product of the educational process which should be learning, the industrial model doesn't fit. However, from the point-of-view of schools being for teachers and where the emphasis is on what teachers do instead of on what learners are learning, the industrial model could be seen as appropriate. As such, anyone who draws on the analogy of the industrial model as applying to the educational process is also revealing that they view the educational process in the traditional sense where the emphasis is on teachers and teaching. An emphasis on the negative aspects of the industrial model reveals that the person (if an educator) is bored teaching the same courses in the same way year after year, of course, the solution for teachers who think of their job as fitting the industrial model is to change their role. Instead of teaching *courses to students*, they should become instructioneers and teach *students* whatever it is they need from *courses*.

During the past fifteen years during which I developed the ideas and concepts contained in this series, I have frequently and consistently used various aspects of what could be called the *medical* model to illustrate my ideas of what the instructional process should be like. Although the medical model is not appropriate in all aspects of the medical process in comparison with the instructional process, it is very appropriate in those aspects in which the industrial model is inappropriate, i.e., recognition of individual differences, open entry and open exit, solving of patient problems, an emphasis on getting the patient *well* (mastery learning). In the medical world, the recognition of individual differences affects the type and length of treatment. These individual differences are identified by diagnostic procedures which always precede the treatment and are used to identify the appropriate treatment. In the industrial model like traditional education, the treatments are given first and for the same length of time. Diagnostic procedures (inspections) in the industrial model occur after the treatment and products not fitting the quality control standards are rejected (in traditional schools, they are *pushed out* or called *drop outs*).[35]

In the medical model, patients start whenever medical services are needed and are considered ready to leave whenever the medical services are no longer needed. A patient who is in need of a treatment at other times of the year is not told to come back September 1st as that is when that treatment is given. Nor does the patient have to take the treatment for a specific length of time regardless of the needs of the patient. However, it is common in traditional education for students to have to wait months and even a year or more because certain courses are only offered at certain times. Similarly, in the industrial model, certain products may be produced only at certain times and only when there is a sufficient demand for the product.

When instruction is individualized, the students in any one classroom may all be involved at different places in the same subject or they may be involved in a variety of subjects. In the medical model, if one were to visit any particular hospital ward, the patients might be at all different stages of the same or similar treatments or they could be

---

[35] Where the industrial model doesn't fit the traditional educational process is in the quality control concept. In industry, quality control is often defined in terms of achieving the desired specifications with *zero defect* (mastery level of learning), whereas in traditional education, there are no specifications (SO's) and the quality control of *passing* is anything above about 60 percent achievement which does not represent very high quality. Also, the emphasis in industry is on maximizing the number of products with *zero defect*, whereas tests in traditional education are designed to eliminate some of the students.

involved in a wide variety of treatments for the same or different problems. One of the first questions raised by teachers when they think of individualizing instruction is *How can I have two or more things going on at the same time?* If the teacher is the only one who can give the instructional treatment, then it is difficult to have two or more things going on simultaneously because teachers only have one mouth. However, if the teacher allows other things and materials to constitute the treatment, then every student could be learning different things. This would free the teacher from presenting the treatments and allow the teacher to perform the more important humanizing role of solving student problems. The old *one-room school* in some respects illustrates what I mean. In these schools, there were from six to ten grades in the same room. No teacher in these schools ever said, *I'm sorry we can't offer fourth grade this year because there is only one or two students!* Teachers in these schools couldn't be the only presenters of course content in all subjects and at all grade levels. The emphasis was on students learning independently. Teacher presentations were only given to get students started or to solve a common learning problem.

In the medical model, the concept of *getting well* is concerned with bringing the person back to a condition of good health which could be similar to instructional efforts in the affective domain in which we may try to develop or change attitudes, values, and beliefs into acceptable or *good* emotional tendencies. In this aspect, the medical model is not appropriate for cognitive and sensory learning. In the industrial model, a product starts from practically nothing and is increased cumulatively as it goes through the process by achieving an increasing number of the prescribed specifications. This is more like what happens to learners in the cognitive and sensory domains.

In reference to the additional learning that a teacher and/or student may select to be learned above and beyond the minimum common core objectives, neither the medical nor the industrial model fits.

One of the most important applications of the medical model concerns the similarity between the role of the professional doctor and his or her strategy in solving patient problems and the role of the professional teacher (instructioneer) and his or her strategy (theory of instruction) in solving student learning problems. Because there are so many known and unknown variables affecting a patient's health and the process of getting well, it is practially impossible for a doctor to be able to select the perfect treatment for each patient. Therefore, given whatever diagnostic information the doctor can gain from the patient and from various laboratory tests, the doctor selects from available treatments that one that works best under the given conditions for most patients having similar problems. If that doesn't work, then the doctor selects the next best treatment. If that doesn't work, then the doctor selects a third best treatment and continues the process until the patient gets well. If the doctor runs out of treatments, he or she calls in a specialist to help. Doctors accept the fact that no one treatment will work successfully for all patients and just because a patient doesn't get well from one or two treatments doesn't mean that the patient can't get well at all. The doctors philosophy keeps them trying until the patients get well.[36]

In a similar manner, the professional teacher in the role as an instructioneer uses the theories of instruction as described in Chapter IV (Volume I) and develops the same strategy of problem solving. Based on whatever diagnostic information the teacher can get from tests and student interviews (the students can usually tell the teacher how they learn best and what they are interested in most), the teacher can select that treatment that works best in helping similar students learn the same GO's and SO's. If that treatment doesn't work, the teacher selects the next best treatment. If that treatment doesn't work, the teacher continues the process until the required learning occurs or until the teacher runs out of available treatments and has to call in a specialist. The specialists could be specialists in treatments (learning resource centers or subject matter specialists) similar to a pharmacist or they could be specialists in various learning problems (psychologists, reading specialists, etc.) similar to heart specialists, skin specialists, etc. The important concept here is for the instructioneer (like the doctor) to develop a hierarchy of treatments ranging from the one that works best for most students down to ones that work only for certain students who have certain unique problems. Equally as important is to share this information with other teachers who are concerned with teaching the same common core objectives.

A second very important application of the medical model concerns the similarity in procedures followed in reference to the very sick patient and the procedures which should be followed in reference to the student with major learning problems. In the medical model, the sicker a patient is and the more health problems the patient has, the more medical service the patient receives, the more personalized service the patient receives, and the more money that is spent to solve the problems. In most hospitals today, there are intensive care wards for the patients who are critically ill. In the instructional model I am proposing in this book, I would like to see the most help (personal and financial) given to the students with the greatest needs on a proportion-

---

[36] Admittedly, some patients are terminal cases and don't get well, but this is not considered a problem of the patient. The problem is that in the present state of medical science, the doctors don't have available the right treatment for the problem, i.e., getting cured from cancer is not a patient problem, it is a problem for medical research and eventually will be solved.

ate basis. Instead of the classes for slow learners, lower abilities, and mentally retarded where all too often the students are just kept busy because it is assumed they can't learn or the GO's and SO's are so compromised that the students can never get out of these classes. What is needed is an *Instructional Intensive Care Ward!* This does not mean that the gifted or student without learning problems would be forgotten. For most of the students who are gifted or don't have learning problems, the best thing that can be done is to let them go on ahead learning the required GO's and SO's of the next unit or course independently or if the students have already achieved the required learning, let them be independent learners who can learn whatever they want. [37] Although in the traditional educational school, it is common to have teachers rejoice when they are assigned to a gifted class, I have never heard of a doctor who was happy about being assigned to a group of well patients who didn't need his or her services!

In the traditional educational approach the better or faster learning students or the students with the least learning problems frequently had also the best facilities and teachers while the students who had the most problems in learning frequently had the worst facilities and the poorest teachers. At the present time, there are multiple efforts aimed at providing *equal opportunity* for education by trying to equalize the facilities and teachers available for all students. Although this is better than the traditional approach, individual differences among students in the presence of equal facilities and teachers does not result in *equal opportunity for achievement* which is a different concept than just equal opportunity. In order to give *equal opportunity for achievement,* the students who need more help will have to be given more help (personal and financial).

> NOTE: The emphasis on the learner learning on an individual basis does not mean that there will be no group learning. An integral part of an instructional design could very well include objectives which could only be learned in the context of a group. As the students achieved the prerequisite GO's and SO's, they would be put into groups of five or more (whatever size is necessary and/or appropriate) to learn the group learning objectives and then they would continue on an individual basis until the next group learning objective. By requiring all students to learn from the same vehicle for learning in the traditional setting, group interaction for learning is

---

[37] As a student achieves the required learning, he or she could be offered five choices: continue on vertically to the next unit or course; go back and delve deeper into previously learned GO's and SO's for horizontal learning; spend time studying and learning GO's and SO's of other subjects; spend time studying as an independent learner in a hobby or other high interest area which is not a subject area normally offered as a course; or spend time relaxing at any other activity.

minimized whereas in a situation where a variety of vehicles for learning have been used, group interaction can be increased. By requiring achievement of the prerequisites GO's and SO's before being involved in the group learning objectives, group interaction is also increased.[38]

b. GUIDELINES FOR DEVELOPMENT OF THE INSTRUCTIONAL EVENT

There are multiple known and unknown factors which affect learning and in turn affect the development of any instructional environment which is designed to facilitate learning. Two key guidelines are: first, no one instructional environment will work for all students; and second, the best instructional environment for any one student is one that facilitates that student learning all of the required GO's and SO's. In addition to these key guidelines, a general overall guideline is to minimize known factors which might interfere with learning for most learners, maximize the known factors which facilitate learning for most learners, and maintain flexibility to reflect individual student learning needs.

Another very useful guideline when developing a new instructional environment or when making major changes in an existing instructional environment, instead of spending the time, effort, and money to develop an entire course, select a unit of the course that is representative of the types of GO's and SO's found throughout the course. Develop the instructional environment for the unit, try it out on a sample of students from the intended or target population and use the results and student comments on learning from the sample unit as guidelines for developing the other units in the course. If the course being developed has a specific sequence for successful learning such that cumulative ignorance in one unit will affect learning in subsequent units, then it may be necessary in the development of an instructional environment for a new course to use the first unit. In the development of an instructional environment of an on-going course or one that has been taught before, the best unit to select as a sample unit for

---

[38]To assume that the only place students ever get together is in school is a mistake. Students get together in many ways and in many places. Some of the most exciting learning occurs for students during group discussions in the hallways of the schools, on street corners, in dormitories, in student union facilities, etc. As an adult, after attending four or five annual regional or national conventions of any organization, you find out that the exciting things to be learned rarely occur during the regularly scheduled meetings or presentations. The most exciting things usually occur in the hallways, coffee shops, hotel rooms, hospitality rooms, and cocktail lounges. To try to defend the traditional use of *classes of students* on the basis of the students' need for group interaction is faulty and is generally used to cover up the teacher's need for the ego involvement of presenting course content to groups which can still be done in Scholarship Sessions.

development is the unit that has been the least successful under the present or previous approach.

NOTE: Most teachers in in-service workshops or when taking courses in which they have to prepare a curriculum unit as a requirement of the workshop or the course, select a unit they already know very well and consequently probably already are able to teach it fairly well regardless of the technique used. As a result, if the teachers try out the newly developed units in their classrooms, they won't be able to identify much change in learning and will conclude that the new techniques or approaches are not that much better than what they are already using. If the teachers will select the least successful unit and use it as a demonstration unit, there is a greater chance for identifying any improvement in learning which might result from the new technique, method, etc. The least successful unit can usually be identified by looking at a grade book or test results. That unit in which the students score the lowest is the least successful unit. In lieu of not having any grades or scores, that unit that the teacher and students like the least is also probably the least successful.

In picking the least successful unit, student errors on the tests for the unit serve as locators for changes to be made. In order to gain the greatest cooperation of other teachers and the greatest application of the development efforts, the minimum common core GO's and SO's of the selected unit should be the emphasis of the developmental efforts. The more teachers involved in identifying the problem unit and the minimum common core GO's and SO's of the unit, the greater use there will be of the sample instructional environment which is developed. By following the procedure of developing a sample problem unit first, the balance of a course can be developed with a minimum of time, effort, and money.

The following guidelines and principles of learning have proven to be useful in the development of successful instructional materials and instructional environments.

(1) Learning proceeds best from the known to the unknown.

(2) Learning occurs best when appropriate for the present abilities of the learner.

(3) Learning occurs best when the student can proceed at his or her own pace.

(4) Learning occurs easiest when the student has all of the prerequisite skills (no cumulative ignorance).

735

(5) Learning occurs faster when the vehicle for learning matches the students major interest areas.

(6) Learning occurs faster when the learning environment (method, language, etc.) used matches the learning environment in which the student learns best.

(7) Learning occurs easier when the student learns in the manner in which what is learned is to be used (relevancy).

(8) Learning occurs easier when the sequence of learning follows some logical pattern and appears logical to the learner.

(9) Learning occurs faster when the learners are actively involved in *doing* what they are supposed to be learning.

(10) Learning and changes in behavior occur more readily when the person is aware of the consequences of his or her actions.

    (a)   If the consequences are positive or rewarding, the probability of the actions being repeated are increased.

    (b)   If the consequences are negative or punishing, the probability of the actions being repeated are decreased.

(11) The sooner the learner is aware of the consequences or results of his or her actions, the sooner the learning or change occurs.

(12) Receiving frequent but intermittent *knowledge of results* keeps the learner working longer at a task.

(13) Student errors or mistakes can be useful in facilitating learning if they are a result of learner deficiences and the teacher views them as learning problems to be solved.

(14) Student errors or mistakes which are a result of designed deception (the detractors used in the so-called objective type test items) or a lack of design or communication on the teachers part are not useful in facilitating learning and should be detected and corrected as quickly as possible.

(15) Minimizing overlaps or potential boredom (pretest scores) and gaps or cumulative ignorance (preentry test scores) in the instructional environment facilitates the maintenance of the student's motivation for learning.

(16) Learning occurs easier when the learners know what they are supposed to learn.

(17) Learning occurs easier when the learner is confident of his or her ability to learn successfully.

(18) Learning occurs easier in an environment where the primary discipline concerns achieving mastery in learning rather than where discipline concerns behaviors other than learning and/ or the appearance of the learners.

(19) Affective domain objectives are achieved more successfully if taught indirectly and are more apt not to be achieved if taught directly.

(20) Where applicable, learning is facilitated when teachers practice what they want students to learn, i.e., *practice what is preached; teachers teach the way they were taught, not the way they were taught to teach;* if teachers are humane, students will tend to be humane; if teachers are good communicators, students will tend to become good communicators; if teachers are honest (let students know what they are to learn — the SO's and tests), students will tend to be honest (won't cheat); etc.

(21) The more concrete the learning experience, the easier it will be for the learner to observe relevance and hence the easier to learn.

(22) The more the learner is involved in the learning experience, the easier for learning to occur.

(23) The more the learner is involved in the selection of the learning experiences, the more likely the desired learning will occur, i.e., the student can select the method and vehicles for learning, the student can select the elective courses, and the student can select the voluntary SO's in most courses. (The teacher's identify, select, and have to be able to defend the required courses and the required minimum common core SO's in all courses).

(24) Learners learn better *how to learn* and are more apt to become an independent learner if the learning environment encourages and facilitates learning independently.

(25) Learning will be increased if changes in the instructional environment are made and guided by incorporating solutions to identified learning problems (previous non-achievement of SO's).

(26) Learning will be facilitated if instructional technology is

utilized to specifically aid in the achievement of desired SO's rather than to illustrate or utilize the technology.

(27) Learning is increased as the instructional environment is increasingly individualized and the degree of potential individualization in an instructional environment is inversely proportionate to the degree that a teacher is involved in presenting the course content (to a group or class of students) i.e., if a teacher presents the entire course content (to a class of students), the potential for individualization is practically zero; if a teacher doesn't present any of the course content (to a group or class of students), the potential for individualization is practically 100 percent.

(28) Learning is facilitated when the unit, block, or size of the learning step is appropriate to that amount that the learner's self-image believes is achievable.

This is not a complete listing of principles and guidelines for facilitating learning and some of these on the list are almost duplicates (worded differently) of others in this list, but these are important enough such that if followed, learning will be facilitated and if an instructional environment contains the reverse of any of these principles and guidelines, learning will be inhibited or suppressed and conducive to the development of learning problems. Obviously, in the case of the latter conditions, the solutions to the learning problems would be to reverse the situation in which one or more of these principles or guidelines were being inversely applied.

c. THE FIRST STEP: SEQUENCING THE OBJECTIVES IN THE INSTRUCTIONAL EVENT

NOTE: The synthesis or development of the instructional environment should not be started until all of the necessary adjustments in the course objectives have been made as indicated by the results of trying out the preentry test, the pretest, and the posttest on a sample of the intended student population.

The first step in the synthesis of the instructional event is the arrangement of the course or unit objectives into the best sequence for learning. Research concerning the need for sequence has been split and the results are dependent upon the objectives in the instructional unit used in the research. If a researcher wants to prove that sequence isn't a relevant concept, the researcher uses a series of objectives or units which are not interdependent and are individually complete. If a researcher wants to prove that sequence is a relevant concept, the researcher uses a series of objectives or units which are interdependent and depend on a certain sequence. What this proves is two things: first, if given the freedom to pick any series of units or objectives, a researcher can prove almost any point-of-view he or she wants to prove; and second, that there is a continuum of dependency on sequence as it affects learning ranging from a series of objectives or units at one end of the continuum in which there is no sequence that is better than any other sequence to a series of objectives of units at the other end of the continuum in which there is only one sequence which will facilitate mastery learning.

In some courses, there is a traditional sequence which has been used in which students are able to learn successfully. However, if a traditional sequence has not been very successful for student learning but has been convenient for teacher presentations, it may be that the sequence should be changed to a learner-oriented sequqnce. An indication of a need for changing a sequence is when students make statements similar to *Now I know what you meant six weeks ago (last month, last semester, etc.).* These statements indicate that whatever is being presented now should have been presented back when the misunderstanding occurred or whatever was presented back when the misunderstanding occurred should have been presented now along with the present material.

If you or whoever is developing the instructional environment followed the steps in the behavioral analysis, the sequence may have already been developed. If the desired terminal behaviors are specified first and then the students' entry behaviors are identified and specified, the listing of the enabling objectives which will take the learner from where he or she is to the goals or terminal objectives of the course or unit also identifies the sequence that the enabling objectives should be in for optimum learning.

If the steps of the behavioral analysis have not been followed very closely, the best first guess as to the most appropriate sequence can be made by a teacher who has taught the course or unit successfully in the past such that most of the students learned most of what they were supposed to learn. This sequence is probably the result of trial and error experiences of the teacher over a period of time.

The ultimate determiner of the best sequence is the learner and under conditions where the learner is able to learn all of the desired course or unit objectives.

In between these two (the teacher and the learner), there is a method of determining the sequence for learning which is based on the learning principle that *learning is facilitated when the learning sequence goes from the known to the unknown.* I call this method the *Matrix Method of Sequencing.*

NOTE: If you are reading this book to gain an awareness of its contents and are not actually involved in developing an instructional event or if you are actually developing an instructional event and you have already identified the sequence of learning you want, then it may be appropriate to skip over the description of the Matrix Method of Sequencing to page 773. The reason for this is that over the years of trying to describe the method, I have found that the best way to communicate the method is to actively involve the person or persons in the sequencing procedures of the method itself. Because of the work involved, the casual reader or the reader who already has identified the sequence he or she wants, may find the following material requires too much effort for what they want to get out of it.

(1) THE MATRIX METHOD OF SEQUENCING OBJECTIVES

The design of this unit is programmed such that a variety of levels of involvement can be utilized. As long as you understand what is happening in each step as you read it, it may only be necessary to be covertly involved. However, if at any step you don't understand what is happening, obtain some sheets of graph paper (about ten sheets will be sufficient to be involved in each step) and follow through this unit or that part you don't understand by performing the tasks as suggested. The format of this unit is such that on a given page where you are asked to perform a certain task on the supplementary graph paper and you complete the task, you can turn the page and you will find a copy of the completed task which can be used to check your work and identify any mistakes you may have made in performing the suggested task on the supplementary graph paper. If you discover differences between your work on the supplementary graph paper and the reinforcement of the task in this unit, then you should to back over the task and eliminate your errors before going on to the next step. Obviously, there will be a temptation to turn the page and not actually get involved in the development of the suggested task, but if you wish to learn how to perform the matrix method and the tasks involved, there is only one best way for most readers to learn the step successfully, and this is to be *actively involved* in the process.

A matrix is a square with "n" columns and "n" rows upon which an array of symbols are placed in order to facilitate the analysis and sequencing of the learning objectives for a course or for an instructional unit. Each column and each row represents one of the learning objectives of the course or unit. The sequence of columns (objectives) from left to right match the sequence of rows (objectives) from top to bottom. The symbols placed in the squares of the matrix indicate a

740

fundamental relationship between the column (objective) and the row (objective). Because of the columns and rows represent the same sequence of objectives, the placement of the symbols in the squares will appear to be symmetrical around the principal diagonal of the matrix from the upper left-hand corner to the lower right-hand corner, i.e., in Figure 74, the "x" indicating a relationship between row (objective) 1 and column (objective) 5 is the same relationship as the "x" indicating a relationship between row (objective) 5 and column (objective) 1, the "x" indicating a relationship between row (objective) 2 and column (objective) 7 is the same relationship as the "x" indicating a relationship between row (objective) 7 and column (objective) 2, etc. The squares making up the principal diagonal of the matrix will always be filled in because any one column (objective) has an identical relationship with its corresponding row (objective).

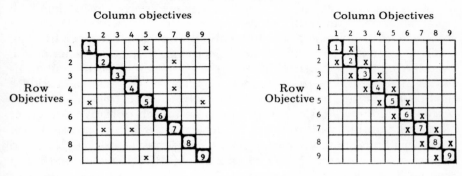

Figure 74 — A Matrix of Nine Objectives

Figure 75 — Matrix of Relationships Going from the Known to the Unknown

If a sequence of objectives has been arranged such that learning could precede from the known to the unknown, then each objective would have a relationship to the next objective and the matrix would look like Figure 75, i.e., objective (row) 1 has a relationship with objective (column) 2, objective (row) 2 has a relationship with objective (column) 3, etc. Because of the symmetrical relationship, the "x's" above the diagonal are duplicated below the diagonal. In a situation where there is no special sequence, the "x's" will be spaced almost at random around the matrix (see Figure 74) and it is not possible to rearrange the sequence to arrive at an eliptical pattern around the diagonal as in Figure 75 or Figure 76. If there is a sequence, the resultant matrix would look more like Figure 76 than like Figure 75 in that there are usually other relationships besides those which are adjacent to the diagonal. These extra relationships provide alternate

741

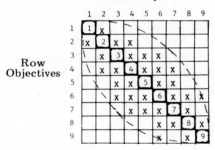

Row
Objectives

Figure 76 — Matrix of Relationships

pathways for learning. For example, in Figure 76, if the student had learned objective 4 and the instructional materials were designed to teach objective 5 in terms of its relationship to objective 4, but for some reason the student was not able to understand this relationship and consequently could not learn objective 5, then the teacher could, by referring to the matrix (Figure 76), try to teach objective 5 in terms of its relationship with objective 3 (there is an "x" indicating a relationship at the intersection of objective 3 with objective 5). The teacher could also skip over objective 5 and teach objective 6 in terms of its relationship with objective 4. The teacher could also skip over objectives 5 and 6 and teach objective 7 in terms of its relationship to objective 4 and then go back and pick up objectives 5 and 6 in terms of their relationships with objectives 4, 7, or 3. Therefore, not only does the matrix method help identify a potential sequence for learning from the known to the unknown, but the method also results in revealing alternate pathways to learning which could be selected because of student interest or as solutions to learning problems.

If the number of objectives to be sequenced approaches 100, the use of the matrix system as described in this unit can be rather cumbersome and very time-consuming. Therefore, it may be easier to sequence subunits or units of a course rather than to try to sequence the SO's. for example, in a given semester course, there may be 350 specific, measurable learning objectives, but the course itself divides quite easily into five units and can be further subdivided into a total of 30 subunits. The use of the matrix with the 350 objectives would be very difficult, unless it is set up for a computer analysis instead of the manual analysis as demonstrated in this section. Where the maximum number of objectives, subunits, or units is determined by and is proportionate to the amount of work involved (unless a computer is used), the minimum number of units, subunits or objectives that can be used in the matrix analysis successfully is determined more by the pattern of interrelationships between these units than by the actual number of units. If in an instructional unit where there are 20 learning objectives and each objective is related to every other objective, then the number of objectives in this case would be too small to utilize the matrix method for sequencing effectively because no matter what the sequence was, all of the objectives would still relate to all of the other objectives and any sequence would fit the pattern of *going from the known to the unknown*. In another situation, there could be five units in a course, in which there were limited interrelationships between the units. In this case, the five units may be successfully sequenced by using the matrix method.

The first step in using the matrix method would be to set up a matrix with as many rows and columns as there are learning objectives

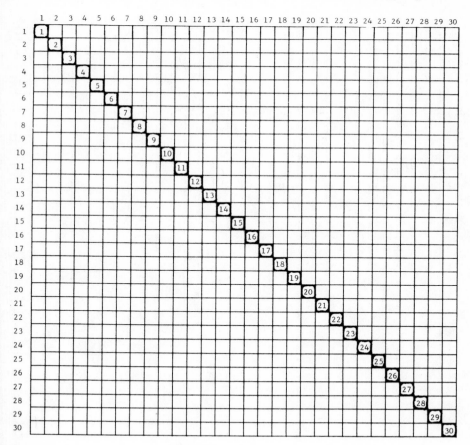

Figure 77 — First Step in Matrix Method of Sequencing Objectives

or subunits that are going to be sequenced by this method. Numbers representing each one of the learning objectives or units are placed across the top of the matrix and down the left-hand side of the matrix as indicated by Figure 77 for a matrix with 30 learning objectives (or it could be 30 subunits in a course). As a convenience, I have found it useful to put the same sequence of numbers (which are across the top of the matrix and down the left hand side of the matrix) down the diagonal from the top left hand square to the bottom right hand square.

The second step in the matrix method of sequencing objectives would be to go row by row and identify all of the different relationships between each of the objectives (or subunits). The symbol used to identify relationships between objectives is purely arbitrary and in this

	1	2	3	4	5	6	7	8	9	10	11	12	13	14	15	16	17	18	19	20	21	22	23	24	25	26	27	28	29	30
1	1											X																		
2		2	X		X							X						X												
3		X	3		X							X		X																
4				4				X	X		X		X		X		X				X									X
5		X	X		5						X	X		X				X												
6						6				X					X	X	X				X	X		X						
7							7				X		X	X				X						X						X
8			X					8			X		X		X	X			X		X			X			X			
9			X						9				X		X		X						X	X			X			X
10					X					10								X			X			X				X	X	
11			X	X		X	X				11				X										X					
12	X	X	X		X							12																		
13			X			X	X	X					13	X	X	X														
14		X		X		X							X	14																
15			X			X		X	X		X		X		15		X	X	X					X	X		X			
16			X			X		X			X		X			16			X			X	X	X	X		X			
17			X					X	X				X				17		X			X	X	X		X	X			X
18	X		X	X		X							X					18												
19								X		X					X	X	X		19		X		X				X			X
20																				20		X			X			X	X	
21			X		X		X											X			21	X	X		X	X				X
22			X						X						X	X					X	22		X	X	X		X		X
23								X							X	X		X	X	X			23			X	X			X
24						X	X	X	X						X	X	X					X		24	X					X
25									X						X	X					X	X		X	25					X
26									X								X			X	X	X				26		X		
27							X	X	X						X	X	X		X				X				27		X	
28																		X			X	X			X			28		
29																		X							X				29	
30				X			X		X								X		X			X	X	X	X	X				30

Figure 78 — Second Step in Matrix Method of Sequencing Objectives

instance the symbol used will be a "X". "X's" in the squares of the matrix indicate a relationship between two objectives, (or subunits), just as the square itself represents the intersection of a column and a row. The numbers associated with the column and the row are the objectives that have the relationship which has been identified by the letter "X". See Figure 78.

As can be identified by examining Figure 78, in the present sequence of objectives as identified by the numbers 1 through 30, there are only four relationships that are adjacent to the principal diagonal of the matrix (along the top or bottom of the diagonal). This type of a relationship pattern and sequence of objectives would be typical of a course in which the learning levels are very low. The greater the percentage of squares adjacent to the principal diagonal that are filled with "X's" indicating relationships between objectives, the greater the tendency for learning to be taking place maong the learners. Therefore, the purpose of the matrix method of sequencing objectives is to rearrange the sequence of the objectives such that the maximum number of "X's" can be placed into the squares adjacent to the principal diagonal. Although the establishment of the relationships between the objectives as represented by the placement of the "X's" on the matrix is subjective, once the relationship is identified, the ultimate sequence based on these relationships is not subjective. As already noted in Figure 78, there are only four "X's" in squares adjacent to the principal diagonal, out of a possible 29 squares on either side of the principal diagonal. In the process to be described, as more and more changes are made in the sequence of objectives such that more and more "X's" are adjacent to the principal diagonal, all of the other "X's" tend to form an elliptical shape around the principal diagonal.

It should be pointed out that the matrix method will not change or affect the first objective in the sequence, so the identification and selection of the first objective is quite important to the overall sequencing of objectives.

The first revised sequence is determined by the order in which the "X's" *first appear in each column*, as the person who is revising the sequence scans each row from right to left, starting at the top and working to the bottom of the matrix. In accordance with this pattern, an examination of the first row of the matrix in Figure 78 reveals that the first two numbers in the revised sequence are 1 and 12 (See Figure 79).

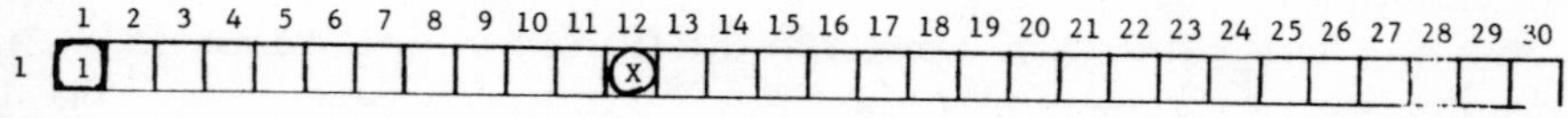

Figure 79

NOTE: To keep track of the revised sequence as it is developed, get a sheet of graph paper with at least 31 columns and 31 rows. As the revised sequence is developed, put the numbers across the top row of the graph paper starting with the second column. The first column is used to put the revised sequence of numbers down the left hand side of the matrix.

The second row of the matrix reveals that the next three objectives in the revised sequence are 3, 5, and 18 (See Figure 80). Number 12 is not used again because it is already in the revised sequence.

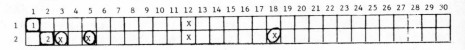

Figure 80

An examination of the third row reveals that the next two objectives in the revised sequence are 2 and 14 (See Figure 81).

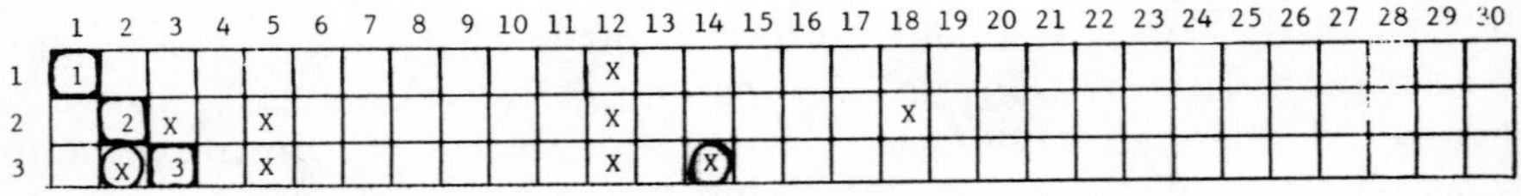

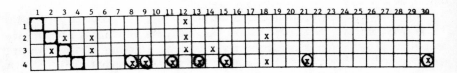

Figure 81

An examination of the fourth row identifies that Objectives 8, 9, 11, 13, 15, 21 and 30 are next in order in the revised sequence (See Figure 82.).

Figure 82

An examination of the fifth row (See Figure 83) reveals that there is no column in which the "X's" appear in the fifth row for the first time. An examination of the sixth row identifies the following objectives as being next in order in the revised sequence: 10, 16, 17, 22, 24 (See Figure 83).

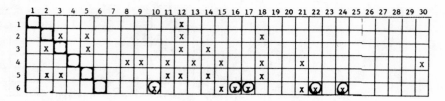

Figure 83

An examination of Row 7 reveals that there are no "X's" which are in any of the columns for the first time (see Figure 84). An examination of Row 8 identifies the following objectives as being next in order in the revised sequence: 4, 19, and 27 (See Figure 84).

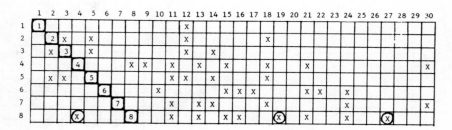

Figure 84

An examination of Row 9 identifies only one new "X" in the column, which would put Objective 23 next in the order of the revised sequence (see Figure 85).

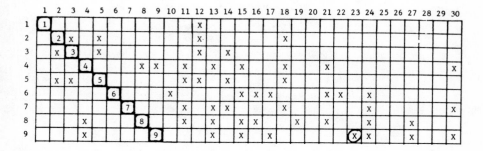

Figure 85

An examination of Row 10 identifies the following objectives to be next in order in the revised sequence: 6 and 26 (see Figure 86).

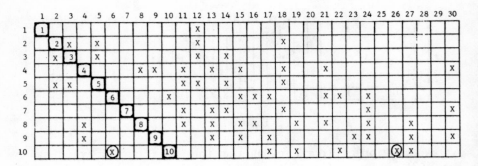

Figure 86

An examination of Row 11 identifies the following objectives as being next in order in the revised sequence: 7, 25, (see Figure 87).

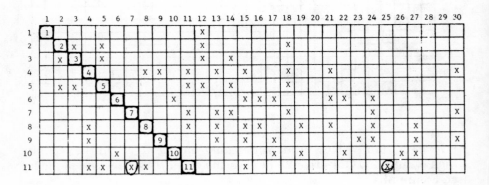

Figure 87

An examination, row by row, of Rows 12 through 19 will not reveal any new "X's" appearing in the column for the first time (see Figure 88). An examination of Row 20 identifies Objectives 28 and 29 as being the next two objectives in the revised sequence (see Figure 88).

748

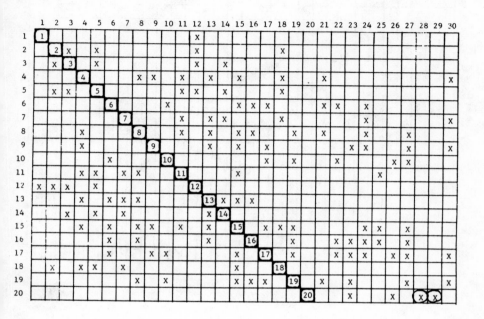

Figure 88

An examination of Rows 21 and 22 reveal no new "X's" which appear in a column for the first time (see Figure 89). An examination of Row 23 reveals an "X" in Column 20 as appearing for the first time, so this is the next objective in the revised sequence (see Figure 89).

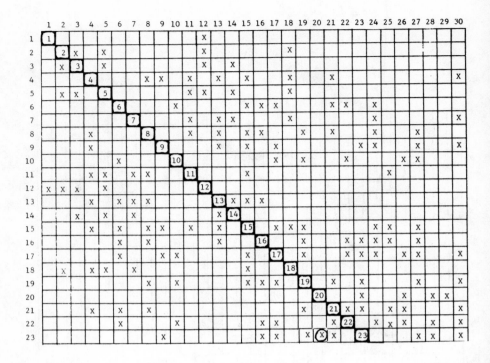

Figure 89

If the new sequence of objectives had been recorded on a piece of graph paper as we progressed row by row through this matrix, it would have been noted as we identified Objective No. 20 as being next in order in the revised sequence, that Objective 20 was also the last objective needed to fill up the 30 columns of the new revised sequence (see Figure 90).

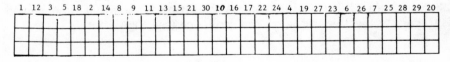

Figure 90

A row by row examination of Rows 24 through Row 30 in Figure 78 will reveal that there are no more new "X's" appearing in any of the columns for the first time, which confirms the fact that the revised sequence is complete.

The next step is to place the numbers indicating the revised sequence across the top and down the left-hand side of a sheet of graph paper. To facilitate the performance of the next step, the same numbers of the revised sequence can be placed along the principal diagonal (see Figure 91).

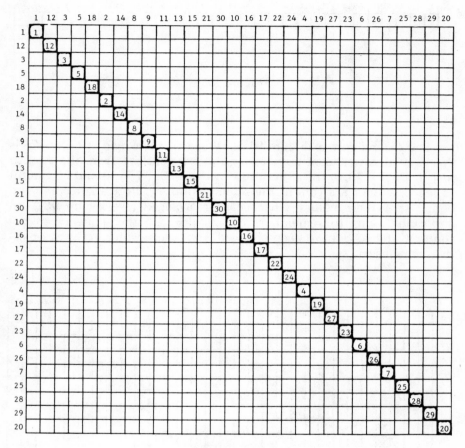

Figure 91

The next step in using the matrix method is to put the "X's" identifying the relationships between objectives on the matrix with the new sequence of objectives. The position of the "X's" is made with reference to Figure 78. For example, in the first row of Figure 78, there is a relationship between Objective 1 and Objective 12, and this relationship is represented by an "X" in Column 12 of Figure 78. In transferring this relationship to Figure 91, the "X" in Column 12 would be placed in Row 1 of Figure 91 as indicated in Figure 92.

751

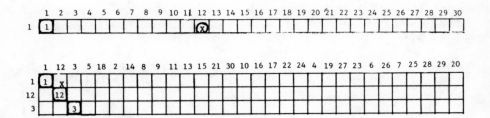

Figure 92

The second row in Figure 91 is Objective 12, which in Figure 78 is the twelfth row and in transferring the relationships from the twelfth row in Figure 78 to the second row in Figure 91, you should be careful to see that the "X's" are in the same columns in both figures, remembering that these columns have been rearranged (see Figure 93). An important point to remember is that, although the sequence of the columns and rows have been changed, the relationships between objectives remains the same.

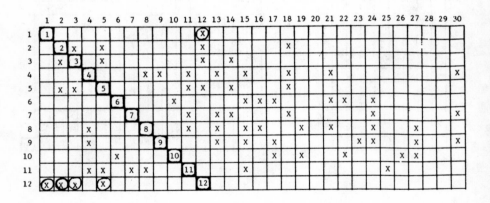

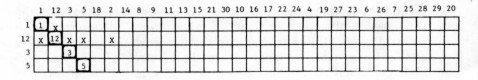

Figure 93

752

In reference to Figure 93 Row 12 in the top matrix (representing the original sequence) has "X's" in Column 1, 2, 3, and 5. These "X's" are now represented in the lower matrix of Figure 93 (representing the revised sequence) and are represented by "X's" in the squares which are intersections between the row numbered 12 and columns numbered 1, 2, 3 and 5.

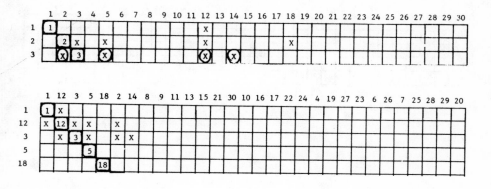

Figure 94

Consider Figure 94. Row number 3 in the top matrix has relationships with Columns 2, 5, 12 and 14, so in transferring this to Row 3 in the lower matrix, the "X's" or relationships are also found in Columns 2, 5, 12 and 14. In order to continue learning the matrix method of sequencing, at this point, it will be helpful to become involved in the sequencing process if you haven't been keeping track of what has been happening. On the supplementary graph paper on which you copied the revised sequence along the top, left side, and down the diagonal, label this matrix as the *First Revised Sequence.* If you haven't already, put "X's" in the top three rows as there are in the lower matrix of Figure 94. From now on, instead of my showing you the changes to be made and then you copy them on your graph, you find the next changes to be made first, record them on your graph and then I'll show you what is right. Therefore, on supplementary graph paper and in reference to the top matrix in Figure 95, transfer the "X's" representing relationships between the Row 5 and the columns numbered 2, 3, 11, 12, 14 and 18 to the Row 5 on your supplementary graph or in the lower matrix on Figure 95. After you have filled in the "X's" in Row 5 on your supplementary graph or in the lower matrix of Figure 95, compare your results with Figure 96.

753

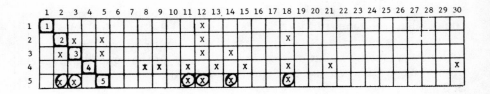

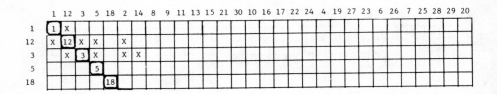

Figure 95

If the "X's" in Row 5 on your supplementary graph paper match the "X's" in Row 5 in Figure 96, then continue on, row by row, of the revised sequence (Figure 91) filling in the relationships with reference to the relationships as they are presented in the original sequence (Figure 78).

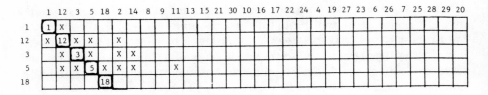

Figure 96

When you have completed filling in all of the relationships as identified in the original sequence (Figure 78) on your sheet of graph paper in accordance with the revised sequence (Figure 91), check your results with Figure 97.

If you find that the second matrix sequence which you have completed on a separate sheet of graph paper is identical to the second matrix sequence, (Figure 97), then you are ready to proceed to the setting up of the third matrix sequence. In looking at Figure 97, notice

754

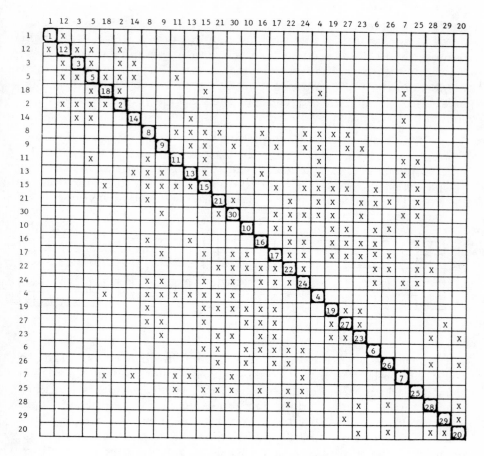

Figure 97 — The Second Matrix Sequence

that in the squares adjacent to either side of the principal diagonal, there are now twelve squares filled with relationships in comparison to the first matrix sequence which only had four squares adjacent to either side with "X's" in them. The development of the next sequence is established in exactly the same manner that the second sequence was developed. On a separate sheet of graph paper, identify the new sequence by locating the columns in which the "X's" appear for the first time as you examine the second matrix sequence (Figure 97) beginning with the top row going from left to right and continuing row by row until you reach the last row of the matrix. In reference to Figure 97, the first row numbered 1, the sequence remains the same, starting with Column 1 and the second column, 12. In the second row numbered 12 the first "X's" in the columns appear in Columns 3, 5, and 2. These are next numbers in the new sequence. In Row numbered 3, "X's" appear for the first time in Column 14 only, so that is the next number in the third sequence. In the fourth row numbered 5, "X's" appear for the first time in columns 18 and 11, so they are the next numbers in the third sequence. Continuing on, row by row, you should be able to identify the sequence for the third matrix and this sequence should be the same as Figure 98.

> NOTE. There will be a temptation to just copy my second revised sequence (Figure 98) rather than doing the work described in the last paragraph. If you really want to understand this process and particularly if you ever want to use it, you have to get involved. If you didn't generate the second revised sequence by yourself, go back and do it now!

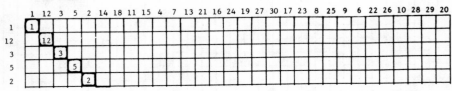

Figure 98 — The Third Sequence

If your third sequence is the same as Figure 98, then you are ready to transfer the relationships between objectives as indicated on the original sequence, Figure 78, to the new matrix which represents the third sequence (this should be done on a supplementary piece of graph paper you are using. Remember to go row by row down the matrix of the third sequence and establish the relationships in the same numbered columns in the third matrix sequence as the relationships are identified in the numbered columns of the original sequence (Figure 78).[39]

When you have completed filling in on the separate sheet of graph paper the third sequence matrix, then compare your results with Figure 99. If the third sequence matrix which you have developed on a separate sheet of graph paper is identical to Figure 99, then you are ready to go on to the next sequence. Notice in Figure 99, that there are now fifteen "X's" in squares which are adjacent to either side of the principal diagonal. In contrast, there were only 12 "X's" on either side of the principal diagonal in the second sequence matrix (Figure 97) and

---

[39] In case there have been any errors in establishing the relationships in the second matrix sequence, Figure 97, it is best to go back to the original sequence, Figure 78, in the placing of the "X's" in the third matrix sequence. In this way, any errors that might have been introduced in the placement of the "X's" in the second matrix sequence will be by-passed and will not affect the ultimate sequence.

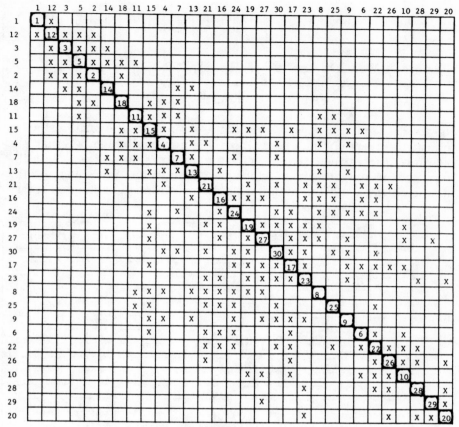

Figure 99 — The Third Sequence Matrix

only four "X's" on either side of the principal diagonal in the original sequence matrix (Figure 78).

As before, the first step in the development of the fourth sequence is by examination of the third sequence matrix, Figure 99, and identifying the sequence of numbers, as represented by the first time the "X" appears in a column, starting with the top row and going row by row through the matrix to the bottom row again, (be sure you identify this fourth sequence on a separate sheet of graph paper). When you have completed the fourth sequence, compare your sequence with the sequence presented in Figure 100.

If the sequence which you have arrived at on the supplementary graph paper agrees with the fourth sequence as presented in Figure 100, then you are ready to go ahead with the next step, which would be to place the "X's" indicating the relationships between the objectives in

757

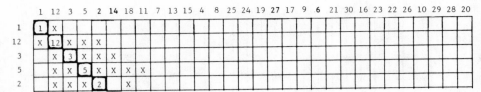

Figure 100 — Fourth Sequence

the fourth sequence matrix, by using as a reference the relationships as indicated in the original sequence, Figure 78. Remember that the relationships between the objectives have not changed; it is just the sequence of the objectives which has affected the placement of the numbered rows and the numbered columns. Using your supplementary

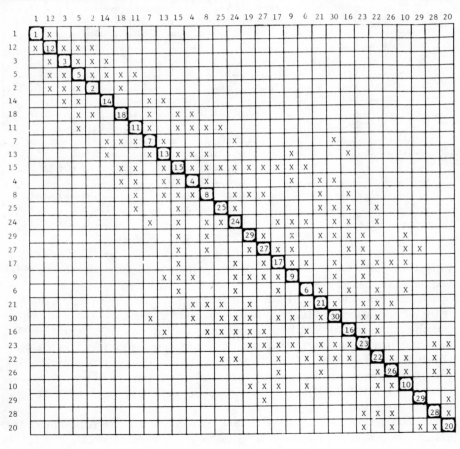

Figure 101 — Fourth Sequence Matrix

sheet of graph paper, place the numbers in the order of the fourth sequence across the top and down the left-hand corner to the lower right-hand corner. In going from the top row of the matrix to the bottom row, transfer the objective relationships indicated by "X's" in Figure 78 to the new fourth sequence matrix. When you are through with the last row, compare your fourth sequence matrix with Figure 101.

If your fourth sequence matrix is identical to Figure 101, then you are ready to go on to the next revised sequence. Notice in the fourth sequence matrix there are now 19 "X's" in the squares adjacent to either side of the principal diagonal. This is an increase of four "X's" over the third sequence matrix (Figure 99). Following the same procedures as were used to develop the revised sequence for the second, third and fourth sequence, use Figure 101 and on a separate sheet of graph paper develop the revised fifth sequence. When you have completed this sequence, compare your revised fifth sequence with Figure 102. If your sequence agrees with Figure 102, then you are ready to go on to the development of the matrix by transferring the relationships between

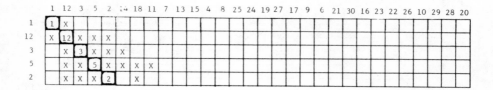

Figure 102 — Fifth Sequence

objectives as identified in Figure 78, on to a separate sheet of graph paper using the new revised fifth sequence and following the same procedures that were used to develop the second, third and fourth sequence matrices. When you have completed the matrix by filling in all of the "X's", compare your fifth sequence matrix with Figure 103. If your fifth sequence matrix agrees with Figure 103, then you are ready to develop the sixth sequence. Notice in the fifth sequence matrix, there are now 20 "X's" in squares along either side of the principal diagonal which is only an increase of one square over the last matrix. Using the same procedures that were used in the development of the other revised sequences and on a separate sheet of graph paper, develop the sixth sequence. When you are through, compare your revised sixth sequence with the sequence on Figure 104. What do you find? Right. They're exactly the same, so at this point, when the revised sequence is the same as the previous sequence, you have arrived at the maximum

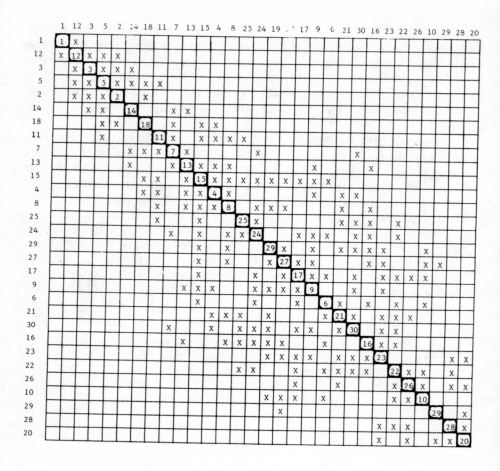

Figure 103 — Fifth Sequence Matrix

number of "X's" in the squares on either side and adjacent to the principal diagonal that can be obtained by the procedures we have been using. Depending on the relationships between the objectives and where these relationships are placed on the matrix, this maximum or ultimate point of this particular technique, may be arrived at after two revisions or after 20 revisions. Although this is the limit of this particular technique which has been used to go from four "X's" in squares on either side of the principal diagonal up to 20 "X's" in squares on either side of the principal diagonal, this is not the limit in the number of "X's" which can be placed in squares adjacent to the diagonal. Depending on the placement of the "X's" in the matrix, it may be possible to gain more "X's" adjacent to the diagonal by observation.

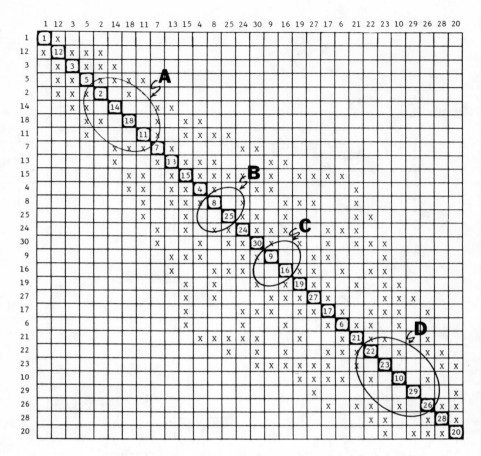

Figure 104 — Four Gaps in Sequencing

Of the 29 squares on each side of the principal diagonal, the previous sequence of activities has been able to fill in 20 of these squares on either side, leaving nine squares on either side of the principal diagonal with no "X's". These nine squares fall into four groups, (A, B, C, and D) as indicated by Figure 104.

In making the changes in the sequence of these four groups such that more "X's" will be adjacent to the principal diagonal, you need a worksheet like Figure 105. If you are using supplementary graph paper, copy the numbers and "X's" on Figure 105 on to your sheet of graph paper.

In order to facilitate the learning of this second set of procedures used in revising the sequence by observation, the first gap to be revised will be Gap "B", then Gap "C", then Gap "A", and the last one to be

761

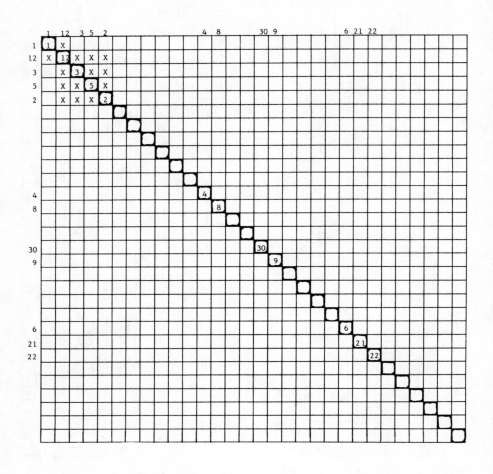

Figure 105 — Gaps in Sequence Worksheet

revised will be Gap "D".

On Figure 104, look at the square which is the intersection between the row numbered 8 and the column numbered 25. Although 8 does not relate to 25 in looking to the right of the empty square, 8 does relate to 24, and 24 in turn, is related to 25, and 25 is related to 30, so by making this change, we can now fill in the square which is the intersection of the row numbered 8 and the column numbered 25 (see Figure 106).

762

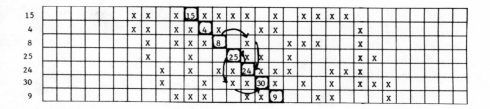

Figure 106 — Revising Sequence of Gap "B" by Observation

After making the changes in sequence as indicated in Figure 106, the new sequence for Gap "B" will be like Figure 107.

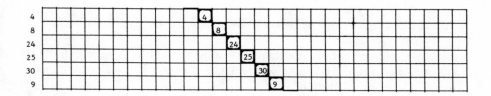

Figure 107 — Revised Sequence for Gap "B"

In changing the sequence of objectives 24 and 25, it is necessary to remember that all of the relationships identified by the "X's" in the squares for rows and columns numbered 24 and 25 will also have to be changed. Because the changes in the sequence of the other gaps will also affect the placement of the "X's", it is best to wait until all the changes in sequence in the other gaps are completed before transferring the "X's" to the new sequence. Fill in the revised sequence for Gap "B" on your worksheet (Figure 105).

In looking at Gap "C" (Figure 104), there is only one empty square. In looking to the right (or below) objective 9 on the diagonal (see Figure 108), notice that 9 relates to 27. By looking above (or to

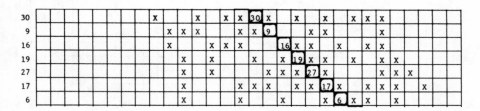

Figure 108 — Revising Sequence of Gap "C" by Observation

763

the left) 27, notice that 27 is related to 16 which was skipped over. Using part of the previous sequence, 16 is related to 19. By looking to the right (or below), notice that 19 relates to 17.

After making the changes in sequence as indicated in Figure 108, the new sequence for Gap "C" will be like Figure 109.

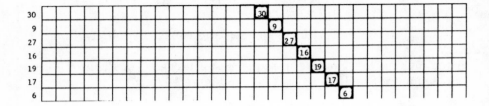

Figure 109 — Revised Sequence for Gap "C"

Again, remember that in changing the sequence, the "X's" will have to be changed to reflect the new sequence. Fill in the revised sequence for Gap "C" on your worksheet (Figure 105).

Gap "A" consists of three empty squares adjacent to the diagonal and involves rows and columns numbered 2, 14, 18, and 11 (see Figure 104). In looking at Gap "A", it can be seen by looking to the right (or below) the first empty square (see Figure 110) that objective 2 relates to objective 18. The first thing to check is if 18 relates to objective 14 which was skipped over. It doesn't. By looking to the right (or below) 18, it can be seen that objective 18 relates to 7. In order to try to pick up the objectives (14 and 11) which were skipped over, check to see if 7 relates to 14. It does, so 14 is next in the sequence. Does 14 relate to 11? No. Does 14 relate to the next objective not yet in this revised sequence? Yes, it does, so 13 is next in this revised sequence. 13 doesn't relate to 11, so leave 13 related to 15. Notice by looking above (or to

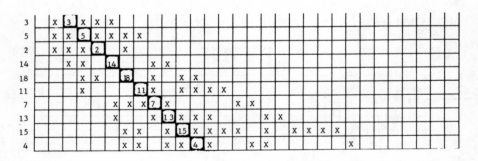

Figure 110 — Revising Sequence of Gap "A" by Observation

the left) of 15 that 15 is related to 11. By looking to the right (or below) of 11, notice that 11 is related to 4. So the revised sequence for Gap "A" is 2, 18, 7, 14, 13, 15, 11, and 4 and will look like Figure 111.

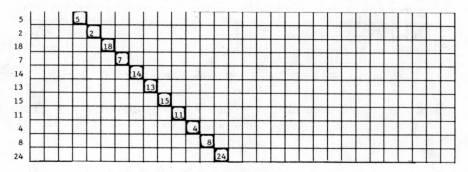

Figure 111 — Revised Sequence for Gap "A"

Fill in the revised sequence for Gap "A" on your worksheet (Figure 105).

The last gap to be revised is Gap "D" (See Figure 104) and consists of four empty squares adjacent to the diagonal (Figure 112), a relationship can be seen between 22 and 10. By looking to the right (or below) objective 10 on the diagonal, a relationship can be seen between 10 and 26. Since 26 does not relate to either 23 or 29 (which were skipped over), then use the previous sequence relating 26 to 28. Notice by looking above (or to the left) that 28 relates to 23 which is one of the objectives that was skipped. By looking to the right (or below) 23, notice that 23 relates to 20 which in turn is related to 29 which is the other objective that was skipped over.

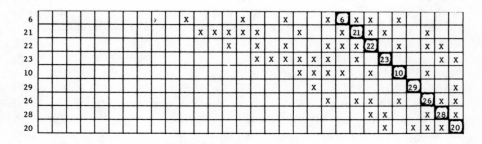

Figure 112 — Revising Sequence of Gap "D" by Observation

After making the changes in sequence as indicated in Figure 112, the new sequence for Gap "D" will look like Figure 113.

765

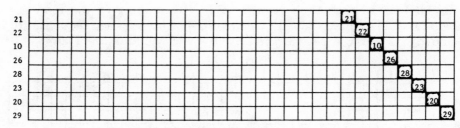

Figure 113 — Revised Sequence for Gap "D"

Fill in the revised sequence for Gap "D" on your worksheet (Figure 105) which should now look like Figure 114 across the top of the matrix.

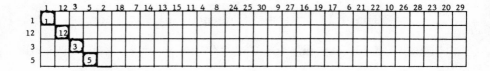

Figure 114 — Sixth Revised Sequence

In order to complete the last sequence, transfer the relationships between objectives as identified in Figure 78 to your worksheet (Figures 105) by using the same procedures that were used to fill in the "X's" in the second, third, fourth, and fifth sequence matrices. When you have completed the matrix by filling in all of the "X's", compare your sixth sequence matrix with Figure 115.

With this last revision of Gap "D", the sixth revised sequence matrix now has every square adjacent to the principal diagonal filled with "X" representing the relationship between the row-numbered objective and the column-numbered objective. Beginning at the top left-hand corver, once the student has learned objective 1, the learner will be able to follow the path way from the *known to the unknown*. Now, does this mean that this sequence is the ideal sequence for learning? No, all this sequence means is that the learner is going to go step by step through the instructional unit represented by these 30 objectives, and by utilizing this sixth revised sequence, the learner will be able to go from the known to the unknown. The major advantage of using the matrix approach to sequencing is that the subject matter specialist is involved in changing the sequence of a set of numbers, and as such, the subject matter specialist will not resist the changes in the sequence, whereas if the subject matter specialist could see the objectives themselves being rearranged, his biases, which may flavor the

766

	1	12	3	5	2	18	7	14	13	15	11	4	8	24	25	30	9	27	16	19	17	6	21	22	10	26	28	23	20	29
1	**1**	X																												
12	X	**12**	X	X	X																									
3		X	**3**	X	X		X																							
5		X	X	**5**	X	X	X																							
2		X	X	X	**2**	X																								
18				X	X	**18**	X		X			X																		
7						X	**7**	X	X					X		X														
14			X	X			X	**14**	X																					
13							X	X	**13**	X		X	X				X		X											
15						X			X	**15**	X	X	X	X	X		X	X	X	X	X									
11			X	X					X	X	**11**	X	X	X																
4						X			X	X	X	**4**	X			X	X					X								
8									X	X	X	X	**8**	X				X	X	X		X								
24						X				X			X	**24**	X	X	X		X	X		X								
25									X	X				X	**25**	X	X						X	X						
30						X						X		X	X	**30**	X		X	X		X	X					X		
9								X	X			X	X	X		X	**9**	X	X			X						X		
27										X				X	X	X	X	**27**	X	X	X	X						X		X
16								X	X	X	X	X		X		X	X		**16**	X		X						X		
19										X		X	X	X		X	X	X	X	**19**	X	X						X		
17										X		X	X	X	X	X	X		X	X	**17**	X	X	X	X			X		
6										X		X				X	X		X	X	X	**6**	X	X	X					
21									X	X	X	X	X			X					X	X	**21**	X	X					
22									X		X	X	X			X					X	X	X	**22**	X	X	X			
10																	X				X	X	X	X	**10**	X				
26																	X				X	X	X	X	X	**26**	X		X	
28																								X	X	X	**28**	X	X	
23														X	X	X	X	X	X	X	X					X	X	**23**	X	
20																										X	X	X	**20**	X
29																		X										X	X	**29**

Figure 115 — Sixth Revised Sequence Matrix

original sequence, would affect the decisions. By taking the last sequence and now attaching the verbal objectives to each of the numbers in the sequence represented by Figure 115, the subject matter specialist should now look for any particular trend that has become apparent because of the change in sequencing. Upon examination of the verbal objectives as they are placed in the last sequence, there are some changes that can be made without leaving any blank spaces in the squares adjacent to the principal diagonal. These changes can only be made when there are four or more adjacent rows intersecting an equal number of columns in which there is a relationship or "X" in all of these squares of the intersecting rows and columns. There are two such places in the 30-column and row matrix with which we have been working (see Figure 116).

767

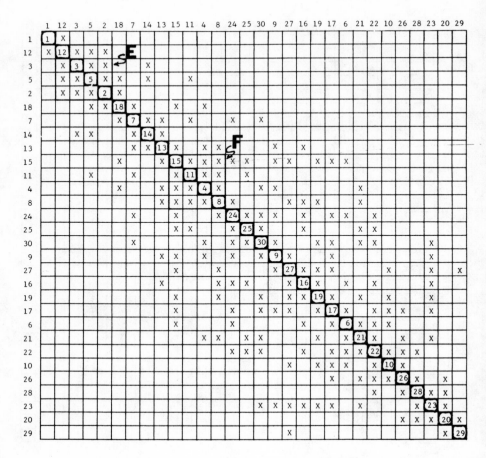

Figure 116 — Arbitrary Sequence Changes

An examination of the four by four square "E" and the four by four square "F" in Figure 116, it can be seen that by changing the sequence of the middle two objectives in square "E" from 12, 3, 5, 2, to 12, 5, 3, 2, and in square "F" from 15, 11, 4, 8 to 15, 4, 11, 8 that this will not affect the number of "X's" in the squares adjacent to the principal diagonal.

In performing this type of matrix analysis and sequencing during workshops which I have conducted several interesting trends were identified. The most significant was the need to reverse the usual approach to the medical education. Most schools follow the sequence followed by the experienced doctor: the student learns how to take patient histories, and then the student learns diagnostic procedures, then how to decide on the right prescriptions, treatments, or manage-

768

ment of the patient's problem, and finally the student works in out-patient clinics to observe how well the medical process works. According to the matrix sequencing approach the usual sequence should be reversed. After looking at the results, medical educators can see why. Although the patient's history is taken first, the actual questions asked are selected on the basis of years of experience which the new student doesn't have. Therefore, the sequence indicated by the matrix suggests that medical students should start out in the out-patient clinic in which they could see the relationships and effectiveness of the professional patient history, the professional diagnosis, and the professional treatment of the patient's problem. Where mistakes in diagnosis or treatment were made or problems were overlooked, the students can be made aware of the correct procedures and can identify why the mistakes or lack of problem identification occurred. Then the students start working in developing proper management or treatment of patient problems based on professional patient histories and professional diagnoses. Then the students start working on diagnostic procedures based on professional patient histories. Finally, the students start taking patient histories, but by this time, the students have had the experience necessary to ask the right questions which will reveal the data needed to make a good diagnosis, a good treatment, and a well patient in the out-patient clinic.

This reversal has implications for almost any occupation in which a similar sequence is followed. For example, in automotive repair, asking the customer questions about what is wrong with a car should really be the last procedure to be learned in a course on automotive repair.

The general implication of this is that the sequence used by professional or experienced people in performing their jobs may not be the best sequence for learning. This would be particularly true when some of the first steps are actually based on prerequisite knowledge and skills which could not have been learned in those first steps but could be learned in later steps or procedures.

Another change which occurred as a result of going through the matrix sequencing procedures concerned the stewardess training program of a major airline. Prior to the workshop, the airline's stewardess training program was made up of a series of units concerned with the stewardess' duties on each type of airplane the airline had in service. As new airplanes were put into service, new units were added to the training program. The result was that some stewardesses got confused and would forget some of their duties and the major problem was the duplication of training time and effort on duties which were the same in several types of airplanes. The matrix sequence suggested that the major training trend should not be the type airplane, but the emphasis is on the procedures the stewardesses perform from the time they arrive at an airport prior to take off to the time they leave the airport after they arrive at their terminal point. In between, where appropriate, the differences in duties depending upon the type of airplane should be covered as they are met while going through the usual procedures.

This change also has implications for any instructional program that might be broken up into a number of units in which each unit contains some duplication. For example, instead of learning to write five or more different types of essays at different times, it might be better to learn well a general procedure for writing an essay and then at appropriate places in the development of the essay, learn where the differences are for different types of essays and what these differences should be.

As indicated at the beginning of this section, the matrix is very useful to the teacher who is performing the role of a *solver of learning problems*. In going from the *Known to the Unknown*, every relationship above (or to the left of) the objective to be learned indicates alternate paths of learning. It should be remembered that the relationships between objectives was originally established by the subject matter specialist or whoever performed the sequence matrix analysis, and that these relationships are based on the background and experiences of the subject matter specialist. Therefore, it is possible for a student to have trouble in learning from a sequence that appears to go from the known to the unknown according to the specialist. The problem may be that the student can't see the same relationships that the specialist sees. For example in Figure 117, the learner has learned objectives 14, 13, 15, 11, and 4 in relationship to the previous objective just learned.

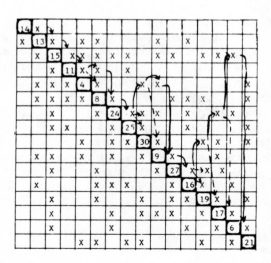

Figure 117 — Alternate Learning Paths for Solving Learning Problems

When the learner is exposed to the relationship between objective 4 and objective 8, the learner experiences difficulty. By looking at the sequence matrix analysis, the teacher can see that 8 also has a relationship with objective 11, and by using this relationship the learner learns. If that relationship didn't work, in looking above objective 8 on the diagonal, notice that 8 is also related to 15 and 13 which have been learned previously. Now once the learner has learned objective 8, he is able to go on to the relationship between objective 8 and 24, and between 24 and 25. In trying to learn the relationship in the intersection between 25 and 30, the student experiences difficulty again, and so the teacher solves the problem by introducing the learner to the relationship between 30 and 4 (the student knows 4 already, so we are still going from the known to the unknown). After learning objective 30, the learner is exposed to the learning objective 9 in its relationship with objective 30. Here again, the student encounters problems in learning. In looking above objective 9 on the diagonal, there are four alternate paths for learning available: the relationship between 9 and 24, 9 and 4, 9 and 15, and the relationship between 9 and 13. In this case, suppose the relationship between 9 and 4 worked and the student was able to learn objective 9. In continuing on through the instructional unit, there are really a wide variety of alternate pathways available to solve student learning problems.

NOTE: In the development of computer-assisted instructional learning paths, the sequence matrix analysis provides alternate paths which the computer can be very easily programmed to switch to, in case of learning difficulties which may be encountered by the learner. The development of these alternate learning paths would have a much stronger foundation and logical basis for existence then is presently the case in the majority of computer-assisted instructional alternate paths which are all too often developed upon the basis of the whims or *gut* feeling of the author who is writing the computer-assisted instructional unit.

Sometimes in the performance of a sequence matrix analysis, it will be revealed by the matrix that there are one or more groups of objectives which do not have any relationship at all with the objectives in other groups. This results in a blank square adjacent to the principal diagonal and between each of the groups and could appear similar to Figure 118. This type of a result in developing the sequence matrix identifies a situation in which it doesn't make any difference which subsequence is learned first as they are interchangeable. However, within the subsequences A, B, and D a sequence of learning the objectives has been identified. In subsequence C where all of the five objectives relate to each other, there is no particular sequence of the

771

five objectives that is any better than any other sequence of the five objectives.

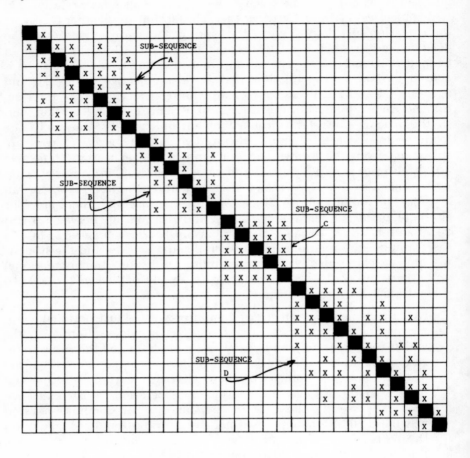

Figure 118 — Multiple Subsequences

In using the two methods, matrix sequencing and observation, it is not always possible to fill every space adjacent to the diagonal. The objective is to be able to maximize the number of relationships between course or unit objectives which can be learned by going from the *known to the unknown*. In cases where there are still a few empty spaces next to the diagonal, remember that it is possible to use one or more of the alternate paths which relate the new objective to one or more of the previously learned objectives which is still within the framework of the principles of going from the *known to the unknown*.

d. DEVELOPMENT OF THE INSTRUCTIONAL EVENT

The second step in the synthesis or development of the instructional event is to examine each objective in the course or unit from the point of view of what would be the *ideal* media, method, etc. to be used in presenting the content of the course or unit associated with each objective, *keeping in mind* why that particular objective is desired, what the learner is expected to do with the learned behavior once it is learned, and how long the learner is supposed to retain the learned behavior (see Figure 119). After identifying the *ideal* media, method,

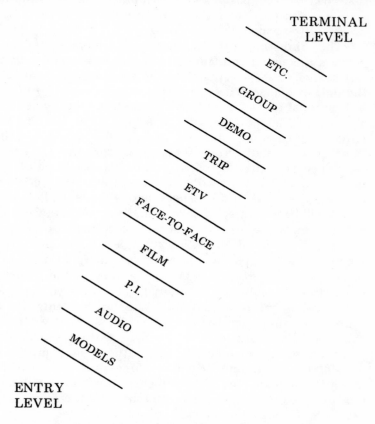

TERMINAL
LEVEL

ETC.

GROUP

DEMO.

TRIP

ETV

FACE-TO-FACE

FILM

P.I.

AUDIO

MODELS

ENTRY
LEVEL

Figure 119 — Determining the *Ideal* Media, Method, etc., for the
Presentation of Each Objective

etc. for presenting each objective, then the objectives should be re-examined from the point of view of the total unit or course, convenience of the learner in learning from the completed course or unit, budget available, materials available, packaging of the course or unit, and the feasibility of using the *ideal* media, methods, etc. The advantage of identifying the *ideal* media, method, etc., first is that in the first trial unit or course that is developed, if learning for most students doesn't occur for one or more of the objectives for which the presentation was a compromise from the *ideal*, then potential solutions are indicated by changing the presentation of the problem objectives to be closer or more similar to the *ideal* media, method, etc. Occassionally, it may be possible that in order to solve a learning problem to the degree desired that the costs and development of the solution make the learning of a particular objective prohibitive. In that case, it may be necessary to change the objectives.

The third step of the synthesis or development of the instructional event is the actual construction and preparation of the materials necessary to help the learner achieve the enabling and terminal objectives of the unit or course. These materials may be in the form of programmed instructional texts (linear, branching, etc.), correspondence instructional materials, learning activity packets (LAP's), learning modules, computer programming, films, video or audio tapes, models, demonstrations, field trips, directions for group discussion or face-to-face lectures, etc. Whenever possible, existing materials should be utilized as long as they do not change the objectives of the unit or course. Remember, because of individual differences among students, it should be assumed that it will be necessary to have more than one pathway (same GO's and SO's) through the instructional unit or course in order to facilitate 90 percent or more of the learners to learn 100 percent of the SO's. Whereas the first pathway through an instructional unit or course is based on a teacher's prior experience as being the best strategy for the most students, subsequent alternate pathways will be based primarily on the needs, interests, and abilities of the students who aren't able to learn successfully by following the first pathway. It should also be expected that most of the alternate pathways will only be partial pathways for learning certain SO's rather than complete pathways for learning the entire unit or course. Some programs have been developed in which there are multiple complete pathways through a unit or course (cognitive learning styles). The alternate pathways in these programs are usually developed on the basis of a teacher's experience and opinions rather than being based on the specific needs (learning problems) of learners and their interests and abilities. As such, the method of having alternate pathways through a course tends to become an objective rather than the learning of the SO's.

NOTE: Because of the traditional emphasis on media, methods, etc., rather than on learning, the most difficult problem to avoid is the trap of letting the media, method, or the vehicle for learning become the objective to the detriment of learning. Anytime the media, method, or vehicle for learning becomes the objective in which all of the students have to use it, the ignoring of individual differences has to have negative affects on learning. In the case where the use of multiple pathways becomes the objective, the selection of the pathway is determined by the learner's cognitive learning style rather than by a specific learning problem. Within a particular pathway, learners are allowed to complete the use of the pathway without learning all of the SO's which indicates that the use *of pathways* has become more important than the learning which was to be facilitated by the pathways.

To help maintain an emphasis on learning, the development of alternate pathways (partial or complete) through a unit or course should be done after the initial pathway has been tried out on a sample of students. Learning problems encountered by a majority of the students indicate changes to be made in the initial or basic pathway. Learning problems encountered only by one or a minority of students indicate the need for alternate pathways for those particular students and, as such, the development of the alternate pathway should be strongly influenced by the student's needs. interests, and abilities (same GO's and SO's).

Because many students have different amounts to be learned (varying cumulative ignorance and varying existing achievement of desired SO's) and many need different partial pathways through a unit or course, it is important to build places in the initial or basic pathway to allow students to branch away to solve learning problems or to skip over previously learned SO's. As such, these branches not only allow students to learn the same SO's in different ways, they also allow the students to use their time more effectively and efficiently by allowing students to enter the unit or course where appropriate to the learner, skipping over portions already learned, picking up missing prerequisite SO's, or offering enrichment pathways where appropriate.

At the places in the basic pathway where there are alternate pathways or branches available, it is necessary to have a kind of check point, evaluation, or diagnosis to help the learner and/or the teacher identify which alternate path or branch should be taken. Hull has written about the tendency for humans to *short circuit* pathways in learning. The inability of the learner to be able to *short circuit* in situations where the learner feels it would be appropriate, creates dissonance and indirectly has negative affects on the learner's motivation to learn. If at these check points there are several realistic answers or common misunderstandings, then branches might be built into the materials to allow the learner to examine the alternatives or to correct misunderstandings before the misunderstanding becomes a learned behavior.

NOTE: These branches should not be confused with the traditional multiple-choice questions. These branches go someplace and are designed to clarify and facilitate learning. The traditional multiple-choice are dead end pathways (right or wrong) which go no place and are designed to trick the students, confuse learning, and to manipulate the results or scores to fit some predetermined view (curve).

(1) INVOLVING THE LEARNER IN LEARNING

Since the learner is the only one that can actually do the learning, the student has to be involved in the instructional event if he or she actually learns the SO's of the instructional event. Of course, in educational systems where non-learning is permitted and actually expected, it should also be expected that many of the non-achieving students are not involved in the educational event: in part because involvement was not part of the design, in part because the students found it was not necessary to be involved to pass (social promotion and other non-learning oriented criteria for passing), in part because the students couldn't become involved as the educational event was inappropriate for the abilities of the students, and in part because the students didn't want to become involved. Under the Behavioral Learning Systems approach where learning 100 percent of the SO's is a part of the system, the student can't help but be involved in the instructional event. However, the degree of involvement of the learner is still a variable and may very well affect the ease with which the SO's are achieved. The guideline suggested by Dewey is still as good today as it was decades ago, *Learners learn best what they do!* This principle prompted a whole movement in which the emphasis was on *doing* via activity objectives which too often were interpreted as doing *anything.* A modern misinterpretation of the same guidelines is the *do your own thing* approach. As should be expected, when the emphasis is on doing anything according to the whims of the students rather than on the specific learning results of doing certain things guided and designed by the teacher, the results indicate that teachers and schools don't make a difference.

There are at least three levels of involvement in learning. The completely covert level of involvement is when the learner's input senses are involved enough to bring about the learning, but there is no observable evidence that the learning took place because there is no overt behavior during or after the instructional event. As such, the teacher cannot be sure that the desired learning even occurred. As independent learners, all of us have learned this way at one time or another. However, in a designed instructional situation, it is at least necessary to ask the student to demonstrate the desired behaviors in

776

order to know whether or not the achievement has occurred. Therefore, a minimal level of overt involvement would be to at least test the student on his or her achievement of the desired SO's. Because of the multitude of potential distractors in an instructional situation which could interfere with learning, if the only overt involvement of the learner is during the evaluation, then a guideline should be to minimize or eliminate as many of the potential distractors as possible. However, the more a student is overtly involved in the instructional event, the lower the probability that potential distractor can interfere with the student's learning. As long as the student is using various single concept media and handling materials, it is easy to build in overt involvement. But, most available instructional materials and the easiest materials to develop are primarily verbal (reading or listening to tapes) which makes it a little more difficult to design overt involvement into the instructional event.

When I first started conducting seminars for faculty on the improvement of instruction, the only involvement I had in the design was for the participants to use a typical adult education evaluation form which evaluates the performance of the seminar leader and the content of the seminar in terms of the opinions of the participants, i.e., Did you like it?, Would you recommend this seminar to a friend?, What didn't you like?, etc. Even though I was finally able to get a high majority of the participants to say that they liked the seminar, I noticed that few of the participants actually changed what they were doing. Then I realized that what the participants thought of me or the seminar was not what was important. What they learned in the seminar was the major reason for even holding the seminars. As a result, I started testing the faculty participants on their achievement of the cognitive SO's which should have been learned during the seminar. Although there were indications that learning increased, the achievement levels were much lower than they should have been. Under the traditional approach and with students, low achievement scores are usually blamed on poor students. Given that the participants in my seminars were faculty, I couldn't blame them. I was forced to blame the instructional environment. In other words, I had identified a critical learning problem in my seminars which were concerned with helping faculty identify learning problems in their classes. In trying to solve the problem, I re-examined all of my seminar materials, the sequencing of concepts, the objectives, and the testing. I found several places for improvement, but nothing that would so drastically affect the learning levels of such a high level group of participants. I then examined the involvement levels of the participants and realized that I was only expecting them to keep their input senses open. Although some of the participants took notes during the seminars, many of them didn't and there appeared to be a relationship between achievement and note taking. In going back through related research literature, I found that there was support for the value of note taking. In contrast, I, like many other teachers, knew that there were times that it would be better if the students or participants listened rather than took notes. Most students have had the experience of a teacher telling them not to take notes and to concentrate on listening instead; but then when the next test was given, the students wished they had taken more notes. The conclusion is that there are times when students (or participants) will learn best when only the input senses are operating and there are other times when students (or participants) will learn best when their involvement level is more overt (taking notes). The problem is that most teachers do not identify for the students when it is appropriate to listen and when it is appropriate to take notes.

As a student, I can remember having a teacher in an engineering physics course who had just started teaching and had a background of experience in industry and with no training in how to teach or test. For some reason, every time he started to talk about something he was planning to test us on later, he would cough. It was as if he was saying, *Pay attention!* Once we caught on to it, it was really great because we knew when to relax and listen and when to take notes. In fact, this teacher's habit was so successful that every student made it through the course. Later on, as this teacher learned the tricks of traditional teaching, I heard that he stopped his habit of communicating what was important and started to get a more negative skewed grading curve (more "D's" and "F's") which was closer to the expected norm in science courses. Lucky for me and my fellow students, we had him as our teacher while he still thought it was *good* that all students have success in his courses.

As a result of the conclusion that it is necessary to have more designed overt involvement in my seminars (and classes), I developed what I call an *Active Involvement Form (AIF)* (see Figure 120). The form looks very similar to a test and has been used for that purpose. At times, you may want the students to write in a specific word or phrase; however, most of the time, the students or participants are asked to write down in their own words their interpretation of what you are saying. In these AIF's, students can also be involved in constructing or completing diagrams, charts, graphs; labeling drawings or photographs; completing problems to be solved; etc. As with programmed instruction, the motivation is to fill in the blanks and as long as what the student or participant is writing down is what the teacher considers important, then the students are learning *what they are doing* and what is important.

In using the AIF's in my seminars and classes I noticed a very significant improvement in initial achievement and a reduction in hav-

778

ing to repeat parts of my presentations in order to maximize achievement.

NOTE: Almost every teacher has felt that the students who should be asking questions hardly ever ask them. The primary reason for

---

D. In testing out units of courses or even total courses, be especially aware of the following six learning variables which contribute to individual learning differences:

1. _____

2. _____

_____

Students	Entry	Terminal
A		
B		
C		
D		

3. _____

  a. Why are there different_____ of learning?

    (1). Can you believe the following statement?

      " _____ "

    (2). Where do " _____ "?

      (your notes)_____

      _____

    (3). A student's academic progress depends upon the

      between the _____ a student _____ and the _____

      a teacher _____ .

  b. The ultimate teacher is _____ :

    (1). Define Positive Simulation:

      _____

      _____

    (2). Define Negative Simulation:

      _____

      _____

4. _____

_____

5. _____

_____

  a. _____

  b. _____

6. _____

_____

_____

Figure 120 — A Page from an Active Involvement Form (AIF)

this in the traditional educational environment is that these students don't know what it is that they don't know and don't know what questions to ask. In using the AIF, the students will know what they don't know and are much more likely to ask questions particularly if they know that sooner or later they will have to achieve it anyway.

In fact, the results of using the AIF were so good that I suspected there was more to it than just improving the communication of what I felt was important. After a period of time spent observing and comparing classes without AIF's and in the use of AIF's, I identified what I think is a second factor in the success in the use of AIF's. The problem that this factor affects is illustrated very commonly in any group gathering where the group is listening to a speaker, teacher, etc. Among elementary and secondary school students this problem is called *daydreaming* whereas among adults (particularly faculty in faculty meetings) it is called *meditation*. There are several reasons for this behavior and one of them concerns the difference between the rates of information receiving and information producing. The input senses of the mind are capable of accepting information at a much greater rate than the human vocal apparatus is capable of producing. Research in compressed speech where 50 minute lectures have been compressed into 20 minutes and less have shown that students can listen to these compressed lectures with no loss of comprehension. Since the input senses and the mind can work much faster than they are asked to in the usual traditional situation, the mind has a tendency to wander to random thoughts floating around in the mind or to thoughts triggered by random stimuli coming in via the input senses. In a situation where a presentation is being made, we also frequently predict what a person is going to say and then purposely let our mind wander to other things. In either case, whether the distraction is accidental or intentional, if the *mental trips* only last a few moments or even a few minutes, when the listener tunes back into what the speaker is saying, nothing is usually lost from the presentation which in a way rewards the listener. The problem is that since these *mental trips* are usually triggered by random thoughts or random stimuli in the environment, if only by chance, sooner or later the listener will run into a *mental trip* that is more interesting than what is happening in the presentation. Then the listener is distracted for five, ten, fifteen, or more minutes and when he or she tunes back into the presentation, the listener is lost. In the traditional educational approach, a lot of non-achievement can be traced to these extended distractions. By using the AIF's, when the listener tunes back in, he or she can very quickly locate the point where the presenter is and at the same time identify what was missed.

NOTE: The structured notes are comparable to the minimum common core of objectives in that most students and participants using the AIF's write down more than is expected and the margins and backs of the pages in the AIF's get filled up with additional comments which reflect the individual differences in the needs and interests of the student or participant. If two or more teachers are using the same AIF, the extra notes may also reflect the individual differences in the teachers.

Not only can the AIF be used with live or recorded presentations, it can also be used in conjunction with reading assignments and, of course, has been used for decades in laboratory experiments and in workshop experiences to record observations and to guide the learner through a designed learning experience. In order to improve class discussions of reading assignments, in a traditional environment, a teacher can design an AIF to go along with the reading assignment in which the student has to record whatever it is that is important in the assignment. The filled in AIF then acts as the student's ticket to participate in the class or small group discussion. To further facilitate discussion, add several opinion type questions at the end of the AIF and then sort students into small groups such that each student in the small group has a different opinion than the others in the group. Start the groups out by having each student in the group state his or her opinions. Most students will spend hours trying to defend their opinions.

If in the design of the instructional environment or even in a traditional setting you plan to give hand-out material, don't have the hand-out complete because it will go in the back of the students' notebooks and they will ignore it until needed for a test. Build in blank spaces for involvement of the learner in those things that are important in the hand-out. By involving the learner in the materials, you indirectly add value to the materials. Whereas completed hand-outs are frequently lost or thrown out when no longer needed, hand-outs and notes which contain the writing or involvement of the learner are kept for a much longer period. For example, many college graduates keep their course notes for years after graduating. Look at the materials you save. Those which reflect your involvement are more apt to be retained than those which only reflect the thoughts and work of others.

The use of an AIF is of particular importance when the students are listening to audio only recorded presentations. If there is nothing for the eyes to do, the chances for distraction are increased. Before television, it was very common for people to listen to their favorite radio programs with their physical eyes open and not actually seeing anthing while their mental *eyes* added visuals to the program based on their piror experiences and the cues and sound effects in the program. The same experience occurs when people read books and the words act as stimuli to awaken and assemble appropriate mental visuals within which the action of the story takes place. After so many years of watching television, the ability or habit of having your eyes open without seeing and developing your own mental visuals has been almost lost. Even people who used to listen regularly to radio programs have difficulty in seeing nothing with their physical eyes and when listening to recordings of their favorite radio programs, they tend to pick up a magazine to look at or do other things that give their eyes something to do. Therefore, in developing audio only materials, it may facilitate learning and minimize distractions if an AIF is provided to be used by the student while listening.

(2) STEP SIZE AND REINFORCEMENT

Step size in learning can be defined in several ways. In general, step size refers to that amount of learning a student can handle at any one time and still be successful. For example, in the primary levels of elementary school, a teacher may not expect a student to pronounce a whole word at once until the student has learned how to pronounce each of the syllables as a step in learning. In high schools, before a student will be asked to do an entire scientific experiment as a learning step, the student may be asked to do each part of a similar experiment as a series of steps. Another way of looking at step size is the amount of learning which is expected to take place before evaluation or diagnosis occurs to see whether or not the learning took place. Some programmed instructional materials have been broken down into such small steps that the learner feels his or her ability to learn is being insulted. On the other hand, it is not uncommon in some high school and college level courses for teachers to go almost a whole semester before any evaluation occurs. If a student thinks that learning in a particular course is easy, it may be that the step size is too small for that student. If a student thinks that learning in a particular course is difficult, it may be that the step size is too large for that student. Lewin has stated that a student's motivation to learn decreases as the learning task is perceived to be either too easy or too difficult.

The problem of step size is compounded in situations where mastery learning (100 percent achievement) is not a part of the process. In traditional situations where students are passed along with a wide variety of achievement levels (even failing students are passed along in most elementary schools), the cumulative ignorance that the students take with them becomes an invisible hitch-hiker on subsequent step sizes. What may appear to be a reasonable step size for learning for an *average* student, may be too small for the student who already knows part of the step and too large for the student who has cumulative ignorance and has to learn prerequisite SO's in addition to the regular learning step. In the traditional approach, step size may have to be changed for each student in a class studying the same SO's because of the differences in their cumulative knowledge and cumulative ignorance. However, in a Behavioral Learning Systems approach where mastery learning is in effect and there is minimum, if any, cumulative ignorance to deal with and skipping ahead is allowed for those students who have already learned part of the steps, step size may not have to be altered at all except in cases of learning problems.

Another view of step size concerns how many SO's can be given to a student at one time. Do you start out a course giving the student the whole package or do you break it down into units and only give the students a unit at a time? The right size of a learning step and the learner's need for reinforcement are both very much affected by a student's prior learning experiences which in turn affect the student's self-image. If a student has had many negative or failure-oriented learning experiences in schools, the student will need short learning steps and constant or frequent reinforcement as to the success of his or her attempts to learn. The same is true of students who are just starting school or just starting a new course or curriculum. As the student's confidence in his or her ability to succeed in learning increases, the step size (number of objectives or difficulty level of objectives) can be increased and the student's need for reinforcement is decreased.

As indicated earlier, many students find the step by step learning and constant reinforcement of programmed instruction very helpful; but once their self-image is restored and they have confidence that they can learn, the step by step learning of programmed instruction may become too slow. Once the method begins to have negative affects on the learner's motivation, the method should be changed for that learner. Changes in method or materials should not be made because a teacher doesn't like them or would not like to learn from them if students are having success learning from the method or materials. Conversely, methods or materials should not be retained and used because a teacher likes them if students are not able to learn successfully from them. All too often a particular method or set of materials becomes the objective which is accepted or rejected without regard to the learning which the method or materials is supposed to facilitate.

A problem to be remembered in reinforcement is that in instructional materials where the answers are provided at some place in the book for all or part of the learning steps, students tend to make *energy decisions*, i.e., does it take more energy to do the learning step or just look up the answer. In traditional situations where non-achievement is acceptable, the students may just look at the answer and not really learn what was in the step. In this situation, the answers which were designed to be a reinforcement for learning become a pathway for partial learning and the real reinforcement comes when the student is passed on without having to learn each step. As such, the students partial learning is rewarded and the student is conditioned to look for further *low energy pathways.* In the Behavioral Learning Systems approach where mastery learning is the only way to complete a step, students who look at the answers without learning have to go back through the same materials or other alternate pathways until the desired learning occurs. In this situation, what appeared at first to the student to the *low energy pathway* (looking at the answers without learning) actually turns out to be a *high energy pathway* because of having to go back through the pathway again and/or through other alternate pathways. As such, students learn very quickly that following the prescribed pathway is more effective and efficient for learning and for energy output.

(3) ASSEMBLY AND VALIDATION

The next step is to put together all of the materials that have been developed into a whole unit (if that was all that was being developed), a complete course (if that was all that was being developed), or a coordinated curriculum (if that was all that was being developed). The purpose in this step is to examine the whole instructional development from sort of a *gestalt* point of view to make sure that all of the pieces fit together, have continuity in content, clarity in the directions for learning and in the materials from the learner's point of view, and a high correlation between the SO's, the evaluation or diagnostic instruments, and the instructional materials.

Of course, the most important step of all is the trying out of the instructional materials on a representative sample of the intended student population for which the instructional environment was being developed. Because of the long standing emphasis in traditional education research of trying to find one method, media, set of materials, etc., which will teach all students (those who don't learn are supposedly incapable of learning!), there is a strong tendency among instructional materials developers to try to make the one pathway be the most successful for the most students. The trouble with this is twofold: first, the concept ignores the basic rule that no one pathway will work for everyone and mastery learning cannot be achieved via one pathway: second, in solving the problems for some, you may create problems for others. In developing programmed instruction and in order to have high achievement levels, the programs frequently were aimed at the slowest potential student with the greatest need for small steps and reinforcement which then make them uninteresting and demotivating for the faster student who could have learned in larger steps and needed less reinforcement. Therefore, in trying out the instructional environment on a sample of students from the intended audience, the following two guidelines may be useful. Learning steps in which 50 percent or more of the students have trouble learning the desired SO's should be considered as representing program problems. As such, changes should be made in these instructional steps until at least 50 percent or more of the learners can achieve the desired SO's. Learning steps in which at least 50 percent or more of the students have success in achieving the desired SO's should be considered as acceptable initial pathways. The non-achievement should be considered a problem of individual differences and indicates a need for one or more alternate pathways which should be developed to reflect the needs, interests, and abilities of the non-achievers and will convert them into achievers. *Remember, the changes are made in the learning pathways not in the GO's and SO's of the learning steps.* The alternate paths which are developed should also be validated by trying them out on another sample of students.

NOTE: The sample of students upon which the alternate pathways are tried out on should *not* be a random sample of the total intended student population for the initial instructional environment. They should represent a sample of students from a population of students who had trouble learning the desired SO's from the initial pathway or subsequent alternate pathways.

The same procedures are followed over again for the alternate paths. If 50 percent or more of the non-achievers in the initial program still cannot achieve in the first alternate pathway, this should indicate changes to be made in the first alternate pathway. If at least 50 percent or more of the non-achievers in the initial pathway were able to achieve the desired SO's via the first alternate pathway, then the first alternate pathway should be considered acceptable. The non-achievement of some students in both the initial path and the first alternate pathway should still be considered a problem of individual differences and indicates a need for a second alternate pathway which should be developed to reflect the needs, interests, and abilities of the non-achieving students. Again, this second alternate pathway should be tried out on a sample of students who were non-achievers on the initial pathway and the first alternate pathway. This process is repeated until at least 90 percent or more of the students have achieved mastery or 100 percent of the SO's. During the process, a hierarchy of learning pathways is developed. Once developed, this heirarchy can guide the teacher in terms of which pathway to use first, second, third, etc. in the process of solving student learning problems.

(4) POTENTIAL SOURCES OF PROBLEMS IN THE DEVELOPMENT OF LEARNING PATHWAYS

As indicated in the last section, there are two major sources of learning problems in the instructional environment or learning pathway; first, there are program problems as indicated when approximately 50 percent or more of the students in the sample of students from the target population are not able to achieve the desired SO's and second, there are those problems which are primarily caused by individual differences among students as indicated when over 50 percent but not 100 percent of the students are able to achieve the desired SO's.

The most common problem concerns a low correlation between the course or unit objectives and the evaluation or diagnostic instrument. In other words, the tests are not testing for the same learning that the objectives indicate should be learned. These correlation problems in turn are caused by one or more of three problem areas: the objectives are not really specific enough to be observable and measurable; the tests are not specific enough in that the evaluation is too subjective or the so-called *objective type* tests are used which may be objective in scoring but very subjective in writing and design and rarely match any specific objective that can be defended in terms of the questions of justification; and just plain ignoring the obvious lack of correlation between a specific objective and a specific test item as indicated by a mismatch in noun and/or verb correlation. In connection with the specification of objectives, if the SO's are not defended in terms of the questions of justification, it is possible to have SO's which are irrelevant and/or superficial and not really what the developers want.

Another common related problem is the tendency to carry over from the traditional curriculum preparation procedures the separation of steps. Traditionally, the course or unit objectives are stated (usually GO's) and then set aside, then the curriculum is developed as a separate procedure, and then the evaluation is designed to give the desired results (some sort of curve) with little if any behavioral (verb) relationship between the objectives, the learning procedures, and the evaluation. As a result, some curriculum developers have accepted the need to have SO's, some have accepted the need to have the evaluation instrument match the SO's, but some haven't quite accepted the fact that the learning procedures or pathways should be developed in terms of the SO's, the tests, and the interests and abilities of the students. In other words, the learning pathway may not actually be designed to teach the SO's and matching test items.

Many problems can stem from an inadequate behavioral analysis such as errors in the identification of the student's actual entry levels which in turn results in a lack of necessary branching for individual differences or a starting point which doesn't match where the students really are.

Problems in step size are frequently a result of the developers being unable to put themselves in the role of the learner, i.e., what is clear to the developers (with their background and experience) is not clear and is ambiguous to the learners (with their limited background and experience). What is assumed and left out by the developers may be necessary and may have been learned easily by the learners. What is easy to learn from the developers point of view may be difficult to learn from the point of view of the learners. What is difficult to learn from the developers point of view may be seen as impossible to learn by the learners. Since curriculum logic is often a very personal thing, what appears logical to the developers may not be logical to the learners. Notice that psychologists and particularly Piaget have identified that children's system of logic changes as they mature and gain experience.

A related problem is that with the developers greater experience, there is a tendency to assume that the learners have had similar experiences and the words which are symbolic of an experience are used when actually visuals, actual materials, or actual experiences should be used rather than the words. This is a problem associated with the belief that *words* have meanings instead of remembering that *words* are just symbols and that only people have meanings. If the meanings are missing in a person, it is because the experiences necessary to develop the meanings are missing, not necessarily something wrong with the person's vocabulary.

Also related to step size is the lack of sufficient and frequent diagnostic procedures to identify the existence of potential cumulative ignorance before it starts causing non-achievement and a loss of motivation.

4. UTILIZING OR ADAPTING READY-MADE SOFTWARE

As emphasized in the prior section on identifying minimum common core SO's, there is not much gained in having every teacher re-invent the curriculum SO's and the instructional environment. Given that most materials in almost every subject matter area are able to help some students learn some things whether or not any SO's have been written and given that a successful instructional design has to involve multiple pathways, the smart developer will use whatever materials are readily available rather than develop new materials from scratch without knowing whether or not they are even needed. In lieu of having SO's in the traditional situation, most traditional teachers tend to teach a book and when they change books the course changes accordingly, but not necessarily the course title. Once a teacher has the SO's and matching tests for a particular course, you can make the books and other materials fit the course rather than making the course fit the books and/or materials. The key is to use what is appropriate and works (helps students learn) and skip over or discard those parts which are not appropriate and/or those parts which even if appropriate don't work!

In evaluating instructional materials which have been prepared commercially or by someone else as to its usefulness in your course, there are a series of questions, criteria, and suggestions which you could ask or use as a guide that will facilitate the evaluation.

(a) If available, what are the GO's and/or SO's of the materials? If not available, examine materials for potential GO's and SO's.

(b) How do the GO's and SO's of the materials compare to the desired GO's and SO's of your unit or course? Those that match, use them. Those that don't match, skip over or discard.

(c) How do the entry requirements for the materials compare with the entry requirements for your unit or course? If the entry requirements for the materials are not available, examine the materials and estimate what they might be. If the entry requirements of the materials are lower than yours, it may be that the materials start at a lower level, so you may need to develop some branching check points to let your students start at appropriate places in the materials. If the entry requirements of the materials are lower than yours and the materials start at essentially the same place, then the materials are aimed at students with lower abilities. If used with regular or higher ability students, you may have to build in some check-points to allow the students to skip ahead faster through the materials when and where appropriate. If the entry requirements of the materials are higher than yours, you may need to develop some brief materials to raise your students to the level where they could have success with the available materials.

(d) Is there any information or data regarding the tryout period of the program or instructional materials? If there is, analyze the data from the point-of-view of the model for instructional design evaluation formulas in the section following this one. Be sure to check if the types of students used in the try-out of the materials are similar to the types of students you will be using the materials with. If the two student groups are different, the data may not be relevant and you may have to act as if there isn't any data. Also, be sure that the SO's and tests used in the try out include the SO's and test items you plan to use. If the SO's are different and/or if the test items are different (particularly if the test items are of the so-called *objective type*), the data is essentially useless and you will have to act as if there isn't any data. If there isn't any information or data and you believe the materials have potential to act as an initial or alternate pathway to learn your SO's, try out a unit of the materials on an appropriate sample of your students, i.e., if for the initial or basic pathway, the sample would be from the total student group; if for an alternate pathway, the sample should be from the group of students not able to learn from your initial pathway or other alternate pathways you are already using, if any. If 50 percent or more of the students sample can learn 100% or your SO's from the materials, then the materials may be useful as an initial or alternate pathway. If you are comparing two or more sets of instructional materials, that set that you get more students to achieve 100 percent of your SO's is the better set for that group of students. Before discarding the other sets of materials, try them out again on a sample of students who were the non-achievers in using the set of materials which appeared to be better. It is possible for a particular set of instructional materials to be very successful with a particular group of students and yet not show up very well with a general mixture of students. This type of program would not be good as an initial or basic learning pathway, but it might be very good as an alternate pathway for non-achievers in the initial pathways or in other alternate pathways.

(e) Are there preentry tests, pretests, and/or post tests available? If none of these three tests are available and there are also no SO's, then you may still want to tryout the materials using your own SO's and matching tests in order to identify which of your SO's, if any, the materials may be useful in facilitating student achievement. If there are no tests, but there are SO's, then it should be relatively easy to make up matching test items (slight changes in the wording of the SO's). Depending upon the correlation between your SO's and the SO's of the program, you may or may not want to try it. If there are only a few of the SO's of the materials that are what you want, then you may not want to use the program unless those few SO's happen to be ones that are learning problems in other sets of materials you are using. The higher the correlation between the SO's and tests of the materials and your desired SO's and tests, the more likely the materials could become a basic or initial pathway. If there are tests, but no SO's, then by slight changes of wording in the test items, you should be able to identify some SO's and then compare these SO's with your desired SO's. If the test items happen to be the so-called objective type (multiple-choice, true-false, and/or matching), neither the test items nor any SO's directly derived by slight changes in wording will probably be relevant, useful, or really represent the potential SO's that could be learned from the materials. In this last situation, it is almost better to assume there are no tests as it would be easier to try out the materials using your own SO's and matching test items in order to find out which ones can be learned from the materials then to try to examine the materials and identify or develop the SO's available in the materials and then compare them with yours.

(f) Is there a teacher's manual available? Frequently, when teachers are teaching a course for the first time, the only difference between the students and the teacher is that the teacher has the manual. Since many teacher's manuals have lists of SO's, sample tests, and suggestions for facilitating learning in them, the easiest way of facilitating students who want to learn independently is to give them copies of the teacher's manuals. The added cost is minimal in most cases.

(g) Do you need a specialized environment in order to use the materials, i.e., slide projector, tape recorders, teaching machine, etc. If yes, be sure that these are available when needed. If there is a need for certain equipment and it isn't possible to obtain sufficient equipment for all of your students to try the materials, then it may be appropriate to try to get enough equipment for a sample group of your students to try the materials. If the materials work and students learn the desired SO's, then it may be worth purchasing the necessary equipment.

(h) Although the primary importance of using instructional materials is to facilitate the learning of desired GO's and SO's, it is also important that the supporting materials and information which represent other potential GO's and SO's (not identified) does not contain misinformation or emphasis which may detract from the learning of the desired GO's and SO's. If there is a potential for distraction in those sections or parts of the materials not related to the learning of the desired GO's and SO's, consider eliminating those parts if possible. If the potentially negative parts can't be eliminated, then a decision will have to be made as to whether or not the value of the materials in helping students learn the desired GO's and SO's is worth exposing the students to the negative aspects of the materials.

(i) An obvious factor in using any ready made materials is the cost. In most situations, the cost of having each teacher re-invent *curriculum wheels* is much more expensive than using ready-made materials. The more students and teachers involved in the same or similar GO's and SO's (same common core), the easier it is to justify making up curriculum materials for the basic or initial pathways which are tailor-made for the desired GO's and SO's. It is more effective, efficient, and economical to use a few good tailor-made pathways which will facilitate 90 percent or more of the students to learn 100 percent of the SO's than to use a larger number of mediocre ready-made pathways to achieve the same level of quality control. As more and more teachers in school districts, colleges, and universities cooperate in the identification of the minimum common core SO's in their courses, the more the development of ready-made materials can be correlated with the common core SO's.

(j) As indicated indirectly in several of the previous questions, the most important criteria for acceptance or rejection of any ready-made materials concerns whether or not your students are able to use them and learn your desired GO's and SO's. Ultimately, the best way to find this out is to try the materials out on a sample of your students (see question "d").

5. *INSTRUCTIONAL DESIGN EVALUATION*

For decades in education, the emphasis in educational research has been on trying to find significant differences between the pretest and posttest of one method or between the posttests of two or more different methods. Most critiques and/or reviews of this type of research were based on what the degree of *significance* was and the power and reliability of the statistics used in the research design. Not much attention has been paid to the instructional situation and test design from which all the data was obtained. In computer terminology, there is a concept called GIGO which stands for *garbage in — garbage out.* The concept refers to a problem of people evaluating the computer output without evaluating the input. If the output is good or bad, the evaluation usually concerns the *goodness* or *badness* of the computer when in actuality, the quality of the output is a direct result of the quality of the input. In applying this concept to educational research, the traditional approach associates the power of the statistical instrument and the degree of statistical significance with the *goodness* or *badness* of the particular method, technique, or technology used as the independent variable in the research. In actuality, if the instructional situation and/or the tests are *garbage*, then any data obtained from the

791

situation or the tests is also *garbage* regardless of the power of the statistical instrument used or the degree of significance. Stop and think, how often have you actually seen a copy of the instructional materials and/or a copy of the test that was used in the research? Given that few, if any, fellow educators will actually see the instructional materials or tests used in research, it is possible to design the materials or tests to give you almost any data you want regardless of what students know or don't know. For example, a high percentage of educational research is based on the use of the so-called *objective type* test items (multiple-choice, true-false, and matching) which are only objective in scoring and are very subjective in writing. A professional test item writer can hold constant the stem and the correct choice of a multiple-choice item and by varying the *distractors* in the wrong choices, the writer can obtain almost any desired percentage of students who will get an item right or wrong regardless of whether or not the students actually know the desired content of the item. As such, the distribution of scores resulting from a test made up of *objective* type test items is much more affected by the design of the test items than by what students know. In addition, the multiple choice format is very unreal in relation to life and it forces the testing of many different desired behaviors into only one behavior — that of discrimination. As a result, *almost all educational research which utilizes the so-called objective type test items in order to obtain data becomes garbage because the tests are garbage!*

An even more important way to evaluate research data concerning a certain set of materials is to examine the instructional situation from three new points of view: The Boredom Factor, the Instructional Effectiveness Factor, and the Instructional Efficiency Factor. Assuming that the test is designed to test for the achievement of what is covered in the instructional materials, then the higher the pretest scores, the more bored the students will be during the instructional process. Under the concept of individualized instruction, students should start an instructional unit from a point which would minimize any overlap in learning and yet not have any gaps in learning. Therefore, the ideal pretest score should be between zero and 10 percent or an average of five percent. Pretest scores that are higher than this indicate a strong possibility that boredom will contaminate the student's motivation to learn from the instructional materials and in turn also contaminate any research based on the use of the instructional materials. In order to calculate the *Boredom Factor*, divide the pretest score (in terms of percentage) by five (the ideal percentage). For example, in a particular research design, the average pretest score was 18 out of a possible 40. Eighteen is 45 percent of 40 and when divided by five (45/5) results in a Boredom Factor of nine which is nine times higher than it should be if boredom is to be minimized. Obviously, a pretest score of 45 percent indicates that almost half of the time the students are involved in the instructional process they are in a non-learning and potentially boring situation.

The second factor is based on the posttest score and concerns the effectiveness of the instructional design. Obviously, if the instructional design is so haphazard that the average learner is only learning "C" (70-85 percent), "D" (60-69 percent), of "F" worth (below 60 percent) of what there is to learn in the instructional unit, then this weakness could very easily contaminate the utility of any data for research. Ideally, a good instructional unit should be effective enough so that students should learn between 90-100 percent of the objectives of the unit with an average of 95 percent. Therefore, the Instructional Effectiveness Factor is the posttest score (in percentage) divided by 95. For example, if in a given research, the average posttest score is 26 out of a possible score of 40 or 65 percent, this would result in an Instructional Effectiveness Factor of 65/95 or .68 which even under a normal grading curve is just "D" achievement. Consequently, any instructional unit that is so badly designed that the average student only achieves "D" worth of the unit objectives is bound to affect the value of the research data in a negative way. As a general rule, the higher the Instructional Effectiveness Factor, the greater the number of students who are achieving 100 percent of the desired GO's and SO's of the instructional materials and the greater the possibility of the materials being useful as a basic or initial pathway for learning.

NOTE: Remember, instructional materials which may have a high Boredom Factor and a low Instructional Effectiveness Factor for a general student audience could have a low Boredom Factor and a high Instructional Effectiveness Factor for a specific group of low achievers. As such, instructional materials which may be inappropriate as an initial or basic pathway could be useful as an alternate pathway for certain groups of low or non-achieving students.

The third factor is based on the efficiency of the instructional unit and concerns the minimizing of the Boredom Factor and the maximizing of the Instructional Effectiveness Factor. In other words, the ideal instructional unit should have pretest scores between zero and 10 percent and posttest scores between 90 and 100 percent which would result in an average gain of 90 percent (from 5 percent to 95 percent). To determine the Instructional Efficiency Factor, divide the percentage gain of an instructional unit (posttest score minus the pretest score) by 90 percent. For example, in the research cited for the first two factors, where the average posttest score was 26 and the average pretest score was 18, the average gain was 8 or 20 percent (8/40). In this case, the Instructional Efficiency Factor is 20/90 or .22 which is so inefficient, it couldn't help but contaminate the learning situation and any research based on the use of the instructional materails would have to be *garbage*. Oddly enough, this same data resulted in significant differences between the pretest and posttest and as such was published in a professional journal as respectable educational research.

In examining the results of using tailor-made or ready-made instructional materials or in examining instructional research (and particularly educational research), check the following before making your own conclusions or accepting anyone else's conclusions (particularly if based on *significant differences*).

— If the so-called *objective type* tests were used, you can't make any conclusions nor can you accept any conclusions based on data from these tests.

— Identify the total possible score in the pretest and posttest. If this information is not available, it is not possible to calculate any of the three factors described in this section. Significant differences based on the number of items achieved without knowing the number of items not achieved makes the significance doubtful.

— If the average pretest score (in percentage) is much over 15 or 20 percent, the resultant boredom will affect the learning situation and any research data based on the learning situation. As a maximum, the Boredom Factor should be less than three or four.

— If the average posttest score (in percentage) is less than 80 percent, the instructional materials are too ineffective to be useful or to result in good research data. The Instructional Effectiveness Factor should be about .90.

— Subtract the average pretest score (in percentage) from the average posttest score (in percentage). The difference should be at least 60 percent otherwise the efficiency of the instructional unit will be so low as to affect the value of the data and any conclusions based on the data. The Instructional Efficiency Factor should be about .90.

Under the traditional approach to research, *significant differences can be obtained from data resulting from a boring, ineffective, and inefficient instructional unit.* Under the Learning Systems Approach to instructional research in which the Boredom Factor is minimized and the Instructional Effectiveness and Efficiency Factors are maximized, *there will always* be significant differences between pretest and posttest scores. When comparing the posttest scores of two different methods for significant differences, the value of the significance is still dependent upon whether or not the instructional design of both methods minimized the Boredom Factor and maxmized the Instructional Effectiveness and Efficiency Factors.

If LEARNING is the *name of the game* in the instructional process which is supposedly taking place in our schools, then these factors which evaluate the instructional design should be much more important than whether or not there are significant differences (particularly when comparing pretest and posttest scores).

NOTE: Because of the differences between 100 percent of test items and 100 percent of SO's, these three factors should ideally be based on the percentage achievement of SO's rather than on the percentage achievement of test items. In evaluating instructional materials where there are SO's and matching test items, the evaluation can be made on the basis of SO's. In evaluating instructional materials or research where there aren't any SO's, the use of test item data can be used but the results aren't as reliable as it would have been if there were SO's.

Television has a great potential for instruction, but as long as instructional television programs are developed without objectives, this potential might just as well be forgotten. As of 1970, the number of instructional television programs that have been developed according to a systems concept with objectives, testing, etc., could almost be counted on two hands. One such program, *Sesame Street*, has been acclaimed as fantastic, the greatest thing in television, and a model for all instructional television! If other television programs use *Sesame Street* as a model, then instructional television will continue to move into the 20th century in a horse and buggy with both the driver and the horse wearing blinders to keep from seeing what is happening around them. Yes, in comparison with other instructional television, *Sesame Street* is great; but so is the horse and buggy great in comparison to walking! To back up these statements, consider the evidence as presented in the evaluation report of *Sesame Street* prepared by the Educational Testing Service. *(The conclusions of the report from the point of view of traditional education were that the series was a success. By looking at the same data from the point of view of a systems approach, the success is pretty empty).* According to their own data, the average pretest score of all children in their study was 42 percent which means that the children already knew almost half of what *Sesame Street* was supposed to teach which would obviously result in a high level of boredom for most children. If the series was designed so that the children could start from wherever they were intellectually, then the pretest score for each child should be somewhere between zero and 10 percent (of course because of individual differences in what they know, some children would have to see more of the programs than others). The Boredom Factor should be 1.0 for an ideal instructional situation. With an average pretest score of 42 percent, the Boredom Factor (42/5) for *Sesame Street* is 8.4 or about eight times higher than it should be.

The average posttest score of all the children was 59 percent which means that the series was only successful in teaching 59 percent of what the series should have been able to teach. In most classrooms, a student achieving 59 percent would recieve an "F" or at best a "D". Under the current concept in designed instruction, the learners should have learned between 90 and 100 percent of the objectives of the series. Therefore, with an average posttest score of 59 percent, the Instructional Effectiveness Factor (59/95) for *Sesame Street* is about .62.

In looking at the efficiency of the series, an ideal program which minimizes the boredom and starts each learner with a pretest score of from zero to 10 percent and maximizes learning by having the learners learning 90-100 percent of the objectives would result in the average learner gaining 90 percent. The average child in the *Sesame Street* study gained 17 percent. Therefore, the Instructional Efficiency Factor (17/90) is only .19, which is pretty bad.

With a little more analysis of the data it is rather easy to uncover that it took the average child *five hours of viewing SESAME STREET to gain the answer to one test item.* As if that isn't bad enough, in isolating the data for the advantaged children in the study, it turns out that they were so bored that it took them an *average of seven hours of viewing Sesame Street* in order to gain enough knowledge to answer one additional test item correctly. Now that is *fantastic!*

E. SELECTING, MODIFYING, AND/OR DESIGNING HARDWARE FOR THE INSTRUCTIONAL EVENT

In selecting, modifying, and/or designing hardware for the instructional event, it is critical to recognize and remember the interdependent relationships between instructional software and instructional hardware:

— The best software is made ineffective if the hardware used with it is ineffective or inoperative;

— the best hardware is made ineffective if the software used with it is ineffective;

— if the use of either the software (as a vehicle for learning) and/or the hardware becomes the objective of the instructional event rather than the learning of the GO's and SO's, the achievement of the desired GO's and SO's will be negatively affected;

— the more flexible the use of the hardware, the more flexible the software can be that is used with it, and the more useful the hardware will be in an instructional event;

— as the design of the hardware exerts limitations on the design of the software used with it, the design also limits its usefulness in an instructional event.

The key guideline to remember in selecting, modifying, and/or designing hardware for an instructional event is that the desired GO's and related SO's are identified *first;* then the software is selected, modified, or designed (depending upon the desired learning and who is to do the learning); the *last step* is to select, modify, and/or design the hardware (depending upon the desired learning, the software to be used, who is to do the learning, where the learners are, when the learners want to learn, and how they learn best). In the traditional educational event where it is rare that the SO's have been identified, it has become traditional to select first either the software (as a vehicle for learning GO's) or the hardware and then hope that learning will take place. If learning didn't occur, it has been and is still traditional in most schools at all levels to blame the students and/or the external environment, i.e., parents, home environment, society, the atom bomb, the Vietnam War, etc.

Of interest is that when a hardware or software specialist is involved in the selection, modification, or design of the instructional event, the resultant instructional event more often reflects their speciality interest area than it does the needs and interests of the intended learners. For example, a librarian will usually recommend the use of books; an audio-visual specialist will usually recommend the use of slides, transparencies, or a multi-media show; a television specialist will usually recommend the use of television; a computer specialist will usually recommend the use of a computer; an educational psychologist will usually recommend some form of programmed instruction or whatever the current educational fad is; etc. What is really needed are learning specialists who will recommend whatever software and hardware combination that will successfully facilitate the learning of the desired GO's and SO's in the most effective and efficient manner.

Some might say, *With all the decisions that have to be made, why even use any hardware?* There is only one way to eliminate the need for and the use of hardware and software in the instructional event and that is for the teacher and life experiences to be the living software and hardware. The trouble is that the same interdependent relationships still exist. The live teacher has only one mouth and as such can only communicate in one way at any one moment. If there are two or more students, that one way may not be appropriate for effective and efficient learning for one or more of the students. Even if the teacher could be limited to only one student at a time, the human being isn't physically equipped to present visuals and the visual life experiences which could be used may not always be available when the student is ready to learn. Consequently, even when the live teacher and life experiences are selected as the software and the hardware of learning, their physical limitations limit the learning that can take place and who can do the learning.

If we are really concerned about the successful learning of each and every student, teachers have to get out of the role as educational software and hardware and get into much more important role of selecting, modifying, and designing software and hardware to facilitate desired GO's and SO's and to solve student learning problems. In changing their role, the flexibility of the instructional event is greatly increased and hence the potential for increased individualization and increased learning is also greatly increased. In selecting, modifying, and designing hardware, remember that hardware can;

- help simulate varying levels of an instructional event;

- help make the instructional event portable so as to be available at the convenience of the learners (across distances);

- record the instructional events for later recall (across time);

- enable the instructional event to be manipulated when necessary to facilitate learning, i.e., speeded up, slowed down, edited, enlarged, etc.

- multiply the event for many students at different places, at different times, or all at the same time.

Given that software and hardware other than the teacher is going to be used and given that the software is going to be designed to facilitate the achievement of certain GO's and SO's for certain students, then the hardware should be selected, modified, and/or designed to facilitate the use of the software which in turn facilitates learning of the desired GO's and SO's. As pointed out earlier in this Chapter, when teaching and teachers are the emphasis, the selection, modification, and design of the hardware and software is to facilitate the teacher in his or her process of teaching which may or may not facilitate the desired learning and certainly ignores the individual differences among students. Therefore, when the emphasis is on learning and learners, the selection, modification, and design of hardware and software has to be learner-oriented not teacher-oriented.

Before discussing the design of new hardware, it is more appropriate to consider the selection and modification of existing and readily

798

available hardware. There are a number of different ways that available hardware can be catagorized. If you can accept that learning can take place almost any place and especially that it can take place away from live teachers and out of school buildings, then it is convenient to divide available hardware into three catagories: traditional information technology (hardware); contemporary information technology (hardware); and new information technology (hardware).

1. Old information technology is defined as technology where *the learner goes to the source* for the necessary learning experiences. This would be like the learner goes to the library for books, or the learner goes to the classroom for the teacher, or the learner may go to a film department to see a film.

2. Contemporary information technology refers to a situation in which *the learner and the source are at the same place.* This would be exemplified by the use of single concept films or video cassettes by the student, by the student having his own textbooks (paperbacks), by the student having his or her own portable hardware, etc.

3. The new information technology refers to a situation in which the *source goes to the learner.* This would be exemplified by dial-access systems, television, computers, etc.

As more and more contemporary and new information technology is introduced into the teaching-learning situation, the more we enable learners to learn at their own pace and at their own site or any other place where learning is convenient for the learner, such as in the homes, offices, dormitories, learning centers, etc. Once we start admitting that learning can take place out of the classroom and away from the school, two factors become apparent, in addition to having teachers managing MORE students, schools should be able to handle more students. For example, a school that is designed for 3,000 students may very well handle 6,000 students of which there may be only 2,000 students in the school at any one time.

To illustrate how some of the old information technology can be converted into contemporary or new information technology, consider the following examples:

— *Textbooks:* If the student already owns the books, this would be the same as contemporary technology. Although there will probably always be a need to store books in a library, when specific books or parts of books which are located in a library are necessary in the instructional design, then it may be of value to consider changing these books or parts of these books from the old information technology into contemporary or new information technology. One of the easiest ways to accomplish this would be to give the student his own microfiche containing the necessary pages and make available individual microfiche readers. Another way that this could be accomplished would be to have a person with good speaking voice record this material on audiotape and in order that the learner would not lose a lot of learning time because he can read faster than the speaker on the audiotape can speak, it may be useful to consider *compressed speech*.[40]

— *Lectures:* One of the values often stated by educators in support of lectures is that the textbooks which are written for a national audience may not be appropriate for a specific regional or local audience, and that the educator is able to adapt the textbook materials through a lecture to the needs of the learners. If this is the case, once the teacher has identified the problem and then gives the lecture, there's really no reason for the learner and the teacher to be together at the same place and at the same time nor is there any reason for the teacher to repeat the lecture many times. If the lecture is recorded, the learner has the opportunity to listen to it two or three times, to stop it, to start it again, to study it as he would a book. The learner could also take the recorded lecture anyplace that is convenient and conducive for learning. When the learner thinks he or she has learned the desired GO's and related SO's he or she was supposed to have learned from the recorded lectures, the learner can see the teacher (who has more time to work with students now instead of spending it repeating the lectures) to ask questions, take the appropriate tests, and receive the necessary prescriptions if needed.[41]

— *16mm Films, Slides, Film Strips:* Although it is possible to convert 35mm and 16mm films to 8mm single concept films and to let the students have their own copies and to let the

---

[40] Compressed speech refers to any one of several different methods of compressing human speech into a time interval that is less than the normal speaking voice of the person doing the recording. Depending on the material and what the listener is supposed to listen for, it is possible to compress speech considerably without loss in comprehension and then play the recorded speech on a regular recorder. The same equipment that can compress speech can also be used to stretch out the speech such that students who are not familiar with the language used in the speech can hear it at a much slower rate than the normal speaking voice of the person doing the recording. As this equipment becomes less expensive, it will be possible for students to regulate the rate of the recorded speech to fit their own needs.

students have their own slides and film strips, for large numbers of students, this duplication process could become expensive, so it may be convenient to convert these permanent visual media into temporary recorded media (television, slow-scan TV, video discs or cassettes, etc.) for easier retrieval and distribution.

— *Three-Dimensional Materials:* In a number of learning situations, it is important for the learner to feel and manipulate three-dimensional materials. If the learning of the desired behaviors is important rather than have the students come to a special laboratory or go to a special place, it may be possible to develop an instructional kit or module in which all of the necessary three-dimensional items are available to the individual student at his own location.[42]

For the time being, as teachers and schools go through the process of identifying the GO's and related SO's of their courses and in particular the minimum common core SO's, as they increase the individualization of instruction with its accompanying change in the role of the teacher, and as more students achieve the required learning on an independent basis, the most popular and useful hardware will be the contemporary information technology with the emphasis on the learner having his or her own individual sources, i.e., cassette or cartridge audio and/or video tapes, paper back books, learning activity packets, instructional modules, etc. Actually this approach to the selection, modification, and design of hardware provides for the maximum of flexibility. However, the duplication of materials for the initial or basic pathways and for multiple alternate pathways in order to achieve 100 percent learning for 90 percent or more of hundreds, thousands, and millions of students may become prohibitive and there will be a need for some type of hardware system in the new information technology which will

---

[41] Whenever a teacher is recorded, there is a tendency on the part of the teacher and particularly the hardware specialists to try to make the best recording possible. Under a traditional approach, in which the educator is going to be evaluated on his ability to *present*, the preparation of the tapes becomes very important. Under a behavioral learning systems approach, the development of the audiotapes or video-tapes from the point of view of *presenting* is not as critical as under the traditional approach because the evaluation is based on whether or not the students learned what they were supposed to learn. Any changes in the audio or video recording are based on a lack of learning results. If the learning can be achieved without the *finishing touches*, then time and money are saved.

---

[42] For example, the Articulated Instruction Media program at the University of Wisconsin developed a take-home instructional module about the size of two shoeboxes end to end, within which they were able to put all of the equipment necessary to perform the traditional experiments required in a first-year college physics course (in addition to the materials in the kit, the experiments made use of some materials readily available in the majority of homes).

minimize the costs of duplication while at the same time maintaining maximum achievement and possibly increasing the flexibility of diagnosis and retrieval of prescribed alternate pathways for learning.

In reference to the new information technology, where the source goes to the learner, there is another differentiation that should be made. There are situations, such as broadcast television and radio, in which the source goes to the learner, but the time for transmission of the message is decided on by the source. In the utilization of most dial-access systems and computer systems, which also bring the source to the learner, the actual transmission of the message takes place under the learner's initiative. Compromises between the two categories — source initiated and learner initiated — have been tried by a number of educational television and radio stations through repetition of a given program, which allows the learner two, three, or more choices of the time for viewing or listening to the program. The number of choices in this compromise are dictated more by the number of program channels available and the number of programs to be broadcast than it is based on the needs of the learners.

At the present time, the three identifiable media that could be considered in the category of new information technology are radio and television, audio and visual dial-access systems, and computer systems. Depending on your point of view, these three could very easily overlap. For example, in large dial-access systems, they almost always include some kind of logic for a computer system. Video dial-access systems include some form of television. In radio and television, from one point of view, the listener is using a form of a *dial* in order to select the video channel or the radio frequency. It would also be possible in the use of a computer for instructional purposes that, at a given moment, the computer could automatically retrieve audio or video information very much like a dial-access system. Although these systems do overlap, it is useful to examine each of these individually.

1. TELEVISION AND THE <u>STEWART ITV</u> FORMAT

Although educational television has been around for over 25 years and almost all students have some form of educational television available to them, it has not really lived up to the great potential for affecting learning that many educators believed was possible back in the early 1950's. This fact is frequently referred to by the educators who resist the advances of technology into education. The important point to remember is that educational television *as it is and has been used* didn't make much of an impact on the educational scene.

In reference to the differentiation between instructional materials and educational materials, the majority of educational television and even instructional television can be classified in the category of educational materials, or chance learning experiences, because most televised learning experiences are not accompanied with SO's and/or tests to identify whether or not learning took place. And if there are no tests, it is possible to draw the conclusion that the televised learning experience was developed without specific, measurable objectives for learning. If television is going to have a measurable impact on education, producers of televised learning experiences will have to start developing these materials from the point of view of facilitating the learning of specific, measurable objectives. In addition, television has to become more flexible in its format and in its availability to the learner. It has been known since the beginning of television that it is a medium which can uniquely transmit sound, live images, film, print, charts, and could serve as a distribution system for all other media. We have assumed that since the TV receiver can receive moving visuals and sound that we should use moving visuals and sound all the time. In fact, the most common criticism of television programs is that the media wasn't exploited to its fullest. Although this point of view is acceptable when thinking of television as a medium for designed instruction, full use of the media may actually interfere with learning. As long as there is action going on the television screen, the learner's attention is concentrated on viewing rather than on acting. If learners learn best by doing, then it may be better to use less action and visual involvement in the television program and require more action and mental involvement in the learners.

In contrast to the present teacher-oriented television, learner-oriented television programs would take on characteristics that are quite radical from the contemporary educational television programming. Since most producers of instructional television programs may claim that their programming is *learner-oriented*, even if there are no tests or objectives available, it is necessary to differentiate between the traditional instructional television and the new format of instructional television, which is designed to achieve certain measurable learner behaviors. For lack of a descriptive title, which would rule out misinterpretations, the new format will be referred to as the *Stewart ITV* format. If you are a producer, director or teacher involved in instructional television, a question to ask yourself is *What do I want the student to learn as a result of viewing this television program?* Answers to this question can serve as guidelines in the development of the program and can also serve as a test to test the effectiveness of the program. A second important question to ask yourself is *What should the learner be doing during the program to facilitate learning?* Answers to this question will help in the design of an instructional television program which will result in measurable learning. For example, if there is a diagram or photograph available in a textbook and yet not appropriate for television transmission because of the need for high resolution, why not go to a black screen on the television and, using only audio, direct the student to take out their textbooks and turn to whatever the right page is, and talk to them while they are examining the photograph or chart. There may also be times in which the teacher may want the learner to think or solve a problem, to study a chart, etc. During these times, it may be best to stop all audio and video transmission, even though the video tape recorder may still be moving. If motion is not required in order to achieve the learning objective, then a series of stills could very easily be used. If no visuals are required at all, then why not use just audio. Television programming developed along these lines (the Stewart ITV Format) would be much easier to edit for the purposes of revision and improvement of instruction, and also would be much easier and cheaper to produce. Not only would this approach to instructional programming improve the instructional value of the programming, but this format is designed to demand involvement of the learner in the learning process.

Harry Skornia, University of Illinois, quotes Otto Neurath, the distinguished Austrian scholar, as saying *the best teacher is he who is best at leaving out.* Skornia further states:

In this source, the various media need to be examined with regard to the extent to which they do what is required, without doing so much more than is needed that they erase what was accomplished — or doing what the student himself must do if learning instead of merely exposure is to take place.[43]

Scornia also states that *television, especially, is frequently being wasted on things which radio can do better.*

John B. Haney, Director of the Office of Instructional Resources, University of Illinois at Chicago, states that:

We have come to the conclusion that the best instructional television not only tells or shows something to the student, but directs his activity toward specified learning outcomes.[44]

In a report[45] of a seminar held by the National Education Association on May 16-18, 1959, one of the guidelines for ETV developed by the participants was that educators should:

[43] *Educational Television: the Next Ten Years.* Stanford University, Stanford University, Stanford. 1962 p. 356.

[44] Griffith, B. L. and D. W. MacLennan, editors, *Improvement of Teaching by Television.* University of Missouri Press, Columbia, Missouri. 1964. p. 74.

[45] Frazier, A. and H. E. Wigren, editors, *Opportunities for Learning: Guidelines for Television.* DAVI, National Education Association, Washington, D. C. 1960. p. 59.

Plan more programs which become *opportunities for learning* . . . To be most effective, programs should require something of learners as well as give something to them . . . Obtain maximum involvement of learners in the televised program.

Fred Hechinger, Education Editor, the *New York Times,* states that:

There is a thin line between learning and entertainment in TV because of the place which TV has in the home. Its appeal is very much to be relaxed. Television in the home very rarely becomes purely instructional unless it makes some specific demands on the viewer.[46]

After a number of instructional television programs have been developed, utilizing the *Stewart ITV Format,* then it will be possible for television to make a greater impact on our educational effort than ever before.

There is a minimum potential need for approximately 300 instructional program channels in elementary and secondary education at any one learning center and at any one time — 12 grade levels times 5 or more subjects per grade times the need for 5 or more lessons per subject because all students will not be ready for the same lesson on the same day or at the same time. The addition of college level programs or adult education programs would necessitate a system with a program capability of 500 or 600 instructional programs.

Under existing conditions the simultaneous transmission of 300 instructional television programs would require 300 video channels. This, of course, would be impossible with available spectrum space, but if the Stewart ITV Format was utilized in the development of the instructional programs, there is a possibility of having 300, 500, or even 1,000 instructional programs available at any one time. This would be made possible because only a certain portion of any one instructional program would need full video or motion television (probably less than 10 percent of a program). Another portion of the instructional programming might necessitate limited video for the transmission of still visuals by utilizing *slow-scan* television.[47] The balance of the instructional program would be audio only or blank spaces, during which the

---

[46] *Educational Television: The Next Ten Years.* Stanford University, Stanford, California. 1962. p. 85.

---

[47] Slow-scan television refers to the transmission of still visuals and the process utilizes a spectrum space of approximately 1/600 of that needed for full video transmission. Although theoretically, 600 slow-scan channels would be equivalent to one full video channel, practically, it would only be possible to obtain between 200 to maybe 400 clear, slow-scan channels, for each video channel. Comparing slow-scan television to regular television would be similar to comparing slides or film-strips to motion pictures.

learner is actively involved in performing some task.

Since slow-scan television and audio messages can be transmitted via audio channels (why should one video channel be used when one audio channel would be sufficient?) and since there are times when motion is necessary for instructional goals, the Stewart ITV Format would combine a number of audio channels with one or more video channels (the number of audio and video channels depends on the total number of programs to be transmitted and the percentage of motion visuals necessary). Although the learners would be receiving via a television set, it is not necessary that the signals transmitted to the set have to be full television band width signals. Instead of using one video channel for one or two instructional programs in a given hour, the *Stewart ITV Format* would basically utilize a pair of audio channels[48] for each one of the five, ten, twenty, or more instructional programs in a given hour; nevertheless, each instructional program would have the capability of video by time sharing a video channel (see Figure 121). The actual number of instructional programs (using the *Stewart ITV Format)* that can share a video channel in a given hour depends on the amount of video time required by the individual instructional programs. It is conceivable that under certain instructional requirements, a single instructional program may need a video channel for the entire hour and it is also conceivable that a large number of instructional programs would not need a video channel at all.

There are two major problems that can be foreseen: How do you switch from audio channel pairs to video and what if two instructional programs require video at the same time? If the switching was controlled by a small logic system or computer, a signal or cue recorded on one of the paired audio channels of an instructional program could notify the computer whenever a video channel is required and the computer would scan available video channels and switch the program source from the paired audio channels to an unused video channel[49] and then back to the paired audio channels when there is no further instructional need for video. The *Stewart ITV Format* would be most effective and efficient when used with multiple video channels so that different instructional programs could utilize the video medium at the same time.

---

[48] One of the paired audio channels would be used for audio transmission and the other would be used for transmission of still visuals (slow-scan television) or any other audio band width communication device, such as the *blackboard-by wire* which transmits written messages over audio channels.

---

[49] The receiving television set would be switched remotely by the computer at the same time the program source was switched through use of audio control cues. This would be similar to the remote control devices used now with television receivers to change channels and volume.

Under the *Stewart ITV Format*, it would be possible to transmit 300 instructional programs, all with the capability of video, over 300 paired audio channels (600 clear audio channels or approximate equivalent of two video channels) and 10-15 video channels. The use of the *Stewart ITV Format* would allow a reduction of up to 95 percent in the use of educational communication wave lengths which are presently using the traditional television formats (full video) for simultaneous transmission of instructional programs.[50]

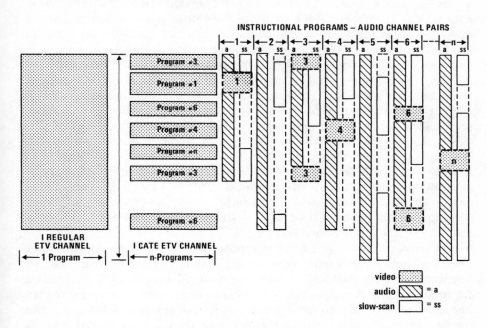

Figure 121 — Time Sharing of ITV Channel Using
the *Stewart ITV Format*

The integration of the *dial-access* concept for random retrieval of instructional programs using the *Stewart ITV Format* eliminates one of the major problems in instructional television. Generally, teachers and students have to receive an instructional television program whenever it is made available by the central source, whether they are ready or not, rather than being able to retrieve the program whenever it is convenient for the teachers and students.

---

[50] If this format proves successful, ETV and CCTV stations around the country could multiple their program capability many times with a minimum increase in additional television channels and audio channels.

2. COMPUTERS IN THE INSTRUCTIONAL EVENT

Computers can be used in any one or more of three ways: they can be used directly in the instructional process, for record keeping, and/or for management of the instructional process.

As usual, the use of computers like the use of other hardware in traditional education is more often prompted by the desire of educators to be thought of as *mod* than by an identified need or learning problem which is being solved by the use of the computer. As with most educational technology, one or more educators get together and write out a proposal for the purchase of the technology and after deciding on the technology and sometimes even after having the technology installed, they decide to try to identify some way to use the technology.

The most common use of computers in education (besides research) is to correct tests and because the easiest test for the computer to correct is the so-called objective type test (multiple-choice, true-false, and matching), most of the tests corrected by computers are of this type. Notice that the format of the test items is controlled by the technology rather than by the SO's of the instructional event. As indicated many times, the use of the so-called objective type test items is a malpractice against the students and as such, this use of the computer should decrease substantially. There are a variety of other testing formats which can be used with computers and are in line with the SO's of the instructional events.

The next easiest use of the computer is as a management or record keeping tool. In changing over to individualized instruction, record keeping for each student's achievement of all course SO's becomes a formidable task. As such, teachers who have to rely on manual record keeping can get discouraged with individualized instruction. At the present time, there are many (probably at least 200 or more) schools who are experimenting with computers as a management device. The minimum use of the computer would be just to keep track of test scores and achievement of course SO's. A management function can be added by having the computer diagnose learning problems (test items missed) and prescribe alternate sources for learning of the necessary SO's.

The fastest growing use of computers in education is in the instructional event. This could be viewed as a good thing if the use of the expensive computer was in learning problem areas in which other technologies were not as effective. However, most projects are designed to use the computer in instruction rather than to solve identified learning problems. As such, the growth of the use of computers in instruction may very well slow to a stop and may actually decrease as it becomes necessary to account for and defend the added expense of the computer without added quantity or quality of learning over other less expensive methods. A common problem is a carryover from traditional education in which every student is supposed to get the same treatment and to let every student use the computer gets expensive. In looking at the instructional event from a systems point-of-view, the computer would only be used with those students who can't learn via some other pathway. In this way, the costs are lower and the results are greater.

Because the computer is easily adaptible to the multiple-choice concept, most computer programming for instruction involves the branching type of programmed instruction. As long as the branches are realistic and each branch discusses the rightness or wrongness of the choices, the multiple-choice format is acceptable as an instructional device in the learning process but the multiple-choice format is still not acceptable as a testing device.

There are eight advantages in using the computer in the instructional event.

a. The computer has the facility to adapt to the individual student BUT only to the degree that the author of the computer program is able to build in this facility. The computer can do no more than what the author wants it to do.

b. The computer can store, retrieve, and present data in different locations and at different times so it is very useful in individualizing instruction.

c. The computer can be used for almost all types of computation and excells at this function.

d. The computer can be programmed so as to involve a variety of other audio-visual media, so it is not a single mode technology.

e. The multiple-choices in the branching part of the instructional programs actually go someplace and the choices are discussed by the computer program as to the rightness or wrongness of the choice.

f. The computer helps to motivate some students to learn and when used with students who have not had much success in the regular classroom, the computer has been able to convince some students that they can learn. So far, the computers and computer assisted instruction have been able to sustain a long-term Hawthorne effect for the learner. With most other educational equipment, after about the second or third time through the equipment the Hawthorne effect starts to drop off, but so far the computer seems to be intriguing enough for most learners what the Hawthorne effect tends to hang on over a much longer period of time than most other equipment.

g. The computer is a very useful device to test out and refine programmed instruction because it is possible to vary the program even while it is being used. Once the program is validated as being able to get 90 percent or more of the students to learn 100 percent of the SO's, the decision should be made as to whether the program should remain in the computer or be published in book form. If there are many points where there are more than four branches, the program might be best left in the computer. If there are only a few choices at these points, then it may be more economical to pull the program out of the computer and publish it in book form.

h. The computer is also being used as a guidance tool in limited ways which releases the guidance staff to work on other problems. The impersonal aspect of the machine (computer) may very well be an advantage for those students who have had negative experiences with educators and other adults.

There are also eight disadvantages in using the computer in the instructional event.

a. Although there are over 1000 instructional programs for computers, there aren't really enough because the programs have been prepared for 30 or more different computers and in over 16 different computer languages. This averages out to only about two instructional programs for any one computer in the same computer language. In order for computers to really be successful in instruction, the companies will have to make their computers more compatible or furnish interface units which will make them compatible. Also, the authors will have to identify a more common computer language such that more of the available programs are really available.

b. As with many *mod* instructional programs, just because an instructional program uses a computer does not mean that the program is effective and efficient. Often the label of a proven technique is applied to similar efforts which have not been proven or validated. This problem is found in programmed instruction, instructional modules, systems, etc. Each instructional program should be made to support itself based on its own effectiveness and/or efficiency.

c. As with most educational programs, the development of most computer instructional programs is done without the benefit of SO's and as such may be a very expensive way of bringing about *chance* learning. Where there are SO's, they are often ignored or compromised because they don't fit the multiple-choice format of the test items used to measure the achievement of the SO's. Computer instructional programs, even more than others because of the cost, should be developed from the basis of SO's and the test items should directly relate to the SO's even if they have to be tested in some other way than by the computer.

d. Although stated before, it is important to overstate and emphasize this disadvantage of the use of the so-called objective type test items in computer instruction. Multiple-choice, true-false, and matching type test items rarely match any desired SO's and if they do, the items become rote memory items with designed distractors.

e. Even though many computer instructional programs have been validated on students, many of these programs have been developed without student input from diagnostic tests to identify where the program should start. Also, when the instructional programs are developed away from students, there is a tendency to develop more alternate branches than are necessary for effective and efficient learning. In one computer instructional program I reviewed, the author wrote 34 possible branches a student could pick and only about 10 of them were ever selected by the students.

f. Although the state of the art of computer instructional programs is beyond that being used practically, the practical state of the art is rather limited in what can be used for input into the computer and for output from the computer. At present, the practical state of the art is primarily limited by high costs of equipment. In particular, typing on a computer keyboard is too slow for non-typing students and most students can read faster than the average computer terminal can type out the messages.

g. Where the average computer can work with 15-30 remote terminals and some computers can handle about 200 remote terminals, in order for computers to really become an integral part of a designed instructional system, the computer should be capable of working with thousands of terminals.

h. Finally, as indicated earlier, most computer instructional projects are designed and utilized to demonstrate the computer rather than to solve student learning problems.

There is a very close parallel between the design and development of computer instructional programs and the design and development of programmed instructional materials. However, many of the authors of

811

computer instructional programs are making the same mistakes which were made early in programmed instruction a decade ago and some of these authors are hardly even aware of programmed instructional materials.

As more and more designed instruction is carried on out of schools and away from teachers, the use of computers in the instructional process will also increase. The management function of the computers will also increase such that the computer may do certain diagnostic and prescriptive tasks and may actually tell students when they need to see a teacher.

3. THE DIAL-ACCESS CONCEPT IN THE INSTRUCTIONAL EVENT

In making the transition from traditional education to the Behavioral Learning Systems Approach to instruction, the easiest way to find release time to perform the various tasks associated with the new role of the teacher is to record the teacher's classroom presentations and then let the audio or audio-visual recording do the subsequent presenting. In order to make these recordings available to the students when and where they need and want them, it is useful to utilize the dial-access concept. The term *dial-access* is usually only used in reference to a telephone type dial retrieval system, i.e., dialing for the weather or the time; dialing for a prayer, for jokes, for flight information; and dialing for the retrieval of recorded instructional programs. However, the concept of *dial-access* is much broader in that it refers to the retrieval of stored information at a time and place convenient for the student. Under this definition even a manual system can be considered as within the *dial-access* concept. A manual retrieval system would be where a student goes up to a desk and asks for a specific cassette or cartridge and then takes the software and necessary hardware to wherever he or she wants to play it back. Dial-Access Information Retrieval Systems or DAIRS are broadly defined as systems involving two or more receivers (learners) who are able to select and receive any one of two or more stored programs (audio and/or visual), from a source which is at a location different from that of the receivers, the transmission from the source to the receiver being wholly or in part electronic.

The first automatic dial-access system was installed in 1961. In 1965 when I first started by Dial-Access Information Retrieval Systems (DAIRS) Newsletter[51] there were still only about 20 installations in the United States of the automatic type dial-access systems being used

---

[51] DAIRS and Systems for Instruction Newsletter was started in July 1965. The DAIRS Newsletter is written and edited by Don Stewart and is currently being published by SLATE Services, Post Office Box 8796, Fountain Valley, California 92708.

for instructional purposes. As a partial result of the DAIRS Newsletter spreading information about the concept, the number of DAIRS installations increased to over 400 during the next three years and the number of companies involved in manufacturing and installing the dial-access equipment when from one company in 1965 to over 15 companies in 1968. As with most of the technologies, most of the schools were installing the equipment in order to be *mod*, not because the equipment would help more students learn more. Where the schools installing the automatic dial-access systems did not take time to train their faculty in their new role, the dial-access systems remained as a supplemental tool on the periphery of the instructional event. Frequently these systems only had demonstration materials stored in them so the administrators could show the system off to visiting educators. Where the schools made an effort to train their faculty on their new role, the dial-access system became an integral part of the instructional event. Whereas up until about 1968, I had put a lot of effort into pushing the dial-access concept, after 1968, I changed my emphasis in my seminars from hardware to software and learning because too many schools were emphasizing the hardware rather than on what the use of the hardware could do for the instructional event.

In the last few years, the installation of dial-access systems for the sake of having a DAIRS has about reached a peak of approximately 1000 installations. As a result, of the emphasis on hardware rather than on learning half or more of the companies involved in manufacturing and installing DAIRS have already gone out of the business.

As with computers, there are advantages and disadvantages in the use of the dial-access concept. From the point-of-view of facilitating learning, there are nine advantages which can be gained by utilizing the DAIRS concept.

a. In the process of developing materials for the dial-access process, most teachers have to be more specific in what they want their students to learn and as a result, more students are able to learn more.

b. Recorded audio or audio-visual presentations are the easiest modes of instruction to prepare as substitutions for the teachers' lectures.

c. Since the materials are pre-recorded, it is possible to incorporate a greater variety of other media and/or modes of instruction. This is an advantage if the other media or modes of instruction are utilized because they facilitate learning. Where other media or modes of instruction are utilized for the sake of having multiple media or modes of instruction rather than for the sake

813

of learning, it is possible for an inappropriate use of media or mode of instruction to actually interfere with learning.

d. In using the DAIRS concept as a substitute for the teachers' classroom presentations, the teacher is released to use the classroom time to individualize instruction even in a traditional environment.

e. Whereas in the typical lecture situation the student has no control over the teacher's presentation and becomes a passive recipient of the presentation, by combining an Active Involvement Form with the DAIRS concept, not only does the student have control over the reception of the presentation (starting and stopping or replaying the recorded presentation), but the student can become an active participant in the instructional event. By involving the student, it is possible to gain greater concentration and hence increased learning.

f. Whereas in the typical lecture situation the students have to be at the same place and at the same time as the teacher who is making the presentation, the use of the DAIRS concept allows the student to receive the presentation at almost any place and at any time that is convenient to the learner. As such, the traditional space and time requirements for learning are eliminated. In an automatic DAIRS, the students may be limited by the locations of the retrieval stations and the hours the system is open for retrieval. In a manual system where the recorded materials and the playback devices are portable, there are no limitations as to where or when learning can take place.[52]

g. With the print medium, it is very difficult to be looking at a photograph, diagram, or chart while at the same time to be reading a description of what you are looking at. With the DAIRS concept, it is possible to be hearing a description or narration at the same time you are looking at something.

h. The DAIRS concept facilitates the use of information and materials not available in print, i.e., speeches by certain people, personalized literature (the author reading his or her own literary works), certain events where audio and/or visual cues are important for learning or motivation, music, etc.

i. Given a verbal message in print, it is possible to misinterpret the message by mentally emphasizing some words, de-emphasizing

---

[52] In a midwestern college that had installed an automatic DAIRS as a part of the local telephone system such that students in the dormitories or in their homes could dial in and receive class lectures at any time, the busiest time for the system was between midnight and 3:00 a.m. Obviously, it would be difficult to get teachers to lecture at that time of night.

other words, and putting in pauses where the source of the message didn't intend for them to be. The DAIRS concept can cut down possible misinterpretations by having the source record his or her own vocal emphasis. The concept also allows for the personality of the speaker to be heard and/or seen and for the inclusion of non-verbal and non-vocal sounds.

As with all educational innovations, there are also some disadvantages and limitations of the DAIRS concept particularly as it is presently being used.

a. There are not enough programs available to make a significant impact on a school's instructional program. This is caused in part because of the lack of identified minimum common core SO's which results in everyone doing their own thing with a minimum of interschool or even intraschool cooperation and sharing. This is also caused by the resistance of faculty in giving up their traditional presenting role and the relative high cost in time, effort, and money to develop materials to the technical quality level demanded by the technologists even when the added technical quality may have no affect on learning.[53]

b. As with the presentations that have been recorded and made available via the DAIRS concept, most of the programs, have not been designed to produce or to facilitate learning so they tend to be teacher or content-oriented rather than learner-oriented. The biggest cause of this problem is a lack of SO's and matching test items which could be used to evaluate the achievement of the learners and the contribution of the materials to the learners achievement. Another factor in this problem is that few of the materials presently available or presently being used under the DAIRS concept have been tried out on learners and edited or changed to reflect the needs of the learners and solutions to their learning problems, i.e., in a multi-lingual class, the same presentation could be made available in several languages and dialects to facilitate learning rather than the traditional single presentation approach where non-achievement of students who speak languages and dialects other than classroom English is blamed on genetics and home environment rather than viewed as a language problem.

---

[53] This refers to the general statements that it takes about 15 hours to make a one-hour audio tape and about 40 hours to make a one-hour video tape. When designed to facilitate the achievement of SO's, the estimates of time to produce effective materials may be overstated. When designed to be technically perfect, the time estimates may be right, but if there are no SO's, the resultant materials may be practically useless as far as facilitating student learning.

c. Most of the DAIRS installations have been put in for the sake of having a DAIRS. As such, the design of the DAIRS hardware and the DAIRS environment is not matched to any identified learning needs of the students. Then, as learning needs are identified and it is recognized that the DAIRS installation does not fit the needs, the blame is placed on the DAIRS concept as being inadequate rather than on the original planning to install a DAIRS as being inadequate.

d. Since most of the DAIRS installations have been installed because of administrative decisions, it should not be too unexpected when teachers resist using the system. The administrative objective is to be up-to-date via use of the system. The faculty objective, too frequently, is to prove that the system won't work. Faculty have to be involved and the emphasis has to be on the solving of a teaching and/or learning problem where DAIRS happens to provide a solution rather than to identify the solution and try to find a problem to fit it! The easiest way to achieve this is to focus on the changing role of the teacher from a presenter of course content (regardless of individual differences) to the humanizer of learning who identifies and solves student learning problems.

Although many educators who have used or are using the audio-tutorial (AT) approach to instruction originated by Samuel Postlethwaite of Purdue University may not be able to think of the AT approach as being a part of the DAIRS concept, it actually is a manually operated DAIRS in that the audio tape acts as the spine of the instructional event. However, in most AT installations, there is a much greater use of other media and materials programmed into the instructional event than is usually found in the typical DAIRS installation. The advantages and disadvantages of the DAIRS concept apply also to the AT systems except that there is a greater effort in the AT systems to reflect the needs of the learner and to facilitate the designed achievement of SO's. For those readers who are not familiar with the audio-tutorial approach, the basic unit is an audio tape playback device (reel to reel, cartridge, or cassette). The teacher then records not only his or her presentations, but directs the student to specific reading assignments, to view certain visuals, to view certain exhibits, and/or to perform certain experiments. The teacher can also record a discussion of what has been just read, viewed, or done while the experiences are still fresh in the learner's mind. Initially, the AT concept was considered just another way of presenting course content. During the past few years, educators who are developing AT units have included the use of SO's such that the AT units have become more learner-oriented and less teacher or presenter-oriented.

A serious disadvantage of both DAIRS and most AT systems which is also reflected in all traditional curriculum materials is that it is assumed that all learners learn best in the same way by having only one pathway through the instructional event. Whereas in the traditional environment where there are few SO's and it is difficult to develop alternate paths to non-existant goals; under the DAIRS concept and the AT approach it is much easier to develop and offer multiple pathways through an instructional event. This is facilitated when a teacher incorporates quality control into the instructional event such that at least 90 percent or more of the students have to learn 100 percent of the SO's of the instructional event. In order to achieve these standards, it is necessary to recognize individual differences in learning by offering multiple pathways to the achievement of the same SO's.

4. SELECTION OF HARDWARE AND THE USE OF CONSULTANTS

As mentioned many times previously, it is a mistake to think that a particular hardware configuration (computer, television, DAIRS, etc.) is the solution to all problems without knowing first what the problems are which need solutions. In selecting hardware, there are at least six areas to consider in identifying the problems and solutions:

a. the format and type of storage medium,
b. the medthods of access and retrieval,
c. the transmission modes,
d. the receiving environment,
e. potential expansion needs, and
f. the writing of software and hardware specifications.

In order to keep the selection as open as possible, think of the resultant hardware configuration as an Instructional Information Retrieval System (IIRS) rather than as a computer, television, DAIRS, etc. Instructional Information Retrieval Systems are broadly defined for the purposes of this book as systems involving two or more receivers (students) who are able to select and receive any one of two or more stored programs (audio and/or visual) from a source which is at a location different from that of the receivers, the transmission from the source to the receiver being wholly or in part electronic (in a manual or partial manual IIRS, the transmission of one or more of the stored programs may be manual or mechanical). A point of view that should also be kept in mind is that in an instructional institution an IIRS should be installed for the purpose of making the learning process more effective and efficient. For this reason, in the planning of such a system, the overriding consideration should be the instructional specifications of the system, not the technical specifications. The technical specifications should be designed to permit the achievement of the specified instructional objectives, plus a reserve margin to take care of the potential deterioration of equipment due to normal use.

If the technical specifications of a proposed system are established without knowledge of the instructional specifications, it may be difficult, if not impossible, to achieve the instructional goals once the system is installed. Also, it is possible that the system could be priced beyond the available budget, and, more than likely, the technical specifications may preclude competitive bids from more than one or two companies. If the technical specifications are established in view of the system functions and the instructional objectives, it is possible that all of the companies manufacturing TV, DAIRS, computers or related equipment could submit competitive bids utilizing diverse equipment to achieve the system's technical and instructional specifications.

While involved in the specification of instructional functions and objectives, it may be of value to estimate the percentage of student use of each of the various functions of the IIRS. These estimates can be very useful in making decisions on whether or not to purchase certain hardware. In a system where only about 10% of the students' use would require visuals, it may be best to use supplementary visual devices. If a significant percentage of the students' use requires visuals, it may be best to build into the system some form of visual display. If a significant percentage of students' use would require individual control of stored program (start, stop, backspace, record, etc.), it may be better to install separate audio or audiovisual recorders at the receiver locations rather than overload the IIRS.

To ensure a successful system, not only is it important to involve the faculty members in specifying the instructional functions of the system, but also to encourage and help the faculty members to develop and use the programs to be stored and presented by the system. Because of the almost inherent resistance of faculty members to any automation of the instructional process, it is important to point out to the faculty that an educational technology exists and is a fact in the modern instructional process and that the use and direction of this technology should be guided by instructional policies for the benefit of the learner and the instructor.

With human guidance controlling the technology, there is no need to worry that the technology will displace, degrade, or regiment teachers and sutdents, or that it will dehumanize the educational process. On the contrary, courses specifically designed to utilize technology for the sake of learning can release teachers from repetitious tasks so that more personal contact with the students becomes possible. Their teaching efforts can deviate from the traditional task of presenting content to the challenging task of helping students turn new knowledge into understanding through application. The teachers can awaken within the students an awareness of the interrelationships of disciplines and, as one of the major goals of education, the teacher will have time to inspire a motivation for continued learning that will persist beyond commencement day.

With reference to the first area to be considered, the type and format of the storage medium, this of course would depend on the results of the development of a number of instructional modules in accordance with the learning systems approach. It would be important to know, do you need audio, audio-visual, video, slow-scan, microfiche, microfilm, and could you use single-track audio recorders, or do you need two tracks, four tracks, eight tracks, etc. should the audio recorders be reel to reel recorders, cartridges, discs, casettes, etc. In the case of video tape recorders, do you need broadcast quality? Do you need high resolution? Do you need color? Do you need the ability to identify specific segments of the videotape, etc. In the case of a computer, are you going to have to retrieve audio and/or visual materials? Could it be integrated with a DAIRS, does it need a cathode ray tube (CRT), is the information for the computer going to be stored on interchangeable disc packs, on tape, etc.

With reference to the methods of access and retrieval, there are essentially three methods of access and retrieval: manual access and manual retrieval, combination of manual and automatic access and retrieval, and automatic access and retrieval. Manual access and manual retrieval refers to the learner selecting manually an audio or video tape cartridge (cassettes, etc.) and placing it into a playback system, or possibly checking out a complete reel to reel audio or video tape recorder, or placing into the system manually a computer disc pack, or the use of almost any other medium in which the learner personally handles the storage medium.

Combination manual and automatic systems are when the learner is at a remote location and by some mechanism, either by dialing a phone or by keying in on a computer console, the learner indicates to some central source that a desired program is wanted, and at the source, the instructional programs are still manually put into the system, even though the learner may dial in automatically or key in automatically to the system and the system may transmit the materials automatically to the learner. Another combination manual and automatic system is when the learner manually operates an automatic system which is located in the same place with the learner. The difference is in the first instance the learner is remote from the storage medium and the access is automatic but the retrieval is manual. In the second situation, the learner is near the storage medium and the access is manual but the retrieval is automatic.

Under automatic access and retrieval, there are four sub-divisions or degrees of access and retrieval:

Scheduled Access — the stored IIRS programs are played back into the system at specific periodic intervals regardless of whether or not there are any students connected to the program.

Non-private Limited Random Access — the stored IIRS programs can be cued for playback into the system on a random basis except when the program is already in the process of being played back. Even then, there is still random access to the program but not to the beginning of the program.

Private Limited Random Access — the stored IIRS programs can be played back to a single receiving station on a random basis except when the program is already in the process of being played back.

Private Random Access — the stored IIRS program can be played back to a single receiving station on a complete random basis.

Generally, systems offering *Scheduled Access* and/or *Non-private Limited Random Access* are priced much lower than systems offering *Private Random Access*. In comparing bids from different companies, be sure that you take into consideration the degree of privateness and random accessibility which in turn should be dictated by the needs of the teachers and students. If your particular needs can be satisfied by a *Scheduled Access* IIRS, then it would be superfluous to install a *Private Random Access* IIRS. On the other hand, if your needs are for a *Private Random Access* IIRS, then you will not be happy or very successful with a *Scheduled Access* IIRS. Actually, based on defined needs and operating schedules, some combination of the four types listed above might provide the most efficient and economical system. In planning for a IIRS, the following suggestions may be helpful in the decision-making process.

If relatively large numbers of students will want access to specific programs, it is better to place these programs on a scheduled access basis which is by far the more economic way of offering automatic access and retrieval. On a scheduled basis, multiple-track recorders can be played into the system, and in the case of the utilization of the *Stewart ITV Format* or integrated audio and video programs, the offering of programs on a scheduled basis (every hour on the hour) offers better opportunities for minimizing the number of channels necessary and maximizing the utilization of time-shared video channels. Scheduled access has been used at a number of schools in their dial-access systems, and although the ideal approach would be to allow the learner complete random access whenever the learner needed the material, the economic advantages of scheduling the instructional programs on an hourly or half hourly, etc. basis are such that they outweigh the disadvantages of having the student wait for up to an hour before getting a particular program that the student may want.[54]

If relatively few students will want access to specific programs, it is better to place these programs on a random access basis. The frequency of retrieval will dictate whether you would use *Private Limited Random Access* or *Private Random Access*. If the frequency of retrieval is especially low, it may be better to utilize a library of tapes such that the requested tapes can be placed into the IIRS manually or issued in cartridges or cassettes for use in individual playback devices.

The random, nonprivate basis of access and retrieval refers to IIRS in which the first student to access a program (where there is only one program on the tape) is the only one that has random access to the beginning of the program. Learners who access the program after the first learner, enter the program wherever the first learner is, and have to wait until the program is over before he or she is able to hear or see the beginning of the program. In the case of multiple tracks, the random access is to the first learner who accesses any one of the multiple tracks. After that, any learner that accesses any one of the tracks enters the program at that point on the tape where the first learner is. In the case of a number of the foreign language drill sessions, it is not too critical for the learner to come in on the middle of a drill; but since most instructional programs in other subject matter areas tend to be sequential and build on a previously-laid foundation, the random, nonprivate method of automatic access and retrieval is not considered a very effective or efficient method of access and retrieval.

A more effective and efficient (and also more expensive method would be an automatic, random access and retrieval system that is private such that any learner that accesses into the central source essentially gets his or her own program to work on. This, of course, is characteristic of almost all computer instructional programs and not characteristic of most other IIRS. In providing random private

---

[54] It should be pointed out that, in a sense, most television programming is on a scheduled basis, but where this schedule offers a given program only once or twice, or at most, three times a day, this is really quite a bit different than offering the program every hour on the hour throughout the day.

access and retrieval, the systems usually have to limit the number of students using the system, and are much more expensive to install initially than the scheduled, or random, nonprivate systems. If in offering to the learner random, private access and retrieval, you also want to give the learner controls over the programs, so that he or she can start, stop, rewind, fast forward, interact, etc., this again increases the cost of the system. Private Random Access can best be obtained from systems utilizing some type of master program recorders (which could be multi-track) and slave or buffer units upon which requested programs are automatically dubbed at high speed, the learner is then connected to the buffer unit while the master recorder is released for other IIRS access signals.

The location of the source of the IIRS could be almost any place on the site of an educational institution, but some advantage in convenience and economy may be gained by locating the source near or central to the majority of the receiver locations; near the recording facility which in turn should be convenient to the faculty who are doing the recording; and/or near the library, learning resource center, or instructional materials center. The physical appearance of the source could range from a small system consisting of two or more tape recorders tied into an existing telephone exchange up to a complex system of computers, audio and video recorders, independent on-site switching systems, interface (interconnecting) equipment between the independent system to the regular off-site telephone exchange system, etc. Depending upon the size, required functions, and other variables of a given IIRS, some form of switching devices at the source in order to connect the receiver with a specific program may or may not be included.

With reference to the various transmission modes, this could include the use of regular telephone circuits (internal and/or external telephone systems), broadcast radio or television, cable radio or television, microwave, etc. The actual transmission mode used would depend on location of the source and location of the receivers, the terrain, the nearness of other similar sources and receivers, the needs of the instructional materials, etc. In future systems, it is possible that satellites and laser beams could be the mode of transmission.

The receiving environment refers to where the learner is, and how he receives the instructional messages. The modes of reception could be audio, audio active, audio record, audio-visual still, audio-visual motion, cathode ray tube, typewriter printout, etc. The receiving environment can be divided into two subcategories, in reference to the number of learners involved simultaneously at one receiving station. For large group reception, the learners could be located in classrooms, in dormitory lounges, in large auditoriums, theatres, etc. For individual or small group reception, you might use study carrels, located in a variety of locations, language laboratories and dormitory rooms, in homes, offices, cafeteria, library, out-of-doors,[55] other nearby educational institutions, or in small learning centers established in remote urban areas to facilitate the necessary learning activities of students who otherwise would have to use some of their limited learning time for commuting back and forth to the main educational institution. These small learning centers could also be used by students whose home environment is not conducive to study and learning, or is not equipped to facilitate the retrieval of the Instructional Information. The receiving environment should reflect the needs of the learner in utilizing the instructional materials to learn the desired SO's. For example, if other media are involved, then the environment should have electrical outlets and space available for the use of the other media. In the case of laboratory courses, if water and/or gas is necessary, then the receiving environment should provide for these needs. If the receivers are supposed to be able to access the instructional materials automatically, a broad definition of IIRS would include typing, dialing, push buttons, digital selection, etc.

An area that is frequently overlooked is the potential for expansion of an IIRS. This becomes very important because some systems can't be expanded, other systems may only be expanded if the same companies equipment is used which limits the bidding for any future expansion. Also, the basic cost of a particular system may be less than some other system, but the expansion costs of the cheaper system may be much higher than the expansion costs of some more expensive systems. Since most IIRS are installed on a pilot or experimental basis with future expansion based on the results of the initial installation, this factor should be considered from the beginning. If there is sufficient doubt as to the need for future expansion of a pilot or experimental IIRS then there should also be sufficient doubt as to the need for even the initial IIRS installation.

In preparing the specifications for hardware or an IIRS, the emphasis should be on the specification of the functions of the system rather than the technical specifications. Technical specifications tend to favor certain manufacturers whereas functional specifications opens up the IIRS to alternate methods of achieving the desired functions which in turn should reflect the instructional needs of the learners, the materials, the teachers, and the institution. The development of these functional specifications should be done with the help of consultants who are specialists in this area in order to increase the chances for a successful

---

[55]At a west coast college, dial-access receiving stations were located out on the campus grounds near the beach, where the students preferred to study.

system. There are two types of consultants that could be used in the development of the functional specifications: hardware consultants, and software consultants. In some cases, the educational institution may already have these consultants on its staff. If not, then consultants can be retained on either a temporary, day-by-day basis, or under a contract basis. The software consultant can be utilized for the following types of activities:

(1) to motivate the faculty and encourage their involvement in the development of an integrated learning system;

(2) to help identify the learning needs of the learners, teachers, and the school;

(3) to help develop the functional specifications for a system, based on the identified needs;

(4) to assist in the development of instructional materials which are learner oriented, will result in learning, and are to be utilized in part, or totally, by the system; and

(5) to assist in the evaluation of the software used in the system.

The hardware consultant can best be used in the following activities:

(1) to assist in the writing of functional specifications from a hardware point of view;

(2) if bids are put out for the installation of hardware, the hardware consultant can assist in the selection of a company or companies which are best able to fulfill the functional specifications of the system;

(3) to supervise the installation of the hardware, being sure that the terms of the contract and the functional specifications are fulfilled;

(4) once the system is installed, to assist in the evaluation of the hardware system before final payment;

(5) to assist in the setting up of the necessary and appropriate maintenance and operating procedures of the system; and

(6) if and when expansion becomes necessary, to assist and coordinate the expansion.

During the past several decades, educational institutions have been able to install a wide variety of educational hardware items and systems, with little if any identified learner needs to substantiate the installation. Because of the increasing costs of the hardware, the increasing costs and difficult development of software, increasing competition from other educational areas for the educational dollar, the growing resistance of the taxpayer against increased school taxes, and the continued inefficiency and ineffectiveness of our school systems, educational institutions are going to have to substantiate investments in hardware items and systems on the basis of what our learners are not learning now that they will learn with the new equipment (hardware and software). Subsequent evaluation of the IIRS will then be based on the original statements and will consist essentially of — did the learners learn what they were supposed to learn. Although there are still many educational institutions that are spending millions of dollars in order to keep up with the *educational Joneses* or for the sake of innovation, the period of the unsubstantiated spending of the educational dollar is fast closing.

It is important to point out that although the primary function of an IIRS is to make a variety of stored educational programs available to receivers, the system could also be used for other purposes: it could be used for student retrieval of daily announcements; students could call the teacher for immediate help on independent study problems; students could dial in for a live lecture; or into a computer for assistance in problem solving. Other uses for the IIRS will be developed as the system is used.

5. QUESTIONS TO BE CONSIDERED WHEN PLANNING FOR AN INSTRUCTIONAL INFORMATION RETRIEVAL SYSTEM (IIRS)

In planning for some type of automated IIRS, it is best to start out with some kind of a manual system where the students actually access and retrieve the necessary instructional information which could be books, kits, audio and/or video tapes, cassettes, programmed units, films, slides, etc. In this way, it is easier to identify the potential needs of any automated system, i.e., where and when do students want to use the materials, how many students need the same materials at the same time, what types of materials are used in the instructional materials, etc. As the duplication of materials and/or the distribution of materials becomes a problem because of high use and/or wide spread use, then it may be appropriate to consider some type of an automated system. In smaller schools and in schools where the teacher involvement and student use are small, there may never be a need for an automated system. However, as smaller schools begin to work together cooperatively rather than each teacher and each school re-inventing *curriculum wheels* on their own, then an automated system may be appropriate and economical.

825

a. SOFTWARE CONSIDERATIONS

Before listing the questions to be considered in the planning for the software considerations in an IIRS, it is of primary importance to consider four factors which will contribute to the degree of success or failure of the total system. Each of these factors can be considered to constitute a continuum with a zero at one end and a maximum effort at the other end.

(a) The degree of faculty involvement in the design, development, and use of software.

(b) The degree to which the software is learner-oriented (this is in contrast with most educational materials which are teacher-oriented.)

(c) The degree of specificity in the stating of instructional goals or objectives.

(d) The degree of availability of support personnel and facilities during the design, development, and use of the software.

If an instructional institution is definitely going to install some form of IIRS (this is also true when installing closed circuit television or other media systems and even when the system is to be manual), it is important that the administrative staff make commitments regarding these four factors. The level of these commitments should be identified and stated before trying to answer the other questions because most of the software considerations are dependent upon one or more of these four factors.

Because the originators of proposals for IIRS are usually technically-oriented, there is a built-in tendency to overlook the costs and the problems of preparing programs or software. If the success of an IIRS does depend on the students and faculty using the system and using it with positive results, then any valid proposal for an IIRS should include plans and costs for the development of the necessary software. In school systems or instructional institutions which are not accustomed to developing course materials on a systematic basis, there is a temptation to minimize or underestimate the cost of developing instructional materials. Depending upon a number of factors, the development cost of the software could account for a third or more of the proposed cost of the total system.

It is difficult to specify the actual costs of software development because of the variation between institutions in faculty salaries, consultant fees, commercial program prices, and the costs of films, printing, models, etc. However, the following questions indicate the areas to be considered and suggest the effects on costs and effectiveness of the resultant software.

1. What is the relationship between the stored programs in the proposed system and the regular curriculum of the educational institution?

    1.1 Are you planning to buy or develop programs of a horizontal enrichment nature on subject areas other than those covered by the regular course materials? (Because of minimal use, this approach will probably cost the least and also have the least affect on the learning of required SO's.)

    1.2 Are you planning to buy or develop programs of an enrichment nature on subject areas covered by the regular course materials? (Although these materials will probably be used more which will increase the costs, there will still not be much affect on the learning of the required SO's.)

    1.3 Are you planning to buy or develop programs which will be integrated into the regular course materials and will substitute for certain parts of the course which are now being presented by some other mode? (There will be higher use of these materials and consequently the costs will rise and so will the potential affect on learning. However, since the teacher is still presenting a lot of the content, there will still be minimal teacher time available to solve learning problems.)

    1.4 Are you planning to buy or develop programs which have been identified by a systematic analysis of curriculum objectives and re-design of learner oriented course materials? (This approach will cost the most initially, but will also result in the greatest amount of release time for teachers to solve student learning problems which in turn will result in the greatest affect on the learning of the required SO's).

2. What is the source of the software?

    2.1 External — Are you going to use *off-the-shelf* audio, audio-video programs, and other necessary instructional materials? (See prices in appropriate catalogues.)

    2.2 Semi-External — Are you going to contract with a commerical company to develop the programs or to work with your faculty in the development of the programs? (Contact several companies that develop instructional materials on contract basis.)

    2.3 Semi-Internal — Are you going to use the services of outside consultants for faculty orientation and training in the development of course materials? (Consultant fees will depend upon who the consultants are and how often they will be used)

2.4 Internal — Do you have a staff member available or are you planning to add a staff member or members to work with the faculty on the development of programs? (Staff member's salary).

3. What are your plans regarding the use of faculty time in the development of programs? (Although faculty can actually make their own release time by minimizing their presenting time, by cooperating with other teachers so they are not re-inventing curriculum wheels which have already been invented, and by minimizing the time spent on classroom activities which can not be defended on the basis of SO's which are learned on the activity, most faculty will be more productive if given some release time.)

3.1 Do you expect faculty to develop programs on their own time or on school time but without changing their teaching schedule? (Little or no extra cost involved but this approach will result in few programs.)

3.2 Do you expect faculty to develop programs on an overtime basis or through a reduction in their teaching schedule? (The cost depends on how many faculty members are involved and how much overtime or release time is needed and will result in a limited number of programs. This approach would be used by an institution which desires to make a slow transition from the present system to the use of IIRS.)

3.3 Do you expect to use some faculty on a full-time basis for the development of the programs? (The cost depends on how many faculty are involved and how long a period and will result in a large number of programs. This approach would be used by an institution which desires to make a moderate transition from the present system to the use of an IIRS.)

3.4 Do you expect to use all or most of your faculty on a full-time basis for the development of programs during summer vacation or in the case of new schools, prior to the opening of the school? (The cost would be the highest, but would probably result in the most successful program construction and with a maximum number of programs. This approach would be used by an institution which desires to make a fast transition from the present system to the use of an IIRS or by a new institution which is developing the necessary instructional materials for the first time.)

4. What audio and video (if required) recording equipment, other production equipment, and facilities do you have available and what will you have to purchase for the development of programs for the proposed IIRS? (Although this cost is for software development, the equipment necessary may be included in the cost of the hardware.)

5. Are you planning to use supplementary materials in connection with the students use of the IIRS? (This cost would vary widely, depending upon the types of supplementary materials involved: 8mm films, slides, mimeographed or printed materials, laboratory kits, etc.)

b. HARDWARE CONSIDERATIONS

One of the first questions that educators ask when contemplating an IIRS is, *How much does it cost?* This is a question which cannot be answered without knowing the specific functions required of the system. The more specific the educator is in listing the required functions of the contemplated system, the easier and more specific can a representative of a company which installs IIRS determine the cost of such a system. There are many variables to consider in trying to estimate the cost of an IIRS. Hardware costs only could range from $10,000 to $1,000,000 or more. For the reader who is looking for rough estimates, the price range of an IIRS installation can be arrived at by using cost figures from $250 — $1,000 for each receiver location, from $100 — $1,000 for each program source (audio only), and from $500 to $10,000 for each A/V source. Depending upon the instructional and technical specifications, the cost of an installation could exceed or be under this estimated price range.

After identifying the instructional functions and instructional specifications required of a system in reference to the learning needs of the students, the facilities needed by the instructional materials, and the teaching needs of the teachers, the following questions concern the considerations which will help identify the potential costs and space needs of the system. More accurate costs and space needs can be determined by giving the list of required instructional functions and the answers to the following questions to several companies involved in this type of system.

1. *Student or Receiver Locations:*

    1.1 How many receiver locations do you want?

        1.11 How many for individual use?

        1.12 How many for small group use (less than five)?

        1.13 How many for large group use (five or more)?

1.2 How many individual study carrels?

 1.21 What kind of carrel do you want or need?

  1.211 Electrical needs (power, audio, video).

  1.212 Communication needs (telephone, cable, etc.)

  1.213 Learning needs (gas, water, etc.)

 1.22 What kinds of storage and workspaces are needed?

  1.221 How large a study space?

  1.222 How large are storage spaces for books and supplementary equipment?

  1.223 What kinds and how large are supplementary work spaces (sink, typing table, etc.)?

1.3 How many of the receiver locations will utilize supplementary recording and playback devices in addition to the program sources?

 1.31 How many of these recorders are audio only?

 1.32 How many of these recorders are audio-video?

 1.33 How many will utilize a remote recorder that is part of the source?

 1.34 How many will utilize a separate recorder located at the receivers' stations?

  1.341 Will the recorders be portable or mounted in the student station?

  1.342 Will the master tracks be recorded from the dial-access system or available as separate tapes?

1.4 How many of the receiver locations will have microphones?

 1.41 How many will only amplify the students' voice in his own earphones?

 1.42 How many will allow recording and playback of the students' responses?

1.5 How many of the receiver locations will have video?

 1.51 How many will be for individual viewing?

  1.511 What size screen?

1.52 How many will be for group viewing?

    1.521 If monitors, what size screen?

    1.522 If projection TV, what size screen?

1.53 How many will be for reception of slow-scan television (slides, filmstrips, etc.)?

1.6 How many of the receiver locations will have computer terminals?

    1.61 How many will have typewriter terminals?

    1.62 How many will have cathode ray tube display?

    1.63 What other supplementary computer equipment will be used?

1.7 What other kinds of supplementary materials will be needed at the receiver locations (tape recorders; film, filmstrip, or slide projectors; microscopes; kits of learning materials; special workbooks; phonographs; etc.)

1.8 Are there any plans to expand the number of receiver stations in the proposed IIRS at some later date?

    1.81 If yes, how many more receiving stations and on what kind of expansion schedule?

2. *Transmission*

2.1 Is the transmission between the source and receivers manual, mechanical, electronic, or some combination of these?

2.2 Is some kind of interface[56] equipment needed at either or both ends of the transmission channels?

2.3 What is the distance between the receiver locations and the source programs?

    2.31 How many locations will depend on coaxial cable connections?

    2.32 How many locations will be served by telephone lines?

    2.33 How many locations already have the necessary telephone or coaxial connections?

---

[56] *Interface equipment* refers to equipment necessary to change or control the input or output signals to be carried through the transmission channels — dataphones, recorder couplers, translators, etc. or between incompatible types of equipment.

3. *Switching System (see Page 820)*

    3.1   How many receivers should have access to the stored programs simultaneously or almost simultaneously?

        3.11 If all receivers require almost simultaneous access *to the IIRS* what is the maximum time allowable between the first and last connection?

        3.12 If all receivers require almost simultaneous access *to the same program,* what is maximum time allowable between the first and last connection?

4. *Source:*

    4.1   How many program sources do you want to have available at any one time for student retrieval?

        4.11 How many programs are audio only?

        4.12 How many programs are video only?

        4.13 How many programs are audio and video?

        4.14 How many programs do you plan to have available on a scheduled basis for group listening?

            4.141 How many receivers can listen to the same program at the same time?

        4.15 How many programs do you plan to have available for individual random access?

            4.151 How many programs will allow remote control, e.g., start, stop, backspace, fast forward, record, playback?

            4.152 How many programs will allow other receivers to dial into a program already in progress?

        4.16 How many program sources do you want to have available for random access by student request to an attendant?

    4.2   What kind of storage medium do you intend to use?

        4.21 How many audio programs will be stored on single-track recorders?

        4.22 How many audio programs will be stored on double-track recorders?

        4.23 How many audio programs will be stored on four-track recorders?

4.24 How many audio programs will be stored on multi-track, highspeed computer controlled access recorders?

4.25 How many video programs will be stored on single program video recorders?

4.26 How many video programs will be stored on multi-program high speed computer controlled access recorders?

4.27 How many video programs will be stored on 8mm film projectors, 16mm field projectors, cartridge filmstrip projectors, or slide carousels, and made available via interface equipment and television cameras?

4.28 How many computer programs will be available?

4.281 How many computer programs will be stored at a local source?

4.282 How many computer programs will be stored at a more distant location?

4.283 How many computer programs utilize visuals?

4.284 How many computer programs utilize audio?

4.3 Are there any plans to expand the number of audio, audio-video, or computer proposed IIRS at some later date?

4.31 If yes, how many more program sources of what type, and on what kind of expansion schedule?

In addition, the decision to install an IIRS should also include consideration of the following factors:

(a) What functions do you want performed by the system?

(b) Assuming that two or three different systems can perform the necessary functions, which one has the better price?

(c) Assuming equal or almost equal prices, what extra flexibility is built into the system to take care of future needs?

(d) Assuming equal or almost equal prices, what extra audio and/or video technical qualities are built into the systems above those specified by the consumer?

(e) Assuming equal or almost equal prices, what are the guarantees or warranties and servicing arrangements?

(f) If you plan to expand the proposed IIRS at some future date, it may be very important to obtain estimates on the costs of expansion. Dependent upon factors such as the size of the initial installation and the size of the projected expansion, it is possible that the company submitting the lowest bid on the initial installation may be forced to submit the highest bid on a projected expansion of the system because of equipment limitations. (Because of the need for compatibility between the initial and the projected installations, it is assumed that the consumer will contract with the same company for both installations.)

(g) An increasingly important factor is the percentage of *down-time* or the number of hours the system is inoperative (closed down to locate problems and correct them) out of the total number of hours the system is supposed to be in operation. In visiting other IIRS installations, a good question to ask and discuss is the problem of *down-time*.